Public Enterprises Today: Missions, Performance and Governance

Learning from Fifteen Cases

Les entreprises publiques aujourd'hui: missions, performance, gouvernance

Leçon de quinze études de cas

P.I.E. Peter Lang

Bruxelles · Bern · Berlin · Frankfurt am Main · New York · Oxford · Wien

CIRIEC
Luc Bernier

Public Enterprises Today: Missions, Performance and Governance

Learning from Fifteen Cases

Les entreprises publiques aujourd'hui: missions, performance, gouvernance

Leçon de quinze études de cas

Social Economy & Public Economy
No. 5

CIRIEC activities, publications and researches are realized with the support of the Belgian Federal Government – Scientific Policy and with the support of the Government of the Belgian French Speaking Community – Scientific Research.

This publication has been peer-reviewed.

© P.I.E. PETER LANG S.A.
Éditions scientifiques internationales
Brussels, 2015
1 avenue Maurice, B-1050 Bruxelles, Belgique
info@peterlang.com ; www.peterlang.com

ISSN 2030-3408
ISBN 978-2-87574-224-7
eISBN 978-3-0352-6499-9
D/2015/5678/01

Printed in Germany

CIP available from the British Library, GB and the Library of Congress, USA.
Bibliographic information published by "Die Deutsche Nationalbibliothek"
"Die Deutsche Nationalbibliothek" lists this publication in the "Deutsche Nationalbibliografie"; detailed bibliographic data is available in the Internet at http://dnb.d-nb.de.

Table of Contents / Table des matières

8

Acknowledgements

CIRIEC's International Scientific Commission Public Services/ Public Enterprise launched the research project with a Research Steering Committee including Gabriel Obermann, President of the Commission (WU Vienna University of Economics and Business, Austria), Philippe Bance (University of Rouen, France), Luc Bernier (ENAP Québec, Canada), Massimo Florio (University of Milan, Italy). These project leaders have been helped and supported in this project by the international secretariat of CIRIEC: Barbara Sak together with initially Maya Abada in the early stages of the project and at the end Lia Caponetti. They should all be thanked for their precious help and time devoted to this project.

The editor of the book would like first to thank the authors of the various chapters for their contribution. He would also like to thank Bernard Thiry and Benoît Lévesque for the improvements they suggested to the book and Jacques Fournier who wrote the preface of the book. It is an honour and a privilege that scholars and practitioners of such a high quality and reputation help us in this endeavour.

Préface

Jacques FOURNIER*

Conseiller d'État honoraire, président d'honneur de la SNCF,
ancien président du CIRIEC international

L'entreprise publique est-elle une espèce en voie de disparition ou une plante vivace porteuse d'avenir ?

Les quinze études de cas présentées dans cet ouvrage ne peuvent que conforter dans le choix de la seconde branche de l'alternative.

Ce livre ne nous présente pas que des réussites. Il ne sous-estime pas les difficultés rencontrées. Il fait par là comprendre les évolutions en cours et permet d'éclairer l'avenir.

Les entreprises concernées opèrent dans neuf pays, en Europe ou sur le continent américain, elles ont des champs d'activité très divers – eau et assainissement, transport, services urbains, finances, énergie, communication –, leurs niveaux d'intervention, national, régional ou local, et leurs modes de gouvernance, plus proches, selon le cas, du droit public ou du droit privé, sont différents. Mais elles ont toutes en commun le service de l'intérêt général, elles sont toutes des organisations hybrides, *entreprises*, agissant sur le marché, mais entreprises *publiques*, contribuant à l'action publique.

L'intérêt de la recherche engagée sous l'égide du Ciriec International est de montrer les problèmes qui se posent à elles en ce début du 21ᵉ siècle, dans le troisième temps de l'évolution qu'elles ont connue depuis la fin du dernier conflit mondial.

Le premier temps fut celui de leur affirmation comme acteur essentiel d'un développement économique fortement encadré par les pouvoirs publics, à un moment où l'intervention de l'État dans l'économie paraissait naturelle. Les entreprises publiques sont alors, à côté des administrations, l'un des fleurons dans la panoplie des acteurs publics. Grands services publics de réseau, établissements de crédits et entreprises industrielles constituent un vaste ensemble, tantôt plus centralisé comme en France

---

* Auteur de *L'économie des besoins*, Éditions Odile Jacob, Paris, 2013.

et au Royaume-Uni, tantôt plus proches de l'échelon local comme en Allemagne ou en Autriche et leur rôle aura été déterminant, d'abord dans la période de reconstruction de l'après-guerre, puis pour mettre en place, au cours des « Trente Glorieuses », les bases du développement.

Est venu ensuite un second temps, celui de la remise en cause, au nom d'un néolibéralisme qui a progressivement envahi la pensée économique. L'entreprise publique est dans le collimateur de la vision dominante. Elle subit les coups de boutoir qui lui sont assénés au nom du consensus de Washington et du *New Public Management*. La supériorité intrinsèque de la gestion privée est érigée en dogme. En Europe la présence de l'entreprise publique reste tolérée mais on lui fait obligation de se banaliser – c'est la doctrine absurde de l'investisseur privé avisé sur le comportement duquel l'État actionnaire devrait calquer son action – et on entretient autour d'elle une suspicion permanente de violation des règles de concurrence. En découlent des programmes massifs de privatisation, parfois voulus, ailleurs imposés, dans les États de l'Union.

Nous sommes entrés maintenant dans un troisième temps, celui de la résilience. L'entreprise publique a résisté. Même si son champ s'est restreint, elle est toujours là. L'intérêt général continue à pointer son nez, au travers de l'enchevêtrement mondialisé des échanges marchands. La crise et la menace d'effondrement des systèmes bancaires ont entraîné un regain momentané de nationalisations. Mais le mouvement est plus profond et il est bien mis en valeur dans les deux volets du projet de recherche du Ciriec pilotée du CIRIEC par Philippe Bance, Luc Bernier, Massimo Florio et Gabriel Obermann. Les études de cas recensées dans ce livre doivent en effet être rapprochées des analyses transversales qui ont été menées parallèlement et qui feront l'objet de publications dans plusieurs revues scientifiques. On voit ainsi se dessiner un tableau complexe et instructif.

Les études de cas nous montrent que l'entreprise publique est un instrument malléable, capable d'évoluer, de s'adapter, de se moderniser, qu'elle est susceptible de répondre à des attentes très diverses et qu'elle peut associer dans sa gouvernance les intérêts de multiples parties prenantes. Loin de constituer pour elle un handicap, son hybridité est une force. La tension qu'elle génère est féconde si elle est bien gérée. La culture que l'entreprise publique a de l'intérêt général, l'engagement de ses personnels, le rapport qu'elle est en mesure d'entretenir avec la société civile sont des atouts valorisables.

Les analyses transversales, de leur côté, révèlent qu'il n'y a pas aujourd'hui dans le monde un mouvement à sens unique de restriction du secteur public. Vues à l'échelle de la planète, privatisations et publicisations se balancent dans un équilibre relatif, variable selon les activités et les pays concernés. On voit la poussée des participations publiques réapparaître là même où l'on s'y attendait le moins, comme aujourd'hui en France dans le domaine de la politique industrielle. Et il est clair que l'entreprise publique reste un recours possible face à de nouvelles crises, qu'il s'agisse d'une crise économique de l'ordre de celle que l'on a connue en 2008 ou de la survenance de dérèglements climatiques majeurs qui rendraient nécessaire le déploiement au niveau mondial de moyens d'intervention nouveaux à rentabilité aléatoire.

L'avenir de l'entreprise publique dépend désormais de sa capacité à maintenir sa spécificité, son originalité. Il lui faut, entre pressions libérales et exigences citoyennes, tenir fermement les deux bouts de la chaîne, savoir faire face aux réalités du marché tout en restant fidèle à sa mission d'intérêt général.

Secteur public et secteur privé ne sont pas deux mondes différents. Ils sont étroitement imbriqués et peuvent s'influencer l'un l'autre. Le public peut trouver des exemples utiles dans les méthodes de gestion du privé. Le privé gagne à reconnaître sa responsabilité sociale. L'un comme l'autre ont aujourd'hui une vision internationale de leur développement. Ils peuvent coopérer, comme le montrent plusieurs des études présentées dans ce livre. L'entreprise publique n'est pas un oiseau rare isolé dans sa cage. Elle vit sur le marché. Elle en connaît les pratiques et doit savoir les mettre en œuvre à bon escient.

Mais, ce faisant, elle ne peut perdre un instant de vue la mission dont elle est investie. Sa vocation, même si l'exigence d'un équilibre dynamique s'impose à elle comme à toute autre entreprise, n'est pas d'enrichir ses actionnaires. Elle a une mission publique, elle fournit des services collectifs, elle est un acteur de l'économie des besoins. À ce titre, et indépendamment des objectifs sectoriels qui lui sont assignés, elle doit toujours être, d'une manière ou d'une autre, en quête de plus d'égalité dans le bénéfice de ses prestations, d'une meilleure qualité des services qu'elle rend aux diverses catégories de la population, d'une plus grande convivialité avec toutes les parties prenantes du monde politique économique et social et de la société civile.

Aucune des entreprises publiques présentées dans cet ouvrage ne réussit sans doute à satisfaire toutes ces exigences. Mais il n'est pas une d'entre elles qui ne s'y essaye d'une manière ou d'une autre, avec des succès bien sûr inégaux. Le panorama ainsi dressé n'est pas exhaustif. Des différenciations peuvent se faire jour. De nouvelles variétés peuvent apparaître. Mais ce qui caractérise l'entreprise publique, association d'une mission d'intérêt général et d'une action sur le marché, est bien une nécessité durable.

La plante reste vivace et continuera sans nul doute à diversifier et enrichir le jardin de l'économie.

The Future of Public Enterprise
Another Look at an Old Idea

Luc BERNIER

ENAP

Massimo FLORIO

University of Milan, Italy

Introduction

Despite the large-scale privatisations over the last three decades (Bognetti and Obermann, 2008), Governments, either at national or local level, still own or partly-own a wide range of organisations providing public services (and of course other functions). They have also created new ones. For several reasons, privatisation policies have left under the control of Government a core of public enterprises. The question arises: how should Governments define the missions, the performance criteria, and the governance mechanisms of the old and newer public enterprises in a changing environment?

CIRIEC's International Scientific Commission on Public Services/ Public Enterprises has launched an international research project to revive the subject of public enterprise as an important field of analysis in the perspective of public economics and of social sciences in general. Special issues of *Journal of Economic Policy Reform* (2014) and of the *Annals of Public and Cooperative Economics* (2015) have been published or will be in the near future in relation to this book that is an essential part of this project. The book includes fifteen cases studies that have been presented at the Milan European Economy Workshop in June 2013 that has been co-financed by the funds of the Jean Monnet Chair of European Union Industrial Policy and CIRIEC.

This introduction presents the context, rationales, concepts, scope of the analysis, methodology of the project that have lead to these cases studies that are presented in the following chapters. At the end of the book, a general conclusion presents the lessons learned.

Context

According to Christiansen (2011), who reports the results of a wide data collection exercise, State-owned or partly State-owned enterprises (SOE) in the OECD Members States employ more than 9 million people, are worth USD 3 trillions in terms of net assets, and are mostly concentrated in the network industries and the financial sectors. In absolute terms, countries as diverse as the USA, Japan, France, Italy, UK, Poland, Turkey, Canada, just to mention some, stand out as the hosts of important SOEs. These include mostly public utilities, but – following the recent global crisis – also temporarily, for example, a major car manufacturer in the USA (General Motors), one of the biggest banks of the world (Royal Bank of Scotland), and other entities as well as insurance companies.

The OECD survey is incomplete in terms of country coverage, and of type of firms. For example, the very large number of municipally-owned utilities in Germany or in the Scandinavian countries are not covered. Some information at country level is provided by CEEP (2010), which focuses, however, on the different issue of mapping the provision of services of general interest in Europe. Thus, the exact definition and statistical information on contemporary public enterprises are relatively un-surveyed.

Nevertheless, it is beyond doubt that Governments in Europe and elsewhere (fully or partly) own a large number of organisations providing public services. These include inter alia electricity and gas supply, telecommunications, postal services, water and sewage, waste collection, local transport, railways, ports and airports, and several others. In many countries, core financial players are under the control of Governments, including major banks, insurance companies, pension funds, etc. Social services, such as health, education, childcare, vocational training, etc. are still widely supplied by public organizations, in some cases as trusts, public corporations, public-private-partnerships (PPPs).

In this book, we shall refer to "public enterprises", in the broad meaning of organisations (a) directly producing public services, either through liberalized market arrangements or under franchised monopoly, (b) ultimately owned or de facto controlled by public sector entities, (c) with a public mission that can be identified in legislation, regulation, statutes, etc., (d) whose ownership in principle can be shifted to the private sector.

This definition excludes from our scope of research several other organisations:

- manufacturing companies owned directly or indirectly by the public sector;
- departments or agencies, which deliver core government functions (defence, law and order, etc.);
- companies which have been put temporarily under Government control following a bankruptcy, or for other reasons, but for which no public mission can be identified (more on this below).

In this perspective, Governments still own substantial productive assets, recruit managers and employees, and accumulate human capital in the public sector, in activities where private investors actually or potentially operate as well. Is this fact a remnant of past history, due to delays in the privatisation agenda, or is it a symptom that public enterprises will remain with us in the future? And, if the latter holds, how can we explain and forecast the survival of these organizations? The case studies presented here illustrate how varied the experience of public enterprises can be and how they can adapt to changing environments in different parts of the world.

Conceptual Framework

Public Mission – Definition

Given our definition of public enterprises, it is important to distinguish two different issues related to public missions of the organizations to be considered: missions of general interest, and public service missions (CEEP-CIRIEC 2000).

General Interest Goals

Governments always have some broad objectives in terms of macroeconomic and other national policy goals. These include for example policies related to employment, containment of inflation, promotion of research and development, of human capital, of fixed capital accumulation, competition and industrial policies. The internalisation of these objectives from public and private enterprises depends upon laws and other forms of regulation. Historically, public enterprises have been involved in these general interest goals in several ways: for example, they had to sustain public investment, to employ labour in certain regions; they were not allowed to increase their tariffs in times of high inflation, etc. Market opening clearly constrains the potential commitment of public enterprises in these areas of Government intervention. And via regulation, the European Union for example also subjects state aid to scrutiny.

The Public Service Mission

Under a more direct mechanism of control, public enterprises are required to perform certain specific tasks. Here Government ownership may act through hierarchical linkages. While issues of principal-agent relations and of asymmetric information have been discussed in the context of any regulated organisation, public enterprises are closer to the public principal, and hierarchy is a more effective mechanism than under private ownership. Specific forms of universal service obligations, in principle, can be applied to any service provider, including the private ones, but the direct linkage between Ministries, regional Governments, Mayors and public service providers is a powerful internalisation mechanism.

Research Object and Proposed Methodological Approach

The traditional normative theory of public enterprise started often from a set of assumptions, such as statutory monopoly at national or local level, the direct relationship between public planning and service provision, symmetric information between principals and agents, departmental regulation of prices, etc. These assumptions are less realistic today. In contrast, contemporary public enterprises are often operating in the context of mixed oligopoly, exposure to international markets, regulation by independent authorities, information asymmetries, and a less close relationship with public policy making. In many cases the legal arrangements for public enterprises have changed as well, from public sector entities subject to administrative law toward corporate entities subject to civil law, applicable in similar ways to privately owned organisations.

If public enterprises are to survive in the next decades, what kind of predictions and prescriptions can be distilled by modern public economics theory, and by the advancement of other social sciences, in order to improve their efficiency and effectiveness? Can we learn from privatisation and re-nationalisation? This book offers a few answers that will have to be completed by future research.

One possible approach to look at these two broad questions (actual missions and normative theory) is to focus on *case studies of contemporary public enterprises*. In an evolutionary perspective, organisations which have been able to adapt themselves to the new post-privatisation/liberalisation environment may suggest lessons to be learned, drawing from their resilience and change in the new context. There is also something to learn from failures in the adaptation process and of mixed results.

The most promising candidate case studies have been selected based on a call for proposals. The number of selected organizations does not always need to be high. Albert Hirschman built his seminal book "Development Projects Observed" around eleven case histories. Elinor Ostrom also used a limited number of case histories in her work on common goods. There are several other examples in social sciences of influential research based on limited, but well-chosen and carefully analysed case studies, and we should be inspired by former research based on this approach.[1] The fifteen case studies presented here can also be supplemented by recent work built in similar fashion (see Lethbridge, 2014; Macdonald, 2014).

The case studies focus on a set of specific themes including at least the six following ones.

Public Mission, Market Opening, and Performance

Under market opening, a plurality of actors enter the arena of public services provision, from multinationals to NGOs, from public-private partnerships (PPPs) to municipally or State-owned enterprises, and compete in some way. They have different performance criteria: financial profitability for private investors, social welfare for public enterprises, or combined criteria for PPPs. Competition can take the form of competition in the market, or for the market (à la Demsetz). How can missions of general interest, and specific public service missions, be accommodated in this environment? Does this plurality of players lead to stable equilibria? Under which conditions does public ownership welfare-dominate other arrangements? Is market opening desirable *per se* or is it wasteful in some cases? Models of mixed oligopoly have tried to answer the questions, and some empirical studies have been carried out in this area. There is however less evidence on the adaptation necessary to the public enterprise to survive the change. Is in fact the adaptation destroying the public missions of the organisation? Or can the general interest and public service missions be preserved within the new environments and strategies? What can we learn from case studies of contemporary and past arrangements under market opening?

Governance

This topic has been widely researched for private organisations in recent years, also because of the perceived wide failures of arrangements in such industries as banking, or in large listed companies, etc. Do we have any evidence that some governance mechanisms are more effective for public enterprises? Is the huge literature on corporate governance of large private firms relevant to public enterprises, with citizens as the ultimate owners instead of shareholders and consumers? The OECD and the World Bank have occasionally suggested corporate governance

---

[1] See for example, World Bank, 2005; Flyvbjerg, 2006.

principle for public enterprises, when privatisation is unfeasible or undesirable. The New Public Management (NPM) literature has suggested quasi-market mechanisms. There are traditional and new questions in this domain. Who appoints managers? To whom are they accountable? How to pay them? How to measure the performance? Should industrial relations be designed to imitate the private sector? To what extent should employees and consumers be represented in the governance of public enterprises?[2]

Regulation

The relationship between public enterprises, regulators and policy makers is now perhaps more complex than it was in the past. Do independent regulators, which after all are public sector employees, bring an added value when public enterprises are concerned, or do they add to the transactions costs of their management? Do managers tend to capture regulators? How do regulators act when they face a mixed oligopoly? The current regulatory economics literature focuses more on the issue of "incumbents" and asymmetric regulation, but often tends to skip the paradoxes arising from different public sector entities, which interact in the market. It would be important to understand the nature of the relationship between regulators, Ministries, and public enterprise managers, as this is perhaps the most important change in the architecture of government that has changed the role of public enterprises, beyond the Morrisonian tradition of arms' length control.[3]

Finance

Public enterprises used to be financed in three ways, according to countries and sectors: transfers from the Treasury (i.e. general taxation), bond finance, and tariffs. One core aspect of the traditional doctrine of public enterprise was optimal pricing, e.g. the Ramsey-Boiteux view of the case of budget constrained firms (which is the normal case under EU state aid legislation). In the Laffont-Tirole framework the optimal pricing mechanism has been widely modified by principal-agent issues. In practice, there is limited evidence that price equilibria in regulated mixed oligopoly have converged towards socially efficient pricing of a sort. Which is or should be the pricing strategy, if any, of public enterprises in the current circumstances? This issue is closely related to the next topic. Transfers from the Treasury are now limited by State aid regulations in the EU, but exceptions are still possible. Bond finance,

---

[2] See for example Palcic *et al., On employees' ownership in the transition from public to private ownership*, 2011.

[3] This is common law term (see e.g. http://www.duhaime.org/LegalDictionary/A/ ArmsLength.aspx), which needs a careful re-thinking today in our context.

assisted or not by guarantees from the state, is also a current opportunity. In some cases, indirect international bond finance is possible (e.g. by the European Investment Bank (EIB), European Bank for Reconstruction and Development (EBRD), World Bank). What should be the optimal financial mix for the future, learning from the experience?

Distribution and Social Welfare

Another core concern of the traditional theory was about distributive issues. Cross-subsidies of tariffs were used to force universal coverage under balanced budget, and other mechanisms were in place to ensure the distributive mission of public enterprises. Do public enterprises still perform a role in redistribution of welfare, or has this role been definitively delegated to taxation/subsidies and other mechanisms? There is considerable literature on these issues,[4] for example related to fuel poverty, but the way social affordability of public services should be achieved is still lacking an adequate frame of analysis.

Implementing the General Interest Goals

Public enterprises, as mentioned, and recently restated by Millward (2011), had also some political functions, related to national or local strategies. This was or still is also a matter of perceptions by users and by decision-makers. Examples are issues of territorial cohesion, security of supply, strategic considerations. Are some of these issues still important today for public enterprises in some sectors?

Others

Additional topics include, for example:

- the consequences for public enterprises when owners or stakeholders are spread over different Government levels and jurisdictions;
- human resources, including education and background of managers, incentive pay, role of trade unions and industrial relations in general;
- corruption and quality of institutions;
- climate change, environmental considerations, sustainable development, etc.

Scope of the analysis

As mentioned in section 2, in this project we use the label "public enterprise" in a broad meaning. We encompass in the scope of the

---

[4]   See for example Clifton *et al.,* 2011.

analysis different levels of Government, including local Government, but in principle also inter-governmental agencies which cannot be considered as belonging to the "State".[5]

Public enterprises analysed in this book cover various sectors such as water, electricity, financing. They are in both Americas and Europe. They also come from very different administrative traditions such as the German and the Italian or the Canadian.

The case studies have been written around a common template which considers the following topics within a unified framework:

- Identification of the enterprise
- History
- Public mission
- Operations
- Performance
- Governance
- Regulation
- Tariffs, Investment, Finance and Distributional Issues with respect to Public Missions
- an Open Section, and
- Conclusions and Lessons Learned.

Methodology

The proposed research approach for the wider project was divided in three. First, critical reviews of literature on the recent advances in the theory and empirical analysis of public enterprise in general (not limited to one sector or country/continent); two, the selection of interesting case studies of contemporary successful or less successful public enterprises, focussing on their internalised public missions, performance and governance, and analysing them according to the annexed template; and synthesis and lessons learned, with a focus on policy implications for the future.

The collection of case studies is the core of the research project and of this book. Participants to the project were asked that each report should focus on the last ten to twenty years of the selected public enterprise, and should achieve a good understanding of the performance of the enterprise, its governance mechanisms, relationships with government

---

[5]   See e.g. Warner, *About inter-municipal entities in the US*, 2011; Bernier, *About federal versus provincial public organizations in Canada*, 2011.

and regulators, competition issues, pricing and finance, management and principal-agent problems, organisation's role in terms of social identity and cohesion, etc. The case studies, crucially, needed a combination of desk research from a variety of sources (including existing studies, company reports and websites, press, etc.) and of interviews of different stakeholders. In some cases this can be evaluated in terms of social costs and benefits in quantitative terms, but in other cases a more qualitative assessment may be necessary (Del Bo and Florio, 2012). The case studies presented in this book reflect these various possibilities.

Organisation of the Book

The book is divided in three sections according to the nature of the industries.

In the first section, the five chapters discuss public enterprises in the water and sewage sector. These enterprises are in four different European countries and in Peru. They present an interesting portrait of the transformation of the industry under various administrative traditions and regulatory frameworks. In Paris, it is the return to the State, two cases of renationalisation, a topic that has to be better studied in the future. In other cases, it is the adaptation to changing conditions with the perpetuation of the necessity of offering the basic service to the population.

In the second series of cases studies, we give an overview of some transportation services. From how local transport is organised in Vienna and Brussels, we move to the essential link offered by British Columbia ferries on the west coast of Canada to the as important economic role played by airports in modern Ireland.

In the third section of the book, we look at various public enterprises that also illustrate the possibilities of the formula. Ontario has created a new agency to deal with pressing infrastructure needs. The French postal service has had to face the difficulties acknowledged by all postal systems around the world and found new solutions to a declining industry. The two Italian cases that follow are indicative of the tensions to adapt to the new reality of their economic sector and the need to be more efficient. In Quebec, a financial institution created in the modernisation drive of the 1960s has redefined itself several times to continue its intervention in the economy. Finally, the *Stadtwerke Köln* is an intriguing case of an integrated public conglomerate that offers many services to the population of the city.

The lessons learned from these cases are summarised in the conclusion of the book and are linked to some of the recent development in the scientific literature on the topic and to the case-study methodology literature. Public enterprises are important in this century as they have been before the privatisation drives that started in the 1980s but they are different from their predecessors, among other things in terms of governance and performance. The cases presented in this book offer a picture from various industries and countries.

As also discussed in the conclusion, although we should not generalise too largely from case studies, important lessons and hypotheses can be drawn from this collective research effort for further studies and public policies of the future.

L'avenir de l'entreprise publique
Revisiter une vieille idée

Luc Bernier et Massimo Florio

Introduction

En dépit des privatisations à grande échelle qui ont eu lieu au cours de ces trois dernières décennies (Bognetti and Obermann, 2008), les gouvernements nationaux ou locaux détiennent toujours l'intégralité ou une partie de toute une série d'organisations fournissant des services publics (mais ayant aussi d'autres fonctions). Ils en ont aussi créé de nouvelles. Les politiques de privatisation ont, pour plusieurs raisons, laissé un noyau d'entreprises publiques sous le contrôle du gouvernement. La question se pose de savoir comment les gouvernements définiront les missions, les critères de performance et les mécanismes de gouvernance des anciennes entreprises publiques ainsi que des plus récentes dans un environnement en mutation.

La Commission scientifique internationale Services publics/Entreprises publiques du CIRIEC a initié un projet de recherche international afin de relancer le sujet de l'entreprise publique comme domaine d'analyse important du point de vue de l'économie publique et des sciences sociales en général. Les éditions spéciales du *Journal of Economic Policy Reform* (2014) et des *Annals of Public and Cooperative Economics* (2015) ont été publiées ou le seront dans un avenir proche dans le contexte du présent livre qui constitue une partie essentielle de ce projet. Cet ouvrage comporte quinze études de cas qui ont été présentées lors de l'atelier Économie européenne de Milan en juin 2013, qui a été cofinancé à l'aide de fonds de la chaire Jean Monnet de politique industrielle de l'Union européenne et du CIRIEC.

Cette introduction présente le contexte, les raisons, les concepts, le champ d'analyse ainsi que la méthodologie du projet qui ont mené aux études de cas présentées dans les chapitres suivants. La conclusion à la fin de l'ouvrage résume les enseignements à retenir.

Contexte

Selon Christiansen (2011), qui présente les résultats d'un vaste exercice de collecte de données sur le sujet, les entreprises partiellement ou totalement détenues par l'État dans les États membres de l'OCDE emploient plus de 9 millions de personnes, elles ont une valeur de 3 milliards de dollars en termes d'actif net et se concentrent principalement dans les secteurs financiers et des industries de réseau. En termes absolus, des pays aussi différents que les États-Unis, le Japon, la France, l'Italie, le Royaume-Uni, la Pologne, la Turquie et le Canada, pour n'en mentionner que quelques-uns, se distinguent par leurs importantes entreprises d'État. Celles-ci incluent surtout des services publics, mais depuis la dernière crise mondiale, elles comptent aussi temporairement par exemple, un grand constructeur automobile aux USA (*General Motors*), une des plus grandes banques du monde (*Royal Bank of Scotland*), ainsi que d'autres banques et compagnies d'assurance.

L'étude de l'OCDE n'est pas complète quant aux pays et aux types d'entreprises étudiés. À titre d'exemple, un nombre significatif de services municipaux en Allemagne ou dans les pays scandinaves n'est pas couvert. Certaines informations nationales sont fournies par le CEEP (2010), qui met toutefois l'accent sur un autre aspect, à savoir la cartographie de la fourniture de services d'intérêt général en Europe. Relativement peu d'études portent donc sur la définition précise des entreprises publiques contemporaines et les informations statistiques afférentes.

Il ne fait aucun doute que les gouvernements – en Europe et ailleurs – détiennent (partiellement ou totalement) un nombre significatif d'organisations fournissant des services publics, parmi lesquels entre autres la fourniture de gaz et d'électricité, les télécommunications, les services postaux, l'eau et les eaux usées, la collecte des déchets, les transports locaux, les chemins de fer, les ports et aéroports, etc. Dans de nombreux pays, les opérateurs financiers clés sont sous le contrôle des gouvernements, parmi lesquels de grandes banques, des compagnies d'assurance, des fonds de pension, etc. Les services sociaux, tels que les soins de santé, l'éducation, les services de garde d'enfants, la formation professionnelle, etc. sont dans une grande mesure assurés par des organismes publics, dans certains cas par des trusts, des entreprises publiques, des partenariats public-privé (PPP).

– Dans le présent ouvrage, nous nous référons aux « entreprises publiques » au sens large d'organisations (a) produisant directement des services publics soit au travers d'accords libéralisés soit dans le cadre de monopoles franchisés, (b) détenues en fin de compte ou contrôlées de facto par des organismes du secteur public, (c) avec une mission publique pouvant être identifiée dans la législation, la réglementation, les statuts, etc., (d) dont la propriété peut en principe être transmise au secteur privé.

Cette définition exclut plusieurs organisations de notre champ de recherche :

- les entreprises manufacturières détenues directement ou indirectement par le secteur public,
- les départements ou agences, qui exercent des fonctions publiques essentielles (défense, ordre public, etc.),
- les entreprises qui ont momentanément été mises sous le contrôle de l'État suite à une faillite ou pour d'autres raisons, mais pour lesquelles aucune mission publique ne peut être identifiée (voir ci-dessous).

Dans cette perspective, les gouvernements détiennent encore d'importants actifs de production, recrutent des gestionnaires et des salariés, et accumulent du capital humain dans le secteur public, dans des secteurs d'activité où opèrent, ou peuvent aussi opérer des investisseurs privés. S'agit-il là d'un vestige de l'histoire dû au retard enregistré sur le programme de privatisation ou est-ce un signe que les entreprises publiques subsisteront à l'avenir ? Dans cette dernière hypothèse, comment expliquer et prévoir la survie de ces organisations ? Les études de cas présentées ici illustrent combien l'expérience des entreprises publiques peut être différente, et la façon dont celles-ci peuvent s'adapter à des environnements en mutation dans différentes parties du monde.

Cadre conceptuel

Mission publique – définition

Vu notre définition des entreprises publiques, il est important de faire la distinction entre deux aspects différents liés aux missions publiques des organisations en question : les missions d'intérêt général et les missions de service public (CEEP-CIRIEC 2000).

Objectifs d'intérêt général

Les gouvernements poursuivent toujours des objectifs généraux sur le plan macroéconomique ou au niveau des autres politiques nationales. Mentionnons à titre d'exemple les politiques d'emploi, de maîtrise de l'inflation, de promotion de la recherche et du développement, les politiques relatives au capital humain, à l'accumulation de capital fixe, les politiques industrielles et de concurrence. L'internalisation de ces objectifs des entreprises publiques et privées dépend des législations et autres formes de réglementation en vigueur. Historiquement, les entreprises publiques ont été impliquées de diverses façons dans ces objectifs d'intérêt général : à titre d'exemple, elles ont dû soutenir les investissements publics, employer de la main-d'œuvre dans certaines régions ; elles n'étaient pas autorisées à accroître leurs tarifs en période d'inflation élevée, etc. L'ouverture du marché restreint clairement l'engagement potentiel des entreprises publiques dans ces domaines où l'État intervient. En outre, l'Union européenne contrôle, par exemple, les aides d'État par le biais de ses réglementations.

La mission de service public

Dans le cadre d'un mécanisme de contrôle plus direct, les entreprises publiques sont priées d'assumer certaines tâches. Dans ce cas, l'appartenance à l'État peut agir au travers des liens hiérarchiques. Les questions de relations principal-agent et d'information asymétrique ont été discutées dans le cadre des organisations réglementées ; les entreprises publiques sont plus proches du principal public, et la hiérarchie est un mécanisme plus efficace que dans le cadre de la propriété privée. En principe, des formes spécifiques d'obligations de service universel peuvent s'appliquer à n'importe quel prestataire de service, y compris privé, mais le lien direct entre les ministères, gouvernements régionaux, maires et prestataires de services publics est un mécanisme d'internalisation puissant.

Objet de recherche et approche méthodologique proposée

La théorie normative traditionnelle de l'entreprise publique partait souvent d'une série d'hypothèses, telles que le monopole légal au niveau national ou local, le lien direct entre la planification publique et la prestation de service, l'information symétrique entre le principal et l'agent, la réglementation des prix, etc. Ces hypothèses sont moins réalistes aujourd'hui. En revanche, les entreprises publiques contemporaines opèrent souvent dans le contexte d'un oligopole mixte, d'une exposition aux marchés internationaux, d'une réglementation par des autorités indépendantes, d'asymétries de l'information et d'une relation moins étroite avec la prise de décision au niveau public. Dans de nombreux cas, les dispositions légales régissant les entreprises publiques ont aussi changé, les entités du secteur public soumises au droit administratif devenant des sociétés relevant du droit civil qui s'applique aussi aux organisations privées.

Si les entreprises publiques doivent survivre au cours des prochaines décennies, quelle prévision ou prescription peut-on extraire de la théorie de l'économie publique moderne ou des progrès des sciences sociales en vue d'accroître leur efficacité et efficience ? Pouvons-nous tirer un enseignement de la privatisation et de la renationalisation ? Cet ouvrage propose quelques réponses qui seront à compléter par de futures recherches.

Pour aborder ces deux grandes questions (missions effectives et théorie normative), une approche consiste à se concentrer sur des études de cas d'entreprises publiques contemporaines. Dans une perspective évolutive, les organisations qui ont été à même de s'adapter au nouvel environnement d'après la privatisation/libéralisation, peuvent proposer des enseignements sur la base de leur résilience et changement dans le nouveau contexte. On peut également tirer des leçons des échecs enregistrés dans le cadre du processus d'adaptation ou des résultats mitigés.

Les études de cas les plus prometteuses ont été sélectionnées suite à un appel d'offres. Le nombre d'organisations sélectionnées ne doit pas toujours être élevé. Albert Hirschman a rédigé son ouvrage de référence « Development Projects Observed » (Projets de développement observés) autour de onze cas. Elinor Ostrom a aussi utilisé un nombre limité de cas dans son ouvrage sur les biens communs. Il existe quelques autres exemples dans le domaine des sciences sociales de recherches influentes basées sur un nombre restreint d'études de cas bien choisis et soigneusement analysés. Nous devrions nous inspirer des recherches antérieures basées sur cette approche[1]. Les quinze études de cas présentées ici peuvent aussi être complétées par des travaux plus récents effectués de façon similaire (voir Lethbridge, 2014 ; Macdonald, 2014).

Les études de cas sont axées sur une série de thèmes spécifiques incluant au moins les six thèmes suivants.

Mission publique, ouverture du marché et performance

Dans le cadre de l'ouverture du marché, une pluralité d'acteurs se lancent dans la fourniture de services publics, depuis les multinationales jusqu'aux ONG, depuis les partenariats public-privé (PPP) jusqu'aux entreprises d'État ou municipales, et se font d'une certaine façon concurrence. Ces opérateurs ont des critères de performance différents : rentabilité financière pour les investisseurs privés, bien-être social pour les entreprises publiques, ou combinaison de critères pour les PPP. La concurrence peut prendre la forme d'une concurrence dite « sur le marché » ou « pour le marché » (à la Demsetz). Comment les missions d'intérêt général et les missions de service public spécifiques peuvent-elles être assurées dans cet environnement ? La pluralité d'acteurs entraîne-t-elle un équilibre stable ? À quelles conditions la propriété publique apporte-t-elle davantage de bien-être par rapport à d'autres modes de propriétés ? L'ouverture du marché est-elle souhaitable en soi ou est-elle peu rentable dans certains cas ? Des modèles d'oligopole mixte ont tenté de répondre à ces questions, et des études empiriques ont été effectuées dans ce domaine. Il existe néanmoins moins de preuve quant au besoin d'adaptation de l'entreprise publique pour pouvoir survivre face

---

[1] Voir par exemple, Banque mondiale, 2005 ; Flyvbjerg, 2006.

à ces changements. L'adaptation anéantit-elle les missions publiques de l'organisme ? Ou bien les missions d'intérêt général et de service public peuvent-elles être préservées dans ce nouvel environnement et face à ces nouvelles stratégies ? Quels enseignements pouvons-nous tirer des études de cas portant sur les accords contemporains ou antérieurs dans le cadre de l'ouverture du marché ?

Gouvernance

Des organismes privés ont procédé à de nombreuses études sur ce sujet au cours de ces dernières années, entre autres en raison des échecs manifestes au niveau des accords dans des secteurs tels que le secteur bancaire ou dans de grandes entreprises cotées en bourse. Est-il prouvé que certains mécanismes de gouvernance sont plus efficaces pour les entreprises publiques ? L'abondante littérature relative à la gouvernance de grandes entreprises privées s'applique-t-elle aux entreprises publiques, avec des citoyens comme propriétaires ultimes à la place des actionnaires et des consommateurs ? L'OCDE et la Banque mondiale ont parfois proposé d'appliquer le principe de gouvernement d'entreprise aux entreprises publiques, lorsque la privatisation n'était pas faisable ou pas souhaitable. La documentation sur la nouvelle administration publique propose des mécanismes de quasi-marché. Des questions traditionnelles ainsi que de nouvelles questions se posent à cet égard. Qui nomme les directeurs ? Devant qui ces derniers doivent-ils rendre compte de leurs actes ? Comment les payer ? Comment mesurer leur performance ? Les relations industrielles doivent-elles être conçues de façon à imiter le secteur privé ? Dans quelle mesure les salariés et consommateurs doivent-ils être représentés au niveau de la gouvernance des entreprises publiques ?[2]

Réglementation

La relation entre les entreprises publiques, les régulateurs et les décideurs politiques est peut-être plus complexe aujourd'hui que dans le passé. Les régulateurs indépendants, qui après tout sont des employés du secteur public, apportent-ils une valeur ajoutée lorsqu'il s'agit d'entreprises publiques ou augmentent-ils les coûts de transaction de leur administration ? Enregistre-t-on une tendance à la capture de régulation de la part des directeurs ? Comment les régulateurs agissent-ils face à un oligopole mixte ? La littérature actuelle relative à l'économie de la régulation se concentre davantage sur les « opérateurs en place » (incumbents) et la régulation asymétrique, mais a souvent tendance à

---

[2]   Voir par exemple Palcic *et al., L'Actionnariat salarié dans la transition de la propriété publique vers la propriété privée*, 2011.

omettre les paradoxes résultant des différentes entités du secteur public qui interagissent sur le marché. Il serait utile de comprendre la nature de la relation entre les régulateurs, les ministères et les directeurs d'entreprise publique étant donné qu'il s'agit peut-être là du changement le plus important au niveau de l'infrastructure de gouvernement qui a transformé le rôle des entreprises publiques au-delà de la tradition morrisonienne du contrôle à distance[3].

Finances

Les entreprises publiques étaient généralement financées de trois façons en fonction des pays et des secteurs : transferts du Trésor (i.e. fiscalité générale), financement par obligations et tarifs. La tarification optimale était un aspect fondamental de la doctrine traditionnelle de l'entreprise publique, par ex. la tarification de Ramsey-Boiteux sous contrainte d'équilibre budgétaire (ce qui est normalement le cas en vertu de la législation de l'Union européenne sur les aides d'État). Dans le cadre d'analyse de Laffont et Tirole, le mécanisme de tarification optimale a été significativement modifié par les enjeux de relation principal-agent. Dans la pratique, il y a peu de données prouvant le fait que les équilibres de prix dans un oligopole mixte régulé ont convergé vers une tarification socialement efficiente. Quelle doit être ou devrait être, le cas échéant, la stratégie de tarification des entreprises publiques dans les circonstances actuelles ? Cette question est étroitement liée au sujet suivant. Les transferts du Trésor sont limités à l'heure actuelle par les réglementations de l'Union européenne relatives aux aides d'État, mais des exceptions sont toujours possibles. Le financement par obligations, assisté ou non par des garanties de l'État, est aussi une possibilité à l'heure actuelle. Dans certains cas, un financement international indirect par obligations est possible (par exemple, par la Banque européenne d'investissement (BEI), par la Banque européenne pour la reconstruction et le développement (BERD), la Banque mondiale). Sur la base de l'expérience, quel serait le mix financier optimal à l'avenir ?

Distribution et bien-être social

Les problèmes de distribution étaient une autre préoccupation fondamentale de la théorie traditionnelle. Les subventions croisées de tarifs ont été utilisées pour imposer une couverture universelle dans le cadre d'un budget équilibré ; on a, en outre, recouru à d'autres mécanismes pour assurer la mission distributive des entreprises publiques. Les entreprises publiques jouent-elles encore un rôle dans la redistribution

---

[3] Il s'agit d'un terme du droit coutumier (voir par ex. http://www.duhaime.org/Legal Dictionary/A/ArmsLength.aspx) qui doit être mûrement repensé dans le contexte actuel.

du bien-être social ou bien ce rôle a-t-il été définitivement délégué à la fiscalité et aux subventions ainsi qu'à d'autres mécanismes ? Ces aspects font l'objet d'une littérature abondante[4], comme par exemple celle sur la pauvreté énergétique, mais il n'y a toujours pas de cadre d'analyse adéquat pour étudier la façon dont les services publics pourraient être socialement abordables.

Mise en œuvre des objectifs d'intérêt général

Comme mentionné, et réaffirmé récemment par Millward (2011), les entreprises publiques exerçaient aussi certaines fonctions politiques liées aux stratégies nationales ou locales. C'était, et c'est toujours une question de perception de la part des utilisateurs et décideurs politiques. Les questions de cohésion territoriale, de sécurité d'approvisionnement, des considérations stratégiques en sont quelques exemples. Certaines de ces questions revêtent-elles encore de l'importance, à l'heure actuelle, pour les entreprises publiques de certains secteurs ?

Divers

Parmi les autres sujets, mentionnons par exemple :

– les conséquences pour les entreprises publiques de la dissémination des propriétaires ou actionnaires sur différents niveaux de gouvernement ou sur différentes juridictions ;
– les ressources humaines, y compris l'éducation et la formation des directeurs, la rémunération incitative, le rôle des syndicats et les relations industrielles en général ;
– la corruption et la qualité des institutions ;
– le changement climatique, des considérations environnementales, le développement durable, etc.

Champ d'analyse

Comme indiqué à la section 2, nous utilisons la notion « d'entreprise publique » au sens large du terme dans ce projet. Le champ d'analyse englobe différents niveaux de gouvernement, y compris le gouvernement local, mais en principe également des organismes intergouvernementaux qui ne peuvent être considérés comme appartenant à « l'État »[5].

Les entreprises publiques analysées dans le présent ouvrage couvrent divers secteurs tels que l'eau, l'électricité, le financement. Elles sont situées aux États-Unis et en Europe. Elles ont également des traditions

---

[4]   Voir par exemple Clifton *et al.*, 2011.

[5]   Voir par exemple Warner, *Les entités inter-municipales aux États-Unis*, 2011 ; Bernier, *Les organismes publics fédéraux et provinciaux au Canada*, 2011.

administratives très différentes telles qu'allemande, italienne ou canadienne.

Les études de cas ont été réalisées sur la base d'un modèle commun prenant en considération les aspects suivants dans un cadre harmonisé :

- identification de l'entreprise ;
- histoire ;
- mission publique ;
- opérations ;
- performance ;
- gouvernance ;
- régulation ;
- tarifs, investissement, finances et aspects distributionnels eu égard aux missions publiques ;
- une section ouverte, et
- conclusions et enseignements tirés.

Méthodologie

L'approche proposée dans le cadre du projet plus large comportait trois parties. La première partie consistait en un examen critique de la littérature relative aux derniers progrès effectués dans le domaine de la théorie et de l'analyse empirique de l'entreprise publique en général (non limitée à un secteur ou pays/continent). La deuxième partie présente une sélection d'études de cas intéressants d'entreprises publiques contemporaines très performantes et moins performantes, en mettant l'accent sur leurs missions publiques internalisées, leur performance et gouvernance, et en les analysant conformément au modèle en annexe ; et enfin, la synthèse et les enseignements tirés, axés sur les implications politiques pour l'avenir.

La compilation d'études de cas constitue la partie essentielle du projet de recherche et de ce livre. Les participants au projet ont été priés d'axer leur rapport sur les dix à vingt dernières années de l'entreprise publique sélectionnée ; ils devaient avoir une bonne compréhension de la performance de l'entreprise, de ses mécanismes de gouvernance, de ses rapports avec le gouvernement et les régulateurs, des questions de concurrence, de la tarification et des finances, de la gestion et des problèmes principal-agent, du rôle de l'organisation en termes d'identité sociale et de cohésion, etc. Il était d'une importance cruciale que les études de cas aient fait l'objet de recherches documentaires dans diverses sources (y compris les études existantes, les rapports et sites internet d'entreprise, la presse, etc.) et d'interviews de diverses parties prenantes. Dans certains cas, ceci peut être évalué en termes de coûts sociaux et d'avantages en termes quantitatifs, mais dans d'autres cas, une évaluation qualitative peut être nécessaire (Del Bo and Florio, 2012). Les études de cas présentées dans cet ouvrage reflètent ces diverses possibilités.

Structure du livre

Ce livre est divisé en trois sections selon la nature des industries.

Dans la première section, les cinq chapitres traitent des entreprises publiques dans le secteur de l'eau et du traitement des eaux usées. Ces entreprises se situent dans quatre pays européens différents et au Pérou. Elles présentent un portrait intéressant de la transformation de l'industrie en fonction des différentes traditions administratives et des différents cadres réglementaires. À Paris comme à Berlin, on assiste à un retour à l'État : deux cas de renationalisation, un sujet qui doit être mieux étudié à l'avenir. Dans d'autres cas, on s'adapte au changement de conditions tout en perpétuant cette nécessité d'offrir un service de base à la population.

Dans la seconde série d'études de cas, nous donnons un aperçu de quelques services de transport. Nous passons de la façon dont le transport local est organisé à Vienne et à Bruxelles aux traversiers en Colombie-Britannique sur la côte ouest du Canada pour ensuite aborder le rôle économique tout aussi important joué par les aéroports dans l'Irlande moderne.

Dans la troisième section, nous analysons diverses entreprises publiques qui illustrent aussi les possibilités qu'offre la formule. L'Ontario a créé un nouvel organisme pour traiter des besoins urgents en matière d'infrastructures. Le service postal français a dû faire face aux mêmes difficultés que les autres systèmes postaux et a trouvé de nouvelles solutions pour ce secteur en déclin. Les deux cas italiens donnent une idée des tensions auxquelles il a fallu faire face pour s'adapter à la nouvelle réalité de leur secteur économique, ainsi que de la nécessité d'être plus efficace. Au Québec, une entreprise financière fondée à l'époque de la vague de modernisation des années 1960 s'est à plusieurs reprises redéfinie pour continuer à intervenir dans l'économie. Enfin, le *Stadtwerke Köln* est le cas fascinant d'un conglomérat public intégré qui offre de nombreux services à la population de la ville.

Les leçons tirées de ces différents cas sont présentées dans la conclusion du livre. Elles sont liées à certains développements récents enregistrés dans la littérature scientifique ainsi qu'à la littérature relative à la méthodologie retenue pour les études de cas. Au cours de ce siècle, les entreprises publiques jouent un rôle important, comme d'ailleurs avant la vague de privatisation qui a commencé dans les années 1980, mais elles se distinguent de celles qui les ont précédées, entre autres en termes de gouvernance et de performance. Les cas présentés dans le présent ouvrage brossent un tableau des divers pays et industries.

Comme élaboré dans la conclusion, même si nous ne pouvons généraliser les études de cas, des enseignements importants et hypothèses peuvent être tirés de cet effort collectif de recherche aux fins d'autres études et de politiques publiques futures.

Références

Bance, P. (1988), « Approche méthodologique de l'économie mixte, propriétés et comportements », in *Annals of Public and Cooperative Economics*, 59, 4, December.

Bance, P. and Bernier, L. (2011), *Contemporary Crisis and Renewal of Public Action : Towards the Emergence of a New Form of Regulation ? / Crise contemporaine et renouveau de l'action publique – Vers l'émergence d'un nouveau mode de régulation ?*, Peter Lang.

Bernier, L. (2011), « The future of public enterprises : Perspectives from the Canadian experience », in *Annals of Public and Cooperative Economics*, vol. 82, n° 4.

Bognetti, G. and Obermann, G. (2008), « Liberalization and privatization of public utilities. Origin of the debate, current issues and challenges for the future », in *Annals of Public and Cooperative Economics*, 79.

CEEP (2010) – Bauby, P. *et al.*, *Public services in the European Union and the 27 Member States. Statistics, organisation and regulations.*

CEEP-CIRIEC (2000), *Services of General Interest in Europe.*

Christiansen, H. (2011), « The size and composition of the SOE sector in Oecd countries », in *OECD Corporate governance working papers*, n° 5.

Clifton, J., Díaz-Fuentes, D., Fernández Gutierrez, M., Revuelta, J. (2011), « Is Market oriented reform producing a "Two-Track" Europe : evidence from electricity and telecommunications », in *Annals of Public and Cooperative Economics*, vol. 82, n° 4.

Del Bo, C. and Florio, M. (2012), « Public Enterprises, planning and policy adoption : three welfare propositions », in *Journal of Economic Policy Reform*, vol. 15, pp. 263-279.

Florio, M. and Fecher, F. (2011), « The future of public enterprises : contribution to a new discourse », in *Annals of Public and Cooperative Economics*, vol. 82, n° 4.

Flyvbjerg, B. (2006), « Five misunderstandings about case-study research », in *Qualitative Enquiry*, vol. 12, n° 2, pp. 219-245.

Golubova, E. (2011), « The impact of greater autonomy on efficiency of work and quality of service providers : a case of vocational education institutions », in *Annals of Public and Cooperative Economics*, vol. 82, n° 4.

Hirschman, A. (1967), *Development Projects Observed*, Brookings Institutions Press.

Kaul, I. (2006), « Une analyse positive des biens publics », in Touffut J.-P., *L'avancée des biens publics, politique de l'intérêt général et de la mondialisation*, Albin Michel.

Laffont, J.-J. and Tirole, J. (1993), *A Theory of Incentives in Regulation and Procurement*, MIT Press.

Lethbridge, J. (2014), « Public enterprises in the halthcare sector : a case study of Queen Elizabeth Hospital, Greenwich, England », in *Journal of Economic Policy Reform*, advanced access.

Macdonald, D. A. (2014), *Rethinking Corporatization and public services in the global south*, London : Z Books.

Millward, R. (2011), « Public enterprise in the modern Western World : an Historical Perspective », in *Annals of Public and Cooperative Economics*, vol. 82, n° 4.

OECD (2005), *Corporate governance of state-owned enterprises. A survey of OECD countries*, Paris.

Ostrom, E. (1990), *Governing the commons : the evolution of institutions for collective actions*, Cambridge University Press.

Palcic, D. and Reeves, E. (2011), « Privatization, Employee Share Ownership and governance : the case of EIRCOM », in *Annals of Public and Cooperative Economics*, vol. 82, n° 4.

Price, D., Pollock, A.M., Brhilikova, P. (2011), « Classification problems and the dividing line between government and the market : an examination of NHS foundation Trust classification in the UK », in *Annals of Public and Cooperative Economics*, vol. 82, n° 4.

Privatization Barometer (2010), *Report 2010*, www.privatizationbarometer.net.

Warner, M.E. (2011), « Competition or cooperation in urban service delivery ? », in *Annals of Public and Cooperative Economics*, vol. 82, n° 4.

World Bank, 2005, « Influential evolution : detailed case studies », The World Bank Operations Evaluation Department, Washington D.C.

PART 1

THE WATER AND SANITATION OR SEWAGE SECTOR

1. Berliner Wasserbetriebe (BWB)

A Story of Privatisation under Financial Stress and Remunicipalisation under Citizen Stress

Christina SCHAEFER & Stephanie WARM

Helmut-Schmidt University/
University of the Armed Forces, Hamburg

1. Introduction

1.1. Introduction and Research Question

Berliner Wasserbetriebe (BWB) is the sole provider of water and wastewater disposal in Berlin. BWB is the largest water supply and wastewater disposal company in Germany and one of the largest employers and investors in Berlin.

After the reunification of Germany, Berlin had to face a lot of challenges causing a growing budget deficit, for example combining the infrastructure of former East and West Berlin, and transferring the employees of East Berlin's public companies and administration.

The late 1980s and 1990s have seen a wave of public fusions and mergers between different public entities in Berlin, such as the different public water and sewage companies. In 1994, the process ended and the BWB was founded as a municipal company including the water infrastructure of East Berlin. In 1999 BWB was partly privatised, so that BWB, as an institution under public law, is part of the privately operating holding *Berlinwasser Holding AG*. In 1999, 50.1% of the shares were held by the State of Berlin, while the international water company Veolia Water and the German energy utility RWE each hold 24.95%. In 2012, the State of Berlin rebought the share of RWE, and in 2013 the negotiations with Veolia Water were completed with the result, that the State of Berlin also buys back Veolia's share with effect on January 2014 – bringing Berlin back the sole ownership of BWB: after a partial privatisation back to a complete remunicipalisation.

Against this background, to launch the deeper analysis of the case, the opening questions are:

What initiated the process of this partial privatisation?

How was this partial privatisation organised and which obstacles were to overcome?

How was the reaction of the system to the partial privatisation, especially considering the discussions, citizens' decisions, Court decisions and a number of open questions between investors, and the State of Berlin as well as the customers and citizens?

The second main point of the case study will deal with the issue of public mission, public goods, and in the case "water" with natural monopolies. This issue must be illuminated under the national and regional conditions and its perception in Germany and Berlin.

The next part deals with operations, performance, and tariffs, providing an overview a historical perspective as well as directing the main and more detailed attention to the tariffs. The investigation of the structure of tariffs, their calculation, the detection of the main cost drivers, and their impacts take the centre of the analysis. This part broaches also the issues of finance, treasury and investment as well as BWB's performance and its development over the last years, thus providing a profound basis to discuss regulation and governance mechanisms, such as investor relations, and competing goals.

The raised sets of questions require both a stakeholder analysis and a theoretical framework. With regard to the complex principal-agent-structures in the Berlin water sector, this study consults the new institutional economics, especially the principal agent theory.

The case of the BWB is an example of privatisation, respectively partial privatisation in the public sector finally ending in a rebuy. What led to the rebuy? Have the aims of the State of Berlin been fulfilled with the partial privatisation, and if not, why? The rebuy suggests evidence that the aims were not fulfilled – which, of course, needs a more in-depth analysis to provide a profound rationale, especially to further investigate and demonstrate that hastily made policy decisions during the election cycle carry the risk of having an irreversible impact on the privatisation performance and its implementation.

1.2. Short Presentation of the BWB and Method

Berliner Wasserbetriebe is an institution under public law. In the meantime the State of Berlin holds 100% of the shares and thus retrieved the sole ownership. The remaining shares held by Veolia Water (24.95% of BWB) were purchased in January 2014.

Figure 1. Commercial Key Data

Shareholder	From 2014 Land Berlin (100%)
Employees	4,500
Annual Investment Volume	Minimum 250 m Euro
Customers	3.5 m
Balance Sheet total in 2012	6,481 m Euro
Income total in 2012	1,290 m Euro
Annual Result in 2012	1,25 m Euro

Source: *Berliner Wasserbetriebe*, http://www.bwb.de/content/language1/html/1097.php

The case of Berlin and BWB has already been made subject to several scientific and practical inquiries so that sufficient material is available to carry out the case study. BWB is a worthwhile case to analyse due to its complexity and multifaceted conflicts thus providing useful findings in times where the European water sector is "in motion".

This study adopts an economical perspective on the case not a judicial or political one. The latter have been dealt with in various other studies, e.g. the dissertations of Klaus Lederer – *Strukturwandel bei kommunalen Wasserdienstleistungen* – (public administration science), Daniela Ochmann – *Rechtsformwahrende Privatisierung von öffentlich-rechtlichen Anstalten* – (judicial science) or Frank Hüesker – *Kommunale Daseinsvorsorge in der Wasserwirtschaft* – (political science).

2. Public Mission

This paragraph pursues the question to what extent the actual public mission for water supply and wastewater disposal can be identified in the BWB, especially with regard to its organisational changes in the course of its existence. In short, considering the history of BWB one can, slightly provokingly, detect that BWB underwent a change from a water supply and wastewater disposal provider to a financial instrument and back. The main resultant questions are: which specific public service missions can be identified? Which objectives of general interest are deliberately pursued by organisations in general and by BWB in particular?

First of all, to answer these questions the terms "public mission" and "public goods" must be defined in general to specify the public mission of the water sector in Germany, especially in Berlin.

The "service for the public" – State ensures the provision of public goods. Public goods are in their basic properties non-excludable and non-rivalrious. Public institutions provide them, since market-like behaviour of individual gain-seeking would not produce efficient results. In this context two conditions have to be questioned: 1. The good is a public good, and therefore it isn't subject to free market rules and 2.[1] Does a public or private institution provide the public good? Generally, whether a good is classified, as a public good is the result of a political decision process. Public missions, resp. public goods, are vague legal concepts. The classification of public and private goods is not exclusively conducted on the basis of technical, economical or other aspects. Due to their importance for the society, which is clearly subject to manifold changes (changes of Government etc.) over time, public goods are only exposed to the markets at the condition that their allocation is not at risk. Public goods are distributed and provided to the citizens on the basis of certain constitutional political negotiated rules for use and restricted access. The public offer of public goods must be politically legitimated premising a public and democratic control.[2] In Germany, for some goods there is a political consensus to classify them as public goods. This is the case e.g. for water supply and wastewater disposal, waste disposal, local public transport, and the provision with hospitals.[3]

The answer to the question, whether such a good should be provided and produced by public companies and/or private companies, depends on historical, technical or economic factors, and should include a discussion on the strategic relevance and specificity of the good or service under consideration. Above all, in the end, the decision is always a political one.[4]

Water supply and wastewater disposal are public goods. The strategic relevance of water supply and wastewater disposal is beyond question.[5] If the provision and production itself is public or private, the question of specificity does no matter at this point.

Since 2000, the European Water Framework Directive (WFD) has provided the central regulatory framework for the use of water bodies and water resources in Europe. It defines far-reaching objectives with regard to the chemico-physical, biological ecological and quantitative status of groundwater, surface water and coastal waters. These objectives are to be achieved by a cross-sector management approach comprising of a series of basic management and protecting principles.

The management and protection of water bodies must look at the boundaries of natural river catchment areas to take the interdependencies of the hydrologic cycle into consideration as far as possible. Combined approaches consist of quality standards for water bodies and limiting values for emissions into water bodies.

---

[1]   Jansen, S. & Priddat, B., 2007, pp. 11-48.
[2]   Hüesker, F., 2011, pp. 49-50.
[3]   Hüesker, F., 2011, p. 50.
[4]   Jäger, A., 2004, p. 38.
[5]   Hüesker, F., 2011, p. 51.

The cost recovery and polluter-pays-principle foregoes the subsidisation of water, prices and charges, taking into account the environmental and resource costs for prices and charges and assigning costs according to the polluter-pays-principle.[6]

The WFD was implemented in German law through the German Water resources management act and the water laws of the German *Laender*. Based on § 29e para. 1 s. 2 *BerlWassG* and § 18a para. 2 s. 1 WHG the BWB is, also after a partial privatisation, obligated to be responsible for the wastewater disposal. BWB exercises this duty by the compulsory connection and usage, which is exclusively and based on § 29e para. 1 s. 3 *BerliWassG*. Furthermore, the BWB's assigned duty is the water supply, § 37a para. 1 s. 2 *BerlBG* because the BWB is the owner of the water supply network.

The German Basic Law (Article 28.2) and most constitutions of the German *Laender* ensure the local self-Government of municipalities. This local self-Government contains all matters concerning the local community. This means autonomy in terms of bylaws, organisational, personnel, financing, regional and planning issues of cities, municipalities, associations of municipalities and administrative districts in accomplishing their tasks. Water supply and wastewater disposal is an obligation of the municipalities by municipal regulations, the constitutions[7] and water laws of the different German *Laender*.[8]

In this legal framework the municipalities are free to decide the organization of water supply and wastewater disposal. This results in a great variety of forms of organisation and practice.[9]

3. History

This paragraph presents an historical review of the BWB and focuses especially on the partial privatisation in 1999 as well as the further developments until today. With regard to the research questions not only the pure history of BWB is important, but also Berlin's political, economical and social environment along the partial privatisation and remunicipilation processes.

---

[6] Directive 2000/60/EC of the European Parliament and of the Council of 23 October 2000 establishing a framework for Community action in the field of water policy.

[7] E.g. Art. 83 Abs. 1 *Bayerische Verfassung*: "The particular sphere of competence of Municipalities (Article 11, section 2) shall encompass the administration of Municipality capital reserves and enterprises; local traffic and road construction; the provision of water, light, gas and electricity for residents".

[8] *Berliner Wassergesetz (BWG)*, BbgWG, HessWG, WG M-V, WG R-Pf, WG S-A, *SächsWG*, *ThürWG* etc.

[9] Lederer, K., 2004, pp. 232-264; *Branchenbild der deutschen Wasserwirtschaft*, 2011, p. 19.

3.1. History of BWB

For over 150 years BWB and its predecessors have been securing the drinking water supply and wastewater disposal in Berlin and the surrounding regions.[10] "Here are a few historical highlights that at the same time were historic turning points in the capital and surrounding area."[11] The following table shows the historical overview of the BWB until today. The dashed and continuous lines symbolise a change of function of the BWB. The dashed ones stand for a private and profit maximising company and the continuous ones for the public company focusing on the service for the public.

Figure 2. Historical Overview

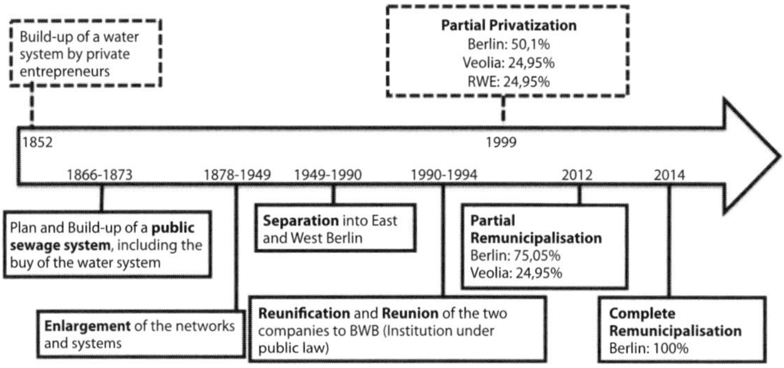

Source: compiled by author, BWB: A company with tradition, http://www.bwb.de/content/language2/html/881.php

3.2. Political, Economical and Social Environment in the 1990s

This paragraph deals with the political, economical and social environment, especially the attitude towards privatisation, in Germany in the 1990s. It will help to get a better understanding of the reasons and rationales for the partial privatisation in 1999.

In the five new *Bundeslaender* the capital investments into facilities and networks of municipal providers and disposal were secured by private capital. This was encouraged by the German politics, granted tax concessions, and implemented by in many cases young inexperienced local affaires. Ministerial task forces and consulting companies supported these processes. However there was a lack of the essential procedural know how. The consequences became apparent in bad planned over

---

[10] BWB: A company with tradition: http://www.bwb.de/content/language2/html/881.php.

[11] BWB: A company with tradition: http://www.bwb.de/content/language2/html/881.php.

dimensioned facilities, asymmetric risk distribution to the disadvantage of the public hand, and extensive transaction costs. Unfortunately these results had long-term effects and came to light delayed in time. Public private partnership (PPP)-initiatives were another new approach during this period. Choosing the PPP-alternative, at first sight the considerable accumulated need of the modernisation of the water and sewage facilities, electricity networks and power stations seemed to be realised without the overload of the underfunded municipal budgets. PPP promised fast and uncomplicated relief on both advantages. Thus the 1990s have seen a wave of privatisations, partial privatisations and PPP in the branch of municipal provider and disposal companies in former East and West Germany. European liberalisation policy for services of general economic interest, municipal lack of public funds, an oversupply of investment-seeking private capital investment and the correspondent spirit of the time created a climate in which many municipalities put their silverware to disposal in a very unbiased and uncritical way.[12]

The special situation after the reunification in Berlin illustrates the following figure:

Figure 3. Berlin's Economic Situation

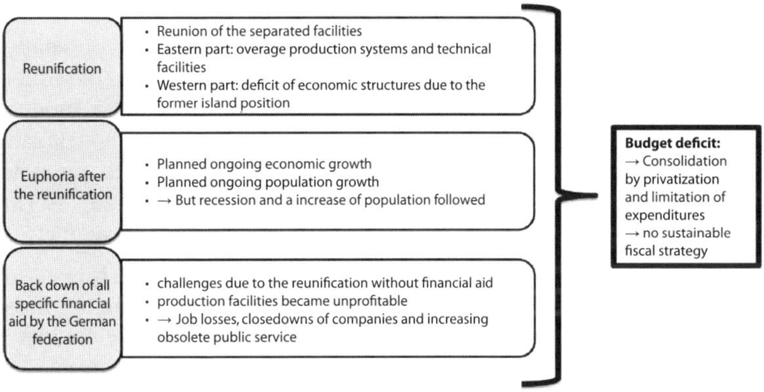

Source: compiled by author, based on: Monstadt, J. and V. Schlippenbach, U., 2005, pp. 9-11, (see also Rupf, W., 1999, p. 396 or Krätke, S., 2004, pp. 512-513), Ochmann, D., 2004, pp. 22-23, Financial affairs Senator Peter Kurth: Abgh.-Ppr. 14/17, p. 928, Lederer, K., 2011, p. 445.

3.3. Partial Privatisation in 1999

Since 1994, the BWB were organised as a public law institution and the *Berliner Betriebegesetz (BerlBetrG)* was effective for the BWB and other public law institutions in Berlin (e.g. public transport company or

---

[12] Lederer, K., 2011, pp. 444-445.

city cleaning). The organisational change was a political aim in order to give the management more entrepreneurial independence and to reduce the political influence and control.[13] The municipality assumes the institutional and guarantor liability for the public law institutions, and in return they should act independent and contribute to the development of the city by entrepreneurial expansion strategies, providing new jobs, and encouraging private investments in Berlin. Critical voices call these public companies "cash machines".[14]

§ 2 para. 7, 8 *BerlBetrG* allowed the public law institutions to assume independent cooperations within their general tasks. The BWB developed a broad portfolio with more than 20 cooperations.[15] Many of these entrepreneurial experiments proved to be unprofitable turning out to be expensive, unsuccessful investments for the BWB and of course for its guarantor Berlin. For many of these cooperations three main problems can be highlighted:

– the relation to the general task of a public company vanished into thin air;

– the bad investments accumulated to a huge amount;

– no politician and no public supervision felt responsible to stop this development.[16]

Though in 1997/1998 the erroneous strategy of the BWB's operations became obvious, Berlin's Government didn't interfere. Instead of reducing BWB's operations back to its core business and generating a moderate revenue for Berlin's budget, e.g. by means of strict supervision, delegating competent representatives as board members, ensuring a competent management, and installation of a corporate governance, Berlin's Government fell back in and sticked to its old patterns of behaviour.

After the full privatisation of its energy companies (Bewag and Gasag) in 1997 and 1998, the only public enterprise left, which promised from the politician's point of view cash inflows to public budget by a privatisation, was BWB. Although Berlin's Government transferred 500 million Euros out of the BWB's equity,[17] both international financial and industrial players were easily mobilised, so that a commitment of well-funded investors was a realistic scenario.

In the face of the fiscal gap in the budget these steps were a matter of emergency. Furthermore, in 1999, elections for Berlin's Government and

---

[13] Preamble of the *Eigenbetriebsreformgesetz* of 09 July, 1993 on Abghs-Drs. 12/2897.

[14] Lederer, K., 2011, p. 447.

[15] *Senatsverwaltung für Finanzen*, 1999, p. 11.

[16] Lederer, K., 2011, p. 447.

[17] Ochmann, D., 2005, p. 21.

the Berlin City Parliament were ahead. The implementation of such an important project was beyond doubt an ambitious aim. Opposition against the privatisation in Berlin's Parliament was not expected; there was a clear consensus of the coalition to cover budget gaps by privatisation.[18,19]

There were no fundamental political oppositions to certain forms of organisation and the area of privatisation. Only the management and the operator model dropped out, since they didn't allow property transfers with correspondent revenues in the budget – at its best they provide continuous revenues on a comparatively low level over a longer period. Berlin's Government found a model, which promised to be enforceable (in the Parliament though against the union) and generate adequate revenues: the BWB should stay a public law company within a holding. In order to create this holding model (a typical silent partnership of a private company in a public law institution) the legal basis had to be established by Berlin's Parliament.[20]

Compared to the transformation into a capital company and its full privatisation this model has some advantages:[21]

Figure 4. Advantages of the Model

Employees	Fiscal Law	Financial Advantages
• 1994: Changing of employment with Berlin to BWB • After another organizational change the employees have the right to return back to an employment with Berlin (BWB preserved as an institution under public law so no organizational change) • No general blockade mentality against the privatization if the employees' interests are guaranteed (abandonment of redundancy and protection of vested rights until 2014)	• Institution under public law as sovereign undertakings are relieved of corporation tax and VAT	• Advantage of institutional liability and guarantor liability can be capitalized by low priced raising of capital (the public hand gets almost impossible insolvent and is unlimited responsible for losses out of the business of the public enterprises) Management supported the partial privatization

Source: compiled by author, cf.: see § 14 para. 6 BerlBetrG, cf.: Lederer, K., 2011, p. 450, cf.: §§ 1 para. 6, 4 KGSt, cf.: Ochmann, D., 2005, p. 31.

---

[18] Hüesker, F., 2011, pp. 120-124.
[19] Plenarprotokoll 13/51, p. 3828 f.
[20] Abghs-Drs. 13/3367.
[21] Lederer, K., 2011, p. 449.

During the preparatory discussions and the whole process some stakeholders were significantly involved. The following table shows the relevant stakeholders and their position and aims.

Figure 5. Stakeholder Analysis

Berlin's Senate	Opposition in the Parliament	BWB
• Aims described in detail in the paragraphs before	• Against the partial privatisation • Instituted a conventions procedure at the Berlin State Constitutional Court	• Management supported the partial privatisation • Investors promised investments • Information were hidden by the BWB (GDR inherit, Schwarze Pumpe)

Employees/ Union	Investors	Consulting Companies	Civil Society/ Population
• Support to the partial privatisation • Broad concessions of Berlin (Job guarantees)	• High interest on BWB • Market entry for international utility companies • Water sector as a future market • Improvement of the reputation	• Were employed by all players at the same time (biding companies and Berlin) • Created the holding model	• General public was more critical against public companies • Privatisation friendly parties won the election • No protest expected or organised

Source: compiled by author, out of Hüesker, F., 2011, pp. 126-132, Frankfurter Allgemeine Zeitung: Noch Hürden bei der Wasser-Privatisierung.

In June 1999, the consortium Vivendi (today Veolia)/RWE/Allianz were awarded to take over 49.9% shares of BWB. The purchase price amounted to 1.7 billions Euros and was the highest of all offers. In addition the consortium also accepted other obligations, e.g. creation of new jobs and a water research centre, guaranteed employment until 2014 for core employees and investments amounting to 5 billion Euros until 2009. The period of validity was 30 years. The partner agreed confidentiality about the contents of the contract of the partial privatisation. This means that due to this secrecy clause the contracts, as the fundamental basis of the cooperation, were neither discussed publicly nor published to the public. In July 1999 the Parliament ratified the contract, which was set up and recommended by a public board, and thus decided on the partial privatisation.

3.4. Further Developments

With the acceptance and conclusion of the contract of the partial privatisation the process of privatisation and its developments have not been completed for a long time yet.

Initiated by the Parliament's opposition there was still the abstract of the judicial review to be performed. First of all they argued that the structure of an institution under public law embedded in a privately organised holding violates the democratic legitimacy. The second point aimed at the partial privatisation law, which provides the basis for the tariff calculation. Especially the imputed interest on the capital employed and the treatment of efficiency measures were starting points for critical comments. Both were created to ensure the profit expectations of the private shareholders. The court followed the objections only for the issue of the calculation of tariffs; all the other points were refused[22]. Paragraph 5.2 "Tariffs" deals with the solution, the liability of compensation of disadvantages.

The tariffs increased ever since 2003. Therefore the former Senator of commerce Harald Wolf recommended an investigation procedure conducted by the cartel office in order to decrease the tariffs. The cartel office followed the idea of the Land Berlin and suggested a price reduction of 16% including a recompense for recent years. The BWB appealed the decision of the cartel office and brought the issue to trial. The argument of the BWB was and has not changed up to now, that the cartel office is not competent, competent is only the local authority[23]. This conflict is ongoing and the Court has not come to a final decision yet.

Yet another development after the privatisation was a petition of a referendum of Berlin's population in 2011. The aim of that petition was to open the consortium agreement and the other contracts to public. Already in 2007 the citizens' initiative started with its activities. It was a difficult procedure because the initiative didn't have the support of any political party. But already in 2010 the amendment of the German freedom of information act came into effect, which allowed the disclosure of the contracts and agreements. Only due to constitutional rules the petition had to be finished and the population had to vote in 2011, although the issue had become obsolete at this time.[24]

---

[22] Lederer, K., 2011, pp. 455-456.

[23] BWB: http://www.bwb.de/content/language1/html/10124.php, Spiegel online: http://www.spiegel.de/wirtschaft/service/kartellamt-zwingt-berliner-wasserbetriebe-zu-preissenkung-a-837084.html.

[24] Citizens' initiative: *Berliner Wassertisch*: http://berliner-wassertisch.net/index.php, Tagesspiegel online: http://www.webcitation.org/5wQWdfQAL, Berlin: Senat legt Verträge zur Teilprivatisierung der Berliner Wasserbetriebe offen: http://www.webcitation.org/5wQX6bBtL, rbb Nachrichten: Wasser-Volksbegehren trotz offener Verträge, http://www.webcitation.org/5w3WOGZ5f.

By far of capital importance were the remunicipalisation-steps in 2012 and 2013.

In 2010, the shareholder RWE signalised its attendance to sell its share of BWB. The pressure of Berlin's Senate became apparently more intensively.[25]

After closing the negotiations the Land Berlin rebought the RWE's share of BWB for 654 million Euros. The Land Berlin holds after the rebuy 75.05% of the BWB's shares. The purchase price is financed by the water revenues. The loan period is not longer than 30 years and financed by a state-owned financial institution. According to Berlin's financial affairs Senator Nußbaum, even if the required tariffs reduction of the Cartel Office must be realised the business is still fully financed.[26]

The rebuy has been accompanied by doubts on part of other stakeholder: The citizens' initiative *Berliner Wassertisch* (Berlin's water table) criticizes that the purchase price is too high and that budgetary principles are violated. The initiative has appealed the Regional Court of Audit to deal with these issues.[27]

In 2013, also Veolia appeared to transfer its BWB's share. So that in 2014 Berlin holds 100% of the BWB, again. The repurchase price for Veolia's share amounts to 590 million Euros. The financing plan is the same as foreseen for the RWE's share.[28]

After the complete remunicipalisation no organisational change is planned, neither the holding structure nor the boards.

For the first time Berlin's Senate considers a reduction of tariffs. Berlin's Senator of Commerce currently negotiates a reduction, which is higher than the Cartel office's demand. The reduction should be reached by a change in the calculation scheme (imputed costs, respectively imputed depreciations) and in consequence a decrease of the distribution of profits. But the negotiations between the parties in Berlin's governing coalition are ongoing.[29]

4. Regulation and Governance

This paragraph broaches governance and regulatory issues of the BWB. For this purpose, after illustrating the holding structure the

---

[25] Schoelkopf, K., 2010.

[26] Thomsen, J., 2012.

[27] Die Linke, 2012; Thomsen, J., 2012.

[28] Verhandlungen mit Veolia abgeschlossen: Vollständiger Rückkauf der Berliner Wasserbetriebe möglich, Pressemitteilung No. 13-020 vom 10.09.2013: http://www.berlin.de/sen/finanzen/presse/archiv/20130910.1400.389076.html.

[29] Anker, J., 2013.

relation between the investors and Berlin are described including a short stakeholder analysis. The stakeholder analysis consults the principal agent theory to highlight the different, in some extent opposing aims of the stakeholder. The second part in this paragraph deals with the regulation issues of BWB.

4.1. Governance

The most important governance mechanism of the BWB and its relations to both, the investors and Berlin, is the consortium agreement. It serves as a fundamental framework of the partial privatisation. In addition to the shared aims of the contract partners the consortium agreement defines among other the determination of business areas, the appointment of persons and bodies, the fundamentals and objectives of the cooperation and arrangements for interruptions, placement of the stock, contract questions of guarantee, merger control and implementation. All other contracts and agreements are annexes of this contract.[30] The consortium agreement was not published in the commercial register because there was no disclosure and, even more important, because of the partners' interest of confidentiality.[31]

The following figure illustrates the structure of the holding model after the partial privatisation.

Figure 6. BWB's Holding Structure

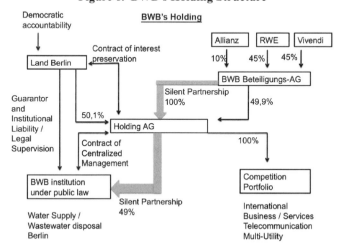

Source: Lederer, K., 2004, p. 344.

---

[30] Abgeordnetenhaus von Berlin: D-13/3367 vom 05.01.1999.
[31] Ochmann, D., 2004, p. 38.

As mentioned before, an institution under public law is characterised by a supervisory board, the management and the guarantors' meeting. Thus it is necessary to consider these organs and explain its relations. Due to the contract of the centralised management between BWB and the Holding AG the Holding AG owns the authority to give directives to the institution under public law. This right is limited by the contract of partial privatisation and is accepted under reserve of the acceptance of the directive committee, in which the Land Berlin owns the majority.[32]

Figure 7. Board of Supervisory and Board of Managers at BWB

Supervisory Board	Board of Managers
• Nomination by guarantor's meeting • Holding AG submit proposals • Consists 16 members • Appointment and Dismissal of the board of managers, refusal only by important reasons • Supervision of the management • Confirmation of the business plan • Determination of the tariffs and charges	• 4 board members • Board members of technology and human resources proposed by Berlin and of finance and development and marketing and sales proposed by Holding-AG, with each consultation of Berlin or Holding-AG • § 9.6 consortium agreement constitutes a committee of the boards, which has 3 members (Berlin, Vivendi, RWE). This Committee has the task to appoint the chairman of the board of BWB after the proposal of the majority. Thus the private shareholders hold the majority in this committee, which is definitely contradictory to § 6 para. 2 BerlBG

Source: compiled by author: Lederer, K., 2011, p. 453, cf.: § 9 para. 1, 2 and § 10 para. 2, 3, 4, 6 BerlBG, Hüesker, F., 2011, p. 155-157, cf.: § 3 para. 2 articles of BWB, cf.: § 9.5 consortium agreement.

Relation Between the Board of Managers and the Supervisory Board.

As shown the representatives of the private investors in the board of managers own a position in which they can enforce their interests against the representatives of Berlin by the voice of the chairman. This provides an opportunity for the private investors of the *Beteiligungs-AG* (Holding-AG) to act against the intentions of Berlin in terms of the business of the BWB as long as the supervisory board is not needed to be involved. In case the supervisory board is involved a consensus between the employees' representatives and the chairman of the supervisory board

---

[32]   Lederer, K., 2011, p. 453; Ochmann, D., 2004, pp. 43-44.

countervail against the private dominated board of managers. The board of managers needs the confirmation of the supervisory board for the following decisions.[33]

Foundation of subsidiaries, disposal and acquisition of companies and participations, disposal and acquisition of assets as well as the disclaimer of receivables and conclusions of compromise agreements unless a limit of 10 million DM (ca. 5 million Euros) is not exceeded etc.

This leads to the following conclusion: the supervisory board is to be involved in important but not in all business decisions. In the case of involvement the supervisory board Berlin has a powerful control instrument. But not to be underestimated is the relation between the board of managers and the supervisory board of the Holding AG: very often the members of the BWB's supervisory board and in the Holding AG's supervisory board are the same persons the same for the BWB's and Holding AG's board of managers. A complicated overlapping of organs with authority is the consequence.[34]

For a deeper analysis of the management and control problems arising as a result of these facts the principal agent theory can be consulted. The main and first principal of any public company is the citizen. By elections the citizen gives power to its representative, its agent, who is in the same time principal, e.g. of the administration, and the public companies. Along this principal-agent-chain it should be ensured that the democratic control is in the citizens' hand. Therefore the citizen needs the possibility to gain information with a minimum of effort, e.g. transactions costs. As the paper has already elaborated, the partial privatisation process featured a lack of transparency, so that a judgement by the citizen was impossible. Even the Parliament did not have full access to the contracts. This gives reason to believe that there were hidden information and actions in terms of the moral hazard phenomenon. The complex structure of the holding, the complicated relation between the supervisory board and the board of managers as a result of the complex contract structure, and different committees with different authorities lead to the obligation to find always consensus and compromises by the boards in order to balance the diverging interest's of the private investors and the Land Berlin.

4.2. Regulation

This paragraph deals with regulation and control issues of BWB. It takes the perspective of the Land Berlin and focuses on the regulation of tariffs as one promising example to show the complexity of regulation in

---

[33] Hüesker, F., 2011, pp. 158-159.
[34] Hüesker, F., 2011, p. 163; Ochmann, D., 2004, pp. 155-156.

the water sector in general and BWB in particular. At first, in the following figure the possibilities of control are described by actors.

Figure 8. Regulation Actors

Berlin's Senate	Senator of Economic	Financial Affairs Senator	Senate's Department for Environment
• Right to change the legal framework for BWB • Distribution of competences for the different senators • Guarantors' committee • Discharge the supervisory board • Appointment of the BWB's auditor	• Chairman of the supervisory board • Control of the institutions under public law and legal supervision • Proposal of imputed interest of the business assets for the calculation of tariffs	• Responsible for the investment management and investment controlling • Definition of fiscal and specialised objectives, they build the basis for the strategic control and the annual objectives for the management	• Implementation of the water law regulation • Approval procedure for water and wastewater works • Approval of tariffs since 2006 (until 2006 Senate's Department of Commerce), this reallocation solves the conflict of interest as the tariffs are also approved by the board of supervisory

Source: compiled by authors: § 14 BerlBG, cf.: § 11 and § 12 para. 2 BerlBG; Hüesker, F., 2011, pp. 209-212; § 3 and § 13 TPrG (*Teilprivatisierungsgesetz*). *Senatsverwaltung für Finanzen*: Hinweise für Beteiligungen des Landes Berlin an Unternehmen (Beschluss des Senats von Berlin of 17/02/2009); *Senatsverwaltung für Finanzen*: Beteiligungsbericht 2006, p. 5.

The political regulation is also difficult because the different Senate departments pursue different aims. The financial department is interested in profits for the budget, the aim of the department for consumer protection and environment has more interest in consumer friendly tariffs and the protection of the environment, and the department for economics has a more general interest in the general development of the BWB and Berlin – all the more since the Economics Senator is the chairman of the supervisory board.

Another point to illuminate is the imposition of tariffs and its control. As already mentioned the representatives to confirm and create tariffs as well as the imputed interest on operating assets are: BWB itself, the supervisory board and the department of consumer protection. In comparison to other German cities the tariffs are too high – obviously the regulation instruments don't operate ideally, even if the Berlin's Senate's aims are stable and fair prices.

At the suggestion of the former and outgoing chairman of the supervisory board and Economic Senator Harald Wolf the Federal Cartel Authority has initiated a procedure against BWB because of too high prices. This was only possible because of the decision of the BGH (Federal Supreme Court), KVR 66/08 of February 2010 deciding on the adaptability of cartel anti abuse legislations of water prices. Until today it is open if the anti abuse legislations are also applicable for public enterprises, because they impose tariffs instead of prices. But nevertheless the procedure is ongoing and the federal cartel office followed the opinion of Harald Wolf.

5. Operations, Tariffs and Performance

In this paragraph the facts of the BWB are highlighted, in particular the economic situation, the tariff calculation and the general performance.

5.1. Operations

The BWB is a water company and provides water supply and wastewater disposal. BWB has 9 water works 6 sewage works and 800 deep wells in order to fulfil its tasks. The drinking water network has a 7,870 km pipeline network for drinking water and 9,606 km canalisation.

There is only an about 2% water loss during the pipeline transportation. This is a low value compared to international and national performance data. It is the result of a consequent maintenance of the pipelines and a sign of high quality, in particular in consideration of the fact, that water is a vital and scarce resource. In addition according to schedule 1% of the network is renewed annually.

During the partial privatisation process the following investments are negotiated and confirmed. In the consortium agreement it is codified that within 10 years 2.5 billion Euros, meaning about 250 million Euros per year, must be used for investments. After the reunification and in the following years the investments were on a high level due to a substantive increase of demand.[35] The BWB's management is in general in favour for investments. Therefore they invested more than the claimed 250 million Euros per year,[36] which can be attributed to two reasons: first, the investments are directly financed by the tariffs and second,

---

[35] Hüesker, F., 2011, p. 298.
[36] BWB: Annual Report 2012, p. 54.

the investments increase the capital employed. An increase of capital employed causes an increase of the imputed interest on the capital employed, which is in line with the interest of the shareholder. Another advantage of investments is an increasing reputation because a company, which invests, stands for innovation and modernity.

The employees are an important stakeholder for the BWB. In the consortium agreement it was confirmed that enforced redundancies are excluded until 2014. Nevertheless it is also clear that the BWB doesn't hire new employees except for the necessary minimum, which is mostly hired from the own trainees.

5.2. Tariffs

The BWB finances itself exclusively from tariffs. Tariffs are public fees, which are imposed by a public regulation authority in return for an individual attributable public good or service. They are supposed to cover the costs of this service or good entirely or at least partly.[37]

This means that the imposition of tariffs is liable to concrete legal requirements. The legal framework on tariffs in Germany is determined by the Community Charges Acts (local rates act) and the municipality codes of the German *Laender*.

Since 2007, after the amendment of the freedom of information act and a Court decision of the Higher Administrative Court Berlin-Brandenburg (OVG), the general basis of the calculation of the water and wastewater disposal tariffs is publicly available. As a consequence of the court decision the BWB published a leaflet with its calculation basis and principles.

The framework for the calculation of tariffs in Berlin is the *Berliner Betriebegesetz (BerlBG*, especially § 16 and § 17 *BerlBG)* and the *Wassertarifverordnung (WTarifVO)*.

The tariffs must follow the principles of equivalence and equal treatment as well as cost recovery. The tariffs are calculated for a maximum period of 2 years (§16 para. 1 *BerlBG*).

The calculation of tariffs is based on basic and variable costs. The fixing of the tariffs can be splitted in basic and variable prices. The basic price can be determined progressively or degressively. Furthermore the BWB can impose a one-time access charge (§16 para. 2 *BerlBG*).

Costs have to be adequate in accordance to the economic principles and subject to economic management. This includes also charges for engaged external labour, imputed depreciations on the basis of replacement

---

[37] BVerfGE 50, 217 (226).

values, imputed single risks, accrued liabilities, adequate imputed interest on capital employed and charges for the economical and technical development (§16 para. 3 *BerlBG*). It is assumed that the replacement costs of assets will be higher in the future than today, respectively in the past, due to general increasing prices.[38]

The capital employed includes operating assets minus the advance payment and first instalments, which are provided free of interest to the institutions under public law by the Land Berlin. The operating assets consist of permanent and floating assets serving the scope of business. Fundamentally the financial asset and manufacturing costs minus the not indexed depreciation are taken as the basis for the calculation of the operating assets (§16 para. 4 *BerlBG*).

The operating assets are included in the calculation via an imputed interest rate determined by the Senate Department for Economics. This imputed interest rate is supposed to comply at least with the average return of German 10-year federal bonds on a calculation base of the last 20 years, plus 2% (§16 para. 5 BerlBG).

Consumers are only allowed to be charged with the actually raised costs. Favourable estimations respectively unfavourable differences are detected by a post calculation. Deviations have to be adjusted within the next two periods (§16 para. 6 *BerlBG*).

In the end, the supervisory board decides on the determination of the tariffs (§17 para. 1 *BerlBG*).

Two general questions arise in this context:

The applied method to determine the imputed interest already includes a profit in the tariffs. But should a profit actually be an element of costs when calculating a tariff for a public good? This leads of course to a follow-up question: in what extent the profit margin is related to the interest rates to be applied?

Depreciation is calculated on the basis of replacement values: does the BWB actually need in the future the same infrastructure, e.g. capacities? Are the dimensions of the facilities well estimated if a reduction of the water consumption is predictable? E.g. there is reliable evidence on decreasing water demand due to technical progress and demographic changes.

Addressing the first question: imputed costs are opportunity costs expressing the monetary value of the investor's opportunity to invest the capital in an alternative investment. In order to consider this fact the imputed interests are a common element in the cost calculations of many

---

[38]   Haberstock, L., 2005, p. 88.

municipalities, permitted by the courts.[39] The other question refers to the interest rate to be applied in relation to the profit. Two facts need to be considered in this context. First, the amount of the capital employed and the way it is calculated. If the private investors pursue the aim of profit maximisation they will have a great interest in a high amount of the capital employed in order to gain more profit due to the higher calculation basis for the interests. This runs the risk that over dimensioned infrastructure is hold available. For this reason the *Berliner Betriebegesetz* regulates the calculation of the capital employed. For this purpose the focus has been shifted on the amount of the imputed interests. Thus, it is permitted to exceed the mentioned amount of interest if it bases on measures, which lead to a permanent increase of the economic performance, especially by new technologies, economisations, increases of efficiency etc. This further amount of interest is valid for 3 years after the assessment. The advantages gained from the adopted measures must be referred to the consumers.[40] As a result of this not clearly defined exceptional rule the BWB's imputed interests are higher than the common 4% in municipalities.[41]

Turning to the second question, the depreciation on replacement values: This chosen method of depreciation bases upon the general assumption that the replacement of facilities in the future will be more expensive than today and assumes an inflation affecting the replacement costs. In the result this leads to increasing water tariffs. Assuming constant revenues, the profit increases because the depreciations – due to their imputed character – are not affected by direct cost increase. The same problem arises when discussing the ordinary useful life of the facilities, which influence the calculation as well.

Although the depreciation on replacement values is economically worthwhile, the risk of its abuse for manipulating tariffs is high because there are too many unclear facts, e.g.: does Berlin need the same facilities and capacities in the future (technological developments, demographic change)? How should future prices be calculated, which price indices are appropriate, in particular since the BWB currently calculates with 21 different, partially to be questioned, indices? For politicians, who are in charge to confirm the tariff calculation, it is difficult to understand and overview all these facts. Thus BWB has an advance of information and can use it against the politicians and the administrative staff.

To get an overview of the elements of costs in the calculation, the BWB has published a leaflet in which these are explained and illustrated.

---

[39] Driehaus, H.-J., 2008, § 6 Rn. 146c.
[40] § 3 para. 4 *Teilprivatisierungsgesetz*.
[41] Hüesker, F., 2011, p. 239.

Figure 9. Overview of the Costs in the BWB's Calculation

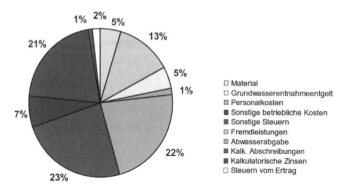

Source: *Berliner Wasserbetriebe*: Grundlagen der Tarifkalkulation, p. 12.

The figure shows that 21% of the calculation is imputed interests and 23% imputed depreciations. This means that almost 50% of the calculation is imputed costs. The BWB is a public company with a natural monopoly. Hence there is no risk that the BWB calculates itself out of the market or that consumers search for substitutes. Having a look at the imputed interest rates currently valid for 2013 6.5% (2012: 6.9%, 2011: 7.1%, 2010: 7.6%)[42] they without a doubt seem over dimensioned comparing the risk.

An increase of the rates serves originally, as pointed out above, the return expectations of the private investors. Today's rate of 10-years German Government Bonds amounts 1.33%.[43] In comparison the BWB's interest rate for 2013 is indeed disputable.

Besides another mechanism influences the amount of the imputed interest: the increase of the imputed depreciation on replacement values. The profits earned via applying this depreciation method remain in the company and turn into equity capital. This increased equity capital must be imputed to the capital employed which is consequently raised by these depreciations. The imputed interests, as mentioned before, are calculated on the basis of the capital employed. With a higher equity capital the company can also save costs for debt capital, which again in turn increases the profit and the return.

---

[42] *Verordnung über die angemessene Verzinsung des betriebsnotwendigen Kapitals der Berliner Wasserbetirebe* (BWB).

[43] http://www.finanzen.net/zinsen/10j-Bundesanleihen.

5.3. Performance

This paragraph deals with the performance of the BWB and points out, why it is difficult to set a benchmark in this context. Although there are two benchmark organisations specialised in the public sector and the BWB is a member of both, one cannot obtain further information on efficiency or other important performance criteria. Thus, it is exceedingly difficult to judge the BWB on the basis of comparative data. At least some facts can be highlighted which influence the BWB's performance.

The overall determining factor is the consumption of water, which has decreased over the last decades.[44]

The decreasing water consumption poses a big challenge for the BWB, in particular its infrastructure. The facilities are already over dimensioned due to the differences in the planned and actual development of Berlin's population. In addition the consumer behaviour changed causing a decreasing demand. Since the tariff calculation in Germany applies absorption costing, as a consequence the maintenance costs (predominant consisting of fixed costs), which are allocated per cubic metre used, have increased, resulting in higher tariffs per cubic metre.

Until 2003 the tariffs were stable due to the contracts and agreements of the partial privatisation. Hence it is interesting to take a look into the further developments until today. For the general water pricing in Germany in the last years an increase of around 0.5-2% per year can be constituted as moderate.[45] In comparison the BWB's tariffs increased remarkably after 2003.[46] There are many reasons for the increase, mainly the general increase of costs (employee, material etc.), the partial privatisation and the distribution of the profits.

After the privatisation the profit transfer conducts to the corresponding shares. In addition there are agreements for deferred liabilities, reserves and the equity capital.[47]

Based on the court decision invalidating the agreement of the tariffs the private investors and the Berlin's Senate have already found a new way to realize the expected and factual guaranteed profits for the private investors: § 23 para. 7 of the consortium agreement guarantees the expected profits for the private investors, even if the Land Berlin (50.1% of the shares) has to abstain from its own portion of the profit.[48] So after

---

[44] *Berliner Wasserbetriebe*: Wasserverkauf: Die Daten seit 1992: http://www.bwb.de/content/language1/downloads/tabelle_wasserverkauf_bis2012.pdf.

[45] BDEW: Wasserfakten im Überblick, p. 6.

[46] BWB: Tarifblatt 2007-2011; Hüesker, F., 2011, p. 254.

[47] Hüesker, F., 2011, p. 240.

[48] Lederer, K., 2011, p. 457; Ochmann, 2004, p. 39.

the change of Government in Berlin and the end of the bondage to stable prices in 2003 the new Government had to negotiate and install new rules for the tariff calculation in order to avoid the funding of the private investors' distribution of profits out of the budget. Berlin's Senate was allowed to determine annually the adequate imputed interest rates on the capital employed. This created a margin for tariff rises. The next measure was to change the basis of the imputed depreciation to replacement values.[49]

During the analysed 10 years the private shareholders received a profit transfer at a total of 1,142.6 million Euros. This means that they received already 67.21% of the invested capital (about 1.7 billion Euros) within 10 years. In the same time the Land Berlin received only 778.1 million Euros.[50] The Land Berlin has resigned about 365 million Euros of its possible share of profit out of its share at BWB during this period. For the private investors it was a good bargain – without any doubt.[51] In the analysed 10 years the shareholders (Berlin and the private) received a profit transfer of 1,920 million Euros out of the BWB. Berlin's portion amounted only to 778 million although the Land Berlin had 50.1% of the BWB. That means that the Land Berlin disclaimed in favour of the private investors' profit transfer.

6. Future Perspectives and Lesson's Learned

This paragraph summarises the conclusions of this case study. This summary includes also future perspectives and ends with the lessons learned.

The confidential contracts and agreements including all amendments and being confidential until 2005 comprise more than 700 pages; adding laws like *Berliner Betriebegesetz* this is a complex and complicate framework. In the end all these aspects led to the presented holding structure affected by governance and regulation problems because of the complicate relation between private investors, the Land Berlin and the BWB. The most important facts from the citizens' perspective are the increasing tariffs and its calculation. The costing scheme is difficult to understand for someone without any economic background. The issues around the imputed costs (imputed interests and depreciations) are complicated, in particular the relation to the capital employed.

After the experience of the BWB's partial privatisation, which was, as already mentioned, a broadly accepted political and social mistake,

---

[49] Lederer, K., 2011, pp. 458-459.
[50] *Beteiligungsbericht of Berlin* 2006-2011 and annual reports 2001-2010.
[51] Hüesker, F., 2011, p. 262.

there is no positive climate for further privatisations in Berlin. There are even ongoing developments for other remunicipalisations in Berlin. In Berlin some citizens' initiatives have been formed dealing with remunicipalisations, for example the *Berliner Energietisch* (Berlin's energy round table) following the aim to remunicipalise Berlin's two energy companies (gas and electricity). Both companies were privatised in the 1990s by Berlin's Government. Now with the gained experiences these companies are up to discussion, especially the Gas AG and Vattenfall's electricity concession. Both concessions expire in 2014 and need to be tendered.

This leads to the following lessons learned:

Transparency

Without transparency, projects such as the BWB privatisation are difficult to legitimate towards the citizens. Citizens don't longer accept the intransparency in political processes. There is a strong request for open Government and more than ever the politicians can't ignore that demand, as well as the demand for participation in serious decisions.

Budget deficits

Budget deficits can't be solved by privatisation. Usually the deficits are not caused by the public companies. Quite the contrary, public companies gaining profits, such as BWB, can – if allowed according to the applicable law – cross-subsidise other public services The short-term view of the public-sector accounting (cash accounting) and budget control favours short-term decisions. For example, one aim of the BWB's partial privatisation was to use the sales revenue to reduce the budget deficit in 1999. But the deficit had and has structural roots and can't be solved by one sales action. To overcome budget deficits overall strategies are necessary and needed.

Strategies

One problem of the politics is the election cycles. Following the findings of the public choice-theory they prevent long-term planning and strategies for municipalities and cities. But long-term strategies are necessary to develop a successful and sustainable municipality, also in terms of competition with other municipalities. The same applies for public enterprises and their function within a municipality. As seen the BWB has changed its instrumental function often during its history. In its beginning the BWB was a privately founded and run company with profit orientation (financial function), after hygienic problems in Berlin the role changed to a service provision orientation and became a public run enterprise (service for the public function). In the 1990s the role changed once again to a financial function due to budget deficits, so that gaining profit dominates again. Due to the public pressure the instrumental function changed in the recent history to a service for the public orientation and function. Often when the function is profit and financial orientated it does not lead to a sustainable success.

If it comes due to election cycles to time pressure, it limits the possibility to get familiar with the complex matter of law and to discuss the actual impacts of projects. In this case study the revenues out of the partial privatisation were already planned in the budget and the next election of the Berlin's Parliament were around the corner. So the Parliament's members didn't have the time to get familiar with this decision and its consequences – but due to the time pressure, a decision was to take.

Politicians' actions

Often political decisions are ascribed to some politicians' "dreams" of realising a certain project or action. In order to get the Parliament's acceptance for the project, sometimes non-realistic estimations are created. In the BWB's case one cannot speak of a "nice dream", actually in order to get the acceptance for the partial privatisation the politicians didn't inform the Parliament about the risks and dangers in an adequate way. Irreversible investment decisions have a long-term influence on the public budget and thus the political capacity to act. Thus more expertise and opinions need to be included in the decision process in order to get more realistic scenarios as a profound base for the decision on the project, respectively investment. Also the aims of the chosen partners (private) must be estimated realistically, especially in terms of the high irreversible character of these decisions. This means it is important always to keep in mind, that the aim of private investors is to realize profits and that the common welfare is only a second aim. If this aim is considered the contracts and regulation of partial privatisations or public private partnerships have to be rethought and politicians should be aware of this during the negotiation process.

As the complete remunicipalisation is only a few months old, deeper analysis and investigations are not possible today. But the first comments can be made:

- the structure and governance mechanisms are the same, this applies also for the management of BWB and the still existing holding.
- the tariffs for drinking water and sewage decreased, respectively will decrease in 2014 and 2015, mainly due to the Cartel Office's demand and the public pressure after the remunicipalisation. The Cartel Office constitutes its decision that one reason of the too high tariffs are the imputed interest and depreciations in the calculation, and thus the hidden profit in the calculation.

- the high investments should persist.
- the remunicipalisation costs about 1.3 billion Euros and could have probably cost less if the Cartel Office's demand would be confirmed by the Court. The Court's confirmation effected in February 2014.[52]

References

Abghs-Drs. 12/2897, (1993): Preamble of *the Eigenbetriebsreformgesetz* of 09/07/1993.

Abghs-Drs. 13/3367, (1999): *Gesetz zur Änderung des Berliner Betriebegesetzes, zur Teilprivatisierung der Berliner Wasserbetriebe und zur Änderung des Berliner Wassergesetzes vom 05/01/1999.*

Abgh-Ppr. (*Plenarprotokoll des Abgeordnetenhauses von Berlin*), 13/51 vom 01/01/1998: Behandlung im Plenum über lfd. No. 6, a) Drucksache 13/3027: Große Anfrage der Fraktion der PDS über: Wer zahlt für die Privatisierung der Berliner Wasserbetriebe (BWB)? And b) Drucksache 13/3028: Antrag der Fraktion der PDS über Wahrnehmung der öffentlichen Verantwortung bei den Berliner Wasserbetrieben (BWB), Berlin, p. 3828-383.

Abgh-Ppr. (*Plenarprotokoll des Abgeordnetenhauses von Berlin*), 14/17 vom 26 Oktober 2000: Behandlung im Plenum über lfd. No. 5, Drucksache 14/701: Große Anfrage der Fraktion PDS über Hoffnungen, Erwartungen, Versprechen – die Realität der Privatisierungspolitik der Großen Koalition, Berlin, S. 927-936.

ATT, BDEW, DBVW, DVGW, DWA, VKU (2011): Branchenbild der deutschen Wasserwirtschaft 2011, Bonn: wvgw Wirtschafts- und Verlagsgesellschaft.

Anker, Jens, (2013): Wasser soll in Berlin 13 Prozent billiger werden, http://www.morgenpost.de/berlin-aktuell/article121165645/Wasser-soll-in-Berlin-13-Prozent-billiger-werden.html, called: 24.10.2013.

BDEW (2012): Wasserfakten im Überblick, http://www.bdew.de/internet.nsf/id/C125783000558C9FC125766C0003CBAF/$file/Wasserfakten%20im%20%20%C3%9Cberblick%20-%20freier%20Bereich%20April%202012_1.pdf, called: 10.05.2013.

Berliner Wasserbetriebe (2007): Grundlagen der Tarifkalkulation. Dokumentation, Berlin.

Berliner Wasserbetriebe (2011): Annual Report 2011, Berlin.

BVerfGE 50, 217 (226).

Coenenberg, A. (2003): *Kostenrechnung und Kostenanalyse*, 5. Auflage, Stuttgart.

Die Linke, (2012): Beschluss 7/1/4, 4. Landesparteitag, 1. Tagung: BWB: Rekommunalisierung statt Rückkauf! Gute Leistung, gute Preise, gute

---

[52] Fahrun, 2014.

Arbeit., 20th October 2012, Berlin, http://www.die-linke-berlin.de/die_linke/ parteitage/4_landesparteitag/1_tagung/beschluss/7/.

Directive 2000/60/EC of the European Parliament and of the Council of 23 October 2000 establishing a framework for Community action in the field of water policy.

Driehaus, Hans-Joachim (1989): *Kommunalabgaberecht. Kommentar*, (39. Erg.-Lfg. 2008), Herne/Berlin.

Fahrun, Joachim (2014): Zu hohe Wasserpreise – Berliner erhalten Geld zurück, *Berliner Morgenpost*, 24.02.2014, source: http://www.morgenpost.de/berlin-aktuell/article125148859/Zu-hohe-Wasserpreise-Berliner-erhalten-Geld-zurueck.html, called: 23.05.2014.

Frankfurter Allgemeine Zeitung (1999): Noch Hürden bei der Wasser-Privatisierung, 10.06.1999, source: http://www.seiten.faz-archiv.de/ faz/19990610/fr11999061091588.html, called: 08.05.2013.

Haberstock, Lothar (2005): *Kostenrechnung I – Einführung*, 12. Auflage, Berlin.

Hüesker, Frank (2011): *Kommunale Daseinsvorsorge in der Wasserwirtschaft – Auswirkungen der Privatisierung am Beispiel der Wasserbetriebe Berlins*, München.

Jäger, Alexander (2004): *Der Zusammenhang von Staat und Infrastruktur und die Privatisierung von Infrastruktur aus staatstheoretischer Perspektive*, in Volker Schneider, Marc Tenbücken (Hrsg.): Der Staat auf dem Rückzug. Die Privatisierung öffentlicher Infrastrukturen, Frankfurt/M., S. 29-52.

Jansen, Stephan, Priddat, Birger, (2007): Theorien der öffentlichen Güter: Rekonstruktionen sozialer Konstruktionen – Politik- und Wirtschaftswissenschaftlich Korrekturvorschläge, in: Nico Stehr (Hrsg.): *Die Zukunft des Öffentlichen. Multidisziplinäre Perspektiven für eine Öffnung der Diskussion über das Öffentliche*, Wiesbaden, pp. 11-48.

Lederer, Klaus (2004): *Strukturwandel bei kommunalen Wasserdienstleistungen – Eine Untersuchung aus verwaltungswissenschaftlicher Perspektive*, Berlin.

Lederer, Klaus (2011): Die Teilprivatisierung der Berliner Wasserbetriebe: Erfolgsmodell oder Abwicklungsfall?, in: *Zeitschrift für öffentliche und gemeinwirtschaftliche Unternehmen* (ZögU), 34 Jg., 4/2011, S. 444-461.

Monstadt, Jochen, v. Schlippenbach, Ulrike (2005): Privatisierung und Kommerzialisierung als Herausforderung regionaler *Infrastrukturpolitik – Eine Untersuchung der Berliner Strom-, Gas-, und Wasserversorgung sowie Abwasserversorgung*, Berlin (netWORKS-Papers, No. 20).

Ochmann, Daniela (2005): *Rechtsformwahrende Privatisierung von öffentlich-rechtlichen Anstalten: Dargestellt am Holdingmodell zur Teilprivatisierung der Berliner Wasserbetriebe*, Baden-Baden.

Pressemitteilung No. 13-020 vom 10.09.2013: Verhandlungen mit Veolia abgeschlossen: Vollständiger Rückkauf der Berliner Wasserbetriebe möglich, http://www.berlin.de/sen/finanzen/presse/archiv/20130910.1400.389076.html called: 24.10.2013.

Schoelkopf, Katrin (2010): RWE will über Anteilsverkauf verhandeln, in: *Berliner Morgenpost*, 21. November 2010, p. 9.

Senatsverwaltung für Wirtschaft (2003, 2004, 2005, 2006, 2007, 2008, 2009, 2010, 2011, 2012): Verordnung über die angemessene Verzinsung des betriebsnotwendigen Kapitals der Berliner Wasserbetriebe (BWB) über die Jahre 2004, 2005, 2006, 2007, 2008, 2009, 2010, 2011, 2012, 2013, Berlin.

Sozialdemokratische Partei Deutschland (2006): *Koalitionsvereinbarung zwischen SPD und Linkspartei.PDS 2006-2011*, Berlin.

Thomsen, Jan (2012a): Senat will das Wasser zurück, in: *Berliner Zeitung*, 17th July 2012, http://www.berliner-zeitung.de/berlin/rekommunalisierung-der-berliner-wasserbetriebe-senat-will-das-wasser-zurueck,10809148,16636818. html.

Thomsen, Jan (2012b): Land soll Wasser zurückkaufen, in *Berliner Zeitung*, 25th October, http://www.berliner-zeitung.de/berlin/rekommunalisierung-land-soll-wasser-zurueckkaufen,10809148,20714388.html.

Webpages

Berliner Wasserbetriebe (BWB): www.bwb.de.

Berliner Wassertisch: www.berliner-wassertisch.net / www.berliner-wassertisch. info.

2. Governance versus Ownership in Jointly Owned Local Government Organisations

The Case of *Va Syd*
(Water and Sewage South)

Ola MATTISSON & Ulf RAMBERG

Lund University

Introduction

The local Government level represents a significant part of the public sector. Local Governments deal with issues close to the people and their operations and performance is an area for continuous debate and discussion. As the demands are increasing the activities are put under growing pressure, both financially and operationally. This call for management attention and the last two decades have shown a great variety of different management techniques to improve performance. In the wake of New Public Management (NPM) the local Government organisations have been subject to extensive reforms in structure and activities, all in purpose to make efficiency gains.

However, many efforts have been made and they are not solely a consequence of NPM. Over the years there have been reforms to merge local Governments, either voluntarily or by legislation, to create more economic viable organisations (Anell and Mattisson, 2009; Jones and Lüder, 2003). However, the impression is that this is not enough as different supplies have different requirements as to size (Byrnes and Dollery, 2002). Therefore local Governments also cooperate voluntarily within single supplies to increase volume and to create efficient conditions. One way for local Governments to cooperate is to form a jointly owned organisation with the purpose of a specific supply in a wider geographical area (e.g. several municipalities). In this way activities previously performed under a municipal department is moved and take place within the framework of a public enterprise. Despite two decades of NPM-inspired reforms, it seems that local Governments are turning back to public enterprises as a suitable form for public activities (Bognetti and

Oberman, 2012). New enterprises are formed resulting in a new thinking on policy, public mission and operations. There is an extensive research about inter-organisational cooperation (Huxham and Vangen 2005; Smith, Carrol and Ashford, 1995). However, less attention has been directed to local Government services provided in jointly owned public enterprises (Mattisson, 2000; Thomasson, 2009).

Few studies have been concerned with the question of what happens in the process after the new enterprise has been established. How can the established enterprise be managed once underway to put expected advantages into effect?

The empirical data steam from a three-years project with some 30 interviews per year (90 in total) about the initiation process and means of governance. VA SYD is owned by four municipalities and provides water and sewage services to some 475,000 inhabitants. The yearly turnover is approximately 100 M Euros.

The rest of the chapter is organised as follows. In the next section we describe the Swedish local Government context. In the next sections the case of VA SYD and its public mission is presented before the history and the regulating context. Then there is a section about governance and performance of VA SYD. Finally some conclusions and lessons learned are presented.

Local Government Cooperation in Joint Organisations

Cooperation between municipalities is currently extensively discussed, both in Sweden and other countries (Anell and Mattisson, 2009; Dollery and Johnsson, 2005; Warner, 2011). When Governments join forces there are high hopes for large-scale advantages and possibilities to share critical resources and competencies.

Swedish municipalities have a long tradition of cooperation and sharing resources and studies show that most municipalities are involved in networks and exchanges with other municipalities (Mattisson, 2000). Similar tendencies can be seen in other countries (Jones and Lüder, 2003). A large part of the municipalities claim that it is more and more difficult to fulfil their obligations and pursue their missions. Too many different tasks require too many different competences which make the small municipal organisation fragmented and less cost efficient. Some municipalities even question if they are able to carry the resources necessary to manage all their assignments (Knutsson *et al.*, 2008). In order to improve the scale of municipal activities the actors put their faith in cooperative initiatives. The rhetoric claims that there is no need for a new structure (merging municipalities) but a higher degree of cooperation within specific supplies will give scale-effects. Inter-municipal cooperation is seen as a central strategy to prepare the municipal sector for the challenges necessary to deal with. Historically, a majority of cooperative efforts have taken place in more or less temporary exchanges of resources (Anell and Mattisson, 2009). Normally it is a matter of networks for exchanging information or expertise of different kinds. However, as local Governments are put under stronger pressure more radical approaches are considered (Lapsley and Skaerbaek, 2012; Mattisson, 2013). It is getting more and more difficult to make both ends meet. To gain even more of large-scale advantages local Governments need more secure and stable institutions to cooperate within. Therefore a dramatic increase in number of joint municipal organisations is seen.

Development of local Government cooperation is considered to be a crucial strategy for the future of the municipal sector. In the infrastructure and technical sector co-operations exist. Common to them all is that they got initiated when several municipalities were experiencing that existing (or non-existent) technical facilities no longer met the formal (legal) requirements in areas such as water, sewage or waste. These organisations were formed to make a capital investment in a joint facility with enough capacity for all municipalities. The joint facility is a run as a separate unit providing the owning municipalities with treatment services for waste, water and sewage. Still, every municipality runs the local distribution etc. within its own geographical area. Large scale advantages have been realised within the plants and works but not in maintenance and operations of the networks. This is a fact that has been questioned in general but it has shown difficult to merge several local organisations.

An increased horizontal cooperation between local Governments is expected to be a crucial strategy for municipalities to develop in the future. To realise large scale advantages a higher degree of mutual adaption and integration is needed. This cannot be done in terms of loose networks, but requires a merger of resources and formation of a joint organisation to take responsibility for the things previously organised by the sole municipality.

VA SYD (Water and Sewage South) – Public Mission

VA SYD (Water and Sewage South) is running all water and sewage facilities in the geographical area of the four municipalities: Burlöv, Eslöv, Lund and Malmö. In total this represents some 475,000 inhabitants. In 2012, the turnover was approximately 895 MSEK (100 M Euros) and the organisation had some 300 employees. The organisation owns water works providing with some 20% of the total freshwater need. However, the major part is bought from Sydvatten AB, a water producing company owned by some 16 municipalities in the Scania region. The wastewater situation is different as VA SYD owns and run all wastewater treatment plants.

When the operations started in a new structural context it was time to establish a completely new organisation with its own procedures, identity and organisational culture. Early in this process, it became important to set long term goals and targets. Between 2008 and 2011 VA-SYD had a business idea describing what they do and a public mission (vision) as follow:

- *we contribute to sustainable development through long-term secure a good supply of fresh water and an ecocyclic sewage and household waste management.*

- *we are known to have cost efficient businesses with quality, safety and service in mind.*

- *we are an attractive workplace that is constantly evolving, find it easy to recruit staff and take advantage of people's differences*

- *we are, through our commitment to the environment, our high competence and cost efficiency an attractive partner to cooperate with and an organisation that more local authorities want to be part of.*

In the business plan for 2012-2014 the vision has been rephrased and shortened:

"VA SYD should be a leading actor in the sustainable society, for the customer and the environment."

It was considered important to state that the ambitions were long term and it was mainly about increasing the performance capacity of the organisation. Cost reduction possibilities were of interest, but mainly as an opportunity to redirect resources and increase performance. The ambition of the political leadership is to create an organisation that proactively could act long-term for sustainability and development.

VA SYD (Water and Sewage South) – History and Main Arguments

The origins of VA SYD can at least be dated back to the early 1990s. The municipality of Malmö was facing a disastrous financial situation and the politician started to sell infrastructural assets, for example the district heating system, to solve the financial crisis. Also the water and sewage business was under consideration for privatisation by the right wing local Government majority, but they decided to put the operation on tender instead. Anglian Water won the tender, but a new political majority decided to call of the tender and continue the operations in-house. Late

1990s the politicians started to discuss the municipality's role as a driving force for the regional development. The chairman of the technical council started to consult the surrounding municipalities to hear of their interest in a regional based water and sewage supply. However it was not until autumn 2002 that the concept of a joint organisation was established. In a formal meeting leading politicians and executives from Malmö and Lund started to talk about a more regional based water and sewage organisation. The short distance between the two municipalities (approximately 20 km) and a fairly large population were regarded as favourable for joint efforts. In each of the municipalities, the conditions and actual operations had been considered to work well before the merger. But politicians, in both municipalities, were aware that the water and sewage sector had gradually become more regulated and complex, making it difficult to meet future standards.

The establishment of VA SYD was preceded by several investigations and projects. At least four extensive reports analysing conditions and prerequisites were published and in the meantime two general city council elections took place. Gradually a consensus evolved about the basic reasons for cooperation and establishing VA SYD. Before the decision there was a clear political majority in both municipalities to view this initiative as the main component in a strategy to secure a competent and skilled public body for water and sewage supply. From interviews and documents it is possible to identify five main arguments behind the decision to form VA SYD:

– A foreseen problem with future *supply of skills* is the most frequent argument. In general, municipalities have low attractiveness as an employer. A large organisation is considered to provide better opportunities to create interesting work conditions in terms of scope and specialisation.

– Another argument is *increased demands on the environment protection and quality*. The requirements for sewage treatment works are continuously increasing, which requires new competencies, skills and development activities.

– *Increases in costs.* It is considered important to be efficient and a larger scale gives opportunities to make structural changes. The individual municipality risks to no longer being capable of bearing all fixed and capacity costs necessary.

– *Customers' view on the water and sewage supply* is an area that requires more attention. A large organisation has better opportunities to organise devoted capacity for external communication and customer support.

– *Changed responsibilities in society*, partly through changes in the Swedish Water act and the Water Framework Directive are also a driving force for change. Both forces require organising the supply of the water and sewage service over a wider geographical area.

All the five arguments are related to scale. As service volume increases it has better ability to bear the fixed costs, and it is easier to reach a critical volume of the activities requiring specialisation. Furthermore, it is also a matter of questioning the idea that each municipal territory is the best geographic area for organising water and sewage supply. A regional organisation is better equipped to initiate development and manage all these challenges. It is clear that collaboration was considered as a strategic measure in order to secure long-term capacity to upgrade the overall water and sewage supply system in the region.

The decision to form VA SYD was taken and it started January 1st 2008. The legal form is a statutory joint authority that was the result of a complete merge of two municipalities' capacities to provide water and sewage supply. A statutory joint authority can be formed by at least two municipalities and is formally regarded as a new individual entity, with the legal status of a municipality. All activities are completely funded by user fees and each municipality set their own user fee and decides upon their investment levels within its own geographical area. Subsequently, two more municipalities, Burlöv (2011) and Eslöv (2012), decided to join.

Regulation – The Empirical Context

The provision of water and sewage services in Sweden is regulated by the Public Water and Wastewater Plant Act from 2006 (SFS 2006:412). The municipalities are responsible for the provision of water and sewage services and for the management of storm water. Both services are usually conducted by the same organisational entity. The municipalities are according to the Local Government Act (SFS 1991:900) autonomous, which means that they to a large extent have the ability to decide how to arrange the provision of public services. As a consequence there are variations between municipalities in Sweden in regards to how the provision of services is organised. In-house solutions or municipally owned corporations used to be the most common solution for organising water and sewage services in Swedish municipalities. The provision of water and sewage is normally financed by fees. Tax subsidies are allowed but only used to a minor extent. The fee is decided yearly by the politicians in the local Government council and it is to be based on operational cost and investment plans for the coming years.

The calculation of the fees are regulated by the Water and Sewage Act (SFS 2006:412) and based upon a cost based price principle meaning that the fees charged for the provision of water and sewage services cannot exceed the actual cost the municipality has for providing the services. You are not allowed to make a profit in this sector and then use that profit in order to finance other public services. If a profit is made for one year, the municipality is required to state in the investment plan, for the three coming years, how the profit is going to be used. Since the fee is based upon the actual costs, this means that the level of the fee is influenced by the level of investments and maintenance as well as geographical conditions within a municipality. Due to differences in conditions between municipalities, the cost for providing the services and, thus also the fee, differs from one municipality to another.

The fee for water supply and wastewater management normally consists of two components: a fixed part and a current price that depends on the consumption (almost all consumers have water meters). The division between the two components varies from municipality to municipality. For example, municipalities with seasonal tourism have decided to almost only base the fee upon a fixed price considering that the consumption of water varies with the season, but cost for the services are constant.

The municipalities are, according to the Water and Sewage Act (2006:412), obliged to separate the financial statement for water and sewage services from the rest of the municipal activities. This in order to be able to account for that the fee does not exceed the necessary cost of providing the services. The level of the fee is decided by the politicians in the municipal council and the decision is based upon information provided by civil servants in the organisation providing for the services.

Governance and Performance of VA SYD

The main reason to initiate VA SYD was to create viable conditions for the future. Increasing demands from regulation and users meant high future investment needs. At the same time the base of resources and competencies were perceived to be insufficient for the future requirements. Apart from facing potential difficulties to organise a stable supply, there was also a risk for dramatic raises of user fees and lost of legitimacy for politicians. However, even if the fees have been raised in the four municipalities since the start of VA SYD, they are still comparatively low compared to rest of Sweden. The on-going growth of VA-SYD makes it too early to value the performance, but the management team has, since 2011, put considerable efforts to better measure different internal processes and goal achievements.

Most of the administrative routines and capacity, as well as the organisational structure came from the former unit in Malmö. However, when merging the activities and the services there were differences in more or less every aspect. It was different size of the operations, different hydraulic conditions and differences in the spatial structure as to the population density and finally also differences of the physical conditions of the assets (works and networks). Even though the ambition was to integrate all operations into one organisational unit it was regarded unfair (and thereby impossible) to merge all this into one single economic entity. Differences needed to be accounted for. Therefore it was decided to create separate economic entities and different user fees. Organisationally, this was arranged by separate ownership councils, one for each municipality. These ownership councils were organised under the VA SYD board and were responsible for the supply in its' own municipality. This ownership council is a forum for the local political involvement as they are responsible for deciding user fees and the capital investments (and the capital costs) within the municipality. (See Figure 1.)

Figure 1. The Chain of Command in VA SYD

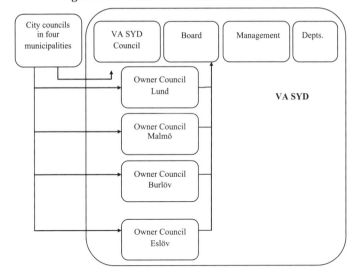

To create a joint-stock company was never an alternative. The politicians feared the risk that political trade-offs and influence would be neglected in favour of professionals seeking efficiency. Therefore, the politicians considered crucial to have overall strong political governance. Representatives from all political compounds stressed that a political organisation requires political governance.

Politicians focused on having a statutory joint authority. It was considered important to have a broad political participation in order to create commitment, transparency and control. By having a joint council there were more seats for elected representatives giving room for involving also the smaller parties, something considered to strengthen the democratic influence in general.

Collaboration means doing things together and there was much support for doing so. The basic idea was to join forces and collect all resources at one place to be able to realise synergies and increase performance. However, even though it was clearly outspoken that a joint organisation (resources for production) was desirable it was also an unconditional political demand to keep separate economic entities. The ambitions for investment in water supply, and the associated fee for it, would be kept separately for each municipality. Besides the physical conditions there were also ideological differences between the municipalities concerning the distribution of fixed and variable components in the water and sewage fee. By introducing an owner-council for each municipality the two water and sewage collectives could be kept apart while the joint authority's resources and capabilities can be used in both municipalities. Revenues and cost could then be allocated to the different municipalities in accordance to use of joint resources and political ambitions for that municipality. In addition, politicians also argue that the owner-councils are important to ensure democratic accountability.

The organisation is reporting to a board governing the organisation. The board is reporting to the VA SYD elected council that is the formal outmost decision maker about policies and operations within VA SYD as a whole. Considering decisions about investments and fees in the different municipalities these issues are decided by the ownership councils. Even though they are not legally regulated, all parties have agreed to respect the ownership councils' directives when decisions are to be made in the general council.

None of the politicians are directly critical to how the governance of the joint authority practically works. They say they have the influence and role one would expect given the design made. One issue, however, reached the boundaries between politicians and officials. When the information to the politicians becomes more overarching and the political decisions more aggregate, there is the risk that certain issues fall away. The view of the extent to which policies should be involved and decide on individual cases varies greatly among the politicians. No one is really critical to the procedure that exists today, but some note that the issue will be discussed more. The organisation still needs to develop its own political culture and form.

The chief officials perceive the statutory joint authority well suited for the task. It is an advantage to have a close relation to the political leadership in a public legal form. As water and sewage is closely connected to other supplies at the local level an open Government form is well suited to its supply with a long-term nature of existence. Fundamentally, the tone is positive as the officials perceive VA SYD as robust and forward looking. Starting from an overall perspective, the politicians state that they sense that the organisation wants to be involved and contribute to future development. Aside from initial problems of integration, the chief officials express that the governance generally works well and provides good conditions to deliver good quality of services.

However good in theory, the chief officials note that the political governance structure have the potential to become a practical and administrative problem. With four owner-municipalities, the number of political fora (and meetings) grows quickly and they all need similar, but slightly different, information. The division into different economic entities with different politicians is perceived to make things complicated (costly) and difficult for the executives. On the other hand, the political insights into operations have to be considered as substantial. The chief officials try to harmonise conditions and operations to save money but are getting endless reminders that there are differences in ambitions and focus. Especially, this is a problem concerning how to invest and its consequences for the daily operations. For example, the condition of the works and networks that came into the joint authority varied greatly. Harmonising the standards requires investment decisions from the owner councils, something they have shown reluctant to so far. Instead, they have being giving priority to rationalise and looking for low costs. Hence, the levels of ambitions are seen to vary between municipalities and between politicians. Primarily this affects the investment levels but in the longer run also the operations budget and operational procedures. Systematic planning gets more complicated when there are differences within one supply. Also on-going operations become more complicated as separate economic entities require different levels of ambition (and actions). In total this may counteract some of the positive effects hoped for. From the lower levels within the organisation there is an expressed demand for a joint vision and an explicit regional configuration (not one for every municipality) as a theme for a new and adapted regional organisation.

Ownership *vs.* Governance – A Discussion

From the interviews, the overall impression is that politicians, as well as chief officials, generally perceive as positive to carry out operations in a larger and more specialised organisation. From time to time it will result in problem of boundaries against other municipal services but the benefits of having a specialised organisation compensate for these problems. Our empirical studies indicate that there are economies of scale to realise. However, there are several difficulties to overcome and many adjustments are needed.

The ownership councils have been introduced to meet the political demands to separate between different municipalities' water and sewage collectives and thus the water and sewage economies. From a political standpoint, it was a crucial prerequisite for the cooperation to take place at all. Two reasons were important. The first is that no one wants to mix money and assets. The other is that no municipality wants to relinquish decision-making power and exclusive political influence over "their own" water and sewage supply. It is clear that the system of ownership councils primarily serves political purposes. Seen from the operational issues, it would be significantly easier with a clearly defined governance board for all operations, i.e. one strong decision-maker. Fewer governing bodies would likely increase the chances of identifying one single aim that define a common quality standard for the entire VA SYD.

The construction of several governing bodies is complicated and not ideal. Some difficulties have been identified even though the study has identified a number of benefits. And there is also a strong belief that cooperation is a way to create opportunities to meet future demand. The complications surrounding the ownership councils (or any possible counterpart) are a consequence of the requirements to have separate decision-making abilities (and economic units). It is not possible to organise away these problems. Instead, the only way to solve the problem is to give up on this requirement. In general, the easiest way is to integrate all activities into one economic unit. If this is not a realistic alternative, the management challenge is to find practical solutions to deal with the diversity and balance of the common and unique for each individual municipality.

By cooperating in a joint organisation, local Governments strengthen their abilities to create stronger organisational forms to enable overview and system thinking and rethinking. Realising the advantages of a larger scale requires a regional vision and strategic direction that guide the municipal decision makers to both think and act on a regional level. It is a balancing act.

The empirical data indicates that several of the main reasons for creating a joint organisation are being realised. A positive attitude towards being part of the organisation is expressed by both the politicians and the management team. The interviews show a lot of commitment to the organisation and on being a driving force to develop and create something new. The general notion is that VA SYD is recognised as an attractive employer. Despite a difficult hiring situation in general, the recruitments works well. Although customers may notice short-term effects, for better or worse, much of the organisation's activities focus on long term. There have been extensive efforts to create uniformity with respect to performance and quality, in many cases at a higher quality level than before. As for cost levels and efficiency, it is too early to say. However, it is worth mentioning that user fees have been increased in all four municipalities since VA SYD started. One explanation is generally higher levels of ambition in terms of common equipment (surveillance of facilities) and joint systems (security, it) but also the purchase cost of water has increased.

Both politicians and senior officials show enthusiasm about the early years. Initially in the process, this was not the case in the lower levels of the organisation where the views were more blended. Critics questioned if VA SYD really was a necessary step to take since major changes was needed anyway and the advantages of the merger difficult to apprehend. Much of the scepticism expressed focused on being part of a much larger organisation compared to the individual municipal units that people worked for before. Since procedures got more formalised, people complained about increased bureaucracy and less focus on professional issues. Both politicians and chief officials stressed the need to attend to hard as well as soft factors in the process. A major effort was made to create systematic procedures and processes (technical systems) for how VA SYD should work. The positive effects are only to be realised when common standards are implemented. However, apart from the technical systems, equally important is the employees and self-image within the organisation.

A programme was introduced to get all employees to feel and commit to the common organisation, i.e. VA SYD. Despite the commitment, still there were differences in preferences about what level of performance was reasonable to aim for and how the operations were to be organised. The situation was accentuated by the fact that the different municipalities had brought their water and sewage assets into VA SYD and the standard of these assets varied greatly. As the different geographical areas (i.e. municipalities) had profound differences in physical standards, it created tensions in daily operations about were to allocate resources, both for maintenance and investments. However, these tensions also created moment of discussions and opportunities to adjust personal views. Gradually, less criticism has been expressed and more of positive observations are expressed. In early 2013, the general impression from the interviews is that VA SYD is considered to be a good idea with great potential for the future. Many of the employees express devotion to be part of creating something new.

From a leadership perspective some observations can be made. Firstly, VA SYD expresses an ambition to create a favourable structure for water and sewage supply that would work long-term and give opportunities to meet the future demands from the society. A bigger scale and being part of an organisation solely focusing on one sector give better conditions to upgrade and adjust for the future. It is described as "crucial" to be able cope with technical challenges and provide a steady and secure supply. The challenge is to show ability to innovate and adapt to new demands at the same time. Present and potential new stakeholders (connected to things as sustainability, ethics, and contributions to society as a whole) are better served by a stronger (i.e. bigger) organisation. This has to be linked to the technical skills that are highly valued historically. A common denominator in the statement from the interviews is that everyone seems to agree that in the long run, this is a matter of survival. The VA SYD initiative was never a project focusing on reducing costs. Instead the emphasis was on organisation's ability to develop for the future and meet raised service standards. However, cost levels and priorities are mentioned in these discussions. In general, people within the organisation acknowledge that development work is taking place (to what extent varies between the units) and that the costs have increased less than was expected (due to issues related to integration and innovation).

A larger structure creates better operating conditions for the organisation. In the interviews it is indicated that economies of scale in planning and production is being realised gradually. It has been possible to identify generic resources and activities that can be used in all municipalities. For activities in operations, it is easy to allocate the cost to the correct entity. Therefore, the costs will be lower as the resources are shared between several collectives.

On the other hand, a condition to set up the joint organisation was to keep the economic entities separate and guarantee that politicians in each municipality may decide upon fees and investments independently from others. Thus it is possible for each municipality to integrate some resources with others, without being fully harmonised. Even though VA SYD is about decision making about water supply in a regional context, a majority of the politicians will continue to primarily work within their own community. They are local politicians with their main obligations towards their local voters. Therefore it is perceived crucial that every municipality decide upon their own fees and investment plans.

When it comes to long-term decision-making the situation is different. Efforts to coordinate and harmonise the organisation can be observed among the chief officials. From a practical point of view the officials claim that it is comparatively easy to coordinate procedures and assets that are possible to use in all municipalities. However, issues close to activities and priorities directly connected to the owner-councils have been substantially different. From the political bodies, statements have been made to preserve unique features for the different municipalities. One example is the user fee and the division in fixed and variable components. The management group suggested a unified structure for all municipalities (still with individually set user fees for each municipality). So far it has shown difficult to agree upon all the details and no change has yet come into effect. There are similar tendencies when it comes to capital investments in physical assets. From the professionals and the management there is a continuous search for technical solutions and establishing efficiency. Establishing norms for general operations and support functions make the activities more cost efficient. The politicians are, however, hesitant to accept minimum standard levels. Since the starting point differs, it is costly for politicians to agree on a minimum standard if the assets are in a weak condition. Therefore politicians are reluctant to accept minimum levels since it may result in raised user fee, something they wish to avoid as long as possible.

Concerning investment plan (and user fees) there is a continuous discussion going on about priorities and directions. In all municipalities, politicians have taken strong action to maintain the sole right to decide about capital expenditures within their own municipalities. The leading municipal politicians clearly express a will to form their own approach and decide on investment priorities, independently from other municipalities. Officials (and leading politicians within VA SYD) on the other hand, seek uniform solutions possible to accept for local politicians in all four municipalities.

To be able to act forcefully, these governance issues need to be sorted out. Until now the process has been handled by a constant muddling through as obstacles are dealt with as they have occurred. Some issues have proven difficult and have been left unsolved. A vast amount of practical issues to deal with have taken attention away from the systematic long-term structural work to realise the vision and the greater motives behind a larger and more forceful joint organisation. To further develop VA SYD there is a need for approach integrating activities in the different municipalities. Without a shared strategy, consented to by all municipalities, the structure which separates economic entities, risks to create political tension and less power to act regionally (as was an initial motive). The potential success in realising the scale effects sought for is entirely determined by the ability to unite the politicians to adapt to one another and decide on one consistent strategy.

Conclusions and Lessons Learned

The process of establishing the new organisation turned out to be a challenging task requiring a lot of time. In hindsight it is clear that the individuals involved never expected to take so long to get things into operation. Initially, a majority of the employees claimed not to know much about the intentions behind the merger, but eventually the potential positive effects of size were spread in the organisation. However, the hopes of potential advantages as a regional player were gradually side-lined as operational and practical things with integration took most of the attention. It was not until 2012, four years after the start that the operations were set in a true regional structure.

Overall, it is perceived as positive to conduct the operations in a larger (and specialised) organisation. Despite problems of boundaries against other municipal functions (such as physical planning, environment) the positive effects are clearly mentioned. There are economies of scale, but they are difficult to implement and realise. Also, each municipality emphasises the importance of its ownership council and ability to act from its own agenda. One reason is not to mix assets and money from different municipalities, another one is unwillingness to hand over decision power for "their own" assets to politicians from other municipalities. It has not proved possible to create a single view on priorities and goals for quality. Overall, this gives a situation where the joint organisation has to work towards ambiguous and shifting objectives.

It is worth noticing that the system of ownership councils primarily serves political purposes. Politicians want to represent their own residents. There is a general resistance towards integrating a single municipal supply (genuinely local in character) into a regional structure. From an executive or professional view it would be significantly easier with one single clearly defined political council. Fewer governing bodies would likely increase the possibility to define a common quality standard for the entire supply.

A number of advantages with a larger scale have been identified and there is a strong belief that the bigger organisation is a mean to meet future demands. However, the design with several governing bodies is complicated and somewhat problematic. The ownership councils are a consequence of the need to separate influence and safeguard municipality's capacity to decide within their areas. This situation creates a complexity that cannot be organised away. The only way to deal with it is to drop the condition of separate economic entities. If it is unrealistic to create a common joint economic entity, the only way is to find practical solutions to deal with the diversity and balance between the joint and the unique.

A key hope was that a larger organisation would increase the attractiveness on an external market. After five years, VA SYD is considered to be a secure organisation that is able to perform its task, although slow and bureaucratic at times. Increased size of operations has brought opportunities to introduce a more structured approach towards both political bodies and users. As things have turned out, the organisation today has a clearer and more uniform contact with their clients.

As for the impact on operating costs, it is difficult today to see these ambitions fulfilled. One important reason for this is all about the difficulty of measuring and comparing cost effectiveness. The development does not indicate that the current operating costs decreased, rather the opposite. However, there is reason to interpret these figures with caution as the supply today is larger and generally performs more activities. The initial years were characterised by inventories and adjustments to lift all the parts into a unified quality. Added to this, there have been special initiatives such as safety and security. It is noted that in several cases these activities were never performed before in a single municipal department. To that extent it is to be considered as cost driving to join the bigger organisation.

As the initial ambitions were to develop the supply system it may be considered as acceptable with initial cost driving investments. However, the challenge to come will be to make these rearrangements quickly and cost efficient so it is possible to enjoy the benefits of the bigger structure.

The interview data indicate that the power of a larger organisation has come into effect. Staffing is today less dependent on single individuals and the operations thus less vulnerable. There are also more opportunities to put up plans and programmes to develop the competence perspective as an individual. Meanwhile, it is also noted that things are more bureaucratic in the larger organisation that relies more on systems and procedures.

It is important to note that the merger into a new and joint organisation has meant an extensive effort to document and consolidate activities and resources, i.e. facilities, personnel and procedures. More and better information about network conditions and weaknesses of the system meant requests for development to "lift" all components to a minimal level. Not infrequently, this has also led to more or less urgent investments. The organisation today delivers much higher quality in terms of systematic information about the facilities and their function. Additionally, the organisation is also better equipped to implement uniform systems to run their facilities ahead. Thus, this has initially driven investments and cost but also gradually increased quality.

A clear impression from the study of VA SYD is a need to enhance efficiency as well as effectiveness. From a strategic viewpoint it is a matter of ensuring that scale and synergy benefits are realised at the same time as legitimacy is secured. For a single (or small) organisation this is a challenging work as it has to be done despite demanding regulation and restrained budgets. By joining forces and a creating a bigger and more resourceful organisation the local Government facilitates for analysis and solutions on the system level. This is an opportunity to influence the vacuum of effectiveness at a system level (Figure 2).

On the local level, acting for object efficiency limits the possibilities to develop the local supply. Instead it is desirable for local Governments to contribute to the regional vision and act on a system level. Short-term improvements of single activities (or facilities) need to be balanced against their impact on the effectiveness on the system level. To improve on the system level consistent actions needs to be taken in every step where investments and reinvestments are made. Step by step the system of facilities will develop and improve in quality and performance.

Figure 2. Different Concepts of Efficiency on the Object and System

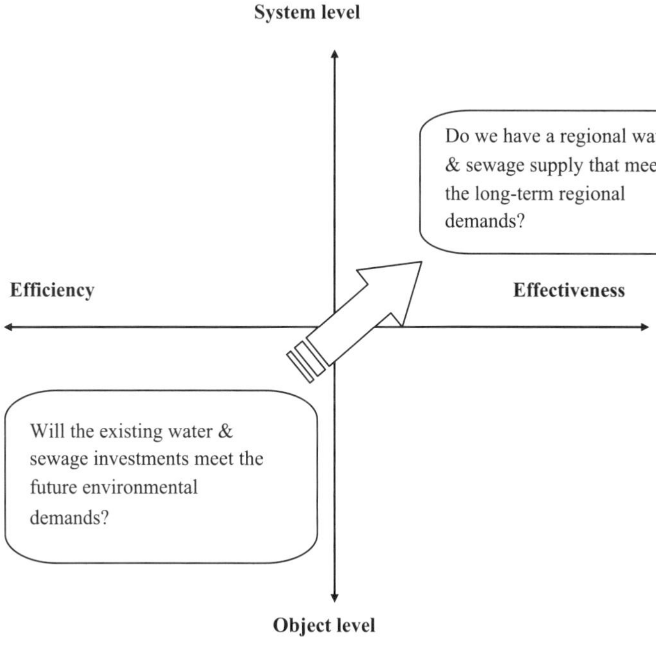

System level

Do we have a regional water & sewage supply that meets the long-term regional demands?

Efficiency   **Effectiveness**

Will the existing water & sewage investments meet the future environmental demands?

Object level

To realise the potentials with the larger organisation it is needed that local politicians are willing to hand over decision-making to the organisation and thereby also adjust to the others parties. Expecting too much of local adjustments within the same organisation results in complicated conditions for management as it will bring different subsets of procedures in each local setting.

Much of the issues discussed in this chapter highlights governance issues and questions to deal with when an organisation is newly initiated and finding its forms. When standards are set and a joint approach is developed and shared it becomes less feasible to request special conditions. For new municipalities to enter, they have to comply in full with the joint approach as it is, and with no room for exceptions. From the view of the professionals this is a desirable situation as it gives stable conditions. However, it raises issues of the politicians' influence and accountability. It may show difficult to act strategically on the regional level and then face political accountability, by other measures, on the local level. Will politicians be able to decide on actions locally to support the performance on the regional (system) level? What types of conditions will this give for the professional (management) to realise the potentials of the bigger organisation? These are issues that certainly need more research attention.

References

Anell, A., Mattisson, O., *Samverkan i kommuner och landsting*, Studentlitteratur, Lund, 2009.

Bognetti, G., Oberman, G., "Local Public Services in European countries: Main Results of a Research project by Ciriec international", in *Annals of Public and Cooperative Economics*, 2012, Vol. 83, No. 4, pp. 485-503.

Byrnes, J., Dollery, B., "Do Economies of Scale Exist in Australian Local Government? A Review of the Research Evidence", in *Urban Policy and Research*, 2002, Vol. 20, No. 41, pp. 391-414.

Huxham, C., Vangen, S., *Managing to Collaborate. The Theory and Practice of Collaborative Advantage*, London Routledge, 2005.

Jones, R., Lüder, K., *"Reforming Governmental accounting and budgeting in Europe"*, 2003, PWC, Berlin.

Knutsson, H., Mattisson, O., Ramberg, U., Tagesson, T., "Do management and strategy matter in municipal organisations?", in *Financial Accountability & Management*, 2008, Vol. 24, No. 3, pp. 295-319.

Lapsley, I., Skaerbaek, P., "Why the Public Sector Matters", in *Financial Accountability & Management*, 2012, Vol. 24, No. 1, pp. 355-358.

Mattisson, O., *Kommunala huvudmannastrategier för kostnadspress och utveckling – En studie av kommunal teknik*, Lund Business Press, 2000.

Mattisson, O., *Organisation och styrning på den lokala samhällsnivån – en forskningsöversikt om förändringar och utvecklingstendenser*, Lunds Universitet, Bilaga till utredningen om en Kommunallag för framtiden, 2013.

Mattisson, O., Ramberg, U., *VA SYD 2008-2012. Framväxt och värdering av ett Kommunalförbund*, Lund University, Institute of Economic Research, 2013.

Smith, K., Carrol, S., Ashford, S., "Intra- and Interorganisational Cooperation: Toward a Research Agenda", in *Academy of Management Journal*, 1995, Vol. 38, No. 1, pp. 7-23.

Thomassson, A., *Navigating in the landscape of ambiguity*, Lund Business Press, 2009.

Warner, M., "Competition or Cooperation in Urban Service Delivery?", in *Annals of Public and Cooperative Economics*, 2011, Vol. 82, No. 4, pp. 421-435.

3. Milan's Water and Sanitation Service after Corporatisation

Metropolitana Milanese Spa

Olivier Crespi REGHIZZI*

CIRED, AgroParisTech & CERTET, Bocconi University

1. Introduction

This case study focuses on of Milan's water and sanitation service (WSS). Since 2003, Milan's WSS has been provided by *Metropolitana Milanese* Spa (MM) which is a joint stock company fully owned by Milan's municipality. Previously, from its creation in 1888 till 2003, Milan's WSS has always been directly provided by Milan's municipality under full direct management (Crespi Reghizzi, forthcoming b; d).

Metropolitana Milanese Spa (MM) runs two different businesses: i) the water and sanitation service for Milan city area[1] (we shall refer to MM-WSS in this case study), ii) civil engineering services mainly in the transportation sector (we shall refer to MM-ENG in this case study).

Both business areas are clearly operated distinctly since MM-WSS is tightly regulated (Section 6) while MM-ENG is unregulated and operated on the market. The present case study focuses particularly on the WSS area of MM even though some aspects of MM as a whole shall be analyzed too.

* An earlier version of this paper has been presented in June 2013 at the Milan European Economic Workshop in the framework of the CIRIEC research project "The Future of Public Enterprise". We wish to thank the Paris water operator *Eau de Paris* and the French *Agence Nationale de la Recherche* (ANR) through the EAU&3E research project (http://eau3e.hypotheses.org) for their financial support. We also thank *Metropolitana Milanese Spa* for all the data and all the interviewees for their availability and kindness.

[1] *Servizio idrico integrato della città di Milano.*

Box 1: Metropolitana Milanese SpA

Metropolitana Milanese SpA – Soggetta a direzione e coordinamento dell'azionista unico Comune di Milano. Codice fiscale/partita IVA 01742310152   Legal adress & headquarters: Via del Vecchio Politecnico, 8 20121 – Milan – Italy – Phone +39 02 77 471   WSS area offices Via Meda, 44 – 20141 Milan – Italy – Phone +39 02 84 77 1   http://www.metropolitanamilanese.it

Source: http://www.metropolitanamilanese.it, February 26 2013.

Box 2: basic information on Metropolitana Milanese in 2011

MM as a whole   – Turnover: 233 M euros   – Number of employees: 714 people   – Area of operation: Water (E36) and sewerage (E37) + civil engineering services (F42)   – Owner: *Comune di Milano*   MM-WSS (Water and Sanitation part of MM only   – Turnover: 123 M euros   – Number of employees: 463 people   – Area of operation: water and sanitation services   – Population served: 1.35 M people   – Number of meters: 47 136   – Water volumes billed: 231 M m³/year

Source: author's elaboration based on data from Metropolitana Milanese SpA.

This case study adopts two perimeters of analysis: i) a company perimeter focused on MM-WSS when one limits the analysis of the water and sanitation service to the company which performs the service and ii) a wider perimeter which includes all the stake-holders of Milan's WSS (see Figure 3).

Section 2 focuses on operations of MM while section 3 analyses the corporatisation process in the water sector in Milan (and in Italy). Section 4 examines the implementation of the public service missions. Technical and financial performances are treated in section 5 while sections 6 and 7 focus on regulation and governance respectively. Section 8 analyses tariff issues.

2. Operations

2.1. Water Supply and Sewer Networks

MM runs entirely on its own the water service of the city of Milan within the regulatory area of the *ATO Città di Milano* (see also section 6). MM runs entirely on its own the sewer network too, while wastewater treatment plants are operated by external companies.

Operations concerning water supply and sewer networks include: running and monitoring of the wells and pumping stations, daily maintenance of all the water supply and sewer infrastructure, water quality control, metering, billing and customer service. It also includes the asset management of the entire infrastructure: investments planning, implementation of the various administrative steps, procurement and monitoring of the public works. Engineering and design studies are made by the engineering services (MM-ENG) of MM itself and their costs are re-invoiced to the WSS area (MM-WSS). Works are tendered through public bids.

2.2. Wastewater Treatment

Until 2005, the city of Milan had no wastewater treatment plants and water was discharge with no treatment into the river system. Three plants are now in operation: Nosedo, San Rocco and Peschiera Borromeo. Although MM does not operate those plants, it bills and collects a wastewater treatment fee from the users and pays the external entity in charge of the plant's operation according to the terms of each specific legal agreement.

Nosedo treatment plant (1,250,000 population equivalent capacity) is operated by a private company *Milanodepur SpA* representing the consortium of companies[2] which built that plant through a project-financing scheme (DBOT). MM pays a yearly fee[3] to *Milanodepur SpA*. MM also pays directly energy and sewage sludge disposal which are not included in the yearly fee.

San Rocco plant (1,050,000 population equivalent) is operated by *Degremont SpA* which was the leading partner of the consortium which built that plant. Milan's municipality owns the plant. MM pays a yearly fee to *Degremont SpA* which is inclusive of all the operating costs (including energy and sludge disposal).

The Peschiera Borromeo line[4] treating Milan wastewater (250,000 population equivalent) is owned by *CAP Holding SpA* and operated by

---

[2]   SIBA SpA (leading partner), Degremont Italia SpA, Pssavant Impianti SpA, Veolia WST Italia SpA, Unieco Scarl, Bonatti SpA, Itinera SpA are shareholders of the consortium. Operations are however delegated to *Vettabbia Società Consortile a responsabilità limitata.* source: http://www.depuratorenosedo.eu, retrieved the 26/2/2013.

[3]   The DBOT agreement was signed by the consortium and by Milan's municipality. However MM pays the yearly fee (*canone g* and *canone f*) to Milano Depur SpA on behalf of Milan's municipality.

[4]   The Peschiera Borromeo wastewater treatment plant treats mainly wastewater coming from the ATO Provincia di Milano sewer system. One line of the plant is dedicated to Milan city's wastewater. Obviously the plant is run as a whole and wastewater from Milan city and from the Milan provincial are obviously mixed and treated altogether.

AMIA Acque SpA (previously *CAP gestione SpA*). MM transfers to *AMIA Acque SpA* all the "waste water treatment" revenues billed to users located in the eastern area of Milan's municipality and connected to the Peschiera treatment plant. MM makes no earnings on the wastewater treatment part of the service with those users (except a small billing fee).

It appears that no capital expenditure or financial costs on the past investments in the wastewater infrastructure are due or currently paid by MM. All these costs were and are covered by Milan's municipality. MM received existing waste water treatment plants as an infrastructure capital stock "granted" with no capital costs, amortization or financial costs induced. Nevertheless nowadays MM is responsible of the investment policy on those assets (maintenance and new investments).

2.3. Engineering

In 2011 the organisational structure of MM was reformed in order to create more integration between the two areas of business (MM-WSS and MM-ENG).

A part of MM-ENG provides engineering services (technical studies, design, procurement, works supervision) for the water and sanitation department of MM. Another part of MM-ENG works on infrastructure engineering projects on behalf of Milan's municipality through an in house contract awarding which does not require open tendering.

Since 2006, new contracts of MM for other Italian public administrations cannot be signed.[5] Therefore activities of the engineering department of MM in Italy can be provided only to Milan's municipality (including other municipally owned companies such as SEA which owns and runs Milan airports) and to other Italian private sector companies (*Società Autostrade*, the highways company, for example). Thus, services provided internally to the MM-WSS department represent a significative percentage of the activities of the MM-ENG department.

It appears from our interviews that an internal accounting reform has been undertaken in 2011 together with the organisational one. MM-WSS and MM-ENG are now considered as autonomous entities from

---

[5]   Indeed the Bersani decree (D.L. 4-7-2006 n. 223 e legge 248/2006) established accordingly to the EU principles that services could be provided to a local public administration by companies owned by the local public administration itself through in-house provision. Conversely companies operating in-house for their owner (local public administration) cannot work for other local public administrations. To comply to the new legislation separate branches (*Metro engineering* srl and *Napoli metro engineering srl*) were created to fulfill previously existing contracts (particularly the Naples underground lines) with other public administrations.

an accounting point of view in order to have a transparent view of the profitability and cost-effectiveness of the two areas of business. We have been told that the services delivered from MM-ENG to MM-WSS are billed at market prices with no cross-subsidies taking place but we have not been able to countercheck such information.

Box 3: The History of Metropolitana Milanese

Metropolitana Milanese SpA was created by the municipal administration in 1955 to design and build the underground. Works started in 1957 and the first line was brought to completion by 1964. In 1969 the first part of the second underground line was completed. In 1990 the first part of the third underground line was completed. MM was responsible of the realization of the underground lines on behalf of Milan's municipality while these are operated by the ATM, the municipal public transport company.

Source: http://www.metropolitanamilanese.it/pub/page/it/MM/storia, retrieved April 23rd 2013.

3. Corporatisation

3.1. A Classification of WSS According to their Legal Status

Despite the great variety of institutional models of the water and sanitation services in Europe (Barraqué, 1995), public water and sanitation entities can be classified in three major categories according to their degree of autonomy and to their legal and accounting rules status as shown in Table 1:

- in the first category (Cat A) water and sanitation services are municipal departments with no legal autonomy, ruled by administrative law and public accounting rules;
- in the second category (Cat B) water and sanitation services are autonomous legal entities ruled by public law and public accounting);
- in the third category (Cat C) there are companies ruled by private law and private accounting rules, fully or partially owned by municipalities or other public bodies.

Table 1: Institutional Status of the WSS in Europe

	Cat. A	Cat. B	Cat. C
	Full municipal provision	Autonomous municipal provision	Corporatised provison
Germany	*Regiebetriebe*	*Eigenbetriebe*	*Eigengesellschaften* et *StadtWerke*
Spain	Existing	Existing	Joint stock company

	Cat. A	Cat. B	Cat. C
	Full municipal provision	Autonomous municipal provision	Corporatised provison
France	Régie simple or régie à autonomie financière	Régie à personnalité morale et autonomie financière, EPIC, EPCI	Société d'Economie Mixte SEM or Société Publique Locale SPL
Italy	Servizi in economia	Azienda municipalizzata / azienda speciale	Società per Azioni
Portugal	Existing	Existing	Holding and subsidiaries Aguas de Portugal
Switzerland	Services municipaux	Some stadtwerkepfliege	
Wallonia (Belgium)	Régie directe	Interco	

Source: author's elaboration.

In Italy, the *Legge Giolitti* on the municipalisation of local public services was approved in 1903 and modified in 1925.[6] The *Azienda Municipalizzata* legal framework was defined together with the legal procedure to be adopted by a municipality wishing to procede to a municipalisation. "In-house" provision of the service was still authorized, particularly for those municipalities which were already directly providing the service[7] (Rotondi, 1997).

Despite various attemps through the decades after WWII to introduce a reform of the 1903 Giolitti act on local public services (Arcangeli, 2000, p. 457), it was only in 1990 that a significant reform of local public services was made (*Legge* 8 giugno 1990 No. 142). According to the 1990 act, local public services could be provided through the following four institutional forms: a) direct provision (Cat A), b) concession to a private partner, c) through an *azienda speciale*[8] (a new name for the *azienda municipalizzata*) (Cat B) or d) through a private plc partially or totally owned by the municipality (Cat C).

In 1994, an ambitious reform of the water sector was launched (*Legge Galli* 36/1994). It implied an autonomisation of Italian WSS, as only the three last institutional models of service provision were allowed while formal direct provision was excluded. In 2001,[9] the *azienda speciale*

---

6   *Legge 29 marzo 1903 No. 103, Regio Decreto 30 dicembre 1923 and Regio Decreto 15 ottobre 1925 No. 2578.*

7   In Milan the water and sanitation services already existed as municipal departments prior to the 1903 lax. Their institutional form was not impacted then by the 1903 reform. Conversely the *Azienda Energetica Municipale (AEM)* was created to operate the municipal power plants.

8   Modifications were made to the 1986 decree DPR No. 902 which fixed the organisation and accounting rules of the *Aziende Municipalizzate*.

9   According to the decree n. 448/2001 (Art. 35).

legal status was not allowed anymore and the joint-stock company was the only legal form allowed regardless of the ownership (public, private or mixed). This was the kick off to the full corporatisation of Italian WSS.

3.2. Corporatisation of Milan's WSS

The Milan's WSS were under direct provision (*gestione in economia –* CAT A) from their creation in 1888 until 2003 (Crespi Reghizzi, forthcoming b; d).

In Milan, as in the rest of Italy, the Galli reform was implemented with a significant degree of inertia. In 1997, the Formentini municipal administration had chosen to transform Milan's WSS from direct provision into an *azienda speciale*. Such a shift never took place and the forthcoming municipal administration (Mayor Albertini) opted instead in favour of a municipally owned joint stock company (Lobina and Paccagnan, 2005).

At first the idea was to create a specific joint stock company (SOGEA) which would have been owned by the municipality (99 % of the shares) with a small share holding by AEM (the municipal power company which had been partially privatised). However the 2001 decree (*decreto* 448/2001) made public tendering compulsory to choose WSS operators with the only exception of WSS operated by fully municipally owned joint stock companies.

In November 2002, Milan city administration decided to award a 3 to 5 year water supply and sanitation concession for the ATO *Città di Milano to Metropolitana Milanese (MM)* which was formerly responsible of the engineering and design services in the urban public transport sector (Box 3). WSS operations were transferred to MM in June 2003.

What were the reasons behind such a decision? According to our interviewees one of the reasons was the need to budget-balance MM-ENG with new activities and revenues.

4. Public Service Mission and General Interest Goals

4.1. Public Service Mission Goals in Watsan

What do we mean by *"public service mission"* for WSS? This is a vast concept and in this paper when talking of "public service mission" we shall refer mainly to the following goals:

- universal provision and equal access to the service by all citizens;
- an investment policy driven by a long run vision and an intergenerational concern;
- water resources conservation and environmental protection.

Central and Local Government also have general interest goals: "these include for example policies related to employment, containment of inflation, promotion of research and development, of human capital, of fixed capital accumulation, competition and industrial policies" (CIRIEC, 2012). Indeed public service entities or companies behaviour might be influenced explicitly or implicitly in order to fulfil these general interest goals.

To what extent and how are Milan's WSS, now provided by MM, committed to clear public service goals? Is it driven by general interest goals too?

4.1.1. Explicit Public Service Obligations

Historically in the decades of full direct provision, the public service obligations were implicit and not formalised. Since 2003 a distinct entity, MM is responsible of the WSS's provision on behalf of Milan's municipality (corporatised model – category B- Table 1). Public service obligations are then formalised through various documents: i) the *Piano d'ambito* (investment plan) theorically set by A-ATO MI, ii) the *convenzione* (contract) between MM and the A-ATO MI, iii) the *regolamento di servizio* (set of rules applying to the WSS) between AATO-MI, MM and the users and iv) the *carta della qualità dei servizi* (quality standards charter applying to the WSS).

The three public service mission goals listed in §4.1 are then included and formalised in the above documents. The first goal (a- Universal provision and equal access to the service by all citizens) is the most obvious and is clearly included in all the above mentioned documents. The second and third goals (b- An investment policy, and c- Water resources conservation and environmental protection) are at least in theory regulated and formalised by the *Piano d'Ambito*. On the contrary general interests' goals are not mentioned in those documents.

4.1.2. Non Contractual Public Service Operations

Apart from the public service goals formalised and made explicit, MM provides some other services although they are beyond its contractual mission and not binding: i) supplying water to Corsico municipality, ii) managing and monitoring the shallow aquifer and iii) surface water and flood control.

When asked upon why they were providing these services though not bound to do so, the interviewees told us that it was for a "commitment to public service mission". These activities are run by MM on a public service mission basis since otherwise "no one else would take care of this essential problem".

4.1.3. Corporatisation and Commitment to Public Service

A part of the Italian civil society movement in favour of reclaiming public water militates for a drawback from corporatised WSSs (category C in Table 1) to a full direct municipal provision (category A in Table 1) or autonomous municipal provision (category B in Table 1) arguing that even if fully publicly owned, corporatised WSSs already implement an unacceptable formal privatisation. Through our interviews we have inquired on how the public service mission commitment and implementation changed when comparing the full direct munciipal provision to the MM's corporatised one. From our interviewees point of view the "public service philosophy" (meaning the commitment to public service goals) driving MM's operations has not changed significantly compared to the one previously driving the fully municipal WSS. Indeed MM's commitment to provide "non contractual public service operations" even if not bound to do so (§4.1.2.) might be considered as a proof that public service awareness is still driving MM's operations. According to our interwiewees what might have significantly improved is that public service goals have been formalised and that the flexibility (in management, in accounting, in finance) allowed by the corporatised legal status is much more efficient and effective in reaching the public service mission goals.

5. Performance

5.1. Financial Performance and Cost-Effectiveness

The WSS provision was transferred from Milan's municipality to MM in June 2003. Indeed, there was a large increase in revenues between the years 2002-2003 and the years afterwards. The two tables in Appendix I show a reclassified Profit & Loss account for MM as a whole and for MI-WSS from 2002 till 2011. The largest part of MM's EBIT is due to the WSS part of the company since MM-ENG's external activities decreased after 2006 (when the possibility for MM-ENG to provide services to other Italian Public Administration was restricted).

The "full cost recovery principle" applies to Italian WSS, which means that MM does not receive explicitly any revenues from Taxes or Transfers (3T's: OECD 2009) neither from the municipality nor from the Central Government. However, the past investment burden is not weighing on MM but on Milan's municipality (as we already mentioned in §2.2), and this might be initially considered as a Tax revenue in the OECD 3T's.

In fact the picture is more complex since some money is also flowing each year from the water and sanitation budget to the general budget of Milan's municipality. Figure 1, here below, shows the financial flows taking place between MM, Milan municipality and other major actors.

Figure 1: Financial Flows of MM

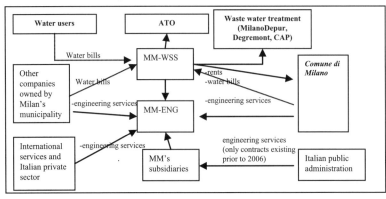

Source: author's elaboration.

Although over the last 10 years MM constantly made a profit, no dividends have been given to the share-holder (Milan's municipality). On the contrary the profits made increase the net assets. As classically done by most municipally owned companies, MM's approach consisted in having a small EBIT for fiscal optimisation purpose. This does not mean however that no financial transfers were taking place between MM and its municipal shareholder. It rather means that financial transfers were taking place using the cost side of the business rather than the income side.

Indeed, from 2003 to 2007, MM paid a yearly concession fee (*canone*) of roughly 23 M euros to Milan's municipality.[10] This is a huge amount (it has the same order of magnitude as all the salaries and wages costs – excluding social security costs); indeed it was overestimated in order to transfer money from the water budget to the general municipal budget to avoid fiscal losses in favour of the central Government.

In 2006, a decree[11] tried to implement more rigorously the "water pays for water" principle and made clear[12] that no concession fees could be paid by the water operators to the municipalities while it was confirmed that the water operator was responsible of the payback of the loans which

---

[10]   *ATO Città di Milano*, 2007 p. 185; *ATO Città di Milano*, 2010, p. 26.

[11]   Decree 152/2006, article 153, http://www.camera.it/parlam/leggi/deleghe/06152dl2. htm, retrieved 4/24/2013.

[12]   According to the CONVIRI the payment of concession fees from water operators to the municipalities was not legal even before 2006 since the *Metodo Tariffario Normalizzato* was not mentioning concessions fees among the acceptable costs. *CONVIRI, Parere n°7625, Aprile 2011.*

had been subscribed by the municipality to finance water and sanitation infrastructure.

To comply with the 2006 decree, in 2008 the concession fee was abolished and replaced by three kinds of financial transfers from MM to the municipality: i) loan's payback, ii) building rent[13] and iii) other costs for various services. After 2010 the three items add up for a total amount of roughly half of the concession fee previously paid. Although this amount might appear more reasonable it is still an over-estimation of the real costs faced by Milan's municipality.

A negotiation between MM and Milan's municipality is taking place now and we are keen to think that the financial transfers from MM to Milan's municipality are very probably bound to decrease in the future.

5.2. Technical Performance

A benchmark comparison of MM versus other Italian operators has been undertaken by Massarutto *et al.* (2011; 2012). Most data show that MM is well above the average technical performances of Italian water services (which are not so high though). MM delivers water which fully complies to quality standards with no interruption while 245 municipalities in Italy (and 24 in the North of Italy) do not fully respect drinking water standards. Unplanned maintenance interventions are not frequent (0.48 interventions/km of network/year) showing a good reliability of the drinking water network. (See also Appendix I).

In terms of cost indicators MM figures are affected by the peculiarities of Milan's WSS (typical of a dense big city): a dense network means that the costs per unit of network are relatively high, a large population served (cost/unit of people served is low) and large sold volumes (cost/volume is low).

Since 2009, relations between MM and its customers are ruled by a *Carta di Servizio* through which MM has made various commitments concerning its customer service. Commitments made by MM appear to be much more ambitious than those made by many other Italian water utilities.

---

[13] The amount paid for "*godimento beni di terzi*" was of 17.6 M Euros in 2008 and 13.5 M Euros in 2009 (*ATO Città di Milano*, 2010, p. 26). After 2010 the rent amount was of roughly 6 M Euros per year. Rent contract (year 2010) between MM and Milan's municipality: http://www.atocittadimilano.it/public/nicola/fck/file/Sotto%20allegati%20dell%27Allegato%20G%20della%20Deliberazione%2013_2013%20del%20CdA%20del%2003%20Aprile%202013/All.%20G%206.PDF retrieved 4/24/2013.

5.3. Sustainability

To better tackle the many intergenerational aspects of the public service mission, the three goals mentioned in §4.1 might also be expressed in terms of sustainable development.

An evaluation framework for WSSs based on the concept of sustainability has been proposed by Massarutto (2002; 2004; 2007): a WSS is sustainable as long as externalities through time and space are avoided. In other words "a WSS is sustainable if it satisfies the present generation without jeopardising the future generation capabilities" (Massarutto *et al.*, 2012, p. 25). In practice to be sustainable, one single generation should not damage the natural capital (water resources, natural environment, biodiversity), but maintain the infrastructure capital (networks, treatment plants, etc.) in order not to transfer the costs on the next generation.

Is MM-WSS sustainable? The research report edited by Massarutto has made such a analysis on various Italian WSSs among which MM (Massarutto *et al.*, 2012).

– Economics: in all the Italian WSS considered by Massarutto *et al.* (including MM) it appears that the undertaken investment allowed by the incomes are still much below what would be needed to reproduce in the long run the infrastructure capital. A first reason for such unsustainability is the complexity of obtaining a digging authorization. Another reason has to be found in the water and sanitation tariff levels which have been set too low, determining too low cash flows to make the investment plans (*Piani d'Ambito*) bankable (Massarutto *et al.*, 2012, pp. 84-92).

– Environment: although after years of postponed investments waste water treatment plan have been brought to completion, the river system around Milan is far from having reached the good ecological status recommended by the European Water Framework Directive (see figure below and Massarutto *et al.*, 2006, p. 27). Somehow the natural capital had been so terribly damaged by the past generations that the present and future ones are/shall be paying the full price of it.

– Ethics: This might be the only point on which Milan's WSS might be considered fully sustainable since its water tariff is low and affordable. However this is largely due to the fact that it is unsustainable on the two previous criteria.

Milan's WSS should not be considered fully sustainable. Indeed if the infrastructure capital was correctly reproduced and a full environmental sustainability was met, the WSS's costs would be much higher and eventually the WSS's tariff deriving from these costs would not be affordable for all users (Massarutto *et al.*, 2012).

6. Regulation

6.1. Legal and Regulatory Framework after 1994

In 1994, an ambitious reform of the water sector was launched in Italy (*Legge Galli – Legge No. 36 1994*). A vast amount of literature[14] has already analysed this reform and it is not the purpose of our work to make a new analysis. However a synthetic summary of the main features of the legal regulatory framework of the Italian water sector might be useful for the reader. The major features of the implemented reform were:

The concept of integrated water and sanitation services (*Servizio Idrico Integrato*) meaning that water and sanitation had to be run jointly by the same entity.

Economies of scale: WSS were to be run at a larger geographical scale, the *Ambito Territoriale Ottimale* (ATO).

WSS could be operated through various formulae: i) direct municipal management, ii) the municipally-owned "*azienda speciale*", iii) the partly municipally-owned PLC and iv) a concession to a private partner.

Regulatory powers were awarded to local regulators to be created for such a purpose (*Autorità d'Ambito Territoriale Ottimale – AATO*). A national regulatory committee the *Comissione Nazionale di Vigilanza sulle Risorse Idriche* (CONVIRI)[15] was also created.

AATO were responsible of the following tasks: i) designing an investment plan (*Piano d'ambito*), ii) choosing how to operate the service (in-house provision, bid for a concession, etc.) iii) signing the contract with the operator (*Convenzione*), iii) approving the business plan and iv) periodic and extraordinary regulatory revision of the ATO investment plan (*Piano d'Ambito*) and of the tariff.

The CONVIRI was mainly responsible of preserving the users' interest and supervising tariff regulation. It was also responsible of an observatory and database on the water services. In practice it was an understaffed institution, suffering from huge information asymmetries and having little regulatory power.

Last but not least the water and sanitation services were to be self-financing and transfers from the central state were forbidden. A revised tariff methodology (*Metodo Tariffario Normalizzato – MTN*) based on the full cost recovery principle was approved in 1996 (*decreto ministeriale*

---

[14] An updated evaluation of the reform has been recently done by Massarutto and Ermano (2013) and by Massarutto *et al.* (2012). Many interesting papers are included in Muraro and Valbonesi (2003).

[15] At first it was called *Comitato Nazionale di Vigilanza sulle Risorse Idriche* (COVIRI).

1 agosto 1996). Exceptions to the MTN were made for concessions existing prior to the Galli act. As a result in 2011 many operators were still applying the former CIPE tariff methodology instead of the MTN one (AEEG, 2012a, p. 25).

The implementation of the reform was left to a large extent to the local authorities (municipalities and regions) resulting in large technical implementation discrepancies. Indeed the ATO were to be defined at the regional level, thus a great variety of choices has been made: from a unique regional ATO (as in Puglia where the *Acquedotto Pugliese* was operating the service) to an ATO limited to a single municipality (as in Milano). In most of the other cases the ATO has been placed at the intermediate scale of the *Provincia* (county division).

Between 1994 and 2011, the Galli reform has been implemented with great inertia and frequent legislative modifications.[16] Legislative changes and debate were particularly frequent concerning the degree private sector participation.

In December 2001,[17] an act imposed de facto the selection of water operators exclusively through competitive tendering, with the only exception being represented by the direct award of a concession to a wholly publicly-owned company provided that within two years of the concession award an equity stake of at least 40% was sold to a private operator selected through competitive tendering.

WSS could not be operated anymore by the municipality and should be delegated to autonomous company. The latter could be municipally owned[18] (in-house provision), private, or partially owned by a municipality and by a private partner. To comply to such a decree the responsibility of Milan's water and sanitation services was given to *Metropolitana Milanese* as a temporary solution at first (Lobina and Paccagnan, 2005).

The 2001 legislation was partially at odds with EU principles and in 2003 the law was modified and this time it allowed only three institutional choices for WSS: i) awarding a concession to a private company selected through competitive tendering; ii) a public-private joint venture whereby the private partner is selected through competitive tendering and iii) a company entirely owned by local authorities (in house provision according to the TECKAL European Court of Justice jurisprudence).

---

[16] *Decreto legislativo 3 aprile 2006, n. 152, decreto legge 112/2008, decreto legislativo 16 gennaio 2008 n°4, legge 26 marzo 2010, n. 42.*

[17] *Legge. n. 448/2001*, (the 2002 Budget act) Art. 35.

[18] Or regionally owned in the case of the *Acquedotto Pugliese*.

In 2009, the Ronchi Decree (decree 135/09) made competitive tendering compulsory to award a concession of the WSS within an ATO. Companies entirely publicly owned could participate to the competition. Although the decree did not exclude WSS run by municipally owned companies (Massarutto, 2009; Scarpa, 2009a; 2009b), it was considered by the public opinion as imposing the privatization of water services. An opposition movement developed[19] and made the legal step to obtain a referendum in June 2011 against the "water privatisation" on two issues: i) did the voters want to abolish the part of the 2009 Ronchi Decree which made compulsory to use competitive tendering to choose the operator for WSS? And ii) did the voters want to abolish the "remuneration of the invested capital" part within the water tariff computed by the MTN? The "Yes" won with an overwhelming majority in both cases.

6.2. The New Regulatory Regime after 2011

The CONVIRI turned out to be very weak and many experts and policy makers argued in favour of a more independent and powerful national regulatory authority. After the 2011 referendum[20] the regulatory power on water services was transferred[21] to the *Autorità per l'Energia elettrica ed il gas* (AEEG), the national regulatory authority for gas and energy.

The AEEG undertook in 2012 a public consultation process[22] in order to reform the WSS tariff regulation. This was a sensitive task since the new tariff regulation should both respect the 2011 referendum outcome (which had canceled the remuneration of the invested capital element in the tariff formula) and guarantee full cost recovery[23] including the financial costs of investments[24] in order to make investments in the water sector again "bankable".

Indeed, after the referendum, uncertainty about the regulatory framework had induced operators to avoid investments and to restrain as much as possible their activity to daily ordinary operations.

---

[19] *Forum Italiano dei Movimenti per l'acqua* – http://www.acquabenecomune.org.

[20] Just prior to the referendum the decree 70/2011 had created the *Agenzia nazionale per la regolazione e la vigilanza in materia di acqua*, which was never effectively in operations.

[21] *Decreto legge 6 dicembre 2011 n°201* enforced with the *Legge 6 dicembre 2011 n°214.*

[22] (AEEG 2012a; AEEG 2012b) available on: http://www.autorita.energia.it/it/operatori/operatori_idr.htm.

[23] Also to comply with EU rules.

[24] "*Un nuovo metodo tariffario per la determinazione della tariffa del servizio idrico integrato... pena la violazione del decreto legge n. 70/11, del diritto comunitario e degli stessi principi affermati dalla Corte Costituzionale (sentenza n. 26/11), la copertura integrale di tutti i costi di esercizio e di investimento, compresi i costi finanziari.*" (AEEG 2012a, 12).

The AEEG approach consisted in both defining a temporary tariff regulation (*Metodo Tariffario Transitorio – MTT*) and working on designing a brand new tariff regulatory method to apply afterwards. The MTT was approved in December 2012 in order to be applied in 2012 and 2013 (AEEG, 2012c).

6.3. Regulation in ATO Città di Milano

In Lombardy the ATO were defined in 2003[25] (more than 8 years after the adoption of the Galli act). An ATO was created for each *Provincia* except for the *Provincia di Milano* where two distinct ATO were created: the *ATO Città di Milano* and the *ATO Provincia di Milano*. According to our interviewees, a unified ATO was not chosen mainly for political reasons in order to preserve the autonomy of the two historical operators (Milan's municipal water service operating within the city and CAP operating in the neighbouring municipalities).

The *Ufficio d'ambito ATO Città di Milano* (AATO-MI)[26] was created as an *Azienda Speciale*[27] of Milan's municipality in 2006[28] and is responsible for the regulation over the ATO *Città di Milano*. According to a 2010[29] act, by 1st January 2011 the AATO have been abolished and it was left to the regions to choose how to confer the responsibilities exerted by the AATOs. Later on,[30] the deadline was postponed to 31/12/2012.

In 2007 the AATO approved the *Piano d'Ambito*[31] for the 01/01/08 – 31/12/2027 time frame. Waiting for such a plan, the most urgent investments (94 millions Euros in sanitation to be spread over 20 years) were inserted in a prior investment plan (*Piano stralcio*) approved in 2001.[32] In 2010 the Piano d'Ambito was reviewed (*ATO Città di Milano 2010*) postponing a significant part of the investments to the second half of the concession period (2018-2027) as shown in Appendix 3. In 2013 MM is proposing to the ATO Città di Milano to adopt a new revision of

---

[25] *La loi régionale 23 du 12/12/03 modifiée par la loi régionale 18 du 08/08/06.*

[26] http://www.atocittadimilano.it.

[27] According to the law the AATO could be established either as a formalised consortium of municipalities or with a lighter formalisation as an agreement between municipalities. The *Azienda Speciale* is a special kind of public law entity created by the art Art. 114 of the decree n°267 of the 18th 2000.

[28] *Delibera del consiglio municipale* 3 aprile 2006 n. 54.

[29] *Legge 26 marzo 2010, n. 42.*

[30] *Decreto legge 29 dicembre 2011, n. 216.*

[31] The *piano d'ambito (ATO Città di Milano 2007)* was approved by the ATO on the 3/08/07 after the municipal council approval on the 26/07/07.

[32] The *Legge 23/12/2000 n°388 (Finanziaria)* had made compulsory to draft a *Piano stralcio* in order to fasten the investment's rhythm concerning the sanitation part of the water cycle.

the *Piano d'Ambito (ATO Città di Milano 2013)* which would modify once again the investment plan. Total figures of the three versions of the investment plan are summarised in Figure 2 and more details are given in Appendix 3. The 2013 revision proposal of the *Piano d'Ambito* is based on a very different investment plan for the 2013-2027. Major differences with the PdA 2010 consist in:

- 153.5 M Euros less investments as a whole than in the PdA 2010.
- a more "reasonable" and "realistic" investment plan based on the idea that MM and Milan's urban system cannot implement more than 40 million Euros of investment per year (due to the risk of congestion and to the contracting out process). As a consequence: more investments in the 2013-2016 years than in the previous version and fewer investments in the 2017-2027 years.

**Figure 2: Yearly Investments in Milan's WSS
According to Various Versions of the Investment Plan**

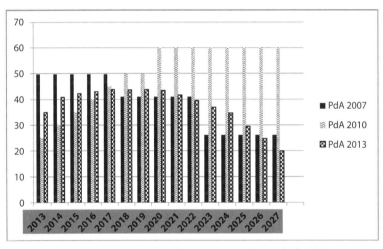

Source: author's elaboration based on data from Massarutto, 2011 and PdA 2013.

Massarutto and Ermano (2013) have pointed out that one of the major weaknesses of the Italian regulatory setting is the subjectivity left to the AATOs for the revision of the ATO's investment plan and their lack of capability to correctly implement such a regulatory process. Indeed in Milan, investment amounts were progressively curbed down in order not to increase the water tariff.

Some other considerations on how the regulation is being implemented in Milan's ATO are given in §7.2.

6.4. Borrowing Constraints

Water and sanitation services are not only concerned with formal regulation of the water sector but might also be constrained by other external factors. In particular from our perspective the borrowing constraints faced by Italian WSS are a key issue in a phase where they have huge investments needs.

From a historical point of view despite the great variety of institutional models of the water and sanitation services in Europe (Barraqué, 1995), investments in water and sanitation services have mostly been the responsibility of municipalities and other local public authorities. If we make reference to the three classical institutional models of direct municipal provision, *affermage* (leasing) and concession, only in the latter model, the concession, CAPEX investments are the responsibility of the private *concessionaire* while on the contrary they are "publicly" driven not only in the direct provision model but also in the *affermage* scheme.[33]

In Italy (Milan included), for decades investments in WSS were undertaken by municipalities. The WSS's budget was not clearly distinct from the global municipal one. Debt[34] issued to finance WSS investments was considered as municipal debt to all means. Now Italian WSS have been corporatised (§3.1) and are provided by joint stock companies. Some of these such as *Metropolitana Milanese* are fully municipally owned. To what extent debt issued by those public entities is accounted for as sub-sovereign debt and *in fine* as sovereign debt? Furthermore, in a normative view, should such a debt be considered as sub-sovereign debt?

In Italy an Internal Stability Pact[35] was approved by law in 1998 (*Legge 448/1998*), making local public authorities (in particular the municipalities) contribute to the goals of the European Stability and Growth pact (SGP) in terms of percentage of consolidated sovereign debt/GDP (Fraschini, 2002, p. 177). This internal stability pact is seen as a major constraint on Italian municipalities'autonomy and is presently

---

[33] Indeed, in *affermage* the contract States which investments are the responsibility of the public entity and which ones are the responsibility of the private operator. In France in most *affermage* contracts, and especially in the most recent ones, the great majority of investment is the responsibility of the local public entity (*autorité organisatrice*) while the private operator is only responsible of maintenance and minor investments.

[34] Debt was subscribed at concessional rates with public lending entities such as the *Cassa Depositi e Prestiti*, the *CREDIOP* or the *Cassa del Mezzogiorno*. More details on these aspects are given in the forthcoming papers (Crespi Reghizzi forthcoming b; d).

[35] Not all European countries chose to approve an internal stability pact in order to apply the European agreement. For example, France did not create such a tool.

criticized for constraining public investments and indirectly slowing down the economic recovery.

However according to the EU legislation WSS's debt should not be considered as sub-sovereign debt. Indeed the European legislation (Council Regulation No. 2223/96 – SEC95) established that "market" public enterprises with Tariff covering at least 50% of the total costs should not be included in national public accounting[36] used for yearly reports to EU institutions in the framework of the European growth and stability pact (SGP).

Italy follows a twofold approach: although it obviously complies to EU guidelines for computing national public debt, the Government also required (decree No. 1/2012) the local public companies owned by local public entities providing "in-house" services (such as WSSs) to fulfill to the internal stability pact previously applied to local public authorities only. One of the ideas behind such a decree was that local public authorities were by definition guarantors of those local public companies' debt in case of financial imbalance (*Corte dei Conti*, 2012). Until now the constraint deriving from the decree No. 1/2012 has not been implemented since no implementation ministerial decree has been published yet. It seems that a second stability pact to be applied to fully publicly owned companies could be created in addition to the existing one which applies to local authorities.[37]

An argument in favour of the corporatisation of Italian WSS was that corporatised WSS would be more autonomous from the municipal administration; but from our perspective considering their debt as sub-sovereign raises a striking paradox. We have shown that the Tariff level of Italian WSS does not allow a high level of self-financing for investments. If their access to debt is also constrained, the critical under- investment in WSS infrastructure is not going to diminish. It is clear that both their economic and environmental sustainability goals (§6.3) shall not be met if their access to debt-financed capital is limited. Indeed how shall the infrastructure capital be reproduced? How shall be undertaken the huge investments to restore the good ecological status in rivers (as required by EU WFD)?

---

[36] National public accounting made by ISTAT in Italy or by INSEE in France apply such a definition and does not include debt of Water and Sanitation services within national public debt.

[37] Press article of Gianni Trovati on *Il Sole 24 Ore* on the 30/01/2013 and 04/02/2013.

7. Governance

7.1. Formal Governance

This section addresses the formal governance of Milan's Water and sanitation. Two aspects shall be analysed: i) MM's formal governance as a company, ii) Milan's WSS institutional mapping and regulatory governance.

MM is a joint stock company fully owned by Milan's municipality. There is a president and a board of directors (4 members) while a general director is responsible of the operations. The president, the members of the board and the general director are appointed by the municipal council. In 2013 an open call[38] for candidates was launched by Milan's municipality in order to renew the president and the board of directors of various municipal companies among which MM.

MM's formal governance as a company is only a part of the story since a significant part of it does not take place within a straight shareholder-company relationship. The institutional mapping is more complex and observing the figure below might be useful. Indeed a regulatory relationship is taking place too. Regulation is exerted by the *Ufficio d'ambito ATO Città di Milano* (AATO-MI) on behalf of Milan's municipality. The AATO-MI employs five people: a director, an engineer, an economist and two employees. The director is a high ranked municipal civil servant. Since it is an *azienda speciale* (autonomous municipal body subject to administrative law and public accounting rules) the AATO-MI is administrated through a board of directors composed of three people. The board of directors is nominated by the municipal council. Presently, the board of directors (nominated the 24th November 2011) is composed of independent "experts"[39] who do not receive any indemnity for their mission. Even if AATO-MI is responsible of MM's regulation, its regulatory power is not that high since major decisions of the AATO-MI have to be approved by the city council.

Since 2011 (and in practice since 2012) the national regulator (AEEG) has also had a key role in the governance of Italian WSS since it defines the regulatory method to be applied and it monitor AATOs' regulatory decisions.

---

[38] Retrieved on April 2013 the 23rd from: http://www.comune.milano.it/dseserver/ webcity/garecontratti.nsf/WEBAll/1475B3CC880A60A8C1257AFA004E10F7?open document.

[39] The president is a professor of economics while the two counselors have been working previously in the water sector and seem to have some political affinity with the left wing Milan administration and with the 2011 water referendum movement.

Figure 3: Milan's WSS Institutional Mapping

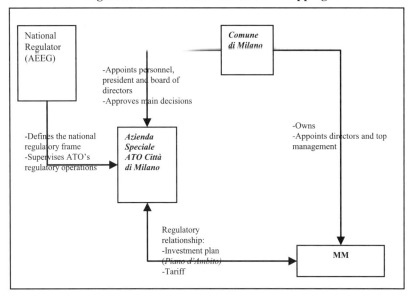

Source: author's elaboration.

7.2. Beyond the Formal Governance

In this section we rely on the various interviews we undertook to go beyond the formal aspects of the governance previously analysed. What are the real relationships between MM and the municipality like? How is the regulatory process between MM and the municipality undertaken in real terms?

One could imagine that the municipality (including the political majority) would try to impose its influence and power on MM on various aspects of the company life. Indeed, as all municipal services, the water and sanitation service can be partially used as an asset in the political arena. Results from our interviews show a twofold relationship. On the one hand the municipality has relatively unfrequent interactions with MM and ignores it as much as possible. Indeed, once MM's board of directors and top management are appointed, the municipality is unaware and does not interfere with MM's daily operations. On the other hand the water price is a political issue and currently Milan municipality (and AATO-MI) is reluctant to adopt the water price increase which results from AEEG new tariff regulation methodology (MTT – §6.2). Another example of political influence is the decision made in 2013 by MM to install public fountains to deliver sparkling water. From our interviews it appears that

MM was encouraged by the municipality although it was not keen on doing that.

Another key aspect to consider is that after WSS's transfer from the municipality to MM (in 2003), all the muncipal human resources having knowledge and experience concerning the water sector were transferred to MM too. Nearly no water sector expert has been left within the municipal administration. That means that the municipality and the AATO are in practice unable to exert by themselves any relevant control on MM. It also means that the Municipality relies on MM for all water related public policies issues.

The pattern is similar within the local regulator, AATO-MI which is in fact not able to truly control and regulate by itself MM'activity. By definition, a classical informational asymmetry takes place between MM which has all the informations and both AATO-MI and the municipality which are "in the dark". What is really striking in Milan's case is the fact that no knowledge at all has been kept within the Municipality and the AATO-MI. In practice MM exerts both the role of regulated entity and regulator.

For example the two past investment masterplans (*Piano d'Ambito*) have been entirely drafted by MM while such a key regulatory document should have been AATO-MI's responsibility (and indeed it bears AATO-MI logo, but only on the front page). In all the key steps of its regulatory mission (ATO's plan revisions, tariff revisions) AATO-MI has recruited private consultants and relied on them to conduct the regulatory process. In our opinion the need for an external help is a clear indication of AATO-MI's weak regulatory capability. The good point might be its awareness of such a weakness and the decision to ask for some external help to compensate the weakness. Unfortunately, no stable partnership has been established with a single consultant but new people have been recruited every time with a continous loss of regulatory knowledge.

More globally speaking Milan's municipality as a whole is not able to express an unambiguous goal function to which MM should comply. Indeed Milan's municipality is composed of many entities which might give contradictories signals to MM. A clear example is with the administrative process required to undertake infrastructure works: on one hand MM has to fulfill the investments targets defined in the masterplan which has been approved by the AATO-MI and by the municipality, on the other hand MM is subject to a complex administrative process for the works implying to dig under the streets. Apparently to have a dig authorisation requires such a high effort that it is the major constraint on MM's investment's level. Indeed from MM's point of view dig autorisations are so hard to obtain that funding is not yet a constraint on the investment policy.

8. Tariffs, Finance and Distributional Issues with Respect to Public Missions

8.1. The Tariff Structure

According to the *Legge Galli* and to the *Metodo Tariffario Normalizzato* (MTN) the water service has to be billed with an increasing block rate (IBR). This charging policy, which started in Italy already in the 1970s, was supposedly designed both to ensure WSS financial sustainability and to apply a discount rate on essential water needs of domestic users.[40] In Milan, IBR has been adopted and a two-part tariff with increasing block rates is in place. Water is mostly billed through collective metering (one bill per residential building). Indeed there are only 47 136 meters in Milan and the majority of the bills are paid by the condominium administrator who is the "user" from the utility's point of view. The user pays both a volumetric tariff (commodity charge) T_{vol} and a fixed charge T_{fixed}. The commodity charge T_{vol} is composed of four volumetric elements (t_w, t_s, t_{ww} and $t_{stralcio}$[41]) charging respectively for water, sanitation, wastewater treatment and the special contribution to the *Piano stralcio's* amortisation. The three last elements are uniform and charged just the same to all users. T_w instead is charged differently to domestic, non domestic and agriculture users. Furthermore T_w is charged according to an increasing block-rate system. The formulas below show how the bill amount is computed:

(1) $T_{total} = T_{fixed} + T_{vol}$

(2) $T_{vol} = T_w + t_s * V_{tot} + t_{ww} * V_{tot} + t_{stralcio} * V_{tot}$

(3) $T_w = t_{w1} * Vol_1 + t_{w2} * Vol_2 + t_{w3} * Vol_3$

(4) Vol A $= 0.350 * n°flat * n°days$

(5) $Vol_1 = min [V_{tot}; Vol A]$

(6) Vol B $= 0.750 * n°flat * n°days$

(7) $Vol_2 = min [V_{tot-}Vol_1; Vol B]$

(8) $Vol_3 = Vtot-Vol_2$

The commodity charge (water + sanitation + waste water treatment) for domestic users varies from a total of 0.53 to 0.80 euro per cubic meter depending on the block of consumption. The fixed part T_{fixed} is not very significant when compared to the volumetric part.

---

[40] *"La ristrutturazione tariffaria deve armonizzare le denunciate ed accertate necessità del graduale ripianamento economico della gestione aziendale con l'esigenza di assicurare all'utenza una tariffa agevolata, limitata ai consumi essenziali."* (Provvedimento CIP n°26/Agosto 1975).

[41] The *piano stralcio* is a special investment plan to undertake sanitation infrastructures (see § 6.3).

From our perspective, Milan's IBR system (in presence of collective metering) has many caveats: i) it can hardly pretend to mimic marginal cost pricing, ii) it does not give a clear price signal incentivising water conservation and iii) it is far from being transparent in the resulting cost-allocation between the various users. In principle all Italian WSS have to apply an IBR and as far as we know many other Italian cities have adopted it in presence of collective metering as in Milan. We think that Milan's IBR system raises many policy questions and that there is the need for further research including data collection on the ground.

8.2. Lower Volumes, Higher Rates

Water consumption is decreasing in many European cities and the case of Milan confirms this general trend as Figure 4 shows. Indeed the yearly water volumes[42] peaked in 1971 (more than 352 million m³) and decreased almost steadily afterwards due to various factors among which the city's tertiarisation.

The tariff revenues are mainly based on the sold volumes of water since the fixed part of the rate is not very significant. On the contrary most of the costs are fixed regardless of the volumes.

In the constrained framework of full cost recovery, when only tariff revenues of the service have to cover its costs, a decrease in sold volumes implies sooner or later an increase in the unitary rate. This is the sustainability dilemma faced by many WSSs in all of Europe.

WSSs might be considered club goods. In cities in developed countries almost everyone is member of the club (Barraqué, 2011, p. 240). Most of the costs of the club are fixed regardless volumes consumed. Club membership dues (total yearly water bills) are then condemned to remain constant regardless of the sold volumes too.

It might be politically slippery however to first incentivise users to conserve water and then to increase their unitary rates in order to collect roughly the same amount of revenues as if the sold volumes had stayed constant. Such a counter-intuitive fact has to be explained to the users. That's one of the reasons for more users participation in the WSS's governance.

---

[42] The values in the figure refer to the volumes withdrawed from the water table and pumped into the network. According to MM these are the only reliable figures in the long run. Volumes metered and billed to the users are lower.

Figure 4: Yearly Water Consumption and Population in Milan (1945-2011)

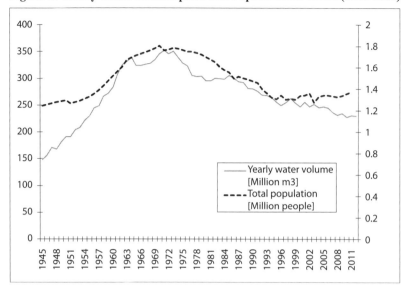

Source: author's elaboration based on *Metropolitana Milanese* internal database.

9. Conclusion and Lessons Learned

In 2002, prior to its corporatisation, Milan's WSS was the largest[43] Italian WSS under full municipal provision. In 2003 the WSS was corporatised to comply with the national legal framework and the WSS's provision became *Metropolitana Milanese*'s responsibility (section 3).

We have presented an in-depth analysis of Milan's WSS after corporatisation. Two perimeters of analysis make sense to fully understand Milan's case study: i) an analysis only focused on *Metropolitana Milanese* as a company and ii) a wider analysis of Milan's WSS institutions as a whole as shown in Figure 3.

9.1. Metropolitana Milanese

From our research MM appears as a well run company with rather good technical and financial performances (section 5). One could wonder however what is the rationality in MM operating two very different business areas (civil engineering especially in underground transport lines, and water and sanitation services); apart from the fact that both areas require knowledge concerning the underground since groundwater is used in Milan. Moreover in this kind of situation, hidden or apparent

---

[43] Metropolitana Milanese, *Bilancio d'esercizio 2003*, p. 15.

cross-subsidies might take place. However in the case of MM, the risk of hidden cross-subsidies should not exist anymore. Indeed, since 2011 both areas of business have clear distinct accounting sections in order to enhance transparency on their profitability and cost-effectiveness (§2.3).

The corporatisation of Italian WSS can be considered as part of the New Public Management (NPM) paradigm (Osborne and Gaebler, 1993; Hood, 1995). Admitting that implementing NPM might improve public sector efficiency and effectiveness, one could wonder then whether the corporatised service might imply a loss in the commitment to public service goals or not (§4.1). From our investigation, it appears that despite being a corporatised entity, MM and its staff are strongly committed to public service goals with no significant differences with what was happening previously under full municipal provision. Our results on this point are consistent with Colon and Guérin-Schneider (2012) who show that in selected case studies in two developing countries NPM implementation did not imply a loss of "Public Value" (as defined by M. Moore, 1994; 1995). In Milan's case, one could even argue that the corporatised WSS is more effective in fulfilling public service goals than the full municipal provision was previously, as the stories of postponed investments tell us (Crespi Reghizzi, forthcoming d).

9.2. Milan's WSS

Enlarging the perimeter of analysis to all the stakeholders (Figure 3) of Milan's WSS is much more interesting than focusing only on MM. The results of such an enlarged analysis raise at least two puzzling issues.

The implementation in Milan of the Italian regulation model implying two regulation authorities at the local and at the national level (respectively AATO and AEEG) is puzzling. On the one hand the formal regulation process is formal, complex and costly;[44] on the other hand both Milan municipality and the AATO-MI lack of knowledge, human resources and capability to truly control and regulate MM (§7.2). The regulatory process in place might be compared to a play in which the two actors (MM and AATO-MI) are forced to perform following a formal and imposed script. Indeed, if it was not for the existence of an expert and powerful national regulator (AEEG see §6.2) which plays the role of the "unwanted third party"[45] one could even wonder whether a regulatory process would be truly performed since the regulatory key documents (such as the *Piano d'Ambito*) were *de facto* drafted by MM on behalf of the regulator AATO-MI (§7.2).

---

[44]   As shown by the quantity of documents required to perform the 2013 regulatory process (available on http://www.atocittadimilano.it/default.asp?pag=22&tipo=3).

[45]   *Il terzo incomodo.*

Milan municipality as a whole is not able to express an unambiguous goal function to which MM should comply. Indeed Milan municipality is composed of many entities which might give contradictories signals to MM. Let's take two examples: i) on one hand MM has to stick to the investments level specified by the *Piano d'Ambito* which has been approved by Milan's municipality, on the other hand digging authorisation are so complex to obtain that they slow down MM investments' rhythm. ii) on one hand the water tariff is a political issue and Milan's municipality push for keeping a low water tariff, on the other hand the municipality still asks MM to pay a significant yearly fee (§5.1).

From the general public point of view, Milan's WSS is seen as a well performing public service delivering the water and sanitation service at an affordable price (the lowest price in Italy). Indeed, if we limit to the first perimeter of analysis our case study confirms that MM-WSS in itself is rather well performing. However an enlarged perimeter of analysis shows that MM is part of an imposed baroque institutional governance system (institutional map in Figure 3) which is neither very effective nor efficient. Indeed, the regulatory architecture at local level is perfectly performed from a formal point of view but does not seem to be truly taking place in substance. This is largely due to the total lack of knowledge and capabilities left to Milan's municipality and AATO-MI after the corporatisation. Luckily, MM's commitment to public service mission balances such a lack of control.

The entry of a national regulator (AEEG) into the water sector regulation arena might be criticised on the basis that it makes the regulatory process more complex and costly. From our perspective however, additional complexity and transaction costs shall be justified if AEEG's guidelines and supervision shall imply a switch from a formal vision of the regulatory process to its substantial implementation.

One might consider that Milan's WSS is effective and well performing, within the short run public service goal consisting in delivering a good quality water and sanitation service to all users at an affordable price. The judgment might be quite different if one adopts a long run and intergenerational point of view using "sustainability" as an evaluation criterion. Is Milan's WSS fully sustainable? Not really. On the contrary it seems that much more effort would be needed both from the environmental and infrastructural point of view to reproduce the infrastructure capital and to restore the good ecological status of the river system (§6.3).

Capital expenditures and investments are crucial in a WSS service. One of the weakest points of the implementation of the Galli reform was that investment plans (*Piani d'ambito*) were too ambitious and often not "bankable". Things got even worse after the 2011 referendum due to the regulatory uncertainty it created (§6.1). The new MTT implemented by AEEG should help restoring the bankability of the Italian water sector. However all efforts made by AEEG will be useless if the Damocles sword of an effective extension of the Internal Stability Pact to the debt of publicly owned companies isn't removed (§6.4). Indeed, the low tariff level of Italian WSS does not allow a good level of self-financing of the planned investments. If their access to debt were to be constrained by the Internal Stability Pact, Italian WSS would be condemned to stay in the under-investment status in which they have been for the last decades. Their sustainability would be challenged even more.

References

AEEG, 2012a, "Consultazione pubblica per l'adozione di provvedimenti tariffari in materia di servizi idrici – documento per la consultazione 204/2012/R/IDR".

AEEG, 2012b, "Consultazione pubblica per l'adozione di provvedimenti tariffari in materia di servizi idrici – documento per la consultazione 290/2012/R/IDR".

AEEG, 2012c, "Regolazione dei servizi idrici: approvazione del metodo tariffario transitorio (mtt) per la determinazione delle tariffe negli anni 2012 e 2013 – deliberazione – 585/2012/R/IDR".

Arcangeli, Rosalia, 2000, *Economia e gestione delle imprese di servizi pubblici*, Padova, CEDAM.

ATO Città di Milano, 2007, "Piano d'ambito dell'ATO Città di Milano", http://www.atocittadimilano.it/default.asp?pag=23&tipo=9.

ATO, 2010, "Primo aggiornamento – Piano d'ambito dell'ATO Città di Milano", http://www.atocittadimilano.it/default.asp?pag=23&tipo=9.

ATO, 2013, "Aggiornamento – Piano d'ambito dell'ATO Città di Milano", http://www.atocittadimilano.it/default.asp?pag=23&tipo=9.

Barraqué, Bernard, 1995, *Les politiques de l'eau en Europe*, 1 Vols, Paris, la Découverte.

Barraqué, Bernard, 2011, "Is Individual Metering Socially Sustainable? The Case of Multifamily Housing in France", in *Water Alternatives*, Vol. 4, p. 2.

CIRIEC, 2012, "The Future of Public Enterprise Mission, Performance and Governance: Learning from Success and Failures a Research Agenda 2012-2014".

Colon, Marine, and Laetitia, Guérin-Schneider, 2012, "L'entreprisation des services publics d'eau potable urbains dans les pays en développement, créatrice de valeurs publiques? Le cas de l'Ouganda et du Cambodge?", in *Actes du colloque AIRMAP*, Paris, http://cemadoc.irstea.fr/oa/PUB00036636-entreprisation-des-services-publics-eau-potable-ur.html.

Corte dei Conti, 2012, "Rapporto 2012 sul coordinamento della finanza pubblica".

Crespi Reghizzi, Olivier, forthcoming b, "Providing and Financing a Municipal Infrastructure: Water and Sanitation Investments in Milan (1888-1924)", in *The Economics of Infrastructure Provisioning – The (Changing) Role of the State*, edited by Arnold Picot, Massimo Florio, Nico Grove, and Johann Kranz. Submitted to MIT Press.

Crespi Reghizzi, Olivier, forthcoming d, "Water, Sanitation and InterGovernmental Relations in Italy after WWII: A Case Study on Milan's Water and Sanitation Service", *Submitted to the Journal of Competition and Regulation in Network Industries.*

Hood, Christopher, 1995, "The 'new Public Management' in the 1980s: Variations on a Theme", in *Accounting, Organizations and Society*, Vol. 20, No. 2-3, pp. 93-109, doi:10.1016/0361-3682(93)E0001-W.

Lobina, Emanuele, and Paccagnan, Vania, 2005, "D33 Water Time Case Study – Milan", on Water Time, www.watertime.net.

Massarutto, Antonio, 2002, "Full-Cost Recovery and Optimal Pricing Rules for Water Supply and Sewerage". Unpublished report, courtesy of the author.

Massarutto, Antonio, 2004, "Water Pricing: A Basic Tool for Water Sustainability?", in *Challenges of the New Water Policies for the XXI Century*, edited by Enrique Cabrera and R Cobacho, Lisse, Balkema, http://ron-griffin.tamu.edu/AgEc677reads/massarutto2004.pdf.

Massarutto, Antonio, 2007, "Water Pricing and Full Cost Recovery of Water Services: Economic Incentive or Instrument of Public Finance?" in *Water Policy*, Vol. 9, No. 6, p. 591, doi:10.2166/wp.2007.024.

Massarutto, Antonio, 2009, "Un sistema che continua a fare acqua", http://archivio.lavoce.info/articoli/pagina1001435.html.

Massarutto Antonio, 2011, "L'affidamento in house del servizio idrico integrato a Metropolitana Milanese – relazione per MM".

Massarutto, Antonio, Antonioli, Barbara, Monacina, Monica, Ermano, Paolo and Graffi, Matteo, 2012, "La riforma della regolazione dei servizi idrici in Italia – L'impatto della riforma: 1994-2011", in *IEFE – Università Bocconi*, http://www.iefe.unibocconi.it.

Massarutto, Antonio, Basoni, Anna, de Carli, Alessandro, Linares, Elisabetta, Lodi, Alessandro, and Paccagnan, Vania, 2006, "Il sistema di depurazione di Milano dall'emergenza alla sostenibilità", in *IEFE – Università Bocconi.*

Massarutto, Antonio, and Ermano, Paolo, 2013, "Drowned in an Inch of Water: How Poor Regulation Has Weakened the Italian Water Reform", in *Water Utility Regulation in Developed Countries*, Vol. 24, No. 0, pp. 20–31, doi:10.1016/j.jup.2012.09.004.

Moore, Mark H., 1995, *Creating Public Value: Strategic Management in Government*, Harvard University Press.

Moore, Mark H., 1994, "Public Value as the Focus of Strategy" in *Australian Journal of Public Administration*, Vol. 53, No. 3, pp. 296–303, doi:10.1111/j.1467-8500.1994.tb01467.x.

Muraro, Gilberto, and Valbonesi, Paola, 2003, *I servizi idrici tra mercato e regole*, Roma, Carocci.

OECD, 2009, *Managing Water for All: An OECD Perspective on Pricing and Financing*, Paris, OECD.

Osborne, David, and Gaebler, Ted, 1993, *Reinventing Government: How the Entrepreneurial Spirit Is Transforming the Public Sector*, Plume.

Rotondi, Claudia, 1997, "La municipalizzazione tra le due guerre : un soggetto anomalo nel governo dell'economia", in *L'acqua e il gas in Italia: la storia dei servizi a rete delle aziende pubbliche e delle Federgasacqua*, by Bigatti, Giorgio, Giuntini, Andrea, Mantegazza, Andrea and Rotondi, Claudia, Collana Ciriec di storie d'impresa pubblica e di pubblico interesse, Milano, F. Angeli, http://www.sudoc.fr/010718206.

Scarpa, Carlo, 2009a, *Comuni S.p.a.: Il Capitalismo Municipale in Italia*, Collana Della Fondazione ENI Enrico Mattei, Bologna, Il mulino.

Scarpa, Carlo, 2009b, "Servizi locali: le regole non possono attendere", http://archivio.lavoce.info/articoli/pagina1001435.html.

Appendix I

Table 1: MM-WSS infrastructure

Water infrastructure	Quantity	Sanitation infrastructure	Quantity
Boreholes	538	Large sewers 3<A<20 m²	101.99 km
boreholes in operation	416	Medium sewers 1<A<3 m²	233.12 km
Pumping stations in operation	27	Small sewers (A<1m²)	1121.89 km
Pumping capacity	9,000 l/s	Total sewers	1457 km
Pumping stations with water treatment units	23		
Storage units	35	Population equivalent capacity of the 3 wastewater treatment plants	2,300,000 inhab
Total storage capacity	229,403 m³		
Pipeline	2,332 km		
Meters	47 136		

Source: author's elaboration based on data from MM and Massarutto (2011)

Table 2: Management of Milan's waste water treatment plants

	Nosedo	San Rocco (ex Milano Sud)	Peschiera Borromeo (2nd line of treatment)
Builder	Consortium lead by SIBA S.p.A.	Consortium lead by Ondeo Degremont	Consortium with Siba S.p.A. –, and Ondeo Degrémont
Contractual scheme	Building and operating (incl. project financing)	Building + operating (no project financing)	Building
Investments	€ 117 milions for the works +. € 17 milioni per concession costs	€ 87 milions for the works and € 48 milioni per the 5 years management and additional works	€ 17 milions for the second line and € 5 milions for the sewer
Lenders	Banca Intesa and Royal Bank of Scotland		
Other donors	Regione Lombardia and Fondazione Cariplo for the public park		
Infrastructure owner	Consortium until 2015, Comune di Milano afterwards	Comune di Milano	CAP Holding S.p.A.
Operations	Milano*Depur* S.p.A.	Degrémont S.p.A.	Amiacque S.r.l. (ex CAP Gestione SpA)
Length of the management (years)	12 + 4 years	5 + 4 + 1 years	26 years
End product disposal costs	MM S.p.A.	Included in the operations fee	Amiacque S.r.l.
Energy costs	MM S.p.A	Included in the operations fee	Amiacque S.r.l.
Gas costs (sludge drying)	MM S.p.A	Included in the operations fee	–

Source: author's translation based on Massarutto (2011)

Table 3: Reclassified Profit & Loss account of MM SpA

Thousand Euro	2002	2003	2004	2005	2006	2007	2008	2009	2010	2011
Revenues	80,828	189,441	279,468	239,943	230,453	248,002	254,292	236,930	260,507	232,792
Operating Costs	75,942	168,980	263,785	227,835	217,517	231,968	237,997	219,967	240,816	201,435
EBITDA	4,886	20,461	15,683	12,108	12,936	16,034	16,295	16,963	19,691	31,357
Depreciation, amortization and write down	2,542	3,986	4,389	5,463	7,314	8,609	9,722	12,522	13,272	15,387
EBIT	2,344	16,475	11,295	6,645	5,622	7,426	5,682	4,442	6,419	11,273

Thousand Euro	2002	2003	2004	2005	2006	2007	2008	2009	2010	2011
Financial income and expenses	-1 168	-806	-386 983	-877 132	-1 697	-2 749	-2 998	-1 970	(2,077)	(3,388)
Result before taxes	1,765	15,563	10,980	6,078	3,910	4,750	2,684	2,760	4,199	7,282
Income taxes	1,474	6,903	5,581	3,956	3,192	3,586	2,545	2,497	3,346	3,390
Profit (Loss) of the year	291	8,660	2,122	5,399	718	1,164	139	264	852	2,766
CASH FLOW	-4,133	25,730	-19,300	-976	-5,851	-9,137	-1,378	-71	1,712	12,787
Leverage[46]			0.42	0.70	1.41	1.91	2.90	3.60	3.30	2.80
ROI [%]			24.29	11.18	6.54	6.94	4.82	3.11	3.96	7.35
ROE [%]			6.46	15.45	2.01	3.16	0.38	0.71	2.24	6.77

Source: Author's elaboration based on data from Massarutto (2011) and from the "*Bilancio d'esercizio*" of MM, various years, all values in thousand Euros.

Table 4: Reclassified Profit & Loss account of MM-WSS

	2004	2005	2006	2007	2008	2009	2010	2011
Revenues	104,962	116,169	117,668	110,796	110,326	113,917	113,464	123,019
Costs	86,648	101,929	107,097	103,726	99,146	101,856		
Ebitda	18,314	14,240	10,571	7,070	11	12,070	15,900	24,715
Depreciation, amortization and write down	8,928	9,032	8,439	3,794	7,767	7,636	10,686	13,908
EBIT	9,386	5,208	2,132	3,276	3,413	4,434	5,214	10,807
Financial income and expenses	538	237	273		1,999			
Result before taxes	8,848	4,971	1,859		1,414	4,277	4,626	8,804
Income taxes	4,566	2,747	1,369		1,397			
Profit (Loss) of the year	4,282	2,224	490		17	2,086		

Source: author's elaboration based on data from three versions (2007, 2010 and 2013) of the *Piano d'Ambito ATO Città di Milano*. The 2013 version is only an internal draft version, courtesy of MM.

---

[46]   Posizione Finanziaria Netta / Patrimonio Netto.

Table 5: Benchmarking of MM – technical performance

		MM	Lombardia	Nord	Italia
Water losses	Water (million m^3)	221	1,408	3,696	8,143
	Water billed (million m^3)	201	1,111	2,727	5,500
	Total losses (%)	-13%	-21%	-26%	-32%
Waste water	Waste water recycled after treatment (%)	33%		0%	0%
	Users connected to a waste water treatment plant	100%	81.5%	84.9%	78.5%
	Users connected to advanced waste water treatment plants	100%	69.9%	68.8%	52.2%
Water non respecting drinking standards	N° municipalities	0		24	245
	Population (millions)	0		0.06	2.1
Network maintenance	Unplanned maintenance intervention on the network (n./km)	0.48		1.25	3.18
Total cost / km network	Euro/km	48.697			23.325
Total cost / inhabitant	Euro/inhabitant	88			135
Total cost / 1000 m^3	Euro / 1000 m^3	543			1475
Total cost / employee	Euro / employee	241.25			222

Source: Massarutto (2011; Massarutto *et al.* 2012) based on data from MM, ISTAT, Mediobanca and IRPET

4. Analysis of SEDAPAL, the Largest Public Water and Sanitation Provision Enterprise of Peru

GISELLA Aragón* & JOSÉ LUIS Bonifaz**

Univerdisad del Pacífico, Perú

Introduction

SEDAPAL is the largest and most important public enterprise in Peru that provides water and sanitation services. Its financial sustainability depends on the financial support of the Peruvian State and, the financial resources that the firm can generate based on the tariffs that users pay for the service.

Even though it has had a good performance in financial terms, the last few years SEDAPAL has had to search for financial support in order to undertake projects and works that are on their agenda, raising its leverage ratios.

Therefore, it is crucial to study the viabilities to improve the firm's financial capacities, governance settlements and regulation schemes, which affect directly to its operative performance.

1. Identification of the Enterprise

Servicio de Agua Potable y Alcantarillado de Lima (SEDAPAL) is a public enterprise owned by the Peruvian State that has been constituted as a corporation and, whose prime purpose is to provide water and sanitation services to Lima Metropolitana and Callao Constitutional Province[1] (defined by Law No. 28696).

SEDAPAL was created by Legislative Decree No. 150, and was founded, based on the transformation of *Servicio de Agua Potable y*

---

* Professor of Economy, Faculty of Economics and Finance, Universidad del Pacífico, Perú. Aragon_gs@up.edu.pe.

** Associate Dean of Economy, Faculty of Economics and Finance, Universidad del Pacífico, Perú. jbonifaz@up.edu.pe.

[1] The districts or areas of the department of Lima that are joined by ministerial resolution of the housing sector are also served by SEDAPAL.

Alcantarillado de Lima (ESAL). Its legal address is Autopista Ramiro Prialé 210, La Atarjea – El Agustino, Lima, Peru.

SEDAPAL is governed by its Statute, the General Corporation Law (Law No. 26887), the State Business Activity Law (Law No. 24984) and the National Fund for Financing State Enterprise Activity Law (Law No. 27170). These laws define the economic, financial and employment status of the company, as well as the relationship with the various levels of Government and administrative systems.

Serving to Lima Metropolitana and Callao Constitutional Province, SEDAPAL is the largest water and sanitation enterprise; and, the most important public enterprise in Peru. Taking in consideration the total number of connections served through water and sanitation supplier enterprises (EPSs) in Peru that is up to 22.1 millions, SEDAPAL's share is 42%. On the other hand, 49 EPSs serve the other 58%.

Then, the importance of SEDAPAL and its influence over the water and sanitation service sector is not trivial. Moreover, SEDAPAL's most important shareholder is Peruvian State. Therefore, any change on this financial support, affects directly to the institution.

Besides of its prime mission of providing water and sanitation services to Lima Metropolitana and Callao Constitutional province, SEDAPAL invests in projects that allow the firm to expand its service's coverage, improve the sanitary system in marginal areas, etc. However, the execution of these kinds of projects is also determined by its capacity to generate financial flows.

SEDAPAL's financial sustainability depends on: (i) the financial support of the Peruvian State; and, (ii) the financial resources that the firm can generate based on the tariffs that users pay for the service. However none of them are under direct control of the enterprise.

The Peruvian Water and Sanitation Regulatory Agency (SUNASS) is in charge of the establishment of the parameters of the tariff formula and tariff scheme SEDAPAL works with. Once SEDAPAL applicates the established tariff formula and proposes the tariff schemes to SUNASS and it is approved, SUNASS defines the strategic goals for SEDAPAL and the application of the resulting tariff scheme. However, in the latter years, the rates determined in the tariff scheme have been very low.

Even under these restrictions settled, SEDAPAL has been able to maintain a solid financial profile generating stable flows that allow it to finance its investments and adequately meet their financial obligations. These financial obligations mainly cover investment projects in the long-term, and are provided by multilateral organisations and the Ministry of Economy and Finances (MEF) of Peru transfers.

SEDAPAL's basic information that supports this discussion can be seen in Table 1.

Table 1. SEDAPAL's Basic Information, 2012

Sectors of activity (NACE Classification)	E "Water supply; sewerage, waste management and remediation services", E36 "Water collection, treatment and supply"; and, E37 "Sewerage".
Operative income	S/. 1,384,421 thousands
Profit of the year	S/. 131,706 thousands
Debt	
Inter debt	S/. 736,430 thousands
Extern debt	S/. 1,636,986 thousands
MEF's debt	S/. 799,119 thousands
Number of employees	2,278 employees.
Population served and area of operation	It gives service to 8,706,000 habitants in Lima Metropolitana and Callao Constitutional Province.
Ultimate owner	State of Peru.

Source: SEDAPAL.

2. History and Framework

2.1. SEDAPAL's History

SEDAPAL's origin as a water and sanitation EPS dates back to the restructuration of ESAL on 1981. Before 1990, the provision of water and sanitation services was in charge of 15 public enterprises that were autonomous (SEDAPAL was one of them), 185 unities of municipal operation and an undetermined number of user's groups.

However, in late 1990s the Government disposed the transference of property and the operation of the EPSs, which were under central Government control to municipalities' control. The only exception was SEDAPAL, who continued working under the direct property of the central Government.

In 1991, through de Private Investment Promotion Law (Legislative Decree No. 697), the Government eliminated the obstacles to the exploitation of the water and sanitation services, letting them to be executed by natural or legal persons, only if they got the municipalities authorisations and respected the tariffs determined by municipalities too. These did not affect SEDAPAL.

By 1992, the Government got SUNASS in charge of supervising the EPSs that formed part of the water and sanitation sector. However, it was not up to 1995 that all the norms that regulate the operation of the EPSs were settled. The most important Law defined was the General Law of

Sanitary Services (Law No. 26338), which made emphasis on the fact that SEDAPAL is a property of the central Government and its shares are issued in the name of the State. It also defines that its General Meeting of Shareholders should be conformed according to the State Business Activity Law (Law No. 24984).

2.2. Peruvian Water and Sanitation Sector Framework

2.2.1. Water and Sanitation Sector Structure

The distribution of the EPSs in Peru is conditioned to its geopolitical division. All EPSs are regulated by SUNASS. As a matter of fact, they have been re-classified[2] considering the number of water connections served. The classification is defined as follows:

Table 2. EPSs Classification

Types	Number of water connections supplied (X)	Number of EPSs	Share of connections served
Small	X < 14,999	20	4.80%
Medium	15,000 < X < 39,999	13	9.60%
Large 2	40,000 < X < 99,000	12	21.00%
Large 1	100,000 < X < 999,999	4	22.60%
SEDAPAL	X > 1,000,000	1	41.90%

Source: SEDAPAL.

Currently, there are 16 large, 13 medium and 20 small water and sanitation services EPSs. SEDAPAL and the groups of large and medium enterprises serve 95% of water connections. Finally, 48 EPSs are public and municipal-owned enterprises. The 2 EPSs remaining are: (i) SEDAPAL, under the responsibility of the Central Government; and, (ii) ATUSA, which is a private company operating under a concession arrangement.

2.2.2. Main Actors and Roles

a. The water and sanitation supplier enterprises (EPSs). The EPSs are public, private or mixed. The mayors of each municipality name the directors of these public EPSs. SEDAPAL is an exception since it is governed directly by central Government.

An important requirement for public EPSs is to be enrolled in the register of the regulatory agency (*Recognition Policy*). Doing so, the EPS agrees to respect the quantity and quality of water and sanitation service standards. Also, the EPS has to define the service's tariffs considering the

---

[2] Previous classification only considered four categories.

principles set by SUNASS and apply them once SUNASS and mayors approve them. Finally, in order to raise their public funds, EPSs have to ensure the accomplishment of certain goals.

b. The municipalities. Municipalities are public institutions responsible for the provision of water and sanitation services. They grant "the right of operation" to EPSs and create municipal owned enterprises. The mayor of a municipality is in charge of approving the EPSs y tariffs. Nevertheless, in order to get the political approval of their voters, most mayors do not support the raise of water and sanitation tariffs, putting in risks EPSs financial sustainability.

c. The National Superintendence of Sanitation (SUNASS). SUNASS is the regulatory agency of water and sanitation services and has full jurisdiction over the *recognised* EPSs. Its most important tasks are to evaluate EPSs plans (master, financial and investment plans as part of a Master Plan), regulate tariff formulas and the achievement of goals, verify the payment for the regulation rate, etc.

d. Other Public Entities. The Ministry of Housing, Construction and Sanitation (MVCS). Through the General Sanitation Office it formulates and executes the national water and sanitation policy.

The Ministry of Economy and Finance (MEF). MEF influences the industry through: (i) the National Fund for Financing State Enterprise Activity (FONAFE), which controls SEDAPAL; and, (ii) the National Public Budget (DNPP) involved in the budget process for the municipalities and the EPSs.

e. Consumers. The consumers are formed by: (i) current consumers, who already have home water and sanitation connection; and, (ii) the potential consumers, who do no receive the services yet.

3. Public Mission

SEDAPAL *mission* is to improve the quality of life of the population of Lima Metropolitana and Callao Constitutional Province, through the provision of drinking water; the collection, treatment and disposal of wastewater; and, the reuse of the same water in order to preserve the environment. SEDAPALs *vision* is to be the best public enterprise, providing a quality service to the population of Lima Metropolitana and Callao Constitutional Province.

In order to follow its mission and vision, SEDAPAL goals are: (i) provide water (drinkable water) and sanitation services, (ii) execute operative, maintenance and control policies related to the services provided that follow the sector policies; and, (iii) elaborate projects, execute works, and give technical advice and assistance.

4. Operations

The core indicators that express SEDAPAL's operations are: (i) the length of water networks, (ii) the length of sewerage networks, (iii) the billed connections, (iv) the produced volume of water, (v) the billed volume of water, (vi) the share of not billed water; and, (vii) the micro metering level. These indicators can be seen in the following table:

Table 3. SEDAPAL Operation Indicators (2005-2013)

Year	Length of water networks *(Km)*	Length of sewerage networks *(Km)*	Billed connec- tions	Volume of water produced *(thousands of m³)*	Volume of billed water *(thousands of m³)*	Non-Billed Water *(percent- age)*	Micro metering level *(percent- age)*
2005	10,431	9,377	1,041,378	669,720	394,600	41	66
2006	10,622	9,534	1,065,275	664,805	410,110	38	68
2007	10,707	9,666	1,089,513	650,762	410,072	37	70
2008	11,308	10,131	1,151,092	658,749	414,912	37	70
2009	11,763	10,553	1,208,356	671,604	415,879	38	69
2010	12,615	11,245	1,238,928	680,819	423,589	38	69
2011	12,898	11,504	1,274,720	683,246	447,010	35	77
2012	13,375	11,987	1,326,717	682,449	472,377	31	82
2013	13,626	12,244	1,351,710	679,940	482,846	29	83

Source: SEDAPAL.

In terms of the length of water and sewerage networks the indicators show that on average, the length of water network has been equal to 11,927 Km, while the length of sewerage networks has been equal to 10,693 Km between 2005 and 2013. It is important to highlight that in this period both lengths have followed a growing path. As a matter of fact, the highest growth of both water and sewerage networks was on 2010 with a 7% rate.

Also, in terms of the connections of water and sanitation services that were billed between 2005 and 2013, it can be inferred that it has also followed a growing path due to the behaviour of the previous variables described. On average, the number of connections billed has been equal to 1,194,188 for this period.

Referring to the volume of water produced between 2005 and 2013 by SEDAPAL, the path of growth has also been positive. It is important to recognise that there have been years were it was not maintained, though. The volume of water produced on average in this period was equal to 671,344 thousands of m³. The highest volume produced was 683,246 thousands m³ on 2011, while the lowest volume produced was 650,762 thousands m³ on 2007.

Together with the volume of water produced, it is important to analyse how much of it was effectively billed by SEDAPAL. From Table 3, it is possible to infer that the percentage of non-revenued water has decreased between 2005 and 2013 at an average rate of 4%. However, it still is relevant since by 2013, it share is equal to a third of the total volume of water produced. SEDAPAL's efforts should focus on this in order to keep the consistent decreasing path that it has had for the last years. (See chart 1).

Chart 1. Relationship Between the Volume of Water Produced and Billed Water of SEDAPAL (2005-2013)

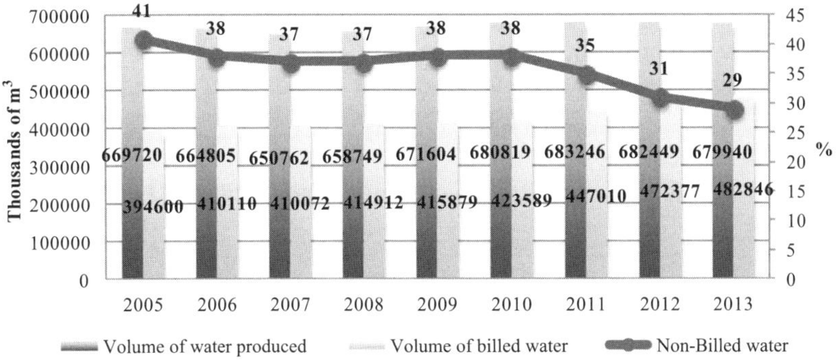

Source: SEDAPAL.

Finally, the last operative indicator that is relevant to examine is the micro metering. The micro metering refers to the proportion of total water connections that have an operating meter installed. As a matter of fact, this indicator has an inverse relation with the non-revenued volume of water because; the higher the share of connections that have the meter measuring, the less connections that are considered as non-revenued. In the period between 2005 and 2013, the micro metering has increased in an average rate of 3%, passing from 66% on 2005 to 83% in 2013. It is still important to work on this since 20% of connections are not still part of the metering system, depriving the generation of revenue to SEDAPAL.

On summary, SEDAPAL operative indicators show that the EPS has improved its service provision standards. But, there is still work to do related to the non-revenued volume of water, which reduces its turnover and puts in risk its financial stability together with the low tariff rates.

127

5. Performance

The financial performance of SEDAPAL is evaluated through the following ratios:

a. Liquidity measurement ratios. These ratios can determine the ability of SEDAPAL to cover its short-term obligations using the most liquid assets held. While by 2008, the current assets of SEDAPAL covered 0.98 times the current liabilities; in 2013 the current assets covered 1.84 times the current liabilities. Moreover, if we consider only the most liquid corporate assets such as cash, the accounts receivable and other short-term investments, all these covered in 2008 0.97 times the current liabilities and in 2013, 1.83 times. Finally, if cash and cash equivalents are the only assets used to meet short-term obligations, SEDAPAL shows that in 2008 this only covered 0.33 times current liabilities while in 2013 reached 1.28 times cover it. In summary, the liquidity measurement ratios have an upward trend, so it can be concluded that the company has improved its liquidity performance throughout the period. (See chart 2).

Chart 2. Liquidity Measurement Ratios (2008-2013)

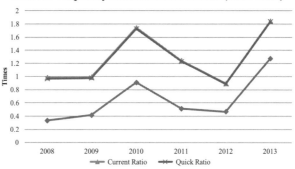

Source: SEDAPAL and Superintencia del Mercado de Valores.

b. Leverage Ratios. The *debt ratio* measures SEDAPAL's level of leverage and its tendency. In this case, the debt ratio shows an upward trend, although in the last it has a slight fall. In 2008, the ratio was 0.49, which means that the liability of SEDAPAL represented half of its own resources. In the following years, the ratio grew, until 2011, were it reached its maximum value of 0.83. Thereafter, the debt ratio starts to fall, and in 2013 it is 0.66, which means that SEDAPAL's debt represents more than half of its own resources.

On the other hand, *the shareholder equity ratio* indicates which portion of SEDAPAL's assets is financed with equity. This ratio shows a downward trend over the period of analysis. In 2008, SEDAPAL financed

67% of its assets with equity. In the following years, the atios falls, reaching its lowest point in 2011 with 55%. Afterwards, it increases and reaches the value of 60% in 2013.

The *total debt to total assets ratio* estimates the part of the total assets that is being financed with liabilities. This ratio has a growing trend. In 2008, 33% of the assets of the company were financed with external debt. In the following years, the ratio increased and in 2012 it was 45%. However, in 2013 it dropped again to 40%.

In summary, it appears that SEDAPAL's leverage has increased throughout 2008-2013, and this debt is being financed primarily with funds from third parties. (See chart 3).

Chart 3. Leverage ratios (2008-2013)

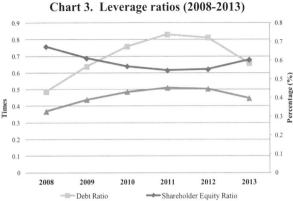

Source: SEDAPAL and Superintencia del Mercado de Valores.

c. Profitability indicator ratios. These indicators are responsible for measuring the value of SEDAPAL as a percentage of its net sales. The *gross profit margi*n was 42% in 2008, which means that SEDAPAL generated a gross profit of 0.42 *Nuevos Soles* for each Nuevo Sol sold. In the following years, the margin followed a downward trend until 2012, were it was equal to 23%. After that, the margin begins to grow and is equal to 39% by 2013. The *operating profit margin* has a similar behaviour. However, the *net profit margin* differs from the previous indicators because it had an upward trend until 2009 and reached a maximum value of 20.28%. Subsequently, it decreases until 2012 and then it increases again taking the value of 16.50% in 2013.

Other indicators that measure the profitability of the EPS are the ones relative to the return value as a percentage of the investment, which is represented by the equity or the total assets of the company. The *ratio return on equity (ROE)* has an increasing trend, which means that the benefit that the company has obtained throughout the study period is greater than the amount of capital invested on it. In 2008, the *ROE* was equal to 0.12%, while in 2013 the *ROE* was 3.74%. Then, the utility per Nuevo Sol invested has increased over the period. Unlike *ROE*, the *ratio return on assets (ROA)* has a decreasing trend, which means that the benefit obtained from the investment in assets has been declining in the course of years. In 2008, the *ROA* was equal to 3.83%, while in 2013 it was 2.14%. Then, the yield on invested assets per Nuevo Sol has decreased over the period. (See chart 4).

Chart 4. Profitability Indicator Ratios (2008-2013)

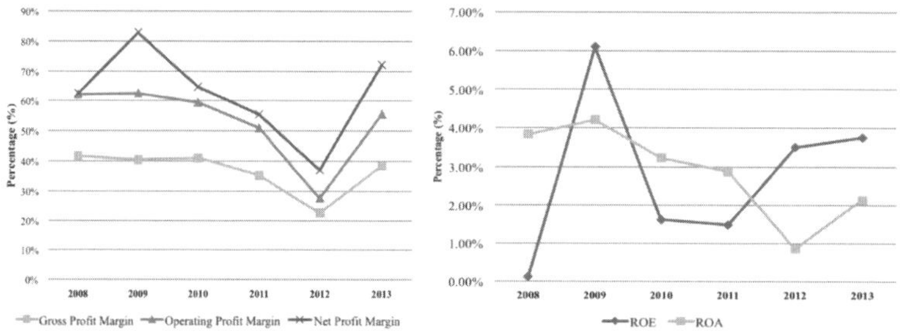

Source: SEDAPAL and Superintencia del Mercado de Valores.

d. Indicator of company's financial performance. The *earnings before interests, taxes, depreciation and amortization (EBITDA)* measures the profitability generated by the operations of a business regardless of how they were financed, the income tax, the depreciation of fixed assets and the amortization of intangible assets. The evolution of the *EBITDA* throughout the period has a growing trend, taking a value of 571.90 million of *Nuevos Soles* in 2008 and a value of 948.00 million *Nuevos Soles* in 2012. Therefore, the profitability of SEDAPAL has increased in 2008-2012. (See chart 5).

Chart 5. EBITDA (2008-2012)

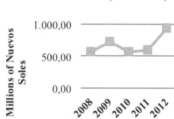

Source: SEDAPAL and *Superintencia del Mercado de Valores.*

In overall, SEDAPAL's performance should be analysed from two perspectives: (i) SEDAPAL's debt is being financed basically through founds from third parties, which implies that the enterprise is gaining obligations that will have to be refunded in the near future; (ii) SEDAPAL's profit development has been positive and its EBITDA has increased. However, the return on actives has not had the same positive trend (it is recovering, though), which implies that the enterprise should improve its investments in order to guarantee sustainability.

Therefore, even when profit is growing, SEDAPAL has to worry about covering its financial obligations. For that, it is crucial to be aware of its investment needs and the results that should be accomplished by them, which are fundamental for its status in the long term. The Balance sheet, Income Statement and Financial Ratios can be seen in Annex.

6. Governance

Nowadays, Peruvian Constitution of 1993 is the principal norm that rules the State and its actions. It establishes from Articles 191 to 197 that it is responsibility of municipalities the provision of public services. This is complemented by Article 2, Section 1 and 22, which stipulates life rights and physical integrity, Article 7 and 9, where health rights and health policy are defined, and Articles 66 and 67, referred to use of natural and water resources.

In accordance to Section 80, No. 2.1 of the Organic Law of Municipalities, provincial and district municipalities have the shared function to manage and regulate directly or grant concession rights for potable water services. Furthermore, the Organic Law of Regional Governments establishes that regional Governments have to (but not force to) technically and financially help local Governments for the provision of sanitation services.

In 1981, the National Service of Potable Water and Sewer Systems Provision (SENAPA) was created by Legislative Decree No. 150, a public utility that was in charge of enterprises in Lima, Arequipa and Trujillo, previously managed by the General Direction of Sanitation Works and had 10 operative units across the country and 15 subsidiary utilities. One of these enterprises was SEDAPAL (which provides potable water and sewer system services to Lima city).

On April 1990, all of the enterprises were transferred from SENAPA to the provincial and district municipalities, according to Legislative Decree No. 574 and No. 601. Moreover, on December 1992, SUNASS was created by Law Decree No. 25965. Some of its duties were the sector's development and the proposal of norms for sanitation services provision, and the solution of users complains as a last resort entity. It marked the dissolution and liquidation of SENAPA.

In 1994, Law No. 26338 and Supreme Decree No. 09-95-PRES were approved. They stated institutions competence in the sector, and rights and duties of users and enterprises, defining also the pricing regime, and establishing private participation conditions.

In 2002, the Ministry of Housing, Construction and Sanitation (MVCS) was created by Law No. 27779, and its functions, competence, scope, and organization were defined by Law No. 27792, published later. Even though the Ministry is the most important organisation, there are several other institutions that play an important role in the sector. The institutional structure of the water and sanitation sector is presented below.

Chart 6. Governance of Water and Sanitation in Peru

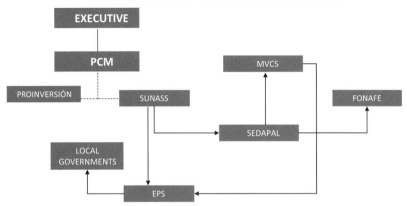

Source: SUNASS, 2010.

The Ministry Council Presidency (PCM) depends on the Executive Government of Peru. PROINVERSION is the Sponsoring Agency of Private Investment and SUNASS, which is the Sanitation Regulatory Agency that regulates EPSs and SEDAPAL. Therefore, SEDAPAL depends on the MVCS and FONAFE (the National Fund for Financing State Enterprise Activity).

Moreover, the Health Ministry (MINSA), through the General Direction of Environmental Health and the Executive Direction of Basic Sanitation (DIGESA and DESAB, respectively), exercises its function in sanitary and quality aspects for human consumption water and environmental protection for health. DIGESA is the responsible authority to norm, regulate, evaluate and authorise the use of sewage waters, and approve effluent treatment system projects. The provincial and local counterparts are the Health Directions and the health centres managed by health networks, respectively (Law Decree No. 17752, General Water Law).

In the rural field, there have been important changes. In 1962, according to Law No. 13997, the Ministry of Public Health was in charge of promoting public services in the rural towns and cities through DISABAR (Direction of Basic Rural Sanitation). Many projects were implemented to cover the basic infrastructure needs for service providing and later were handled to users' associations named Management Committees, conformed by local townspeople who manage, operate and maintenance these facilities.

The National Sanitation Plan 2006-2015 (PNS), approved on March 2006, is oriented to achieve Millennium Development Goals. These objectives mostly consider an increase in coverage, better quality of service and service sustainability. Therefore, investments are centred in restoring and expanding water and sanitation systems. The following objectives were proposed:

- management modernisation of sanitation sector,
- increase services sustainability,
- improve services' quality,
- achieve service providers' financial viability; and,
- improve service access.

Despite having planned actions and policies for achieving these goals, these are presented without any prioritisation, which difficults its application. Moreover, even though this plan establishes general strategies to be implemented, a sector integral reform concept is required and should be incorporated in the plan.

Water resources management is another important issue, concerning mostly in the agriculture sector. There is a need to implement an integral approach oriented to water multi – purpose exploitation but considering water as an economic good, managed with efficiency, equity and sustainability criteria.

In 2004, Ministries of Agriculture, Energy and Mines, Production, Defence, Health, Economy and Finance, and Housing, Construction and Sanitation took initiative to prepare a National Strategy for Water Resources Management, with many principal aspects like the rational and sustainable exploitation of water, the integration of water basins as a managed units, the multipurpose characteristic of water and the protection of the resource. In 2009, the National Law of Water Resources was published and; in 2010, Regulation of this Law was approved by Supreme Decree No. 001-2010-AG. The importance of this Law and its regulation resides on regulating the management and use of water resources that comprise continental, superficial, underground water and associated goods.

In summary, the governance of the sector is inadequate. In the case of EPS, municipalities have been unable to provide the right governance framework to companies and rather have been influenced by the political power of the mayors. For SEDAPAL, MVCS has made an acceptable driving company which has reached levels of good service through the years. However, investments are carried out mostly under political guidelines rather than business ways, which has weakened the governance of the company as a consequence.

7. Regulation

Regulatory Organisations Law (Law No. 27332) refers to the nature, functions and scope of regulatory organisations. Among a regulator functions are: to supervise, regulate, norm, audit, sanction, solve controversies; and, to solve users claims. These functions will be exercised within the established scope of each regulatory agency laws and rules.

According to this law, the Director Board must be composed by five directors for each sector's regulator. Two members are designed by Ministry Council Presidency, one from the Sector's Ministry, one from Ministry of Finance and Economy and, finally, one from INDECOPI.

SUNASS, a decentralised organisation from Ministry of Presidency, is the sector's regulator, with legal capacity for public law and with economic, financial and official autonomy for proposing water and sanitation service provision norms. Also, the Basic Sanitation Direction (created by Legislative Decree No. 574) got dismissed and, since activation of Sector's General Law, SUNASS would count with 1% of turnover contribution from private and public sanitation service providers.

In 1994, General Law of Sanitation Services was approved, and later regulated by a Supreme Decree (DS No. 09-95-PRES) in 1995. It established involved institutions competences and stated users and service providers' duties and rights. It also defined the tariff regime and designated SUNASS as the organisation who implement tariff formulas and its legislation. Conditions for private participation in the sector were also considered.

Utilities under municipalities control must wait for its corresponding Mayors to approve the tariffs proposed by SUNASS. In case they disapprove these prices, EPS can appeal to SUNASS as a last resource. Moreover, municipalities must approve the tariffs after a formula modification.

Municipalities must also concede rights for sanitation services exploitation to any private or mixed (public – private association) service providers. Also, municipal EPSs can promote private participation for improving their business management.

As mentioned before, SUNASS is the organisation that regulates water and sanitation sector. This function is exercised by its Board of Directors and, in accordance to the General Tariff Regulation Rule, it considers:

– tariff determination (price formulas and tariff structure) of water and sanitation services provided by EPS;

– establishment of performance goals for the EPS, in line with approved tariffs;

– approval of activities costs of collateral services;

– approval of contractual clauses about tariffs and quality and coverage levels to be incorporate in concession contracts for provision of sanitation services.

SUNASS has the autonomy and authority to sanction and apply corrective measures (in the scope of its responsibility and competence) for non-fulfilment of duties derived from legal and technical norms, and for non-fulfilment of obligations by concessionaries. It can also solve claims and controversies between users and service providers, authoring SUNASS organisations to do it by an administrative procedure.

8. Tariffs, Investment, Finance and Distributional Issues with Respect to Public Missions

Theoretically, EPSs should be able to auto finance the provision of water and sanitation services through an efficient tariff scheme. However, they have not succeeded on it. Even though tariffs are still low, SEDAPAL is the only EPS that has been able to auto finance its investment projects. Nevertheless, it has also received public financial assistance and international contributions in order to achieve this status.

Tariff regulation is ruled by different principles, specified in the General Tariff Regulation Rule:

– *Economic efficiency principle.* Prices charged by EPSs for service providing must incentive optimal resources allocation, so maximum social welfare is achieved.

– *Financial feasibility principle.* Tariffs applied by EPSs must recover required investment for service provision, while achieving quality and service levels stated by SUNASS. Furthermore, it should allow the utilities to broaden service coverage.

– *Social equity principle.* SUNASS will implement a sanitation service access policy that will include and cover the great majority of persons.

– *Simplicity principle.* Tariffs should be easy to understand, apply and control.

- *Transparency principle.* Tariff system will be published.
- *No discrimination principle.* SUNASS acts are held without discrimination, treating everybody the same way in terms of the tariff system and resolving according with the legal system and social interest.

SUNASS tool for tariff formulas, structures and management goals implementation for water and sanitation services is PMO (Optimized Master Plan). PMO is a tool for long-term planning horizon of thirty years that contains the schedule of investments in terms of economic efficiency and financial projections of the efficient development of the operations of the EPS. Also, SUNASS can determine maximum costs for activities within collateral services. A PMO must be formulated and presented by applicants. Exceptionally, SUNASS will formulate a PMO, according to Article No. 96 from General Sanitation Services Law Rule TUO.

SUNASS, in line with Article No. 20 from Tariff Regulation Rule, issues a resolution accepting EPSs application, once verified that it meets the requirements. After this, SUNASS Director Board publishes a resolution that approves tariff and structure formulas and management goals. According to Article No. 25, utilities are notified by SUNASS and have 30 calendar days to issue some commentary. Once this period is over, in accordance with Article No. 30, after evaluating utility's opinion (if it was presented), a final tariff study is made by Tariff Regulation Management, which contains SUNASS final opinion and proposal for investment programmes, management goals, tariff and structure formulas.

Also, it is worthy to note that after the first resolution, there must be obligatory Public Audiences. These "public hearings" are called by SUNASS generally in the municipality served by the EPS and the assistance and participation of civil society is through user associations or professional associations of the locality. In the "public hearings" SUNASS supports the draft rate study with the proposed pricing formula, tariff structures and management goals, drawn up based on PMO presented by the EPS and would be applied for is for the next five years in the area of responsibility.

Furthermore, Article No. 94 from TUO of Law No. 26338 specifies that tariffs must be guided by above principles. In line with this, the approved tariff formula must ensure the five years medium term average costs recovery according to Articles No. 96 and No. 98. Article No. 101 and No. 102 specifying that the tariff formula can be adjusted by inflation and for updating management goals achievement in the PMO, which will be revised every 5 years. From Article No. 100, tariff formula general expression is as follows,

$$T_t = T_{t-1} * (1+x) * (1+Kt)$$

Where,

T: Service tariff

x: Growth rate for price index, corresponding to cost structure for service providing

Kt: Annual adjustment factor to express real increments in tariffs.

In relation to capital base for tariff calculation, assets acquired by the company will be part of it, as a component of the economic costs, and hence the tariff. Fixed assets that didn't meant costs for utilities must be deducted, for not representing own resources disbursements for acquisition. To accomplish this, revaluations and capital contributions have been withdrawn from the recoverable capital base that the company has received as a donation for the service.

8.1. The Actual Tariff Scheme (2010-2015)

8.1.1. Fundaments

The tariff scheme is established based on financial, operative, investment and commercial performance indicators evaluated by SUNASS and determined for 5 years. SEDAPAL's actual tariff is programmed to rule until April 2015. The estimations that fund it are:

a. Demand of water and sanitation services estimation. The demand estimation considers: (i) the population growth rate, (ii) the number of family members per household, (iii) the distribution of active connection by consume ranges, (iv) the under record factor; and, (v) other factors that account characteristics of users whose consume is not measured or that do not receive the service. On the other hand, the estimation of the sanitation services considers: (i) the required volume of water per user category; and, (ii) the required volume of water in order to cover the losses that are consequence of non-revenued water consumed. (See table 4).

Table 4. Water and Sewerage Connections Estimation

Years	2010	2011	2012	2013	2014	2015
Water connections	1,293,348	1,356,418	1,413,450	1,483,252	1,560,540	1,627,308
Sewerage connections	1,160,235	1,225,403	1,284,991	1,357,060	1,435,612	1,504,742

Source: SEDAPAL.

b. Investment programme. The investment programme in order to expand the supply capacities of the EPS and to cover the deficits of the water and sanitation services provision is founded by Government contributions, leverage, SEDAPAL resources and the sale of financed connections. (See table 5).

Table 5. Investment Programme by Financial Source

Years	Government contributions (S/.)	Leverage (S/.)	SEDAPAL resources (S/.)	Sale of financed connections (S/.)	Total (S/.)
2011	132,287,706	397,727,534	171,554,472	25,628,579	727,198,291
2012	188,840,385	240,758,867	218,445,651	20,349,441	668,394,344
2013	82,281,771	351,422,792	189,579,764	124,604,375	747,888,702
2014	-	336,623,025	225,201,664	79,937,597	641,762,286
2015	-	254,813,614	246,489,364	96,496,003	597,798,981
Total	403,409,862	1,581,345,832	1,051,270,915	347,015,995	3,383,042,604

Source: SEDAPAL.

c. Exploitation costs estimations. The exploitation costs are determined by: (i) the operative costs; and, (ii) the sunk costs. The costs of exploitation follow the demand's growing trend. This trend is also supported by the investment projects that are programmed to develop in order to increase the quality and integrity of the services.[3] (See table 6).

Table 6. Exploitation Costs Estimation

Year	2011	2012	2013	2014	2015
Exploitation costs *(Thousands of S/.)*	598,706	660,941	704,879	715,835	729,191

Source: SEDAPAL.

d. Income estimation: The estimation of income considers: (i) the income from water and sanitation service provision (which represent on average 93% of the total income); and, (ii) the income generated from the connection fees that are charged to new users and defaulter users. (See table 7).

Table 7. Income Estimation

Year	2011	2012	2013	2014	2015
Income *(Thousands of S/.)*	1,201,033	1,250,089	1,357,978	1,453,160	1,525,258

Source: SEDAPAL, www.sedapal.gob.pe.

---

[3] The estimation of the costs does not include depreciation, provision for losses or the regulatory contribution.

138

The expected increase in income from the provision of water and sanitation services is a result of both the *tariff increment rate* and the *increase of the volume of billed water*. *Tariff increment rate* is determined considering the financial evaluation that tariff proposal study that SEDAPAL elaborates. For 2010-2015, the tariff increment rate is equal to: 2.0% in 2011, 2.0% in 2012, 2.3% in 2013, 0.0% in 2014 and 0.0% on 2015.

8.1.2. The Tariff Scheme

Considering the tariff formula (determined by the General Sanitation Services Law No. 26338); and, the tariff increment rate (that is conditioned to management goals), the tariff scheme is established for the period 2010-2015. It contemplates 2 types of consume: *residential*, with social and domestic categories; and, *non residential*, with commercial, industrial and public categories. Additionally, each category is classified within ranges of water and sewerage consume. For each range of consume there is an established tariff in *Nuevos Soles* (S/.) per m³, and a fixed charge. (See table 8).

Table 8. SEDAPAL's Tariff Scheme

Type of Consume	Category	Ranges (m³)	Tariffs (S/. per m³)		Fixed charge
			Water	Sewerage	
Residential	Social	0 – more	0.875	0.382	4,444
	Domestic	0 – 10	0.875	0.382	4,444
		10 – 25	1.004	0.438	4,444
		25 – 50	2.234	0.975	4,444
		50 – more	3.796	1.657	4,444
Non Residential	Commercial	0 – 1,000	3.796	1.657	4,444
		1,000 – more	4.067	1.775	4,444
	Industrial	0 – 1,000	3.796	1.657	4,444
		1,000 – more	4.067	1.775	4,444
	Public	0 – more	2.125	0.928	4,444

Source: SEDAPAL.

8.1.2.1. The Management Goals Achieved by 2013

The management goals that SEDAPAL has to achieve in the period 2010-2015 are fixed in order to guarantee the efficiency of the EPSs and its users. These goals are mostly referred to operative facts of the enterprise.

By 2013, the only management goals that SEDAPAL did not achieve were referred to: (i) the annual increment of residential water connections, (ii) the annual increment of residential sewerage connections; and, (iii) the annual increment of new meters.

The principal results of goal achievement for 2012 and 2013 are resumed in Table 9.

Table 9. SEDAPAL's Management Goals achieved

Management Goals	2010	Goals 2012	Goals 2013	Executed 2012	Executed 2013	Compliance Rate (%)
Annual increment of residential water connections	-	27,340	41,897	6,858	14,520	21.0%
Annual increment of residential sewerage connections	-	27,127	41,395	6,893	14,555	21.2%
Annual increment of new meters	-	154,617	126,083	31,563	64,191	22.9%
Non-revenued water *(%)*	38.1%	31.9%	30.0%	-	29.9%	100%
Average continuity *(hours/day)*	21.6	21.8	21.9	-	21.9	100%
Average pressure *(m.c.a)*	22.6	22.8	22.9	-	23.6	100%
Employment relationship *(%)*	-	60.0%	58.0%	-	56.0%	100%
Active water connections *(%)*	93.0%	94.1%	94.6%	-	95.7%	100%
Update of the technical registry of water and sewerage *(%)*	98.5%	99.0%	99.5%	-	99.7%	100%
Update of the commercial registry of water and sewerage *(%)*	100%	100%	100%	-	100.0%	100%
Average flow of wastewater treatment *(m³/sec)*	2.5	2.7	2.8	-	8.1	100%

Source: SEDAPAL.

8.2. Tariff Structuration and Focalisation Problems

The current tariffs of SEDAPAL are determined in order to set a *cross-subsidy scheme* that is based in an increasing stepped blocked tariff. This scheme works charging higher rates per cubic meter consumed to users of water and sanitation services who have a large volume of water consumption, and subsidising those users who have a lower volume of consumption (who are charged with a much lower rate per cubic meter). Then, its main purpose is to generate a cross-subsidy to benefit users unable to pay for the service (poor and extreme poor households) and maintain the resources needed by the EPS to operate and expand their networks, promoting the rational use and preservation of water resource.

However, the cross-subsidy scheme has problems when determining which consumers should be subsidised and which consumers should be charged with a higher rate in order to finance the subsidy. As a consequence, targeting issues (of inclusion and exclusion) affect the cross-subsidy scheme, basically because the scheme does not consider the supplied household socioeconomic characteristics in order to determine which is the group of consumers that should be subsidised and which are not.

According to Aragón and Bonifaz (2013), if the actual scheme is analysed considering that the target population of the subsidy is households on *extreme poverty;* the proportion of households that are benefited by the subsidy erroneously is 50% of total non-extreme poor households. On the other hand, 9.55% of the extreme poor households are excluded of the subsidy.

In conclusion, despite the actual tariff scheme follows SUNASS's tariff formula and has been granted with its approval, the focalisation problems underneath it should be resolved. It is not only the way that the cross-subsidy on the tariffs does not recognise the desired population to be benefited, but also its low values.

Conclusions and Lessons Learned

SEDAPAL is the largest EPS in Peru and serves to the capital, providing water and sanitation services to 42% of the total population of the country. Since its service impact is so vast, the central Government of Peru is its owner and determines its public budget. Even when SEDAPAL is well supported, its financial budget is not enough and has to receive contributions from both central Government through the MVCS budget and multilateral investment agencies like the World Bank. Despite all this assistance, the operative results of SEDAPAL's exercise are not good enough in order to guarantee its financial sustainability.

From the operative perspective, SEDAPAL has improved many of its indicators, but it is still a great concern the one third of the water volume is considered as non-revenued. This has a direct affection over its income generation.[4] Together with this, the fact that not all users have the meter installations urges SEDAPAL to improve these indicators.

The previous indicators have a great effect in the financial development of the EPS. As it has been analysed, SEDAPAL has an acceptable financial

---

[4]   The company is mandated to generate sufficient revenue to meet its investment and operating costs by Optimised Master Plan (PMO).

profile. However, it is been necessary for the EPS to raise its leverage, especially through external debts rather than domestic debt.

Regarding the prices, we can say that in general the level of charges is relatively low compared with other countries that have the same income in Latin America. As a matter of fact, these levels of fees are not enough to maintain a high level of water coverage provided by SEDAPAL in Lima. The reasons for the low coverage are primary due to the lack of constant investment planning and to the improper execution of them. In other words, SEDAPAL has serious limitations in their ability to make investments to expand coverage because of their own bureaucracy. Thus, the amount of water supplied by SEDAPAL is insufficient both in terms of uptake and distribution of water, which determines the coverage problems of the company.

Finally, considering the approved tariff scheme, SEDAPAL has accomplished most of the management goals established by SUNASS. However, the tariff formula determined by the regulatory office does not allow increments that permit its sustainability without having to go on leverage. On the other hand, the cross-subsidy scheme that is established on the actual tariff scheme does not work, mainly because of its focalization problems. Nevertheless, these results are not only consequence of the EPS performance but also of the mandatory regulation of SUNASS.

References

Angel-Urdinola, D., Wodon, Q., "Do utility Subsidies Reach the Poor? Framework and Evidence for Cape Verde, Sao Tome, and Rwanda", in *Economics Bulletin*, 2007, Vol. 9, No. 4 pp. 1-7.

Aragón, G. and Bonifaz, J., "The water and sanitation service provision in Peru", in CIRIEC, Working Paper No. 2013/06.

Barde, J. and Lehmann, P., "Distributional effects of water tariff reforms – An empirical study for Lima, Peru", Helmholtz-Zentrum für Umweltforschung GmbH – UFZ, 2013.

Barrantes, R., *Diagnóstico institucional del sector de servicios de saneamiento y propuesta de políticas regulatorias*, 2003.

Battese, G., and Coelli, T., "A model for technical inefficiency effects in a stochastic frontier production function for panel data", in *Empirical Economics*, 1995, Vol. 20, No. 2, pp. 325-332.

Bonifaz, J., *Definición de la visión y alcance de la función reguladora*, 2012.

Corton, M., "Benchmarking in the Latin American water sector: The case of Peru", Public Utility Research Centre, 2003.

Espinoza, B. and Krmelj, L., "Informe de clasificación de *Sedapal Servicio de Agua y Alcantarillado de Lima*", *Equilibrium Clasificadora de Riesgo S.A.*, 2014.

Fernández-Baca, J., "La experiencia regulatoria en Perú II: Los casos de la electricidad y el agua potable", in *Apuntes 43*, 1998, pp. 89-105.

SEDAPAL, "Plan Maestro Optimizado", Vol. 1-3, 2009.

SUNASS, "Benchmarking Regulatorio de las EPS, 2013", 2013.

SUNASS, "Determinacion de la fórmula tarifaria, estructura tarifaria y metas de gestión aplicables a la empresa de servicio de agua potable y alcantarillado – sedapal s.a.", 2010.

SUNASS, "La EPS y su desarrollo, 2013", 2013.

World Bank, "Financiamiento Local de Empresas de Agua: Retos y Oportunidades – El Caso de Perú", 2008.

Yepes, G., "Los subsidios cruzados en los servicios de agua potable y saneamiento", Washington D.C., Banco Interamericano del Desarrollo, Publicaciones IFM, 2003.

Web pages

Superintendencia Nacional de Servicios de Agua y Saneamiento, Peru: http://www.sunass.gob.pe (consultation date: 1st march, 2014).

Servicio de Agua Potable y Alcantarillado de Lima: http://www.sedapal.com.pe/ (consultation date: 1st march, 2014).

Annex 1: Balance sheet

SEDAPAL
BALANCE SHEET
As of December 31, 2008, 2009, 2010, 2011, 2012, 2013
(Amounts in thousands of Nuevos Soles)

Accounts	2008	2009	2010	2011	2012	2013
Assets						
Current Assets						
Cash and cash equivalent	130,193	191,548	308,229	230,314	395,762	885,602
Accounts receivable	202,734	213,731	223,132	239,139	275,561	269,825
Other accounts receivable	44,882	46,831	53,941	84,186	78,929	114,575
Inventories	4,437	5,539	5,099	4,012	4,998	4,765
Prepaid Expenses	2,266	468	661	1,369	1252	0
Other current assets	0	0	0	0	0	3,049
Total Current Assets	384,512	458,117	591,062	559,020	756,502	1,277,816

Accounts	2008	2009	2010	2011	2012	2013
Non-current Assets						
Accounts receivable	35,243	56,662	53,271	48,774	68,339	55,929
Other accounts receivable	0	541	1,500	147,398	173,140	36,472
Property, plant and equipment	5,031,748	5,474,584	5,804,062	6,004,562	8,231,698	8,399,703
Intangible assets	2,247	359	933	315	22,845	832
Deferred taxed assets	23,114	56,403	92,842	127,539	2,565,046	932,151
Other non-current assets	868	0	0	0	0	0
Total Non-Current Assets	5,093,220	5,588,549	5,952,608	6,328,588	11,061,068	9,425,087
TOTAL ASSETS	5,477,732	6,046,666	6,543,670	6,887,608	11,817,570	10,702,903
Liabilities and Equity						
Liabilities						
Current Liabilities						
Financial liabilities	123,964	245,231	122,226	150,108	127,216	123,572
Accounts payable	80,208	110,420	92,146	147,315	155,422	173,437
Income tax and current holdings	18,027	31,408	5,695	0	25,973	39,004
Provisions for employee benefits	0	0	0	6,727	5,689	5,496
Other accounts payable	153,419	72,589	81,003	93,698	142,488	128,064
Provisions	15,224	2,935	38,253	51,522	388,198	224,402
Total Current Liabilities	390,842	462,583	339,323	449,370	844,986	693,975
Non-Current Liabilities						
Financial liabilities	1,399,545	1,832,877	2,404,988	2,540,493	3,045,319	2,068,299
Deferred income tax	0	58,416	78,328	79,932	1,274,732	475,173
Provisions for employee benefits	0	0	0	0	49,287	51,076

Other accounts payable	0	0	0	54,087	57,873	172,428
Deferred income	43	84	8	0	23,035	786,817
Total Non-Current Liabilities	1,399,588	1,891,377	2,483,324	2,674,512	4,450,246	3,553,793
Total Liabilities	1,790,430	2,353,960	2,822,647	3,123,882	5,295,232	4,247,768
Equity						
Capital stock	5,309,298	5,309,298	5,309,298	5,309,298	3,408,208	5,486,687
Additional capital	294,280	383,650	435,857	510,308	422,341	13,197
Statutory reserves	42,956	42,956	0	0	0	0
Retained earnings	-1,959,232	-2,043,198	-2,024,132	-2,055,880	2,691,789	955,251
Total Equity	3,687,302	3,692,706	3,721,023	3,763,726	6,522,338	6,455,135
TOTAL LIABILITIES AND EQUITY	5,477,732	6,046,666	6,543,670	6,887,608	11,817,570	10,702,903

Source: SEDAPAL.

Annex 2: Income Statement

Sedapal
Income statement
For the year ended December 31, 2008, 2009, 2010, 2011, 2012, 2013
(Amount in thousands of *Nuevos Soles*)

Accounts	2008	2009	2010	2011	2012	2013
Net sales	1,003,083	1,108,674	1,113,286	1,232,856	1,384,420	1,471,680
Cost of sales	-584,494	-660,541	-656,737	-798,839	-1,072,129	-904,703
Gross Income	418,589	448,133	456,549	434,017	312,291	566,977
Selling expenses	-110,741	-114,311	-150,786	-147,552	-159,469	-180,363
Administrative expenses	-89,685	-84,180	-99,163	-121,220	-101,708	-141,651
Other operating income	10,419	16,407	12,858	31,799	19,025	53,394
Other operating expenses	-24,033	-19,540	-14,524	-2,701	0	-46,397
Operating income	204,549	246,509	204,934	194,343	70,139	251,960
Financial income	147,655	267,383	0	21,992	35,926	64,763
Financial expenses	-356,865	-190,249	-31,370	-70,510	-118,407	-61,847
Net exchange difference	0	0	-97,983	-81,962	211,672	69,187
Net Profit Before Taxes (Pretax Income)	-4,661	323,643	75,581	63,863	199,330	324,063

Accounts	2008	2009	2010	2011	2012	2013
Employee participation	1,307	-14,744	0	0	0	0
Income tax	7,448	-84,042	-16,070	-8,589	-67,624	-79,958
Net Income	4,094	224,857	59,511	55,274	131,706	244,105

Annex 3: Financial Ratios

FINANCIAL RATIOS	2008	2009	2010	2011	2012	2013
LIQUIDITY MEASUREMENT RATIOS						
CURRENT RATIO	0.98	0.99	1.74	1.24	0.90	1.84
QUICK RATIO	0.97	0.98	1.72	1.23	0.89	1.83
CASH RATIO	0.33	0.41	0.91	0.51	0.47	1.28
LEVERAGE RATIOS						
DEBT RATIO	0.49	0.64	0.76	0.83	0.81	0.66
SHAREHOLDER EQUITY RATIO	67.31%	61.07%	56.86%	54.64%	55.19%	60.31%
TOTAL DEBT TO TOTAL ASSETS RATIO	0.33	0.39	0.43	0.45	0.45	0.40
PROFITABILITY INDICATOR RATIOS						
GROSS PROFIT MARGIN	41.73%	40.42%	41.01%	35.20%	22.56%	38.53%
OPERATING PROFIT MARGIN	20.39%	22.23%	18.41%	15.76%	5.07%	17.12%

146

NET PROFIT MARGIN	0.41%	20.28%	5.35%	4.48%	9.51%	16.59%
RETURN ON EQUITY	0.12%	6.10%	1.61%	1.49%	3.50%	3.74%
RETURN ON ASSETS	3.83%	4.21%	3.23%	2.88%	0.86%	2.14%
INDICATORS OF COMPANY'S FINANCIAL PERFORMANCE	2008	2009	2010	2011	2012	2013
EBITDA	571.90	728.40	571.10	594.00	948.00	

5. The Remunicipalisation
of the Water Service in Paris

Pierre BAUBY

PhD in Political Science

Mihaela M. SIMILIE

Phd in Law

This chapter deals with the factors, stages and preliminary effects of the process of remunicipalisation of the water service in Paris during the late 2000s.

The responsibility for water and sanitation of the 36,000 French *communes* dates back to the 1789 Revolution. Unlike developments in other network services, French local authorities were always acknowledged the right to organise their own water supply in their community (Duroy, 1996; Bauby & Lupton, 2004; Bauby, 2009). However, water and wastewater services are usually organised and function separately in France. Paris is no exception. This chapter presents the case study of the Parisian water service.

1. Parisian Specificities

1.1. A Small, Densely Populated Municipality

With a small area (105 km²) and 2,257,981 (2011) inhabitants, the city of Paris is very densely populated: it has 21,504 inhabitants per km². Most of its habitat has a collective nature. That is one of the characteristics explaining why, in comparative studies on water prices, the city of Paris often comes in below the average prices noted in other big French cities. It also has the lowest price level in the region *Île-de-France*. Incidentally, since the beginning, a collective water service subscription system exists in Paris (per building) and not an individual subscription and individual contract with each household.

1.2. A Predominance of Collective Housing

In Paris, the collective subscriber is the contractor of the water distribution service. In most cases, the collective subscriber is the association of the co-owners of the building (*Syndicat de copropriété*) or a social housing rental company (*bailleur social*). In 2000, a Parisian water subscriber represented, on average, a building of about 24 consumers. At the beginning of 2013, there were 93,920 water subscriptions for most of the 2 million inhabitants. The relationship regarding water provision is thus established between the water distribution operator and subscriber who is, in few cases, the final consumer.

Individual subscriptions and bills exist for some professionals only. The joint ownership may decide to introduce individual meters for households. But water charges are more often than not included in the collective charges of the joint ownership (*charges de copropriété*), which are calculated for each household according to the area of its apartment. This creates a series of difficulties in individualising the relationships with final users and accessing individual data.

1.3. Multiple Extra Muros Water Resources

For its drinking water provision, the city of Paris uses only water resources coming from territories situated beyond its area. More than half of the water resources used by the city are groundwater; for a long time, their treatment was low-cost. However, the city has maintained its autonomy as regards the organisation of the municipal water service. Around Paris, most suburban municipalities are part of the *Syndicat des eaux d'Île-de-France (SEDIF)*, which was created in 1923. 149 municipalities now belong to SEDIF.

1.4. Two Easily Accessible Water Distribution Networks

Unlike many other cities in the world, Paris has two distribution networks, one for non-drinking water and the other for drinking water. Most of these networks were planned and built between 1855 and 1874.

In early 2000 the non-potable mains supply was about 1,600 km of pipes for almost 400,000 m³ of water used each day of which only one quarter was used for non-commercial purposes (cleaning of sewers and streets, watering of public parks and yards).[1] The network does not cover the whole city and, in the past, its maintenance was questioned. The network situation was re-examined by the current municipality

---

[1]   The city also uses drinking water for most of its public parks and gardens.

which decided to maintain and improve it. An investment programme is planned.

The drinking water network is about 1,990 km. In the subdued relief of the city 18 water plants and three water towers raise water.

1.5. A Tradition of Public Water Supply and Wastewater Management Services Involving Private Operators

In Paris the municipal water service was traditionally provided in public management. At the same time and to a certain extent, private players were always involved in the management of water service. Thus, since 1860, the management of billing and invoices (including taxes), collection and customer relations (*contrat de régie intéressée*) was delegated to the *Compagnie Générale des eaux* (recently known as subsidiary of *Véolia*).

2. History

Eleven years before the Revolution, in 1778, Charles-Auguste Perier and his brother Jacques-Constantin created the *Compagnie des eaux de Paris* to provide water in Paris. This was the first company to provide large-scale water distribution in France, inspired by the London model. In 1788, the city of Paris had to buy 80% of the shares of this company as their value on the stock exchange declined sharply. The service thereby became a municipal entity (*régie*), which deserved about 600,000 Parisians.

During the middle of the 19th century the city of Paris expanded its territory and redesigned its public water service to give its inhabitants broader access to drinking water and to meet public health objectives. The customer management service was however delegated to the *Compagnie générale des eaux*, a private company that ensured water service management in the communes that became part of the city of Paris.

The public service for water production and distribution was long managed by a public entity (*régie*) in Paris. Apart from some amendments in 1910 and 1924, the organisation of the Parisian water service remained unchanged until the mid-1980s, when delegated management was decided. But, during the late 2000s, a second important change triggered complete public management of the water service for the first time since 1860.

2.1. The Chirac Era

The organisation of the water service in Paris became more complex during the three terms of office of Mayor Jacques Chirac (1977-1995).[2]

---

[2] The position of Mayor was abolished between 1871 and 1977, Jacques Chirac becoming the first elected Mayor on 20 March 1977.

Jacques Chirac was elected Mayor in 1977. The customer management contract concluded by the city with *Compagnie Générale des eaux* in 1924 for a period of 60 years came to an end in 1984. The new municipality decided new arrangements and directly conferred the management of water service distribution to two private operators on the basis of two lease contracts concluded on 29 December 1984 for a period of 25 years (until 31 December 2009).

The territory covering the right bank of the Seine (the river that flows through Paris), representing about two thirds of Parisian water consumers, was conferred to the *Compagnie Générale des eaux* (subsidiary of *Vivendi Cie générale des eaux*, now part of *Véolia*). The network of drinking water on the right bank was about 1,200 km. In 1999, it was managed by 148 employees and served 63,414 subscribers for a volume of about 164 million m³ per year.

The left bank of the Seine, representing about one third of consumers, was allocated to the *Société Eau et Force de Paris* (subsidiary of *Cie Suez-Lyonnaise des eaux-Dumez*, now part of *Suez-Environnement*). The drinking water network on the left bank was about 576 km. In 1999, it was managed by 73 employees and served 25,577 subscribers for a volume of about 81 million m³.

This contract enlarged the historical presence of the *Compagnie Générale des eaux* (Véolia) in the capital city of France. However, it had to share this local monopoly with its historical national competitor, the *Société Eau et Force de Paris* (*Lyonnaise*), which entered this local market for the first time. The entry of the latter company on the Parisian market can only be explained by the close relationships between the Mayor of Paris, Jacques Chirac and the President General Director (PDG) of *Lyonnaise*, Jérôme Monod, who was director of its cabinet between 1975 and 1976, when Jacques Chirac was Prime-Minister. Then, between 1976 and 1978, J. Monod became General Secretary of RPR, the party of Chirac with which he became President of France in 1995. In 1980 J. Monod became President General Director of *Lyonnaise des eaux*. He held this position until 2000.[3] Several authors emphasise the proximity between the Mayor of Paris and the PDG of *Lyonnaise des eaux* (Stefanovich, 2005, p. 225), in a broader context of public life financing, in particular of the financing of presidential campaigns by private operators involved in the provision of various public services (Hall & Lobina, 2001; Barraqué, 2012, pp. 904-905).

The municipality advanced several reasons to justify the delegation: the need to renew a water plant and to reduce leakages, the need of investments which were considered too high for the budget of the city.

---

[3]   Jérôme Monod was a political adviser to the President of the Republic, Jacques Chirac, since 2000 until 2007.

According to the contract concluded with *Générale des Eaux* (Véolia) the city of Paris considered that "it is desirable (…) to implement a mode of management of the distribution network offering the best guarantees of efficiency".

The contracts concluded with the two private operators had the legal nature of lease contracts in which the obligations of distributors to finance investments was limited. Thus, the realisation of large distribution works and investments regarding the extension of networks remained the responsibility of the city of Paris. However, it seems that few distribution or extension works were realised by the city during the period of the delegated management of the distribution.

In February 1987, the production and transport of water in Paris (until then ensured by a municipal department) was delegated to a mixed society created to this end on 26 January 1987: the SAGEP – *Société anonyme de gestion des Eaux de Paris* (later to become *Eau de Paris*, limited liability company, transformed in industrial and commercial public enterprise – EPIC – in 2010). 70% of its shares were owned by the city of Paris, 14% by the two private drinking water providers, the rest being owned by the *Caisse des Dépôts et Consignations*. The contract with SAGEP was concluded for a period of 25 years and had the legal nature of a concession contract.

In 1987, the Cleanliness and Environment Department (*Direction de la Propreté et de l'Environnement* – DPE) was created within the public administration of the city to replace the previous Department for Industrial and Commercial Services (*Direction des Services Industriels et Commerciaux* – DSIC). The Water Control Service of the city (*Service de Contrôle des Eaux de la Ville de Paris* – SCEVP) became the Centre for Water Research and Control (*Centre de Recherche et de Contrôle des Eaux de Paris* – CRECEP). These were the city's services which should allow the local authority to exercise its responsibilities as organising authority in relation with, on the one hand, the two private operators and, on the other hand, the mixed company. In fact, these contracts, have created a new situation. The management of water service distribution was conferred to two distinct private operators while control and monitoring responsibilities were conferred by the city to the mixed company in charge of water production and transport – SAGEP. Progressively, the city had lost the knowledge and expertise necessary to play its role of organising authority, to orient and control the delegates. A series of asymmetries appeared that led to the phenomenon of capture of the city by its operators (in the terms of the "principal-agent relationship")[4] and to governance

---

[4] This case study does not proceed to an indepth analysis of this concept; we are only presenting the practical impact of the remunicipalisation process.

problems. Thus, the contracts and their implementation became subject of two special reports following controls and audits initiated in 2000, one by the municipal authority (Mairie de Paris, Inspection générale, 2003), and the other by the Regional Chamber of Accounts (Chambre régionale des comptes, 2000).

During 2000-2001, water became an issue of the municipal electoral campaign. In October 2000, on the occasion of the debates within the Council of Paris, Bertrand Delanoë, President of the Socialist Group of the Council and candidate for the function of Mayor of Paris in the municipal elections of 2001, announced his aim of a thorough review of the water management system. At the same time, according to the duration established by the three contracts, eleven years of delegated management still lay ahead.

2.2. The First Mandate of Delanoë

In the elections of 2001, the socialist-green-communist coalition won and, for the first time in the history, a mayor from the left wing was elected in Paris. His aim was to take over the public control of the water public service and to review the contracts with the private operators. The municipal coalition was also concerned about the fact that private operators did not respect their contracts in terms of leakage level (Barraqué, 2012, pp. 907).

The delegation of the water service management has become one of the priorities of the new municipality. Shortly after taking office, it noticed that in fact there was no real expertise left within municipal services to ensure the orientation and control of water services and delegates. A first objective of the city was to reassemble the capabilities and means to assume its responsibilities as organising authority. The Report of the General Inspectorate of the city of Paris (*Mairie de Paris, Inspection générale,* 2003) commissioned by the former mayor noticed numerous governance problems. Certainly, SAGEP had a degree of control but the presence of the two big private operators gave rise to suspicions of conflict of interest.

New positions were created in the administration of the city to rebuild and reinforce the necessary human resources. A first audit of the commercial service in charge of the GEI (group of economic interest, in charge of client management service) of the two delegates was initiated in 2001 and a water annexed budget was realised starting with 2004.

In 2002 the CRECEP was organised as a public entity with legal personality and financial autonomy in charge of water research and control.

The city could not end existing contracts without penalties. However, the context was favourable for the municipality to open negotiations with operators to review some of the contractual provisions.

In 2003, following negotiations, amendments to the three contracts were concluded with the two water distributors and the water producer. They included in particular their engagement to complete investments to control leakages and to replace all meters with intelligent meters before the end of the contract:[5] complementary investment for water conducts and to replace all lead pipes,[6] the development of wireless readout system; to divest distributors of the capital of SAGEP-*Eau de Paris* (in favour of the *Caisse des dépôts et consignations*); reinforcement of the control of the city on the three delegates; disclosure of performance objectives (to limit leakages).

At the same time, since the adoption of the Sapin Law of 1993,[7] any delegate mandated by a public authority with the management of a public service must give account of the exercise of this delegation in an annual report.

In 2005, the SAGEP decided to start to prepare the end of contracts, which had their expiry date in 2009. Thus, it created a participatory group aiming to define the vision, the studies to determine different hypotheses of the future organisation of the water service.

In 2007, the SAGEP was renamed "*Eau de Paris*". It was the subject of personnel and financial reductions and redeployment of tasks. France Nature Environment, the main representative of the French environment associations, has become member of the Management Board of *Eau de Paris*, as qualified person entitled to one vote.

2.3. The Municipal Elections of 2008 and the Beginning of the Second Mandate of Delanoë

Two years before the end of the two lease contracts by which the city delegated the water distribution service in Paris and four months before the municipal elections of 9 and 16 March 2008, the Mayor of Paris, Bertrand Delanoë announced in a press release his intention to reform the Parisian water service. He announced that the municipality will not renew the public service delegations that were granted to the private operators and that it will grant to a single public operator the responsibility for the entire water cycle, from production to distribution. This operator could take the legal form of a public entity (*régie*).

---

[5] Barraqué, 2012, p. 907.

[6] In 1998, there were 93,370 water connections in Paris of which about 18,000 of lead on the left bank of the River Seine. By the end of 2001, 13,532 water connections were subject to works from a total 71,761 connections.

[7] Law No. 93-122 of 29 January 1993 concerning prevention of corruption and the transparency of economic life and of public procedures.

This choice was placed at the centre of the electoral campaign of the municipal elections of March 2008. It was first explained by political reasons. The majority of the former municipal council rested on an alliance between the socialist party, the communist party and the green party. Water remunicipalisation was one of the very few topics which could be the subject of the common agreement between all of them for the elections of 2008, even if some socialist elected officials, administrative and technical agents, city engineers and trade unions were rather reluctant about remunicipalisation. Water remunicipalisation became a key tool for the renewal of the political alliance and for the electoral campaign.

The inclusion of the proposal of water service remunicipalisation in the electoral programme of the mayor for the municipal elections of March 2008 created a framework for public debate and then for legitimating this decision.

The change of the management mode involved several steps:

1) The creation of the public entity (*EPIC*) "*Eau de Paris*",

2) The takeover of production and transport activities and of CRECEP activities,

3) The takeover of the distribution activity.

In France, water services are qualified as industrial and commercial services and cannot be organised as an administrative public entity. From this point of view, the city had only two possible models for organising the remunicipalised water service: via public entity (*régie*), either with financial autonomy,[8] or with legal personality and financial autonomy;[9] the city chose the latter. According to the deputy mayor in charge of water affairs, this choice was made "because we want to have some autonomy in the management, with our own management board. We want the governance of this management board to be opened beyond the representatives of the elected officials in the council of Paris to representatives of employees, to users and associations" (Locher and Marx, 2011). Our interviews revealed the need of a new governance and regulation model to build a coalition of the "public policy community" around water. This led to changes in the governance of the water issue in the city as this community concerns not only public water service but all the aspects regarding the relationships between water and the city (drinking and non-drinking water, waste water, rain water, channels,

---

8 The management of the EPIC by the local authority with its own budget and eventually an operation council and a director. The accounts are presented in a specific budget, annexed to the budget of the local community.

9 In the second case, the *régie* enjoys legal autonomy, its own budget, a management board, a director and a president. It can operate with or without a contract of objectives (or framework contract) with the city.

ports, climate change, biological diversity, etc.). The aim was therefore to associate stakeholders formerly excluded from water issues (private and social housing, transport stakeholders, etc.) and create working interrelationships between corresponding city departments; this would have been previously unimaginable (Henri Coing, 2013).

Initially, the public entity *Eau de Paris* took over only the production activity from the former SAGEP. A new step of the reform was accomplished on 1 January 2010 with the transfer of employees and activities of the two private companies in charge of water distribution to *Eau de Paris*. Certain responsibilities, such as the relationships with clients, the call centre and the maintenance of the wireless readout system were integrated in the activities of the public entity in autumn 2011. CRECEP, the public centre in charge of water research and control, was also incorporated in *Eau de Paris*.

A contract of objectives binds the city of Paris and its public water entity. It defines both a series of ten main objectives and a series of performance objectives.

We could suppose that in exchange for the non-renewal of lease contract with the two big private operators the city has enlarged by public procurement their participation in other activities for the city and thus the possibility of some counterparts (externalisation in water field or in other sectors, such as waste collection). However, public procurements managed by *Eau de Paris* in the field of water represent only a minor part, and it seems difficult to establish a direct relationship with other markets of the large groups.

The members of the opposition in the municipal council have criticised the lack of transparency in the preparation of the decision of remunicipalisation. In particular, they emphasised the late communication of the studies commissioned by the city (two days before the meeting of the Council of Paris which decided the reorganisation of water service) and the lack of debate on the different scenarios envisaged to analyse the reasons of the proposals of creation of an EPIC and thus the absence of a genuine *ex ante* evaluation.

The different sources that we were able to consult converge towards the main reason of the choice of the remunicipalisation: it was a political choice, included in the electoral programme for the municipal elections of 2008 which is seen as the democratic act that validated and legitimated this choice. At the same time, this decision follows the failures of the way the local public authority had exercised its responsibilities as organising authority while it proclaims the virtues of public management. The following electoral cycles could revise this choice. Nevertheless, remunicipalisation could also offer the city new capacities for the management of the service. The interviews we had in the framework of this case study seem to conclude that the hypothesis of a return to delegated management of the water public service is rather implausible on the occasion of municipal elections of 2014, whatever the results, even if such a decision would not be so difficult to implement as there would be no time or contractual constraints.

3. Public Missions

The city, organising authority of the water public service, defines water policy, sets the main objectives and controls the activity of the operator it has created to implement water policy. In Paris, the specific definition of objectives, aims, tasks of the public service, which constitutes the basis of the activity of any organising authority, represent areas that were considerably affected by remunicipalisation.

The two lease contracts for water distribution signed in 1984 and the concession contract concerning water production signed in 1987 were very different as regards the definition of the tasks whose management was granted to the operators. Thus, only the concession contract signed with SAGEP explicitly indicated "the tasks" of the company in charge of water production and transport (Title II of the contract of 1987). SAGEP's tasks were merged in three categories that concerned "water provision" (quantity, water sources, points of distribution, pressure, quality and security), "heritage development and management" (maintaining works, renewal and modernisation works, new works, infrastructure modification) and improvement of water supply (improvement of the resource, sanitary protection, representation and information of the city, relationship with surrounding networks, research).

On the contrary, the two lease contracts did not contain similar provisions. Even if a range of specific public service obligations were provided for by these contracts, most of their provisions concerned the organisation of the service and financial arrangements.

Following remunicipalisation, the statutes of *Eau de Paris* clearly define the main tasks of the public enterprise. Moreover, a contract of objectives was concluded between the city and *Eau de Paris* for a period of 4 years (2010-2014). It was first amended in March 2012.

The contract[10] allows the city to define more precisely the tasks with which it mandated, as organising authority,[11] its enterprise and to define the means given to the city to monitor the activities of the public operator.

---

[10] 50 pages and 10 annexes, monthly, quarterly and annual scoreboards.

[11] From an operational point of view by the *Direction de la Propreté et de l'Eau et la Direction des Finances* and from a political point of view by the Council of Paris.

The tasks of *Eau de Paris* are divided into "10 principal objectives, of a technical, economic, social and environmental nature" concerning the continuous supply of quality water; the role of users, the management of the relationships with users and the information service; the transparent management of the service, water price stability and the cost recovery of the service; access to water (in particular for the most modest users); network and infrastructure performance; investment policy; a prospective vision of the water supply system base on a public centre on research and expertise; the social model of the public enterprise (professional equality between women and men, diversity, professional evolutions, a social dialogue, internal quality communication); the certification of the management system and ecological responsibility; the evolution of the non-drinking water service.

We should notice that this "contract of objectives" gives a reductive definition of the role of the organising authority that "the city intends to fully play (…) by its direct presence in four domains". It reduces its role to the representation of the service to the administrative and local authorities, the strategy of communication towards users and subscribers, the management of crisis situations and international relationships and solidarity for access to water and wastewater.

Each objective is divided into performance indicators, defined by levels and intermediary objectives resulting in more than 130 indicators (40 in the contract and more than 90 in annexes). They are considered tools of regulation, monitoring and evaluation of the service according to its results. Some of them have a regulatory nature, in particular those defined by ONEMA (National Office on Water and Aquatic Environment). A quarterly and an annual activity report are delivered by *Eau de Paris* to the city. The former contains 47 data and indicators, the later 68, provided for in annexes 7 and 8 of the contract of objectives.

The performance indicators for the monitoring of water and wastewater services have known an important development in France since the end of the 1990s (Guérin-Schneider, 2001). However, a regulatory list of indicators to be included in annual reports on the price and quality of service was not adopted until 2007.[12] This approach was part of the LOLF (legislation governing public finance)[13] process of 2001 in force since 2006 which requires the evaluation of public policies by indicators.

The representatives of the city often emphasise that there was no obligation to conclude such a contract. It is the results of "the willingness to agree in common objectives and to give us means to verify together

---

[12] Decree No. 2007-675 of 2 May 2007.

[13] It organises essential governmental functions of the state through (more than 600) programmes, missions and actions.

that these objectives can be met or should be modified".[14] Most of the public water enterprises do not have such contracts. It was considered not only as a new element but also essential in the reorganisation of the public water service, for the monitoring and evaluation of the efficiency and quality of the service. At the same time, the contract is not seen as the equivalent of the delegation contracts even if they provided for many public service obligations (the contracts contained 90 articles and 8 annexes) and sanction powers for the city. These were seen as too technical in nature and with no precise objectives, therefore allowing delegates considerable room for manoeuvre during their intervention on the network (Anne Le Strat, deputy mayor in charge of water). Still, it seems that since the 2000s French water service delegation contracts evolved to answer new needs of local authorities and to integrate more precise objectives and indicators.

The objectives of the contract were also the subject of criticism. It was rather considered as "a catalogue of good intentions than a real contract of objectives, because its effects have nothing contractual in nature", "a simply formal contractualisation, with no effective sanction in case of non-respect of the pre-established objectives".[15] For the representatives of the city and *Eau de Paris* such criticisms are not justified because the public operator was created and is owned by the city that mandated it to ensure the provision of public water service. The nature of the relationships between the city and the public operator is particular and different from the nature of those existing between the city and a private operator who would provide such a service as delegate. It is a co-construction relationship for the development of the public service where any sanction would be counter-productive. The control and monitoring by elected officials and users are sufficient to determine the needed measures to adapt the service. Thus, this contract is the subject in particular of an internal and regular evaluation by the technical services of the city and an annual evaluation by the Council of Paris and the Parisian Water Observatory. It should (Sinaï, 2013, p. 98) facilitate the control of the *régie* by its citizens.

Users may inform themselves on the results of the service through the annual activity report of the public enterprise and the annual report of the city on the quality and price of the public water service. They are freely accessible on the website of the public enterprise. They are also

---

[14] M. Denis Penuel, (*Service Technique de l'eau et de l'assainissement*) at the OPE meeting of 11 January 2012. See the minutes of the meeting on http://www.paris. fr/pratique/eau/l-observatoire-parisien-de-l-eau/l-observatoire-parisien-de-l-eau/ participez-a-la-prochaine-reunion-de-l-observatoire-parisien-de-l-eau/rub_10062_ dossier_107477_port_25216_sheet_19468.

[15] See the meeting debates of the Council of Paris, March 2012.

complementary to each other on several points. In exchange, the city did not make available on its website the annual reports presented in the past by the delegates.

Do all these elements allow users to have tools of evaluation of the service? According to a representative of the *régie*,[16] "there is an evolution of the content [of the contract of indicators] (…) as we certainly had too many indicators. These are above all useful information for the city which is the organising authority. They have a limited interest for the majority of observers of the sector".

Furthermore, it seems that the contracts of delegation of water service management have evolved in the last decade to meet the new needs of the French municipalities and integrate more precise objectives and indicators.

4. Operation and Performance

Following the remunicipalisation, a single operator – *Eau de Paris* – is in charge of the production and distribution of water and the relationship with subscribers and users. For the representative of the city and the *régie*, it is "a considerable advantage in terms of organisational visibility. We share some functions (…) Thus, we have a better technical efficiency and even a better traceability of the water supplied (…) We had an excessive organisational complexity" (Anne Le Strat in Locher & Marx, 2011). But for the representatives of the former private operators this rationalisation could be made without remunicipalisation in the framework of a new call for tender (Véolia and Suez Environnement).

The EPIC is subject to a mixed legal regime: *Eau de Paris* is a legal person and its main activity consists of public service tasks whose operations are realised in a public law regime. The application of the private law rules concerns the relationships with users and the statute of the employees. The latter are subject to private law rules, with some exceptions: a public law regime for the general director named by the local authority, for the accountant appointed by the Prefect on the proposal of the local authority and for other employees whose transfer towards private law regime is in progress. Public servants may be detached or seconded to the new EPIC. The public law rules govern the organisation of the service (the administrative regime of the normative acts; the principles of equality, continuity, adaptability; the public procurement rules).

---

[16] Jean-François Collin (Eau de Paris), at the OPE meeting of 11 January 2011. See the minutes of the meeting on http://www.paris.fr/pratique/eau/l-observatoire-parisien-de-l-eau/l-observatoire-parisien-de-l-eau/participez-a-la-prochaine-reunion-de-l-observatoire-parisien-de-l-eau/rub_10062_dossier_107477_port_25216_sheet_19468.

Eau de Paris has a distinct budget, autonomous from the budget of the local authority. It is adopted by its management board. It is subject to public accountability rules and it has a separate treasury, according to activities. Commercial taxation (corporation tax, VAT) applies only to activities on the market.

4.1. Network Performance

Unlike the situation of the "Glorious Thirties", when access of all citizens to water service increased and the quantity of water consumed doubled almost every fifteen years (Godot, 2013, pp. 3-4), in the 1990s, the volume of water sold start to drop for the first time in the French cities (Barraqué, 2012, p. 906). In Paris, there was a drop of about 17% between 1991 and 1998; consumption then stagnated but dropped again after 2003; in 2011 consumption was 27% below the quantity of water consumed in 1991. There are many explanations for this situation: more efficient domestic equipment, less network leakages, changed behaviour,[17] the decrease of the Parisian population, reduced industrial and economic activities, and a more economical management of the water consumption by the large consumers because of the increase in the water price. The water infrastructure therefore appears oversized today.

On average, 70% of water is consumed by households and 30% by enterprises. "This is an estimate because *Eau de Paris* does not know precisely the users behind its subscribers. Thus, a co-ownership may group both professionals and households".[18]

The level of water production has decreased from 1% to 2% per year.[19] Because of the structural decrease of consumption,[20] the municipality decided to raise the price to balance the accounts (excepting the stagnation and the decrease of water price in 2009, 2009-2011 and 2011-2014) (Barraqué, 2009, pp. 82-93).

---

17 François Poupart, General Director of *Eau de Paris*, at the OPE meeting of 13 February 2013. See the minutes of the meeting on http://www.paris.fr/pratique/ eau/l-observatoire-parisien-de-l-eau/l-observatoire-parisien-de-l-eau/participez-a-la-prochaine-reunion-de-l-observatoire-parisien-de-l-eau/rub_10062_dossier_107477_ port_25216_sheet_19468.

18 François Poupart, General Director of Eau de Paris, at the OPE meeting of 13 February 2013. See the minutes of the meeting on http://www.paris.fr/pratique/ eau/l-observatoire-parisien-de-l-eau/l-observatoire-parisien-de-l-eau/participez-a-la-prochaine-reunion-de-l-observatoire-parisien-de-l-eau/rub_10062_dossier_107477_ port_25216_sheet_19468.

19 *Id.*

20 At the same time, compared to other French counties, Paris registers the highest annual consumption per inhabitant (86.6 m^3 in 2009) (Observatoire des services publics d'eau et d'assainissement, 2012, p. 61).

The variations of the level[21] of the network performance are an important factor for the economic out turn of the activity and of the price of the service. In Paris, the difference between the production and consumption has known significant variations during the last decades.

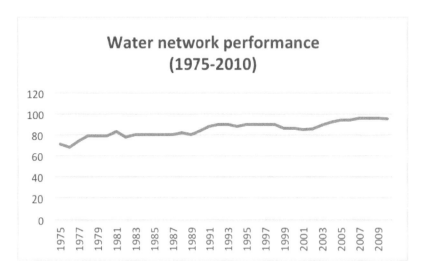

In 2010, the drinking water network performance was still high (95.1%) but current performance, after remunicipalisation, is about 92%; for some, this decrease is because the mode of calculation has changed (to meet the requirements established at national level by ONEMA). However, this is a high level when compared with that of many other French water services.[22]

4.2. Quality

According to the deputy mayor in charge of water, as regards the quality of water there is in reality no difference between the old system (delegated management) and the current system (direct management). Aims are now to favour a preventive approach that is the protection of the resource upstream rather than a curative approach that always involves the implementation of increasingly expensive treatments schemes (Anne Le Strat in Locher and Marx, 2011). This led progressively to new modes and means of action and a profound redefinition of the relationships

---

21 French law requires the respect of a performance level of at least 85% (Decree 2012-97 of 27 January 2012).

22 The average national level of performance of drinking water networks is estimated at about 78% (Levraut, 2013, p. 36).

between the city and the territories from which water is extracted, which impacts not only the public enterprise but also the organising authority (Henri Coing).

4.3. Other Performance Indicators

More generally, the performance of the operators is based on the contractual and regulatory terms established among the organising authority and operators; it is not about an absolute "high level". However, weaknesses are not excluded. For instance, if we analyse the indicators concerning the pipe branch replacement we see that of more than 90,000 pipe branches existing in Paris at the end of 1990 the delegates replaced more than 2,000. Compared to the total number of pipe branches (and their quality) this is a low level of replacement. Nevertheless, this is double the obligation provided for in the lease contracts. Most often, the tasks granted to operators in fact represent the core of the main obligation monitored by the organising authority. Thus, following the renegotiations of the lease contracts in 2003, pipe branch replacement has increased. Currently only about 2,000 old pipe branches still need to be replaced.[23] At the same time, this is not a level to be ignored. In fact, it could in some cases mask difficult problems that are not yet solved; they may be caused by access problems (ownership) or unwillingness or other, objective, reasons.

5. Governance and Regulation

We are using here the framework of the governance of local public services that we proposed earlier (Bauby and Similie, 2014), which rests neither on a linear nor hierarchical, but rather circular, and based on partnership to question some of its dimensions.

It involves combining:

- organising the systematic and regular expression of needs, and using them to define service objectives and tasks through a participative process;
- defining the optimal geographical areas and organising authority responsible for "driving" the service governance process;
- organising cooperation and partnerships between the organising authority with all other levels and actors;
- implementing non-hierarchical cooperation relationships between all levels and with all actors;

---

[23] For the progress realized on the left bank of the Seine river during the delegated management, Suez Environnement, 2012.

- locating service operations as close as possible to users, according to the principle of proximity;
- regulation and control based on the participation of all stakeholders;
- the development of multiple criteria and multi-actor evaluation processes;
- adaptation to evolving user needs and preferences.

This process is continuous.

5.1. The Current System of Governance

Following its reorganisation, the Parisian water service was structured around two essentials poles:

the city, the organising authority of the water service, which defines water policy and sets the main objectives that are implemented by the operator it controls;

Eau de Paris, the single public operator in charge of the commercial and industrial water service.

Remunicipalisation has essentially led to a relationship between two actors, a principal-agent relationship, which could raise the question of asymmetry of information, competences and expertise of the two actors, therefore of the complementary risks of bureaucratic control and the capture of the organising authority by the operator. This challenge is accentuated by the fact that the same person is both Deputy Mayor in charge of water and President of the Management Board of *Eau de Paris*.

The city of Paris as organising authority of the water public service was constantly subject of changes after 1980. The operators in charge of the provision of the service and their relationships with the organising authority entail substantial overturning.

Moreover, while the water bill that subscribers receive also covers wastewater service and taxes, the water service governance system does not cover other activities. This situation creates a certain imbalance of governance among these different services billed together.

5.2. The Organising Authority, the City of Paris

The organising authority of the water service is clearly identified: the city of Paris, whose territorial area has remained stable for 160 years. But this stability raises two questions. First, the fact that water resources come from relatively distant territories, which explicitly raises issues of cooperation with concerned communities and authorities and with residents and farmers from catchments areas. Second, future challenges could not be taken care of within the single territorial area of the city of

Paris. The "big Paris" or the "metropolitan area" is progressively linked with more and more fields and it could be envisaged as an appropriate area for water service as is already the case for wastewater service.

To meet its organising authority responsibilities, the city of Paris should allow for the needs of all users (in particular of household users) to be expressed, and foresee the modalities to do so. But, as we saw, it does not have direct access to all inhabitants and it has little information on their characteristics, situation and aims. Of course, the inhabitants are also "citizens" and can be asked to participate in that capacity in the governance of the water public service. In a way, this was the case in the municipal elections of 2008, when remunicipalisation was one of the main issues on the electoral programme of the lists led by Bertrand Delanoë. But it has to be said that water issues no longer seem to be at the heart of the municipal political agenda. Most of the Parisian population thinks that it is satisfied with the situation and the water issue has become in some ways common.

The city has created the Parisian Water Observatory, a consultative body, which meets regularly and gives opinions. But it seems that its meetings have become rather "routine" assemblies that help little for the emergence of challenges.

The governance of the public water service in Paris faces ambivalent relationships between the two major actors that are, on the one hand, the city, as organising authority and, on the other hand, *Eau de Paris*, the operator of the service. The same person, today Anne Le Strat, speaks of representing both parties in her capacity as Deputy Mayor in charge of water and President of *Eau de Paris*. Certainly, she is only President of the Management Board and a general director manages the current operations of the enterprise. Moreover, most of the members of the Management Board of *Eau de Paris* consist of elected officials from the local council of Paris, including two representatives from the opposition. Even so, risks of confusion or even conflict of interests do exist.

This potential confusion between the political control and the management of the service could be questioned as it leaves little room for manoeuvre for an independent control of the performance of the new institutional system (Barraqué, 2012, p. 912).

Anne Le Strat justifies this situation by emphasising on the one hand that the Deputy Mayor is not the sole representative of the city to control; the Deputy Mayor in charge of financial affairs and the departments of the city in charge of financial affairs exercise a "co-supervision". Moreover, the contract of objectives defines precise and quantified indicators which allow evaluation. This double function is of interest as it allows a single person to decide the municipal orientations and to chair the management board of *Eau de Paris* without managing the enterprise. This favours the coherence and continuity of direction of the enterprise approaches and their implementation.

More generally, the governance encounters the existence of a face-off between the two major actors that can be either paralysing or unbalanced. Binary relationships are often unbalanced and profit only one participant, most often the operator which benefits from more knowledge, information, expertise and means than the organising public authority. Experience shows that asymmetries cannot be totally cleared out but they can be reduced by moving from a two-player to a multiple-player governance (by involving in particular users and employees), from a regulation of experts to a regulation of actors (Bauby, 1998).

5.3. The Operator, Eau de Paris

On the basis of its statutes, *Eau de Paris* develops in-house relationships with the city of Paris, organising authority to supply the public water service. *Eau de Paris* has the statute of a public industrial and commercial enterprise (*EPIC*), *régie* with financial autonomy and legal personality.

The statutes of *Eau de Paris* provides for a management board including 18 members entitled to one vote (most of them are representatives of the city council, two from the opposition), two representatives of the employees and three representatives of the civil society (associations active in the field of environment, consumer protection and a representative of *Eau de Paris*). Two qualified persons in the fields of water and governance participate, too (they have consultative vote). The representatives of the Council of Paris own the majority of voices in the Management Board of *Eau de Paris*. Their mandate cannot exceed the duration of their mandate as elected officials. On the one hand, this situation may benefit the governance of the service which can adapt to new political orientations following the electoral cycle. On the other hand, this could disturb the stability of the governance system.

The agenda of each management board meeting is drafted by the *régie* but the city may request the organisation of a previous preparatory technical meeting when it finds this necessary.

The city must ensure not only the definition of the water policy and the objectives of the service but should also avoid any possible risk of being dispossessed of its powers to control the service (according to the preamble of the contract of objectives). If it finds necessary, the city could command technical or financial audits of the whole of part of the activities of the *régie*.

Transparency and access to information are important aspects of the governance of the service as they allow the city to evaluate it. In this respect, the contract of objectives provides for a general obligation of "regular" information of the city regarding the operation of the service, the evolution of the consumption and demands from subscribers, as well as the progress of works programme. The public *régie* can also provide information on its own initiative. It has to transmit all data needed for the monitoring by the city of its activity, monthly information on the main aspects of the activities of the previous month and a quarterly review of activities as well as annual reports on the main areas of activity. A monitoring committee of the contract of objective organises meetings twice a year; it associates elected officials and the corresponding departments of the city. Monthly technical meetings are also organised.

Are there any evolutions before and after remunicipalisation? The minutes of the meetings of the Council of Paris before remunicipalisation contain critical positions from the opposition regarding the lack of transparency on the delegation which has prevented local elected officials from precise evaluation. The SAGEP, the mixed society whose majority of shares were owned by the city (70%), should realise technical and financial control over the delegates but it seems that it did not fulfil its role. As regards the two delegates, their lack of communication and/ or partial or unclear communication of accounts[24] were also subject to criticism. Moreover, a lack of control of information provided by the delegates was emphasised while the contractual provisions enabled the city to exercise such control.

The governance also involves transparency towards users and the civil society stakeholders.

5.4. The Role of Users

As noted above, Parisian users are in a peculiar situation. Not only because collective housing and collective subscriptions are widespread but also because most of the principal residences are often occupied by tenants (61% of households in 2007,[25] most often for a temporal occupation) and more than half of the Parisian households are formed by a single person. Furthermore, for tenants, no obligation to publish the collective taxes and charges exists (water is often part of the rent costs). The water service therefore remains rather invisible for its users and there is no real citizen movement around water issues.

The relationships between the public water service and the subscribers and users are governed by the "Regulation of the public water service in

---

[24] See the observations of the Regional Chamber of Accounts (*Chambre régionale des comptes*) of 2000 on the management of the production and distribution of drinking and non-drinking water in Paris.

[25] http://www.cartesfrance.fr/Paris-75000/logement-Paris.html.

Paris" (*Règlement du service public de l'eau à Paris*).[26] Therefore, all the rights and obligations of the parties are provided for by law and regulation. Users participate through their representatives in the Consultative Commission of Local Public Services which gives consultative opinions on some normative decisions (for instance, on the regulation of the public water service).

This consultative commission was created by Law No. 92-125 of 6 February 1992. Is has competences over one or several local public services either managed in-house or by delegation. Among others, representatives of user associations are members of such commissions. But the obligation to set up a consultative commission only applies for local services covering communes of more than 3,500 inhabitants or associations of communes having more than 3,500 inhabitants. In Paris, the Consultative Commission of water and wastewater services was created in 1998. It received for discussion reports from SAGEP and from the two private water distributors before releasing them to the public (on demand) via the town halls. Each year the Commission submits a report to the Municipal Council to present its views and proposals.

In 2001, after the election of the new mayor, the structure of this commission changed. Sectoral commissions were created, including a water commission chaired by an association of users active in water services. It was meant to give citizens real means of control of an asset that concerns their daily life.[27] In 2003, it was suppressed due to the creation on 23 March 2003 of the Consultative Commission on Local Public Services (*Commission consultative des services publics locaux* – CCSPL), on the basis of Law 2002-276 on neighbourhood democracy (Chapter on the Participation of users and inhabitants in the life of public services). Unlike the legislative act of 1992, the obligation to create such commission applies only to regions, departments and municipalities of more than 10,000 inhabitants, to inter-municipal public entities having more than 50,000 inhabitants and to mixed unions having at least one municipality of more than 10,000 inhabitants. On 5 November 2008 this commission gave its opinion on the reform of the Parisian water public service. Because it had no sectoral water commission, in 2006, the city decided to create the Parisian Water Observatory (*Observatoire parisien de l'eau – OPE*). Nevertheless, the CCSPL remains in charge of examining the annual reports of the city on the price and quality of the public water

---

[26] The current regulation was adopted by the Council of Paris in February 2013 and entered into force on 1 April 2013. It repeals the regulation adopted in June 2012.

[27] Communication from the Mayor of Paris at the meeting of 19-20 November 2001, www.paris.fr.

service and any project regarding the delegation of the management of a local public service or the creation of a *régie* with financial autonomy, as well as the annual reports of other public services managed by public entities (*régies*), etc.

The CCSPL includes members of the local council, designated according to the principle of proportional representation, and representatives of local associations, appointed by the local council. However, the composition of the commission gives more voices to the representatives of the city (the Mayor or his representative as Chair of the Commission, the Chairman's alternate, ten local councillors as titular members and ten as alternate members) than to the eleven representatives of users' associations who are likewise appointed by the local council. Furthermore, its activities do not seem to play an important role in the decision-making process (for instance, in 2011, the Commission held two meetings, on 15 and 22 September, attended by only 10 and 11 members). The Secretariat of this Commission is ensured by the Mission on Local Democracy (*Mission Démocratie Locale*) of the Users, Citizens and Territories Department (*Direction des Usagers, des Citoyens et des Territoires*) of the Centre for Services to Parisians (*Pôle Services aux Parisiens*) of the city hall. But, unlike the Parisian Water Observatory, CCSPL has no special internet page and the minutes of its meetings are not available online. Moreover, the annual reports of 2011[28] and 2010[29] of the city hall's services made no reference to this commission, which seems relevant as regards its importance in the decision-making process at city level.

The Parisian Water Observatory (*OPE*) developed a new dynamism in the years around the time of the remunicipalisation. The public steering of the Observatory remains obvious even if the *ex post* transparency of debates is ensured. According to the contract of objectives binding the city and the water *régie*, the local authority will guarantee the autonomy of the Observatory as regards choice of the issues that its representatives decide to discuss to make it an organ of initiation of public policies. Until April 2013, its presidency was ensured by the representative of the city, the Deputy Mayor in charge of water. Since then, a representative of users is the chair of the Observatory. The Observatory has the task of evaluating the services supplied, transmitting users' aims and their complaints and proposing questions that should be addressed in matters of water and wastewater (Art. 2 of the Mayor's decision of 19 June 2006). Unlike the

---

[28] http://labs.paris.fr/commun/rapport_activite_2011/pdf/paris_rapport_activite_ services_2011.pdf (accessed on 10 May 2013). See also http://labs.paris.fr/commun/ rapport_activite_2011/direction-usagers-citoyens-et-territoires.html.

[29] http://labs.paris.fr/commun/rapport_activite_2010/direction-usagers-citoyens-et-territoires.html (accessed on 10 May 2013).

CCSPL, the Secretariat of the *OPE* is ensured by the Department on the Protection of Environment of *Eau de Paris*.

The preamble of the contract of objectives which binds the city and its *FPIC* provides for the presence of users' representatives in the management board of the *régie*, which is meant to ensure their larger involvement in the decision-making process concerning them. The text underlines that the Water Observatory should play a central role in the definition and monitoring of the municipal orientation. As we saw, this is an instance born of the municipal willingness, not the legislator's will, which continues to require the City to consult the CCSPL for opinions on water service.

Another question appears useful:[30] In France, water services have developed in different ways. Why should users be involved in these systems which have developed without them? These services did not need them until now. Is it not rather a technical opposition between, on the one hand, a system that has existed for one hundred years which gathers water and other sectoral industries? Today, the water treatment chain in France is developed end-to-end by private operators. Are elected officials truly free to regain water management and can then count on the entire involvement of citizens?

5.5. The Integration of Staff

Before remunicipalisation the staff involved in the management of the water service were subject to different statuses even within a single enterprise.[31] Wage costs of the employees of *Eau de Paris* were lower than those of distributors' employees (according to an estimate, in late 2008, the difference was about 10%). In addition to these disparities, they had different experiences and organisational cultures. However, according to French law the operator that takes over the activity of the water service must also take over the staff and their employment contracts. The law also guarantees staff the right to maintain their statuses and remuneration on the occasion of integration in the new operator.

During the remunicipalisation process a reduction of about 6% of the staff of SAGEP (*Eau de Paris*) was decided to accompany the reduction of consumption and revenues. It was implemented before the end of the

---

[30] Question of Julien Souriau – PhD candidate *Eau de Paris* at the OPE meeting of 27 June 2012. See the minutes of the meeting, http://www.paris.fr/pratique/eau/l-observatoire-parisien-de-l-eau/l-observatoire-parisien-de-l-eau/participez-a-la-prochaine-reunion-de-l-observatoire-parisien-de-l-eau/rub_10062_dossier_107477_port_25216_sheet_19468.

[31] In fact, the strikes led by the employees of CEP in 1999 and *Eau et Force* in 2000 mainly originated from differences of status with the same companies.

production concession contract. The city was also committed to take over the whole staff from the two private delegates and CRECEP. In total, about 830 persons from the mixed company, CRECEP and the two private operators were transferred to the new public entity, of which 228 former employees of the two delegates.[32] It seems that some employees of the private operators did not wish to join the new public operator, in particular the managers. Some observers consider this as leading to a loss of competence, a loss in terms of service quality. In 2013, the *régie* had 930 employees, thus becoming the largest public enterprise for production and distribution of water in France (Sinaï, 2013, p. 31). Under French law the management board of the EPIC has full competence as regards staff employment.

Different stakeholders we met while conducting this study case incline to agree that integration of the staff coming from the four different structures and the new staff was one of the most difficult aspects in the process of remunicipalisation. The transfer of employees from the private delegates gave rise to several social conflicts.

To ensure staff transfer and integration, *Eau de Paris* initiated a social audit in 2008 and then implemented a new method of social dialogue by associating all interested parties. A first harmonisation social agreement was negotiated with all social partners. In 2009, two methodological collective agreements were signed, followed by four harmonisation agreements signed between June 2010 and March 2011. They concern trade union rights and social dialogue, annual and special leaves, a uniform health and welfare costs coverage, early retirement, rest days and complementary retirement for all employees.

The staff of the industrial and commercial public service is subject to the private law system (in Locher and Marx, 2011).

5.6. Regulation and Evaluation

Two particular governance issues deserve attention: the regulation and evaluation of the service.

In France the water sector operates in an environment marked by largely informal regulation. A report by the High Council of the Public Sector (*Haut Conseil du Secteur Public*, 1999) recommended creating a regulatory authority on water and urban services that should be in charge of setting up technical standards, indexation price rules, etc. In 2000, the Competition Council[33] suggested creating a monitoring authority to

---

[32] *Id.*
[33] Communication No. 00A12 of 31 May 2000 relating to a request for opinion from the Commission of Finance, Economy and the National Assembly Plan on water prices in France.

gather and distribute information owned by different administrations or organisations active in the sector. It should play a role of observation, information and advice and could submit the Competition Council investigation request regarding prohibited practices. In June 2001 the Government introduced a bill that provided for the creation of a High Council on a Public Water and Wastewater Service. The project was suspended after the 2002 elections. The only successful initiative was the creation through the Water Law of 30 December 2006 of the ONEMA to accompany the implementation of water policy in France (promotion of research and development, coordination of information on the water system, etc.), but without any real functions of market regulation. At that time it was considered that the existence of the Competition Council allowed efficient protection of consumers' rights (Conseil d'Etat, 2010).

During the interviews we conducted for this study, the necessity of establishing a national regulatory authority for the national market was shared by very few of the stakeholders we met. The recent Lesage report (Lesage, 2013, p. 17) proposes the creation of an independent National Water Authority, of a genuine regulatory tool, whose guarantees of independence and powers could largely inspire the existing Independent Administrative Authorities. This authority could thus be given powers of investigation and sanction (in particular on prices, delegation contracts, implementation of equalisation of subsidies granted by water agencies). The report emphasises that, in France, water is the only network sector which does not have a regulatory authority. The risk of conflict of interest is very high in this field considering the structure of actors involved and their financing (Lesage, 2013, pp. 68-70).

Despite some progress, governance of water sector has been found wanting in two key functions: multi-actor regulation and multi-criteria evaluation.

6. Tariffs and Financing

The Framework Water Directive of 2000 provides for the full cost recovery principle in water public services (Bauby, 2011; 2012). Under French law "water pays water". This principle concerns extraction, treatment, distribution, storage, collection and sanitation. Thus, in principle, users (households, services, industry and agriculture) must ensure the financing of water and wastewater services. Water agencies and county councils may however grant subsidies (Levraut, 2013, pp. 115-117).

The mode of calculation of water prices is defined by the State and the price is fixed by the municipalities or organising authorities. However, there are appreciable differences between the price of this service since local circumstances, quality of resource, number and density of inhabitants, required investment and quality of service vary throughout France.[34]

Consumers have to pay the quantity of water consumed and the corresponding taxes and subscription. The water bill is divided into three parts:

- the "drinking water" fraction pays for the production and distribution of water (on average, 46% in France, 33.8% in Paris);[35] the water price includes a fixed component (rental and maintenance of meters) and a variable component according to the quantity consumed;

- the "wastewater" fraction pays for the collection, transport and treatment of wastewater (it represents on average about 40% in France, 38.8% in Paris);[36]

- the "taxes and charges" fraction is paid to the State and water agencies (on average, 14% in France, 26.9% in Paris and VAT at 5.5% applies to the whole bill (VAT on the wastewater fraction is 7.5%).

The current structure of the water bill mirrors a transmutation that is observed not only in Paris but also in the rest of France: the distribution fraction in the water bill has been reduced significantly over the last two decades. However, the level of taxes and royalties (for pollution, extraction, etc.) collected by water agencies[37] has been increased to ensure the protection of water resources and the maintenance of quality of aquatic systems. Thus, the water fraction dipped from about 62% in 1984 to 42% in 1997. In 1998, the water fraction of the bill was about 50% in Paris (36% for production and 14% for municipal wastewater collection). About half of the water resources provided by the public water service was extracted from underground areas far from the city. But they also needed treatment as they were polluted as a result of recent agricultural practices.

---

34 See data gathered by the national Observatory on water and wastewater services on http://www.services.eaufrance.fr/observatoire/rpqs.

35 François Poupart, General Director Eau de Paris, at the OPE meeting of 13 February 2013. See the minutes of the meeting on http://www.paris.fr/pratique/eau/l-observatoire-parisien-de-l-eau/l-observatoire-parisien-de-l-eau/participez-a-la-prochaine-reunion-de-l-observatoire-parisien-de-l-eau/rub_10062_dossier_107477_port_25216_sheet_19468.

36 Regarding Paris, this fraction also pays the SIAAP, the inter-county water purification body.

37 On the basis of the Grenelle 2 Law of 12 July 2010 the annual water service report must contain an annex presenting a note produced by the water agency on the allocation of royalties among water users, their redistributors and intervention. For a critical analysis of the royalties system, see Levraut, (2013), p. 20.

Pollution charges are therefore also encourage farmers to rethink their practices. Paris and Île-de-France remains the first agricultural French region, a major exporter, and the foremost grain producer in the European Union (IAU, 2011). Negative water externalities of agricultural activities and green economy objectives could also allow the development of organic farming. Otherwise, for public water services, one solution might be to ensure water resources direct from isolated hydrological natural parks where water resource will be preserved (De Marsily, 2010, p. 121).

The price structure raises real governance issues as the management of the different components is not the sole responsibility of a single actor.

6.1. Evolution of the Average Bill and the Fraction and Price of Drinking Water

The price of water in Paris has increased considerably since 1985. In the first decade of delegated water management, the price of water almost doubled, rising from 2.50 F to 4.65 F per m³. Between 2004 and 2011 the price of water rose about 4.78% each year against an increase of the consumer price index of 1.79% per annum. In the context of remunicipalisation, the city decided an 8% water price reduction (representing about 18 million per annum). The city also decided not to increase water charges until 2014 (date of municipal elections). This reduction was adopted by the Management Board of *Eau de Paris* on 22 March 2011. It was presented as the first result of remunicipalisation and the decrease of the costs determined by this process.[38]

Movement of Water Prices Between 2008 and 2012

	2008	1.01.2009	1.01.2010	1.01.2011	1.01.2013
Price of the service with taxes	2.94 €/m³	3.07 €/m³	3.10 €/m³	3.18 €/m³	3.29 €/m³

Source: Mairie de Paris, Rapports annuels sur le prix et la qualité des services publics de l'eau potable et de l'assainissement 2008-2012.

In fact, this reduction, then the stagnation of the price of water, seems rather symbolic. It had only a limited impact on consumers. The global price even rose because of a crossed effect between: reduction of the price of drinking water, a slight increase in the extraction tax, a stable municipal

---

[38] In fact, as was observed in one of our interviews, the remunicipalisation of water in Paris has produced visible effects outside Paris, in the Parisian suburbs which have used it to renegotiate their delegation contracts (SEDIF with Véolia).

price for wastewater collection and a significant increase of the treatment costs due to the implementation of EU water directives.

In this context, various stakeholders (elected officials, experts, representatives of the operator) consider that increasing the price of water cannot be ruled out in the future: *Eau de Paris* has not only reduced water price but it also saw its revenues fall because of decreased consumption. In 2008 fixed costs represented about 85% of the water price while investments were needed. Added to this there were higher costs of production and distribution of water due to pollution of the resource[39] and the evolution of technical, sanitary and environmental norms and the movement of the price of energy. The question is what part of the price will be raised to ensure the needs of the city? What new distribution of costs between users and tax) payers (for instance to finance some investments from the general budget)? This also raises the question of the future of the French principle "water pays water". Would it be appropriate to set up a more flexible mode of calculation of tariffs to include social or environmental criteria (criteria evoked by the representatives of the city but not yet defined)? Other solutions are also proposed: cost control, setting up new modes of operation, either by enlarging the area of activity or the geographical area of operation (including by the creation of a "Big Paris of Water" (Sinaï, 2013, 104, 107, 109; Garrigues, 2013), which is still a "delicate", sensitive subject).

Are there water cuts due to non-payment of water bills? Such a practice is not usual in Paris. The level of water bill arrears has remained around 0.2% in Paris in recent years.[40] This ensures a less expensive billing cycle. At the same time, a Solidarity Fund for Households (*Fonds de Solidarité pour le Logement – FSL*) is used to manage the arrears or non-payment of public services bills by households. It was set up in 1990 (Law of 31 May 1990 implementing the right to housing for the most vulnerable). It is managed by the County Councils at county level. It is constituted by funds coming from public networks services, social housing entities and the county council budget but only aids households who have a direct contract with the service providers. A part of this fund is directed to water payments. The Law 2011-156 of 7 February 2011 on the solidarity in the field of water and wastewater allows the setting up of a levy which cannot exceed 0.5% of the water and wastewater royalties (tax not included) to finance the FSL. This subsidy is not compulsory. But we should note how difficult it is to measure the effect of this intervention for social cases in Paris where metering is not individualised. More generally, in the case of collective housing, water cuts would usually affect all households and

---

[39] In Paris, pollution from agriculture affecting underground water resource.
[40] http://services.eaufrance.fr/sispea/showSpeaIndicatorsAction.action.

such a practice would not be realistic. In this context, how make effective the provisions of Article 21-1 of the Public Water Service Regulation is Paris, which provides that water bills are calculated on the basis of criteria which incite consumers to control their consumption if the billing system and the consumption are not individualised and if most users do not know how much they pay for the water service?

On the other hand, the Water Framework Directive and the French Law 2000-1208 of 13 December 2000 on urban solidarity and renewal allow the individualisation of meters (Article 93 of the French Law). But in Paris studies show that implementing individualisation is too expensive and the corresponding expenses are not recovered by the individualisation of bills (Barraqué, 2009; Euzen, 2004). Furthermore, the passage from a division of costs among users on the basis of the surface of their apartment to a division based on their water consumption does not favour large families[41] and households who live in small apartments. For the moment, the collective subscription establishes a system of equalisation between different users of each building.

In the context of remunicipalisation a preventive policy was designed to support the most vulnerable households in paying their household charges. This consists of creating a specific "water" label for a part of previous household aids granted by the city (44,000 households benefited from these aids which represented in total about 5 millions euros per year). An amendment to the public water service regulation allows those living in squatter settlements (if the building is not in danger and in conditions established by convention with the water provider) to have continuous water provision. More recently, a part of the social housing (HLM) benefited from a campaign and subsidies for the installation of water saving kits (15,000 kits in 2010, 30,000 up to March 2013). This should allow a 15% reduction of water consumption and a reduction of about 50 euros on the annual water bill (for a household composed of two persons) against an investment of about 7-8 euros per apartment.

Moreover, 18 public bathrooms-showers (in free use since 1 March 2000) continue to be managed by the city and offer about 900,000 uses per year.

In 2008 at the beginning of the new mandate of Bertrand Delanoë the objective of setting up a social tariff system was evoked. But no consensus was found on this topic. Different opinions expressed different approaches that could be followed to this end, ranging from price mechanisms reserved to the most vulnerable households, to larger systems, also covering typical households.

---

[41] In Paris, according to recent statistical surveys of INSEE, they represent a minority of households.

At the same time, the collective subscription system makes difficult (or even impossible) the implementation of a social tariff or of personalised social aid schemes. Other sources of information exist (such as the housing tax, which depends on the income of inhabitants) but they present the disadvantage of a time lag of several months between the obligation of payment and the intervention of social mechanisms.

We should also point out that, in Paris, there are still persons that have access to drinking water only in public areas. Taking into account this reality, the city monitors the maintaining and development of water points in the city as well as an indirect action through social aids.

At national level, the Brottes Law of April 2013 allows experimentation as regards the modulation of tariffs according to the size of households and their incomes as well as the introduction of economic incentives to reduce water consumption. It allows the implementation of a progressive tariff which can include a first part of free consumption (derogation from the water pays water principle). But the interest of these new provisions could not be so high considering the part of water in the invoice received by subscribers. Municipalities are in any case free to adopt a progressive pricing system. On the other hand, this recent French law does not make any specific reference to the affordable character of the service provided for in the EU law since the Lisbon Treaty and does not precise a uniform water quantity to be considered as meeting essential needs. Furthermore, the fact that the law concerns only household consumers raises the question of the Parisian case where many buildings gather different categories of water users (households and economic or non-economic entities).

According to a recent report (Lesage, 2013, p. 133), the city of Paris considers that a progressive pricing system would be inappropriate in densely populated urban areas where collective subscription is dominant because it would not favour large families. In exchange, it would favour single non-married families, whatever their incomes, with no redistributive effect for the most vulnerable. The city has therefore chosen to act by preventive and curative aids.

Some evoke the need to consider new systems of pricing: the first cubic meters free of charge, a progressive pricing system to discourage overconsumption, a new equalisation system. In March 2012 the Observatory of Wastewater Users of Ile-de-France proposed the creation of a new social right in the form of a specific water aid to be granted by the Family Allowance Fund (*Caisse d'allocations familiales* – CAF) to aid all families whose water charges exceed 3% of their resources. A bill aiming at the creation of a water social benefit was initiated.[42]

---

[42] http://www.assemblee-nationale.fr/13/propositions/pion2973.asp.

In fact, the decrease of water consumption impacted operators' revenues while investment needs remain high. This also raises the question of the economic balance of the *régie*. The current system of pricing and organisation cannot ensure the increasing needs of service financing. In a medium-term perspective higher prices or a different organisation should be set up. Current and future water policy challenges also raise the question of new financing schemes for investments. The city of Paris is exploring new instruments of intervention (Albert, 2012, p. 6). It takes into account a new (environmental) water pricing system with two possible ways of analysis until June 2013: seasonal tariffs (more expensive when water is in short supply and/or consumption higher) to be applied to all or part of the users, and a green pricing system or on green cubic meter with a segment linked to the environmental service provided by farmers to preserve the quality of water resources (Lesage, 2013, pp. 131-132).

Conclusion and Lessons

France has traditionally developed the delegated management of the public water services. However, in recent years, the number of decisions of water service remunicipalisation has increased and, consequently, the number of inhabitants supplied by services managed under the delegated model has decreased. At the same time, it is too soon to conclude on the existence of a general tendency of remunicipalisation. Sometimes, even the proposal of nationalisation of these public services is evoked.[43] But water services were never subject to nationalisations in France, neither in 1940 nor in 1980. They have the characteristics of a local public service subject to the powers and responsibilities of local public authorities and not of the central State.

Many delegated water and wastewater service management contracts will be nearing an end in coming years. In this context, the exercise by local authorities of their power of reversibility of the management mode of water services, as in Paris, creates references that inspire not only the choice of the management mode but also new conditions for the negotiation of the new contracts of delegation and, more generally, the issues of organisation, regulation and governance of these public services.

The remunicipalisation of water in Paris, whose conditions and modalities were analysed in this case study, allows us to provide some conclusions and lessons that may be summarised below by examining the effects of this process on the main actors.

---

[43] See in particular the legislative proposal of 2007 (http://www.assemblee-nationale. fr/13/propositions/pion0430.asp) aiming to create a public water service.

For more than 150 years now the city of Paris has been the organising authority of the water public service. Even if it is not the most relevant economical and technical area to organise the service, it is at city level that the objectives and tasks of the service, its organisation and management model, its control, evaluation and regulation are set up.

The elected officials play a key part in this field, in particular as the function of mayor has become again an elected position since the end of the 1970s. The decision concerning delegation of the management of the Parisian water service was adopted by the elected officials in the 1980s. In the 2000s they decided the complete remunicipalisation of the service and the integration of all its components in a single public operator. First, to rebuild its capacities as organising authority by creating the conditions for renegotiation of contracts, then to be able to remunicipalise, etc. As shown above, remunicipalisation allowed the elected officials to take back control of the public service which they considered to be an essential power. They are the institutional winners of this new deal.

The city is also represented by the technical and administrative services, which saw their means clearly reinforced in quantity and quality. They have also gained recognition.

The second key actor is the operator *Eau de Paris*, which now operates of the whole value chain, of the management of the resource and of relationships with subscribers. Today, it is the first public enterprise in France in the water sector and a national and international reference. The *régie* has gained a key position which seems to be rather consensual, as no political calls it into question in the process of preparation of municipal elections of March 2014.

Eau de Paris could also be apprehended in relation with its employees. The integration of employees coming from four different entities and having different statuses seemed to be difficult and accompanied by social conflicts. However, it seems that the means of *Eau de Paris* allowed finding solutions and making its employees beneficiaries of the remunicipalisation process.

The large groups, Véolia and Suez-Environnement, experienced remunicipalisation as a setback both for their presence in the water sector in Paris (they seem only to be active as contractors of certain public procurement contracts) and for their image in France and at international level. "Losing" water management in Paris is highly symbolic, even if these global leaders (Bauby, 2010) of the water sector have to a certain extent accepted the decision as based on a political choice rather than questioning their efficiency. They stress that if the city would have organised a bid allowing them to compete with *Eau de Paris* instead of deciding a direct remunicipalisation of the service, they could have been able to make more interesting proposals on prices, quality and service than what has been decided[44] and this would have been of benefit to consumers, etc.

The benefits that users have received from remunicipalisation it is much more difficult to assess. Certainly, the municipality decided an 8% reduction of the water price in 2011, but this decision went unnoticed by users, on the one hand because the total amount of water bill did not reflect it as the taxes and royalties and the wastewater fraction had increased and because the Parisian inhabitants are almost unaware of water bills.

Thus, the change of management mode and the new distribution of roles have generally passed by unnoticed by Parisian inhabitants. This is a real paradox considering that this reform is supposed to be made for them.

More generally, we should note that in relation to the framework of the partnership governance of the public services shown above there are – or there continue to be, as no significant change has appeared in this field – real deficits: on the one hand, as regards the expression of needs and their evolution, the existing participatory procedures benefit from only a limited interest; on the other hand, as regards the multi-actors regulation, which is concentrated in a face-to-face relationship between the City and *Eau de Paris;*[45] finally, as regards the multi-criteria evaluation, it seems to be limited to the monitoring of a number of mainly technical and economical indicators, and the existence of an Observatory which still appears mainly to associate experts.

In a way, it seems that this major reform has stopped along the way: conditions were created for setting up a real partnership governance system. But the inhabitants are still little involved while meeting their needs is the aim of the public service. Similarly, the reform is limited to the area of the City of Paris. Water issues must be treated in terms of multi-level governance – water resource coming from external areas – and by taking into account the projects of setting up a Parisian metropolis and/or a Big Paris which will lead to the development of cooperation and partnerships with suburban areas.

Remunicipalisation will therefore be confronted with several essential challenges, such as the management of water consumption, which led to the decrease of the revenue of the EPIC, without easily reducing prices. One hypothesis would be to sell water to neighbouring communes; but

---

[44]   Similar to certain of the contracts that were renewed in recent months and years.

[45]   Any face-to-face relationship of this type is unbalanced, the operator benefiting from asymmetries of knowledge, skills and expertise. The phenomenon is complicated in Paris by the fact that the Vice Mayor in charge of water – in charge of defining the objectives and aims of the service – is at the same time chair of the Management Council of Eau de Paris which must ensure their implementation.

these are essentially grouped in the SEDIF, which renewed on January 2011 the delegated management contract with Véolia for 12 years. Could the water service remain in future within the sole competence of the city of Paris? The resource is extracted from remote areas, which involves protection policies; references to the "Big Paris" are multiplying and the Paris metropolis was created by law. This metropolis could in future have both water and wastewater competence, the latter being already organised at supra-communal level. Therefore, a possible scenario could in future lead to integrating the Parisian water service in SEDIF and subjecting it to the same type of management, which could then lead to the dissolution of the EPIC or to its transformation. In such a case, remunicipalisation may have been no more than a parenthesis.

References

Monographs, Studies, Articles

Laurence, Albert, "Le plan de Paris pour mieux gérer son eau", in *Les Echos* No. 21147, 19 March 2012, http://www.lesechos.fr/19/03/2012/ LesEchos/21147-022-ECH_le-plan-de-paris-pour-mieux-gerer-son-eau.htm.

Bernard, Barraqué, "Return of drinking water supply in Paris to public control", in *Water Policy*, No. 14, 2012.

Bernard, Barraqué, "Abonnements individuels à l'eau en appartements à Paris: éclairages international et national", in *Revue Flux*, No. 2, 2009, pp. 76-77.

Pierre, Bauby, Mihaela M., Similie, "Europe" chapter in UCLG (ed.), *Basic Services for All in an Urbanizing World*, Routledge, 2014.

Pierre, Bauby, "Local services of general economic interest in Europe. Water services: What are the challenges?", in *Annals of Public and Cooperative Economics*, Vol. 83, No. 4, December 2012, Ciriec International, Willey-Blackwell.

Pierre, Bauby, *Service public. Services publics*, La Documentation Française, Paris 2011.

Pierre, Bauby, "Les deux 'majors' françaises de l'eau: une 'valse à trois temps' (intégration, internalisation, environnement)", in Graciela Schneier-Madanes (dir.), *L'eau mondialisée. La gouvernance en question*, La Découverte, 2010.

Pierre, Bauby, *The French System of Water Services*, CIRIEC Working Paper No. 2009/03. http://www.ciriec.ulg.ac.be/fr/telechargements/WORKING_ PAPERS/WP09-03.pdf.

Pierre, Bauby, Sylvie, Lupton, Euromarket Work Package 4 (Phase 2), Report France – Analysis of the legislation and emerging regulation at the EU country level, 2004.

Pierre, Bauby, *Reconstruire l'action publique*, Syros, 1998.

Conseil d'Etat, Rapport Public 2010 "L'eau et son droit", http://www. ladocumentationfrancaise.fr/var/storage/rapports-publics/104000255/0000. pdf.

Henri, Coing, "Nuevos desafíos en la gestión municipal des agua. El caso de Paris", *Ciudades*, No. 99, July-September 2013, RNIU, Puebla Mexico.

Stéphane, Duroy, *La distribution d'eau potable en France. Contribution à l'étude d'un service public local*, LGDJ, Paris, 1996.

Agathe, Euzen, "Vers une décentralisation de la gestion de l'eau froide en habitat collectif: la question de la généralisation du comptage individuel à Paris", *Cybergeo: European Journal of Geography*, Dossiers, Séminaire de recherche du GDR Rés-Eau-Ville (CNRS 2524), "L'eau à la rencontre des territoires", Montpellier, France, 27-28 and 29 May 2004, online 15 October 2004. URL: http://cybergeo.revues.org/1306.

A., Garrigues, "Luttes d'influence avant la construction d'un Grand Paris de l'eau", in *La Gazette des communes*, 21 January 2013, http://www. lagazettedescommunes.com/151520/luttes-dinfluence-avant-la-construction-dun-grand-paris-de-leau/.

Clélia, Godot, *Centre d'analyse stratégique, Analysis Note No. 326*, "Pour une gestion durable de l'eau en France", April 2013.

Laetitia, Guérin-Schneider, *Introduire la mesure de performance dans la régulation des services d'eau et d'assainissement en France*, PhD Thesis, 11 May 2001, ENGREF.

David, Hall, Emanuele, Lobina, *Private to Public: International Lessons of water remunicipalisation in Grenoble, France*, August 2001, www.psiru.org.

Fabien, Locher et Raphaelle, Marx, entretiens avec Claude Danglot et Anne Le Strat, "L'eau comme bien commun? Un retour sur l'expérience parisienne de remunicipalisation", in *Revue Contretemps*, 23 March 2011, http:// www.contretemps.eu/interviews/leau-comme-bien-commun-retour-sur-lexp%C3%A9rience-parisienne-remunicipalisation.

Institut d'aménagement et d'urbanisme (IAU), *Nourrir 12 millions de Franciliens*, 2011, IAU, Paris. www.iauidf.fr/fileadmin/Etudes/etude_787/NR_535.pdf.

Ghislain, de Marsily, in *Les cahiers de l'eau – Valeur et prix de l'eau dans le 21ᵉ siècle*, Lyonnaise des eaux (ed.), September 2010.

Myriam, Chauvot, "Contrat sur l'eau: le Grand Dijon prendra sa part des bénéfices dégagés par la Lyonnaise", in *Les Echos*, No. 21097, 9 January 2012.

Agnes, Sinaï, *L'eau à Paris, retour vers le public*, publié par l'Eau de Paris, July 2013.

Yvan, Stéfanovitch, *L'empire de l'eau: Suez, Bouygues et Vivendi, Argent, Politique et Goût du Secret*, Ramsay, 2005.

Suez Environnement, *Water Stories, Paris. Contrat d'affermage. Distribution d'eau potable*, February 2012, http://www.suez-environnement.com/wp-content/uploads/2013/01/Water_Stories_Paris_VF.pdf.

Lao, Tseu, "L'eau en France, un état des lieux", in *Les cahiers de l'eau – Valeur et prix de l'eau dans le 21ᵉ siècle*, Lyonnaise des eaux (ed.), September 2010.

Communications, Public Documents and Reports

Chambre régionale des comptes, *Sur la gestion de la production et de la distribution de l'eau potable et non potable à Paris*, September 2009 http://www.ccomptes.fr/index.php/Publications/Publications/Commune-Paris.

Chambre régionale des comptes, *Observations sur la gestion de la production et de la distribution de l'eau potable et non potable à Paris*, 7 September 2000. http://www.ccomptes.fr/index.php/Publications/Publications/Commune-Paris.

Conseil de la Ville de Paris – débats et délibérations, 1996 – February 2013.

Bertrand Delanoë, *Pour une gestion citoyenne et durable de l'eau à Paris.* Communication de M. le Maire de Paris 37-2001, DPE 147, 19 November. Paris, Mairie de Paris.

Eau de Paris, *Rapports annuels d'activités*, 2009-2012.

Michel Lesage, *Rapport d'évaluation de la politique de l'eau en France*, Rapport au Premier-ministre, June 2013.

Anne-Marie Levraut (coord.), *Evaluation de la politique de l'eau, Rapport d'analyse*, June 2013.

Mairie de Paris, Service technique de l'eau et de l'assainissement, *Rapports annuels sur le prix et la qualité des services d'eau potable et d'assainissement*, 2008-2012.

Mairie de Paris, Inspection générale, *Le contrôle par la Ville de Paris de la filière eau (production-distribution)*, June 2003.

Observatoire Parisien de l'Eau – minutes of the meeting, 2006-2013.

Ville de Paris, *Gestion du service commercial des Eaux de Paris.* Fascicule 0: Synthèse et conclusions, October. Paris, October 2003.

PART 2

TRANSPORTATION

6. *Wiener Linien*

Governance and Provision of Services of Local Public Transport in Vienna

Thomas Kostal, Verena Michalitsch & Gabriel Obermann

WU Vienna University of Economics and Business, Austria

Introduction

The public enterprise *Wiener Linien* is an interesting subject for an analysis by which it can be shown how, over a long period, the provision of an important public service in a large city can be organised and structured. In particular, it can be shown in detail how the public mission in providing local public passenger transport services was fulfilled and developed over time.

For decades, the local public passenger transport (LPT) services in the City of Vienna were provided by various institutions that, in organisational and legal terms, were part of the administration of the municipality.

The subject of this case study, *Wiener Linien GmbH & Co KG*, is the biggest company in Austrian local and regional transport. As a formally independent enterprise under private law and owned by the city, it has been the sole provider of local public passenger transport services in the City of Vienna since 1999. The organisational model applied in Vienna is an in-house solution in accordance with EU law, with *Wiener Linien* acting as an integrated operator, although it has subcontracted bus transport services partly to private enterprises.

Public transport enterprises traditionally have important tasks to perform in the general interest and, as experience shows, in general tend to be deficit-prone. By virtue of its public transport service obligation, *Wiener Linien* partly relies on public subsidies.

The quality of the transport services provided by *Wiener Linien* consistently receives high ratings in international comparisons and rankings. In a framework that has changed considerably over recent years, *Wiener Linien* has generally followed a successful line of development.

Wiener Linien is at present a 100%-owned subsidiary of the *Wiener Stadtwerke Holding AG* which, in turn, is a 100% property of the City of Vienna. The formal organisation is explained in section 5. Table 1 shows the key data.

Table 1. Key data for *Wiener Linien*

Name	*Wiener Linien GmbH & Co KG*
Office address	1031 Vienna, 202 Erdbergstraße
Website	www.wienerlinien.at
NACE sector	49.31 – Local passenger transport (excluding taxis)
Net transport revenues (2012)	484 m. Euros
Public transfers (incl. Capital transfers, 2012)	723 m. Euros
Workforce (2012)	8,322
Catchment area	Vienna – 1.73 m. inhabitants

Source: *Wiener Linien*, Budget of the City of Vienna, own compilation.

The present case study endeavours to analyse the structures and strategies which can be regarded as relevant factors for successful provision of public services, and to draw conclusions for the governance of public enterprises in a dynamic environment, entrusted with the provision of key services of general economic interest and with a clear public mission. The paper utilises company documents and studies. Some insights on informal processes are based on interviews with involved persons.

The next section provides a short history of the development of LPT in the City of Vienna. Section 2 describes the legal framework and the way how the public mission is specified and prescribed in different stages within the institutional setting. Important features of operations, performance and finance are presented in the following two sections. Section 5 is dedicated to a more detailed analysis of the structure and function of the governance system of *Wiener Linien* from a legal and organisational perspective. The key players and other stakeholders are identified, and their relationship is sketched in brief. This section focuses on the role of *Wiener Linien* in its capacity as the sole responsible operator of Vienna's LPT, and the manner in which the public mission to render LPT services is shaped and implemented in practice. Tariff related matters and distributional aspects are highlighted in section 6. The paper concludes with a summary of main findings and conclusions, as well as a few lessons learned derived from the Viennese experience.

1. History of Local Public Transport in Vienna

The creation of local public transport in Vienna dates back to the 19th century. The first horse-drawn tramline was inaugurated in 1865. The subsequent years saw the development of "professional" local public passenger transport. The first licence was issued in 1867 and successively expanded (*Wiener Tramway-Gesellschaft* – the Vienna Tramway Corporation). The 1872 founding of the *Neue Wiener Tramway-Gesellschaft* (the New Vienna Tramway Corporation) brought about the expansion of the route network into Vienna's suburbs. In 1881, the precursor of bus service, *Erste Pferdestellwagen-Gesellschaft* (First Horse-Drawn Bus Corporation) was established.

In 1899, the City of Vienna was granted its first licence to operate electric trams, following the commencement in 1897 of the electrification of the tram network. The last horse-drawn tramline went out of operation in 1903 and the electrification of the last steam-powered tramline was completed by 1922.

The development of LPT in Vienna began to gather pace during the early 20th century. In 1902, the City of Vienna under Mayor Lueger purchased the entire transport network and rolling stock of the (privately owned) New Vienna Tramway Corporation, and established the *Stadt Wien-Städtische Straßenbahnen* (City of Vienna-City Tramways). The takeover by the Municipality was completed in mid-1903. The founding of the city bus service dates back to 1907-1909. The bus service was incorporated into the City Tramways in 1922 (Frank, 1960, pp. 368).

The massive post-World War II investment requirements, next to organisational and staffing considerations, led to the consolidation of the hitherto independently operating service enterprises of the City of Vienna (power utility, gas utility and LPT) into one single service entity, the *Wiener Stadtwerke* (the Vienna City Utilities). Furthermore, the *Städtische Bestattung* (the City Funeral Services) was subsequently incorporated into the City Utilities in 1952 (Frank, 1960, p. 382). The consolidated Vienna City Utilities ranked third among Austrian service enterprises (Reisinger, 1982, p. 351).

The history of the underground train starts in 1968 with the resolution of the Municipal Council to build an underground network. Work began at *Karlsplatz* in 1969. The first route sections were inaugurated between 1976 and 1980 (lines U4, U1 and U2). The continuous expansion of Vienna's underground network is still going on.

Until the 1990s, the *Wiener Stadtwerke-Verkehrsbetriebe* (Vienna City Utilities-Transport Services) was part of *Wiener Stadtwerke*, which, in turn, was run as a (legally non-independent) municipal department of the City of Vienna. In 1999 *Wiener Stadtwerke* was split off from the city administration and transferred to a newly-established, joint-stock company, *Wiener Stadtwerke Holding AG*, in the sole property of the City. *Wiener Linien GmbH* and *Wiener Linien GmbH & Co KG* were founded as LPT subsidiaries.[1]

2. Public Mission

2.1. General Interest in Local Public Transport

Local public passenger transport has always been one of the infrastructural administrative tasks of all larger urban centres and municipalities and within the scope of responsibility of each respective municipal economy.[2]

For a multitude of reasons, public interest, expressed via political processes, requires that the provision of such key service tasks satisfies certain quantitative and qualitative standards.

In practice, this means that the political authorities responsible for provision of public services are required, within the framework of their responsibility, to guarantee functional organisation and satisfactory development of the range of services rendered.

The relevant political institution, usually a regional authority, is responsible for setting the main goals and general quantitative and qualitative standards, and has to take care of allocating a public mission (public service obligation) to an entity or enterprise of its choice, which is entrusted with the fulfilment of the political task at hand. In these cases, according to Thiemeyer (1975), the public enterprise can be regarded as an instrument of the public owner used to contribute to economic, social and other political objectives.

The political task of providing various transport services is in practice usually only generally and vaguely described by the responsible authority. The required public services must therefore be clearly defined, in later stages, in terms of quantity and quality, with regard to specific public missions and obligations, and must furthermore be made operational. Often expectations, demands and technological standards change over time. This results in differently specified targets and formal objectives, as well as commitments for strategic development goals to be pursued over the longer term.

---

[1]   Reasons for this organisational reform are explained in sections 2 and 4. Some general trends of corporatisation of public service provision on municipal level in Europe are discussed in Wollmann and Marcou, 2010; Grossi, Marcou, and Reichard, 2010.

[2]   In the case of the City of Vienna the primary mission is defined as "the provision of a frictionless, high-quality, financially efficient LPT". See in more detail section 4.

In reality, a complex system of governance has developed in LPT in Vienna in which numerous players and stakeholders are active. This structure is supposed to meet widespread, and partially opposed, social, economic and technical interests and demands of the players and stakeholders in this sector.

The municipality or township, as the responsible guarantor of a functional LPT, is required, especially by means of appropriate steering and monitoring mechanisms, to ensure that the participating enterprises abide by the politically formulated public interest in the transport services they provide, i.e. that they fulfil predetermined public service obligations (Obermann, 2007).

2.2. Legal Regulations

In Austria, LPT responsibilities are stipulated in the federal law which regulates local and regional public passenger transport (ÖPNRV-Gesetz). The Federal State is merely responsible for guaranteeing a basic range of services. The actual demand-driven planning of the local and regional public passenger network is done by the (nine) *Länder* (federal provinces) and by local authorities.[3]

The process of awarding and financing LPT contracts was reformed under European Union Directive 1370 in 2007. With a transition period until December 2019, the Directive sets forth in what manner public authorities can contract out limited awards for LPT services in accordance with EU contract-law regulations. Direct contracting-out of LPT services is possible under exceptional circumstances, on condition that only transport service providers are selected over which the local authority "exercises a control that corresponds with the control of its own departments".

These instructions are directly relevant to municipal LPT in Austrian cities and towns. Furthermore, financial settlement for LPT services which are ordered in the public interest but cannot be rendered for profit must be subject to transparent contracts and not exceed compensation for the costs incurred, plus an adequate gain.[4]

The regulation stipulates no (explicit) instructions regarding the quality of the LPT services to be provided. Rather, according to the principle of subsidiarity, it allows the Member States to establish minimum quality criteria in national law, and to enact them in national legal regulations. These may concern, for example, passengers' rights, the needs of persons

---

[3] For more details of the legal framework for LPT and the relation to regional public transport in Austria see Loser, 2009; Wieser, 2002.

[4] For details of the requirements by the European Union see Greiling, 2014; Zatti, 2012, p. 539.

with restricted mobility, protection of the environment, safety and labour law regulations.

2.3. Contractual Regulations

Wiener Linien GmbH & Co KG was assigned by contract the task of providing LPT services for the first time in 2001. The local public transport and financing agreement (*Öffentlicher Personennahverkehrs-und -finanzierungsvertrag, ÖPNV-Vertrag*) between the City of Vienna as the client or contracting authority and *Wiener Linien GmbH & Co KG* as the contractor, defines as the primary objective "(the ability) to provide an optimally integrated, all-inclusive transport service as an attractive alternative to private motorised transport in Vienna".

Accordingly, the enterprise is explicitly obliged by contract to integrate the entire LPT range of services. In Vienna, these include buses, trams and underground trains. Access to LPT is required to be consistently customer-oriented, as well as to enable and/or facilitate transition from individual motorcar traffic to public transport. The Vienna transport network at the time the contract took effect (2001) represents the benchmark for the transport service obligation and, as such, the 2001 quality level is required to be maintained, as a minimum requirement.

In addition to this primary objective, the agreement also lays down a series of detailed objectives for the provision of the service. Securing high quality in all areas concerning the customer is an explicitly set detail objective for the enterprise. The defined criteria pertain to availability, accessibility, information, travel time, customer care, comfort and safety, and containment of negative effects on the environment.

The tasks assigned to *Wiener Linien* include not only the operation and maintenance of the transport network and system, but, furthermore, traffic planning activities subject to agreement with the municipal authorities of the City of Vienna and the district administration authorities. Any necessary changes in the range of LPT services, up to certain pre-defined threshold parameters, can be operated autonomously by *Wiener Linien*. In accordance with the EU-wide instructions in force stipulating the obligation of municipal authorities to only award temporary LPT service contracts, the validity of the current LPT contract expires in 2016.

By contract, *Wiener Linien* is granted autonomy regarding fare-setting, whereby price increases are required to consistently satisfy the principles of fairness and necessity. There is, however, need for harmonisation throughout the tariff system of *Verkehrsverbund Ostregion* (regional transport association).

Besides the LPT agreement, there is a supervision and control agreement between the City of Vienna, *Wiener Stadtwerke Holding* and *Wiener Linien*. In this way, the conditions promulgated in the EU directive concerning direct awards (in-house allocations) of LPT service contracts to cities' own operators (in this case *Wiener Linien*) can be adhered to.

2.4. Other Standards and Documents

Major dimensions of the public mission assigned to it, such as service quality standards, are defined and realised by *Wiener Linien*, as the appointed municipal operator, autonomously and under its own responsibility. The formulation of specific objectives and operational service standards is accomplished internally and described in different documents of *Wiener Linien* (corporate mission, strategy paper, integrated and certified quality management).

The range of services offered by *Wiener Linien* was assessed periodically by citizen surveys within the framework of the European benchmark study BEST. 1,000 people in each of the participating cities (Barcelona, Berlin, Geneva, Helsinki, Copenhagen, Manchester, Oslo, Prague, Stockholm, and Vienna) are polled on their degree of satisfaction with their respective LPT. The customer satisfaction criteria are route density and distribution, reliability, passenger information, staff conduct, safety, comfort and the price-performance ratio. Further factors investigated are the image of public transport and customer loyalty towards the LPT service provider. Not only did the City of Vienna achieve good results in 2010, with a high rank among European LPT enterprises, but it has also continually improved its ranking over the years (see Table 2).[5]

Table 2. BEST Report 2010 – Results for Vienna

Quality criterion	% Satisfaction/Approval
Citizen satisfaction	72
Route density and distribution	64
Reliability	53
Passenger information	53
Staff conduct	56
Safety	74
Comfort	60
Price-performance ratio	42
Image of LPT	81
Customer loyalty	72

Source: BEST Report 2010.

---

[5] For earlier year's results see Unfried, 2005, p. 150.

Furthermore, Vienna's LPT was included in another benchmark study of big cities in 2010, commissioned by the European motoring clubs within the framework of the Europe-wide mobility sector test series *Eurotest*. The data collected by test passengers and the cities' passenger information systems were assessed in terms of the following criteria: travelling time, ease and duration of transfers to connecting routes, information before and during travel, and availability and price of tickets. The City of Vienna achieved the general mark "good" and topped that with a "very good" in the criterion "ease and duration of transfers to connecting routes" (EuroTest 2010 Local Public Transport).

2.5. Quality Assurance through External Certification

An additional measure, not explicitly required by the local public transport and financing contract, that *Wiener Linien* has been taking to ensure further development and improvement in the quality of its services, not least of all by comparison to other public and private transport enterprises, is certification.

Wiener Linien is currently certified with respect to the specifications of the following bodies of standards:

- EN ON 13816:2002c (Transport-Logistics and Services – LPT);
- EN ISO 14001:2009 (Environmental management systems);
- OHSAS 18001:2007 (Occupational safety and health protection management systems);
- EisbG §39 (Safety management systems, relevant for tramways and subways).

3. Operations and Performance

Wiener Linien is the provider of LPT services in Vienna, a 415 km² city with a population of 1.73 million inhabitants. The strategic traffic policy decisions are made by the City of Vienna and are stipulated in the LPT contract with *Wiener Linien* (see section 2.3). The enterprise pursues as primary objectives:

- increased public transport share in the modal split;
- increased cost-effectiveness;
- guaranteed quality of the services provided.

The current modal split for Vienna shows that 39% travel by means of public transport (private motor vehicle 27%, pedestrian 28%, bicycle 6%). Since the early 1990s, the share of public transport has risen markedly, by 10 percentage points. The Transport Master Plan of the City of Vienna envisages an increase of the LPT quota to 40% by 2020. The 2012 passenger count amounted to slightly more than 900 million.

The core tasks of *Wiener Linien* include:

– operating the trams, buses, and underground railway and

– traffic management:

• planning timetables and intervals;

• planning routes and stops for all carriers;

• coordination and integration of carriers;

• sales and marketing for LPT in Vienna;

• operational guidance through control centres or mobile monitoring;

• development and implementation of a comprehensive quality management system.

As already mentioned, *Wiener Linien* is an integrated operator. It provides most of the transport services itself, with the exception of bus services. About one third (seat kilometres) and half of the bus lines, respectively are run by (private) companies, mainly on the outskirts of the city.

Table 3 shows the key performance data for the year 2011. The aggregated length of the *Wiener Linien* network is almost 900 km with a total of nearly 4,500 stops and stations. More than 2,000 vehicles, with a total capacity of almost 260,000 passengers, run on 123 lines. While the bus network is the most extensive, the underground network offers by far the highest capacity (nearly 2/3), both in terms of seat-kilometres and passenger count.

Table 3. Performance Figures 2011

	Underground	Tram	Bus	Total
Network length (in km)	75	172	648	895
Total lines	5	28	90	123
Total stops	101	1,031	3,320	4,452
Railcars	780	520	480	1,780
Carriages	82	240	–	322
Total vehicles	862	760	480	2,102
Vehicle use km (in m.)	78	33	29	140
Seat-kilometres (in m.)	11,792	4,028	2,361	18,181
Available seats	129,098	89,104	40,196	258,398
Passengers (in m.)	568	194	114	875

Source: *Wiener Linien*, own compilation.

Having reached an all-time high at the end of the 1950s, the total number of vehicles went on to drop significantly, before stabilising at around 2,000 in 1980 (Reisinger, 1982, p. 358). While the number of vehicles has remained approximately constant ever since, the vehicle-kilometre and seat-kilometre performance has been rising continuously, most notably due to the expansion of the underground network and service (see diagram 1).

Besides these core tasks, principles of social and ecological sustainability are also important considerations (e.g., barrier-free mobility). As a member of the *Union Internationale des Transports Publics*, *Wiener Linien* became a cosignatory of the UITP Sustainable Development Charter in 2008.

The quality of the services rendered has been enhanced gradually since the early/mid 1990s. Hours of operation were expanded: 22 lines of daily, blanket-coverage night bus service were introduced in 1995, and underground train night operation at weekends and on the eve of public holidays was introduced in 2010. In addition, the rolling stock has been gradually upgraded to low-floor vehicles.

**Diagram 1. Seat-Kilometre and Vehicle-Kilometre Performance,
2003-2012**

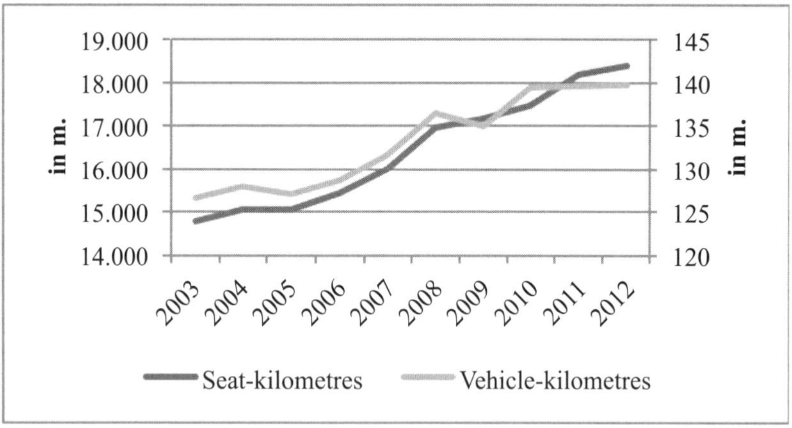

Source: *Wiener Linien*, own representation.

For the future, *Wiener Linien* is planning to continue the strategies initiated in the 1990s and the 2000s. The concrete measures envisaged are:

- expansion of the route network, most notably of the underground;
- boosting of the service quality (QM certification);

196

- expansion and upgrading of the passenger information system (notably mobile phone and internet);
- focus on safety concerns;
- further modal split shift towards public transport (see details above).

4. Finance and Investments

Wiener Linien, like its precursor *Wiener Stadtwerke-Verkehrsbetriebe* and other LPT operators in comparable cities, has always been marked by operating deficits. Despite internal cross-subsidisation within *Wiener Stadtwerke* at the time and in spite of the City of Vienna taking over the pension burden from 1970, investments have had to be covered through external financial resources. Consequently, the volume of debt of the former *Wiener Stadtwerke-Verkehrsbetriebe* has been increasing continuously ever since (Reisinger, 1982, p. 354).

The rule against the previous common practice of municipal cross-subsidisation,[6] coupled with other EU regulations, resulted in the splitting of the company (often labelled "corporatisation") and a new regulation for the financing of *Wiener Linien* (Faber, 2002, p. 190).

In its capacity as the LPT service contracting authority and the policy-maker, the City of Vienna defines strategic traffic policy decisions. The primary mandate is clearly defined by the City. "The provision of a frictionless, high-quality, financially efficient LPT. Given that the proceeds obtainable from the current tariff system do not suffice to cover the running costs and, most notably, the significant investments in infrastructure, *Wiener Linien* is granted – as are all other comparable service providers – running cost and investment subsidies from public funds" (Wiener Stadtwerke Annual Report 2010, p. 26).

Currently, financing is regulated by the LPT contract between the City of Vienna and *Wiener Linien*, which was signed in 2001 and is valid until 2016 (see section 2.3). Said contract contains both the assignment of LPT services in Vienna to *Wiener Linien* and the financing arrangements in the fields of infrastructure and operation.

Wiener Linien is essentially financed from two sources: the transport revenues (including compensation from the City of Vienna and the Federal State for various pupils' and students' free travel) and subsidies

---

[6] Although having multiple services within an organisational entity allows more financial flexibility, separation of services is required by the European Union in order to strengthen competition and transparency.

from the City of Vienna. The Federal State pays a subsidy of 50% for new construction of the underground railway. Revenue from compensation payments from *VOR*, the Eastern Region Transport Association, for through-ticketing losses is not significant for *Wiener Linien* (see section 6). It is common that in LPT, full cost recovery cannot be achieved through fare revenues. For *Wiener Linien*, cost recovery of about 50% was reported for the late 1990-years (Wieser, 2002, p. 174).

To compensate for the operating losses, the City of Vienna pays an annually negotiated lump sum (256 million Euros in 2012). The City's investment subsidies, on the other hand, are increased each year (including 467 million Euros in federal underground-building subsidies in 2012). While the operating cost subsidies in absolute figures have been relatively stagnant since the early 2000s, investment subsidies have been rising from one year to another.

**Diagram 2. Transport Revenue and Operating Cost Subsidies
from the City of Vienna, 2001-2012**

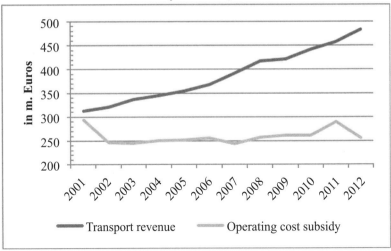

Source: City of Vienna, Budget Estimate, own representation.

A comparison between the development of operating cost subsidies from the City of Vienna and that of transport revenues (see diagram 2) reveals a markedly divergent pattern. While operating cost subsidies remain relatively constant, the average gradient of the transport revenues is approximately 4.1% per year. In 2001, the transport revenue per passenger amounted to 0.43 Euros; by the year 2012, that same parameter had risen to 0.53 Euros. Currently, that corresponds to almost 50% of the enterprise's aggregate revenues. The operating cost subsidies contribute 29% of the aggregate revenue of *Wiener Linien*.

Table 4. Operating Figures 2001, 2006 and 2011
(in millions of Euros)

	2001	2006	2011
Transport revenues	312.0	367.3	458.4
Operating result	-130.0	-124.9	-127.4
Financial result	13.4	36.8	7.7
EGT	-116.6	-88.1	-119.8
Equity ratio (%)	89.1	90.3	86.7
Investment intensity (%)	92.3	96.3	92.6

Source: *Wiener Linien*, own compilation.

Table 4 shows important operating parameters. Despite the significant operating cost subsidies from the City of Vienna and positive financial results, *Wiener Linien* reports a markedly negative operating income as a sole result of capital depreciation and other non-liquid expenditures.

Over the past ten years, the total annual investment volume of *Wiener Linien* has oscillated between nearly 300 and just over 450 million Euros.

The development of the enterprise's workforce clearly shows increasing productivity in the course of time. While approximately 13,000 people were employed at *Wiener Linien* in the early 1960s, staff was much reduced in the following years, mainly by the introduction of one-man operated trams in the early 1970s and due to the higher capacity of the underground system. Since the early 2000s, *Wiener Linien* has employed an average of 8,200 people.

With regard to the workforce, a severe problem arises from administrative spin-offs to new companies.[7] In many cases, far-reaching fragmentation and decentralisation of public labour relations are observed as an effect of liberalisation and privatisation measures (Hermann and Flecker, 2012, p. 199). Like other publicly owned enterprises under private law, in recent years (i.e. since 2002), *Wiener Linien* has employed workers under different forms of labour contracts and with different

---

[7]   Shifting the supply of a service to separated publicly owned legal entities (corporatisations) is a widely observed trend in LPT in European countries (see Zatti, 2012, p. 553). Recent empirical evidence on various economic and social effects of changing working conditions due to liberalisation and privatisation is discussed in Flecker and Thörnqvist, 2012.

salaries schemes.[8] This creates increasing problems within the enterprise between old and new staff. The cost-pressure on public providers is obvious and became a growing political issue for LPT authorities with possible negative effects on service quality (Hermann and Flecker, 2012, p. 201; Wieser, 2002, p. 69).[9]

5. Governance and Regulation

5.1. Formal Organisation – Players and Responsibilities

Until the 1990s, as described above, the planning and provision of important public services used to be carried out by the Vienna City Administration and its utilities, which were organised as owner-operated municipal enterprises, with a subdivision, *Wiener Stadtwerke-Verkehrsbetriebe*, carrying the responsibility for LPT. As part of the reorganisation at the end of the 1990s, this subdivision was spun off and renamed *Wiener Linien.*[10]

Diagram 3. Key Actors

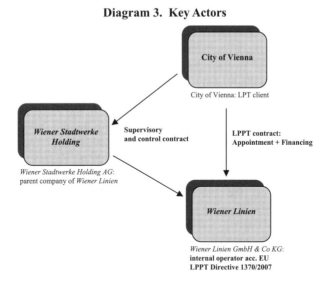

---

8   "New employees who are no longer employed under public law have to accept wages which are about 13% lower than those of their co-workers hired before the spin-off" (Loser, 2009, p. 24).

9   It is reported that publicly owned companies in LPT incur 30-50% higher labour costs than private companies (Loser, 2009, p. 13).

10 For a detailed description of the LPT-regime in the late 1990s see an empirical analysis of the system of governance of LPT in Vienna by Faber, published in 2002; more recent studies are Unfried, 2005; Loser, 2009.

The present governance structure of *Wiener Linien* is characterised by the interplay between three main actors (see diagram 3):
- the City of Vienna, the contracting authority for the transport services;
- *Wiener Linien*, the public contractor providing the specific services and;
- *Wiener Stadtwerke Holding AG*, involved in the governance as the parent company of *Wiener Linien*.

City of Vienna

According to the Austrian federal constitution, Vienna has a special status. It is a municipality as well as a *Land*, hence the political institutions of both authorities exist.

As a *Gebietskörperschaft* (legal authority), the City of Vienna has regional and local tasks to attend to and is – *de jure* and *de facto* – responsible for the functioning of LPT in Vienna.[11]

The provincial parliament (*Landtag*) numbers 100 delegates who are also members of the Municipal Council of the City of Vienna. The City Senate, which is also the provincial Government (*Landesregierung*), with the mayor and eight Executive City Councillors (*Stadträte*) topping the pyramid, constitutes the city Government, and manages the administration. A City Council Committee for Traffic is in place, consisting of representatives of the political parties elected into the provincial parliament.

Austria's Social-Democratic Party enjoyed a comfortable majority both in the provincial parliament and in the City Council for several decades, thus being in a position up to 2012 to form the City Government. Following the 2012 elections, Vienna is currently – for the first time ever – governed by a coalition of the leading Social-Democrats and the Green Party, with the junior coalition partner contributing in a major way in the shaping of the city's traffic policies.

Both parties pursue largely congruent LPT policies: advancement and expansion of the public transport network, as well as reduction of private motor car use in the city. Nevertheless, they sometimes advocate measures and priorities that differ in details.

The administration (*Magistrat*) is divided into administrative city groups. Within the administration of the City of Vienna, there are two entities which are responsible for LPT matters: Municipal Department 18 – Urban Development/City Planning (*Magistratsabteilung 18*

---

[11] See in more detail Loser, 2009, p. 23.

Stadtplanung) and Municipal Department 5 – Financial Management (*Magistratsabteilung 5 Finanzwesen*).

The strategic targets assigned to *Wiener Linien* by the City of Vienna are stipulated in the current Strategy Paper of Vienna Municipal Development (Municipal Department 18). For example, the current Transport Master Plan of the City of Vienna 2003 (*Masterplan Verkehr 2003*), adapted and expanded in 2008, sets forth concrete modal split targets for reducing individual motor car traffic up to the year 2020 (see section 3).

Municipal Department 5 is responsible for the financing of the LPT services ordered from *Wiener Linien*. Besides its contractual obligations, the City of Vienna also exerts influence on the strategic planning of the enterprises through the representatives it appoints to the supervisory committees of *Wiener Linien* and *Wiener Stadtwerke Holding AG*.

The City of Vienna acts both as the purchaser of LPT services and, in its capacity as a policy maker, makes strategic transport policy decisions. It is responsible for transport and environment policy objectives, financing (tariff structure) and strategic planning functions, partially through the involvement of *Wiener Stadtwerke Holding AG*. In practice, the main area of competence of the local authority is the (longer-term) traffic planning for the new links with urban expansion districts and the development of underground railway lines. The tasks of organisational traffic planning (route acceleration, route planning, intervals and timetables, etc.), however, devolve *de facto* upon *Wiener Linien*.

Wiener Linien

Wiener Linien GmbH & Co KG, a limited liability corporation, was formed in 1999 by the reorganisation of *Wiener Verkehrsbetriebe*.[12] The enterprise is a fully owned subsidiary of *Wiener Stadtwerke Holding AG*, which, in turn, is the sole property of the City of Vienna.

All managerial functions are carried out by three directors. The Supervisory Board consists of six members, two of whom are nominated by staff (Wiener Linien Jahresbericht, 2010).

The explicit appointment of *Wiener Linien* with the tasks of planning and execution of LPT services dates from 2001. For the first time, such appointment was done by means of an agreement between the City of Vienna and *Wiener Linien GmbH & Co KG*.

Wiener Linien has the role of contractor for all the relevant functions of traffic management, provision of infrastructure and operational tasks.

---

[12] In particular, *Wiener Linien* is a special legal construction, combining two companies; the operative business is the responsibility of *Wiener Linien GmbH & Co KG*, while *Wiener Linien GmbH*, in its general partner capacity, takes over the management tasks.

As the integrated operator of the Vienna LPT network, the company bears the sole responsibility for the quantity and quality of the entire municipal line system. Only in the bus sector a substantial portion is operated by (private) subcontractor entities commissioned by the licence holder, *Wiener Linien* (see section 3).

The contractual structure implies that *Wiener Linien* assumes the operating risk, since its revenues depend on the extent to which its transport services are actually used. The City of Vienna merely grants a previously agreed financial compensation for specific public service obligation efforts in connection with the quality and quantity of the service. Key determinant risk factors are, consequently, the market acceptance of the transport services provided and the amount of their compensation during the term of the contract.

Wiener Stadtwerke Holding AG

Wiener Stadtwerke Holding AG, legally a stock corporation, is operationally active in Vienna in the business areas of energy, transport, funeral services and cemeteries, and the management of investments. As the parent company and owner of *Wiener Linien*, it can set general objectives and is contractually responsible for supervisory and monitoring functions.

The Managing Board of *Wiener Stadtwerke Holding AG* consists of three members (until 2013 four members), one of whom is responsible for *Wiener Linien*. The Supervisory Board comprises eleven members (twelve until 2013), four of which are nominated by the Works Council.

The three leading actors are thus, in practice, bound by close organisational and economic relationships, mainly determined by company legislation (see diagram 3). Said close relationships are further reinforced by the right of the City of Vienna, as sole proprietor, to appoint the top managers of those companies.

5.2. Cooperation Between the Key-Players

In practice, the interplay between the three key actors displays the following basic pattern:

The City of Vienna – to a certain extent in cooperation with *Wiener Stadtwerke Holding AG* – is responsible for traffic and environment targets, financing (tariff structure) and functions of strategic planning.

Responsible for finance, Municipal Department 5 draws on the budget competence of the Administration of the City of Vienna and in the context *Wiener Linien* assumes the role of the owner's representative. Notably, it is not responsible for traffic policies. In spite of that, Municipal Department 5 has a crucial role in LPT, since it negotiates directly and, to a large extent, independently of other Municipal Departments with *Wiener Linien* the range of services to be included in the LPT contract and, furthermore, regulates financial matters.

Municipal Department 18 (City Development and Planning) is responsible, as part of its city planning tasks, for Vienna's traffic planning. The Department is part of the business group for urban development, transport, climate protection, energy planning, and citizen participation in the Administration of the City of Vienna. In practice, the main responsibilities of this Department lie with (longer term) traffic planning for the connection of newly developed urban expansion zones and with the extension of underground lines. On the other hand, organisational measures of traffic planning are *de facto* left to *Wiener Linien* (Faber, 2002, p. 197). It is therefore incumbent upon *Wiener Linien* to perform all key operative tasks, such as operation and maintenance, infrastructure, marketing and communication, as well as assignment of contracts to subcontractors.

The catalogue of requirements of which the public LPT interest must now take account includes items regarding the size and scale of the transport operation (lines, connections, intervals, etc.) and ever more importantly, the parameters defining the quality of task execution. The LPT-agreement addresses the matters of availability, accessibility, information, travel time, client care, comfort, safety and the containment of negative effects on the environment. The implementation of operational quality criteria, defined by suitable indicators, is effected by the appointed operator *Wiener Linien*. The City of Vienna receives regular reports and has the right to order quality audits.

On the one hand, the organisational structure described above is meant to be conducive to the realisation of the traffic policy targets pursued by the City of Vienna. On the other hand, the same structure is designed to safeguard the direct assignment of LPT service provision contracts to the internal operator *Wiener Linien* without public tendering process, while still complying with the requirements of the EU-Directive 1370/2007. In practice, there exist direct contractual obligations of *Wiener Linien* towards the City of Vienna (LPT-contract), contiguous with the supervision and control contract between the City of Vienna, *Wiener Stadtwerke Holding* and *Wiener Linien*. The key contents of the LPT contract concluded between the City of Vienna and *Wiener Linien* regard the explicit assignment of LPT services to *Wiener Linien* (excepting municipal railway) and the regulation of financing models for both operation and infrastructure.

In the past ten years, numerous planning, coordination and decision-making processes have been worked out and established between the three key actors and other stakeholders in Vienna's LPT system. This organisational structure enables a good response to transport-specific assignments. Moreover, it allows *ad hoc*, specific, higher-priority interests of party politics to be taken into consideration (e.g. economic and social policy demands, political election cycle considerations, etc.).

Based on the experience accumulated to date, *Wiener Linien* regards the previously described organisational model as appropriate for the optimum implementation of its public service mission. This opinion is also shared by the Government of the City of Vienna.

In practice, the operation of the specific "Viennese organisational LPT model" is significantly marked by the mission assigned to *Wiener Linien*, as well as by its self-conception as an integrated operator. The desired integration of functions is meant, from the perspective of the enterprise, to bring about important advantages for travellers, as well as economic benefits to the enterprise itself.

In this model of close legal and informal relations between the three key players and their institutional representatives, the danger of exploiting information asymmetries, particularly by *Wiener Linien*, appears to be negligible or non-existent. Indeed, there is no evidence that this occurs in practice.[13] Moreover, from a transaction cost perspective, the realised institutional arrangement also seems to be advantageous.[14] Looking at similar cases, this general assessment seems justified. Swarts and Warner, 2014, examine the restructuring of public transport in Berlin, where a mixed firm with private subsidiaries was created. They find that "The Berlin case confirms the conclusion prevalent in the literature assessing public transit service delivery that a strong regulatory regime with well-defined roles and limitations of the public and private actors is essential to the success of mixed delivery models" (p. 141).

As already mentioned, *Wiener Linien* assumes the operating risk, since its revenues depend upon the degree of utilisation of its transport services (Unfried, 2005, p. 149). The key parameters in this context are the market acceptance of the range of services it offers, as well as the fares it charges. The City of Vienna only provides a predetermined financial compensation for general interest requirements which define the quality and quantity of the services offered.

---

[13] Some theoretical arguments on this topic are discussed by Cruz *et al.*, 2014.

[14] In the recent discussion on re-municipalising of public services lower transaction costs are an important argument in favour of in house-provision against outsourcing to private providers (Hall, 2012, p. 7). With respect to the consequences of necessary regulation of corporatisations, Zatti, 2012, (p. 563) addresses trade-offs in terms of transaction costs, public control and accountability; see also Grossi, Marcou, Reichard, 2010, p. 237.

The functions to be integrated, with a view to fulfilling the enterprise's public mandate, include especially bus, tram and subway route offerings (network coverage, number of nodes offering transfer possibilities), ticket and tariff architecture (consistent ticket standards and tariff structures), the provision of passenger-relevant information (consistency, accessibility, comprehensiveness), as well as marketing and communication. Furthermore, LPT services are required to be reconciled with other city planning measures and user-relevant facilities (city bikes, car sharing, and park & ride garages).

From the point of view of the enterprise a relevant consideration is that complex and comprehensive LPT services enhance the value-added ratio of the coordination activities and network management to the transport performance.

5.3. Other Stakeholders and Interest Groups

Besides the previously sketched (close) framework of the formal organisational structure of the inner-city transport services provided by *Wiener Linien*, other actors are also involved in the provision and operation of LPT services in and around Vienna (see especially Faber, 2002, section 3.2.3).

Some of the institutions and interest groups involved seek to acquire influence to further their (partial) interests in specific areas. Other organisations and enterprises are directly or indirectly involved in the governance or operation of regional transport in the Greater Vienna area.

The important stakeholders and interest groups are the Federal State (Republic of Austria), *VOR* (regional transport association), *Wiener Lokalbahnen* (Vienna Local Railways), the Vienna Chamber of Commerce, the Federal Chamber of Labour, and the employees of *Wiener Linien*.

The Federal State

The Republic of Austria is involved, in various capacities, in LPT issues. By virtue of the allocation of responsibilities stipulated in the Constitution, the Federal State is in charge of the railway system, which also includes the legislation concerning the subway and tramway network. Furthermore, the Federal State pursues superordinate traffic policy interests.

However, as the owner of the Austrian railway company *ÖBB*, which with its municipal railway lines covers approximately a quarter of Vienna's transport performance (Faber, 2002, p. 297), the Federal State also pursues its own economic interests. The City of Vienna concluded a service contract with *ÖBB* which complies with the EU-Directive 1370/2007 EG; the current version of which is valid until 2019.

Through various conduits (e.g. Family Burdens Equalisation Fund – *FLAF*, Fiscal Equalisation Law – *FAG*), the Federal State grants important subsidies to LPT, which are motivated by distributional goals and social policies. By the same token, the Federal State carries fifty per cent of the underground extension programme's investment costs.

VOR – Eastern Region Transport Association (Verkehrsverbund Ostregion)

The Eastern Region Transport Association (*VOR*) is responsible for the customer-oriented coordination of LPT in Eastern Austria, while also taking into consideration the interests of the three *Länder* in the region.[15]

The Vienna Local Railways (Wiener Lokalbahnen)

Wiener Lokalbahnen AG is a fully owned subsidiary of *Wiener Stadtwerke Holding AG*, and is essentially responsible for the passenger and freight transport on its own railway track connecting Vienna with the town of Baden.

The Vienna Economic Chamber (Wirtschaftskammer Wien)

The Vienna Economic Chamber represents, in the context of LPT, the interests of its member enterprises, and is involved in numerous topics and individual issues (e.g. construction measures, route planning). Private bus operators acting as contract partners, i.e. subcontractors of *Wiener Linien*, can also make their voices heard through the Vienna Economic Chamber.

Federal Chamber of Labour (Bundes-Arbeitskammer)

In keeping with the Austrian system of social partnership, the Federal Chamber of Labour is institutionally involved in all important issues and decision-making processes, as is the Vienna Economic Chamber. The Federal Chamber of Labour represents the interests of all employees who work in Vienna or use *Wiener Linien* to commute to and from work. The interests of LPT and of *Wiener Linien* employees are usually represented internally by the *Wiener Linien* Works Council.

Wiener Linien Employees

Specific interests of the approximately 8,000 employees of *Wiener Linien* are primarily represented internally by the Works Council and the members of the Supervisory Board, who are nominated by the staff.

---

[15] The important role of transport associations in the organisation and coordination of local and regional public traffic services is described in Loser, 2009, p. 7.

Vienna LPT Passengers

One important group of stakeholders are the passengers and users of *Wiener Linien*. The interests of this heterogeneous group of customers are represented, at least partially, by different organisations. In this regard, a special role is played by the *Fahrgastbeirat* or Passengers' Committee, set up by *Wiener Linien* in 2004 as an institutionalised passenger representation body. The Passengers' Committee is tasked with relaying customers' concerns and criticisms directly to the company management.

As a public enterprise with an extensive public service obligation in LPT matters, *Wiener Linien* regards itself not least as a representative of the interests of its passengers. It interprets its service provision mandate based on its own expertise and strives to map out concrete performance-related customer needs.

5.4. Interplay between Stakeholders

The available information and empirical findings reveal the following configuration of the formal and informal relationship structures (see diagram 4).

On the whole, *Wiener Linien* has a position of dominance in the governance system of LPT and enjoys remarkable freedom of manoeuvre in the provision of its transport services.[16] In the past, it has used these structuring possibilities extensively, primarily with an eye to satisfying customer needs and to the further development of the range of its transport services. The other institutions and organisations primarily have (partial) interests of their own in LPT. Either institutionally or informally, such stakeholders are involved in particular phases of transport policy decision-making, whether regularly or on an *ad hoc* basis.[17]

To sum up, it may be said that, despite the changes seen in recent years in the organisational, contractual and informal framework and web of relationships around *Wiener Linien*, the leading actors, power potential and basic pattern of governance have changed only little, if indeed at all.

Regarding performance the transport services provided by *Wiener Linien* function well and LPT in Vienna – even by international comparison – meets quite high quality standards (see section 2.4).

---

[16] Faber, 2002, pp. 191-197 calls it a "quasi-monopoly on traffic services in Vienna".

[17] These findings are in general consistent with the overall results of an empirical analysis of the system of governance of LPT in Vienna (Faber, 2002). His study was carried out about 15 years ago and describes in detail the mechanisms of the LPT-regime. It highlights also the prehistory of transport service provision and is based on numerous interviews with stakeholders and involved parties. On the whole, the statements of the study on essential features of the governance regime remain appropriate for the present time.

Diagram 4. Players and Stakeholders

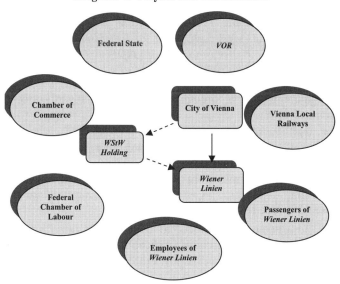

As confirmed in a comparative study of the cities of Lyon, London, Stockholm and Vienna, Wiener Linien shows above-average efficiency in the provision of service (Jansa and Sedeek, 2005). More particularly, Vienna scores best for direct efficiency (passengers per carriage) and costs per journey. The authors conclude that there is no evidence that sharper competition due to the liberalisation or privatisation of LPT would improve efficiency.[18] Current tariff developments (price reduction for annual tickets 2012) and the increasing share of journeys by annual ticket will by no doubt secure this leading position.

Similarly, the level of public subsidies is below average. The financing regulation makes a considerable contribution in this respect, with the enterprise's operating costs subsidised by the City of Vienna. The net profits per passenger are relatively low, but steadily rising. The study also shows that sharper competition due to the liberalisation or privatisation of LPT would do little to improve efficiency.

---

[18] This statement seems to be supported by findings of the LPT-case of Berlin, where Swarts and Warner, 2014 reaches the conclusion "that the potential benefits of competition were not worth risking increased transaction costs and reduced accountability, and in confidence that achieving cost savings would be possible without a competitive bid" (p. 141). The case of the partly privatised Berliner Wasserbetriebe BWB, analysed by Schaefer and Warm 2014, provides an example how political and organisational shortcomings in the implementation has led to negative results. A re-municipalisation of the BWB is currently in discussion.

6. Setting of Tariffs and Distributional Aspects

During the 1950s and 1960s, the setting of tariffs and decisions regarding investments were matters for the City Council. The powers of the management of *Wiener Linien* were greatly restricted, especially in terms of financial and personnel policy, by the bodies of the Municipal Administration (City Council and Mayor). The creation of *VOR* in 1984 and the unbundling in 1999 brought clear changes as regards price-setting (see section 5.3).

VOR was founded at the nexus of *ÖBB, Wiener Stadtwerke-Verkehrsbetriebe* and the Vienna Local Railways. The main aim was mutual acceptance of tickets (through-ticketing) and revenue-sharing. The allocation of revenues from *VOR* is currently regulated in the so-called revenue distribution agreement (*Einnahmenaufteilungs-Vertrag*) (see Loser, 2009, p. 18).

Tariff adjustments are subject to approval by the *Wiener Linien* Supervisory Board and also require ratification by the other *VOR* partners. *Wiener Linien* enjoys tariff autonomy, but tariff consistency within *VOR* is a requirement.

Hereby, *Wiener Linien* needs to take into consideration market requirements, the interests of municipal traffic policies and those of *VOR*. "Tariff hikes are only acceptable within the limits of economic requirements and under consideration of reasonable rationalisation and cost-reduction potentials" (Kontrollamt der Stadt Wien, 2010, p. 5). Tariff changes need to follow changes in objective parameters, for instance rising labour costs or quality improvements.

Diagram 5. Passenger Distribution by Tariff 2012

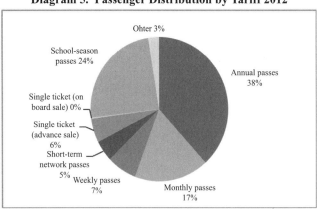

Source: *Wiener Linien*, own representation.

Social and environmental aspects are not specifically addressed in the price-setting process. Nonetheless, the socially and/or physically disadvantaged are granted special fares. The Social-Democratic-Green coalition forming the city Government since 2012 has created a task force mandated with the optimisation of the tariff structure, considering social, temporal, performance-oriented and climate protection parameters. As a first step, the price of the regular annual pass has been brought down. Currently, the annual pass costs 365 Euros, the monthly pass 47 Euros, the weekly pass 15.80 Euros and the individual or single ticket, if bought on board the vehicle, 2.20 Euros. The tariff reduction on annual passes has brought about a marked increase in passenger numbers. Diagram 5 shows the distribution by tariff of the slightly more than 900 million passengers in 2012.

Conclusions and Lessons Learned

Kept very general in the early days of the takeover of trams and buses in Vienna, the objective of provision of adequate LPT services was given concrete form and further developed in many respects over the decades. The past ten to fifteen years have witnessed the development of particularly detailed plans for the expected fulfilment of the specific public mission of LPT.

The primary objective agreed between the City of Vienna as the client and *Wiener Linien* as the contractor is to make available an optimally integrated, comprehensive range of transport options, as an attractive alternative to motorised private transport in Vienna.

The catalogue of requirements of which the public LPT interest must now take account includes items regarding the size and scale of the transport operation (lines, connections, intervals, etc.) and, ever more importantly, the parameters defining the quality of task execution. The LPT-agreement specifically addresses the matters of availability, accessibility, information, travel time, client care, comfort, safety and the containment of negative effects on the environment.

Wiener Linien aspires to maintain its position as an integrated LPT operator in Vienna in the future. It is explicitly interested in the conservation of what is, from its own perspective, the successful "Vienna model", even in the context of future LPT reforms. *Wiener Linien* wishes to avoid being reduced to the role of a "carrier" – now, and in the future.

This target is to be secured through further, enhanced integration of traffic planning, traffic management, infrastructure and operation. In 2010, *Wiener Linien* set its strategic orientation for the following decade. Central to this strategy are the targets set in agreement with the City of Vienna, as owner and contracting body, of boosting passenger numbers and thus further enhancing the market position of the enterprise. Next to quality and performance requirements, the strategy is geared towards consistent improvement of cost-effectiveness and the revenue-to-cost ratio, thus enhancing the competitiveness of *Wiener Linien*. Furthermore, efficiency-boosting measures concerning rail-vehicles and other energy-relevant investments are envisioned (Wiener Linien Jahresbericht, 2010, p. 27).

Conclusions

Vienna's precursor LPT-companies acted, *de facto*, as integrated operators, but under fundamentally different legal and economic conditions as regards governance, financing responsibility and risk. In the past, local public passenger transport companies were steered by means of internal regulation, within the municipal administrative organisation. The financial flows were not transparent, acquisition was secured by internal subsidies from other business fields (municipal cross-subsidising) and deficits were covered from the local authority's budget and borrowed money. Price decisions were not taken autonomously by *Wiener Linien*, but rather by the Municipal Council of the City of Vienna.

Strategic questions of business management, investment policy and transport-related development prospects in Vienna were – and to a great extent still are – discussed and decided by (only) three key players. In this governance model, very much imbued with a spirit of cooperation, there is broad consensus among the key players regarding the general public interest in LPT and central elements of the related public mission. All concerned actors have a basic interest in the realisation of an efficient, modern, safe, user-friendly, need-driven local public transport system. Practical operational tasks are jointly identified, based on the essentially corresponding, undisputed interpretation of the Vienna LPT's public mission. The operator is obliged to fulfil specific, contractually stipulated, long-term assignments.

Wiener Linien is contractually obliged to guarantee a range of services with specific standards as regards quantity and quality, and to stay within the financial limits agreed to that end. Hereby it enjoys considerable *de facto* autonomy in the execution of its service mission, in its price-setting, as well as with regard to the development of an obligatory quality management. The company can also make its own decisions as to which routes it wishes to entrust to private operators. It is further responsible for the EU-wide award of contracts, selection, contract formulation, and for monitoring the performance of the appointed subcontractors. Responsibility for all local public passenger transport services (except for the municipal railway *Schnellbahn*) rests solely with *Wiener Linien*.

Wiener Linien is making great efforts to provide new, specific transport services and enhance its customer orientation. In the same vein, various initiatives are now aimed at boosting the quality of its services. Comparisons with national and foreign transport enterprises serve as a signpost towards the further development and implementation of innovative services, as does international LPT quality benchmarking. These measures contribute to the fulfilment of the enterprise's public mission and are, occasionally, taken on its own initiative. In part, they go beyond concrete, contractual tasks and, to that extent, may be regarded as services provided on a voluntary basis. One important motive for these endeavours may well be the market position of *Wiener Linien* in relation to the goal of further tilting the modal split towards public transport usage and improving its image as an efficient, successful enterprise.

It is quite probable that *Wiener Linien* will be reappointed as the integrated LPT operator after the expiry of the current contract, which is valid until 2016. In the event of a new award of contract, however, it can be expected that the agreement will presumably contain more restrictive, more detailed rules and regulations, following the trend toward greater transparency and objectivity. The grantee will consequently enjoy less room for manoeuvre in the autonomous operationalization of specific transport services and quality matters.

A comparative study of the cities of the LPT in Lyon, London, Stockholm and Vienna reveals for *Wiener Linien* above-average efficiency in the provision of service. There is no evidence that sharper competition due to the liberalisation or privatisation of LPT would improve efficiency.

Although considerable changes have been made in recent years to the organisational, contractual and informal framework and web of relationships around *Wiener Linien*, mainly triggered by the policies and directives of the EU, the leading actors, the power potential and basic pattern of governance essentially remain much the same and have changed little, if indeed at all. Unlike the other actors and stakeholders who, as a rule, follow their own partial interests in LPT, *Wiener Linien* has a decisive *de facto* advantage of information in the planning and operation of transport services. This advantage greatly strengthens the enterprise's bargaining position against partial interests. This results, *de facto*, in a certain dependence of the politically responsible local authority on *Wiener Linien*, which, through its near-monopoly position, can exert great influence on transport policy.

On a more critical note, the traditionally strong position of *Wiener Linien* in this constellation of the LPT governance system does entail the risk for the City of Vienna that it offers (too) few possibilities for effective assertive action in case of severe conflict. Although this issue was not relevant in the past, it could become a challenge in the future, resulting from institutional changes, tensions within the workforce or cost cutting demands.

Another critical point may result in future from the actual allocation of the operational risk. It should be noted that under the LPT contract, *Wiener Linien* bears, at least in principle, the exclusive operating risk, since its revenue depends on the extent of use of its transport services. The City of Vienna merely grants a previously agreed financial compensation for specific public service obligation efforts in connection with the quality and quantity of the service. In a changing environment, with rising expenditures for employees and higher costs for services *Wiener Linien* faces new challenges and difficult management decisions.

Lessons Learned

Considering the evidence and experience of the past, it can be stated that, on the whole, the transport services provided by the public enterprise *Wiener Linien* function well and LPT in Vienna meets – even by international comparison – quite high quality standards. Furthermore, the governance system of Vienna's LPT services may certainly be regarded as a reasonable effective solution in terms of the transaction and organisational costs resulting from the realised institutional arrangement. Indeed, it allows the involved players properly execute the public service obligation.

This seems valid concerning the provision of modern and affordable traffic services as well as concerning the fulfilment of social and ecological demands and of sustainability requirements. In this regard the public enterprise *Wiener Linien* is designed and effective used as an instrument to contribute to various objectives of its public owner (according to the idea of the *Instrumental these* by Thiemeyer, 1975).

Like in other cities, interplay between the actors in LPT takes place in a complex relational system. In the past ten years, various planning, harmonisation and decision-making processes have been worked out and established between the three leading actors and with other stakeholders in the Vienna LPT. This partially informal structure of relations is also secured through interpersonal connections. As a result, the adopted formal and informal governance structures facilitate and promote the creation of consensus between the local authority, *Wiener Linien* and *Wiener Stadtwerke Holding AG*. The coordination effort required for various factual and policy issues, e.g. for the harmonisation of tariffs or for new transport services, is likely to be much less daunting than with alternative organisational models.

Moreover, the risk of misuse of information asymmetries seems low, due to close interpersonal relations. This particular setting further allows, if need be, consideration of specific higher-priority political (party) interests (e.g. economic and social policy desiderata, election considerations, etc.).

The generally high standard and the favourable assessment of Vienna's LPT are probably due to the fact that *Wiener Linien* pursues its public mission in the politically desired manner – that is, in an altogether satisfactory manner. In the past, *Wiener Linien* used, as far as possible, its (considerable) room for manoeuvre in the planning of its services according to its own interpretation of the specific public service mission.

To sum up, the history of LPT in Vienna shows clearly that over decades the model of organisation and governance of services is characterised by public ownership and political responsibility by the city, which both were never seriously questioned.

Since 2000, the public enterprise *Wiener Linien* is the responsible provider of LPT services, in the succession of the former *Wiener Stadtwerke-Verkehrsbetriebe*. *Wiener Linien* benefits from a quasi-monopolistic position within the LPT governance system. It has consistently used the freedom of manoeuvre granted to it to enhance its customer orientation and to further develop the range of transport services it offers. From this perspective, the institutional setting described above has stood the test of time and is likely to prove its achievement potential in the future, as well. There is no evidence or convincing indication that an institutional arrangement for service provision privatised to a higher degree, or in total, would lead to better governance, performance or quality of the specific public service mission in local public transport in the City of Vienna.

References

Cruz, N. F., Marques, R. C., Marra, A., Pozzi, C., "Local mixed companies: The theory and practice in an international perspective", in *Annals of Public and Cooperative Economics*, 2014, Vol. 85, No. 1, pp. 1-9.

Faber, C., *Governance-Regimes im Öffentlichen Verkehr*, Dissertation, Wirtschaftsuniversität Wien, 2002.

Flecker, C., Thörnqvist, C., "Outsourcing, Competitive Tendering and Changing Working Conditions in Local Public Traffic", in C. Hermann, J. Flecker (eds.), *Privatization of Public Services – Impacts for Employment, Working Conditions, and Service Quality in Europe*, New York, Routledge, 2012, pp. 74-88.

Frank, F., "Der öffentliche städtische Verkehr in der Bundeshauptstadt Wien und anderen österreichischen Städten", in *Handbuch der österreichischen Gemeinwirtschaft*, herausgegeben von der Arbeitsgemeinschaft der österreichischen Gemeinwirtschaft, Wien, 1960, pp. 367-383.

Greiling, D., "Stadtwerke Köln: a market-based approach towards public service provision", in this book, 2014.

Grossi, G., Marcou, G., Reichard, C., "Comparative aspects of institutional variants of local public service provision", in H. Wollmann, G. Marcou (eds.), *The Provision of Public Services in Europe*, Cheltenham UK, Edward Elgar, 2010, pp. 217-239.

Hall, D., *Re-municipalizing municipal services in Europe*, PSIRU, London, 2012.

Hermann, C., Flecker, J. (eds.), *Privatization of Public Services – Impacts for Employment, Working Conditions, and Service Quality in Europe*, New York, Routledge, 2012.

Hermann, C., Flecker J., "Conclusion – Impacts of Public Service Liberalization and Privatization", in C. Hermann, J. Flecker (eds.), *Privatization of Public Services – Impacts for Employment, Working Conditions, and Service Quality in Europe*, New York, Routledge, 2012, pp. 192-205.

Jansa, E., Sedeek, S., *Vergleichende Analyse zur Effizienzentwicklung des ÖPNV zwischen liberalisierten Märkten (Lyon, London, Stockholm) und Wien unter Beachtung von Qualitätsstandards*, Diplomarbeit Wirtschaftsuniversität Wien, 2005.

Loser, P., *Austrian Local and Regional Public Transport*, Working paper CIRIEC No. 2009/08.

Obermann, G., "The role of the state as guarantor of public services: Transaction cost issues and empirical evidence", in *Annals of Public and Cooperative Economics* 2007, Vol. 78, No. 4, pp. 475-500.

Reisinger, K., "Die Wiener Stadtwerke", in *Die österreichische Gemeinwirtschaft*, herausgegeben von der Arbeitsgemeinschaft der österreichischen Gemeinwirtschaft, Wien, 1982, pp. 351-359.

Schaefer, C., Warm, S., "Berliner Wasserbetriebe (BWB) – Water and sewage company in Berlin", in this book, 2014.

Swarts, D., Wagner, M. E., "Hybrid Firms and Transit Delivery: The Case of Berlin", in *Annals of Public and Cooperative Economics* 2014, Vol. 85, No. 1, pp. 127-146.

Thiemeyer, T., *Wirtschaftslehre öffentlicher Betriebe*, Reinbeck bei Hamburg, Rowolt, 1975.

Unfried, D., "Öffentlicher Personennahverkehr (ÖPNV)", in Kammer für Arbeiter und Angestellte für Wien (Hrsg), *Zur Zukunft öffentlicher Dienstleistungen*, Wien, 2005, pp. 145-158.

Wieser, R., "Wettbewerb im öffentlichen Personennah- und Regionalverkehr", in *WIFO Monatsberichte* 3/2002, pp. 167-178.

Wollmann, H., Marcou, G. (eds.), *The Provision of Public Services in Europe*, Cheltenham UK, Edward Elgar, 2010.

Wollmann, H., Marcou, G., "From public sector-based to privatized service provision. Is the pendulum swinging back again? Comparative summary", in Wollmann, H., Marcou, G. (eds.), *The Provision of Public Services in Europe*, Cheltenham UK, Edward Elgar, 2010, pp. 240-260.

Zatti, A., "New organizational models in European local public transport: From myth to reality", in *Annals of Public and Cooperative Economics* 2012, Vol. 83, No. 4., pp. 533-559.

Official reports and documents

BEST *Benchmarking in European Service of public Transport*: BEST Results of the 2010 survey. Copenhagen 2010.

EisbG: *Bundesgesetz über Eisenbahnen, Schienenfahrzeuge auf Eisenbahnen und den Verkehr auf Eisenbahnen*, BGBl. 60/1957, Fassung vom 01.02.2014. Bundesrepublik Österreich.

EN 13816/2002: *Transport-Logistik und Dienstleistungen – Öffentlicher Personenverkehr – Definition, Festlegung von Leistungszielen und Messung der Servicequalität*. European Committee for Standardization.

EN ISO 14001/2009: *Umweltmanagementsysteme – Anforderungen mit Anleitung zur Anwendung*. European Committee for Standardization.

EuroTest 2010 *Local Public Transport*; http://www.eurotestmobility.com.

KfLG: *Bundesgesetz über die linienmäßige Beförderung von Personen mit Kraftfahrzeugen*, BGBl. 203/1999, Fassung vom 01.02.2014. Bundesrepublik Österreich.

Kontrollamt der Stadt Wien, *Wiener Linien GmbH&Co KG, Prüfung der Tarifstruktur*, KA IV-GU 230-2/10, 2010.

OHSAS 18001/2007: *Occupational safety and health protection management systems*.

ÖPNRV-G: *Öffentlicher Personennah- und Regionalverkehrsgesetz*, BGBl. I No. 204/1999, Fassung vom 01.02.2014. Bundesrepublik Österreich.

ÖPNV-Vertrag: *Öffentlicher Personennahverkehrs- und -finanzierungsvertrag*, Stadt Wien und Wiener Linien.

StrabVO: *Verordnung des Bundesministers für Wissenschaft und Verkehr über den Bau und den Betrieb von Straßenbahnen*, BGBl. II No. 76/2000, Fassung vom 01.02.2014. Bundesrepublik Österreich.

VO (EG) 1370/2007: *Verordnung über öffentliche Personenverkehrsdienste auf Schiene und Straße und zur Aufhebung der Verordnungen (EWG) No. 1191/69 und (EWG) No. 1107/70 des Rates*. Europäisches Parlament und Rat der Europäischen Union.

Wiener Linien, *Jahresbericht* 2010.

Wiener Stadtwerke, *Annual Report* 2010 and 2012.

7. L'opérateur de transport public à Bruxelles (STIB) et la Région de Bruxelles-Capitale

25 ans de vie commune

Christophe GOETHALS

*Coordinateur du secteur économie au Centre de recherche
et d'information socio-politiques (CRISP), assistant
à l'Université libre de Bruxelles (ULB) et chercheur associé
au Centre Émile Bernheim (SBS-EM – ULB).*

1. Introduction

Cette contribution porte sur la Société des transports intercommunaux de Bruxelles (STIB), l'opérateur public de transport en commun dans la Région de Bruxelles-Capitale. Cette société créée en 1953 a dû s'adapter à un environnement en constante évolution et aux multiples facettes. Alors que ses résultats d'exploitation n'avaient cessé de se détériorer entre 1960 et 1990 – années pendant lesquelles la société a subi à la fois une réduction des recettes du trafic, un accroissement des dépenses d'exploitation et une désaffectation croissante de la clientèle – la STIB affiche aujourd'hui des résultats en nette amélioration. De 1990 à 2012, sa dette a diminué de 65 %, son taux de couverture est passé de 35 % à plus de 55 % et la fréquentation a augmenté de 164 %.

Ces résultats seront analysés et mis en perspectives à la lumière des évolutions contextuelles, organisationnelles et institutionnelles. Une attention particulière sera apportée aux aspects relatifs aux missions de service public, à la régulation et aux processus de prise de décision en matière de transports publics à Bruxelles.

2. Identification de l'entreprise

La STIB est l'opérateur de transport public urbain à Bruxelles. Financé par la Région, il exploite des lignes de bus, de tram et de métro essentiellement au sein de la Région de Bruxelles-Capitale. La STIB dessert également partiellement 11 communes de la périphérie. Certaines lignes des opérateurs de transports publics des deux autres régions

(Région flamande et Région wallonne) pénètrent sur le territoire de la Région de Bruxelles-Capitale. Voici les principales caractéristiques de l'opérateur.

Nom de l'opérateur	Société des transports intercommunaux de Bruxelles (STIB)
Adresse du siège social	Rue Royale 76 1000 Bruxelles Belgique
Date de création	1953
Site Internet	www.stib.be
Secteur d'activités	Code primaire NACE BEL 2008 : Transports urbains et suburbains de voyageurs (49310)
Chiffre d'affaires (2012)[1]	244 601 000 euros
Transferts publics (2011)	417 743 000 euros
Effectif (2012)[2]	6 717 ETP
Population desservie (2013)[3]	1 400 000 habitants (dont 243 700 pour les 11 communes de la périphérie)
Aire géographique desservie	254,7 km² (Région de Bruxelles + 11 communes de la périphérie)
Fréquentation (2013)[4]	355 millions de voyages
Actionnariat	La STIB est détenue à 100 % par la Région de Bruxelles-Capitale
Autorité	Le gouvernement de la Région de Bruxelles-Capitale est l'autorité responsable de l'organisation des transports publics sur son territoire. La Région de Bruxelles-Capitale est l'une des 3 régions qui, avec les 3 communautés et l'État fédéral, interviennent dans la composition de l'État belge
Forme juridique	Association de droit public

3. Historique

Le paysage organisationnel des transports collectifs urbains en Belgique a subi de profondes modifications au cours du temps, marquées par plusieurs périodes caractéristiques. Le début du 20ᵉ siècle correspond à l'âge d'or des transports en commun à Bruxelles. Le tramway est alors le principal moyen de transport urbain, tandis que l'automobile ne fait

[1] STIB, *Comptes annuels*, 2012.
[2] STIB, *Comptes annuels*, 2012.
[3] Statistiques de population de droit par commune au 1ᵉʳ janvier 2013. Sources : SPF Économie.
[4] De Schrijver, M., Voogt, F., « Stib : le bus a reculé en 2013, le tram et le métro ont patiné », in Le Soir, 13 janvier 2014.

que balbutier. À cette époque, l'exploitation des lignes est confiée à l'initiative privée qui, après en avoir fait la demande auprès des autorités compétentes et moyennant le paiement d'une rente, dispose sur certaines lignes de toutes les prérogatives d'une concession de monopole de services publics.

Partagé entre plusieurs concessionnaires privés, le réseau va ensuite subir un incroyable mouvement de concentration motivé par la perspective de l'introduction de la traction mécanique, rendue possible par l'électrification du réseau. En 1925, ce mouvement aboutit au monopole de la Société de tramways bruxellois. Exploiter les tramways est alors une entreprise profitable, à tel point que l'intervention publique n'est pas jugée nécessaire et les prix sont ponctuellement revus à la baisse.

Le 31 décembre 1945, les concessions accordées par les pouvoirs publics à la Société des tramways bruxellois arrivent à expiration. Une convention est conclue avec l'État et la province de Brabant afin d'assurer la poursuite des activités au-delà du délai prévu. En 1953, la Société des transports intercommunaux de Bruxelles (STIB) est créée. Elle prend alors la forme d'une société de droit public dotée de la personnalité juridique et qui présente toutes les caractéristiques d'une régie mixte. Le capital est détenu à parts égales par les pouvoirs publics (État, provinces et communes) et par l'entreprise des Tramways bruxellois qui font tous deux apport de leurs biens immobilisés[5]. Elle reçoit l'autorisation d'exploiter le réseau pour une période de 30 ans minimum[6].

Dans les années 1960, les transports en commun perdent progressivement du terrain et le véhicule particulier s'impose en tant que mode de transport dominant. À Bruxelles, malgré le développement de lignes de bus et la construction du métro, le déclin des transports en commun ne peut être jugulé, si bien que le pouvoir de tutelle doit soutenir financièrement les sociétés de transports publics. Cette situation amène les investisseurs privés à réduire leurs participations dans ce secteur au début des années 1970. En 1978, la gestion des transports urbains tombe totalement sous le contrôle des pouvoirs publics et plus particulièrement de l'État central.

Sous régime public, les sociétés de transports urbains continuent comme par le passé de disposer d'une certaine latitude de gestion au niveau de l'entretien et de l'exploitation du réseau. Les travaux d'infrastructure dont ceux de type métro, les mises en site propre, etc. sont quant à eux directement financés par l'État qui, logiquement, prend les décisions en la

---

[5] Suite aux négociations, les Tramways bruxellois et les pouvoirs publics sont parvenus à admettre un capital de 700 millions pour chacun des partenaires. Pour ce faire, l'apport du privé a été sous-estimé et celui des pouvoirs publics surestimé.

[6] Loi du 17 juin 1953, art. 3, *Moniteur belge*, 21 juin 1953.

matière après consultation et négociation avec la société. À cette période, l'État investit largement dans le réseau de métro à Bruxelles. À partir de 1982 et malgré les déficits d'exploitation successifs, les budgets mis à disposition de la société par l'État sont réduits notablement. La STIB est obligée d'élaborer des plans d'assainissement pour la période 1983 à 1988.

En 1989, la troisième réforme de l'État élargit considérablement les compétences des communautés et des régions. La politique des transports urbains est alors transférée au niveau des régions, et la Région de Bruxelles-Capitale nouvellement créée devient le nouveau pouvoir de tutelle et l'unique actionnaire de la STIB. À ce titre, la Région de Bruxelles-Capitale fixe dorénavant les objectifs qui s'imposent à la STIB dans le cadre de la politique de transports en commun à Bruxelles. Les relations entre l'autorité organisatrice et l'exploitant sont contractualisées par le biais d'un contrat de gestion négocié. Parallèlement, la société reçoit une plus grande autonomie de gestion et un pouvoir d'initiative accru pour adapter l'offre de transport à l'évolution des besoins de ses clients.

4. Les enjeux des transports publics à Bruxelles et les missions de service public

La régionalisation des transports, et plus particulièrement du « transport en commun urbain et vicinal »[7], est l'occasion pour la Région de Bruxelles-Capitale de confirmer sa volonté de disposer d'un réseau de transports en commun urbains qui allie l'efficacité, la rapidité, la sécurité et le confort. La politique de déplacement qu'entend mener la Région accorde en effet la priorité aux transports publics en vue de contribuer à l'amélioration de la qualité de vie en ville[8]. À cette époque, les enjeux qui s'imposent à la jeune Région sont déterminants. Un mouvement de périurbanisation vide progressivement la région de sa population, la fréquentation des transports en commun observe une baisse régulière depuis une dizaine d'années, les déficits d'exploitation se succèdent, la dette de l'opérateur se creuse et l'insuffisance des nouveaux moyens financiers alloués à la Région la contraint à une inéluctable rigueur budgétaire. Concernant ce dernier point, la STIB apparaît dès le début comme un risque financier important pour la Région puisque l'aide qui lui est apportée représente, déjà en 1992, 23,6 % du budget régional.

---

[7]   Loi spéciale de réformes institutionnelles du 8 août 1980 modifiée par la loi spéciale du 8 août 1988, *Moniteur belge*, 15 août 1980.

[8]   Gouvernement de la Région de Bruxelles-Capitale, Déclaration de politique générale de l'Exécutif présentée au Conseil Régional le 18 octobre 1989.

Avant la régionalisation, l'État, la province, l'agglomération et les communes flamandes ne parvenaient qu'à un contrôle grossier de l'offre de transport car l'initiative dans cette matière restait, dans une large mesure, entre les mains de la STIB elle-même[9]. Les obligations qui incombaient à la STIB consistaient alors à exploiter le réseau existant sans que des missions claires en matière de service public lui soient explicitement imposées.

Avec la régionalisation, la Région de Bruxelles-Capitale entend imposer sa légitimité auprès de ses interlocuteurs par une plus grande « explicitation » de l'action publique, notamment par l'intermédiaire de la contractualisation[10]. Elle entend également reprendre le contrôle en matière de responsabilité stratégique et notamment le pouvoir de définir le plan de réseau en intégrant cette réflexion dans un contexte plus large, conforté par les nouvelles compétences dont elle a été dotée (mobilité, urbanisme, aménagement du territoire, etc.).

L'ordonnance du 22 novembre 1990[11] fixe alors le nouveau cadre juridique de l'organisation des transports publics à Bruxelles. Les statuts de la STIB sont modifiés. Elle prend la forme d'une association de droit public *sui generis*. Les relations entre l'autorité organisatrice et l'exploitant sont contractualisées. Le contrat de gestion régit dorénavant pour une période de cinq ans les objectifs imposés aux parties et le calendrier prévu pour leur réalisation.

Dans ce contexte, les missions de service public définies par le pouvoir de tutelle vont recouvrir deux finalités bien distinctes. La première consiste, du moins théoriquement, à assurer un droit à la mobilité, c'est-à-dire à satisfaire par le biais des transports publics les besoins sociaux de tous les Bruxellois. Le cahier des charges de la STIB rappelle les grands principes (égalité, continuité, neutralité) que doivent respecter les missions de service public qui lui incombent et les principes d'application qui en découlent (transparence et responsabilité, simplicité, accessibilité, confiance et fiabilité, participation et adaptation)[12], mais de manière générale, la notion de « droit à la mobilité » restera floue. La deuxième finalité consiste à promouvoir une utilisation efficace et équilibrée des

---

[9]   Stratec, Étude d'organisation, de gestion et de commercialisation de la Rapport de synthèse, Bruxelles, 1987, p. 18.

[10] Tellier, C., Sacco, M., *La régionalisation de Bruxelles à l'épreuve de la contractualisation. Vers de nouvelles manières de gouverner la ville ?*, Acte du XLVI colloque de l'ASRDLF des 6, 7 et 8 juillet 2009 à Clermont-Ferrand.

[11] Région de Bruxelles-Capitale, Ordonnance du 22 novembre 1990 relative à l'organisation des transports en commun dans la Région de Bruxelles-Capitale, *Moniteur belge*, 28 novembre 1990.

[12] Conseil de la Région de Bruxelles-Capitale, Cahier des charges de la STIB du 18 juillet 1996, art. 2, *Moniteur belge*, 24 septembre 1996.

transports publics à l'échelon régional compte tenu des ressources disponibles. La Région cherche à transformer l'opérateur, tant du point de vue de son organisation et que de ses modes de gestion, en l'amenant sur la voie du client-centrisme : modernisation de l'entreprise, amélioration de la performance, développement d'une logique commerciale orientée clients, meilleure satisfaction des besoins, etc.

Cette dichotomie entre efficacité et universalité du service apparaît clairement dans les différents documents qui fixent le cadre juridique de l'organisation des transports publics à Bruxelles et qui réglementent les relations entre la Région et la STIB, à savoir l'ordonnance du 22 novembre 1990, le cahier des charges de la STIB, le contrat de gestion et les statuts de la STIB.

L'objectif d'une gestion efficace va se faire de plus en plus contraignant au début des années 2000, au moment précis où est discutée au niveau européen la possibilité d'une ouverture du secteur à la concurrence. L'objectif affiché par la Région est alors de préparer la STIB au nouveau cadre réglementaire européen mais aussi d'en faire un acteur solide sur le marché pour lui permettre de faire face, le cas échéant, au défi de la concurrence[13]. C'est pour cette raison que le contrat 2001-2005 accorde une importance non négligeable aux normes de qualité, à l'autonomie de l'entreprise, à la transparence du financement et à la réduction de la dette. Bien que le mouvement ait été initié dès 1990 avec l'entame d'une démarche qualité (cf. section sur *La démarche qualité*), la perspective d'un marché libéralisé va pousser la société de transport en commun bruxelloise à réaliser une profonde transformation de ses modes de gestion et de ses processus internes. La volonté affichée à cette période est de transformer la STIB, entreprise publique bureaucratique, hiérarchique et monopolistique, en une entreprise moderne et performante. La société recrute entre autres des cadres issus du privé, restructure son organigramme et met en place de nouvelles techniques de management.

5. Le cadre réglementaire européen

À Bruxelles, la Région de Bruxelles-Capitale est l'autorité chargée de l'organisation de la politique de transport public sur son territoire. La STIB est l'opérateur désigné, par voie législative et donc sans mise en concurrence, pour l'exploitation du réseau de bus, de tram et de métro. Détenu à 100 % par la Région, il constitue un opérateur interne (également appelé opérateur *in house* ou quasi-régie). En 2000, ce type

---

[13] Lauwers, K., Colla, O., « De contractuele relaties tussen Brussels Hoofdstedelijk Gewest en de MIVB », in Huygens, Ch. (coord.), « Les contrats de gestion : un facteur de performance pour les entreprises publiques de la Région de Bruxelles-Capitale ? », *Cahier de Sciences Administratives*, n° 12/2007, Bruxelles, Larcier, 2007, p. 45.

particulier d'organisation fait l'objet d'une profonde remise en question par la Commission européenne dans sa proposition de règlement relatif à l'action des États membres en matière d'exigences de service public et à l'attribution de contrats de service public dans le domaine des transports de voyageurs par chemin de fer, par route et par voie navigable[14]. Après les débats qui ont suivi au sein du Parlement européen et au sein du Conseil, et suite aux oppositions de nombreux États et autorités locales, des modifications substantielles sont apportées au texte initial et le règlement CE 1370/2007[15] est finalement adopté le 23 octobre 2007.

Le règlement 1370/2007[16] relatif aux services publics de transport de voyageurs par chemin de fer et par route entre en vigueur le 3 décembre 2009 et se substitue aux règlements 1191/69 et 1107/70.

L'autorité locale compétente peut dorénavant opter pour différentes formes d'attribution. Celles-ci ne sont plus présentées comme des exceptions mais bien comme des décisions entièrement discrétionnaires pour l'autorité compétente. Cette dernière peut ainsi :

– déléguer l'exécution des missions de service public de transport de voyageurs à un tiers avec l'obligation de mise en concurrence ;

– attribuer directement ces missions à un opérateur interne sous certaines conditions ;

– exécuter elle-même ces missions sous certaines conditions.

Dans tous les cas, la contractualisation est la règle. Dans le cas de l'attribution des missions de service public à un opérateur interne, ce dernier doit limiter ses activités de transport public de passagers à l'intérieur du territoire de l'autorité locale compétente. De plus, il ne peut participer à des appels d'offres à l'extérieur de ce territoire (« spécificité géographique »). Les grands opérateurs publics des métropoles se voient donc fortement limités dans leurs velléités d'expansion au-delà des périmètres du monopole, stoppant leur conquête des réseaux de province[17].

---

[14] Commission européenne, Proposition de règlement du Parlement européen et du Conseil relatif à l'action des États membres en matière d'exigences de service public et à l'attribution de contrats de service public dans le domaine des transports de voyageurs par chemin de fer, par route et par voie navigable [COM (2000) 0007 final, 26 juillet 2000], in *Journal officiel de l'Union européenne*, C 365E, 19 décembre 2000, pp. 169-178.

[15] Règlement (CE) n° 1370/2007 du Parlement européen et du Conseil du 23 octobre 2007 relatif aux services publics de transport de voyageurs par chemin de fer et par route, et abrogeant les règlements (CEE) n° 1191/69 et (CEE) n° 1107/70 du Conseil, in *Journal officiel de l'Union européenne*, L 315, 3 décembre 2007.

[16] Règlement (CE) n° 1370/2007, *op. cit.*

[17] Pflieger, G., *Entre échelle locale et communautaire, les nouvelles régulations croisées des politiques de transports urbains*, Section thématique 12.1. Regard critique : le local comme objet global ?, Congrès AFSP 2009, p. 11.

Le règlement définit les opérateurs internes comme étant des entités juridiquement distinctes, sur lesquelles l'autorité compétente exerce un contrôle semblable à celui exercé sur ses propres services. Il n'est cependant pas obligatoire que l'autorité compétente détienne 100 % du capital de l'opérateur, ce qui permet la création de partenariats publics-privés.

Le règlement précise en outre les conditions pour lesquelles une contrepartie financière pour la réalisation d'obligations de service public peut être accordée à l'opérateur[18].

Enfin, le règlement impose à chaque autorité compétente de publier, une fois par an, un rapport global sur les obligations de service public relevant de sa compétence, les opérateurs de service public retenus ainsi que les compensations et les droits exclusifs qui leur sont octroyés en contrepartie, afin de permettre le contrôle et l'évaluation de l'efficacité, de la qualité et du financement du réseau de transport public.

Cette adaptation souple de la première version du règlement est le fruit d'un processus itératif, dans la mesure où le processus d'européanisation, qui est généralement perçu comme un processus *top-down*, a également résulté d'une démarche *bottom-up* par laquelle les collectivités locales se sont saisies de l'Europe[19]. Le cadre de référence réglementaire qui a été défini a contribué à une normalisation qui n'est néanmoins pas sans effet au plan local, en particulier pour les régies françaises, allemandes et italiennes[20].

---

[18] Rendu en juillet 2003, l'arrêt de la Cour dans l'affaire *Altmark* (Cour de justice des Communautées européennes, 24 juillet 2003, *Altmark Trans*, C-280/00, *Rec.*, I-7747.) a mis fin au débat juridique sur la qualification d'aide d'État en définissant clairement la notion d'avantage financier. La Cour précise dans cet arrêt quatre conditions auxquelles une compensation relative à une obligation de service public ne constitue pas un avantage financier et ne peut dès lors pas être qualifiée d'aide d'État : (1) l'entreprise a été expressément chargée d'obligations de service public clairement définies par un acte officiel (« mandat ») ; (2) des paramètres objectifs de calcul de la compensation ont été clairement établis avant son versement (exigence de transparence) ; (3) cette compensation n'occasionne pas de surcompensation (exigence de nécessité et de proportionnalité) ; (4) la mission de service public a été confiée à l'entreprise à l'issue d'une procédure de marché public ou, en l'absence d'une telle procédure, le niveau de la compensation repose sur une analyse des coûts que pourrait réaliser « une entreprise moyenne, bien gérée ». Les trois premières conditions de cette décision ont été transposées dans le Règlement (CE) n° 1370/2007.

[19] Pflieger, G., *op. cit.*, p. 10.

[20] *Ibid.*, p. 10.

6. Performance opérationnelle

À Bruxelles, la STIB exploite directement l'entièreté du réseau de bus, de tram et de métro sans faire appel à la sous-traitance. Il existe néanmoins une certaine forme de concurrence sur le marché puisque l'opérateur public doit faire face à la présence des autres opérateurs sur certains tronçons : l'opérateur ferroviaire national (SNCB) et les opérateurs de transport public des deux autres régions (TEC pour la Wallonie et De Lijn pour la Flandre). Cette concurrence est pour le moins théorique puisque TEC et De Lijn proposent des liaisons entre la Région de Bruxelles-Capitale et les deux autres régions. La SNCB, quant à elle, possède de nombreuses gares ferroviaires à Bruxelles mais son objectif prioritaire reste le transport « inter-city ». Elle est donc complémentaire à la STIB, ces deux sociétés « s'échangeant » mutuellement des passagers[21].

Au-delà de son activité de base, la STIB s'est progressivement vu confier d'autres activités, pour la plupart attachées à des missions particulières de service public :

• Transport à la demande pour les personnes à mobilité réduite (PMR) ;
• Taxis collectifs ;
• Voitures partagées Cambio.

En termes de performance opérationnelle, le fait le plus marquant est sans doute l'augmentation spectaculaire de la fréquentation des transports en commun observée depuis la fin des années 1990[22].

Après une première période de stagnation dans les années 1990, la fréquentation des transports publics à Bruxelles a littéralement explosé à partir des années 2000. Le nombre estimé de voyages a augmenté de 119 % entre 1999 et 2012. Plusieurs facteurs permettent d'expliquer cette augmentation spectaculaire de la fréquentation estimée. Les rapports analysant les résultats de la STIB[23] imputent la croissance du nombre d'usagers pour une part importante aux politiques d'accompagnement mises en œuvre par les pouvoirs publics et à l'influence de facteurs

---

[21] Chaque jour, 350 000 personnes se rendent à Bruxelles, en voiture ou en transports en commun, pour y travailler ou étudier.

[22] Pour plus de détails concernant les indicateurs de performance opérationnelle de la STIB, lire : Goethals, C., *Relation entre l'opérateur de transport public à Bruxelles (STIB) et l'autorité organisatrice : entre asymétrie et coopération*, CIRIEC, Working Paper n° 2014/06, 2014.

[23] Cf. Gouvernement de la Région Bruxelles-Capitale et la STIB, *Rapport quinquennal du contrat de gestion 2001-2005 : Cinq ans d'amélioration des transports publics à Bruxelles*, Bruxelles, 2006, p. 14 ; PWC, *Rapport quinquennal sur l'exécution du contrat de gestion 2007-2011 liant la Région de Bruxelles-Capitale et la STIB*, Bruxelles, 2011, p. 11.

externes sur lesquels la STIB a peu ou pas de maîtrise : politique de stationnement, l'introduction de tarifs préférentiels, hausse du prix du carburant, accroissement de la congestion, croissance de la population, croissance économique, conscientisation croissante de la population aux enjeux environnementaux, etc. Parmi les facteurs explicatifs, d'autres études évoquent également l'augmentation générale de la mobilité des personnes et la construction de complexes de bureaux à proximité des stations[24].

Figure 1. Évolution de la fréquentation estimée de la STIB (1970-2012)

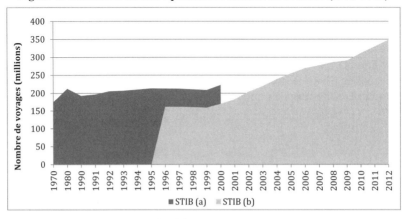

Sources : Bureau du plan et rapport d'activités STIB.

Remarques : Les statistiques de fréquentation sont calculées sur la base des oblitérations enregistrées, des ventes et du nombre d'abonnements vendus, chaque catégorie d'abonnement étant assortie d'une hypothèse de taux de fréquentation[25]. Sur la base des résultats d'une enquête réalisée auprès des utilisateurs, les coefficients ont été ajustés à partir de 2000. Ceci explique la présence de deux courbes dans le graphique : STIB (a) pour les hypothèses de calcul prévalant avant 2000 et STIB (b) pour les hypothèses de calcul prévalant après 2000.

Parmi les facteurs ayant contribué à l'augmentation de la fréquentation, la STIB, dans ses rapports d'activités, met également en avant l'accroissement de l'offre et de la qualité des services. Or,

---

[24] Corijn, E., Vloeberghs, E., *Bruxelles !*, VUB Press, Cahiers urbains, 2009, p. 75.

[25] Pour de plus en amples détails sur la méthodologie de calcul, voir : Lebrun, K., Hubert, M., Huynen, P., De Witte, A., Macharis, C., *Les pratiques de déplacement à Bruxelles*, Cahiers de l'Observatoire de la mobilité de la Région de Bruxelles-Capitale, pp. 72-74.

l'offre globale de la STIB, exprimée en véhicule-kilomètres, n'a que très légèrement augmenté depuis 1993 (+3,9 % au total entre 1993 et 2012). L'offre a certes subi de nombreux changements ces vingt dernières années, mais ceux-ci sont le fruit de réorganisations successives visant à allouer les ressources différemment : certaines lignes sont rallongées de quelques arrêts, d'autres sont scindées en deux pour renforcer la ponctualité, les fréquences sont augmentées sur certaines lignes à certains moments de la journée et elles sont réduites dans d'autres cas. L'analyse de l'offre kilométrique a montré que ces réorganisations privilégiaient le développement du métro et du tram au détriment de celui du bus (cf. figure 5, annexe 1). Quant à la qualité, les enquêtes de satisfaction de la clientèle montrent au mieux des notes relativement stables (cf. figure 9, annexe 1).

Il est par conséquent difficile de juger si les différents plans de restructuration du réseau et l'évolution de la qualité ont réellement eu un effet d'induction sur la demande – la dégradation de la vitesse commerciale n'y a certainement pas contribué[26] – mais le mérite de la STIB relève sans conteste de sa capacité à avoir pu absorber le surplus de demandes par l'achat, avec le financement de la Région, de nouveaux véhicules plus capacitaires. En acquérant de nouveaux véhicules, en favorisant le rabattement de lignes secondaires sur des lignes à haute capacité (tram et métro essentiellement) et en augmentant les fréquences sur ces lignes[27], la STIB est en effet parvenue à considérablement augmenter le nombre de places disponibles tout en diminuant les coûts opérationnels associés à chaque voyage. Le nombre de places-km a augmenté de 55 % tous modes confondus entre 2000 et 2012. La plus forte augmentation est à mettre au compte du mode métro (+95 %), suivi par le mode tram (+47 %) et dans une moindre proportion par le mode bus (+6 %).

7. Les aspects financiers

7.1. Taux de couverture

Dans le domaine des transports publics urbains, les recettes tarifaires ne permettent généralement pas de couvrir l'ensemble des coûts

---

[26] De manière générale, la vitesse commerciale, surtout sur le réseau de surface, se dégrade depuis une vingtaine d'années, et ce peu importe le mode de transport analysé. Ce constat s'explique notamment par la saturation des voiries et la congestion du trafic automobile.

[27] Dobruszkes, F. *et al.*, « Réorganisation d'un réseau de transport collectif urbain, ruptures de charge et mobilités éprouvantes : l'expérience bruxelloise », in *Journal of Urban Research*, 7, 2011, 16 p.

d'exploitation. En fonction de la politique tarifaire définie, une aide financière plus ou moins importante est allouée par les autorités publiques pour compenser la différence entre les recettes issues des ventes et le coût réel d'exploitation.

Le taux de couverture indique le pourcentage des recettes commerciales qui couvrent les coûts d'exploitation. Défini selon les normes comptables européennes, le taux de couverture SEC 95 a subi à Bruxelles une forte augmentation depuis 2000. Il atteint 55 % en 2012 alors qu'il se situait aux environs de 35 % entre 1990 et 2000. Ce résultat est la conséquence des effets conjugués de l'augmentation continue des tarifs et de la fréquentation, et depuis 2007 d'une maîtrise des coûts d'exploitation[28].

Depuis plusieurs années, la STIB et la Région affichent clairement l'objectif d'atteindre et de maintenir le taux de couverture (au sens européen) au-dessus de 50 %[29]. La réalisation de cet objectif rendrait possible, en conformité avec la réglementation européenne et si les autorités le souhaitent, de déconsolider la dette de la STIB de celle de la Région. Actuellement, les comptes de la STIB sont toujours globalisés avec ceux de la Région avec pour conséquence évidente de limiter le taux d'endettement de l'entité fédérée. Cette globalisation pèse par ailleurs sur les capacités d'investissement régionales, tant pour assurer l'avenir à long terme des transports publics à Bruxelles que pour mener à bien d'autres politiques urbaines prioritaires.

7.2. Endettement de long terme

L'endettement de l'entreprise bruxelloise a subi une explosion entre 1990 et 1995 due au besoin de rattrapage des retards d'investissement accumulés avant la régionalisation (cf. figure 2). Dès les premiers contrats de gestion, la Région a donc exhorté la STIB à assainir sa dette et, ainsi, à diminuer sa dépendance aux finances publiques. Pour ce faire, la STIB est invitée à accroître ses recettes propres et à retrouver une situation financière viable. Pour lui permettre d'atteindre ses objectifs, la STIB reçoit une large autonomie dans la fixation de ses tarifs (cf. la section sur *La politique tarifaire*). Cette politique tarifaire, combinée à une maîtrise des coûts, a incontestablement porté ses fruits, puisqu'en 17 ans, la STIB a réduit sa dette de 75 %, la faisant passer de 500 millions d'euros en 1994 à 125 millions d'euros en 2011. Comme pour l'évolution du taux de couverture, ces résultats ont été rendus possibles

---

[28] Les coûts d'exploitation par unité produite (places-km) sont restés globalement stables sur la période 2007-2012, alors qu'ils avaient augmenté de 23 % sur la période 2000-2006 (calculs de l'auteur).

[29] STIB, *Rapport d'activités*, 2006, p. 12.

par l'augmentation de la clientèle et une plus grande contribution financière de la part des usagers.

Figure 2. Dette à plus d'un an de la STIB (millions d'euros courants)

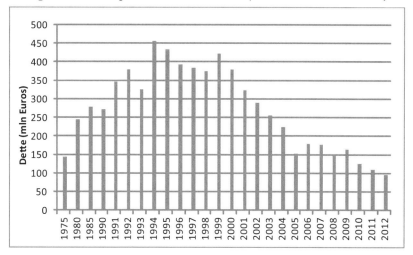

Sources : STIB, rapports d'activités, plusieurs années.

7.3. Transferts publics

Le montant des transferts publics est composé, d'une part, d'un financement régional qui inclut :

- une dotation globale qui comprend :
- une dotation de base répartie en une dotation de fonctionnement et une dotation d'investissement ;
- un facteur correcteur des gains ou pertes de vitesse commerciale ;
- une contrepartie financière des gains de productivité ;
- une dotation pour les travaux réalisés par la STIB pour le compte de la Région ;
- une dotation spéciale à titre d'intervention pour les tarifs préférentiels ;
- une dotation pour l'amélioration de l'offre ;
- une dotation spéciale pour le financement des efforts particuliers en matière de sécurité ;
- une dotation spéciale pour couvrir les coûts liés aux mesures extraordinaires prises en cas de pic de pollution ;

- des compensations spécifiques pour missions particulières de service public (intermodalité, transport de personnes handicapées, etc.).

Ces subsides sont complétés, d'autre part, par un financement de l'autorité fédérale, soit à titre exceptionnel, soit destiné à des investissements spécifiques (matériel roulant, infrastructure, etc.)[30].

En outre, la Région finance directement une partie des dépenses pour les travaux d'investissement, d'entretien et de renouvellement des ouvrages et des équipements métro et prémétro, ainsi que pour l'amélioration de la vitesse commerciale du réseau de surface.

De manière générale, l'intervention financière des autorités publiques dans les transports en commun est en constante augmentation. Elle augmente de 64 % entre 2003 et 2009, soit 7 % de plus que l'évolution du budget régional sur la même période et 51 % de plus que l'évolution de l'indice des prix à la consommation (cf. figure 7, annexe 1). Toujours entre 2003 et 2009, la part du total des dépenses régionales allouée à la construction et à la gestion des transports en commun oscille entre 18 % et 23 %, soit une proportion proche de celle enregistrée en 1990 (cf. figure 8, annexe 1). Ce calcul ne tient pas compte de l'intervention financière de l'autorité fédérale.

On observe par ailleurs que le budget public alloué aux transports en commun est de plus en plus ciblé. Les subsides à l'exploitation sont aujourd'hui complétés de dotations affectées directement à l'amélioration de l'offre ou de la sécurité, qui sont octroyées en fonction de l'atteinte des objectifs fixés dans le contrat de gestion, etc. Dans l'ensemble, l'intervention financière publique à destination des transports en commun demeure soutenue à Bruxelles. Malgré l'évolution du budget général de la Région supérieure à l'évolution de l'inflation, la part du budget public allouée aux transports en commun reste relativement stable au cours du temps et représente environ 20 %.

8. La politique tarifaire

8.1. *Évolution des prix*

Les tarifs sont réglementés par l'AO. Ils ne peuvent être modifiés qu'une seule fois par an. Pour lui permettre d'atteindre ses objectifs,

---

[30] Depuis 1993, un accord de coopération (BELIRIS) signé entre l'État fédéral et la Région de Bruxelles-Capitale permet l'intervention financière de l'État pour la réalisation d'une série de travaux d'infrastructure à Bruxelles visant ainsi à promouvoir son rôle national et international.

la STIB reçoit une large autonomie dans la fixation de ses tarifs. Alors que l'augmentation des tarifs en Flandre et en Wallonie ne peut dépasser l'évolution de l'indice des prix à la consommation, à Bruxelles, l'évolution globale des tarifs peut théoriquement atteindre l'indice des prix à la consommation majorée de 2 %, même si, en pratique, un accord a été établi sur une hypothèse de croissance moyenne annuelle des tarifs de 1 % au-dessus de l'indice des prix à la consommation[31]. Les marges de manœuvre données à la STIB lui permettent d'opérer une adaptation tarifaire différenciée en fonction du type de titre de transport. L'indicateur de l'évolution globale des tarifs est en effet calculé sur la base de l'évolution moyenne du prix de chaque type de titres existants, pondéré par le nombre de titres vendus.

En analysant l'évolution des tarifs (cf. figure 3 ci-dessous), la STIB semble avoir mis ce mécanisme à profit en concentrant les hausses tarifaires les plus prononcées sur les formules les plus prisées, à savoir les abonnements classiques et MTB[32]. Le prix de ces abonnements a augmenté presque deux fois plus que l'inflation depuis la régionalisation. Or, ces formules d'abonnement concernent une proportion importante de clients captifs, soit parce qu'ils bénéficient d'une prise en charge des frais d'abonnement par leur employeur ou par l'État, soit parce qu'ils n'ont pas d'autre choix que de se déplacer en transports en commun. Dans les deux cas, une augmentation des prix n'aura que peu d'incidence sur leurs choix et comportements en matière de transport. L'autorité semble donc avoir choisi de faire porter le coût davantage sur l'usager que sur la collectivité. Notons que, sur la période analysée, le prix de l'abonnement scolaire a été maintenu à un niveau relativement bas.

La STIB a donc pleinement saisi la plus grande autonomie accordée par la Région en matière de tarification. Rappelons que le gouvernement bruxellois conserve néanmoins le droit, en dernier ressort, de refuser le plan tarifaire proposé par les organes de gestion de la STIB.

---

[31]   Gouvernement de la Région Bruxelles-Capitale et STIB, *Contrat de gestion 2007-2011 entre la Région de Bruxelles-Capitale et la STIB*, Bruxelles, 2007, p. 56.

[32]   Ces abonnements représentaient 68 % des voyages effectués par les usagers de la STIB en 2011 et plus de 50 % des recettes propres de l'opérateur.

**Figure 3. Évolution des prix des principaux titres de transport
STIB – indice 100 = 1992**

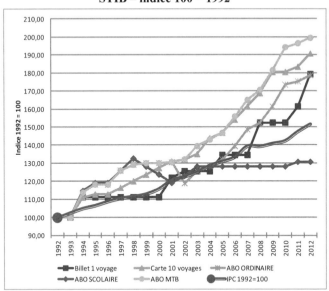

Sources : Arrêtés ministériels du gouvernement de la Région de Bruxelles-Capitale depuis 1990.

8.2. Les aspects redistributifs de la tarification

Depuis 1990, un éventail de titres de transport a été créé. Ceux-ci se différencient en fonction de la fréquence d'utilisation (occasionnel, régulier, intensif) et du profil de l'utilisateur (âge, statut social, etc.). Des réductions (tarifs préférentiels et gratuités) sont offertes à certaines catégories de citoyens. La charge financière des réductions et des gratuités est assurée par le budget régional ou communautaire (dans le cas des abonnements scolaires). La compensation versée par l'autorité publique est censée couvrir le manque à gagner de l'exploitant, à savoir la différence entre la valeur tarifaire réelle et le prix effectivement payé par l'usager.

Il existe également un système dit du « tiers payant » qui permet d'offrir à l'employé, sous certaines conditions[33], une réduction sur son titre de transport en commun grâce à une participation de l'employeur aux

---

[33] L'intervention de l'employeur dans les frais de déplacements de ses employés en transports en commun à Bruxelles est soit prévue dans les conventions collectives de travail, soit prévue par la loi lorsque la distance entre le domicile de l'employé et le lieu de travail est de 5 km au moins. En dehors de ces obligations, l'employeur reste libre de conclure une convention tiers-payant avec ses employés.

frais de déplacement. Ce financement se situe entre 60 % et 100 % du prix effectivement payé par le travailleur.

La politique tarifaire dans son ensemble révèle certaines inégalités car les réductions sont en général accordées indépendamment du niveau de revenus du bénéficiaire. La tarification spéciale sur la base de critères sociaux est réduite et ne concerne que les personnes à très bas revenus (OMNIO) ou ayant un statut social spécifique (ex : VIPO, anciens combattants, etc.)[34].

9. Régulation et processus de prise de décision

9.1. Les instruments de contrôle ou de régulation

La Région de Bruxelles-Capitale est, par l'intermédiaire du gouvernement et du ministre ayant les transports publics dans ses attributions, à la fois l'unique actionnaire de la STIB et le pouvoir de tutelle de cette dernière. Elle porte donc une double casquette. En tant qu'actionnaire majoritaire et propriétaire de l'opérateur, la Région de Bruxelles-Capitale est censée diriger et contrôler les activités de l'exploitant dans l'intérêt commercial du groupe. En théorie, ce pouvoir de gestion est délégué au conseil d'administration qui se voit accorder la responsabilité de la bonne gestion financière et du développement de l'entreprise. En tant qu'organe de tutelle et co-contractant du contrat de gestion, son rôle est de s'assurer de la bonne exécution des missions de service public. Ces dernières doivent s'inscrire dans la politique globale de transport menée par le gouvernement.

Ce double rôle assuré par la Région apparaît à certains égards comme contradictoire, ou tout au moins difficilement conciliable. L'objectif de bonne santé financière de l'entreprise est en effet purement économique alors que les missions de service public sont bien souvent déficitaires. Ce double rôle est néanmoins caractéristique de la gouvernance des entreprises publiques, où les objectifs poursuivis par les autorités publiques dépassent généralement les logiques purement économiques. L'expérience montre que la finalité de l'autorité publique n'est pas forcément d'opérer un choix entre ces deux objectifs mais bien de canaliser les facteurs qui vont influencer l'atteinte de ces objectifs.

Dans le cas de la STIB, la manière de canaliser les facteurs qui vont influencer ses objectifs se traduit par différents types de contrôle, *a priori* et *a posteriori*, mis en œuvre par la Région. Le contrôle de la Région porte aussi bien sur les objectifs financiers que sur le respect des missions

---

[34] Hubert, M., Dobruszkes, F., Macharis, C., « États généraux de Bruxelles. La mobilité à, de, vers et autour de Bruxelles », *Brussels Studies*, Note n° 1, 5 janvier 2008, p. 4.

de service public et de la réglementation. En outre, l'implication du personnel et des usagers dans le processus de décision par le biais de la consultation et de la concertation constitue un mécanisme de contrôle *a priori* permettant de légitimer davantage les décisions qui seront prises.

9.1.1. Les organes d'administration et de gestion

En tant qu'actionnaire, le gouvernement exerce son pouvoir de contrôle, *a priori*, en siégeant à l'assemblée générale des actionnaires et en faisant usage de son droit de nommer les membres de deux des principaux organes d'administration et de gestion de la société, à savoir le conseil d'administration et le comité de gestion.

9.1.1.1. Le conseil d'administration

Le conseil d'administration constitue essentiellement un organe de contrôle et d'approbation des décisions de la direction. Il agit très souvent sur proposition du comité de gestion. Il est composé de 23 membres. Parmi eux, 15 sont des administrateurs « ordinaires ». Ceux-ci ont en règle générale une affiliation aux groupes politiques qui forment le gouvernement. Ils jouent le rôle d'intermédiaires entre la direction de la STIB et leur parti, à qui ils rendent le plus souvent des comptes. Ils sont attentifs à l'avancement des dossiers et s'assurent que les décisions qui sont prises au sein de la STIB sont conformes aux grandes orientations données par le gouvernement. Dans ce cadre délimité, ils laissent une grande autonomie de gestion à l'administrateur-directeur général et à son adjoint.

L'administrateur-directeur général et son adjoint sont nommés par le gouvernement. Ils n'ont pas forcément d'affiliation à un parti politique. Ils sont chargés, chacun pour ce qui le concerne, de la gestion journalière de l'entreprise[35] et siègent au sein des trois principaux organes de gestion : ils dirigent l'*executive committee* (comité exécutif) composé des cinq seniors vice-présidents et sont membres de droit du conseil d'administration et du comité de gestion au sein desquels ils participent à la prise de décisions.

Concrètement, ils ont pour rôle de définir la stratégie de l'entreprise, d'assurer la gestion quotidienne, de négocier le contrat de gestion liant l'entreprise à la Région, de veiller à sa mise en œuvre, de contribuer durablement à l'atteinte des objectifs fixés, de rapporter au comité de gestion et au conseil d'administration, etc. L'administrateur-directeur général et le directeur général adjoint sont responsables de leurs décisions devant le conseil d'administration et le gouvernement, qui seul a le pouvoir de les sanctionner ou de les révoquer.

---

[35] Région de Bruxelles-Capitale, Ordonnance du 22 novembre 1990, *op. cit.*, art. 29.

En outre, trois administrateurs nommés sur présentation des trois organisations syndicales, deux commissaires du gouvernement et un chargé de mission assistent aux réunions avec voix consultative. Les deux commissaires du gouvernement et le chargé de mission sont nommés par l'Exécutif pour assurer le contrôle des décisions prises pour le compte de l'autorité de tutelle. Ils peuvent introduire un recours contre toute décision qu'ils estiment contraire à la loi, à l'intérêt général ou au contrat de gestion. Le chargé de mission dispose en outre d'un pouvoir délibérant au sein du comité de gestion.

9.1.1.2. Le comité de gestion

Le comité de gestion exerce les pouvoirs de haute direction dans la gestion de la société[36]. Il est composé de 12 membres. Sur proposition du conseil d'administration, le gouvernement de la Région de Bruxelles-Capitale désigne parmi les membres du conseil d'administration deux administrateurs pour siéger au comité de gestion de la STIB. Les cinq personnes qui viennent compléter le comité de gestion en sont membres de droit. Il s'agit de l'administrateur-directeur général, du directeur général adjoint, du président et du vice-président du conseil d'administration, ainsi que du chargé de mission du gouvernement. En outre, les trois administrateurs nommés sur présentation des trois organisations syndicales et les deux commissaires du gouvernement assistent aux réunions avec voix consultative.

9.1.1.3. Collège des commissaires aux comptes

Le Collège des commissaires aux comptes surveille les opérations comptables de la société. Il est composé de trois membres nommés (tous les trois ans) par l'assemblée générale, sur proposition de l'Exécutif. Les commissaires peuvent prendre connaissance des livres, de la correspondance, des procès-verbaux et généralement de tous les documents et de toutes les écritures de la société. Il leur est remis chaque semestre un état résumant la situation active et passive de celle-ci. Ils reçoivent annuellement, un mois avant l'assemblée générale ordinaire, toutes les pièces nécessaires à la vérification des écritures. Parmi les commissaires, le commissaire-réviseur atteste que les documents comptables sont établis selon les exigences légales et, s'il s'agit de comptes annuels, qu'ils donnent une image fidèle de la société.

9.1.2. Le contrôle parlementaire

Le contrôle parlementaire est l'une des missions dévolues au Conseil de la Région de Bruxelles-Capitale (également appelé Parlement

---

[36] Région de Bruxelles-Capitale, Ordonnance du 22 novembre 1990, *op. cit.*, art. 27.

bruxellois). En réponse aux questions orales et aux interpellations qui lui sont adressées, que ce soit en séance plénière ou en commission de l'infrastructure, le ministre compétent est amené à se justifier à propos d'un acte politique, à expliquer une situation précise ou à préciser des aspects, spécifiques ou généraux, de la politique du gouvernement dans les matières dont il est responsable. Lorsque les questions ou les interpellations touchent directement aux activités de la STIB, le ministre consulte généralement la direction de la STIB pour apporter les éléments de réponse nécessaires. Dans certains cas particuliers, à propos de dossiers ou de questions sensibles, l'administrateur-directeur général ou certains membres de la direction viennent répondre en personne aux questions posées en commission[37]. Ils n'en ont cependant pas l'obligation puisque, pour rappel, l'administrateur-directeur général et son adjoint ne sont tenus de rendre des comptes que devant le conseil d'administration et le gouvernement. En dépit de l'autonomie de gestion accordée à la STIB, il arrive que, suite à des interpellations des députés[38], le gouvernement, par l'intermédiaire du ministre compétent ou du conseil d'administration, intervienne directement ou indirectement dans la gestion opérationnelle de la société. Cela constitue en quelque sorte un système de régulation « à chaud » : le gouvernement s'intéresse à un problème donné à partir du moment où ses répercussions atteignent la sphère politique (c'est-à-dire que le ministre ou le gouvernement ne peuvent plus l'ignorer). Le problème est alors analysé et traité de façon isolée et ponctuelle, afin de le résoudre le plus rapidement possible.

9.1.3. Les lieux de concertation et de consultation

Au-delà du contrôle exercé par les responsables politiques à travers les organes de gestion de la société ou les débats parlementaires, de nombreux lieux de concertation et de consultation permettent d'impliquer

---

[37] Le 22 juin 2005, Alain Flausch (administrateur-directeur général de la STIB), Christian Dochy (directeur du développement réseau) et Jean-Michel Mary (attaché à la direction développement réseau) ont présenté la restructuration du réseau de surface devant la commission infrastructure et ont répondu aux questions des commissaires (Conseil de la Région de Bruxelles-Capitale, *Projet de Plans tram et bus de la STIB. Rapport fait au nom de la Commission de l'infrastructure, chargée des Travaux publics et des Communications*, 22 juin 2005). Le 22 juin 2011, Alain Flausch a été entendu en commission infrastructure suite à la divulgation dans la presse d'une note interne jugée indélicate par bon nombre de députés (Sources : *Le Soir*, 23 juin 2011).

[38] En 2009, la diffusion d'un message audio dans les stations de métro invitant les usagers de la STIB à ne pas encourager la mendicité provoque l'indignation d'un grand nombre de députés. Suite aux discussions parlementaires qui s'ensuivirent (en commission des affaires sociales et en commission infrastructure), à la demande de la ministre de tutelle Brigitte Grouwels ou à l'initiative de la STIB, la diffusion du message est interrompue.

dans le processus de décision d'autres acteurs directement concernés par les activités de la STIB. Il s'agit en premier lieu du personnel de la STIB, notamment à travers le conseil d'entreprise et le comité de prévention et de protection au travail. Il s'agit ensuite de Bruxelles Mobilité, l'administration de la Région de Bruxelles-Capitale chargée des équipements et des déplacements, qui assure à la fois un rôle de coordination et de contrôle. Enfin, il s'agit des usagers, dont l'implication dans les décisions était clairement souhaitée par le gouvernement et la STIB elle-même au lendemain de la régionalisation. Cette intention se manifeste en effet dans l'ordonnance du 22 novembre 1990 et se concrétise par la mise en place de la commission régionale de la mobilité, du comité consultatif des usagers, des comités tripartites pour la qualité de service et d'un service de médiation. Ces lieux de concertation et de consultation constituent des opportunités d'amorcer un dialogue en amont des décisions. Ils constituent en quelque sorte des mécanismes de contrôle *a priori*.

La multiplication des lieux de concertation et de consultation témoigne d'une prise en compte croissante par les décideurs des publics destinataires des politiques publiques de transports en commun. Ceux-ci font l'objet d'une certaine attention. Ces lieux ne constituent cependant pas des lieux de décision, mais plutôt des lieux d'expression, où la possibilité est donnée à différents acteurs de la politique de transports d'interpeller les décideurs.

9.1.4. La planification

Depuis la régionalisation et le transfert des compétences en matière de planification, on voit apparaître une multiplication des plans de toutes sortes déclinés thématiquement et géographiquement à partir des deux plans régionaux hiérarchiquement les plus importants, à savoir le Plan régional de développement (PRD), qui définit la stratégie de planification globale du développement du territoire régional, et le Plan régional d'affectation du sol (PRAS), qui est le plan réglementaire définissant l'usage des différentes zones du territoire de la Région.

En matière de mobilité, le Plan Iris constitue le plan stratégique de référence. Il traduit concrètement le volet « déplacements » du Plan régional de développement (PRD) et consigne les objectifs de la Région en matière de mobilité. Il n'a pas de statut réglementaire.

Les deux générations du Plan Iris (les Plans Iris 1 et 2) montrent que le processus d'élaboration dure entre 6 à 8 ans. La réalisation de l'étude, qui fait intervenir une collecte colossale de données et l'élaboration de modèles complexes, n'est évidemment pas immédiate. Mais indépendamment de cela, on observe que le processus de décision politique menant à l'adoption du plan fait l'objet de longues négociations entre les partis de la majorité. L'explication réside notamment dans le fait que le contenu du plan constitue aux yeux des décideurs le champ des possibles[39]. Les projets qui ne s'y retrouvaient pas auraient selon cette logique des difficultés à voir le jour. Le travail de planification tel qu'il est perçu n'intègre pas la possibilité de changer d'avis, de s'adapter à de nouveaux enjeux ou de revenir sur des propositions précédemment écartées.

Ce long processus d'élaboration du plan a des conséquences directes sur le timing de mise en œuvre des mesures préconisées par celui-ci. Au moment où le texte est approuvé et compte tenu de la répercussion du retard enregistré dans l'élaboration du plan, le délai devient d'emblée insuffisant pour mettre en œuvre toutes les mesures nécessaires à l'atteinte des objectifs fixés à l'horizon déterminé. De plus, la mise en œuvre de certaines mesures préconisées ne dépend pas directement de la volonté de la Région. C'est par exemple le cas du développement du réseau RER ou de la mise en œuvre des plans communaux de mobilité. Enfin, compte tenu du caractère ambitieux des plans et des moyens budgétaires limités, la Région ne peut procéder que par arbitrages successifs dans l'hypothèse où elle ne peut trouver de sources de financement complémentaires.

Pour tenter de pallier ces problèmes de mise en œuvre, le Plan Iris 2 lui-même prévoit l'amélioration de la gouvernance du plan par la création au sein de l'administration d'organes *ad hoc* chargés de piloter la mise en œuvre du plan, une plus grande implication et coordination des acteurs, une mise en cohérence des différents plans régionaux et autres textes de référence avec le Plan Iris, etc.[40] En outre, dans le cadre de la mise en œuvre de la sixième réforme institutionnelle de l'État, le gouvernement de la Région de Bruxelles-Capitale a approuvé le 26 juillet 2013 une ordonnance instituant un Plan régional de mobilité (PRM) qui s'impose à tous, y compris aux communes, sans qu'il puisse y être dérogé[41]. Le but affiché est d'assurer sur l'ensemble du territoire régional et entre les communes la cohérence et la coordination des politiques de mobilité. Nous y reviendrons plus loin.

---

[39] Tellier, C., *Corps technique et techniques du corps. Sociologie des ingénieurs du souterrain bruxellois (1950-2010)*, thèse de doctorat en sciences sociales et politiques, Bruxelles, Université Libre de Bruxelles, 2012, in Hubert, M., Lebrun, K., Huynen, P., Dobruszkes, F., *op. cit.*, p. 16.

[40] Région de Bruxelles-Capitale, *IRIS 2. Plan de mobilité de la Région de Bruxelles-Capitale*, Bruxelles Mobilité-AED de la Région de Bruxelles-Capitale, 2011, p. 135.

[41] Conseil de la Région de Bruxelles-Capitale, Ordonnance du 26 juillet 2013 instituant un cadre en matière de planification de la mobilité et modifiant diverses dispositions ayant un impact en matière de mobilité, *Moniteur belge*, 3 septembre 2013.

9.1.5. La contractualisation

La STIB est le premier organisme para-régional à avoir conclu un contrat de gestion avec la Région bruxelloise. Depuis, la procédure s'est généralisée et systématisée, tant dans le domaine des transports comme dans beaucoup d'autres domaines de l'action publique en Belgique. Les autorités et les opérateurs de transport public en sont aujourd'hui à leur cinquième génération de contrats. Le contrat de gestion est négocié entre les parties, précisant les droits et les devoirs de chacune des parties en matière de politique de transports publics à Bruxelles. Outre les objectifs imposés aux parties, le contrat de gestion fixe également les principes relatifs à la construction et à la transformation du réseau, le plan d'investissement, l'ampleur des subsides, la régulation des tarifs et les bénéfices ou les sanctions qui sont fonction du respect des objectifs. Chaque année, un plan d'entreprise est établi, destiné à assurer la réalisation effective du contrat. Le suivi des engagements et des obligations établis dans le cadre du contrat de gestion est confié à un comité de suivi composé des délégués du ministre chargé des Transports publics, de Bruxelles Mobilité et de la STIB.

En analysant le contenu des différentes générations de contrat de gestion, on remarque que ceux-ci ont évolué, témoignant sans doute d'une plus grande maîtrise de l'outil et d'un apprentissage par l'expérience. Les contrats de gestion de première génération visent à recadrer la relation entre les co-contractants, les responsabilités de chacun et les objectifs à atteindre. Les contrats de gestion de troisième et de quatrième génération apportent leur lot de nouveautés[42]. Ils introduisent en effet un mécanisme de récompenses/sanctions appliqué en fonction du degré de réalisation des objectifs. Ce mécanisme couvre un nombre limité d'objectifs et le montant des bonus/malus ne dépasse pas 2 % de l'ensemble des subsides alloués à la STIB. Cela provient sans doute de la difficulté de définir et d'évaluer la part de responsabilités de l'opérateur dans les résultats, mais aussi du caractère potentiellement imprévisible de l'impact budgétaire des incitants, s'ils venaient à être conséquents, sur les finances des autorités publiques[43].

L'analyse du processus d'élaboration des contrats montre également certaines évolutions. La première génération de contrats correspond à une logique de conquête de la Région, désireuse d'imposer son autorité dont

---

[42] Voir Lauwers, K., Colla, O., « De contractuele relaties tussen Brussels Hoofdstedelijk Gewest en de MIVB », *Cahier de Sciences Administratives*, Larcier, Bruxelles, 2007, p. 34.

[43] Mattijs, J., « Belgique, terre des contrats : contexte managérial, juridique et économie politique du mouvement de contractualisation », in *Cahier de Sciences Administratives*, Larcier, Bruxelles, 2007, p. 15.

la légitimité était encore fort récente. Cela explique pourquoi le premier contrat de gestion a été rédigé par la Région de manière quasi unilatérale. L'intervention de la STIB plus tôt dans le processus d'élaboration des contrats suivants[44] s'explique sans doute par sa volonté de faire partager à la Région sa vision tactique et stratégique de la politique de mobilité à Bruxelles.

De plus, entre le projet de contrat et la signature, les négociations semblent prendre de plus en plus de temps, de sorte qu'il est maintenant devenu la règle de proroger d'un an le contrat en cours avant d'arriver à un accord sur le contrat suivant. Si certains articles constituent des passages « obligés » (objet et périmètre du contrat, rôle et objectifs des parties, etc.), chaque nouveau contrat est cependant différent du précédent. De nouvelles dispositions sont ajoutées (notamment pour tenir compte de l'évolution de la législation), les mécanismes de financement se perfectionnent et se diversifient, les missions se complexifient, etc. Les négociations entre les partis de la majorité, sous forme de réunions inter-cabinet, portent essentiellement sur le montant des investissements et les projets de développement du réseau à inscrire dans le contrat. De la même manière que pour l'élaboration du plan régional de mobilité, une partie de l'explication réside dans le fait que le contenu du contrat constitue aux yeux des décideurs le champ des possibles. Il importe donc que les projets jugés essentiels pour une famille politique apparaissent dans le contrat, même s'ils ne sont garantis ni en termes de financement, ni en termes de calendrier.

Enfin, il n'est probablement pas inutile de préciser que, de manière générale, le contrat de gestion conclu entre l'autorité de tutelle et l'organisme d'intérêt public ne constitue pas en Belgique un contrat de droit commun régi par le Code civil. Il s'agit en effet

> D'un instrument de gestion créateur de normes juridiques contraignantes mais dont la nature ne peut être rangée dans une catégorie d'acte juridique classique. Il s'agirait en quelque sorte d'un contrat (…) mais de type administratif (…) et dont les sanctions en cas de non-respect de ses clauses ne sont pas forcément judiciaires mais administratives et/ou financières[45].

Si sa nature ne permet pas de le classer dans la catégorie des contrats de droit commun, il n'est pas pour autant dénué de tout effet contraignant.

---

[44] Burhin, F., « Contrat de gestion en Région de Bruxelles-Capitale : dernière génération », in Huygens, Ch. (coord.), « Les contrats de gestion : un facteur de performance pour les entreprises publiques de la Région de Bruxelles-Capitale ? », *Cahier de Sciences Administratives*, n° 12/2007, Bruxelles, Larcier, 2007, p. 30.

[45] Mareschal, M., *Les contrats de gestion en Belgique, exemple d'une déjuridicisation*, Contribution au séminaire de droit public « L'État doit-il être efficace ? », ULg, 18 septembre 2009, disponible sur Internet : http://dev.ulb.ac.be/droitpublic/fileadmin/telecharger/theme_3/contributions/MARESCHAL-3-20090803.pdf.

Le processus organisant le dialogue entre l'entreprise et sa tutelle prime sur la valeur légale du contrat. Il oblige en effet les deux parties à présenter des objectifs et des politiques cohérents, à discuter sur la base de ceux-ci et à s'engager publiquement. Cet accord oblige chacune des parties à avoir une attitude réfléchie et cohérente avec la rationalité économique. De par sa nature, il constitue un instrument organisationnel de régulation. Par les garanties qu'il apporte, son bénéfice est réel pour les deux parties : pour la Région, car elle assure de la sorte le développement d'une politique de transports en commun inscrite dans la durée, et pour la STIB, car elle diminue l'incertitude financière à laquelle elle peut être confrontée.

9.2. L'intervention de la STIB dans la sphère stratégique

Les modes théoriques d'organisation du marché des transports publics locaux font généralement état de différents niveaux de décision bien distincts, dont la responsabilité incombe soit à l'autorité de tutelle, soit à l'opérateur. Ces niveaux de responsabilité se différencient eux-mêmes par le type et la portée des décisions[46]. Il s'agit des niveaux stratégiques, tactiques et opérationnels, tels qu'illustrés dans la figure 2 ci-dessous.

En pratique, les décisions se rapportant à un thème ne sont pas toujours attribuées en totalité à un seul acteur et des glissements sont apparus par rapport aux intentions du départ. On observe par exemple l'immixtion, tantôt ponctuelle, tantôt durable, de la STIB à des niveaux qui ne sont initialement pas les siens. Ainsi, la STIB a partiellement investi le champ de la stratégie. La Région est quant à elle associée aux décisions tactiques concernant les tarifs, les itinéraires et le choix de la flotte de véhicules. Seul le niveau opérationnel semble être entièrement de la responsabilité de la STIB.

Les glissements de responsabilité peuvent être observés à plusieurs niveaux. En ce qui concerne les tarifs par exemple, le premier contrat de gestion indique que la STIB définit la politique tarifaire à condition que l'augmentation globale, qui ne peut avoir lieu qu'une seule fois par an, ne dépasse l'évolution de l'indice des prix à la consommation. Ils sont par ailleurs soumis à l'accord préalable du gouvernement. À partir du troisième contrat de gestion, la STIB se voit accorder une plus grande autonomie dans la fixation de ses tarifs puisqu'elle est autorisée à les augmenter jusqu'à 2 % au-dessus de l'évolution de l'indice des prix à la consommation. De surcroît, ceux-ci sont dorénavant le plus souvent automatiquement acceptés par la Région.

---

[46] Coppe, A., Gautier, A., « Régulation et concurrence dans le transport collectif urbain », *Reflets et perspectives de la vie économique*, 43(4), 2004, p. 66.

Figure 4. Les différents niveaux de responsabilité dans l'organisation des Transports publics[47]

Niveau de responsabilité	Description générale	Décisions	
STRATÉGIQUE Long terme	*Que veut-on réaliser ?*	**Objectifs généraux** • Politique des transports • Parts de marché • Profitabilité/budget	
TACTIQUE Moyen terme	*Quels sont les services qui permettront d'atteindre les objectifs ?*	**Caractéristiques détaillées des services** • Tarifs • Routes • Véhicules	• Horaires • Fréquences
OPÉRATIONNEL Court terme	*Comment produire ces services ?*	**Ventes** • Activités de vente • Information au public	**Production** • Gestion de l'infrastructure • Maintenance du matériel • Recrutement et gestion du personnel

Le fait le plus marquant est probablement celui lié à l'évolution du rôle accordé par la Région à l'opérateur. De pur exploitant, rôle désiré à l'origine par les pouvoirs publics, la STIB se voit offrir de plus en plus de responsabilités dans la sphère stratégique, dont les objectifs sont théoriquement exclusivement définis par la Région au travers de l'ordonnance, du cahier des charges, du Plan Iris, du contrat de gestion et des orientations du gouvernement.

En 2001, la Région de Bruxelles-Capitale accorde en effet à la STIB « un pouvoir de proposition » et l'invite à « un devoir de participation et de conseil » en matière de stratégie régionale de mobilité pour les aspects qui concernent le transport public urbain et le bouquet de services y associé[48]. La note d'orientation relative au contrat de gestion 2001-2005[49] appelle la STIB à se substituer peu à peu au rôle de la Région dans sa tâche

---

[47] Adapté de Van de Velde, D. *et al.*, « Contracting in urban public transport », Amsterdam, European Commission – DG TREN, p. 32.

[48] Gouvernement de la Région Bruxelles-Capitale et STIB, *Contrat de gestion 2001-2005 entre la Région de Bruxelles-Capitale et la STIB*, Bruxelles, 2001, p. 95.

[49] Note d'orientation relative au contrat de gestion STIB 2001-2005 adoptée par le gouvernement de la Région de Bruxelles-Capitale le 20 juillet 2000.

de planification tactique et, à terme, à évoluer vers une entité chargée de l'encadrement des entités productrices, dont certaines pourraient être externes à la société régionale.

Cette évolution est à remettre dans le contexte de l'évolution de la réglementation européenne. Le moment coïncide en effet avec la volonté de la Commission européenne d'ouvrir radicalement le secteur à la concurrence. En confiant à la STIB un rôle stratégique, la Région parvient à faire de l'entreprise publique un acteur incontournable à Bruxelles et conforte ainsi sa position d'opérateur exclusif dans un contexte de marché en cours de libéralisation.

L'implication de la STIB à différents niveaux de la politique régionale pose question compte tenu de la rente informationnelle dont l'entreprise dispose. Cette situation est d'ailleurs à l'origine de nombreux débats entre les élus politiques, qui relancent régulièrement la question de la confiance envers l'opérateur ou celle de son allégeance envers l'autorité de tutelle. La Région est néanmoins soucieuse de ne pas se laisser imposer n'importe quelles conditions par la STIB. Le dernier contrat de gestion 2013-2017 tente à cet effet de renforcer le rôle du comité stratégique constitué en 2001. Celui-ci est composé de huit membres distribués paritairement : quatre représentants de la Région et quatre représentants de la STIB. Ce comité stratégique de haut niveau constitue l'instance de coordination entre la STIB et Bruxelles Mobilité pour les études stratégiques et tactiques ayant un impact sur les transports publics ainsi que pour les investissements dans les infrastructures de transports publics. Par ailleurs, il a été décidé de renforcer la Direction Stratégie de Bruxelles Mobilité par l'engagement de personnel nouveau et par l'attribution de nouvelles missions et de nouveaux outils de *monitoring*. Enfin, la Région s'appuie, lorsqu'elle l'estime nécessaire, sur l'expertise de bureaux d'étude qu'elle mobilise, comme nous l'avons vu, notamment pour la confection du plan régional de mobilité.

10. Conclusions

Dès la création de la Région de Bruxelles-Capitale en 1990, le gouvernement bruxellois affichait deux finalités bien distinctes en matière de politique de transports en commun : (1) donner la priorité aux transports publics en vue de contribuer à l'amélioration de la qualité de vie en ville et (2) promouvoir une utilisation efficace et équilibrée des transports publics à l'échelon régional compte tenu des ressources disponibles. L'étude des données statistiques montre à cet effet un net renversement des tendances observées par rapport à la période précédant la régionalisation. L'augmentation de la fréquentation a littéralement explosé à partir des années 2000 et la dette de l'opérateur a été réduite de 75 %, diminuant ainsi le risque que représente l'opérateur pour les finances régionales.

Une analyse plus fouillée des résultats montre que tout n'est cependant pas parfait. L'offre exprimée en termes de kilomètres-convois n'a augmenté que de 3,9 % et la vitesse commerciale diminue un peu plus chaque année. Tout semble montrer que la priorité ait été donnée à une gestion plus efficace des ressources dont dispose la STIB, en laissant secondaire l'objectif de garantir aux Bruxellois un droit universel à la mobilité. Le développement du réseau s'est fait à un rythme lent et modéré, témoignant sans doute par là de l'héritage d'un maillage déjà relativement bien développé au moment de la régionalisation. L'analyse a également montré que la forte augmentation de la fréquentation est davantage attribuable aux actions et aux mesures d'accompagnement réalisées par la Région, ainsi qu'à des facteurs externes (coût du pétrole, conscientisation croissante, phénomènes démographiques, etc.) qu'à un effet d'induction des actions menées par la STIB. Le mérite de la STIB relève néanmoins de sa capacité à avoir pu absorber le surplus de la demande par l'achat, avec le financement de la Région, de nouveaux véhicules plus capacitaires tout en maintenant la qualité des services à des niveaux acceptables. Le plus grand mérite de la STIB tient sans doute au fait qu'elle ait pu maîtriser sa gestion financière en réduisant radicalement son endettement et en augmentant de manière substantielle le taux de couverture. Elle a pu y arriver en s'appropriant pleinement l'autonomie que lui a accordée la Région en matière de gestion et de politique tarifaire.

Avec la régionalisation, le mode de régulation des transports publics a profondément été modifié. Le choix a été fait de garder l'opérateur dans le giron public et d'en faire une entreprise « *in house* » régulée par le biais du contrat de gestion. Si son caractère réellement incitatif peut être mis en doute et si sa nature ne lui confère pas de force juridique au sens du droit commun, nous avons vu que le contrat de gestion n'était pas pour autant dénué de tout effet contraignant. Le processus organisant le dialogue entre l'entreprise et sa tutelle oblige les deux parties à présenter des objectifs et des politiques cohérents, à discuter sur la base de ceux-ci et à s'engager publiquement. Cette étude de cas nous apporte ceci d'intéressant que par les garanties que le contrat apporte, son bénéfice est réel pour les deux parties : pour la Région, car elle assure de la sorte le développement d'une politique de transports en commun inscrit dans la durée, et pour la STIB, car elle diminue l'incertitude financière à laquelle elle peut être confrontée. La contractualisation a en outre permis une clarification des rôles à un moment où la Région ne disposait que de peu de légitimité.

Une autre leçon intéressante se dégage de cette étude : l'analyse du processus décisionnel a montré que, malgré un cadre strict répartissant les responsabilités de chacun, les décisions étaient rarement prises par un seul acteur et que de nombreux dossiers étaient traités de concert. Indépendamment des textes réglementaires, le périmètre d'action des acteurs n'est pas totalement figé, ni dans l'espace, ni dans le temps. La perspective de la libéralisation du secteur et l'expertise manifeste développée par la STIB ont en effet mené à une intervention de plus en plus marquée de l'exploitant dans la sphère stratégique. Face à cet état de fait, par ailleurs initié par la Région, l'autorité régionale tente aujourd'hui de rééquilibrer le rapport de force. Cette réalité réfute la conception classique qui verrait le pouvoir politique exercer ses fonctions en toute indépendance, et l'opérateur disposer de prérogatives uniquement dans les limites concédées ou tolérées par l'autorité de tutelle. Cette vision semble en effet peu réaliste et purement formelle.

Enfin, une des clés de la bonne collaboration entre l'autorité organisatrice et l'opérateur réside dans leur intérêt commun à travailler ensemble. À la lecture du cas présenté ici, la Région et la STIB semblent être, en effet, liées par une destinée commune. Les décisions du gouvernement (fiscalité, financement, aménagement des voiries, etc.) ont un impact évident sur les résultats de l'exploitant. L'expression d'un fort intérêt politique pour les transports collectifs et la mobilisation de ressources financières conséquentes ne peuvent qu'inciter l'opérateur à s'impliquer en prenant acte des priorités régionales. Inversement, les responsables politiques doivent montrer qu'ils agissent efficacement par le biais de l'institution qu'ils dirigent. Les transports publics sont une compétence visible, touchant aux préoccupations concrètes et quotidiennes de nombreux usagers-citoyens. La mise en circulation de matériels neufs, l'information aux voyageurs, l'accessibilité pour les PMR, etc. participent aux politiques « d'image ». L'interdépendance entre les actions de la Région et celles de la STIB implique des pratiques que l'on peut qualifier de partenariales. Dans le cas qui nous occupe, la convergence des intérêts n'est ni naturelle ni automatique : elle est construite. Cette construction se déroule à plusieurs niveaux au sein d'un système complexe faisant intervenir une multitude d'acteurs dont l'analyse n'a pu rendre compte qu'imparfaitement.

Bibliographie

Commission des communautés européennes, *Les services d'intérêt général en Europe*, COM(2000) 580 final, 20 septembre 2000.

Commission européenne, Proposition de règlement du Parlement européen et du Conseil relatif à l'action des États membres en matière d'exigences de service public et à l'attribution de contrats de service public dans le domaine des transports de voyageurs par chemin de fer, par route et par voie navigable [COM(2000) 0007 final, 26 juillet 2000], in *Journal officiel de l'Union européenne*, C 365E, 19 décembre 2000, pp. 169-178.

Conseil de la Région de Bruxelles-Capitale, Cahier des charges de la STIB du 18 juillet 1996, in *Moniteur Belge*, 24 septembre 1996.

Conseil de la Région de Bruxelles-Capitale, Ordonnance du 26 juillet 2013 instituant un cadre en matière de planification de la mobilité et modifiant diverses dispositions ayant un impact en matière de mobilité, *Moniteur belge*, 3 septembre 2013.

Conseil de la Région de Bruxelles-Capitale, *Projet d'ordonnance relatif à l'organisation des transports en commun dans la Région de Bruxelles-Capitale. Rapport fait au nom de la Commission Infrastructure, chargée des travaux publics et des communications*, A-71/2-90/91, 7 octobre 1990.

Conseil de la Région de Bruxelles-Capitale, *Projet de Plans tram et bus de la STIB. Rapport fait au nom de la Commission de l'Infrastructure, chargée des Travaux publics et des Communications*, 22 juin 2005.

Coppe, A., Gautier, A., « Régulation et concurrence dans le transport collectif urbain », in *Reflets et perspectives de la vie économique*, vol. 43, n° 4, 2004.

Corijn, E., Vloeberghs, E., *Bruxelles !*, VUB Press, Cahiers urbains, 2009, p. 325.

Courtois, X., Dobruszkes, F., « L'(in)efficacité des trams et bus à Bruxelles : une analyse désagrégée », in *Brussels Studies*, n° 20, 2008, p. 25.

De Sadeleer, N., Martens, M., « La mobilité à la croisée des droits », in Castaigne, M., Hubert, J.-P. *et al.*, *Droit et mobilité*, Actes du Colloque du 18 octobre 2002, Presses universitaires de Namur, 2003, p. 58.

De Schrijver, M., Voogt, F., « Stib : le bus a reculé en 2013, le tram et le métro ont patiné », in *Le Soir*, 13 janvier 2014.

Decreet van 20 april 2001 betreffendede organisatie van hetpersonenvervoer over de weg en de oprichting van de Mobiliteitsraad van Vlaanderen, *Moniteur Belge*, 21 août 2001.

Dobruszkes, F. *et al.*, « Réorganisation d'un réseau de transport collectif urbain, ruptures de charge et mobilités éprouvantes : l'expérience bruxelloise », in *Journal of Urban Research*, 7, 2011, p. 16.

Dreyfus, M., « Subsidiarité et service public européen sous l'éclairage des transports publics locaux », in Potvin-Solis, L. (dir.), *Les effets du droit de l'Union européenne sur les compétences des collectivités territoriales*, L'Harmattan, coll. Grale, Paris, 2013, pp. 363-389.

Goethals, C., *Relation entre l'opérateur de transport public à Bruxelles (STIB) et l'autorité organisatrice : entre asymétrie et coopération*, CIRIEC, Working Paper n° 2014/06, 2014.

Gouvernement de la Région Bruxelles-Capitale et STIB, *Contrat de gestion 2007-2011 entre la Région de Bruxelles-Capitale et la STIB*, Bruxelles, 2007, p. 75.

Gouvernement de la Région Bruxelles-Capitale et STIB, *Contrat de gestion 2001-2005 entre la Région de Bruxelles-Capitale et la STIB*, Bruxelles, 2001, p. 95.

Gouvernement de la Région Bruxelles-Capitale et STIB, *Rapport quinquennal du contrat de gestion 2001-2005 : Cinq ans d'amélioration des transports publics à Bruxelles*, Bruxelles, 2006.

Gouvernement de la Région de Bruxelles-Capitale, *Déclaration de politique générale de l'Exécutif présentée au Conseil Régional*, 18 octobre 1989.

Gouvernement de la Région de Bruxelles-Capitale, *Exposé préliminaire du contrat de gestion 1991-1994 approuvé par l'Exécutif de la Région de Bruxelles-Capitale*, 25 octobre 1990.

Gouvernement de la Région de Bruxelles-Capitale, *Note d'orientation relative au contrat de gestion STIB 2001-2005*, 20 juillet 2000.

Hubert, M., Dobruszkes, F., Macharis, C., « États généraux de Bruxelles. La mobilité à, de, vers et autour de Bruxelles », in *Brussels Studies*, Note n° 1, 5 janvier 2008, p. 15.

Hubert, M., Lebrun, K., Huynen, P., Dobruszkes, F., « Note de synthèse BSI. La mobilité quotidienne à Bruxelles : défis, outils et chantiers prioritaires », in *Brussels Studies*, n° 71, 18 septembre 2013, p. 29.

Huygens, Ch. (coord.), « Les contrats de gestion : un facteur de performance pour les entreprises publiques de la Région de Bruxelles-Capitale ? », in *Cahier de Sciences Administratives*, n° 12/2007, Bruxelles, Larcier, 2007, p. 125.

Lauwers, K., Colla, O., « De contractuele relaties tussen Brussels Hoofdstedelijk Gewest en de MIVB », in Huygens, Ch. (coord.), « Les contrats de gestion : un facteur de performance pour les entreprises publiques de la Région de Bruxelles-Capitale ? », *Cahier de Sciences Administratives*, n° 12/2007, Bruxelles, Larcier, 2007, pp. 25-37.

Lebrun, K., Hubert, M., Huynen, P., De Witte, A. *et al.*, *Les pratiques de déplacement à Bruxelles*, Cahiers de l'Observatoire de la mobilité de la Région de Bruxelles-Capitale, p. 112.

Loi du 17 juin 1953, art. 3, *Moniteur belge*, 21 juin 1953. Loi spéciale de réformes institutionnelles du 8 août 1980 modifiée par la loi spéciale du 8 août 1988, *Moniteur belge*, 15 août 1980.

Mareschal, M., *Les contrats de gestion en Belgique, exemple d'une déjuridicisation*, Contribution au séminaire de droit public « L'État doit il être efficace ? », ULg 18 septembre 2009.

Mattijs, J., « Belgique, terre des contrats : contexte managérial, juridique et économie politique du mouvement de contractualisation », in Huygens, Ch.

(coord.), « Les contrats de gestion : un facteur de performance pour les entreprises publiques de la Région de Bruxelles-Capitale ? », *Cahier de Sciences Administratives*, n° 12/2007, Bruxelles, Larcier, 2007, pp. 11-24.

Pflieger, G., *Entre échelle locale et communautaire, les nouvelles régulations croisées des politiques de transports urbains*, Section thématique 12.1. Regard critique : le local comme objet global ?, Congrès AFSP, 2009, p. 15.

PWC, *Rapport quinquennal sur l'exécution du contrat de gestion 2007-2011 liant la Région de Bruxelles-Capitale et la STIB*, Bruxelles, 2011.

Région de Bruxelles-Capitale, *IRIS 2. Plan de mobilité de la Région de Bruxelles-Capitale*, Bruxelles, Bruxelles Mobilité-AED de la Région de Bruxelles-Capitale, 2011, p. 146.

Région de Bruxelles-Capitale, Ordonnance du 22 novembre 1990 relative à l'organisation des transports en commun dans la Région de Bruxelles-Capitale, *Moniteur belge*, 28 novembre 1990. Règlement (CE) n° 1370/2007 du Parlement européen et du Conseil du 23 octobre 2007 relatif aux services publics de transport de voyageurs par chemin de fer et par route, et abrogeant les règlements (CEE) n° 1191/69 et (CEE) n° 1107/70 du Conseil, in *Journal officiel de l'Union européenne*, L 315, 3 décembre 2007.

STIB, *Comptes annuels*, 2001.

STIB, *Comptes annuels*, 2002.

STIB, *Comptes annuels*, 2003.

STIB, *Comptes annuels*, 2004.

STIB, *Comptes annuels*, 2005.

STIB, *Comptes annuels*, 2006.

STIB, *Comptes annuels*, 2007.

STIB, *Comptes annuels*, 2008.

STIB, *Comptes annuels*, 2009.

STIB, *Comptes annuels*, 2010.

STIB, *Comptes annuels*, 2011.

STIB, *Comptes annuels*, 2012.

STIB, *Rapport d'activités*, 1992.

STIB, *Rapport d'activités*, 2006.

STIB, *Rapport d'activités*, 2007.

STIB, *Rapport d'activités*, 2008.

STIB, *Rapport d'activités*, 2009.

STIB, *Rapport d'activités*, 2010.

STIB, *Rapport d'activités*, 2011.

STIB, *Rapport d'activités*, 2012.

STIB, *STIB 2020 : Visions d'avenir pour le transport public urbain à Bruxelles*, Bruxelles, 2004.

Stratec, *Étude d'organisation, de gestion et de commercialisation de la S.T.I.B.*, Rapport de synthèse, Bruxelles, 1987.

Tellier, C., Sacco, M., *La régionalisation de Bruxelles à l'épreuve de la contractualisation. Vers de nouvelles manières de gouverner la ville ?*, Acte du XLVI colloque de l'ASRDLF des 6, 7 et 8 juillet 2009 à Clermont-Ferrand.

Thiry, B., Tulkens, H., *La performance économique des sociétés de transports urbains*, CIRIEC, 1988.

Van de Velde, D. *et al.*, *Contracting in urban public transport*, European Commission – DG TREN, Amsterdam, 2008.

Vandenbulcke, G., *Accessibility indicators to places and transports*, Final Report, recherche effectuée dans le cadre du programme « Action en soutien aux priorités stratégiques de l'autorité fédérale » mis en œuvre et financé par le SPP Politique scientifique, en appui à la politique du SPF Mobilité et Transports, 2007.

Vincent, P., *Benchmarking and Quality Management in Public Transport*, PORTAL teaching material, 2003, p. 69.

Annexe 1

Figure 5. Nombre de véhicules-km parcourus par les véhicules de la STIB

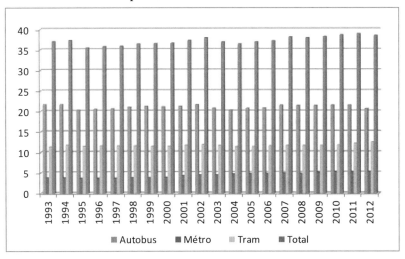

Sources : STIB.

Figure 6. Évolution du parc de la STIB – Indice 100 = 1991

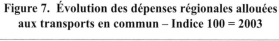

Sources : STIB.

**Figure 7. Évolution des dépenses régionales allouées
aux transports en commun – Indice 100 = 2003**

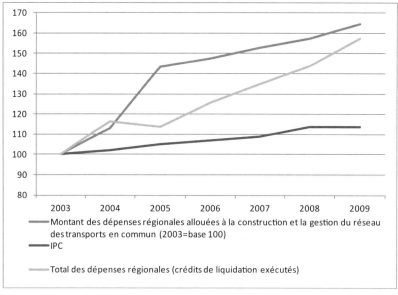

Sources : STIB.

Figure 8. Part des dépenses régionales allouée aux transports en commun

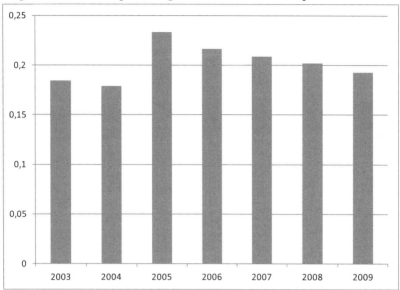

Sources : STIB.

Figure 9. Satisfaction des usagers des transports en commun à Bruxelles

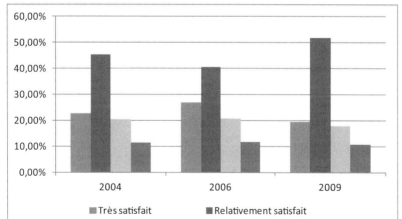

Sources : Eurostat – Urban Audit – Perception Survey.

8. Dire Straits Ahead

British Columbia Ferries, 1985-2014

Malcolm G. BIRD

University of Winnipeg

British Columbia Ferry Services Incorporated – BC Ferries – has strived to improve the service it provides to its customers: polite on-board announcements mark each departure, new restaurants, clean bathrooms, travel reservations and even offering vacation packages, are just a few notable examples of tangible efforts to improve the consumer value this public enterprise provides to its users. These operational enhancements accompanied changes to its governance model and its relationship to the Government of British Columbia in an attempt to create a more independent, self-supporting, and "commercially-oriented" public firm. Initiated in 2003, the changes were brought about by a new piece of governing legislation and an externally chosen American CEO, and were partly done in response to a failed attempt to build three high-speed ferries in the late 1990s. But these changes, as we will see, will not alter the fundamental – structural – problems that this firm faces, the most crucial of which is its shrinking user rates – it carries fewer passengers and vehicles today than it did in the early 1990s. Consider, too, the essential character of its services, over one-third of the province's population is dependent on it, and the inherent political nature of allocating such an important, often times, essential service, coupled with inflexible operational costs, extremely high capital costs, and one has a better sense of the challenges that face this public enterprise.

This chapter is an analysis of BC Ferries from 1985 to the present day.[1] Its central premise is that BC Ferries is a public enterprise under

---

[1] This chapter's finding are derived from primary and secondary source materials, but its most critical insights, particularly those pertaining to the political dynamics surrounding its operations, come from 12 personal interviews with senior current and former executives of this Crown and its stakeholder community. The author would like to thank all participants for their time and insights since without their contribution this type of analysis would not be possible, but readers are reminded that all arguments,

a considerable amount of stress. Both it, and its political superior, the Government of British Columbia, are charged with allocating marine transportation services, and the burden of associated costs of provision, in a sector where a private market is unable to provide sufficient levels of service. Several factors are of note. User rates of passengers and vehicles have been in decline for over twenty years, due largely to a host of structural factors beyond this firm's control. Its operational costs, not surprisingly, have grown considerably over this time and are both relatively high and inflexible, given stringent maritime regulations and an organised work force, for instance. Further complicating the matter is that both its costs and service levels are highly politically salient issues for the public at large as well as the Government since it provides an essential service to over one third of the province's population, and is an organisation with a high popular familiarity and visibility. Both its public ownership and its monopoly position providing coastal ferry services, as will be explained, is the only politically viable option for the province, but such an institutional arrangement means that it is the Government left to balance competing interests in this sector, most notably, between raising fares, offloading costs onto users, or conversely, providing a subsidy from the public coffers, offloading costs onto all BC residents. This is the central trade off that is at the heart of all of the political and policy dynamics that surround this public firm.

In terms of its evolution, this chapter will argue that BC Ferries was created to expand the province's infrastructure and that a market mechanism was unable to provide adequate levels of service to achieve this task. Built for the political purpose to ensure adequate levels of service, significant Government control over its affairs was to be expected, however, over the course of its 54 year lifecycle, we have witnessed a gradual decline in the level of direct political control over its business operations. Ostensibly, such a division was formalised when in 2003 the Government revamped the governance arrangement of this firm by enacting a new piece of legislation that shifted BC Ferries from a Crown corporation to an independent operating entity. The new CEO, David Hahn, also set out to modernise much of its internal operations and focused on improving the customer's experience. While tangible efforts were made to separate this firm from the Government of BC through a revised system of governance and reporting, as well as the use of complex operating contracts, and using an external entity to set fares, these efforts were not, nor are not, able to fully separate this firm, and its

statements, errors, and omissions are the sole responsibility of the author. While this work respects individual anonymity, a complete list of research participants is available from the author, upon request, the author can be reached at: m.bird@uwinnipeg.ca.

operations, from the Government of the day. Declining user rates have further exacerbated its challenges, and exacerbated its need for higher public subsidies and higher fares to meet its operating costs. Despite these efforts to remake this institution and the manner in which it is governed, it is still, for all intents and purposes, dependent on the Government of BC since all pertinent financial and political liabilities lay with decisions made by the Government; these changes in governance and operations, in short, are unable to alter the fundamental economic and political factors that underpin this collective action problem in this province. This new independent model of managing this firm, as will be clear by the end of the chapter, is simply not sustainable and the Government will need to reconsider the current arrangement. Providing ferry service in BC, as the Government knows all too well, is an essential public service that must be provided in a manner little different from other public goods such as highways, universities and the like.

To thoroughly examine this public enterprise, this chapter's first three sections will briefly identify this firm, provide a short history as well as explain its public mission. It will then examine its physical operations, its financial performance, its relationship with the BC Government and the role of the federal Government in terms of regulating its ocean going vessels. Its concluding sections will shed light on the challenges this firm faces, some potential solutions to its problems as well as some additional lessons that can be gleaned from analysing this enterprise. There is a table in the appendix that provides some of its pertinent operational and financial statistics.

Identification

2013 (Financial and operational numbers are stated in 000's)

Head Office	User Rev ($)	Operate Cost ($)	State Subsidy ($)	Capital Cost($)	Employ (2006)
Victoria, BC	576,195	701,557	210,200	96,600	3,406

Ships	Passengers	Vehicles	Routes
35	19,900	7,700	25

BC Ferries is a provider of marine transportation services for passengers and vehicles on Canada's Pacific west coast in the province of British Columbia. It is headquartered in Victoria, British Columbia, Canada and it provides three types of ferry services: its three major routes connect two highways between the Vancouver area, the province's main commercial city on the mainland to Vancouver Island where the capital city, Victoria, is located; second, it provides ferry services to small and remote communities located on both the mainland and small islands in the southern part of the province and finally it provides service to more northern communities and the Queen Charlotte Islands. It has 47 terminals on its 25 routes served by its 35 ships. It receives over \$210 million in subsidies from the public sector which, in addition to \$576 million in revenues, goes towards meeting its \$701 million operating expenses. 19.9 million people used its services in 2013 as it moved over 7.7 million vehicles.

A Short History of BC Ferries

BC Ferries started service in 1960 and was the creation of W.A.C. Bennett's Social Credit Government. First announced in a speech by Premier Bennett on July 17, 1958 when he made public his Government's intentions of building and operating its own ferry service. Ostensibly, his actions were spawned by labour unrest at the two previously operating private firms, American-owned Black Ball Ferries and Montreal-based Canadian Pacific (CP) Ferries, which provided services between Vancouver and Vancouver Island. That summer CP Ferries' workers had been on strike for over two months and the federal Government was unwilling to intervene to end the strike. Its reluctance to act on such a critical matter for a maritime province as British Columbia infuriated Bennett, and when workers at Black Ball threatened a sympathy strike, Bennett invoked the *Civil Defence Act*, which empowered the province to seize the ships and operate them in the event of a strike.[2] While labour unrest, and federal Government's indifference, are the commonly attributed reasons for Bennett's bold actions[3] and that he was reluctant to create this public enterprise, a closer analysis reveals an entirely opposite motivating factor.

Bennett sought to use a public enterprise to provide ferry service since this was the only viable means to provide reliable and effective marine transportation to the citizens of the province. The creation of BC Ferries was one key component of his efforts to engage in "province building"[4] and its creation illustrated his strong belief in the need for the provincial Government to build and maintain transportation infrastructure in order for the province and its people to flourish. Bennett was a very successful businessman before becoming the province's visionary leader from 1951-1971 and, despite discussions – and pleas – with ferry executives for more frequent service and improved terminal infrastructure, they refused his requests. He understood, better than most, that these private firms had no intention of investing capital into their operations, as the costs would

---

[2]   Obee, 2008.
[3]   Mitchell, 1983.
[4]   Black and Cairns, 1966.

simply not be recoverable, let alone a means for maximising profits. The creation of BC Ferries was not a default action, but rather was to be an activist state-owned enterprise, a central component of his post-war reconstruction efforts whereby the provincial Government was to act as a state developer, investing in the province for the benefit of its people and the business community.[5]

In terms of operations, BC Ferries started providing ferry service in June of 1960 with two specifically built ships, MV Tsawwassen and MV Sidney. In its first full-year of service in 1962, BC Ferries carried 2.04 million passengers and 697,000 vehicles.[6] Throughout the 1960s and 1970s, BC Ferries expanded its service area through the development and acquisition of new routes and new vessels, as well as the necessary terminal infrastructure required for such expansion. Rising user rates were characteristic of this time period and by 1969, for instance, it carried 4.77 million passengers and 1.73 million vehicles; ten years later in 1979 those numbers more than doubled with BC Ferries carrying 10.4 million passengers and 3.76 million vehicles.[7] These strong numbers were both the result of and a key factor for further expansion of its services, and corresponding vessels and infrastructure required to meet those demands.

In terms of governance, initially BC Ferries operated as a division of the British Columbia Toll Highways and Bridges Authority and was subject to a relatively high degree of political interference in its business operations. This would include the setting of its schedules and its fares as well as capital expenses in the arenas of building new ships and new terminal infrastructure. Such a fact was both characteristic of Canadian provincial Governments and their Crown appendages for this time period, but might have been also relevant to BC Ferries since its specific purpose was to build transportation infrastructure and marine transit services as part of its role in building the province. Its operations were under the direction of Premier Bennett who was known for his close interest in much of the Government's policies and such a fact is congruent with Canadian provincial Governments where key decision-making power is focused in the Premier's office.[8] There was good reason, in other words, to refer to BC Ferries as "Bennett's Navy". Officially, BC Ferries became a Crown corporation on January 1, 1977 with the introduction of the *British Columbia Ferry Corporation Act 1976* and it thus gave the Crown its own board of directors, an official legislated mandate which, in the abstract, should have made it, and its operations, more independent of the

---

5   Leonard, 2002.
6   British Columbia Ferry Corporation, 1986, p. 32.
7   British Columbia Ferry Corporation, 1986, p. 32.
8   White, 1988.

Government and the Cabinet. But, right up until the 1990s most of the key decisions regarding service levels and especially fares, prior to the introduction of the new 2003 *Act* still lay with Cabinet, and not with the ferry corporation itself. As a number of participants have reported, it also had little capacity to engage in long-term strategic thinking as its capital outlays were covered by the Government in the year they were incurred (much like building a highway) and any annual shortfalls in its budget were covered by the Treasury Board. Correspondingly, any surpluses it generated, it was allowed to keep to fund new capital projects. Such an informal arrangement worked well when user rates were rising and as long as the Government was willing to continue funding its capital needs, but it stymied the corporation's ability to make long-term plans and investments, and became problematic as user rates began to fall.

Also noteworthy, is that in 1985, BC Ferries took over the ferry routes and ships of the Saltwater Branch of the BC Ministry of Transportation and Highways that consisted of a number of short, coastal routes and a number of smaller ferry vessels. The two central points to note regarding its history: First, is that for its initial quarter century from 1960 to 1985, with the exception of one year, BC Ferries enjoyed strong and consistent year-over-year growth in its passenger and vehicle user rates. This helped to keep both its fares and required subsidy amounts relatively low. Second, the creation of this public enterprise was in response to the market's failure to provide adequate service levels and to invest in ferry and terminal infrastructure. The creation of a public enterprise to redress this deficiency meant that it is ultimately the provincial state, through its Crown appendage, that must be the arbitrator that allocates ferry services; it was the political needs of the Government that created this public firm and its fundamentally political character is as pertinent today as it was fifty years ago.

The Public Mission of BC Ferries

The public mission of BC Ferries is relatively straightforward and has changed little over the course of its 54 year lifecycle. Its public mission is stated as: "To provide safe, reliable and efficient marine transportation service which consistently exceed the expectations of our customers, employees and communities, while creating enterprise value".[9] To do this, it operates and manages an ocean going fleet of ferry vessels and terminals to move people, vehicles and the goods they carry around the province of BC in a manner that is as cost effective as possible, dependable and safe. To some extent, it can be considered to be an extension of the highways

---

[9]   British Columbia Ferry Services Inc., 2013.

and road system that forms a central component of any regions' ground transportation infrastructure. In terms of cost effectiveness, its goal is to provide the lowest cost to both ferry users, who pay direct costs via fares, and the BC taxpayers, who pay for ferry services via the provincial and the federal Governments' contributions to its operations.

In order for BC Ferries to be able to provide transportation services it had to build the required infrastructure and vessels to be able to carry out its mandate. Such large-scale public investment created some significant economic activity in terms of direct and indirect jobs and business opportunities. But while these were most welcome positive side effects of such investments, it was not the primary goal of this firm. More specifically, however, BC Ferries is a major component in developing and maintaining a strong BC-based shipbuilding industry employing individuals constructing new ships and refurbishing existing ones. (This is mutually reinforcing since BC Ferries has a vested interest in maintaining a sustainable BC shipbuilding industry and at the same time the work it requires is a catalyst for much of the industry itself). Up until the early 2000s, it was the Government's policy to have all ships built within the province even though this added to the initial upfront cost to the Government for the procurement of ships as when compared to having the same ships built in a foreign shipyard. Governments at the time rationalised slightly higher upfront costs because all of the initial expenditures would be recovered through the increased economic activity and resultant taxes paid by ship workers, for instance, that could be derived from such a project; the so-called multiplier effect of such a project was at least three times its upfront costs. The Liberal Government elected in 2001 ended the buy-BC policy in the aftermath of the failed Fast Ferry Project and the significant political fallout from it, and they did this by ignoring or excluding from the discussion the value of any residual multiplier effects derived from domestic industrial production. Three "Coastal" class ships where built in Germany on fixed price contracts and delivered in 2007 and this was a conscious effort by the Liberal Government to ensure that they were built in a foreign country so that there would be sufficient distance between the Government and the construction of these ships so as to mitigate any potential negative fallout that could emanate from this process.

An additional component of BC Ferries' mission is to provide safe, i.e. incident-free, marine transportation services to the citizens. Obviously such a goal is understandable for any firm, public or private, but it has a particular resonance for a public enterprise such as BC Ferries since it is under a heightened amount of public and media scrutiny, any accidents or incidents are well-publicised in the popular press, for example. Finally, like all public firms, a key part of its mandate is to not bring any unneeded

261

or unnecessary attention to its operations, particularly its relations to its organised workers, into the public sphere.

The Operations of BC Ferries

BC Ferries is a large and complex organisation. In terms of its evolution, the most prominent feature of this firm is that its user rates have stagnated, and in some cases, declined, over the last twenty years. This downward trend, as we will see, is at the root of the problems that face this public enterprise. To provide some context, in 1992 BC Ferries carried 20.52 million passengers and 7.97 million vehicles and to provide service to these customers its total operational cost were $281.1 million and it earned $250.9 million from its operations. It also received $28.5 million in roughly equal proportions from the federal and provincial Governments to cover its operational shortfall and to fund its capital investments; it employed 2,945 full-time individuals. Twenty-one years later in 2013 it carried 19.9 million passengers and 7.7 million vehicles and the cost of providing these services was $701.5 million from which it earned a total of $576.2 million from its operations. From the provincial Government it received $182.1 million and from the federal Government $28.1 million, for a combined total of $210.2 million, to aid in covering its operational expenses, capital costs and service its debt. These numbers, and the policy and political realities that they illustrate, are very significant in the evolution of this public firm. Not surprisingly, this has meant that user fares have had to rise at rates far in excess of inflation: since 2003, for instance, fares on the northern, major and minor routes have increased by 80%, 40% and 70% respectively.[10]

In 2006 (the last year statistics are available), BC Ferries employed 3,406 people and they are represented by The British Columbia Ferry and Marine Workers' Union. They are a relatively militant group of workers, willing to use labour disruptions to improve their contracts, and over the years they have secured strong collective agreements. Aided by the fact that the provincial Government, regardless of its partisan stripe, have been unwilling to permit long work stoppages, and as a result BC Ferries' labour-related cost structure is relatively high and inflexible.

BC Ferries owns and operates 35 vessels, and its fleet is relatively old. While the acquisition of three new large Coastal class of ships in 2007 reduced the age of its ships on major routes from 33 years to 19 years, its small and intermediate vessels that serve on its minor and northern routes have an average age of 36 years.[11] Acquiring ships,

---

[10] Ferry Advisory Committee Chairs, 2011, p. 2.
[11] British Columbia Ferry Service Inc., 2012, p. 38.

not surprisingly, requires considerable resources. Its latest three Coastal class ships cost just over $108 million each when purchased from their German ship builder. Even the smaller ships are expensive to acquire, the Island Sky, for instance, which carries 125 vehicles cost $45.5 million in 2008.[12]

At the core of the challenges facing BC Ferries is its declining user rates and while the reasons for this are difficult to causatively pinpoint, a few are noteworthy. A high Canadian dollar and difficult economic times in the United States, particularly since 2008, have reduced the number of American tourists coming to the province and their use of a ferry to move about.[13] Difficult economic times, more generally, have reduced the number of foreign tourists from other nations and as well as have had an effect on the number of BC residents using the ferry system, particularly for recreational purposes. Changing demographics, population growth (or lack thereof) and land use restrictions, likewise, are also key contributing factors. As populations age, retirees replace daily commuting workers, many of whom when they were working, resided on coastal islands and commuted to larger metropolitan centres for work on daily basis. Restrictive land use development policies which is the official mandate of the Island Trust (a Government appointed regulator of land-use throughout much of the Gulf Islands) has helped to contribute to soaring land values on many coastal communities. This phenomenon has been exacerbated by wealthy individuals purchasing vacation homes on these islands, all of which has reduced the number of young, working families on many of these islands and coastal communities. Full-time residents with children, not surprisingly, are more likely to be regular users of BC Ferries than part-time residents.[14]

Some groups blame rising fares themselves for reducing the number of travellers on BC Ferries,[15] and that ferry consumers, like all consumers, respond through actions to increases in price. As cities on Vancouver Island have grown, they are better able to serve all the needs of their residents, and so there is less incentive to visit the mainland to take advantage of specific services. Structural changes in the trucking industry, coupled with alternative service providers (particularly for commercial operators) as well as a reduction in the number of tour and travel buses using the firm's services, are additional contributing factors to why its numbers have been in a slow and steady decline for the last twenty years. The central point, however, is that BC Ferries' ridership rates are dropping and the causes

---

12 British Columbia Ferry Services Inc., 2008.
13 British Columbia Ferry Services Inc., 2010, p. 32.
14 Vancouver Sun, 2009.
15 Island Trust, 2011.

for the decline are diverse and, for the most part, structural in nature and, therefore, largely out of the control of this public firm.

The Performance of BC Ferries

BC Ferries is not able to fully recover either its operational or capital costs through the revenues that it earns from its operations. It has made efforts to increase its non-tariff revenues over the past ten years, but it is not possible, nor would many argue, desirable, for this to be a self-financing public agency. To cover its shortfalls, it receives an annual subsidy from both the federal and provincial Governments, and carries a significant amount of debt on its own books. In 2013, those amounts were $28.1 million from the federal Government and $182.1 million from the province, totalling 210.2 million, whose contributions served to fill in its operational deficit of $125.3 million and its capital expenditures that same year of $96.6 million. It also carries a significant amount of debt and in 2013 its total liabilities were approximately $1.48 billion of which $1.14 billion was owed in loans, mostly outstanding bonds.[16]

BC Ferries cross subsidises its lower use services from revenues earned from its major routes. For instance, route one from Victoria (Swartz Bay) to Tsawwassen is responsible for 40% of its revenues and route two between Horseshoe Bay and Nanaimo contributes 22% of its total operating revenues. Its two other most popular routes, likewise, contribute an additional 21% to its bottom line.[17] Only routes one and two produce operational positive revenues while the other 23 operate at a loss. Such cross subsidisation is the most critical reason for maintaining the firm in its whole form since without BC Ferries the Government would still be obligated to provide a route-by-route subsidy.

The subsidies to BC Ferries come from two sources. The federal Government provides an annual subsidy to BC Ferries in the form of an annual grant, stemming from a 1977 agreement, which replaced a previous arrangement where the federal Government provided funds directly to private ferry providers and whose routes BC Ferries acquired. Initially, the grant started at $8 million annually and it is indexed to the Consumer Price Index for Vancouver, B.C.[18] The terms of the agreement are set in perpetuity and can only be altered with the mutual consent of both Governments. The grant is a general payment and is not earmarked for a particular purpose. Without this agreement, the federal Government

---

[16] British Columbia Ferry Services Inc., 2013, p. 81.
[17] Coastal Ferry Services Contract, 2003, pp. 1, 7, 12 and 17.
[18] Transport Canada, 2005.

would eliminate the grant entirely since it is in contradiction with its National Marine Policy, and would replace it with targeted funding for meeting the transportation needs of specific remote communities,[19] but it is unable to do so. Its continuation, then, is partly justified by the political need to aid BC Ferries in providing effective and reasonably priced marine transportation services and their partial obligation to aid remote communities.

BC Ferries receives the bulk of its public subsidy from the provincial Government and this amount has grown exponentially over the last twenty years. Such an increase in required revenues not only constitutes a significant financial burden on the Government, but this amount of public funds is at the heart of all discussions regarding all aspects of its operations, principally the setting of fares and schedules and the procurement of capital assets. The amount provided to the firm has grown in absolute and relative terms when compared to both its operational costs and moneys received from the federal Government. In 1994, the province provided BC Ferries with $17.9 million or 49% of its total subsidy, with the remainder, $18.4 million, coming from the federal Government. Both levels of Government in that year provided funding that was equal to 13.1% of the amount the enterprise earned from its users through its operational revenues which totalled $277 million.

In 2013, things looked much different. The provincial subsidy of $182.1 million comprised 87% of the firm's total state subsidy of $210.2 million with the remainder, $28.1 million coming from the federal Government. Public funding was equal to 36.5% of the revenues it earned from its operations which totalled $576.2 million. Recall that the federal subsidy amount is tied to the Vancouver Consumer Price Index, making it a reasonable proxy for inflation, and as such it has grown by approximately 53% since 1994. The provincial subsidy, however, has grown by over 900% during this same time period. Remember too that the system served fewer people: moving 21.5 million passengers and 8.3 million vehicles in 1994 versus 19.9 million passengers and 7.7 million vehicles in 2013; it also had approximately 300 more full-time employees.

Governing BC Ferries

The governance regime of BC Ferries can be divided into two distinctive phases that reflect the evolution of this public firm. The first period started from the time of its inception in 1960 and runs until 2003, and the second phase runs from this year till the present day. Such a sharp demarcation in the evolution of the governance regime of this firm is

---

[19]   Transport Canada, 2005, p. 9.

possible since in 2003 it received a new piece of governing legislation, *The Coastal Ferry Act 2003* that set out to completely overhaul how this enterprise related to both the provincial Government and its citizen customers. Such a fundamental change was an attempt to establish distance between the Government and this Crown entity by reducing the degree of political interference in its operations and to improve its customer focus and the quality of service it provides with the overall goal to turn it into a self-financing commercial entity that would resemble a private firm and would be less dependent on public subsidies. While such a goal may have been a laudable objective for the Government of BC, as we will see, turning BC Ferries into a quasi-independent commercial entity is neither possible nor plausible given the structural challenges it faces and the political significance of its operations.

Before moving forward it is important to examine one particular event, the attempt to build three high-speed catamarans, the Fast Ferries Project (FFP), which was a catalyst for radically altering BC Ferries' governance structure. Please note, however, that there is a major divergence between the public perception and political significance of this project, that it was a complete failure and lead to the reorganisation of this firm, on one hand, and a more empirically focused view of this event currently being conducted by this author whereby it is now coming to light that this project was not a failure due to technical and financial shortcomings, but rather because of both poor political management and blatant political opportunism within the partisan sphere of the province, on the other (see, Newman and Bird, under review). Regardless of the empirical realities of this project, the (mis)perceptions surrounding it helped to reshape the governing structure of this public firm. The acute effects of this project was that it motivated the incoming Liberal Government of Gordon Campbell, who replaced the previous New Democratic Party (NDP) Government, to fundamentally alter the governance structure of this Crown to ensure that such an event would not occur again by insulating the firm from political influence. Such a motivation was derived from the intense political blowback from the overwhelmingly publicised perception that this was deeply troubled project that contributed to ending the NDP's ten-year rule of the province from 1991 to 2001.

The FFP was a project initiated in 1994 to build three high-speed, aluminum-hulled, catamaran vessels that would provide service from the mainland to the mid-point of Vancouver Island (Nanaimo), as well as be a means through which to revitalise the BC ship building industry. It was a plan that was a Government initiative endorsed strongly by Glen Clark, the minister responsible for this Crown, despite objections from BC Ferries' senior management and engineering department. As the Morfitt report later argued: "The decision to proceed with the fast ferries was, we believe, more a ministerial directive than a board decision".[20] The three ferries were delivered late and their costs had more than doubled the original projections, and the reported total cost for the project was $463 million for the three completed ferries. It was argued that the ferries had some significant technical limitations (however, others debate these claims): they were not able to operate at a significantly higher speed than conventional ferries; they used up to twice the fuel of a traditional vessel; they had limited space for commercial vehicles and they were not able to operate out of the Tsawwassen terminal, among other deficiencies. As far as the public and political spheres were concerned, they did not work as promised, and after little debate or thoughtful analysis, they were sold for $19.4 million by the Liberal Government in 2003.[21] At the time and in the terms of popularised perceptions of this project, the FFP was a total and complete policy, fiscal, technical, political, as well as a governance disaster for both BC Ferries and the provincial Government.

The new governance model for BC Ferries was largely motivated by the political fallout from the FFP and the need to further separate this Crown from interference from the political sphere. Fred Wright, summarising the findings of two reports on the project, noted that despite BC Ferries' efforts to implement some of the recommendations of the 1999 Morfitt Report, "BC Ferries remains vulnerable to influence that is inspired by decidedly non-commercial motives", his central recommendation was for the Government to write a new piece of legislation that would enshrine BC Ferries as an independent entity from the Government, with its own a non-partisan board of directors, a clear operational mandate from the provincial Government and would report directly to the legislature and would produce robust annual business plans, among other recommendations.[22] The Liberal Government followed the spirit of these recommendations when it passed the *Coastal Ferry Act 2003* which came into effect on April first of that year.

Prior to the introduction of this new *Act*, BC Ferries' was governed by *The British Columbia Ferry Corporation Act 1977*, and it was a relatively short and vaguely worded piece of legislation that did not have much on the specific operational or governance components of this firm. For instance, the *Act* had no provision for how long a board member could serve nor how the CEO of the Crown corporation was to be selected.[23] This, not surprisingly, meant that these decisions, as well as many of its operational decisions from fares to service levels to capital acquisitions

---

20   Wright, 2001.
21   Stewart, 2008.
22   Wright, 2001, p. 10.
23   Stewart, 2008.

were made by the ruling Government, either by the premier's office or the Cabinet. Such forms of political interference in a firms' operations were typical for this era, but made running a modern firm, particularly one that is facing declining ridership levels, considerably more difficult since they often were extended to include direct political involvement in collective bargaining processes; the creation of fare categories to favour very specific groups of users; irrational discount structures; weak business cases for new routes and under investments in infrastructure, among other problems.[24]

The new governing regime was specifically intended to create a truly independent operating firm that would be insulated from any undue political interference in its operations. To do this, the new governance regime had four major components: an independent ferry authority (The British Columbia Ferry Authority); a commercial operating company (The British Columbia Ferries Services Inc.); an independent regulator (The British Columbia Ferry Commissioner) and a long-term service contract (The Coastal Ferry Services Contract). The general theme of this arrangement is that BC Ferries is now owned and managed by and reports to the BC Ferry Authority, which is regulated by the BC Ferry Commissioner who sets and monitors fares, routes and service levels as they are outlined in the service contract between the provincial Government and BC Ferries.[25] The BC Ferry Authority holds one voting share in BC Ferries which was converted to a commercial company (hence the change from British Columbia Ferry Corporation to British Columbia Ferry Services Incorporated). It is through the use of a holding company that helps to ensure that BC Ferries operates independently from the Government, particularly as it pertains to the selection and composition of its board of directors.[26] It has nine directors, two of whom are appointed by the province, four of which are selected from nominees from communities heavily-dependent on ferry service, two at-large members are appointed by the board and one member is from the union that represents BC Ferries' workers. The members can only be removed by a vote of their fellow board members and they are all limited to two, three-year terms. The board selects one member to be the Chair and it is the authority which is responsible for hiring and evaluating the performance of the CEO of BC Ferries.[27]

Next, the operating company, British Columbia Ferries Service Inc., has its own board of directors which are appointed by the authority. The authority's nine members must "… select individuals in such a

---

[24] British Columbia Ferries Services Inc., 2011, pp. 10-11.
[25] Stewart, 2008, p. 14.
[26] Stewart, 2008, p. 15.
[27] Stewart, 2008, p. 16.

way as to ensure that, as a group, the directors of BCFS are qualified BCFS candidates who hold all of the skills, and all of the experience needed to oversee the operation of BCFS in an efficient and cost effective manner".[28] The *Act* also stipulates that an officer of the company may not be Chair of the board and the CEO cannot be a director on either board. The Government owns 75,000 non-voting shares which entitles it to an annual "dividend" of $6 million from BC Ferries. BC Ferries is now permitted to access private capital via the bond market without the Government's specific approval. It is also worth noting that in 2000, $1.08 billion in BC Ferries debt was assumed by the province[29] and that in 2003 the new firm started its operations with no significant debt. This new governance regime was specifically intended to insulate BC Ferries from direct political interference in its day-to-day operations.

The BC Ferry Commissioner is a quasi-judicial regulatory agency which is comprised of two individuals, the Commissioner and the Deputy-Commissioner, whose central responsibility is to regulate ferry fares of BC Ferries.[30] Its four guiding principles are to balance the interests of ferry users, taxpayers and BC Ferries; encourage a "commercial approach" to BC Ferries; encourage alternative providers of service on ferry routes and finally to encourage innovation without compromising safety. Its other functions are to monitor BC Ferries' adherence to the Coastal Ferry Services Contract, approve capital expenses and handle customer complaints.[31] It issues rulings/decisions and publishes an annual report. In political terms, the function of the Commissioner is to offload difficult and unpopular decisions regarding fares and service levels to an entity that is at arms-length from the ruling Government.

The Coastal Ferry Services Contract (CFSC) is 60-year formal operating agreement between the province and BC Ferries. It is a comprehensive 163 pages document that outlines most of the pertinent components of the relationship between the province and BC Ferries. While under the previous governance regime and the relatively brief *BC Ferries Act 1977* much of the relationship was unspecified and informal, and thus leaving room for politicised interference in the firm's operations; this is an attempt to formalize every aspect of the relationship and to eliminate as much discretion as possible. It reads much like a piece of legislation with general provisos and definitions, and outlines key aspects of BC Ferries' operations, such as: required service levels on designated ferry routes; terminal leases and vessel management; service fees (provincial

---

28 *Coastal Ferries Act*, Section 21.1, 2003.
29 British Columbia Ferry Service Inc., 2001, p. 3.
30 British Columbia Ferry Commissioner, 2013.
31 British Columbia Ferry Commissioner, 2013.

subsidies) and federal subsidies; price caps; processes for "service adjustments" (read: reduction in services) and route discontinuance; service schedules and the requirement of BC Ferries to conduct customer service surveys, among many other key points of BC Ferries' operations. It then goes through each of BC Ferries' 25 routes, providing an overview of the route, specifying service levels (schedules) and complete route-specific vessel information. It provides a comprehensive breakdown of the passenger and vehicle utilization rates, annual demand variations, and a comprehensive outline of pertinent financial information on each route: costs, fare prices, profits, losses and utilization rates and the like. It also includes a listing of major capital expenditures for each route in terms of ship and terminal maintenance and renewal. It is an earnest attempt to both quantify and make public all of the costs of providing ferry service in terms of operational and capital needs of each individual ferry route.

The entire new governance regime, but particularly the operating contract, is an attempt to formalise the relationship between the Government and BC Ferries through the use of quantifiable cost, price and service measurements in a legal document. It is an effort to bring an open and transparent, rational process to the central question that plagues both this enterprise and the BC Government: how to fairly and effectively allocate ferry service? Under a private, market-based system, of course, supply and demand are determined by the market place, but it is much different when it is a monopoly and the one firm is state-owned. Over the first thirty years of its lifecycle when its user rates and operational revenues were rising, it was relatively easy to allocate the ferry service, even though it was a partially politicised process – after all few people complain when more service is provided. With declining user rates and revenues, however, coupled with the political fallout of the FFP, these illustrated to the Government the potential political liabilities emanating from this Crown, particularly those regarding raising fares and reducing service, and thus the need to attempt to distance itself from the operations of BC Ferries. Since its user rates have declined, it has put much more – upward – pressure on fares and has further restricted resources such that it is sometimes necessary to reduce service levels. Both of these are extremely unpopular policies to implement and they cause significant problems for the provincial Government. One way to proactively address this issue is to establish a governance regime whereby culpability for change is distributed amongst a host of non-partisan actors that are guided by a set of rational, and quantifiable policies and procedures in order to further insulate the Government from any potential negative responses to the actions of BC Ferries.

At its core, the *Act* provides a legal framework for the breakup of BC Ferries' operations and the contracting out of its ferry routes. It specifies, for instance, that the terminals are owned by The British Columbia Transportation Financing Authority (section 30), and empowers it to enter into leases with third parties (read: private ferry service providers, section 31). It also has special provisions for private operators of ferry services to use these facilities and even to cross over private property, if need be, in order to fulfil their contractual obligations (section 31). Other provisions allow for the transfer of employees between BC Ferries and potential new providers of ferry services (section 22), and for BC Ferries to establish a refit and maintenance subsidiary (section 23). This is why BC Ferries is rarely mentioned specifically in the *Act* and instead is referred to as a "ferry operator" (even the title of the *Act* itself further reinforces this notion). The goal of the new *Act*, and the new governance regime in general, was to try to establish a system whereby private firms could bid to operate specific ferry routes, while the Government would operate the terminals and regulate the prices, schedules and service levels. Such a regime had all the hallmarks of a "neoliberal" inspired partial-privatisation. Only one route, a small passenger-only route, was contracted out to a private firm (which operates a BC Ferries-owned vessel, however). For a host of economic and political reasons the goals of this *Act* were not, nor could ever be, implemented, the most critical reason being the fact that BC Ferries cross-subsidises almost all of its routes from revenues from its two most popular services that link Vancouver Island to the Mainland.

G: Regulating BC Ferries

While the provincial Government owns and operates BC Ferries, it is the federal Government that dictates the safety regulations that determine minimum staffing levels onboard all of its ships. This is a result of the division of powers sections in Canada's founding piece of legislation, the *British North American Act 1867*, that allocates to the federal Governments all matters concerning "navigation and shipping". The regulations concerning BC Ferries are significant in that they prescribe the minimum number of crew members required to operate a vessels and these requirements are based on the ship operating at 100% of its capacity, even though they rarely operate at full capacity. Staffing levels of new ships that are entering the fleet are also made in in conjunction with BC Ferries' union that, not surprisingly, seeks to have higher numbers of crew members on a ship than BC Ferries' management thinks is an appropriate number. Regardless of how the staffing levels are determined, once they are established, they add considerably to BC Ferries' operating costs and restrict its discretionary decision-making powers in determining the allocation of its labour force. BC Ferries staffing levels when compared to its close American counterpart, Washington State Ferries, are relatively onerous. For instance, two identical ships operating in these two jurisdictions will have significantly different minimum crewing levels: a Canadian mid-sized ferry will require 30 crew members to operate in protected, coastal waters while its American counterpart will only need a staff of 14 to operate in the same sea conditions.[32]

Investing and Financing BC Ferries: Conclusions and Lessons Learned

In competitive markets, dominated by private firms, the state still has responsibilities to ensure that they operate effectively, but the allocation of resources required for the goods and services provided, are not for the state to decide, these are left to the supply and demand curves of the marketplace. But once a collective action problem has been adopted by the public sector, through a public enterprise monopoly, it is the state, and the Government that is charged with running it, that must decide how to allocate scarce resources. This is a difficult task that is fraught with much potential risk of all sorts. The decision to use a publicly owned mechanism to provide ferry services to BC residents was made by Premier Bennett over fifty years ago, and operating BC Ferries has been left to successive Governments ever since. His decision to create BC Ferries thus brought all aspects of its operations, and the allocation of resources in this sector into the political sphere, and no amount of reorganisation of either its operations or how it is governed will change this fundamental reality; it is impossible for both it and the BC Government to escape the politicised nature of its operations.

BC Ferries is under a tremendous amount of pressure and it is seriously constrained in its ability conduct its business. The most basic source of which is that its users demand ferry services and, like most citizens, are unwilling to pay the full cost of its provision and are largely unaware of (and unconcerned with) the full cost for providing it. Its user rates are declining year over year, due to structural factors outside of its control, yet its costs structure is both high and extremely rigid. Its crewing levels are dictated by federal regulators as if its ships are operating at full capacity, which they rarely do. Its workers are unionised, governed by a collective agreement, and are relatively militant which, when combined with the fact that the provincial Government is unwilling to permit any interruptions in ferry service, results in relatively rich collective bargaining settlements. The service that it provides is absolutely essential to over one-third of the province and many of its users are politically cognizant, organised into vocal user and interest groups, as well as being represented on the its political superior's board of directors. It must always adhere to its

---

[32] Roueche, 1976, p. 7.

schedule, even when its ships are woefully under-utilised, and cannot cancel sailings on such grounds. Any service reductions are met with stern and organised resistance. Any fare increases, likewise, are not only well publicized, but are met with intense opposition. Its capital stock, exposed to harsh maritime weather, likewise, is prone to decay and it must maintain all of its terminals and ships to first-rate standards.

The Government's efforts to create an independent commercial entity in 2003 will not alleviate these pressures and, in fact, as BC Ferries continues to acquire debt, it is unable to cover either its operational shortfalls, nor is it able to service its debt load with operational revenues; hence its need for growing revenues from the provincial public purse. Recent attempts to reduce some sailings, introduce gaming on vessels and ending free weekday travel for seniors[33] will not significantly alter its financial bottom line nor resolve the structural problems that it faces. Ultimately, the Government of BC will have to reconsider its current approach of having BC Ferries operate as an independent commercial entity and might have to return this entity to the public utility model where by the Government declares BC Ferries' services to be a public good, provides full funding from the treasury for its capital acquisitions and investments and provides an operational subsidy for its annual shortfalls; much like how highways or universities are presently being supported.

Regardless as to how it is governed, ultimate responsibility and political culpability for its condition lies with the BC Government. This is because it is the Government that determines the subsidy amount to BC Ferries and since its operational revenues are in a relative decline – they are only increasing because fares are rising at rates far in excess of inflation – it is that subsidy amount which determines the fares that individuals pay and the level of service that they receive. Its rigid and high cost structure ensures that this is the case no matter how the governance regime is organised nor how open, transparent, rational, legal and quantifiable are its input costs and output prices. Like many decisions that must be made in this world, they are matters of allocating scarce resources amongst a diverse and never satisfied set of consuming groups. The service contract, the decisions of the Ferry Commissioner on schedules and fares are ultimately beholden to the financial bottom line of BC Ferries, and the provincial Government and the amount of revenue it provides determines that bottom line.

This leaves the Government, and us, with a simple political calculation that occurs annually in the premier's office of British Columbia. It is here where all of the pertinent political considerations come to a nexus and this is where the vast majority of key decisions are made in a Canadian

---

[33] Shaw, 2013.

province. The decision-makers in the premier's office, then, are left to make a difficult political calculation: they must balance the political value of the financial cost that the subsidy imposes on all taxpayers of the province with the political costs associated with the burden that BC Ferries' fares impose on the one-third of the province that are dependent on its services. It is here that the rubber hits the proverbial sea. With a subsidy that has increased over nine folds in twenty years and fares that are rising far in excess of inflation, it is unlikely that anybody will be satisfied with the outcome. Such choices and the evolution of BC Ferries more generally is yet another example of the tough decisions and difficult resolutions to collective action problems that are left in the hands of the state and its publicly owned appendages.

Yet, despite all of the challenges that it faces and the divergent set of interests that are acting on this firm – all making demands on its limited resources – BC ferries continues to provide the province's residents with a safe, secure and consistent level of marine transportation service. (The recent ferry tragedy in South Korea reminds us not to underestimate the importance of technical and professional competency when operating commercial vessels). But, the predicament that BC Ferries faces in general and the plurality of demands made on it also illustrates why state-owned enterprises are such fascinating public policy creatures. They are not merely mandated, like their private sector counterparts, to simply maximise profits, but rather, while financial concerns are always paramount to their operations, they must balance simultaneously a whole host of additional, and sometimes outright conflicting demands, that are being made on them from a variety of sources. Providing services to various groups of citizens or supporting jobs and specific industries – irrespective of the cost of doing so – are but a few examples of the types of demands they must meet, and they must do this while being subject to intense scrutiny from the media, stakeholder groups or the Opposition as well as having to adhere to transparency requirements that are unheard of in the private sector. Canadian state-owned enterprises – and BC Ferries is no exception – continue to fulfil their multiple policy functions well and are yet further testament to the incredibly successful governance mechanisms that rule every aspect of our daily lives.

References

Black, Edwin R., and Cairns, Alan C. (1966), "A Different Perspective on Canadian Federalism", in *Canadian Public Administration*, Vol. 9, Issue 1, March, pp. 27-44.

British Columbia Ferry Commissioner (2013), *Introduction to the Commission*, Victoria: BC Ferry Commissioner, (available at: http://www.bcferrycommission.

com/about-the-commission/introduction-to-the-commission/, accessed May 21, 2013).

British Columbia Ferry Corporation, Various Years, Annual Reports, Victoria: British Columbia Ferry Corporation.

British Columbia Ferry Corporation (1986), Annual Report 1985/86. Victoria: British Columbia Ferry Corporation.

British Columbia Ferry Services Inc. (2012), British Columbia Ferry Services Inc. and B.C. Ferry Authority, Annual Reports 2011/2012, Victoria: British Columbia Ferry Services Inc. and B.C. Ferry Authority.

British Columbia Ferry Services Inc. (2013), Corporate Profile: Our Mission, Victoria: British Columbia Ferry Services Inc., (Available at: http://www.bcferries.com/about/More_Information.html#growing, accessed May 13, 2013).

Coastal Ferry Services Contract Between British Columbia Ferry Corporation [sic] and The Province of British Columbia, 2003, Victoria: 1 April, (available at: http://www.bcferries.com/files/AboutBCF/Coastal_Ferry_Services_Contract.pdf, accessed May 21, 2013).

Ferry Advisory Committee Chairs (2011), *Ferry Governance: A Matter of Ideology*, Presented to the BC Ferry Commissioner, 20 October.

Government of British Columbia (1977), *The British Columbia Ferry Act*, 1977, Victoria: Government of British Columbia.

Island Trust (2011), *News Release: Trust Council asks BC Ferry Commissioner to Help Restore BC's Marine Highway*, 19 September, (available at: http://chly.ca/news-release-islands-trust-council-asks-province-to-invest-in-ferries-islandstrust/, accessed May 15, 2013).

Leonard, Frank, Edward (2002), "W.A.C., Bennett and His Choice of State Enterprise: The 1958 Case of British Columbia Ferries", Victoria: University of Victoria, Unpublished MA Thesis, History.

Mitchell, David, J. (1983), "W.A.C., Bennett and the Rise of British Columbia", Vancouver: Douglas and McIntyre.

Newman, Joshua, and Bird, Malcolm, G. (2014), Under Review. "British Columbia's Fast Ferries and Sydney's Airport Link: Partisan Barriers to Recovery from Policy Failure", in Policy and Politics.

Obee, Dave, 2008, "The Birth of B.C. Ferries", *Dave Obee's Family History Page*, available at: www.daveobee.com/victoria/20080720.htm (accessed 25 February).

Roueche, Leonard (1976), "Economic Pricing of Transportation: The Case of British Columbia Ferries", Victoria: BC Institute for Economic Policy Analysis.

Transport Canada, (2005), "Evaluation of Transport Canada's Grant to the Province of British Columbia for the Provision of Ferry Services", Ottawa: Departmental Evaluation Services.

Shaw, Rob (2013), "Gambling on BC Ferries being Considered as Government Makes Cuts", *Times Colonist*, 18 November, (available at: http://www.theprovince.com/news/Gambling+Ferries+being+considered+Government+makes+cuts/9180696/story.html, accessed Dec. 11, 2013).

Stewart, Gayle, Lorraine (2008), "Repositioning BC Ferries: From Crown Corporation to Administrative Hybrid", Vancouver: Unpublished MA Thesis, Department of Political Science, UBC.

Vancouver Sun, (2009), "BC Ferries Blames Island Trust for High Fares", 12 December, (available at: http://www.canada.com/vancouversun/news/westcoastnews/story.html?id=bee9a475-40bf-44ca-b906-e6aa7a52b1db, accessed May 15, 2013).

White, Graham (1988), "Governing from Queen's Park: The Ontario Premiership", in *Prime Ministers and Premiers: Political Leadership and Public Policy In Canada*, Leslie, A., Pal, and David, Taras, editors, Scarborough: Prentice-Hall.

Wright, Fred, R. (2001), *Review of BC Ferry Corporation and Alternative Uses for the Fast Ferries*.

Appendix A

Table 1. Operations

Year	Pass. Carried (000s)	Vehicle traffic carried – AEQs (000s)	Expenses Operat, $ (000s)	Expen., Cap., $ (000s)	Revs., Operat., $ (000s)	Prov. Subsidy, $ (000s)	Fed. Subsidy, $ (000s)	Total Sub., $ (000s)	Employees
1985	11,912	4,460	125,308	12,456	125,530	43,000	Included	43,000	N/A
1986	12,169	4,524	146,245	68,219	134,900	40,000	Included	40,000	N/A
1987	18,235	6,525	182,616	1,817	166,573	57,000	Included	57,000	2,300
1988	17,014	6,491	176,083	9,292	168,488	57,000	Included	57,000	2,352
1989	17,919	6,885	181,830	7,559	187,599	51,000#	Included	51,000	2,537
1990	19,229	7,499	246,189	17,117	215,212	51,000#	Included	51,000	2,657
1991	19,775	7,707	256,740	101,286	230,419	48,450#	Included	48,450	2,808
1992	20,518	7,965	281,169	217,767	250,901	28,147#	Included	28,147	2,945
1993	20,533	8,029	313,970	178,360	265,249	36,300	Included	36,300	3,097
1994	21,529	8,383	355,983	64,171	277,122	17,900	18,400	36,300	3,140
1995	22,021	8,398	350,535	20,251	320,336	15,947	18,005	33,952	3,159
1996	22,512	9,053	374,568	60,251	340,487	9,352	21,322	30,674	3,272
1997	22,269	8,910	388,828	136,178	333,846	4,700	21,800	26,500	3,292
1998	21,799	8,779	396,650	128,187	356,810	4,700	21,931	26,631	3,374
1999	21,379	8,579	423,273	166,602	362,078	24,000	22,040	46,040	3,389
2000	21,381	8,668	389,084	114,590	356,169	64,913	22,150	87,063	3,390
2001	21,369	8,709	396,021	55,148	361,425	72,519	22,438	94,957	3,339
2002	21,251	8,890	453,381	54,805	376,889	71,706	22,953	94,659	3,380
2003	21,624	9,126	463,855	58,114	391,163	74,243	23,377	97,620	3,345
2004	21,367	8,292	481,699	59,649	403,950	105,806	23,975	129,781	3,261
2005	22,026	8,557	499,471	119,855	433,141	106,971	24,343	131,314	3,375

Year	Pass. Carried (000s)	Vehicle traffic carried – AEQs (000s)	Expenses Operat, $ (000s)	Expen., Cap., $ (000s)	Revs., Operat., $ (000s)	Prov. Subsidy, $ (000s)	Fed. Subsidy, $ (000s)	Total Sub., $ (000s)	Employees
2006	21,729	8,543	504,116	130,181	446,049	108,223	24,890	133,113	3,406
2007	21,665	8,521	528,363	248,316	462,574	108,396	25,309	133,705	N/A
2008	21,788	8,578	569,649	428,292	492,171	122,702	25,856	148,558	N/A
2009	20,727	8,130	624,143	530,269	531,021	124,485	26,294	150,779	N/A
2010	21,035	8,255	660,003	84,166	555,874	149,508	26,924	176,432	N/A
2011	20,746	8,119	672,147	122,180	561,323	151,023	26,924	177,947	N/A
2012	20,170	7,838	682,651	115,304	555,731	154,959	27,487	182,446	N/A
2013	19,900	7,700	701,557	96,600	576,195	182,100	28,100	210,200	N/A

9. Balancing Commercial and Wider Economic Objectives

The Case of the Dublin Airport Authority

Catriona CAHILL, Donal PALCIC & Eoin REEVES

Privatisation and PPP Research Group,
Department of Economics, University of Limerick, Ireland

Introduction

As the State owned enterprise (SOE) that has the statutory mandate to manage, operate and develop Ireland's main airports, the Dublin Airport Authority (DAA) plays an important role in the economic performance of the country's small open economy. Until recently the DAA (which was originally established as Aer Rianta in 1937) held responsibility for Ireland's three principal airports (Dublin, Cork, Shannon). However, this ownership model has been under review since the early 2000s and the *State Airports Act 2004* provided for the establishment of the three airports as fully independent autonomous organisations under State ownership. Moves to implement these changes have, however, been slow, with the separation of the Shannon Airport Authority as an independent SOE only finalised in December 2012. While Shannon airport now operate independently, the other two larger airports will remain under the ownership of the DAA.

These changes mark a critical juncture in the history of DAA and will have important implications for the operation and performance of the company as well as the new SOE responsible for Shannon airport. Moreover, the changes are likely to have consequences for airport policy and wider regional and national economic performance. It is against this background that this chapter examines the history of the DAA in terms of the evolution of its functions and objectives as well as its economic performance and its contribution to the Irish economy.

Rationale for DAA Establishment, Objectives and Activities

Following national independence in 1922 the task of economic development fell largely to the apparatus of the fledgling Irish State.

Among the new SOEs to emerge in the early stages after independence were *Aer Rianta*[1] (established as a limited company in 1937) and the national airline *Aer Lingus* (established in 1936). Both companies were charged with the task of contributing to the development of the Irish aviation sector. Aer Rianta (hereafter the Dublin Airport Authority (DAA)) originally acted as a holding company for the state's shares in Aer Lingus – a role it held until 1966. It was later given responsibility for the management of Dublin airport, which was built in 1940, and its portfolio expanded to cover the management of Shannon and Cork airports, which were constructed in 1947 and 1961 respectively.

The DAA originally operated on an agency basis on behalf of the Minister for Industry and Commerce. In this role it operated the following services: airport management; design and planning; construction and maintenance; security; fire fighting and rescue; car parking facilities; and shops and general catering facilities. The DAA also operated a number of ancillary activities including mail order and tourism services. There were also several aspects of the aviation business that lay outside of the DAA's management. For example, *Aer Lingus* controlled ground handling of aircraft and passengers, and cargo handling services, on behalf of the DAA. Also, the Department of Tourism and Transport provided air traffic controls and communication services, while the Revenue Commissioners and the Department of Justice provided customs and immigration services respectively.

Compared to other Irish SOEs the DAA's "agency status" was unusual. Although agency status was under on-going review since the 1960s significant change did not materialise due to the sizeable capital burden that a newly incorporated SOE would have to bear. The company did achieve greater autonomy in the 1980s when it was delegated authority arrangements for capital projects. The funding system was also changed from one where grants were paid by the Exchequer to one where the DAA funded all capital expenditure from its own resources or borrowings. In addition, the company was permitted to create a capital reserve fund for surpluses, which were not paid over to the Minister. The *Air Navigation and Transport (Amendment) Act 1998* terminated the agency relationship and granted asset ownership and management rights to the DAA.

The objectives of the DAA have evolved gradually since the late 1970s. In 1979, the *Oireachtas (Parliament) Joint Committee on State Sponsored Bodies* (JOCSSB) articulated the DAA's objectives as follows:

---

[1] The *State Airports Act 2004* renamed Aer Rianta as the Dublin Airport Authority (DAA). From this point onwards Aer Rianta shall simply be referred to as the DAA.

- generate sufficient revenue to cover costs and provide efficient investment funds;
- manage the three major airports;
- maximise revenue earning potential of commercial activities;
- develop a properly skilled and satisfied workforce and
- promote good relations with local communities.
- (JOCSSB, 1979).

The on-going requirement for SOEs to operate on a commercial basis was evident over the following years and a later (1992) report by the JOCSSB articulated similar objectives with the noteworthy addition of international expansion. These objectives remain largely in place and were similarly articulated in the *Air Navigation and Transport (Amendment) Act 1998* and the *State Airports Act 2004*.

Up until the late 1980s the DAA classified its operations under two headings: traffic operations and commercial activities. In the second report on the company, the JOCSSB (1992) categorised the DAA's activities as; (1) Operational (i.e. aircraft landing and parking); (2) Commercial (tax free and duty free shops); (3) Overseas (including *Aerofirst*, a joint venture with the Soviet airline *Aeroflot* established in 1988, in which *Aer Rianta International* held a 49% stake. *Aerofirst* provided technical advice on planning, design and construction projects in the airport sector; (4) Technical and (5) Ancillary (including painting and refurbishment services provided to *Aeroflot* and sub-contracted services provided to third parties). In summary, the ownership structure, objectives and activities of the DAA have developed significantly over the last several decades. Since the early 1980s there has been a sharper focus on commercial activities but the efficient delivery of aviation services remains at the core of the DAA's objectives.

Objectives of General Interest

Traditionally, SOEs have pursued objectives of general interest such as employment, investment and regional policy. The development of airports and the wider aviation sector have played a pivotal role in the economic development of Ireland's small, open, island economy. Ireland's status as a small export-dependent economy means that international connectivity by air and sea is of considerable importance to national economic performance. Wider economic development therefore requires that the DAA pursue general interest goals and this is encouraged in the company's mission statement, which articulates the aim "to manage our airport business profitably, meeting customer needs and creating

281

gateways for 21st century Ireland" (DAA 2013). The following sections consider how the DAA has pursued objectives of general interest in terms of investment, affordability, customer service and security.

Investment in Airport Infrastructure

Investment in transport infrastructure is considered not only essential for economic growth but also for the future vitality and survival of the transport industry (Thatcher, 2011). Over the last 25 years the DAA has committed more and more resources to developing airport infrastructure. In one sense these increases can be attributed to the need to compensate for historically low levels of investment and to meet the needs of a growing economy. Whereas just €66 million was invested at the three airports over the period 1984-88, the DAA's average capital investment spend per year at Dublin Airport alone averaged €20 million over the period 1990-1996. This was followed by a further total capital spend of €455 million between 1998 to 2001 which was used to invest in projects including a new pier building and terminal extension at Dublin; a pier and apron extension at Shannon; and a new passenger terminal at Cork.

The establishment of the Commission for Aviation Regulation (CAR) in 2001 brought considerable change to the governance of DAA's investment plans. Although severely constrained by the regulator over the period 2001 to 2004, the company announced a 10-year investment programme in 2005 in response to the perceived need to service increasing passenger numbers. The plan to spend €2 billion over this period was based on non-exchequer sources including revenues generated from commercial activities such as retailing, car parking and property rentals; airport charges levied on passengers for use of terminal and airfield services; and borrowings. Although justified by the company on the basis of the need to compensate for years of under-investment there has been considerable debate about the necessity or otherwise of the scale of investment, particularly the construction of a second passenger terminal (T2) at Dublin.[2]

Affordability

State owned airports face the difficult task of delivering high levels of quality of service to customers (passengers and airlines) at affordable

---

[2] Osbourne A., 2010, "Dublin's flight of fancy is cancelled, and bank's governor saw it coming". (Available at: http://www.telegraph.co.uk/finance/comment/alistair-osborne/ 8144530/Dublins-flight-of-fancy-is-cancelled-and-banks-governor-saw-it-coming. html).

prices. The charges levied on airlines operating in Dublin Airport have been regulated by CAR since 2001 and are reviewed on a four-year basis. Shannon and Cork Airports are not subject to price cap regulation. CAR's first determination was published in August 2001 and a maximum passenger charge of €5.60 was permitted at Dublin Airport. This maximum charge has increased over time with the maximum passenger charge permitted for Dublin Airport for the period 2010 to 2014 set at €8.93 with an additional €2.33 charged when T2 became fully operational at the end of 2010. In 2011, the DAA announced that the average passenger charge for 2012 would remain at the 2011 figure of €10.40 which is 17% lower than the average passenger charge of €12.50 levied in 2009 by comparable European airports such as Stansted, Gatwick, Brussels, Vienna and Munich.[3] Passenger charges at Cork and Shannon are set by their respective Boards with the approval of the Minster for Transport. The passenger charge at both airports is currently €12.65 (€7.15 of which is attributed to passenger services and €5.50 to security charges).

Affordability is also an important element in attracting airlines to airports. As part of the 2009 EC Directive airports must consult with airlines annually unless otherwise stated and must exchange a range of information as part of that process, including forecasts of airport charges. This process allows for the airports to participate in a forum of discussion with service providers and to effectively monitor affordability and performance within the airport. In comparative terms it appears that the DAA has kept charges to service providers at affordable levels. Between 1987 and 2001 the company's airport charges were below the average charges levied at other European airports of a similar size during the same period (DAA Annual Report 2005).

Continuity, Safety and Security

The DAA's quality of service objective includes the assurance of continuity of operations for its customers. However, this goal of continuity is increasingly threatened, not only by aviation disasters but also natural disasters, accidents, pandemics, civil disturbances, terrorism and war. Events such as the two Gulf wars (1990 and 2003), the outbreak of Foot and Mouth disease in Ireland and the UK (2001) and the eruption of the Icelandic volcano (*Eyjafjallajokull*) and subsequent ash cloud have all caused major disruptions for the wider European aviation sector and the DAA. For example the problem of ash cloud resulted in a six-day crisis and the cancellation of 3,200 flights at Dublin, Cork and Shannon,

---

[3]   DAA, 2011, Press Release. (Available at: http://www.daa.ie/gns/media-centre/press-releases/2011/11-11-11/Dublin_Airport_Charges_To_Remain_Flat_in_2012.aspx).

affecting 400,000 passengers.[4] Like other airports the DAA has also responded to security threats especially in the wake of the September 11th (9/11) terrorist attacks in the US. Security measures adopted by the DAA include the establishment of a Group Aviation and Standards function which monitors and reports on aviation safety and security standards and operational procedures at the airport; a Health and Safety Committee that monitors and reviews matters in relation to aviation safety, and health and safety at work at the airports; and a Security Committee that monitors and reviews matters in relation to security at the airport.

Operations

The DAA's operations have evolved in various ways over the last four decades. Traffic operation was, and continues to be, the company's primary function but the company is also engaged in a host of commercial, international and ancillary activities. With regard to traffic operations the company has experienced steady growth since the early 1980s with total passenger numbers increasing from 3.18 million in 1980 to a peak of over 30 million in 2007. Although numbers subsequently declined to 22 million in the context of the global financial crisis in 2008, small increases were recorded in 2011 and 2012. Passenger traffic is heavily concentrated in Dublin airport, which accounted for 83% in 2012.

Table 1. DAA General Overview 2012

Turnover	Total €574.6 m	Aeronautical €234.2 m Commercial €203.8 m International €136.6 m
Employee Numbers	Total 3,016	Airports 2,458 International 558
Passenger Numbers	Total 22,834,545 Transatlantic 1,932,077 Britain 8,774,890 Continental Europe 11,494,525 Other International 478,471 Domestic 66,744 Transit 142,838	Airports Dublin 19,099,649 Cork 2,340,115 Shannon 1,394,781

Each of the three Irish airports offers a variety of destinations through various airlines. In 2011, 62 airlines operated 171 routes out of Dublin Airport with over 80% of seat capacity attributable to *Aer Lingus* and

---

4   RTE News, 2010, "Government will not compensate airlines" (Available at: http://www.rte.ie/news/2010/0427/130327-travel/).

Ryanair. Cork Airport had 25 airlines operating 53 routes and 90% of seat capacity was attributed to *Aer Lingus* and *Ryanair*. Shannon Airport had 16 airlines operating 33 destinations and the major airline customers were *Aer Lingus* (38%) and *Ryanair* (26%), US military transit (14%) and US carriers *Continental* (7%) and *Delta* (5%) (Booz and Company 2011).

Commercial activities have, for long, constituted a significant element of the company's portfolio of operations. Significant features of these activities include the establishment of joint ventures with public and privately owned entities (e.g. bar and catering services and coach tours) as well as the internationalisation of some commercial activities. One service in which the company has successfully internationalised its services is duty-free shopping. In 1987 the company established *Aer Rianta International (ARI)* as a wholly owned subsidiary for the purpose of promoting commercial activities outside of Ireland through a number of joint ventures and management contracts. *ARI's* first joint venture was with *Aeroflot* in 1988. The DAA and *Aeroflot* had been closely connected since the 1970s through a unique barter arrangement involving reduced airport charges in exchange for oil. This relationship created a platform for the DAA to expand internationally and led to its first joint venture, *Aerofirst*, which established the first duty-free shop in Moscow. This was followed by further joint ventures with Aeroflot to run duty-free shops at Leningrad, Kiev and Torfionovka (on the Russian-Finnish border). In 1997, ARI secured a 40% shareholding (with its partner NatWest) in Birmingham International Airport. It also signed a number of management contracts including the deal to manage a duty-free complex in Bahrain Airport; the contract to assist in the management of all operational and commercial activities at Warsaw Airport; and the contract to run the new duty-free shop in Karachi Airport in Pakistan. These developments provide illustrative examples of how the DAA has operated as a commercially oriented SOE that has an established track record in exporting its expertise and internationalising its activities.

Performance

This section analyses the financial performance of the DAA from 1986 to 2010 using standard financial performance indicators. Before presenting the results from our analysis it is important to highlight some of the key exogenous factors that can impact on the performance of airports and airlines and which can lead to considerable volatility. These include natural disasters, political instability, war, terrorist attacks and health epidemics that can often have a significant negative impact on the financial and operating performance of airports and airlines. Before turning to our analysis of the financial performance of the DAA from

1986-2010 we provide a brief overview of the main negative shocks that affected its performance during that timeframe.

The Gulf War in 1990-1991 and the Iraq War in 2003 both had a significant negative impact on the global aviation industry's financial performance. During the Gulf War airlines were hit particularly hard as insurance brokers increased premiums and the price of aviation fuel per gallon more than doubled. This initially led to a surge in airline charges, however, during the same period passenger traffic decreased due to a global economic downturn and, in an effort to stimulate growth, airlines were forced to offer discounts on fares. While some airlines managed to survive the negative exogenous shock, others (including major airlines such as Pan Am) collapsed. This had a knock-on effect for airports throughout the world as many routes were severely disrupted causing multiple delays and cancellations. In the DAA's case, passenger numbers declined for transatlantic flights and the majority of freight consignments could not be sent by air for security reasons. During the same period, the global recession contributed to reduced consumer spending, which in turn, impacted negatively on the DAA's commercial activities. Similar effects occurred following the Iraq War in 2003.

The 9/11 terrorist attacks in New York in 2001 caused chaos for the US aviation industry and, to a lesser extent, the global aviation industry. According to Ito and Lee (2005), 34% of US businesses cancelled international travel for its employees for a sustained period of time following the tragedy. While the initial panic subsided after several months there were long-term ramifications for the aviation sector. The attacks caused a massive blow to consumer confidence in relation to air travel and, in the aftermath, security measures in airports throughout the world underwent a major overhaul. However, the stringent security measures implemented made travel more burdensome and time consuming than ever before, and the high costs associated with the security enhancements were reflected in the aviation sectors reduced profits.

The aviation industry has been hit by several health pandemics in recent years, the most notable being, *Foot and Mouth* in 2001, *SARS* in 2003 and *Bird Flu* in 2005. Passenger traffic for certain routes fell in each instance due to consumer fears and Government imposed restrictions on travel. The Irish Government received much criticism in 2003 for their lack of response to the threat of *SARS*. It was reported by several newspapers that hundreds of migrants from China, Hong Kong, Shanghai, Thailand and Vietnam were entering Ireland without any health checks. Therefore, during the *Bird Flu* outbreak in 2005 monitoring systems and increased security were put in place at Irish airports, resulting in increased costs for the DAA.

Weather phenomena can reduce the efficiency of aviation operations by adversely affecting the traffic handling capabilities of airports. Heavy rain, ice and snow are just some of the meteorological conditions that can render an airport non-operational for certain periods of time. The closure of runways can result in significant delays and cancelations, which in turn will affect the operational revenue of the airport. Hurricane Katrina in 2005 and Hurricane Ike in 2008 caused major disruption to the aviation sector when they made landfall in the US. On both occasions, airlines operating in the three Irish airports were forced to cancel flights to and from the US over a three-day period. In 2010, the DAA was forced to suspend flights on two occasions: the first in April because of the volcanic ash cloud from the eruption of *Eyjafjallajokall* in Iceland, and the second in December because of heavy snowfall. On both instances operations were suspended for several days and as a result thousands of passengers were stranded.

Financial Performance

The DAA's financial performance is analysed using the following standard financial indicators: Profit before Interest, Tax and Exceptional Items (PBITE); Return on Sales (ROS); Return on Capital Employed (ROCE); and Turnover per Employee (T/E). Figure 1 displays the trend in each indicator for the period 1986-2010. In general, the PBITE indicator displays a strong upward trend over the 25-year period, apart from a small number of periods where profitability was negatively impacted on by external shocks that were highlighted in the previous section. While the trend in ROS is less impressive, it somewhat mirrors the changes in PBITE, recovering strongly after the negative shock from the First Gulf War as revenue from aviation and commercial activities grew following the full liberalisation of the European air transport market in 1993. Both the ROS and PBITE indicators also rebound considerably after the impact of the outbreak of Foot and Mouth Disease in Ireland and the UK in 2001 along with the 9/11 terrorist attacks in the USA. Revenues and profits increased significantly between 2003 and 2007 as the Irish and global economic boom resulted in passenger traffic reaching record levels. The global financial crisis that erupted in 2008 and the subsequent global recession led to a significant decline in profitability for the DAA although this recovered slightly in 2010 due to an increase in aeronautical charges (DAA Annual Report 2010).[5]

---

[5] Prior to 1998, the DAA managed the three State airports on an agency basis. The *Air Navigation and Transport (Amendment) Act 1998*, allowed the DAA full ownership rights of the Group's assets. The decline in ROS/PBITE in the 1998 to 2000 period is largely due to increased costs following the transfer of ownership as the Group became liable for increased corporation tax.

Before discussing the trend in ROCE it is worth noting that prior to 1985 all capital expenditure was financed by the Exchequer, so no fixed assets were included on the DAA's balance sheet. Following a structural review in 1986 the Minister decided that expenditure on certain long term fixed assets should be financed directly by the DAA and this decision was further extended in 1988 to include all new assets. Consequently, the ROCE analysis begins in 1989 as this was the first year that the company did not receive a grant from the Government towards capital expenditure and instead financed all assets from its own resources and borrowings.

In contrast to the other indicators, ROCE displays a sustained downward trend over the period of analysis. The sharp fall in ROCE between 1989 and 1992 was largely the result of major investment (the DAA invested heavily in infrastructure through the expansion of its three airports and the purchase of the Great Southern Hotel Group) coupled with the reduction in PBITE resulting from the First Gulf War. After recovering somewhat from 1992-1996, ROCE again declined considerably from 1996-2003 with this decline mainly driven by a substantial five-year capital development programme worth €152 million launched in 1996 and a deterioration in profitability as a result of the transfer of ownership in 1999 and external shocks in 2001. As with the ROS and PBITE indicators, ROCE improved during the 2003 to 2007 boom period before declining again with the onset of the recession.

Turnover per employee (T/E) increased continually for most of the period analysed due to a steady increase in turnover along with minor changes in employee numbers. Fluctuations in T/E can mostly be attributed to the Great Southern Hotel Group (GSHG). The minor decrease in T/E in 1990 and 1998 was due to an increase in employee numbers from the purchase of the GSHG and the addition of a new hotel respectively, while the substantial increase in T/E in 2007 was caused by a reduction in employee numbers following the sale of the GSHG. T/E was negatively affected in 2008-2009 due to a reduction in turnover caused by the global economic downturn.

Overall, the DAA performed well over the period of analysis. With the exception of a number of years where the aviation sector experienced negative exogenous shocks, all three airports were successful in increasing passenger numbers and attracting airlines. The DAA's achievement in terms of its commercial activities is noteworthy, as the success of Aeroflot and ARI have established the company as leaders in their relevant global industries. This strong performance in both airport and commercial activities is reflected in the DAA's financial results (i.e. PBITE, ROS and T/E). However, it is clear from the ROCE results that the company has not been efficient in terms of capital investment. Rather, capital spending during the period of analysis was far in excess of what would be considered productive in terms of the company's output. This level of investment can, to a certain extent, be explained by significant historical underinvestment in the airports throughout the late 1980s and early 1990s; however, recent investment (in particular the construction of T2) cannot be justified in a similar manner at this point in time.

Governance

Governance refers to the framework of practices and rules that are applied to institutions in an effort to ensure accountability, fairness and transparency. According to Armstrong *et al.* (2005), the purpose of good governance is to add value to the organization, reduce risk (financial, business and operational), strengthen shareholder confidence and assist the prevention of fraudulent behaviour. Ultimately, governance should not only protect the interests of investors but also achieve fairness and transparency for other stakeholders (e.g. employees and service users). Whereas governance is an important issue for organisations in both the public and private sectors two important issues that arise for SOEs are the dangers of political interference and the possibility of rescue in the case of financial underperformance (soft budget constraint). According to the OECD therefore, the major challenge with regards to governing public enterprises is to:

> "(...) Find a balance between the States responsibility for actively exercising its ownership functions, such as the nomination and election of its Board, while at the same time refraining from imposing undue political interference in the management of the company" (OECD 2005, p. 3).

In order to maintain high standards of corporate governance, the DAA voluntarily apply principles contained in the *UK Corporate Governance Code 2010* and the *Irish Corporate Governance Annex*, as they believe that the "application of these principles assist the Group to comply with the ethical and other considerations implicit in the *Code of Practice for the Governance of State Bodies* published by the Department of Finance" (DAA Annual Report 2011, p. 31). The governance mechanisms applied by the DAA can be examined in the context of the company's stakeholders (i.e. management, employees and consumers).

Board of Directors and Top Management

The Minister for Transport appoints the members of the DAA's Board of Directors with the approval of the Minister for Public Expenditure and Reform. The members may serve for a maximum period of five years but they are eligible for reappointment. Four of the directors are appointed under the *Worker Participation (State Enterprises) Act, 1977 to 2001*, for a maximum term of four years and are eligible for re-election. The

Chief Executive Officer (CEO) of the DAA is appointed by the Board of Directors and acts as an *ex officio* director of the company.

The CEO's remuneration is governed by Government policy and has two elements: basic pay and performance related pay. The relevant Ministers decide upon the range of pay and the Board is informed of the upper limit. The appropriate level of basic pay that the Board may set is considered to be 80% of the maximum level, while performance related pay should not exceed an annual limit of 25% of the basic pay. In order to avoid any potential conflict when determining the salary level, the Board must establish a remuneration sub-committee containing at least three non-executive directors along with individuals with the appropriate private sector experience. In 2011, the CEO of the DAA received a salary of €445,400.

The governance mechanisms applied by the Board are clearly outlined in the Group's most recent annual report, and at the forefront of these mechanisms is performance measurement. The DAA has an audit committee who assists "the Board in its oversight responsibility relating to internal control and risk management; financial reporting; external audit; and internal audit" (DAA Annual Report 2011, p. 33). The committee carried out a self-evaluation in 2011 and were "satisfied that it understands and fulfils its obligations, with the commitment and contribution of members and its effectiveness" (DAA Annual Report 2011, p. 34). The performance of the CEO is monitored annually by the Board and is assessed in line with financial results and the achievement of company objectives. Under Section 29(2) of the *Air Navigation and Transport (Amendment) Act 1998*, the Board have the power to remove the CEO from office should they fail to meet certain criteria as set out in their contract of employment

Employees

The DAA has full autonomy with regards to the hiring of staff. There is no quota set in relation to employee numbers and as such the DAA hires staff on the basis of necessity. As of 2011, the DAA had 3,032 employees (with 2,513 working at the three state airports and 519 working at international activities). Between 1987-2009 public sector pay in Ireland was set out in a series of social partnership agreements negotiated by the Government, employers and trade unions. In 2011, in response to the economic downturn, the DAA were forced to implement a *Cost Recovery Programme* which included redundancies as well as pay reductions. The pay reductions set out in this programme were agreed between the DAA and the relevant trade unions and as such, this agreement stands separate from any wider partnership agreements.

According to the DAA, the company has a detailed performance measurement structure in place encompassing KPIs, scorecards and performance reviews. On a general level, the DAA uses key performance indicators (KPIs) to evaluate their performance. These are applied to various areas of the Groups strategic framework including network expansion, financial stability and company growth. In relation to the evaluation of staff performance, the DAA apply a balanced scorecard method where managers can keep track of all the activities carried out by staff in accordance with the wider KPI framework.

Consumers

With regards to their classification as stakeholders, passengers can be viewed in two ways: (1) as participants in the economic system both as business travellers or tourists; and (2) as individual travellers that have expectations about receiving quality service. According to Scharr and Sherry (2010), these two perspectives have different implications on the goals of an airport.

As participants in the economic system, the most important factor for consumers is the cost of travel. One of the DAA's main objectives is affordability and as part of this the airports goal is to provide access to low airfares. The majority share of airfares is decided upon by airlines and fuel prices but the charges implemented by airports can have a substantial effect on the overall cost. In the DAA's case airport charges are decided upon by the Commission for Aviation Regulation (CAR) and their determination is published every four years. Since 2010 quality of service is included in the overall determination of charge and the CAR can impose a maximum reduction of 4.5% if certain targets are not met.

Local residents could be considered as another category of stakeholders, notably concerning potential complaints, on their side, on the noise of aircrafts; however, no such complaints were noted in the research.

Regulation

There is both a pragmatic and theoretical rationale for the regulation of airports. Pragmatically, most airports have no close geographical substitutes and therefore have significant market power in their catchment areas. In theoretical terms, the natural monopoly characteristics of airports provide a strong rationale for their regulation. In the Irish context, Dublin Airport effectively operates as a monopoly given the importance of Dublin as a destination and its distance from other airports (McLay and Reynolds, 2006). Cork and Shannon Airports are situated in close proximity to several regional airports and therefore face some competition in attracting airlines (in particular Low Cost Carriers (LCCs)). The structure of costs faced by airlines has transformed with the emergence of LCCs. Traditionally airlines had little bargaining power with regards to charges, however, the increasing prominence of secondary airports has allowed LCCs to reject high charges at hub airports in favour of lower charges at competing secondary airports. Since Dublin Airport faces no such competition, the regulator is tasked with ensuring the airport operator acts in a fair and efficient manner.

In addressing the question of how airports should be regulated, it is necessary to examine the following approaches: price cap regulation (single-till and dual-till); and light-handed regulation. When analysing the appropriateness of regulatory frameworks several factors must be taken into account, the most important of which is whether or not the airport is classified as congested or non-congested. For example, reducing the charge level at an airport is usually considered beneficial for both the consumer and airport operator, as a reduction in price will increase demand. However, if the airport is congested then a reduction in price will instead increase excess demand and therefore: "(…) Regulation of airports faces the additional problem of rationing demand efficiently and setting incentives for investment. Hence the structure of charges, the allocation mechanism and the incentives for investment become a major issue for airport regulation" (ITF, 2009, p. 24).

Price-cap regulation is a form of incentive regulation, whereby a cap on the total revenue per passenger that the airport may collect is announced in advance of the applicable regulatory period. The single-till approach considers both aeronautical and non-aeronautical activities when setting airport charges. The dual-till approach separates the aeronautical and non-aeronautical business into income and expenditure accounts, thus ensuring that income from each sector is invested in the corresponding infrastructure. The key difference between single-till and dual-till regulation lies in the allocation of revenues to cover costs. As part of the single-till approach, commercial revenues cover a portion of overall fixed costs so the price cap for aeronautical services is reduced accordingly. In contrast, the dual-till approach separates the aeronautical and commercial sectors and as a result, the price cap for aeronautical services is increased in order to ensure that the airport's aeronautical costs are completely covered by revenues from aeronautical activities.

The single-till approach has been widely used in Europe (e.g. Austria, Belgium, France, Spain); however, this traditional approach is being increasingly challenged by the dual-till approach, with airports such as Brussels and Paris recently adopting dual characteristics (Gillen and Niemeier 2007). It should be noted that within Europe, only four countries currently have an independent airport regulator (Austria,

Ireland, the Netherlands and the UK). However, more countries are set to follow as the European Commission promotes its Single European Skies initiative, aimed at changing legislation to create a unified airspace along with greater efficiency and transparency. A key recommendation of this initiative is the establishment of independent regulators in each Member State.

Dublin Airport is currently regulated on a single-till basis, however, Ireland's Commission for Aviation Regulation (CAR) has committed to reviewing whether or not there is merit in changing from the single-till regulation to dual-till regulation (CAR 2010). The CAR acknowledge that, because it has excluded the costs and revenues of certain activities that it considers not to have commensurate links to the airport (i.e. Cork and Shannon Airports; Aer Rianta International; and International Investments), then the distinction between single-till and dual-till is not as blatant as certain explanations suggest. Following their most recent consultation process, the DAA noted that the adoption of a dual-till approach was unlikely as this would increase charges (thus negatively affecting the Groups affordability objective) and that they "did not see the single-till changing anytime soon". However, the DAA did acknowledge that it might be possible to exclude certain activities, as "in the future, there may be projects that airlines are not in favour of" and therefore "don't want them to be part of what is coming under the umbrella of the single-till".[6]

The Commission for Aviation Regulation

Prior to 2001, airport charges were regulated by the state and under this regime it acted as shareholder, regulator and policy-maker. However, such extensive roles potentially placed conflicting demands upon the state. From 1987 to 2001 airport charges remained static, however, during the period 1995 to 2000 the DAA implemented several changes that resulted in increased airport charges. The DAA gradually withdrew a deep discount scheme that had been applied in the early 1990s to attract airlines to operate in the three Irish airports. The Group also introduced new charges for both airlines (e.g. check-in and ground handling fees) and the travelling public (car park fees). These actions resulted in considerable conflict between the DAA and Ryanair (Ireland's largest airline with passenger numbers of 76.4 million in 2011), as Ryanair argued that the withdrawal of discounts would double airport charges. In protest the airline froze the development of new routes at all three airports in 2001 and publically criticised the Government for a lack of transparency and consultation in setting charges (McLay and Reynolds, 2006).

---

[6]   Interview with members of the DAA management team, January 2013.

A politically independent sectoral regulator, the CAR, was established on the 27ᵗʰ February 2002 under the Aviation Regulation Act 2001. A number of functions previously exercised by the Minister were transferred to the Commission, the most significant of which was the control of airport and aviation terminal charges. The Commission's functions include: the regulation of airport charges and aviation terminal service charges; the granting of licenses to airlines, tour operators, travel agents and ground handling service providers; and slot allocation.

The Commission originally regulated charges for all three of the state airports; however, this was altered under the State Airports Act 2004 to include only Dublin. In attempting to separate the airports under the 2004 Act, it was decided that charges at Cork and Shannon would be set by the relevant airport authorities. When regulating the revenue that Dublin Airport collects in airport charges levied on users, the Commission considers all revenue sourced from: runway and landing; aircraft parking; air bridge usage; and passenger processing. In determining airport charges, the Commission employs price-cap regulation applied to a single till. The cap lasts for a period of four years or more and if the DAA can effectively reduce its costs below the level of the cap then they keep the value of these savings until the cap is reset. The Commission will also consider the reduction in costs realised by the operator when setting the next cap; thus price cap regulation can be beneficial to both the DAA and airport users.

The relationship between the DAA and the CAR was initially characterised by discord, with the DAA publically criticising the regulator on a number of occasions and taking legal proceedings on one occasion. However, over time a more "cordial relationship"[7] has developed between the two entities. The CAR has experienced a far more hostile relationship with Ryanair who have brought legal cases against the CAR seven times within the last decade (six of which were unsuccessful). The most recent was in 2008 when the company challenged the CAR's decision to allow the DAA to increase check-in charges by roughly 50 per cent. The unusually high number of legal cases taken against the CAR (eight in the last ten years) has often frustrated the work of the CAR, and is in stark contrast to the experience of other airport regulators, for example the UK airport regulator has only been challenged once in court in the last twenty-five years (CAR Annual Report 2010).

Conclusions

The aviation sector is a key enabler of economic growth in the Irish economy, contributing approximately €4.1 billion towards GDP and

---

[7] Interview with members of the DAA management team, January 2013.

employing 26,000 individuals across a range of aviation services. Ireland's international trade, including its tourism industry, depends greatly upon its connectivity with the rest of the world. To facilitate the optimum level of service, air transport requires a high standard of airport infrastructure in terms of capacity and quality. This task of providing and operating this infrastructure has largely fallen to the DAA since its establishment (as Aer Rianta) in 1937.

The company has remained under state ownership over the last 65 years and although its general objectives have evolved over time to allow for a greater focus on the commercial side of the business the core objectives of the Group have remained consistent. Its primary objective is to manage its airports in an efficient manner so as to ensure the continued delivery of high quality services. An important factor in achieving this objective is continued investment in airport infrastructure. While capital investment was relatively low throughout the 1980s and 1990s, the DAA has invested heavily in the last decade with the construction of new terminals at Cork and Dublin Airports. An important feature of the DAAs investment record is that since the mid-1980s it has been entirely self-funded with all investment funded from borrowings and revenues from operations.

The Irish aviation industry has been exposed to a number of exogenous shocks in the form of warfare, terrorist attacks, pandemics and weather phenomena. These events have negatively impacted the DAA's financial performance on several occasions. However, when consideration is taken of these exogenous shocks we find that the financial performance of the DAA has followed a largely positive trend across most indicators during the period of analysis.

An important feature of the DAA's history is the Groups successful expansion into international markets. The world's first duty free shop was established at Shannon Airport in 1947 and since then the DAA has developed its international business portfolio to include airport shops throughout the world. *Aer Rianta International*, which is a wholly owned subsidiary of the DAA, can be considered a ground-breaking venture within the aviation industry, and has given the DAA a reputation as one of the world's leading experts in airport retail services.

The most significant development in recent years has been the development of plans to separate the three main airports in the DAA as fully independent commercial entities. The *State Airports Act 2004* paved the way for this, with the main rationale underpinning the legislation being the development of competition in the sector along with the objective of reducing the company's overall cost base. While full separation was delayed for several years, Shannon Airport was finally separated from the DAA and established as a debt free entity on the 31st of December 2012. No decision has yet been made regarding the separation of Cork Airport from the DAA. The introduction of competition in the Irish airports sector therefore remains at an early stage. It is however reasonable to expect that Cork Airport will eventually separate from the DAA and the company will no longer resemble the SOE that was originally established in 1937. It remains to be seen whether this re-structuring will ultimately be beneficial for the Irish airport sector and the wider economy.

References

Airports Council International (2007), "ACI Position Brief", (available online at: http://www.aci.aero/aci/aci/file/Position%20Briefs/position%20brief_AIRPORT%20BUSINESS.pdf).

Armstrong, E. (2005), "Integrity, Transparency and Accountability in Public Administration: Recent Trends, Regional and International Developments and Emerging Issues", United Nations, (available Online at: http://unpan1.un.org/intradoc/groups/public/documents/un/unpan020955.pdf.

Australian Productivity Commission (2012), "Economic Regulation of Airport Services", (available online at: http://www.pc.gov.au/__data/assets/pdf_file/0003/114645/airport-regulation.pdf).

Aviation Business Development Task Force (2012), "Shannon", Dublin: Stationary Office.

Baumol, W. (1982), "Contestable Markets: An Uprising in the Theory of Industry Structure", in *The American Economic Review*, 72, 1-15.

Baysinger, B. and Hoskisson, R. (1990), "The composition of boards of direction and strategic control: Effects on corporate strategy", in *Academy of Management Review*, Vol. 15, pp. 72-87.

Beesley, M. E. (1999), "Airport Regulation", in M. E. Beesley (ed.), *Regulating Utilities: A New Era*, London: Institute of Economic Affairs.

Booz and Company (2012), *Options for the future ownership and operation of Cork and Shannon Airports*, (available online at: http://cdn.thejournal.ie/media/2012/02/Booz-report.pdf).

Braithwaite, V. and Levi, M. (eds.) (1998), *Trust and Governance*, New York, Russell Sage Foundation.

Central Statistics Office (2013), *Aviation Statistics*, (available online at: http://www.cso.ie/px/pxeirestat/Database/eirestat/Aviation%20Statistics/Aviation%20Statistics_statbank.asp?SP=Aviation%20Statistics&Planguage=0).

Chen, T., Chen, S., Hsieh, P., and Chiang, H. (1997), "Auditory Effects of Aircraft Noise on People Living Near an Airport", in *Archives of Environmental Health*, Vol. 52, pp. 45-50.

Cohen, B., Bronzaft, A., Heikkinen, M., Goodman, J. and Nádas, A. (2008), "Airport related air-pollution and noise", in *Journal of Occupational Environmental Hygiene*, Vol. 5, No. 2, pp. 119-29.

Commission for Aviation Regulation (2001), *Response to CP2*, Dublin: Stationary Office.

Commission for Aviation Regulation (2009), "Determination on Maximum Levels of Airport Charges at Dublin Airport 2009", Dublin: Stationary Office.

Commission for Aviation Regulation (2010), "Defining the Regulatory Till", Dublin: Stationary Office.

Crew, M. and Kleindorfer, P. (2001), *Regulation for privatized airports: Single-till versus multi-till pricing methodologies for Sydney airport*, (UNPUBLISHED).

Czerny, A. (2006), "Price-cap regulation of airports: single-till versus dual-till", in, *Journal of Regulatory Economics*, Vol. 30, pp. 85-97.

Department of Finance (2006), "Contracts, Remuneration and other conditions of chief executives and senior management of commercial state bodies", Dublin: Stationary Office.

Department of Finance (2006), "Towards 2016", Dublin: Stationary Office.

Department of Finance (2009), "Code of practice for the governance of state bodies", Dublin: Stationary Office.

Doganis, R. (1992), The Airport Business, Routledge, London.

Dublin Airport Authority Annual Reports 1986 to 2010, (available online at: http://www.daa.ie/gns/media-centre/annual-reports.aspx).

Dublin Airport Authority (2010), "Strategic Plan", (available online at: http://www.daa.ie/Libraries/Presentations_and_speeches_2011/The_DAA_s_Strategic_Plan_2010-2014.sflb.ashx). [accessed September 2012].

Fauver, L. and Fuerst, M. (2006), "Does good corporate governance include employee representation? Evidence from German corporate boards", (available online at: http://corpgovcenter.utk.edu/Research/FauverandFuerstJFEGermanLaborPaper.pdf). [accessed February 2013].

Gillen, D. and Niemeier, H. (2007), "Comparative political economy of airport infrastructure in the European Union: evolution, regulation and slot reform", Centre for Transportation Studies, University of British Columbia, Working Paper 2007-6.

Gorecki, P. (2011), "Economic Regulation: Recentralisation of Power or Improved Quality of Regulation?", in *The Economic and Social Review*, Vol. 42, No. 2, pp. 177-211.

Grossman, S. and Hart, O. (1986), "The costs and benefits of ownership: a theory of vertical integration and lateral integration", in *Journal of Political Economy*, Vol. 94, pp. 691-719.

Hillman, A. and Daziel, T. (2003), "Boards of Directors and Firm Performance", in *Academy of Management Review*, Vol. 28, No. 3, pp. 383-96.

Hulten, C. and Wykoff, F. (1996), "Issues in the measurement of economic depreciation: Introductory remarks", in *Economic Enquiry*, Vol. 24, pp. 10-23.

International Transport Forum, 2010, *Airport Regulation, Investment and Development of Aviation*, (available online at: http://www.internationaltransportforum.org/2010/pdf/Fraport.pdf). [Accessed January 2013].

Irish Stock Exchange (2010), "Irish Corporate Governance Annex", (available online at: http://www.ise.ie/ISE_Regulation/Equity_Issuer_Rules_/Listing_Rules/Appendix_4.pdf). [accessed March 2013].

Ito, H. and Darin, L. (2005a), "Comparing the impact of the September 11th terrorist attacks on international airline demand", in *International Journal of the Economics of Business*, Vol. 12, No. 2, pp. 225-49.

Jorge, J. and Rus, G. (2004), "Cost-benefit analysis of investments in airport infrastructure: a practical approach", in *Journal of Air Transport Management*, Vol. 10, pp. 311-26.

Kay, J. (2010), *Better a Distant Judge Than a Pliant Regulator*, (available online at: http://www.ft.com/intl/cms/s/0/9d5357d0-e6b5-11df-99b3-00144feab49a.html#axzz2VHrQnvMn). [accessed February 2013].

Lu, C. and Pagliari, R. (2004), "Evaluating the potential impact of alternative airport pricing approaches on social welfare", in *Transportation Research Part E*, Vol. 40, pp. 1-17.

Macaulay, S. (1963), "Non-contractual relations in business: a preliminary study", in *American Sociological Review*, Vol. 28, pp. 55-69.

MacCartaigh, M. (2009), *The corporate governance of commercial state owned enterprise in Ireland*, (available online at: http://www.cpmr.gov.ie/Documents/The%20Corporate%20Governance%20of%20Commericial%20State-owned%20Enterprises%20in%20Ireland.pdf). [accessed March 2013].

McAteer, D. (1935), "Suggested airport for Dublin", in *Irish Quarterly Review*, Vol. 24, pp. 73-84.

McLay, P. and Reynolds, A. (2006), *Competition Between Airport Terminals: The Issues Facing Dublin Airport*, (available online at: http://airbridge.bangor.ac.uk/competitionbetweenairportterminalstheisssuesfacingdublinairport.pdf). [accessed November 2012].

Niemeier, H. (2004), "Capacity Utilization, Investment and regulatory reform of German Airports", in P. Forsyth, D. Gillen, A. Knorr, O. Mayer, H-M. Niemeier & D. Starkie, *The Economic Regulation of Airports: Recent Developments in Australasia, North America and Europe*, Aldershot, Ashgate, pp. 163-192.

O'Brien, P. (2011), *Collier bows to pressure in bonus dispute*, (available online at: http://www.irishexaminer.com/text/ireland/kfojsnkfidey/). [accessed March 2013].

O'Carroll, M. (2010), *The Requirement for Airport Competition in Dublin*, (available online at: http;//www.tcd.ie/Economics/SER/sql/download. php?key=299). [accessed November 2012].

OECD (2005), "Corporate governance of State-owned enterprises", (available online at: http://www.oecd.org/daf/ca/corporategovernanceofstate-ownedenterprises/34803211.pdf). [accessed March 2013].

Oireachtas, 1979, "Committee Report", Dublin: Stationary Office.

Oireachtas, 1992, "Committee Report", Dublin: Stationary Office.

Oireachtas 2004, "States Airport Bill: Second Stage", (available online at: http://debates.oireachtas.ie/dail/2004/06/24/00011.asp). [accessed November 2012].

Oireachtas (2012), "Joint Committee on the Environment, Transport, Culture and the Gaeltacht", (available online at: http://debates.oireachtas.ie/TRJ/2012/01/11/printall.asp). [accessed November 2012]

Oireachtas (2012), "Shannon Airport Motion", (available online at: http://oireachtasdebates.oireachtas.ie/debates%20authoring/debateswebpack.nsf/takes/dail2012121100006). [accessed March 2013].

Oireachtas (2013), "Discussion with Shannon Airport", (available online at: http://oireachtasdebates.oireachtas.ie/Debates%20Authoring/DebatesWebPack.nsf/committeetakes/TRJ2013012300004?opendocument). [accessed March 2013].

Oum, T., Zhang, A. and Zhang, Y. (2004), "Alternative forms of economic regulation at airports", in *Journal of Transport Economics and Policy*, Vol. 38, No. 2, pp. 217-46.

Portmarnock Community Association (2006), "Cost Benefit Analysis", (available online at: http://www.norunway.com/t2a/appt2.htm). [accessed February 2013].

Schaar, D. and Sherry, l. (2010), "Analysis of Airport Stakeholders", (available online at: http://catsr.ite.gmu.edu/pubs/ICNS_Schaar_AirportStakeholders.pdf). [accessed January 2013].

Social Economy Centre (2006), "Substitution Effects of Formal and Informal Corporate Governance Mechanisms in the Nonprofit Sector", (available online at: sec.oise.utoronto.ca/english/project.../Substitution_AOM_2006.ppt). [accessed March 2013].

Starkie, D. (2001), "Reforming UK Airport Regulation", in *Journal of Transport Economics and Policy*, Vol. 35, pp. 119-135.

Thatcher, T. (2011), *A guidebook for the preservation of public-use airports*, Washington: Transportation Research Board.

Westphal, J. and Khanna, P. (2003), "Keeping directors in line: Social distancing as a control mechanism in the corporate elite", in *Administrative Science Quarterly*, Vol. 48, No. 3, pp. 361-98.

Williamson, O. (1975), *Markets and Hierarchies: Analysis and Antitrust Implications*, New York: The Free Press.

Figure 1. DAA Financial Performance 1986 to 2010

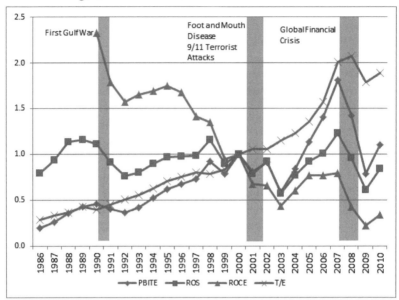

Source: Authors' calculation from annual report data. Note: PBITE and ROS were normalised to equal 1 in the year 2000.

PART 3

SERVICES AND MULTI-SERVICES ENTERPRISES

10. Infrastructure Ontario

The Agencification of Public Works
in a Canadian Province

Patrice DUTIL[1]

Ryerson University, Canada

A long-standing Anglo-Saxon dictum encouraged brides to bring "something old, something new, something borrowed and something blue" to their weddings. The idea was to link the bride's family to the past, but also to symbolize the reality of new relations and beginnings. The display of "something old" (like a piece of inherited jewellery) was to illustrate continuity. The notion of bringing "something new" was to represent good luck and success and the bride's hopes for a bright future in her new married life. "Something borrowed" was to show that sometimes help is needed in order to help a married life. Finally, "something blue" harked back to ancient times when that colour symbolized faithfulness, purity and loyalty.

The saying serves to illustrate the Government of Ontario's approach to agencies, and has particular meaning in the case of Ontario Infrastructure Corporation and Lands (IO), an organization created in 2005 to build new state facilities and expanded in 2011 to oversee the Government stock of real estate. To shape this agency, the Government followed an established past (the State's assumption of public works is something *old*), it brought innovative regulations and structures (something *new*), it adopted methods of real estate funding and management from the private sector (something *borrowed*), and pursued a manner of policy that is more commonly favoured by the right (something *blue*). For a centre-left (red) Liberal Government, this indeed presented a departure.

This practice is genuinely unique. Elected politicians typically wish to control the building of infrastructure for a number of reasons. The first is that political gain is usually associated with the tangible success of building a health centre, a courthouse, a school, a sport or cultural

---

[1] I am very grateful for the research assistance of Ms. Kathryn Barber.

centre, a road, or a multi-purpose Government building. The second has been attributed to the process of construction itself. It is no secret that the political campaigns of political leaders have benefitted from cash-rich contractors. For this reason, the various ministries of "public works" were always as popular as they were necessary.

Yet the Government of Ontario has walked away from this practice. For sure, there still exists a Ministry of Infrastructure, and politicians heading line ministries approve the final decisions on the location and priority of various works and appear at ribbon-cutting ceremonies. But otherwise, they (and the traditional bureaucracies dedicated to public works) have largely removed from the actual construction of new infrastructure. What does this phenomenon reveal about the nature and process of agencification that leads to the creation of public enterprises and indeed about the future of such entities?

IO is revealing of many phenomena in public administration, both in Canada and abroad. Agencification is not new to Ontario, but the practice has grown dramatically in the past decade. There are now more than 600 agencies, board, commissions and tribunals in Ontario that are mandated to pursue a public good, and 259 of them are controlled directly by the provincial Government. It is in this context that IO was created in 2005 with a relatively new structure and a clear mandate, yet displayed clear indications of a path dependency in the sense that it emerged as the product of a slow but steady process of creating an "arm's length" distance between the Government and its infrastructure organization. It is deserving of study because it brings to light a number of features in the study of the birth and development of Government agencies and because it was trumpeted as representative of a new generation of public enterprises.[2] It widely boasts of a reputation as a successful organization, but the metric to prove this claim is not offered. Has IO succeeded in its mandate? The answer is mixed. It has certainly brought a rigor to the process of working with contractors and funders, but could considerably improve its performance in public reporting. The Government committed in 2005 to a five-year, $30B infrastructure plan. IO could not alone reach this objective, but it certainly has gone a long way in meeting it.

---

[2] An exception is Gervan Fearon, "'Guardian' as 'Spender': Infrastructure Investment, 1960-2005", in Patrice Dutil (ed.), *The Guardian: Perspectives on the Ministry of Finance of Ontario* (Toronto: University of Toronto Press, 2011), pp. 287-319. See also P. Antunes *et al.*, *Economic Impact of Public Infrastructure in Ontario* (Ottawa: Conference Board of Canada, 2010) and *Dedicated Public-Private Partnership Units: A Survey of Institutional and Governance Structures* (OECD, 2010).

IO aims to facilitate the building of any public infrastructure in the province by bringing together public and private sector expertise in financing and project management, and by working outside the traditional public service culture. Its mission is reflective of the central tenets of the New Public Management, but is equally rooted in the bureaucratic traditions of the Government of Ontario. This new approach is considered vital at a time when Ontario's public infrastructure is perishing fast (older facilities are unable to cope with current demand, let alone future needs) as the province tries to service a rapidly growing population with an infrastructure that was designed for half the current number. Recent budgets in the province have awarded less than four per cent of expenditures to infrastructure. By its own admission, the Ontario Government needs to spend up to $100 billion to make the necessary repairs and to prepare the province for the future.[3] To that effect, one could say that IO was "built for speed", but one could also argue that it was built for easy collapse. In other words, once the wave of building is completed, Governments could be in a position to wind down the agency relatively quickly and politically painlessly.

Section A: Identification of the Enterprise

The Ontario Infrastructure and Lands Corporation, known simply as "Infrastructure Ontario" (IO), is a crown corporation of the Government of Ontario, the largest province of Canada, with over 13.5 million inhabitants.[4] It employs over four hundred full-time employees (who participate in the Public Service Pension Fund – the cost of post-retirement and non-pension employee benefits are paid by the Government of Ontario), and has an operating budget of over $70M. This number, however, does not convey the complexity of the organization as its employees lead the creation and management of the Government of Ontario's real estate and an important portion of its infrastructure. It is important to note that IO has not been involved in transportation infrastructure or power-generation facility construction which are two key components of the Government's public works engagement.

Infrastructure Ontario is one of two agencies of the Ministry of Infrastructure Renewal and as such is accountable to the Government

---

[3] Government of Ontario, *ReNew Ontario, 2005-10: Strategic Highlights*, p. 2.

[4] Infrastructure Ontario is located in two office towers in downtown Toronto, the provincial capital, at 777 Bay Street, Toronto, Ontario and 1 Dundas St. West, Toronto, Ontario. The Real Estate Management division is based at 900 Bay Street, Toronto, Ontario and has offices in Guelph, Sudbury, Thunder Bay, Ottawa and Kingston. The website is www.infrastructureontario.ca.

through that Department (the other agency is the much smaller and narrowly focused Waterfront Toronto). The Government department sets infrastructure policy and conducts key strategic planning operations to manage the Government's response to infrastructural needs. As such, there is an on-going creative tension between the department and its agency as to who genuinely sets policy and programs. In 2011, Infrastructure Ontario was merged with another Government agency, the Ontario Realty Corporation, an entity that managed the Government's buildings and land. The provincial Government merged the two agencies to oversee the development and management of provincial infrastructure projects, provide loans to various public sector clients (municipalities, universities and colleges, schools and hospitals), and manage the province's real estate. The agency now manages 4,366,443 m^2 (1,021,933 m^2 rented from the private sector and 3,335,219 m^2 owned by the province) in 6,400 buildings and structures. It also manages 97,123 acres of land owned by the province.[5]

The new entity, The Ontario Infrastructure and Lands Corporation, still known as "Infrastructure Ontario," was created by the *Ontario Infrastructure and Lands Corporation Act* (2011). Infrastructure Ontario is economically dependent on the Province of Ontario as the majority of revenue is from services provided to various Ministries of the Province and clients in the sector of municipalities, universities and colleges, schools, and hospitals and long-term care facilities.[6]

The act states the functions of IO as:

- to provide financing for infrastructure purposes to municipalities and to eligible public organizations;

- to provide the Government with advice and services, including project management, contract management and development, related to public works;

- to provide financial management for public works managed by the Ministry or by a Crown agency for which the Minister is responsible;

- to carry out the powers, duties and functions delegated by the Minister to the Corporation under the Ministry of Infrastructure Act, 2011;

---

[5] Government of Ontario, *Public Accounts of Ontario, 2011-12, Financial Statements of Government Organizations, Government Business Enterprises, Trusts and Miscellaneous Statements, Vol. 2b*, pp. 1-231.

[6] *Ibid.*, pp. 1-242.

- to provide advice and services related to real property to public sector organizations when directed to do so in writing by the Minister;
- to advise the Minister on infrastructure projects in Ontario, when directed to do so in writing by the Minister;
- to advise the Minister on financial, strategic or other matters involving the Government, when directed to do so in writing by the Minister;
- to implement or assist in the implementation of transactions involving the Government, when directed to do so in writing by the Minister;
- to provide project management and contract management services related to infrastructure projects in Ontario that are not public works, when directed to do so in writing by the Minister; and
- to undertake any additional objects as directed by the Minister of Infrastructure.

Infrastructure Ontario has been expanding the scope of its activities rapidly, but its aims and structure are not entirely original.

Section B: History

The responsibility to build and maintain publicly owned infrastructure such as provincial roads, hospitals, colleges and universities, and electricity-generating plants has changed hands over the history of Ontario. For most of period since Confederation (1867), individual departments were authorized to build and manage their physical assets. The Ministry of Health, for example, built its own hospitals and the Ministry of Corrections erected its own jails. The result was a patchwork of practices, successes and failures. Each department had its own real estate division, designed its own facilities, hired contractors and managed its properties. Consequently, department developed its own expertise and culture around project management.

The process worked fairly well, but after a rush to build in the 1950s and 1960s, the Government of Ontario slowed dramatically its funding of hospitals, roads, courthouses, schools and universities. The 1970s saw a dramatic increase in the cost of medical services and education and the once healthy portion of the budget that was attributed to building the public infrastructure was gradually whittled to a minuscule proportion of annual expenditures. Indeed, after twenty years of frenetic spending on public infrastructure, the provincial treasury – ever conservative in its fear of debt – balked at the sky-high rates of borrowing in the 1980s. To bring more execution and accounting discipline to the task of building infrastructure the Ontario Government developed a multi-purpose agency to infrastructure expenditure. The creation of the Board of Industrial Leadership and Development (BILD) in 1980 replaced a variety of small single-purpose agencies such as the Ontario Housing Corporation, the Urban Transportation Development Corporation, the Ontario Energy Corporation and the Ontario Universities Capital Aid Corporation that had been established through the 1970s to help prioritize infrastructure building. Building in the 1980s was anaemic, however, as the state coped with inflation and sluggish economic growth.[7]

Finance department officials also slowly came to the conclusion that the "pay-as-you-go" cash accounting method for infrastructure building could no longer work and that its bookkeeping had to reflect the productive life of the asset. The Government started adopting a new way of accounting for its infrastructure building. In the past, the province's investments were made on a year-by-year basis. There was little need to coordinate capital projects and the principal source of funding was simply the provincial treasury, drawn from current revenues, with the entire cost of the project accounted for in the years of building, not over the more realistic life of the asset. By the early 1990s, pressures to move to accrual accounting became difficult to resist. By the end of the century, the habit of expensing the full cost of the tangible capital assets in the year of acquisition or construction was abandoned. Instead, accrual methods of accounting allowed the Government to spread the representation of cost over the life of the asset (15 years for a highway, for example, and 40 years for a building).

In 1990, the left-leaning New Democratic Party was elected and two years later collapsed the BILD, and instead created a "super agency" to stimulate building: the Jobs Ontario Capital Fund. At the same time, new agencies were created to give a clear focus for the construction of assets in discrete areas: The Ontario Transportation Capital Corporation (for rail, roads and urban transit), the Ontario Realty Corporation (to manage Government property). The Ontario Financing Authority was also created to rationalize the Government's borrowing activities.

Government ministries, for the most part, were unaffected by these developments, and the provincial Government financed projects of all sorts with little control on how they would be funded. The problems with this practice grew more evident as infrastructure demands grew more urgent

---

[7] See Neil Bradford, "Public-Private Partnership? Shifting Paradigms of Economic Governance in Ontario" *Canadian Journal of Political Science*, Vol. 36, No. 5 (Dec., 2003), pp. 1005-1033. More positive is Murphy, Tim. "The Case for Public-Private Partnerships in Infrastructure" *Canadian Public Administration*, Vol. 51, No. 1, 2008, pp. 99-126.

in the 1990s and as cost overruns and construction delays became daily fodder for the media. In 1995, a conservative Government was elected and undertook a massive (and highly controversial) redevelopment of the aging hospitals of the province. The Government created an agency, the Jobs and Investment Board, and published a blueprint for infrastructure investment, *A Road Map to Prosperity*. One of its recommendations was the creation of a more permanent agency that would steer Government ministries into new approaches for funding and construction and bring some consistency across Government construction operations. At the end of 1999 the Government created a new crown agency, the Ontario SuperBuild Corporation (OSC), or "SuperBuild", to spearhead new construction.

The intention of the Government was to invest $20B in the 1999-2004 period and pledged $2.9B for the first year of the plan.[8] The objective was plain: the Government wanted a more strategic approach to the financing and management of its physical assets. SuperBuild was made responsible to approve all the capital plans of the Government departments and it, in turn, would submit recommendations to the Cabinet Committee on Privatization and SuperBuild. Within a year, the president of SuperBuild boasted that "already we are having an impact on the way Government thinks about infrastructure. Our mandate is to help the provincial Government and its broader public sector partners be more strategic and be more creative in the financing and management of its physical assets."[9]

In effect, the Government of Ontario had placed an agency in a centralizing role and gave it, and its board of directors, a direct link to cabinet. The Board of Directors of SuperBuild Corporation had a distinct feature in that at least half were public service executives. Their role was explicitly to provide advice on "new public-private partnerships [P3s] and on approaches to privatization."[10] The president of SuperBuild was a long-time advisor to the Premier and a member of the Progressive Conservative Party, David Lindsay.

The core mandate of SuperBuild was clear, as were its activities:

- providing leadership and central coordination for policy development, planning and Cabinet approvals relating to the Province's capital envelope;

---

8   Ontario Ministry of Finance, Backgrounder, "Ontario Budget 1999 Superbuild Grown Fund will Renew Infrastructure", 4 May 1999.

9   Ontario SuperBuild, "Building Ontario's Future: A SuperBuild Progress Report" December 2000, p. 4.

10   *Ibid.*, p. 5.

- focusing on developing public-private partnerships for infrastructure investments and supporting the Government's review of privatization candidates;
- coordinating the implementation of two major SuperBuild partnership initiatives delivered through ministries: investments in infrastructure critical to the future growth of rural areas, including small towns and cities; and projects for developing recreational, cultural and tourist attractions throughout the province.
- managing the "Millennium Partnership Initiative" through various ministries that support infrastructure projects in major urban centres outside the greater Toronto area including:
  - projects that address gridlock
  - environmental protection including sewer and water upgrades and improvements
  - access to strategic highway corridors and international border crossings.
- working with the Ministry of Transportation in implementing the Government's Transit Initiatives including the Golden Horseshoe Transit Investment Partnership (GTIP) and the Transit Investment Partnership (TIP).
- coordinating the Ontario Government's involvement in the revitalization of the Toronto Waterfront through the Toronto Waterfront Secretariat, which reports through SuperBuild.

SuperBuild was thus more focused on policy development regarding P3s than in actually delivering the construction. It would prioritize projects and make recommendations to the Cabinet, but then would step back and allow the Government departments to manage their projects themselves. Within three years, SuperBuild had proven most aggressive: $11.5B of works were started, including $5B for highways and bridges, $4.5B in healthcare infrastructures, $1B in colleges and universities, and $1B scattered among 650 community projects.[11]

During the election campaign of 2003, the Liberal Party promised a vigorous public infrastructure building plan that would specifically reevaluate the practice of P3s. Upon its election, the new Liberal Government of Ontario created the Ministry of Infrastructure Renewal to signal its priority and within ten months published *Building a Better Tomorrow*, to guide the Ontario Government, municipalities, and broader public sector partners in choosing the best options for planning, financing

---

[11] Ontario SuperBuild, *Progress Report 2003* (Toronto: Queen's Printer, 2003).

and procuring public infrastructure assets.[12] SuperBuild ended its operations.

The new framework, released in July 2004, established guidelines for infrastructure planning, financing and procurement of Government real estate. It articulated five fundamental principles:

> *Protection of the Public Interest*: The public interest is paramount in the Government's infrastructure renewal plan. All public infrastructure initiatives should be delivered efficiently; protect and promote public health and safety; ensure high-quality public services; and be accessible to all Ontarians.

> *Value for Money*: Ontarians expect and deserve value for their tax dollars. All public infrastructure investments should be cost-effective, optimize risk allocation, and be completed on time and within budget. There must be safeguards against financial returns that are not proportional to the associated risk where private financing is involved in the delivery of public infrastructure initiatives.

> *Appropriate Public Control/Ownership*: Appropriate public control/ ownership of public assets must be preserved. In particular, consistent with the principle of appropriate ownership/control, the framework states that public ownership of assets will be preserved in the hospital, water/sewer, and public school sectors.

> *Accountability*: Stakeholders involved in delivering public infrastructure initiatives must be accountable. Public infrastructure initiatives should have clear lines of responsibility and accountability, rigorous and transparent reporting and oversight requirements, and clear, measurable performance measures.

> *Fair, Transparent and Efficient Processes*: The processes facilitating the development of public infrastructure initiatives must be fair, transparent and efficient. All public infrastructure initiatives should have efficient and fair bidding processes, and contractual agreements that are based on clear, comprehensive guidelines and full public disclosure.[13]

The Government document outlined the major types of infrastructure expenditure covered by the Infrastructure Planning, Financing and Procurement Framework and proposed the accounting treatment for each form of investment.[14]

---

[12] The Ministry of Infrastructure Renewal was merged with the Ministry of Energy in 2008. That experiment was short-lived, and the small ministry is now known simply as the Ministry of Infrastructure.

[13] *Building a Better Tomorrow: An Infrastructure Planning, Financing and Procurement Framework for Ontario's Public Sector*, Queen's Printer for Ontario, 2004, p. 10. http:// www.moi.gov.on.ca/pdf/en/BBT-Framework_EN.pdf.

[14] *Ibid.*, p. 12.

Investment Classification	Description	Accounting Treatment Guidelines
Maintenance	Maintenance includes the costs of maintaining assets for their intended purpose and service life, and repairs that do not prolong an asset's original life expectancy.	Infrastructure asset-related expenditures that are considered maintenance expenditures should be expensed.
Deferred Maintenance	Deferred maintenance refers to the accumulated value of normally required maintenance investments that have been deferred from prior years. This amount should reflect the amount of investment required to bring the asset into normal operating condition at the beginning of the period (i.e., excluding current-year maintenance investment) to the extent possible.	If the deferred maintenance meets the criteria for rehabilitation and refurbishment, expenditures may be capitalized. If the deferred maintenance meets the criteria for maintenance, expenditures should be expensed.
Rehabilitation and Refurbishment	Rehabilitation and refurbishment are those initiatives that result in any of the following material changes to an existing asset: • increased physical output or service capacity; • lower operating costs; • extended life; or • improved output quality.	Expenditures on rehabilitation and refurbishment initiatives may be capitalized.
Renewal and New Infrastructure Assets	Construction of new assets or the replacement of existing assets.	All direct acquisition, construction and/or development costs related to new infrastructure assets may be capitalized and amortized.

The Government was also clear as to what factors it would recognize in identifying projects:

Factors	Description
Demographics	Entities should consider both current and future indicators, such as population change by age cohort; impacts of births, deaths, immigration and emigration; and issues specific to program areas.
Program Changes	These include new initiatives, program terminations or changes in program parameters.

Factors	Description
Technological Changes	Examples include the impact of Web-based technologies on distance learning, new medical technologies on the delivery of health care or e-business opportunities.
Economic or Business Changes	These include current and projected financial or economic/ market trends and opportunities – in general or specific to the service sector.
Environmental Factors	These include the impact of any potential changes to environmental standards.
Social Changes	Entities should consider any trends that could affect service delivery needs, including the changing needs of consumers of public services.
Legislation	Factors to consider here include any new statutory requirements affecting the entity.
Economic or Business Changes	These include current and projected financial or economic/ market trends and opportunities – in general or specific to the service sector.
Environmental Factors	These include the impact of any potential changes to environmental standards.
Social Changes	Entities should consider any trends that could affect service delivery needs, including the changing needs of consumers of public services.
Legislation	Factors to consider here include any new statutory requirements affecting the entity.

The policy framework even outlined roles and responsibilities for a wide range of actors. Other ministries, for example, were identified as having a role. The Ministry of Finance of the province clearly was to have oversight on expenses to ensure that the ministry's commitments were consistent with what the state could afford. The Government's Management Board Secretariat would have a role in assessing and approving the "financial aspects of annual infrastructure plans, including the linkage of capital and operating expenditures". For instance, the Ministry of Public Infrastructure Renewal was identified as the "central agency" for all aspects of planning, coordinating and financing projects. It was declared to be the "repository of the Government's expertise in the area of infrastructure financing, capital procurement, initiative management, related financial analysis and asset management".[15] Most interestingly, line ministries, clients like hospitals, universities and municipalities would continue to identify and prioritize infrastructure needs. In the first year of its operations, IO worked with the Ministry of Health to develop "Generic Output Specifications" for all hospital projects financed by alternative funding plans (AFPs). These provided

---

[15] *Ibid.*, p. 40.

313

a basic design criteria and performance requirements. The private sector was accorded a role in investment, financing and delivering infrastructure, but on a case-by-case basis.

The document was entirely silent on any possible role for a "SuperBuild" type of agency and yet the Government created – almost in the same month – the Ontario Strategic Infrastructure Financing Authority (OSIFA) to spearhead the funding of public infrastructure assets, particularly in cash-strapped municipalities. OSIFA was endowed with three sources of funds: It was given a $1B endowment that was due to the province in 2053, and another $120M from the Ontario Clean Water Agency. It also sold Ontario Opportunity Bonds for $323M. Its long-term debt amounted to $1.4B. OSIFA was mandated to use the interest from these debts to pay for operations and to begin funding projects.[16] It was also mandated explicitly to pursue a "pooled financing" approach that would aggregate the infrastructure investment needs of many municipalities into one fund. It was expected that this strategy would lead to lower costs and longer term financing, but progress was slow and news of cost overruns and delays in construction continuously embarrassed the Government. By 2006, OSIFA had loaned over $1B to municipalities, educational institutions and not-for-profit long-term care service providers. It is worth noting that Government agencies were not covered by this arrangement. The agency that oversees the regulation and production of electricity, for example, could not use the services of OSIFA.

A year later, the Government of Ontario launched a study of the issue and in 2005 published *ReNew Ontario 2005-2010*, a plan that aimed at adopting more efficient methods of building as well as alternative public financing methods involving the private sector. *ReNew Ontario 2005-2010* indicated that a new agency would be created to operationalize a strategic investment plan to improve Ontario infrastructure and to manage complex infrastructure renewal projects.[17] The notion here was that a new approach was necessary to leverage private financing and expertise to approach more expertly the rebuilding and maintenance vital infrastructure.

ReNew Ontario 2005-10 announced an ambitious five-year strategy to spend $30B on infrastructure. It highlighted key areas where investment was particularly needed. The average age of hospitals, it pointed out, was over 40 years. Many jails were older than 75 years and some dated back to the 19th century. Road transportation remained a constant challenge as highway 401, which traverses the province, remains among the busiest in North America. The seminal document also reinforced the intention

---

16 Ontario Public Accounts, 2003-04, Vol. 2, p. 141.
17 Infrastructure Ontario (2008), *Annual Report 2007-2008*.

that all infrastructure projects would be subject to the principles of the Government's planning, financing and procurement framework:

In Health, $5 billion was to be spent on:

Completion of 39 projects;
Initiation of 33 new projects by 2008;
Start of 33 more projects by 2010.

In Education, $10 billion was to be spent on:

$9 billion in elementary and secondary schools;
$1 billion in college and universities.

In Public Transit and Transportation, $11.4 billion was to be spent:

$3.1 billion in urban transit in metropolitan areas;
$1.4 billion in support for transit in smaller communities
$1.8 billion to upgrade roads, bridges and water treatment in Northern Ontario;
$6.2 billion in highway maintenance and expansion;
$638 million to relieve congestion at border crossings.

In Affordable Housing:

$600 million throughout the province.

For Justice-Sector Infrastructure, $1 billion was to be spent on:

Two new adult correctional facilities;
Two new detention centres for youth;
One new centre for forensic sciences;
Two new courthouse facilities.

It projected that the first $16B would be invested on particular priorities such as hospitals, highways and transit systems, new affordable housing, key infrastructure in northern Ontario and improving municipal water systems, bridges and roads. It also committed to transferring $5 billion to school boards and long-term care facilities and another $5 billion would be dedicated to support repairs and construction in the school system and to fund university expansions. Finally, $1.5 billion would be sent on public transit in Ontario's big cities. Most significantly, the Government anticipated $2.3 billion to be raised through AFP methods. Indeed, *ReNew Ontario* re-articulated the defence of Alternative Financing and Procurement that had first been made by the SuperBuild Corporation. This method, the paper assured readers, would allow the Government "to take advantage of private-sector capital, expertise and efficiencies to do far more in the next few years than we have done in the past, and to do it on time and on budget." It was inspired by the United Kingdom's Private Finance Initiative (PFI) whereby the private sector is charged with responsibilities – and the risks involved – to finance and deliver public infrastructure. Sensitive to public concerns, the document assured that only ten per cent of projects would be funded by AFP methods and that "core assets such as hospitals, schools and water systems will be publicly owned; all public assets will be under control," and reaffirmed the "principled approach" to building infrastructure that had been articulated in the 2004 *Building a Better Tomorrow. ReNew Ontario* was as remarkably silent on the new agency it was creating as it was ambitious about its objectives. A few months, later, in November 2005, some two years after its election, the Government of Ontario established the Ontario Infrastructure Projects Corporation, informally known as Infrastructure Ontario (IO), to implement Ontario's major infrastructure projects. Headed by J. David Livingston, who was appointed by the Government, IO set out to recruit individuals in both the public and private sector who had deep experience in the management of financing and managing the building of infrastructure. Within a year, 130 employees (some inherited from OSIFA) were hired with the ambition to be known by industry to be "tough (but fair) negotiators, acting in the public interest. We want our clients to recognize us as knowledgeable and helpful, working to meet their needs. And we want our shareholder – the Government of Ontario – to see us as the organization that responsibly delivers valuable assets to taxpayers on a timely basis".[18] This was a critical step in decades-long process of agencification of public works. In effect, the Government announced that it had lost confidence in the public service's ability to manage public works, and that it was comfortable in entrusting a team of experts working outside ministries with its most visible accomplishments.

IO also assumed the 50-year loan of a $1B that had been given to OSIFA and its endowment was supplemented by another $120M 20-year loan. The two combined with a new issue of "Infrastructural Renewal Bonds" of $650M provided a Reserve Fund of $2,113,284,000 from which IO was to invest, pay interest on, and fund its operations.[19] IO has also received special funding annually from the Ministry of Infrastructure to help defray the cost of salaries, benefits and general administration for both operations and its loan program.

In 2006, IO merged with OSIFA so as to ensure, as the announcement put it, that "the new Ontario Infrastructure and Lands Corporation will

---

18   Infrastructure Ontario (2007), *Annual Report 2006-07*, p. 4.
19   *Ontario Public Accounts, 2006-2007*, Vol. 2, p. 205.

ensure stronger oversight, transparency and accountability while saving Ontario taxpayers over $10 million over three years".[20]

The primary goals of the new Ontario Infrastructure and Lands Corporation were to provide a financing vehicle to support the municipalities, universities and other public sector entities. It would serve two essential functions: 1) Procurement and project management though the Alternative Financing and Procurement (AFP) model, and 2) Pooled Financing.[21]

Figure B.1. IO Salary and Benefits, 2006-12

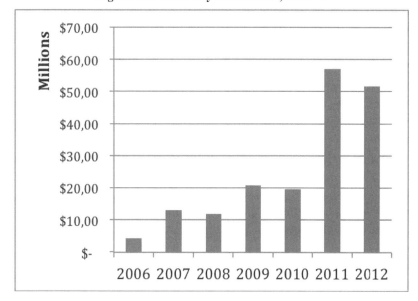

(Source: Government of Ontario Public Accounts)

In 2011, IO was merged with two other agencies. The oldest was the Stadium Corporation of Ontario Limited (StadCo), which had been incorporated in August 1984 under the *Business Corporations Act*.[22] This Crown Corporation was responsible for the construction and operation of the SkyDome, the controversial baseball stadium built in downtown

---

20 Government of Ontario, (June 6, 2011), "OIIPC Merger Announcement", Retrieved from: http://www.infrastructureontario.ca/uploadedFiles/OIPC-Merger-Announcement-fact-sheet.pdf.

21 Government of Ontario, (June 6, 2011), OIIPC Merger Announcement. Retrieved from: http://www.infrastructureontario.ca/uploadedFiles/OIPC-Merger-Announcement-fact-sheet.pdf.

22 Ontario Infrastructure and Lands Corporation Act, 2011, S.O. 2011, c.9, Sched. 32.

Toronto with Government funds in the 1990s. In addition to being the target of multiple lawsuits, it incurred several million dollars worth of debt to the Ontario taxpayer[23] as well as generated tension between provincial and municipal bodies.[24] While the SkyDome was sold to private interests in 1994, StadCo remained operational in order to look after liabilities and obligations that had resulted from construction, operation, maintenance and ownership of the structure.[25]

The merge with the Ontario Realty Corporation (ORC) was far more significant. It was first established by the *Capital Investment Plan Act, 1993*[26] replacing the Ontario Land Corporation and many of the functions of the Ministry of Government Services.[27] It was an initiative of the New Democratic Party Government to generate income, generate jobs and improve Ontario infrastructure at a time of severe economic recession.[28] The ORC continued to provide the Ontario Government with real-estate, property and project management services. Its main duties were the development of policies, strategies and implementation plans to maximize use of existing real-estate portfolios; sales and acquisitions of land and buildings; property leasing as needed to augment the inventory of owned space; property management, including day-to-day maintenance and repair of owned and leased facilities; and project management of large capital projects.[29]

Indeed, the Corporation was responsible for one of Canada's largest real estate portfolios. In 2006, this included: 35,000 hectares of land and 6,000 buildings. The Ontario Government owned 81% of the portfolio and the remainder was leased.[30] The ORC required approximately $600 million in revenue in order to offset the expenses of managing its portfolio. It employed approximately 300 full time employees.

It, too, was no stranger to controversy, something that followed the ORC through three different administrations as opposition parties accused

---

[23] Van Alphen, T., "Final dome tally: $263 million lost", Toronto Star, 29 September 1994; Van Alpen, T., "Bickering, lawsuits the order of the day" *Toronto Star*, 2 August 1992.

[24] Byers, J., "Toronto demands Skydome pay taxes", Toronto Star, 13 August 1991.

[25] Ontario Ministry of Finance, Published Results-Based Plan, 2006-07. Toronto, Ont., 1997. Retrieved from: http://www.ontla.on.ca/ Its main responsibility was the operation of the bus parking facility beside the stadium.

[26] *Ontario Infrastructure and Lands Corporation Act, 2011*, S.O. 2011, c.9, Sched. 32.

[27] Brennan, R., "Ontario land agency in trouble over sales; Property flips, cries of cronyism dog its operation", *Toronto Star*, 18 March 2000.

[28] *Ibid.*

[29] Office of the Auditor General of On, *2006 Annual Report. Chapter 3: Ontario Realty Corporation – Real Estate and Accommodation Services*. Retrieved from: http://www. auditor.on.ca/.

[30] *Ibid.*

the Government of developing the agency simply as a way to conceal Government deficits.[31] During the 2000s, under a Progressive Conservative Government, the ORC was accused of land deal irregularities – namely selling provincial land at prices well below market value to buyers who subsequently resold the properties at significantly higher prices within a number of weeks or months.[32] The Ontario Provincial Police (OPP) anti-rackets branch was called in to investigate as well as an independent audit and a civil suit.[33] This culminated in a 2010 OPP raid on the ORC offices as part of a corruption probe when ORC was under Liberal leadership.[34] These investigations appear to be ongoing (certainly, the results have not been publicized).

Section C: Public Mission

The public mission of IO has thus evolved rapidly in its short history. Its main objectives are to "modernize and finance the renewal of public infrastructure, to maximize the value of public real estate and managing Government facilities."[35] It is not designed, or mandated to generate a surplus (or profit); in fact, IO has been entirely dependent on funding from the state to conduct its activities. These can be classified into four major areas: Realizing Projects, Providing Loans, Maintaining Building and Managing Lands. Under the Projects area, IO addresses Ontario long-term infrastructure renewal and building plans.[36]

The IO manages its own loan portfolio. The money is provided by the Government of Ontario and the issue of bonds. In its loan services, IO offers long-term financing to eligible public sector clients such as Aboriginal Health Access Centres, Community Health and Social Service Hubs, Hospices, Housing Providers, Local Services Boards, Long-term Care Homes, Municipal Corporations, Municipalities, Professional Arts Training, Sport & Recreation Organizations and Universities/Colleges.[37]

[31] Brennan, R., "Ontario land agency in trouble over sales; Property flips, cries of cronyism dog its operation", *Toronto Star*, 18 March 2000.
[32] Brennan, R., "Police probe land deals Critics accuse Tories of political cover-up", *Toronto Star*, 1 April 2000.
[33] Ferguson, R., "Another day, another scandal at Ontario Realty; As much as $11 million may have gone astray", *Toronto Star*, 13 May 2000.
[34] Moore, B., "Realty Corp. axed days before OPP raid", *Toronto Star*, 29 July 2010.
[35] Infrastructure Ontario, "FAQ: What is Infrastructure Ontario (IO)?" Retrieved in March 2013 from: http://www.infrastructureontario.ca/About-Us/Frequently-Asked-Questions/.
[36] http://www.infrastructureontario.ca/templates/Projects.aspx.
[37] http://www.infrastructureontario.ca/What-We-Do/Loans/.

The agency brings a sophisticated approach to managing risk. Its annual reports consistently identify the interest rate risk, the liquidity risk, credit risk and operational risk (such as adequacy of financial systems, adequacy of policy and procedures, legal liability and potential for fraud, error or manipulation). These are revised on occasion and informally audited by outside organizations. IO recently adopted a Business Continuity Plan, including Disaster Recovery, to prepare for major crises such as systems failures, loss of physical office space or extended power outages. IO has adopted a management policy that requires continuous monitoring and reporting of the interest rate risk position to the Board of Directors. As such, IO manages a strict interest rate risk limit that specifies expected losses at specific shifts in interest rates. It also works closely with the Ontario Financing Authority to coordinate and executive borrowing activities. The financial statements of IO are audited by external auditors.

Infrastructure Ontario also manages the province's Alternative Financing and Procurement Program; in other words, it spearheads efforts to find funding for projects, but not from the Government treasury. IO had attached a particularly sophisticated risk assessment and risk management component to its AFP projects so that it considers the construction industry's capacity risk, the actual construction risk, transition risk and operational risk. Most important is the concern for "risk events" that could impede project completion. To identify and manage these risks, IO organizes various project work committees, joint building committees, AFP Construction Committees. The latter are held monthly to review project status, risk issues, schedule performance, contingency status, stakeholder issues and budget/cost issues. It is clear in examining the list of contractors doing business with IO that there is a wide range of actors involved – clearly the reflection of a risk-management approach that would avoid concentrating too many projects in select hands. IO has adopted a reporting template so as to ensure consistency of reporting. No least, the financing risk of the organization is consistently under review.

Under its "building" mandate, IO runs three separate real estate management divisions: Asset Management, Realty Services and Client Program Delivery. Asset Management is responsible for working with private sector service providers in order to deliver services to clients and tenets. The Client Program Delivery division develops real estate accommodations and capital program planning.[38] The Realty Services division addresses the needs of Ontario's broader commitments by developing, recommending and implementing real estate programs and

---

[38] http://www.infrastructureontario.ca/templates/Buildings.aspx.

initiatives. The Lands division is responsible for managing provincially owned and leased real estate in a way that maximizes benefit for Ontario taxpayers.[39]

IO has also created a formal industry outreach program called the "Strategic Opportunities Committee" (SOC) that meets quarterly basis. The committee includes IO executives in addition to representatives from the Ontario Association of Architects, the Ontario General Contractors Association, Consulting Engineers of Ontario and Association of Registered Interior Designers of Ontario as well as IO's project service providers: CB Richard Ellis, MHPM Gestion, and SNC Lavalin O&M.[40] A review of annual reports also reveals collaborations with groups such as the Ministry of the Attorney General, City of Toronto, Humber Regional Hospital, Ministry of Community Safety and Correctional Services, the former Ministry of Energy and Infrastructure, and its sister agency, Waterfront Toronto.[41] It is worth noting that IO's mission keeps expanding beyond brick-and-mortar projects. It recently embarked on the creation of a diabetes registry,[42] and has been assisting an electricity generator with a request-for-proposals on a nuclear procurement project.

Section D: Operations

The structure of IO is relatively flat. Over the years, the operations have evolved according to executive capacity and IO's growing mandate. The CEO currently oversees seven subalterns.

The Executive Vice-President of Commercial Projects and Lending. This office of approximately forty employees is focused on delivering projects that have a commercial dimension and that may thus lend themselves to AFP practices. The focus here is in realizing commercial and municipal projects. This department of about thirty people essentially conducts the banking operations of IO. It is concerned with maintaining stakeholder relations (noted as "customers" in IO documents), and in marketing IO to potentially new clients.

The Chief Administrative Officer.

This office oversees Corporate Services, a group of approximately sixty people. This division regroups the Chief Financial Officer and

---

[39] http://www.infrastructureontario.ca/templates/Lands.aspx.

[40] http://www.infrastructureontario.ca/About-Us/Partnering-with-Industry/.

[41] Ontario Realty Corporation, *Annual Report 2009-2010*, Toronto, Ontario, 2010.

[42] This project was inherited from e-health Ontario, a scandal-prone agency. IO's performance and progress on this file has come under some criticism. See Paul Christopher Webster, "Diabetes Registry Overdue, If not Obsolete", *Canadian Medical Association Journal*, Vol. 184, No. 9, 14 May 2012, pp. 4109-12.

the Office of Human Resources and Information Technology. IT alone has over 25 employees. It also manages the logistics and affairs of the Board of Directors, and the liaison with the MOIR. This office oversees Risk Management and Internal Audit, as well as all aspects of cash management.

The Executive Vice-President of Major Projects

This office supervises the largest division of IP, almost one hundred full-time employees. It is divided in to multiple teams of "civil infrastructure" and "project delivery" teams, each with approximately project managers and coordinators.

The Executive Vice-President of Corporate Development.

This is essentially a one-person department that advises the CEO.

The Executive Vice-President of Real Estate Management.

This individual rallies offices concerned with asset management, client program delivery and realty services. The management of assets is divided into three regional offices: Central (based in Toronto, with twenty employees), North and East (with offices in Kingston, Ottawa, Sudbury and Thunder Bay and thirty employees), and South (with an office in Guelph, and fifteen employees). The "client delivery" section of about thirty employees is divided into five branches, each managing a portfolio of buildings. Finally, the Realty Services branch is composed of forty professionals who manage leases and contractual obligations as well as any environmental issues arising from the properties of the Government of Ontario. This division also has a team to ensure that the buildings owned by the Government are energy efficient.

The Executive Vice-President of Realty Planning and Development

This office directs approximately 45 employees. It is concerned with the variety of issues arising from acquisitions and sales, as well as strategic planning. While half the staff is divided among commercial projects and land development, the other half is devoted to strategic asset planning.

The Executive Vice-President of Transactions Structuring

This office directs almost a hundred people. The team includes legal services (over thirty attorneys and their assistants), business strategy officers of all ranks (including twenty procurement specialists, a dozen financial transaction analysts and ten program coordinators and business analysts), asset optimization division, communications, business relations and Government relations.[43]

---

[43] This structure as of May 2013.

A typical project starts with an idea born elsewhere: in a ministry or a municipality, university, school or hospital. The entity is not forced to approach IO on a project, but there is enormous pressure to do so because ministries have been stripped of the ability to conduct such undertakings and IO has a clear capacity to manage a project from its inception to its completion. IO's Corporate Development and Major Projects teams will first examine the viability of the project and recommend a structure for funding. The Commercial Projects and Lending division will then analyse a range of building and financing possibilities, ranging from simple Design-Build to more complex arrangements. This can include a straight loan or an APF arrangement. As a consequence, IO may request to borrow money from the Government of Ontario, issue debentures of its own, and/ or engineer a strategic partnership with a private sector lender under an AFP framework. IO's Transactions Structuring team will then conduct a competition to attract potential contractors and select the winner based on a range of criteria, ranging from cost to quality of work.

As the project begins construction, IO will continue to monitor progress until it is delivered to the client. Issues involving unexpected delays are brought to its team and arrangements are made to manage the situation so as not to extend the project or increase its cost. IO's team of engineers, architects and project managers will monitor construction until it is completed.

A key function of IO's operations is to attract interest in new project by offering its services. It can make moneys available to municipalities and other eligible clients. Finally, it consistently monitors client and stakeholder satisfaction indices through surveys. It also polls employee opinions on the organization's strengths and weaknesses. The latest survey made public (2010) reported an approval rating of 75% in the top two categories for the Loan Program on the Customer Satisfaction Survey question relating to "Understands customer needs and objectives". It indicated that 93% of current clients viewed IO as an ideal partner for their infrastructure projects and that over three-quarters of all non-clients (76%) are aware of the Loan Program offered by IO. Remarkably, only 37% of respondents would consider an IO loan as a method for financing their "very next capital investment". IO offers no comment as to why this result would be so disappointing.

Section E: Performance

It is difficult to gauge the performance of IO. On one measure of success – the ability to stay away from newspaper headlines – IO has been very successful at a time when many agencies in the Ontario Government have been the object of gross mismanagement and accused of wasting billions of dollars. IO has also been successful in quelling concern about private sector preferential treatment in the management of P3s.

Building Performance

The latest full annual report (2009-10) indicated that IO had 21 projects under construction, and that ten other projects had been substantially completed. It had closed on one financial transaction and closed five requests for proposals. It had opened seven Requests For Proposals in 2009-10, made two requests for qualifications, named one short-list for bidders, and three projects were in pre-tendering stages. In other words, IO managed 53 files in a given year, meaning that each project required an average of 7.5 employees per year. This, of course, does not count the informal advising IO provides on myriad issues. While it does provide a metric, it also opens the question of the efficiency of this agency of Government. It is not evident that ministry operations were any less efficient.

Certainly, the public reporting of IO leaves a great deal to be desired. Since its creation (and at the time of writing in late 2013), it has only delivered four full annual reports (2006-7, 2007-8, 2008-9, 2009-10) and financial statements for the years 2010-11 and 2011-12. Presumably the full annual reports for 2010-11 and 2011-12 are ready to be made public but have been held up by the provincial parliament. In its 2009-10 annual report, it indicated that it had "committed to providing more than $3.54 billion in loans, of which over 2.6 billion had been extended to support over 1,200 infrastructure projects".[44] The current website also notes that "more than $4 billion in affordable loans for municipalities and other eligible recipients".

This is only part of the story, and the greater part of it is not told. The current website indicates that "since its creation, IO has brought to market 52 infrastructure projects worth more than $21 billion. This includes 35 hospital projects; the rest are scattered among justice, transportation, and green infrastructure projects." There is only a partial listing of the infrastructure projects of the Government, or of the role and contribution made to these projects by IO. In the end, one is left to guess that about 22.8 per cent of the infrastructure projects undertaken for the Government of Ontario have been done so by AFP methods, far more than the 10 per cent promised in 2005.

As of 2012, IO had financial assets of $4,861,125,000 and issued loans worth $2.3 billion, a fraction of what was anticipated.

---

[44] Infrastructure Ontario, *Annual Report 2009-10*, p. 16.

a. Financial Breakdown

**Figure E.1. Assets of the Ontario Strategic Infrastructure Agency/
Infrastructure Ontario**

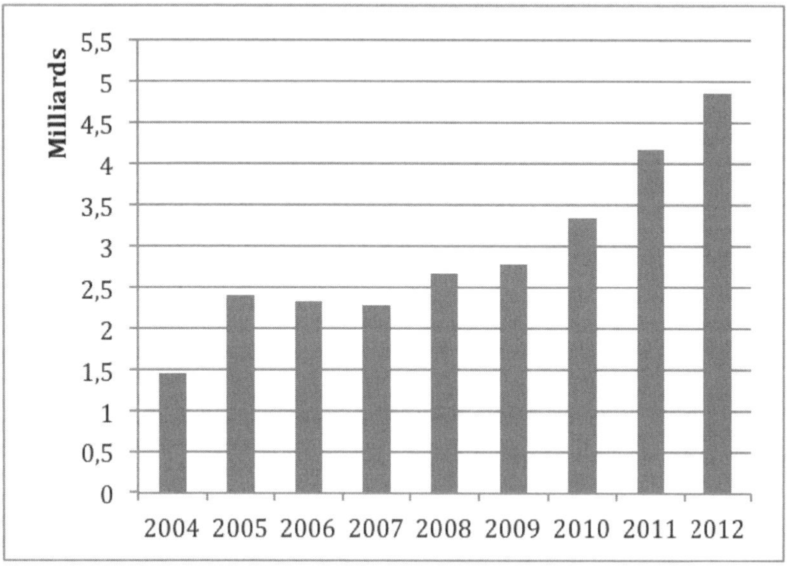

Source: Ontario Public Accounts, 2004-2012.

In its annual report for 2009-10, IO included and "Estimated Value for Money Savings" in its reports on completed projects. The Courthouse in Durham, for instance, which cost $334M, included a "savings" of $49M. There is no accounting for these savings.

The list of projects managed by IO is incomplete (according to Annual Reports 2006-7, 2007-8, 2008-9, 2009-10) but provides a perspective on the range of projects it undertakes.

Year	
2009/10	Credit Valley Hospital, Hamilton Health Sciences – Henderson General Hospital, Kingston General Hospital, Lakeridge Health Corp., London Health Sciences Centre, Montfort Hospital, Niagara Health System, North Bay Regional Health Centre, Ottawa Hospital Regional Cancer Program, Rouge Valley Health System, Royal Victoria Hospital, Sarnia Bluewater Health, Sault Area Hospital, Sunnybrook Health Sciences Centre, Toronto Rehabilitation Institute, Woodstock General Hospital, Bridgepoint Health, Windsor Regional Hospital, Toronto South Detention Centre, CAMH, Ontario Highway Service Centres

Year	
2008/09	Credit Valley Hospital, Durham Consolidated Courthouse, Hamilton Health Sciences, Kingston General Hospital, Lakeridge Health, London Health Sciences Centre, Montfort Hospital, New Data Centre, Niagara Health System, North Bay Regional Health Centre, Ottawa Hospital Regional Cancer Program, Quinte Health Care, Rouge Valley Health System, Ron McMurtry Youth Centre, Royal Victoria Hospital, Runnymede Healthcare Centre, Sarnia Bluewater Health, St. Joseph's Health Care, Sudbury Regional Hospital, Sunnybrook Health Sciences Centre, Toronto Rehabilitation Institute, Trillium Health Centre, Woodstock General Hospital
2007/08	Sunnybrook Health Sciences Centre, Durham Consolidated Courthouse, Trillium Health Centre, Sarnia Bluewater Health, Runnymede Healthcare Centre, Hamilton Health Sciences.
2006/07	Hôpital Montfort (Ottawa), Quinte Health Care, North Bay Regional Health Centre, Sudbury Regional Hospital

Design Quality

Quality builders pride themselves on developing innovative, award-winning designs. This has not been a priority for IO. None of the buildings completed under its tutelage have won design awards.

Operations

Financially, IO has for most of its short history, in a substantial debt position. In 2010, IO was given $200M as a remission on the $1B loan that was granted in 2005. The grant was recorded as revenue, thus effectively wiping out the debt situation.

Figure E.2. IO Financial Position

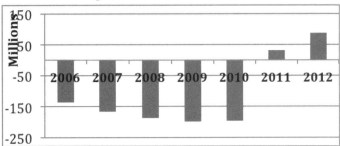

Source: Public Accounts, Government of Ontario.

Section F: Governance

It is in this area that IO marks the strongest departure from past practices. The Board of Directors can be composed of five to thirteen members, or a number prescribed by regulation by the Lieutenant Governor in Council. In effect, the Prime Minister of Ontario appoints the chief executive officer responsible for the operation of the Corporation as well as the Board of Directors and thus has a direct control over the agency, while at the same time ensuring enough distance to allow the "blame" to reside on the agency should any of its operations come under bad publicity.[45] The Board is made of individuals with experience in one of the following areas: finance and investment banking, alternative procurement approaches, accounting, commercial law, labour relations, real estate development, improvements, construction and infrastructure development and Government finance and policy.

The Board of Directors, drawn from members of the community, provides strategic oversight. It is also responsible for approving policies regarding risk assessment and management, approves projects, assesses senior managements, monitors internal control, audit procedures and reporting requirements. Ultimately, the board provides advice to the Minister responsible. Each member of the board receives a $5000 annual retainer and $500 for each meeting. Directors are reimbursed for travel to attend meeting or to perform other duties as part of their tasks.

The Board has, since 2005, been fairly consistent in terms of its composition. The IO board members collectively represent broad experience in all aspects of construction: finance, design, build, the workforce as well as some experience in Government. All the members of the board have extensive experience in the management of non-profit and community organizations. The overwhelming majority have, like the two CEOs who also sit on the board (David Livingston, 2005-12 and Bert Clark since 2012) much experience in the banking industry. For instance, Anthony D. Ross, the chair since 2005, is a former banker and business consultant. The board also features strong female representation. Karen Weaver is Executive VP and Chief Financial Officer at First Capital Realty and was the Chief Financial Officer of Brookfield Properties, one of the largest business property owners in Canada; Isabel Meharry is a chartered accountant and CFO for a major insurer; Darija Scott is an architect and Managing Principal in an design firm that works around the world; Linda Robinson is a retired partner in one of the city's largest law firms.

The rest of the board has included Lawrence Kelly, an Ottawa-based lawyer; Jim Schwindt, a retired engineer and builder; Gadi Mayman, the

---

[45] See Christopher Hood, *The Blame Game: Spin, Bureaucracy and Self-Preservation in Government* (Princeton, NJ: Princeton University Press, 2011), esp. chapter four. See also Peter Aucoin, "Decentralization and Public Management Reform" in Patrick Weller *et al.* (eds.), *The Hollow Crown: Countervailing Trends in Core Executives* (London: MacMillan Press, 1997).

CEO for the Ontario Financing Authority, the Government agency that manages the province's borrowing; Anthony Salerno, now a consultant, who has had a career in both the public sector and in banking; David Leith, a former banker, currently the Chair of the Board of Directors of Manitoba Telecom; John Swinden is a retired accountant and former director of risk management for Ernst and Young International; and Patrick Dillon, an executive with the Building and Construction Trades Council of Ontario.[46] The Board's work is divided among three committees: Audit, Credit and Risk Management, Governance and Compensation. The two people have left the board since 2005, Felix Chee and Harry Swain, had broad experience in banking, financial services and public service.

The executives of IO also were selected on the basis of their wide experiences. David Livingston, the first President and Chief Executive Office, had worked in the banking sector for thirty years before taking his position with IO (he left his position to become the Chief of Staff to the Ontario Premier). His successor, Bert Clark, divided his still young career between banking and the public service. Many executives also have significant Government experience, familiarity in governing non-profit organizations, and in accounting. This form of governance is a net advantage to the Government. The prime minister of the province can effectively control the board through the power of nomination and thus may be in a better position to "manage" the organization from far behind the scenes. The creation of a separate board also fits into a purpose of blame avoidance. Should something go wrong, the board and the staff that supports it can be clearly identified.[47]

Section G: Regulation

There is little doubt that IO must live within the rules and regulations set out by the Government. These were laid out in *Building for Tomorrow* and were reinforced by the law that created it. The "home department" for IO is the relatively small Ministry of Infrastructure (MOI), and it plays a key role in setting out the regulatory framework for IO's operations. It is interesting to note that the enabling legislation for IO specifically indicates that Government intervention is limited to "when directed to do so in writing by the Minister." The meaning of this stipulation is to indicate a measure of the "arm's length" separating the ministry and the agency. This phrase was presumably inserted in the legislation to limit

---

46   Ontario Public Appointments Secretary (2013). Ontario Infrastructure and Lands Corporation. Agency Details. Retrieved from: http://www.pas.gov.on.ca/scripts/en/BoardDetails.asp?boardID=142640.

47   See Christopher Hood, *op. cit.*

informal consultations at the staff level, thus freeing the agency to pursue its affairs as unfettered as possible.

MOI sets out the general policy on infrastructure and planning. In this regard it plays an oversight role on capital planning. Its economic policy and planning division advises the Government on economic infrastructure policy as well as municipal infrastructure policy.

It sets out the parameters by which "growth" will take place: where and when. This office will monitor strategic partnerships and will lead public consultations on what might be acceptable for "growth" to take place. It also sets the tone on the strategic management of real estate and crown land. In this regard, relations with first nations assume importance. What is most important for this ministry is ensuring that other departments act in line with Government policy and advising the central agency, Cabinet Office, of the potential for policy conflict.

MOI is critical in ensuring that IO is successful, and it is clear that there is work division between the ministry and its agency. MOI is consumed entirely with policy work: ensuring compliance with law and with the strategic objectives of the Government. As such, most of its work is in conducting liaison with other ministries and, to some degree, with stakeholders. But the relationship is driven by policy in this case, not by the actual realisation of public works.

Section H: Conclusions and Lessons Learned

In many ways, IO fits the classic definition of a public enterprise, commonly known in Canada as a crown agency or a public agency, in that it is owned by the provincial Government, has a public policy mission, enjoys considerable budgetary autonomy, and can set its managerial standards. What makes IO different is its unique mission in pursuing one of the Government's most popular activities, showing that even some of the core activities of Government can be handed off to an agency.

Frustration with the pace and budget of building infrastructure was the impetus for this public enterprise, but the process of creation was remarkably slow. IO's developmental path was traced in the late 1990s with the creation of the Ontario SuperBuild Corporation. SuperBuild saw itself as a catalyst for investment and a driver of change using the best practices in public asset management. IO has gone much further, however, in "agencifying" all the contracting and technocratic roles required to arrange financing and overseeing contracts. After seven years of operation, it is fair to say that IO has been successful in delivering assets on time and on budget, but there is little demonstrable proof of actual value for money, except that no one is complaining. Without a doubt, credit must be given where it is due: IO has succeeded by practicing excellent project management skills and by ensuring that it has the capacity to assess risk and to respond to it.

There remains the question of sufficiency. To what degree is IO capable of realizing Ontario's ambition of investing $100B over the next decade to meet the province's infrastructure needs? It would have to spend close to $75B in the foreseeable future, and this will not happen. The reality is that IO has not met the Government's goal of spending $30B between 2005 and 2010 – at a time when the province was spending inordinate amounts on economic stimulus projects. Clearly, the shortfall in Government revenue accounts for this reality, as has the reduction in the Province's credit rating. The Government of Ontario has to bring more money to the table in order to really demonstrate the effectiveness of the model. It is notable that most of the funding for infrastructure that is expended from IO comes from Government; and only a minute portion is financed through AFP methods.

One could make the case that IO has done very little to attract investors to the public sphere. Institutional investors are looking for assets that have stable cash flows, constant demand and can generate uncorrelated returns that are linked to inflation (such as highways). The reality is that few of IO's projects generate cash flow.

IO is also doing little in term so of offering a suitable rate of return for institutional investors. Clearly, this is difficult to realize. Governments must ensure affordability and quality service – items that are costly and necessarily reduce the net income of a property that can be passed on to investors. Certainly, the energy utilities and the labour-funded investment bodies, could be attracted to this form of financing, but IO is not legally in a position to offer help.

So, has IO genuinely made a difference? Until 2010, it ran its operations in a deficit situation and was only rescued by a Government grant that placed it in a positive financial state (see chart E.2). It has created a bureaucratic structure that rivals the size of many of the largest departments in the provincial Government, and pays its executives' salaries that are dramatically higher than their counterparts who work in ministries. There is no concrete evidence that IO buildings are less expensive than ministry-built infrastructure, nor can there ever be: the experiments in parallel building that would be needed to demonstrate this have not been tried.

Has IO made a difference in design? It is worth mentioning that the works undertaken by IO have not attracted particular attention by the boldness or innovation of their design: None of the buildings have won praise for their architecture or for originality. It could be said that IO has taken a very instrumental view of infrastructure. Buildings, for instance, are amortized over forty years, indicating that there is little conviction that they will be suitable for the uses of future generations. Indeed, there is a "collapsibility" to the buildings that, in a way, reflect the choice of the Government in agencifying public works. IO is "collapsible" also: an irony for a Government activity that is as old as governance itself. It is important to observe that the Government has so little confidence in the public service that it has invested some of its most important activities to an agency whose oversight is provided almost entirely by members of the business community. Only the premier of the province, through the power of appointment, has a control on the board of directors and senior management.

It is still not clear whether IO has been a success, though it has been a bold experiment in the building and management of hard state assets. The current Government is proud to boast of the achievement to the point where it is actively marketing the IO "model" as an exportable management approach to infrastructure building, particularly in the United States. As this chapter goes to print, the Government of Ontario has yet again announced that it is committed to funding more infrastructure building. For astute observers who will remember that, at one point in time, the dictum that brides bring "something old, something new, something borrowed and something blue" to their weddings also included "bring a Silver Sixpence in her shoe", such Government announcements will ring familiar. Debates over public enterprises aside, IO is dependent on public coffers to realize its projects, and the Government of Ontario must pay many a "silver sixpence" to IO's shoe to fund infrastructure.

References

Antunes, P. *et al.*, *Economic Impact of Public Infrastructure in Ontario*, Ottawa: Conference Board of Canada, 2010.

Aucoin, Peter, "Decentralization and Public Management Reform", in Patrick Weller *et al.*, (eds.), *The Hollow Crown: Countervailing Trends in Core Executives*, London: MacMillan Press, 1997.

Bradford, Neil, "Public-Private Partnership? Shifting Paradigms of Economic Governance in Ontario", *Canadian Journal of Political Science*, Vol. 36, No. 5, (Dec., 2003), pp. 1005-1033.

Brennan, R., "Ontario land agency in trouble over sales; Property flips, cries of cronyism dog its operation", *Toronto Star*, 18 March 2000.

Brennan, R., "Ontario land agency in trouble over sales; Property flips, cries of cronyism dog its operation", *Toronto Star*, 18 March 2000.

Byers, J., "Toronto demands Skydome pay taxes", *Toronto Star*, 13 August 1991.

Fearon, Gervan, " 'Guardian' as 'Spender': Infrastructure Investment, 1960-2005", in Patrice Dutil (ed.), *The Guardian: Perspectives on the Ministry of Finance of Ontario*, Toronto: University of Toronto Press, 2011, pp. 287-319.

Ferguson, R., "Another day, another scandal at Ontario Realty; as much as $11 million may have gone astray", *Toronto Star*, 13 May 2000.

Government of Ontario, *ReNew Ontario, 2005-10: Strategic Highlights*, Toronto, Ont: 2011.

Government of Ontario, *Public Accounts of Ontario, 2011-12, Financial Statements of Government Organizations, Government Business Enterprises, Trusts and Miscellaneous Statements, Vol. 2b.*

Government of Ontario, "OIIPC Merger Announcement", June 6, 2011. Retrieved from: http://www.infrastructureontario.ca/uploadedFiles/OIPC-Merger-Announcement-fact-sheet.pdf.

Government of Ontario, *Building a Better Tomorrow: An Infrastructure Planning, Financing and Procurement Framework for Ontario's Public Secto*r, Queen's Printer for Ontario, 2004. http://www.moi.gov.on.ca/pdf/en/BBT-Framework_EN.pdf.

Hood, Christopher, *The Blame Game: Spin, Bureaucracy and Self-Preservation in Government*, Princeton, NJ: Princeton University Press, 2011.

Infrastructure Ontario, *Annual Report 2007-08*, Toronto, Ontario, 2008.

Infrastructure Ontario, *Annual Report 2006-07*, Toronto, Ontario, 2007.

Moore, B., "Realty Corp. axed days before OPP raid", in *Toronto Star*, 29 July 2010.

Murphy, Tim, "The Case for Public-Private Partnerships in Infrastructure", *Canadian Public Administration*, Vol. 51, No. 1, 2008, pp. 99-126.

Office of the Auditor General of Ontario, 2006 Annual Report, Chapter 3: Ontario Realty Corporation – Real Estate and Accommodation Services. Toronto, Ont: 2006. Retrieved from: http://www.auditor.on.ca/.

Ontario Ministry of Finance, Backgrounder, "Ontario Budget 1999 Superbuild Grown Fund will Renew Infrastructure", 4 May 1999.

OECD, *Dedicated Public-Private Partnership Units: A Survey of Institutional and Governance Structures*, OECD, 2010.

Ontario SuperBuild, "Building Ontario's Future: A SuperBuild Progress Report", December 2000.

Ontario SuperBuild, *Progress Report 2003*, Toronto, Ont.: Queen's Printer, 2003.

Ontario Public Accounts, 2003-04, Vol. 2.

Ontario Public Accounts, 2006-2007, Vol. 2.

Ontario Ministry of Finance. Published Results-Based Plan, 2006-07. 2007.

Ontario Infrastructure and Lands Corporation Act, 2011, S.O. 2011, c.9, Sched. 32.

Ontario Realty Corporation, Annual Report 2009-2010, Toronto, Ont., 2011.

Van Alphen, T., "Final dome tally: $263 Million lost", *Toronto Star*, 29 September 1994.

Van Alpen, T., "Bickering, lawsuits the order of the day", *Toronto Star*, 2 August 1992.

Webster, Paul Christopher, "Diabetes Registry Overdue, If not Obsolete", in *Canadian Medical Association Journal*, Vol. 184, No. 9, 14 May 2012, pp. 4109-12.

11. La Poste

Emblème du service public à la française ou futur groupe leader européen ?

Philippe BANCE

Directeur Adjoint du laboratoire CREAM, Université de Rouen, Normandie Université

Nathalie REY

Directrice adjointe de la Faculté d'économie et de gestion et membre du laboratoire CEPN, Université Paris 13, Sorbonne Paris Cité

Introduction

La Poste est en France en charge du service universel postal, et un important acteur financier. Le groupe est le premier employeur français après l'État, comptant 266 618 salariés fin 2012. Il figure en 2012 parmi les 25 premiers groupes français, le courrier représentant la moitié de son chiffre d'affaires, le reste se répartissant en part presque égale entre les colis express et la banque. La Poste est également devenue un opérateur virtuel de téléphone mobile depuis 2011.

Avant l'ouverture à la concurrence du secteur postal, La Poste était une administration qui disposait du monopole de la distribution du courrier en France. La loi de 2010 a transformé l'administration publique en une société publique à responsabilité limitée. Des craintes de privatisation et de remise en cause à terme des missions de service public ont dès lors suscité des vives tensions et diverses formes d'action : grève nationale, votation citoyenne, amendements du Sénat français pour garantir la permanence de la détention à 100 % de La Poste par l'État. L'ouverture à la concurrence du secteur postal, qu'a impulsé l'Union européenne depuis les années 1990, a suscité de profondes inquiétudes pour l'emblème du service public à la française[1] que représente la Poste. La notion de service

---

[1] Voir ci-après ses principales caractéristiques.

public dit à la française renvoie à un système de valeur, devenu en France élément clef de compromis social, et s'appuyant sur un mode de gestion protéiforme. La conception française du service public doit beaucoup à la doctrine juridique qui le voit comme indispensable à la réalisation et au développement de l'interdépendance sociale (Duguit, 1923). Le service public s'y justifie par le service rendu dans le cadre de missions d'intérêt général, porteuses de solidarités sociales. La légitimation sociétale place l'autorité publique au centre du système de représentation et « le service public à la française peut être considéré comme la mise en forme juridique de prérogatives de puissance publique » (Valette, 2000). L'approche renvoie à une idéologie de l'intérêt général, située dans la tradition rousseauiste de la volonté générale et du jacobinisme (Rangeon, 2001).

Trois principes essentiels de fonctionnement du service public fondent sa spécificité dans la doctrine juridique, selon les lois dites de Rolland. Le premier est celui de la continuité, c'est à dire d'un fonctionnement permettant la satisfaction régulière et continue des besoins, sans pour autant en faire une limitation du droit de grève. Le second principe est celui de l'égalité entre les usagers (les citoyens), qui interdit la discrimination mais non la différenciation. Le troisième principe est celui d'adaptation (de mutabilité), c'est-à-dire d'évolution du service public face aux transformations des besoins sociaux et de l'intérêt général.

L'attachement culturel au « service public à la française » a pour origine le compromis social qui s'instaure à partir de 1945 après la Seconde Guerre mondiale. Les autorités nationales font jouer au service public un rôle essentiel dans la relance de l'économie nationale, la réduction des inégalités, l'aménagement du territoire et la cohésion territoriale, la création d'emploi. Cette action n'ancre pas seulement dans l'imaginaire social l'idée d'un État bienveillant qui remédie aux insuffisances ou aux abus du marché mais aussi la représentation d'un service public vecteur de solidarité et de progrès social. L'attachement majoritaire au service public trouve ses raisons tant du côté des salariés, des usagers que du corps de la haute administration d'État.

Du point de vue des usagers, malgré la pénurie de moyens de certaines activités, le service public permet de satisfaire des besoins sociaux insuffisamment pris en compte par le marché et l'intégration sociale des catégories défavorisées. Il donne l'image de l'intéressement à la personne plutôt qu'à celui du profit. L'action de la haute administration d'État joue également un rôle important dans la légitimation du service public auprès de la population, des politiques et dans l'analyse académique. L'efficacité du management de certaines entreprises du service public marchand est largement reconnue tant en France qu'à l'étranger. La réussite de grands programmes technologiques y contribue, tels le nucléaire ou le TGV. Cette reconnaissance tient également aux innovations du management des monopoles publics pour « internaliser les missions de service public » et promouvoir la cohésion sociale et territoriale.

Dans la sphère marchande, deux modèles français de services publics sont à distinguer. Le premier, qui est sa composante dominante du compromis d'après-guerre, repose sur la propriété publique. Sa dominance de l'après-guerre au début des années 1980 a pu susciter une confusion entre service public et secteur public. Le second, le plus ancien, est celui de la gestion déléguée. Le secteur de l'eau incarne notamment ce second modèle français. Les grands groupes privés y occupent une place prédominante à travers des concessions de service public octroyées par les collectivités locales. Le modèle du mode de gestion publique a été remis en cause au profit de celui de la gestion déléguée, largement porté par les politiques de l'Union européenne (UE) et la libéralisation des services publics.

L'ouverture progressive à la concurrence a modifié les conditions d'exercice du service public postal, questionnant sur l'accessibilité au service, la densité de la présence postale dans les zones rurales et le rôle de l'entreprise pour le développement des territoires. C'est dans ce contexte de changements structurels mais aussi de nette contraction de l'activité du courrier, qu'un débat de fond s'est engagé concernant l'évolution des missions de service public, les transformations du modèle social, la nouvelle gestion des personnels avec la contraction du nombre des fonctionnaires, le rôle de cohésion sociale et territoriale de l'entreprise.

Le groupe vise à déployer une approche fondée sur une logique de développement et d'innovation tournée vers le service à la clientèle et aux territoires. Il entend devenir une référence en matière de performance publique, être un opérateur multi-activités, fondé sur des valeurs sociales et le développement durable en exerçant pleinement ses missions de service public.

L'objet de cette contribution est dès lors d'étudier les transformations en cours et l'impact de l'ouverture à la concurrence sur la stratégie du groupe et sa performance dans les objectifs qui lui sont assignés.

1. Une organisation issue d'une très longue histoire

1.1. Une origine ancienne sur des fondements protéiformes

Dès le Moyen Âge, la fonction de convoyeur de fonds (physiques, lettres de change) avait été associée aux transports des messages ou des objets en 1464. Sous le règne du roi Louis 11, « l'Édit de Luxies » instaure sur le territoire français un réseau de relais de poste pour transporter de manière régulière les lettres royales. En 1603, lorsque la Poste royale est érigée en service public d'État, les services postaux entretiennent des liens étroits avec les activités financières. Les missions publiques de service postal apparaissent dès le 17ᵉ siècle : il s'agit d'assurer par la mise en place d'une administration postale la fiabilité d'un service jugé essentiel pour le fonctionnement de la société.

Au 19ᵉ siècle, l'administration postale est la norme en France comme dans les autres pays. Des obligations de service public voient le jour pour couvrir l'ensemble du territoire à tarif réduit. La péréquation tarifaire est également devenue une pratique commune de facturation du service indépendamment du coût généré par l'usager et donc de sa localisation géographique. Les transferts inter-clientèles, les subventions croisées entre les différents types d'activités permettent de financer les productions non rentables. Pendant le 19ᵉ siècle et jusqu'à la seconde moitié du 20ᵉ siècle, les services postaux ont joué un rôle moteur dans le développement des activités financières sans rencontrer une réelle concurrence. En un siècle et demi, les innovations postales en matière de services financiers ont été nombreuses et les pratiques relèvent d'une conception de l'intérêt général fondée sur l'égalité de traitement, l'accès universel des citoyens au service public, le service rendu aux populations et à la nation[2]. La socialisation des usagers démunis ou isolés, le maintien du lien social dans les espaces ruraux, l'aménagement du territoire national, la contribution au développement économique sont au cœur des missions postales au 20ᵉ siècle. La garantie de l'emploi et l'absence de contrainte de rentabilité sont jugées porteuses d'une « culture de service public », de la disponibilité de l'agent public pour servir les usagers citoyens, la cohésion économique et la solidarité sociale.

Jusqu'aux années 1980, l'administration publique reste dès lors en charge du monopole postal en France, comme dans tous les pays de l'OCDE. L'administration des Postes et Télécommunications (nommée selon les périodes P&T ou PTT) exploite le secteur postal et des télécommunications. Les PTT disposent cependant (depuis 1928) d'une comptabilité séparée auprès du budget de l'État, qui permet d'analyser finement son activité propre. Plus tard, à partir de 1969, les comptes de la Poste et des télécommunications (la Direction générale des télécommunications ou DGT) vont être séparés, et la comptabilité analytique est développée en s'inspirant de celle d'une entreprise (Dang-Nguyen, 1986).

---

[2]   Les juristes français, dans la tradition initiée par Léon Duguit, ont formalisé les missions de service public dans les fameuses lois de Rolland, autour des principes d'égalité, de continuité, de mutabilité (ou d'adaptabilité) du service.

Il n'en reste pas moins que dans le cadre du système de comptabilité nationale française, instauré après la Seconde Guerre mondiale et jusqu'aux années 1990, les PTT figurent dans l'agrégat des Grandes Entreprises Nationales, GEN[3]. Les GEN sont des « entreprises publiques » en situation de monopole dont la dépendance directe vis-à-vis de l'État et les missions de politique économiques sont si étendues, notamment en matière de régulation macroéconomique, qu'on les traite à part. L'action contracyclique des GEN est intense, en particulier durant les années 1973-1980, mais l'activité postale est cependant moins directement concernée que d'autres par la politique de relance. L'effort des PTT s'est tout particulièrement exercé par des investissements massifs demandés par les pouvoirs publics pour développer le réseau téléphonique. Par-delà la mise en place d'un réseau téléphonique dense, performant et couvrant l'ensemble du territoire national, les PTT développent durant les années 1970 un service télématique original (le minitel) et en font une diffusion large en offrant à l'ensemble des usagers le matériel permettant l'accès en ligne aux services attachés (gratuits ou commerciaux), qui se verra cependant dépassé par le développement de l'internet dans les années 1990.

Son action en matière de régulation macroéconomique va disparaître dans les années 1980 du fait de la nécessité pour l'entreprise publique de récupérer des efforts massifs consentis en matière de politique d'investissement, puis structurellement par changement de paradigme économique (Bance et Monnier, 2000). Les réformes menées sous l'impulsion de l'UE vont y contribuer en impulsant une dynamique d'ouverture à la concurrence.

1.2. Les transformations du cadre institutionnel : la libéralisation postale européenne

Comme pour d'autres Services d'intérêt économique général (SIEG), les objectifs de l'Union européenne sont « d'achever le marché intérieur des services postaux et de veiller, par un cadre réglementaire approprié, que des services postaux efficaces, fiables et de bonne qualité soient fournis dans l'Union européenne à tous ses citoyens à des prix abordables ».

Trois directives postales (97/67/CE ; 2002/39/CE ; 2008/6/CE) ont ainsi progressivement suscité l'ouverture totale à la concurrence. Après avoir spécifié les caractéristiques minimales du service universel et ses principes tarifaires applicables, les normes de qualité et l'obligation de créer des autorités nationales indépendantes, la réglementation européenne a dans un second temps ouvert certaines activités à la concurrence (et notamment

---

[3] Les GEN regroupent les Charbonnages de France, EDF, GDF, la SNCF, la RATP, Air France, Air Inter, et les PTT (La Poste et France Télécom).

les lettres pesant moins de 100 puis de 50 grammes), pour abolir enfin tous les domaines réservés. Il s'en est suivi en France des réformes postales adaptatives étape par étape. La transposition de la directive de 2002 est faite par la loi du 20 mai 2005, relative à la régulation de l'activité postale[4], qui procède à des réformes institutionnelles et redéfinit les missions de service public assignées à La Poste. Une nouvelle Autorité de régulation des communications électroniques et des postes (ARCEP) remplace l'ancienne Autorité de régulation des télécommunications (ART). Cette nouvelle autorité est chargée de délivrer les autorisations permettant à des opérateurs de concurrencer La Poste. Elle veille également au bon accomplissement des missions de service public qui sont assignées par la loi française et plus extensives que celle de la simple application des directives européennes.

1.3. L'émergence et la consolidation du groupe La Poste depuis le début des années 1990

Pour préparer les réformes, l'administration des PTT a tout d'abord été scindée en 1991 en deux entreprises : France Télécom et La Poste. La loi n° 90-568 du 2 juillet 1990 donne ainsi naissance à La Poste. Les pouvoirs publics dotent La Poste (tout comme France Télécom) d'une personnalité juridique et d'une autonomie de gestion[5]. La Poste peut dès lors gérer librement son patrimoine en veillant à l'équilibre de ses comptes. Son statut juridique est celui d'un Établissement public industriel et commercial (EPIC). La Poste est ensuite transformée en société anonyme par la loi n° 2010-123 du 9 février 2010. Depuis cette date, La Poste est « soumise aux dispositions légales (…) de la loi relative à la démocratisation du secteur public ». La loi dote ainsi l'entreprise d'un conseil d'administration tripartite : une majorité de représentants des actionnaires publics (État, Caisse des Dépôts et Consignations) ; de représentants des communes et des usagers ; enfin de représentants des personnels (pour un tiers). L'entreprise mère est aujourd'hui possédée à 100 % par l'État. La loi précise que la totalité du capital peut être détenue par l'État, des personnes morales appartenant au secteur public ou par les salariés. La durée de la Société est de 99 ans à compter du 1er mars 2010.

Concernant l'activité bancaire, La Poste est qualifiée, au tournant du 21e siècle, de « banque des pauvres » et de « banque des vieux » (40 % des encours sont détenus par des clients de plus de 70 ans)[6]. La présidence

---

[4] http://www.legifrance.gouv.fr/affichTexte.do?cidTexte=JORFTEXT000000446769& dateTexte=&categorieLien=id.

[5] Voir pour détail, Tigoki Iya N.-E., *La politique de modernisation de la Poste*, L'harmattan, 2011, p. 190 et s.

[6] Rapport du Haut Conseil du secteur financier public et semi-public, 2001.

de La Poste et les autorités publiques ont alors œuvré pour faire accéder les services financiers de la Poste au statut de banque de plein exercice : développement d'une activité de gestion d'actif ; création d'une entreprise d'investissement, Efiposte en 2000 ; création de la Banque Postale le 1er janvier 2006 par transfert des services financiers de La Poste dont elle est la filiale à 100 % et qui chapeaute à présent l'ensemble. Elle est un établissement public devenu en mars 2010 une société anonyme qui se distingue d'une banque commerciale par son actionnariat mais aussi par les missions qui lui sont confiées par l'État français. En 2008, elle crée un réseau de conseillers en gestion de patrimoine. Elle obtient l'autorisation de la part de l'État d'étendre sa gamme de produits à l'assurance dommages en 2009 et à l'assurance santé en 2012. En septembre 2011, elle obtient l'agrément de l'Autorité de contrôle prudentiel pour le financement aux personnes morales (PME, TPE, associations, bailleurs sociaux, etc.). Depuis le 25 mai 2012, elle est autorisée à financer le secteur public local (collectivités locales, SEM, entreprises publiques locales, établissements publics de santé).

La politique de filialisation active déployée par La Poste depuis les années 1990 a permis à La Poste d'échapper au principe juridique de spécialité qui prévalait pour les entreprises de service public puis pour asseoir sa stratégie de développement d'une activité multi-métiers. Avec ses filiales, La Poste est aujourd'hui l'un des quatre grands opérateurs du secteur postal en Europe avec l'allemand, le britannique et le néerlandais. Il s'agit du second opérateur du colis-express en Europe. En 2012, le groupe a également 11,7 millions clients dans la banque. Enfin, en mai 2012, La Poste, a créé une filiale La Poste mobile (51 %, SFR 49 %), est devenu un opérateur virtuel dans le téléphone mobile (MVNO). Le plan stratégique d'avril 2011 « Ambition 2015 » se fixe pour objectif de moderniser l'entreprise autour d'une gestion publique moderne performante au service du client et proches des Français[7]. Les missions de service public, développement durable, qualité de service, innovation et nouvelles activités sont censés incarner cette « ambition ». En 2012, un dialogue social a été lancé auquel ont participé 125 000 postiers et est mise en place une commission dont le rapport (Kaspar) identifie des priorités et fixe des chantiers concernant le dialogue social, l'organisation du travail, la santé et de sécurité[8]. Un accord est signé en janvier 2013 avec des organisations syndicales sur la qualité de vie au travail.

---

[7] http://www.laposte.com/Everything-about-La-Poste/Press-releases/Latest-articles/2010-press-releases/La-Poste-Group-unveils-Ambition-2015-strategy.

[8] http://www.cgcgroupelaposte.org/public/vie_autravail_rapport_kaspar_11092012_3.pdf.

2. Les missions publiques actuelles et leur financement

Si les missions de régulation conjoncturelle et d'investissement à caractère contracyclique des GEN ont été abandonnées depuis le début des années 1980, quatre types de missions de service public n'en restent pas moins d'actualité pour la Poste. La loi du 1er mars 2010 relative aux activités postales les explicite : le service universel du courrier et du colis ; la distribution de la presse ; la contribution à l'aménagement du territoire ; l'accessibilité bancaire.

2.1. Le service universel du courrier et du colis

La loi de 2010 confère pour quinze ans à La Poste la responsabilité de prester le service universel postal sur le territoire français. La définition française du service universel postal s'inspire de l'approche européenne mais, tradition oblige, en retient une conception élargie, déjà précisée par la loi de 2005[9]. Par-delà la directive européenne (caractères universel et abordable des services, normes de qualité), s'y trouve réaffirmée l'approche traditionnelle à la française autour des principes juridiques d'égalité, de continuité et d'adaptabilité (lois de Rolland) tout en visant la meilleure efficacité économique et sociale. Cela « fait de la France l'un des pays européens bénéficiant du service universel le plus large »[10].

Les critères d'accessibilité au service universel postal sont fixés par le décret n° 2007-29 du 5 janvier 2007 qui dispose « qu'au moins 99 % de la population nationale et au moins 95 % de la population de chaque département soit à moins de 10 km d'un point de contact et toutes les communes de plus de 10 000 habitants disposent d'au moins un point de contact par tranche de 20 000 habitants ». L'article R.1-1-10 de ce même décret dispose que « La Poste établit et tient à jour le catalogue des prestations relevant du service universel et du secteur réservé ainsi que des tarifs en vigueur », à partir duquel l'ARCEP peut émettre son avis dans un délai d'un mois.

Avant l'ouverture à la concurrence, La Poste pouvait financer le service universel par son monopole légal, appelé en droit communautaire le « secteur réservé », mais plus à présent avec l'ouverture totale à la concurrence intervenue le 1er janvier 2013. Le « surcoût net » de cette mission de service public vis-à-vis d'une optimisation purement commerciale de l'activité a été estimé en 2007 par la Poste à près de 1 milliard d'euros par an sur

---

[9] Article L1 du Code des postes et des communications électroniques (Loi n° 2005-516 du 20 mai 2005 art. 1, Journal officiel du 21 mai 2005).

[10] Sénat, *Rapport Hérisson, n° 50, sur le projet de loi relatif à l'entreprise publique La Poste et à l'activité postale*, session ordinaire 2009-2010. http://www.senat.fr/rap/l09-050/l09-050.html.

les quelque 10 milliards que représente le chiffre d'affaires du courrier[11]. Par la loi du 9 février 2010 relative à l'entreprise publique La Poste et aux activités postales[12], la gestion comptable et financière d'un fonds de compensation du service universel postal est assurée par un établissement public. Ce fonds est abondé par des contributions de l'ensemble des opérateurs prestataires de service postal, proportionnellement à leur activité, du moins au-delà d'un seuil minimum, via une Agence de services et de paiement, instituée par un décret en 2012[13].

L'ouverture à la concurrence de l'activité du service postal universel n'étant cependant pas pour l'heure effective, les dispositions adoptées introduisent un mécanisme complexe, qui pourrait dans un premier temps être pris en charge très directement par l'opérateur La Poste. Ce mécanisme pourrait par ailleurs s'avérer difficile à gérer, du fait notamment des contentieux qui pourraient naître dans les estimations du coût du service universel de l'abondement du fonds.

Il reste enfin que l'absence de prise en charge directe du service postal universel par l'État ou autres collectivités publiques interroge sur les répercussions du financement actuel du fonds dans un contexte d'adaptation face à la compétition entre grands opérateurs postaux étrangers. Ces derniers fourbissent en effet leurs armes pour se déployer à l'international, sont souvent plus avancés dans ce processus que La Poste, tout en étant soumis dans leur pays d'origine à de moindres contraintes de service public.

2.2. La distribution de la presse

La loi du 2 juillet 1990, dans son article 2, inclut le service public du transport et de la distribution de la presse dans le service public des envois postaux. Ce service, qui vise à contribuer au pluralisme des opinions et faciliter l'accès à l'information par la diffusion la plus large possible de la presse, s'inscrit dans le régime prévu par le code des postes et des communications électroniques (CPCE), dans son article 1-1-17. On y précise que les conditions du service universel postal s'appliquent également aux envois de périodiques qui bénéficient de l'agrément de la commission paritaire des publications et agences de presse.

---

[11]   Selon le rapport Hérisson, précité, p. 26.
[12]   http://legifrance.gouv.fr/affichTexte.do;jsessionid=E91222945EF1CC08E07ADC051
       7E9655A.tpdjo03v_2&dateTexte=?cidTexte=JORFT EXT000021801431&categorie
       Lien=cid.
[13]   Décret n° 2012-1072 du 20 septembre 2012 relatif au fonds de compensation du
       service universel postal et portant diverses modifications du Code des postes et des
       communications électroniques http://legifrance.gouv.fr/affichTexte.do?cidTexte=
       JORFTEXT000026395026&categorieLien=id.

La mission de distribution de la presse se caractérise par un « surcoût net » « qui a pu être évalué à 670 millions d'euros en 2006, les tarifs spécifiques associés à cette mission ne couvrant que 37 % des coûts »[14]. En fait, depuis les années 1980, des accords pluriannuels entre l'État, La Poste et les syndicats d'éditeurs de presse précisent les modalités de prise en charge de cette mission de service public et de son surcoût net. L'accord en vigueur, dit Schwartz, qui couvre la période 2009-2015, se fixe cependant pour objectif l'équilibre financier de la mise en œuvre de cette mission de service public. Cet équilibre doit être réalisé grâce à :

- l'attribution d'une subvention mais dégressive de l'État pour couvrir le coût de l'obligation de service public : de 242 millions d'euros de 2009 à 2011 à 180 millions en 2015 ;

- un accroissement progressif des tarifs sur la période : 20 % pour la presse d'information politique et

- 30 % pour les autres titres ;

- la réduction progressive des coûts de la Poste, pour un montant atteignant 200 millions d'euros en année pleine en 2015.

En 2015, la Poste devra supporter le déficit résiduel qui pourrait résulter de l'accord. Mais, après 2015, aucune subvention de l'État n'est prévue pour couvrir le surcoût de cette mission publique.

2.3. La contribution à l'aménagement du territoire

Cette mission de service public est fixée par l'article 6 de la loi du 2 juillet 1990 précitée : « La Poste contribue, au moyen de son réseau de points de contact, à l'aménagement et au développement du territoire national ». Selon les termes du contrat de service public signé entre l'État et la Poste « la France est le seul pays d'Europe dans lequel l'opérateur prestataire du service universel des envois postaux est chargé de contribuer à l'aménagement du territoire, au-delà de sa mission d'accessibilité du service universel »[15]. Il s'agit d'assurer la cohésion sociale et territoriale française en desservant notamment les quartiers urbains périphériques et les zones rurales en cherchant à garantir une présence de proximité, l'égalité des chances des citoyens pour l'accès aux services publics, à réduire les écarts de richesses entre collectivités territoriales par une péréquation des ressources. Cette mission s'inscrit d'ailleurs dans le cadre de la loi d'orientation pour l'aménagement et le développement des territoires (LOAD) de 1995[16], dont les notions clefs sont « unité de la

---

[14] Projet de loi de finance 2012 : Économie http://www.senat.fr/rap/a11-111-3/a11-111-323.html#toc225.

[15] Contrat de service public 2008-1012.

[16] Loi n° 95-115 du 4 février 1995 d'orientation pour l'aménagement et le développement du territoire, article 1.

La Poste

nation », « solidarités entre citoyens » et « intégration des populations ». Des contrats de présence territoriale sont également signés pour trois ans par l'État, La Poste et l'Association des maires de France, qui précise les modalités de répartition du fonds de péréquation.

La présence territoriale se caractérise par la présence de 16 135 bureaux de poste sur le territoire métropolitain français et par 142 000 autres points de dépôt. Mais, comme le souligne le rapport sénatorial Hérisson[17], la pérennité du maillage territorial peut être remise en question du fait de l'insuffisante couverture par les autorités publiques des charges correspondantes, dans un environnement de plus en plus concurrentiel pour l'opérateur. Le fonds postal national de péréquation territoriale apporte en effet un financement à hauteur de 170 millions d'euros (le montant antérieur de 140 millions ayant cependant été relevé sur le dernier contrat 2011-13)[18]. Mais l'ARCEP estime par ailleurs, dans sa décision du 23 octobre 2012, que « le coût net du maillage territorial complémentaire de La Poste répondant à sa mission d'aménagement du territoire est de 247 millions d'euros pour l'année 2011 »[19]. Le décalage entre le coût estimé et le financement réalisé se situe donc à 77 millions d'euros pour l'année 2011. Et le nouveau contrat se traduit par une simplification : un seul critère y est à présent pris en compte, celui du nombre de points de contact situés dans les zones prioritaires de chaque département, quel que soit le statut de ces points de contact (bureaux de poste ou partenariats). Cela pourrait initier une réduction du nombre de bureaux de poste pour les années à venir.

La Commission européenne a cependant validé début 2012 une subvention de 1,9 milliard d'euros pour financer le service public de distribution de la presse et sa présence dans des zones difficiles d'accès entre 2008 et 2012. Comme l'a indiqué le commissaire européen, M. Alumnia, cette aide a été accordée car « les compensations reçues par La Poste ont seulement couvert en partie le coût net de la mission

---

[17] Sénat, n° 50, sur le projet de loi relatif à l'entreprise publique La Poste et à l'activité postale, session ordinaire 2009-2010, pp. 27-29

[18] Alors que le fonds postal national de péréquation territoriale géré dans un compte spécial de La Poste était abondé pour un montant prévisionnel de 140 millions d'euros par an dans le cadre du contrat de présence postale territoriale entre l'Association des maires de France et le groupe La Poste sur la période 2008-10, ce montant a été porté à 170 millions de 2011 à 2013 http://www.dgcis.redressement- productif.gouv. fr/files/files/directions_services/secteurs-professionnels/services/la-poste/contrat-de-presence-postale.pdf.

[19] ARCEP, Décision n° 2012-1311 de l'Autorité de régulation des communications électroniques et des postes en date du 23 octobre 2012 relative à l'évaluation pour l'année 2011 du coût net du maillage complémentaire permettant à La Poste d'assurer sa mission d'aménagement du territoire, http://www.arcep.fr/uploads/ tx_gsavis/12-1311.pdf.

de service public ». Les postes allemande et belge ont par contre été condamnées à rembourser les aides apportées par leur État[20].

2.4. Le service bancaire

La loi fait de La Banque Postale « un service public national ». La loi de modernisation de l'économie de 2008 confie ainsi à la Banque Postale une mission d'accessibilité bancaire qui s'exerce à travers le Livret A[21]. Les obligations réglementaires spécifiques sont les suivantes : l'obligation d'ouvrir un Livret A à toute personne qui en fait la demande, d'effectuer gratuitement sur ce livret les dépôts et les retraits à partir de 1,5 euro (contre 10 euros pour les autres banques), d'accepter les domiciliations de virement (les prestations sociales et les pensions des agents publics) et de prélèvements (ceux relatifs au paiement des impôts et taxes, des quittances d'eau, de gaz et d'électricité et aux loyers des logements sociaux – HLM) de certaines opérations et, d'octroyer gratuitement des chèques de banque. En permettant à chacun, et donc aux démunis, de domicilier les revenus, de retirer de l'argent liquide et d'émettre des titres de paiement, la Banque Postale joue un rôle important dans la lutte contre l'exclusion bancaire. En 2011, près de 2 millions parmi ses 26 millions de clients sont en situation de fragilité financière et en sont bénéficiaires. Le bon accomplissement de cette mission se fait grâce au maillage territorial de la Poste : 60 % de son réseau est situé dans des communes de moins de 20 000 habitants, 859 bureaux de poste desservent des zones urbaines sensibles ; 6,80 % de ses 6 350 distributeurs automatiques de billets (DAB) sont implantés en zone rurale et plus de 18 % en zones urbaines sensibles[22].

Pour remplir au mieux sa mission de lutte contre l'exclusion sociale, la Banque Postale a établi des liens étroits avec des partenaires locaux et en particulier depuis 2006 avec l'Union nationale des centres communaux d'action sociale (UNCCA). Le projet REFLEX (Réagir ensemble et fédérer la lutte contre l'exclusion) adopté en 2010 avec ce partenaire a été reconnu en décembre 2012 comme une bonne pratique en matière de lutte contre l'exclusion bancaire au niveau européen par la conférence européenne annuelle de lutte contre la pauvreté et l'exclusion sociale.

3. Une stratégie expansive et de mise en synergie des diverses activités

La Poste est un groupe multi-activités, le courrier représentant en 2012 la moitié de son chiffre d'affaires, les colis express près de 26 %

---

[20] http://lexpansion.lexpress.fr/entreprise/bruxelles-avalise-les-subventions-publiques-a-la-poste_280088.html#SHkRvZqg1wY6buw4.99.

[21] Article 145 de la loi n° 2008-776 du 4 août 2008 de modernisation de l'économie.

[22] Rapport annuel de l'Observatoire de l'épargne réglementée, 2011.

et la banque 24 %. L'ambition de La Poste est de devenir un opérateur leader en Europe. Les réorganisations successives des dernières années ont pour objet de faire face à une ouverture croissante à la concurrence tout en répondant aux missions de service public. Le modèle vise à éviter le repli sur le réseau des bureaux de poste, pour développer une approche s'appuyant sur un « écosystème », fondé sur la proximité vis-à-vis des clients, misant sur des synergies entre les différentes activités pour assurer leur développement réciproque et la pérennité du réseau.

3.1. Le courrier

La stratégie du groupe consiste à compenser la baisse prévue des volumes par une politique de renouvellement de l'offre et à se préparer à l'intensification de la concurrence par des réductions de coûts. Plusieurs facteurs suscitent en effet la baisse des volumes de courrier que La Poste estime à près de 30 % sur la période 2008-2016. Le premier est la mauvaise conjoncture économique et par la forte corrélation de l'activité courrier aux échanges économiques. Le second est le développement du e-commerce qui suscite un repli des échanges tout « papier ». Enfin, l'usage croissant et la forte appétence, tant chez les particuliers que dans les entreprises pour des nouvelles technologies suscite une forte expansion de la numérisation des échanges. L'activité courrier est par ailleurs centrée sur des organisations de grande taille et très concentrée sur quelques secteurs (bancaire, public, vente à distance et télécommunications) et les 100 plus gros clients représentent en 2012 près 39 % du chiffre d'affaires de la maison mère du groupe.

Les mutations de la demande conduisent La Poste à chercher à compenser la baisse d'activité en se déployant à l'international et en cherchant à réduire les coûts, d'autant que les tarifs ne peuvent qu'évoluer de manière modérée, du fait de leur encadrement et de la forte élasticité-prix de la demande. L'activité courrier, et notamment celle de la maison mère du groupe, reste largement une « industrie de main d'œuvre » malgré le développement de l'automatisation des traitements. Du fait des obligations de service universel et des objectifs de qualité de service, les coûts fixes sont élevés : plateformes de tri de proximité (frais induits par l'immobilier, l'encadrement), distribution du courrier six jours sur sept (frais de tournée et de temps de déplacement), densité des points de contact.

L'étape suivante, menée depuis la mi-2011 consiste à focaliser sur les relations d'affaires. Il s'agit d'enrichir la gamme par le développement d'une offre innovante en ligne (conseil pour le courrier publicitaire, envoi et réception des lettres recommandées en ligne, etc.). Il s'agit encore de placer dans une perspective d'un courrier responsable intégrant la dimension environnementale (par exemple par la collecte des papiers de bureau des entreprises en vue de leur recyclage, en faisant du courrier neutre en carbone, en lançant par sa filiale Mediapost un programme de compensation de l'intégralité des émissions de CO_2).

Au-delà des activités de la maison mère, le groupe a mené une politique de filialisation active : le pôle Mediapost prend ainsi en charge la communication relationnelle, Docapost pour les échanges professionnels, Viapost pour la logistique et le transport (presse, tri et éco-mobilité), le pôle Asendia, une joint-venture créée en 2012 avec Swiss Post le courrier international en vue d'élargir la couverture internationale. La filialisation se poursuit très activement depuis 2012 pour renforcer le caractère multi-métiers du groupe en cherchant à faire jouer les synergies commerciales, faire partager les innovations et partager les coûts.

3.2. Le colis

En 1984, La Poste fut le premier opérateur postal européen à s'engager dans le colis postal express. Aujourd'hui, le groupe occupe le segment du colis par son département ColiPoste, qui est spécialisé dans la livraison rapide en France des colis de moins de 30 kg (essentiellement en CtoC) et par sa filiale Géopost, dont l'activité est centrée sur la livraison express de ces mêmes colis de moins de 30 kg, d'entreprise à entreprise (BtoB) mais sans négliger pour autant le BtoC. Cette filiale contrôle également les sous-filiales françaises et étrangères du groupe en charge de l'activité du colis (essentiellement express) et connaît une croissance importante (plus de 7 % en 2012) du fait du développement du e-commerce. L'offre de services s'est enrichie par différenciation afin de répondre aux attentes particulières des clientèles : possibilités de choix de créneaux de livraison, produits suivis avec délais de livraison garantis, flashage des produits pour en assurer le suivi. Le marché connaît de plus une forte segmentation, 200 clients représentant près de 70 % de l'activité entreprises dans le secteur du colis. Des plateformes d'opérateurs du e-commerce tendent de plus en plus à jouer un rôle d'intermédiaire entre La Poste et les consommateurs.

Ce marché du colis connaît déjà une assez forte concentration au niveau européen puisque les quatre premiers opérateurs postaux (l'Allemand DHL, le Français La Poste, le Néerlandais TNT et les Britanniques GLS et Parcelforce) détiennent plus de la moitié du marché européen. En ajoutant le cinquième opérateur étasunien UPS, cinq groupes desservent près de 60 % de ce marché. Et la concentration pourrait encore s'accentuer dans les années à venir sur ce marché dynamique.

3.3. La banque

L'activité de la Banque Postale est centrée sur la banque de détail en France (un produit net bancaire, PNB, de 5,015 milliards d'euros en

2012 soit 95,7 % du PNB du groupe la Banque Postale), l'assurance (vie, prévoyance, dommages et santé) ne représentant que 2 % de son PNB et la gestion d'actifs (sociétés de gestion d'actifs et gestion privée), 2,3 %.

La Banque Postale s'appuie sur le réseau de la Poste, sur 35 filiales (qui emploient 3 000 salariés) et participations stratégiques et a mis en place un dispositif de relation multicanaux (relation directe avec les clients dans les bureaux de poste, relation indirecte par téléphone, par internet) afin d'assurer une relation de proximité avec ses clients. Une politique de partenariat très active, initiée depuis 1989 avec la CNP Assurances dans le domaine de l'assurance vie, a pour double objectif de mieux couvrir les besoins des clients et d'étendre l'éventail de ses activités et de ses compétences. En 1998, CNP Assurances et les Services financiers de la Poste ont créé une coentreprise, renommée la Banque Postale Prévoyance en 2007, pour proposer une gamme de produits de prévoyance.

Si la clientèle des particuliers reste le cœur de métier de la Banque Postale, elle commercialise, depuis septembre 2011, une offre de crédit auprès de l'ensemble des personnes morales. Fin 2012, la Banque Postale comptait 446 000 clients personnes morales dont 306 000 associations. Le 25 mai 2012, elle a obtenu l'autorisation d'octroyer des crédits au secteur public local. Elle a développé un nouveau modèle du financement local reposant sur des produits simples, adossés en liquidité et accordés dans le cadre d'une politique tarifaire transparente. À travers sa filiale la Banque Postale Asset Management, elle gère pour sa clientèle des particuliers une large gamme d'OPCVM investis sur les classes d'actifs traditionnels (actions, obligations, monétaires) et elle propose à sa clientèle de personnes morales une gamme d'OPCVM, de fonds dédiés et de mandats de gestion. L'acquisition en avril 2013 de la Banque privée européenne (BPE) auprès de la banque mutualiste Crédit Mutuel Arkéa permet à la Banque Postale de développer son activité de banque patrimoniale.

Entre 2006 et 2012, le nombre de ses clients actifs a augmenté de 17 %, celui de ses conseillers et gestionnaires de clientèle de 46 %, de ses distributeurs automatiques de 35 %.

Tableau 1. L'évolution de l'activité de la Banque Postale depuis 2006

	Nombre de clients actifs (millions)	Nombre de comptes courants postaux (millions)	Nombre de conseillers et gestionnaires de clientèle	Nombre de DAB/GAB	Nombre de points de contact
2006	9	11,2	6 620	4 955	17 043
2009	9,9	11,3		5 343	17 000
2012	10,6	11,6	9 700	6 700	17 000

Source : Rapports annuels de la Banque Postale.

Tableau 2. L'évolution des encours (en milliards d'euros) de la Banque Postale depuis 2006

	Dépôts et Épargne bilantielle	Épargne Financière	Crédits immobiliers	Crédit à la consommation	Crédit au PMO	Crédit au Secteur public local
2006	91,2	148,6	21			
2009	145,4	131,9	33			
2012	157,5	131,1	45	2,6	0,7	0,1

Source : Rapports annuels de la Banque Postale.

Le modèle de la Banque Postale fait preuve d'une certaine résistance à la crise économique. Entre 2006 et 2012, ses encours totaux augmentent de 20 %, son PNB de 14 %, son résultat d'exploitation de 59 % et son résultat net de 54 %. Ces évolutions matérialisent le rôle croissant de la Banque Postale dans le financement de l'économie française. Les évolutions par catégories de placement sont cependant contrastées. Les encours des dépôts et d'épargne bilantielle enregistrent une progression de 73 % tandis que les encours d'épargne financière (assurance vie et OPCVM) baissent de 12 %. Dans un contexte de marché morose, la Banque Postale parvient à développer ses activités de crédit et notamment celle des crédits immobiliers dont les encours ont été multipliés par 2,1 entre 2006 et 2012.

4. Les performances de La Poste dans la mise en œuvre des missions publiques

Le groupe connaît une déformation structurelle de son portefeuille d'activités du fait de leurs dynamiques différenciées, marquée notamment par une contraction sensible des volumes dans le courrier. De plus, il est contraint depuis 2006 par un encadrement global des tarifs. Dans ce contexte, son chiffre d'affaires consolidé connaît depuis 2007 une très faible progression. En 2012, ce chiffre d'affaires s'établit à 21 658 millions d'euros, en progression de 1,5 % par rapport à 2011. Il reste impacté par la baisse marquée du chiffre d'affaires Courrier, la poursuite de la croissance du Colis-Express et l'augmentation du produit net bancaire.

4.1. Le service postal universel et le maillage territorial

La Poste fournit depuis 2006 un rapport annuel[23] précisant la bonne exécution des missions qui lui sont assignées et la qualité du service public universel. Ce rapport établit ainsi des critères de qualité portant sur trois points : les délais d'acheminement, l'accessibilité et le traitement

---

[23] Pour le rapport de l'année 2011 : Résultats de la qualité du service universel 2011.

des réclamations. Concernant les délais d'acheminement, les résultats se situent à des niveaux élevés, ils sont tous supérieurs aux objectifs que La Poste s'est fixée et ils se sont souvent améliorés depuis la première année de diffusion des résultats.

Concernant l'accessibilité, le rapport annuel fait état du respect des critères fixés par la loi. Ce critère renvoie également à la mission publique de maillage territorial complémentaire. Les 17 000 points de contact permettent à La Poste de justifier du respect de ces obligations de desserte. Comme le précise le contrat de présence postale territoriale 2011-13 précité, « sont ainsi appelés "points de contact" : les bureaux de poste, les agences postales communales (APC), les agences postales intercommunales (API), les relais poste (RP) ». Au regard du premier critère fixé par la loi, qui veut qu'au moins 99 % de la population nationale soit à moins de 10 km d'un point de contact, La Poste précise que le taux reste depuis 2006 à 99,9 %. Sur le second critère, voulant qu'au moins 95 % de la population de chaque département soit à moins de 10 km d'un point de contact, le rapport annuel précise également que tel est le cas. Enfin, sur le troisième critère, selon lequel toutes les communes de plus de 10 000 habitants disposent d'au moins un point de contact par tranche de 20 000 habitants, La Poste fait état d'un accroissement du nombre de communes disposant d'un point de contact, qui est passé de 877 en 2008 à 891 en 2011. Le phénomène apparaît largement imputable à l'urbanisation croissante que connaît la France.

Cependant, les données manquent pour analyser l'évolution des caractéristiques des points de contact sur les dernières années ou de manière prospective. Il s'agit pourtant d'un aspect important pour juger des modalités de mise en œuvre de la continuité, de la diversité et de la qualité du service fourni. Il serait en effet utile de pouvoir disposer de données détaillées sur les transformations en cours ou à venir d'un déploiement des bureaux de poste en autres points de contact (notamment relais postes) et de faire une étude du coût d'opportunité, du point de vue de la prestation de service public, du remplacement des bureaux de poste.

Enfin, le rapport 2011 sur la qualité du service postal universel présente l'évolution du nombre de réclamations pour les services du courrier et des colis, la proportion de celles-ci qui sont traitées dans les 21 jours et de celles qui ont donné lieu à indemnisation. Pour le service du courrier, les réclamations se sont fortement accrues depuis 2009 en passant de 628 à 927 mille. Pour le service du colis, la proportion des réclamations par apport au flux total des colis connaît une augmentation sur les deux dernières années respectivement 1,52 et 1,40 % contre moins de 1 % en 2008 et 2009. Les réclamations sont, depuis 2009, traitées à plus de 99 % dans les 21 jours sur les dernières années. Reste que, comme le soulignait en 2008 le rapport Ailleret[24] de la Commission sur le développement de La Poste, et malgré des progrès enregistrés depuis lors, l'affirmation selon laquelle « la satisfaction du client est en demi-teinte » est toujours d'actualité. Les délais d'attente au guichet, les difficultés rencontrées sur les périodes de pointe et dans certains bureaux de poste de zones péri-urbaines, les fermetures de postes en milieu rural durant les périodes restent les premiers facteurs de mécontentement.

4.2. Le service bancaire

Selon le palmarès 2012 du Grand Livre des marques, La Banque Postale est depuis 2010 la marque préférée des Français dans la catégorie banque et assurance. En 2012, un Français sur trois épargne à la Banque Postale. Elle est la 3e banque en France en termes d'encours, sa part de marché tendancielle en encours sur les ménages est de 15,4 % sur les comptes de dépôts, de 24,8 % sur le Livret A, de 20 % sur les trois dépôts réglementés (Livret A, Livret Développement Durable et Livret d'Épargne Populaire) et de 8,5 % sur l'assurance vie[25]. Elle détient un tiers du marché français des associations. Deux de ses filiales ont affiché de bonnes performances en 2012 : la Banque Postale Prévoyance, créée en 1998 (sous le nom d'Assurposte), est le deuxième acteur du marché français de la prévoyance et, la Banque Postale Asset Management est la cinquième société de gestion d'actifs en France.

4.3. Les résultats financiers du groupe

En 2012, le résultat d'exploitation consolidé du groupe est de 816 millions d'euros, en hausse de 21,8 % par rapport à 2011. Le résultat du courrier de la maison mère est cependant en chute de 9,6 % en 2012 du fait d'une baisse de 5,9 % du volume d'activité, de l'inertie des coûts fixes et de hausses modérées de tarifs. Le résultat net du Groupe est quant à lui stable à 479 millions d'euros. Ce résultat permet à La Poste de proposer la distribution d'un dividende de 171 millions d'euros à ses actionnaires. La dette nette régresse, notamment sur l'année 2012, grâce aux dotations en capital de l'État et de la Caisse des Dépôts et Consignations, ainsi qu'avec l'acceptation par la Commission européenne d'une subvention pour compenser le surcoût net du service universel. Par ailleurs, du fait de l'ampleur des missions de service public, la Commission européenne a autorisé en 2012 la couverture partielle de leur coût sur la période 2008-12 par une subvention de 1,9 milliard d'euros.

---

[24] http://www.ladocumentationfrancaise.fr/var/storage/rapports-publics/084000771/ 0000.pdf, page 18.

[25] Source : Banque de France.

Pour consolider sa situation financière, le groupe a également pu bénéficier d'un renforcement de ses fonds propres par une augmentation de capital suite au contrat de souscription signé le 11 février 2011. L'augmentation de capital est d'un total de 2,7 milliards d'euros, octroyé par l'État et la Caisse des Dépôts et Consignations. Au terme de cette opération, la Caisse des Dépôts et Consignation détient 26,32 % du capital de La Poste et l'État 73,68 %. Le groupe a également émis en novembre 2012 un emprunt obligataire de 750 millions d'euros. La dette nette[26] est ainsi d'un niveau relativement peu élevé : en 2012, le ratio de flux de trésorerie des opérations sur dette nette est ainsi de 27,7 %.

Tableau 3. Les indicateurs de performance financière de La Poste de 2005 à 2012 (en millions d'euros)

Année	Chiffre d'affaires	Résultat d'exploitation	Résultat net	Dette nette
2012	21 658	816	479	3 460
2011	21 341	670	478	4 544
2010	20 939	784	550	4 822
2009	20 527	757	531	5 535
2008	20 829	886	529	5 760
2007	20 819	1 285	943	5 800
2006	20 100	949	789	5 917
2005	19 274	777	557	3 800

Source : Rapports annuels de La Poste.

La création de la Banque Postale a été en partie financée par une levée de fonds sur le marché obligataire de la Poste pour un montant de 1 800 000 euros et par la banque elle-même pour un montant de 500 000 euros soit un total de 2 300 000 euros. La crise financière ne semble pas avoir affecté le financement de la Banque Postale par émission sur le marché obligataire. Les dégradations de la notation long terme de la Poste et de la Banque Postale par les agences de ratings dont Standard & Poor's, que l'on peut relier au moins partiellement aux moindres garanties pour les prêteurs de la transformation de La Poste en entreprise autonome et ouverte à la concurrence, semble ne pas avoir eu un effet négatif sur l'intérêt porté par les investisseurs sur les obligations émises par le groupe la Poste. Depuis 1991, Standard & Poor's a dégradé quatre fois sa note attribuée à la Poste, de « AAA » (aucun risque de défaut, solvabilité financière jugée très bonne par Standard & Poor's) du 07/11/1991 au 18/11/2003, elle est « A » depuis le 02/04/2010. En 2013, Standard & Poor's semble

---

[26] La dette nette ne prend pas en compte l'activité bancaire pour laquelle la notion n'est pas pertinente.

considérer que La Poste est plus risquée que sa filiale la Banque Postale (note « A » contre « A+ »). Standard and Poor's a confirmé en juillet 2012 la note « A » de La Poste et a modifié à la hausse la perspective, qui passe de stable à positive pointant des progrès accomplis en termes de génération de trésorerie.

Tableau 4. Évolution des ratings long terme de Standard & Poor's de 1991 à 2013

Date de la notation	La Poste	La Banque Postale
07/11/1991	AAA	
18/11/2003	AA+	
16/12/2005	AA-	AA-
20/01/2009	A+	A+
02/04/2010	A	

Source : Six Financial Information.

5. Les modes de gouvernance d'une « entreprise publique emblématique »

Les actionnaires de La Poste sont l'État qui détient, en 2013, 73,68 % du capital et la Caisse des Dépôts et Consignations, les 26,32 % restants. Cette dernière est une très ancienne institution publique (créée en 1816) dont les missions sont de promouvoir pour le compte de l'État et des collectivités territoriales des missions d'intérêt général. Le fait que le capital de La Poste soit intégralement public n'est ni un détail ni un hasard. Elle a suscité une mobilisation d'une ampleur sans précédent pour éviter que l'entreprise puisse être privatisée après sa transformation en 2009 en société anonyme à capitaux publics. La Poste est très emblématique de l'attachement de la société française à un service public de proximité dans lequel la propriété publique est perçue comme une garante du modèle social fondé sur des missions sociales. La propriété publique y apparaît ainsi comme un moyen de préserver un mode de gouvernance des services publics qui caractérisait le modèle français institué après-guerre.

5.1. La gouvernance institutionnelle : un conseil d'administration tripartite

Le conseil d'administration de La Poste est composé en référence à la loi n° 83-675 du 26 juillet 1983 relative à la démocratisation du secteur public qui veut qu'il comprenne, comme pour les autres entreprises publiques concernées,

1° des représentants de l'État nommés par décret et, le cas échéant, des représentants des autres actionnaires nommés par l'assemblée générale ; 2° des personnalités choisies, soit en raison de leur compétence technique, scientifique ou technologique, soit en raison de leur connaissance des aspects régionaux, départementaux ou locaux des activités en cause, soit en raison de leur connaissance des activités publiques et privées concernées par l'activité de l'entreprise, soit en raison de leur qualité de représentants des consommateurs ou des usagers, nommées par décret pris, le cas échéant, après consultation d'organismes représentatifs desdites activités ; 3° des représentants des salariés élus.

Toutefois, par dérogation à l'article 5 de cette même loi, le conseil d'administration de La Poste est composé de vingt et un membres. Le président du conseil d'administration est nommé par décret. Le conseil d'administration est composé de 8 représentants de l'État et de 3 de la CDC. Un représentant des communes et de leurs groupements figure parmi les personnalités choisies en raison de leurs compétences. Un représentant des usagers de La Poste figure également parmi les personnalités choisies pour ses compétences. Les 7 derniers membres sont les représentants des salariés. Par ailleurs, le conseil d'administration a, en 2001, créé trois comités spécialisés, qui apportent un éclairage sur des questions spécifiques. Ils émettent des avis qui sont présentés en séance au conseil d'administration par leurs présidents respectifs[27].

5.2. La gouvernance des missions postales territoriales

Les règles de gouvernance dans la mise en œuvre des missions territoriales sont également fortement institutionnalisées. Un contrat de présence territoriale est signé périodiquement, qui précise notamment les modalités d'utilisation du fonds de péréquation de présence postale sur le territoire national. Ce contrat est négocié conjointement par La Poste et l'Association des maires de France (AMF). Il précise également les conditions de mise en œuvre des aménagements qui touchent à l'exécution des missions publiques et aux modalités de concertation entre les élus et la Poste. Ainsi, comme le précise le dernier contrat de présence postale portant sur la période 2011-13, « un bureau de poste » peut être transformé en APC (Agence postale communale), API (Agence postale intercommunale), ou en RP (Relais poste) : sur la base d'un diagnostic partagé entre La Poste et la commune concernée, préalable et formalisé ; avec l'accord préalable du maire et du conseil municipal, qui valident le changement de statut du point de contact et la nature du partenariat (APC, API ou RP). Le contrat 2011 de présence postale territoriale a

---

[27] http://www.laposte.fr/LeGroupe2/Nous-connaitre/Gouvernance-d-entreprise/Comites-specialises-du-conseil-d-administration.

de plus explicité de nouvelles règles de gouvernance, qui impliquent au-delà de La Poste, deux institutions : l'Observatoire national de présence postale (ONPP) et les Commissions départementales de présence postale territoriale (CDPPT). Ces dernières ont notamment pour objet d'émettre des avis sur les projets de La Poste, concernant notamment le nombre de points de contact ou la modernisation du service, en relatant les besoins exprimés par la population. Elles veillent encore au respect des engagements pris par La Poste[28].

5.3. La gouvernance de l'entreprise et les salariés

Le groupe La Poste est le premier employeur français après l'État. Ses effectifs tendent cependant à régresser depuis une décennie, mouvement qui s'accompagne d'une nette contraction du nombre des fonctionnaires. Depuis 2003, l'intégralité des recrutements s'effectue sous statut privé. De plus les départs à la retraite n'ont pas été totalement remplacés ce qui a conduit, malgré la poursuite du mouvement de filialisation du groupe, à ce que ce dernier ait, fin 2012, 266 618 salariés en équivalent temps plein (dont 83,1 %, soit près de 221 300, dans la société mère du groupe), le nombre de fonctionnaires poursuivant progressivement sa décrue.

Ce contexte général de baisse tendancielle des effectifs, de particularité de la coexistence (et de baisse) des fonctionnaires issus de l'ancienne administration des postes et télécommunications et de salariés de droit privé, et enfin de transformation de la culture de l'organisation avec l'ouverture à la concurrence sur le service universel, pose en des termes sensibles la relation de la direction de l'entreprise avec ses salariés.

La direction de l'entreprise fait état d'une politique de renforcement des emplois stables par une forte contraction des emplois au temps partiel imposé et de réduction significative du nombre de contrats à durée déterminée (CDD). Elle souligne également l'encouragement à l'évolution professionnelle au sein du groupe, la promotion du développement continu des compétences et de l'accès de tous aux emplois. Face à l'extinction progressive des fonctionnaires, le Contrat à durée déterminée (CDI) à temps complet ou partiel est présenté comme le cœur du modèle social du groupe. Ce dernier précise ainsi que, de 2003 à 2009, le taux d'emploi à temps plein à La Poste a ainsi progressé de 20 points : 88,9 % des salariés travaillent à temps plein en 2009. S'agissant des personnes en CDD, le

---

[28] En 2011, sur les 170 millions d'euros du fonds de péréquation postale territoriale, les CDPTT en ont négocié 29,9 dans le cadre du programme départemental en métropole, près de 5 en outre-mer, 18,4 pour les zones urbaines sensibles. S'y ajoutent 57, 3 pour les bureaux de poste situés en zone rurale, 53 pour les APC et API et enfin 6,1 pour la rémunération des relais poste. http://www.laposte.fr/collectivites-et-territoires/sites/default/files/posteo_contrat_de_presence_postale_1.pdf, Posteo, février 2011.

groupe indique qu'elles ne représentent plus que 3,29 % de l'effectif total de 2009, qui est un très faible niveau pour une entreprise de services à l'activité saisonnière. L'intérim ne représente quant à lui que 1,17 % des effectifs.

Les positions d'organisations syndicales sont par ailleurs réservées, voire radicalement critiques, vis-à-vis du « modèle social » et du mode de gouvernance de l'entreprise vis-à-vis de ses salariés. Les tensions proviennent principalement des transformations de la culture d'organisation que nombre de salariés et de syndicats critiquent fortement. Au-delà de la mise en extinction des fonctionnaires, on retrouve ici les critiques à l'encontre du développement de la culture commerciale au détriment de la culture traditionnelle de service public. Une pression commerciale s'exercerait sur les personnels pour qu'ils se recentrent sur la valorisation commerciale, ce qui susciterait un malaise profond du fait du sentiment de changer de métier, l'optimisation de leur temps de travail et la recherche de la productivité se faisant au détriment du lien social. Cela a pu être mis tout particulièrement en avant concernant les facteurs dont le temps est compté et qui ne peuvent plus, notamment en milieu rural, apporter des services connexes, marqués du signe du désintéressement, du fait d'un manque de disponibilité lié aux nouveaux modes d'organisation du travail.

5.4. La gouvernance bancaire

La Banque Postale a adopté les principes d'une gouvernance conforme à son statut d'entreprise publique. Elle a choisi une structure duale permettant une dissociation entre les pouvoirs de gestion et de contrôle et garantissant une séparation entre les pouvoirs. Les pouvoirs de direction et de gestion assumés par le Directoire sont ainsi différenciés des pouvoirs de contrôle et de décision exercés par le Conseil de surveillance.

Le Directoire définit la stratégie et les orientations opérationnelles du groupe et il informe régulièrement le Conseil de surveillance des résultats de la Banque, de ses projets de développement et de l'évolution de sa stratégie. Il assure son management dans le respect des dispositions légales et réglementaires. Il est composé de trois membres, le président, le secrétaire général et le directeur finances et stratégie. La gouvernance interne de La Banque Postale est rythmée par la tenue du Directoire et de plusieurs comités. Le Conseil de surveillance contrôle la gestion de La Banque Postale et s'assure du bon pilotage de sa stratégie.

6. Une architecture multiniveaux de la régulation publique

Bien que les missions publiques de La Poste soient plus étendues en France que dans les autres pays européens, la régulation publique n'en est pas moins très radicalement différente de ce qu'elle était avant l'ouverture à la concurrence, en perdant ses dimensions de politique industrielle ou de régulation conjoncturelle. Le contrat de plan pluriannuel qui, dans la tradition française de l'après-guerre, incarnait le lien étroit qui prévalait entre politique publique et organisations publiques a ainsi été abandonné avec le renoncement de la France au début des années 2000 à la planification indicative.

6.1. La stratégie de La Poste en tant qu'expression d'une régulation économique et sociale nationale

La Poste signe avec l'État un contrat d'entreprise, conformément à la Loi n° 2010-123 du 9 février 2010 – art. 6. On y dispose que

l'État conclut avec La Poste le contrat d'entreprise mentionné à l'article 140 de la loi n° 2001-420 du 15 mai 2001 relative aux nouvelles régulations économiques. Ce contrat détermine en particulier les objectifs des quatre missions de service public et d'intérêt général visées au I de l'article 2 de la présente loi.

Ce contrat d'entreprise remplace le traditionnel contrat de Plan entre l'État et La Poste qui avait été maintenu au titre de l'article 9 de la loi du 2 juillet 1990 qui créait cette dernière. Cela reflète le changement du mode de régulation initié par l'ouverture à la concurrence.

Par-delà l'objectif d'efficacité économique visé dans l'exercice de l'activité, en tant qu'entreprise publique La Poste revendique l'internalisation d'autres missions qui rencontrent l'intérêt général et qui, sans être formalisées, contribuent à la régulation économique d'ensemble. Cette forme d'internalisation renvoie à la doctrine de l'État stratège, qui a émergé en France durant les années 1990 et 2000. Par cette doctrine, l'État central se veut le maître d'œuvre d'une stratégie d'ensemble que mettent notamment en œuvre des opérateurs. Ces derniers disposent d'une autonomie de gestion et sont incités à inscrire leurs actions conformément aux orientations stratégiques de l'État. L'organisation publique apparaît dès lors comme un vecteur privilégié de mise en œuvre de ce type de stratégie.

6.2. Les déclinaisons locales de la régulation publique dans le périmètre postal

Par-delà la mise en œuvre de sa mission clairement formalisée de contribution à l'aménagement du territoire, La Poste fait état de sa contribution aux politiques structurantes de développement économique local. Les modalités d'ajustement de la régulation s'opèrent notamment par un dialogue en continu sur l'aménagement du territoire avec les élus locaux. Le groupe indique ainsi participer à la mise en place de politiques structurantes des territoires : schémas régionaux Climat Air Énergie, Plans Climat, Agenda 21, d'urbanisme et schémas locaux d'accessibilité. Des actions de développement local renvoient également à des mesures prises pour faciliter l'accès des TPE et PME locales aux marchés fournis par La Poste. Cela s'accompagne ici encore d'actions de sensibilisation sur les achats solidaires concernant notamment le secteur dit « adapté et protégé »[29], à fort impact environnemental, et au secteur de l'insertion par l'activité économique. Il s'agit également de créer des « écosystèmes dynamiques » dans l'intérêt mutuel des différents partenaires et de la Poste.

Ces dispositifs de cohésion sociale et territoriale au plan local n'en restent pas moins dépendants, comme les missions publiques formalisées de contribution à l'aménagement du territoire, à la question de la capacité du groupe à les financer à l'avenir dans un environnement plus concurrentiel.

6.3. Le rôle et l'action de l'instance indépendante de régulation postale : l'ARCEP

L'Autorité de régulation des communications électroniques et postales (ARCEP) a succédé en 2005 à l'Autorité de régulation des télécommunications (ART). L'ART était une autorité administrative indépendante de régulation, créée en 1996 pour assurer la régulation du secteur des télécommunications qui s'ouvrait totalement à la concurrence à l'échéance du premier janvier 1998. Après la directive européenne de 2002 relative au secteur postal, le législateur français a étendu les compétences de l'ART au secteur postal par la loi 2005-516 du 20 mai 2005, créant à cette occasion l'ARCEP. Il s'agit à cet effet d'instaurer une régulation sectorielle visant à assurer la viabilité du service universel postal dans le cadre d'une ouverture progressive du marché à la concurrence et de veiller à ce que cette concurrence soit libre et non faussée.

Après sa création en 2005, l'ARCEP va remplir sa mission dans ses différentes facettes et s'attacher à délivrance d'autorisations qui permettent d'ouvrir le marché à la concurrence[30]. Les autorisations sont délivrées pour 10 ans renouvelables, attachées à la personne du bénéficiaire et sans possibilité de cession. Le 13 juin 2006, une première autorisation est délivrée à l'opérateur Adexo, puis trois supplémentaires le sont le

---

29 En 2012, le secteur adapté et protégé représente 8,5 millions d'euros pour La Poste et plus de 800 mille euros pour la Banque Postale.

30 Pour précisions concernant l'ensemble des décisions prises par l'ARCEP depuis sa création, consulter : http://www.arcep.fr/index.php?id=3.

7 septembre 2006. En mai 2008, trois ans après la création de l'ARCEP, l'autorité avait délivré 20 autorisations, dont 12 à des prestataires de courrier domestique pour l'envoi de correspondances de plus de 50 grammes et 9 à des opérateurs de courrier transfrontalier sortant (dont l'une commune aux deux champs précédents pour La Poste). Comme le montrent C. Gallet-Rybak *et al.*[31], il s'agit de marchés de niche. Pour le courrier domestique, on est alors en présence de courriers de plus de 50 grammes sur des services à valeur ajoutée, complétant les prestations de La Poste (à un prix de 10 à 15 % moins cher), dans des zones locales et liées à l'activité d'origine du prestataire. Pour le courrier transfrontière sortant, la concurrence s'est développée (en débutant dès 1995) sous l'égide, le plus souvent de filiales, d'opérateurs historiques allemand, belge, néerlandais et suisse pour l'envoi de correspondances, de colis, de presse vers le monde entier. La concurrence reste alors marginale ne représentant qu'un pour cent du marché postal dans son ensemble. Au 18 avril 2013, ce sont 33 opérateurs qui bénéficient d'une autorisation d'exercice : 22 sur tout le territoire national ou sur certaines zones délimitées ; 10 pour la correspondance transfrontalière sortante à destination du monde entier et 1 (La Poste) pour les deux types d'activités. Si le nombre d'opérateurs s'accroît, la part de l'activité des opérateurs alternatifs reste très faible et le marché est, dans les faits, quasi monopolistique. À l'instar de ce qui a pu être observé sur les autres marchés postaux européens qui ont été ouverts à la concurrence, le taux de pénétration sur le marché des opérateurs alternatifs est faible. Les études faites sur l'ouverture à la concurrence des marchés postaux européens (WIK, 2008 ; ITA&WIK, 2010 ; Copenhagen Economics ; 2010) ont en effet pointé la faiblesse de la concurrence effective, à l'exception du courrier international. Les opérateurs historiques restent dès lors très dominants sur leur marché et c'est seulement en Allemagne, en Espagne, et aux Pays-Bas que les niveaux de concurrence ne sont pas marginaux. La faible dynamique du marché fait que la menace pour les opérateurs historiques provient, tout particulièrement pour le courrier, du tassement de la demande et du développement d'une concurrence par substitution plutôt que de la concurrence directe des autres opérateurs du secteur.

Reste que pour assurer au mieux la régulation du marché et accroître la concurrence, l'ARCEP a cherché à mettre en place des outils qui lui permettent d'accéder à une information pertinente et fiable concernant l'activité des opérateurs exerçant sur le marché postal. L'Observatoire des activités postales produit ainsi chaque année des données statistiques sur l'activité du secteur. Cette quête d'information et les analyses

---

[31] http://www.arcep.fr/fileadmin/reprise/secteurpostal/article-rutgers-postal-mai2008.pdf.

qui en émanent sont indispensables car, comme le précise lors de la 17ᵉ conférence sur l'économie postale³², J. Tolédano, membre de l'ARCEP et présidente en 2011 du Groupe des régulateurs postaux européens, l'accès à l'information est difficile pour le régulateur dans le secteur postal. Bien que la relation de confiance puisse amener les opérateurs à transmettre une information satisfaisante, les asymétries d'informations entre opérateurs et régulateur sont potentiellement fortes dans le secteur postal pour plusieurs raisons : faible concurrence et donc manque d'enseignements sur des comportements alternatifs ; incapacité à effectuer du benchmarking du fait de l'absence de définition et de principes homogènes et harmonisés d'un pays à l'autre ; analyses financières peu fournies du fait de l'absence en général de cotation sur les marchés financiers ; faiblesse des innovations et donc d'enseignements à en tirer.

Pour tenter de réguler au mieux le marché dans le contexte spécifique du secteur postal, d'autant que les opérateurs sont multi-produits, l'ARCEP a donc travaillé à la mise en place d'instruments comptables et financiers susceptibles de mesurer de manière rigoureuse les coûts (et notamment de l'allocation des coûts de La Poste, du calcul du service universel, du maillage territorial) pour définir, conformément aux orientations européennes des tarifs orientés vers les coûts. L'ARCEP contrôle également périodiquement les tarifs du service universel et approuve depuis 2006 la tarification de type price cap des services de La Poste.

Pour l'heure, dans l'ensemble, La Poste a été assez peu affectée par les décisions de l'ARCEP concernant l'évaluation du coût du service universel ou de la tarification des services. On peut cependant se demander si la volonté de sensiblement renforcer la concurrence et les analyses en cours sur les avantages induits du service universel ne sont pas de nature à changer la donne.

6.4. Les spécificités de la régulation bancaire

Comme l'ensemble des établissements de crédit et des entreprises d'investissement, la Banque Postale est soumise aux mêmes autorités de réglementation et de contrôle et organise son contrôle interne à partir des dispositions du Code monétaire et financier, du règlement CRBF-97-02 modifié, de la réglementation prudentielle, du cadre de référence de l'AMF sur le contrôle interne. Le contrôle interne de la Banque

---

32 Discours du 27 mai 2009 figurant sur le site de l'ARCEP : http://www.arcep.fr/index.php?id=2124&tx_gsactualite_pi1[uid]=1174&tx_gsactualite_pi1[annee]=&tx_gsactua lite_pi1[theme]=&tx_gsactualite_pi1[motscle]=&tx_gsactualite_pi1[backID]=24&cHash=ce914cf8c4.

Postale repose sur trois principes : « responsabilité de tous les acteurs », « la proportionnalité des contrôles au niveau du risque à maîtriser » et « l'exhaustivité du périmètre de contrôle » et s'effectue sur trois niveaux :

- un dispositif de contrôle au plus près des activités (contrôle de 1er niveau), contrôles réalisés par les opérationnels et par des contrôleurs ;
- des fonctions de contrôle interne qui recouvrent le dispositif de contrôle permanent piloté par la Direction de la conformité, la surveillance et la maîtrise des risques assurées par la Direction des risques et le contrôle périodique réalisé par l'Inspection générale ;
- de Comités de gouvernance relatifs au contrôle interne (Comité d'audit, Comité conformité et déontologie, Comité des risques).

Le Comité de coordination du contrôle interne rassemble autour du membre du Directoire responsable du contrôle interne les quatre directeurs pour lui permettre d'assurer la cohérence et l'efficacité du contrôle interne.

Quatre banques françaises, parmi lesquelles la Banque Postale, figurent dans le classement annuel des 50 banques les plus sûres du monde publié en 2012 par « Global Finance ». Le développement de la Banque Postale s'appuie sur un bilan solide et une solvabilité élevée : au 31 décembre 2012, son ratio Core Tier 1 Bâle 2.5 est de 12,1 %, le « noyau dur » des capitaux propres de la Banque Postale représente plus de 12 % de son activité de crédit.

7. Des choix stratégiques de tarification et d'investissement

La Poste a eu pendant les années 1990 une politique d'augmentation très modérée de ses tarifs qui a abouti à une forte distorsion entre les coûts supportés et les tarifs appliqués. Entre 1996 et 2002, La Poste n'ayant pas augmenté ses tarifs, les prix du courrier ont diminué de 7 % par rapport à l'indice des prix[33]. Sur cette même période, La Poste a vu ses coûts d'exploitation augmenter en raison notamment de la mise en place de l'aménagement et de la réduction du temps de travail sans aucun allègement de charges sociales. Début 2003, le tarif lettre de la Poste se situait 8 % en dessous de la moyenne des tarifs lettre appliqués dans les pays européens bien que la superficie et la densité de la France renchérissent les coûts d'exploitation.

---

[33] Larcher G. (2003), Rapport d'information n° 344, Session ordinaire de 2002-2003 du Sénat.

Contrairement à ce qui s'est produit dans d'autres pays européens, et notamment à l'Allemagne, La Poste ne s'est pas servi de sa position de monopole sur l'activité courrier pour augmenter sa « rente »[34]. Entre 1996 et 2002, la poste allemande a augmenté de 92 % le tarif prioritaire de la lettre de 20 g tandis que La Poste n'a pas modifié son tarif. Elle n'a pas utilisé le prix du timbre comme moyen d'accumulation de richesses, se privant ainsi de ressources pour financer sa modernisation industrielle. Après 2003, La Poste opère un « rattrapage » en augmentant à deux reprises ses tarifs puis, elle adopte à partir de 2006 un contrat d'encadrement tarifaire pluriannuel du panier des offres du service universel, price cap, sous le contrôle du régulateur, l'ARCEP. Depuis la loi du 20 mai 2005, c'est l'ARCEP qui fixe le price cap dans le cadre duquel La Poste fait des propositions d'évolution tarifaire. En 2006, l'ARCEP définit l'encadrement des tarifs de la Poste pour la période 2006-2008 en considérant que cet encadrement doit notamment : permettre le maintien de la marge de La Poste ; donner une visibilité pluriannuelle à partir d'analyses des marchés, des charges et de l'inflation ; être incitatif pour La Poste ; tenir compte de l'effort d'investissement et des mutations industrielles que La Poste a engagés depuis 2003, du contexte de stagnation des volumes sur les marchés du courrier et du risque qu'il représente pour La Poste[35]. En janvier 2012, le régulateur français, confronté à plusieurs incertitudes dont celle sur l'évolution de trafics, décide de prolonger en 2012 l'encadrement pluriannuel des tarifs relatif à la période 2009-2011. L'évolution des tarifs du service universel demeure donc fixée à inflation plus 0,3 % mais compte tenu des mouvements antérieurs, la hausse tarifaire que peut pratiquer La Poste en 2012 a été limitée à 1,5 %. Il décide, le 6 novembre 2012, l'encadrement du service universel postal pour la période 2013-2015 : l'évolution du prix moyen du panier des offres du service universel de la période est limitée à l'inflation plus 1 %. Cette décision est suivie d'un avis favorable de l'ARCEP à la demande de La Poste d'augmenter le prix moyen du service universel de 2,6 % au 1er janvier 2013.

Les évolutions tarifaires contribuent au financement de la modernisation de l'appareil de production de La Poste, qui s'est engagée en contrepartie à accroître son efficacité économique au service des entreprises comme des particuliers. Face à la contraction des volumes sur le courrier et au niveau élevé des coûts fixes inhérents à une industrie

---

[34] J. Tolédano estime que depuis 1992 en moyenne la concurrence est extrêmement marginale en France avec moins de 1 % de part de marché « courrier ». http://www.arcep.fr/fileadmin/reprise/secteurpostal/intervention-j-toledano-conf-Rutger-juin2012.pdf.

[35] http://www.arcep.fr/fileadmin/reprise/secteurpostal/slidesposte-confl30606.ppt.

de main d'œuvre soumise à des missions publiques contraignantes, la préservation des résultats peut également être obtenue par deux autres moyens : l'augmentation de la productivité et la baisse de la qualité de service. Les gains de productivité dépendent pour une bonne part de la capacité du groupe à rationaliser son activité (mais avec quel impact sur les missions de service public et sur le climat social au sein du groupe ?) et à développer ses investissements. La baisse de la qualité de service est particulièrement surveillée par l'autorité de régulation qui, comme on l'a indiqué, a pointé la détérioration temporaire des résultats de l'année 2010 et veille à répondre aux réclamations des usagers.

La tarification bancaire peut constituer une source d'exclusion financière. La loi de régulation bancaire et financière du 22 octobre 2010 étend les compétences du Comité consultatif du secteur financier, CCSF, en lui demandant de suivre les pratiques tarifaires des établissements bancaires. La Banque Postale propose des tarifs aux particuliers en deçà des pratiques du marché pour des opérations liées au fonctionnement de compte. À la Banque Postale, les prélèvements et l'abonnement au Service de gestion par Internet sont gratuits et le coût de l'assurance des moyens de paiement est inférieur à la moyenne du marché.

Le groupe La Poste a pour sa part engagé dans les années 2000 un grand programme d'investissement visant la modernisation du processus industriel du Courrier. Depuis la création au 1er avril 2005 de la filiale Poste Immo, cette dernière réalise une part importante des investissements du groupe pour les activités postales en France. La filiale gère les investissements en infrastructure concernant les centres de tris et la rénovation des bureaux de poste ainsi que le patrimoine immobilier. Le plan de modernisation de l'appareil de production de La Poste a conduit à un investissement total de 3,4 milliards d'euros sur la période 2004-12 et permis la création de 42 plateformes industrielles de courrier (PIC) permettant de couvrir 88 % du trafic. Ce programme a sensiblement amélioré la productivité du courrier par une massification des flux et accru la qualité de service, notamment par l'amélioration observée des délais d'acheminement.

Ce processus étant aujourd'hui largement arrivé à terme et le contexte économique étant celui de la baisse d'activité pour le courrier, le montant des investissements bruts des activités hors banque du groupe a été réduit en 2012 de 1,37 million d'euros. Les investissements restent néanmoins à un niveau relativement élevé (864 millions d'euros pour les activités hors banque) pour plusieurs raisons : poursuite de la rénovation du réseau de bureaux de poste ; maintenance du parc immobilier et de l'outil industriel ; renforcement du réseau européen et international de l'activité Express ; acquisition de véhicules ; développement des systèmes d'information.

Conclusion

En 2004, avant qu'elle soit dotée d'un statut d'entreprise publique, La Poste employait près de 310 000 personnes en équivalent temps plein. Les effectifs sont cependant tombés, fin 2012, à moins de 267 000 salariés, après un effort drastique pour réaliser des gains de productivité.

La production du groupe, dont la valeur progresse faiblement depuis le milieu des années 2000, est répartie sur trois pôles d'activités de maturité différente : le courrier et le colis-express essentiellement en Europe, la banque (et plus précisément la banque de détail, l'assurance et la gestion d'actifs) sur le territoire français. Au début de la décennie 1990, l'activité courrier représentait les deux tiers du chiffre d'affaires. Elle n'en représente plus aujourd'hui qu'un peu moins de la moitié, les activités du colis-express et de la Banque Postale, plus dynamiques, se répartissant à parts presque égales l'autre moitié.

La Poste fait des bénéfices depuis plusieurs années sans aides publiques ou de l'État actionnaire. En 2012, elle a cependant bénéficié d'une subvention pour compenser le coût net du service universel durant la période 2008-12, et d'une augmentation de capital pour consolider sa structure financière. Depuis la création de la Banque Postale en 2006, le produit net bancaire et les bénéfices de l'activité bancaire du groupe La Poste ont été respectivement multipliés par un peu plus de 1,1 et de 1,5 soit un taux de croissance annuel respectivement supérieur à 2 % et 7 % en euros constants.

Le groupe développe depuis plusieurs années une stratégie active de filialisation pour renforcer sa spécificité de groupe multi-métiers. La Poste cherche ainsi à accroître les synergies commerciales en partageant en son sein les savoir-faire, les innovations et les coûts. Elle a organisé son activité courrier entre la maison mère qui est chargée de la commercialisation et de la distribution et la filiale Sofipost qui, par l'intermédiaire de plusieurs sous-filiales, est chargée de la communication relationnelle, de la logistique et du transport, du courrier international. Elle occupe le marché du colis par son département ColiPost et par sa filiale Géopost qui développe son activité de livraison express de colis en contrôlant des sous-filiales françaises et étrangères. En quelques années, les services financiers de La Poste sont par ailleurs devenus le sous-groupe La Banque Postale structuré autour de trente-cinq filiales et participations. La stratégie de croissance externe se poursuit activement aujourd'hui.

Le schéma organisationnel de La Poste a été fortement impacté par le processus de libéralisation impulsé par l'Union européenne, qui débouche aujourd'hui dans les textes sur une ouverture totale du marché postal à la concurrence. En vingt ans, La Poste est passée du statut d'administration en 1990 (formant alors, avec l'actuel France Télécom, les PTT) à celui d'établissement public industriel et commercial doté d'une personnalité juridique et d'une autonomie de gestion, puis à celui de société anonyme à capitaux totalement publics depuis 2010. La récente transformation en entreprise a provoqué de fortes inquiétudes chez les élus (notamment au Sénat et à l'Association des maires de France) et dans la population (suscitant même une votation citoyenne) sur la capacité future de l'entreprise à assumer ses missions de service public et sur les risques de privatisation résultant du nouveau statut.

La loi a dès lors chargé l'entreprise publique de remplir quatre missions de service public : le service universel du courrier et du colis ; la distribution de la presse ; la contribution à l'aménagement du territoire ; l'accessibilité bancaire. Bien que le financement de trois premières missions prête à interrogations, du fait des limites de la capacité contributive des autorités publiques à le couvrir à l'avenir (la distribution de la presse apparaissant dès à présent comme une mission dont le financement public est en voie d'extinction), on est en présence d'un modèle national spécifique. L'attachement français au service public se concrétise par l'ampleur des missions publiques, les plus étendues au plan européen, telles qu'elles ont été fixées dans le cadre de la transposition nationale des directives postales. Il confère également pour l'heure à l'entreprise publique un rôle éminent pour internaliser ces missions de service public. Cela se traduit notamment par de fortes contraintes de maillage territorial, par une couverture dense (plus de 17 000 points de contact garantis par la loi) du territoire national pour fournir un service postal de proximité. L'entreprise publique est l'opérateur incontournable pour prester le service universel postal. La loi en fait également la garante nationale, via La Banque Postale, de l'accessibilité bancaire (c'est-à-dire de l'accès à un compte bancaire pour toute personne qui en fait la demande).

Par-delà ce rôle dévolu formellement par la loi, La Poste affiche sa volonté de jouer un rôle éminent d'entreprise citoyenne. Dans le cadre d'une gouvernance multi-niveaux (faisant intervenir notamment les différentes parties prenantes de la société), elle entend ainsi assumer de multiples actions qui participent d'une bonne régulation économique et sociale. L'entreprise publique s'inscrit dans une logique d'intérêt général impulsée dans la société par les autorités publiques nationales et locales : intégration des préoccupations environnementales relatives au Grenelle de l'environnement (par la gestion des parcs automobile et immobilier, en incitant personnels et usagers aux comportements responsables, en développant les énergies renouvelables, en optimisant la gestion des déchets) ; mise en œuvre de mesures à vocation sociétale (contribution au développement de nouvelles filières économiques et des TPE-PME, contribution à des dispositifs d'inclusion sociale) ; participation au financement de travaux sur la responsabilité sociale d'entreprise. Elle accorde également à présent des crédits aux personnes morales et aux collectivités locales pour financement l'économie en favorisant l'aménagement territorial : financements simples et non risqués, apport aux entreprises de modes de financement adaptés et ne reposant pas sur le seul critère de rentabilité immédiate.

La revendication de La Poste d'être une entreprise citoyenne n'est pas pour autant exempte de critiques émanant de centrales syndicales ou d'organisations de consommateurs. Celles-ci soulignent des discordances entre discours et réalités du fait notamment de tensions qui existent entre, d'une part, objectifs à vocation commerciale et, d'autre part, missions sociales ou de service public : dans certains bureaux de poste, la pression peut notamment s'exercer sur les salariés et sur les consommateurs afin d'améliorer fortement les résultats financiers.

Les tensions existent entre missions publiques et objectifs commerciaux qui visent notamment à faire de La Poste un des principaux opérateurs européens. On les retrouve dans le cadre de la régulation postale exercée par l'autorité indépendante de régulation (l'ARCEP). Cette dernière veille à la bonne exécution par La Poste de ses missions (notamment de service universel) et contrôle les tarifs de l'entreprise. Comme les autres opérateurs européens, La Poste est confrontée à une baisse d'activité pour le courrier, ce qui tend à accroître les coûts fixes unitaires. Pour La Poste, les répercussions en sont cependant particulièrement importantes du fait de ses obligations de maillage territorial. Ces réalités l'incitent donc à accroître fortement ses gains de productivité afin de limiter les pertes sans avoir à dégrader la qualité du service (soumise aux contrôles annuels de l'ARCEP) ni à augmenter les prix au-delà des limites autorisées par le régulateur dans le cadre d'une tarification « price cap » La Poste utilise dès lors trois leviers pour accroître sa productivité : la restructuration des réseaux de bureaux de poste (sous contrainte de respect du maillage territorial mais aussi avec un risque de tension avec les collectivités territoriales rurales et certains usagers notamment), l'augmentation du taux de mécanisation du tri (par des investissements conséquents) et la baisse des coûts salariaux (source de conflits avec les salariés du fait de la réduction des personnels, de la modération salariale et de risques de souffrance au travail).

Le contexte reste cependant pour l'heure celui d'une très faible pénétration par la concurrence du marché postal français, comme d'ailleurs généralement en Europe. La concurrence directe n'ajoute donc pas ses effets à ceux de la concurrence par substitution (qui, pour le courrier, suscite la baisse d'activité). On peut cependant s'interroger sur les tendances à venir. Si, sous l'influence de la norme de concurrence européenne, l'ARCEP en venait à mener une politique très active en la matière, consistant notamment à prendre en compte pour la tarification du service universel l'ensemble des avantages qui lui sont associés (comme le préconisent dès à présent un cabinet-conseil mandaté pour en faire l'étude par l'autorité) et à pratiquer la concurrence asymétrique, le modèle développé par La Poste de mise en complémentarité et en synergie des différents métiers ne s'en trouverait-il pas profondément remis en cause ? Les autres opérateurs postaux européens, préparés à la conquête de segments de marchés rentables, ne seraient-ils pas amenés à y conduire une guerre de prix fortement déstabilisatrice pour le modèle de La Poste ? Les missions de service public dont La Poste a la charge pourraient-elles dès lors continuer à être assumées, les financements publics risquant fort d'apparaître comme des aides d'État condamnées par le droit européen ? N'assisterait-on pas rapidement à un phénomène de banalisation comportementale de l'entreprise qui ferait perdre au mode de gestion publique sa raison d'être ?

Bibliographie

Ailleret, F., « Oui, La Poste a un bel avenir devant elle… », Commission sur le Développement de La Poste, *La Documentation Française*, décembre, 2008.

ARCEP, *Observatoire des activités postales en France – année 2011*, Les Actes de l'ARCEP, 25 octobre 2012.

ARCEP, *Le traitement par l'ARCEP des réclamations des utilisateurs des services postaux – Bilan pour l'année 2012*, Les Actes de l'ARCEP, avril 2013.

Bance, P. et Monnier, L., « Entreprises publiques et construction communautaire. Rupture d'un mode de régulation », in Conseil d'État, « Le service public aujourd'hui en France », de Jean-Marc Bélorgey, *La documentation française*, 1995.

Commission du Grand Dialogue de La Poste, *Rapport*, septembre 2012.

Conseil d'État, « Le service public », rapport au Premier ministre de Renaud Denoix de Saint Marc, *La documentation française*, 1996.

Dang-Nguyen, G., « État et entreprise publique : les PTT européens et leur environnement », *Politiques et management public*, vol. 4, n° 4-1, 1986, pp. 119-152.

Duguit, L., *Traité de droit constitutionnel*, Ancienne libraire Fontenoy & Cie, 1923.

Journal officiel de la République française, *Loi n° 2005-516 du 20 mai 2005 relative à la régulation des activités postales*, 21 mai 2005.

Journal officiel de la République française, *Loi n° 2010-123 du 9 février 2010 relative à l'entreprise publique La Poste et aux activités postales*, 10 février 2010.

La Banque Postale, *Tarifs au 1ᵉʳ juin 2012. Conditions et tarifs des prestations financières applicables aux particuliers*, 2012.

La Banque Postale, *Document de référence et rapport financier annuel*, 2012.

La Banque Postale, *Rapports annuels de la Banque Postale*, 2000-2012.

Larcher, G., *Rapport d'information n° 344*, Session ordinaire de 2002-2003 du Sénat, 2003.

Le Groupe La Poste, *La Poste*, Document de référence, *2012*.

Le Groupe La Poste, *Responsabilité sociale et environnementale*, Document de référence, 2012.

Lehmann P. J. et Monnier L. (ed.), *Politiques économiques et construction communautaire. Le choc européen*, L'Harmattan, avril 2000.

Observatoire de l'épargne réglementée, *Rapport annuel*, 2011.

Official Journal of the European Communities, *Directive 97/67/EC of the European Parliament and of the Council, on common rules for the development of the internal market of Community postal services and the improvement of quality of service*, 1997.

Official Journal of the European Communities, *Directive 2002/39/EC of the European Parliament and of the Council*, 10 juin 2012.

Official Journal of the European Communities, *Directive 2008/6/EC of the European Parliament and of the Council*, 20 février 2008.

Rangeon, F., *L'idéologie de l'intérêt général*, Economica, 2001.

Sénat, *Projet de loi relatif à l'entreprise publique La Poste et aux activités postales*, Rapport Hérisson, n° 50, 2009-2010.

Tigoki Iya, N.E., *La politique de modernisation de la Poste*, L'Harmattan, 2011.

Tolédano, J., *Où en est le secteur postal, vingt ans après le livre vert : une perspective franco-européenne*, 20ᵉ Conférence d'économie postale, Centre de recherche sur les industries régulées, juin 2012.

Valette, J.P., *Le service public à la française*, Éllipses, 2000.

12. *Et Lux Non Fuit*

The Privatisation of ENEL and the Structure and Performance of the Electricity Market in Italy

Bruno Bosco, Lucia Parisio & Matteo Pelagatti[*]

DEMS, University of Milan-Bicocca, Milan (Italy)

Introduction

In the last 30 years, privatisation of State-Owned Enterprises (SOEs) has been a pervasive phenomenon worldwide and private entities have now replaced previous public firms/agencies. This is the case of the vast majority of the so-called public utilities created immediately before, and at the end of, World War II (electricity, gas, telephone, transport, etc.), which are nowadays in the hands of private investors. In some cases the privatisation process has taken the form of a direct selling of companies' stock to private stockholders whereas in some other cases – generally in post-Soviet Russia and other East European countries – it has been realised by means of the bonus system. In the first case, a minority quota of public firms' shares was already listed in the stock market after a previous IPO of part of the equity capital, which was followed by a series of seasoned public offers. In these cases, initial partial listing and the consequent regular activity of buying and selling of a minority quota of stocks was just a first policy step before Governments decided to fully (or almost fully) privatise the firm. In some cases, however, the privatisation of a SOE has remained partial and the State has retained a fraction of the capital somehow sufficient to ensure a significant control of the firm and a leading role in management (this phenomenon has been called "reluctant privatisation" (Bortolotti and Faccio, 2004).

What motivated these enormous shifts in property rights on public resources has been the subject of an extensive and still open debate (see Bosco, 2011 for a review and some data). Allocative efficiency seems

---

* With the usual disclaimers we want to thank participants of XII Milan European Workshop, 13-14th June 2013, for comments and suggestions.

371

the most popular reason. SOEs, it was claimed, were endemically misusing resources because they were not challenged by market competitors. As a result, prices were abnormally high as well as production costs. This frequently induced huge budget losses which in turn required the use of government subsidies. The financing of the subsidies created additional allocative distortions. Hence, firms had to become private and operate under strong budget discipline. To prevent consumers' exploitation on the part of firms operating in natural monopoly markets, in many cases the new private firms have been subjected to some form of regulation to ease the establishment of competitive conditions between incumbents and the new entrants and/or to have a ceiling to pricing policy. In some cases, e.g. in Italy, privatisation was also motivated by the desire to induce households' portfolio reshuffling from Treasury Bonds or bank deposits to equity and by the aspiration to reduce the stock of the national public debt.

Have all the above commendable goals been accomplished? To approximate an answer one should conduct – at least – a twofold study. On the one hand, the behaviour of (totally or partially) privatised firms should be analysed considering the peculiar structure of the new shareholding and its consequences in terms of goals pursued by the firms in all the relevant markets in which they operate (primarily, the market for its goods and services but also the stock market). In a regulated environment and with the State disappearing from shareholding – or becoming just one shareholder among others and just one residual claimant, among others, of the profits generated by the firms' activity – it is not obvious whether the goals of the firms would correspond to either the welfare maximising targets that characterised the firms when they were entirely in the public hands or to pure profit maximisation as one would expect from a private firm.

On the other hand, since privatisation has been generally concomitant to some market oriented restructuring of the sectors involved, it is consequently necessary to analyse the behaviour of the privatised firms operating in those sectors in the lights of the new market architecture introduced together with or immediately before privatisation. Only in so doing, can one evaluate whether or not the combination of these two "innovations" (privatisation plus "competition" and new market design conceived to accommodate "competition") has led to an improvement in the allocation of resources. The electricity sector is therefore an interesting case to be studied since it illustrates how a government may still be an influential shareholder in a privatised firm and use its special powers to regulate the liberalised industry from inside.

In this paper we analyse one such a case of former public monopoly privatisation: ENEL, the Italian former public electricity monopolist, which is nowadays a formally private enterprise listed in the Italian stock exchange, but "ultimately or *de facto*" partially controlled by the Ministry of Economics and Finance of the Italian Government. In the perspective of the book, this represent an interesting case since the privatisation of ENEL did not involve a dramatic change in the ownership structure of the former SOE. Following the double analytical perspective outlined above, this study will jointly consider the effects of the shifting of property rights of productive assets from public to private hands and the opening and functioning of a wholesale electricity market (Italian Power Exchange, IPEX) where competition among producers is expected to lead to Pareto efficient outcomes. Hence, what characterizes this research is the attempt to analyse the history, conduct and performance of a previous public and now semi-public enterprise and the regulation framework in which it now operates. At the same time, the research will investigate the architecture and functioning of the newly created electricity market that has been designed to coordinate the activity of independent producers that nowadays compete with what has remained after the unbundling of the former vertically integrated public monopolist. We believe that firm's conduct and market design and functioning are two sides of a same coin and that the mission, conduct, performance and policy of the (new) ENEL cannot be understood without the analysis of the new wholesale electricity market created after the privatisation/liberalisation measures were introduced. This will affect also the analysis of the possible public mission of the enterprise and the price and investment policy that might be motivated by the new mission/s.

The paper is organised as follows. Section 1 outlines the early establishment of the Italian electricity industry and the history and role of ENEL; Section 2 describes the new market oriented mission of the firm; Section 3 describes the new market regulation and Section 4 is devoted to the study of the role and behaviour of ENEL and the impact on consumers of the first ten years of the new market architecture.

1. The History of ENEL

ENEL was constituted as a new public enterprise on the basis of a Parliamentary Bill approved in December 1962 after a long and intense political debate and it was organised on the basis of a peculiar legal structure. It incorporated the previous private, and then nationalised, companies (more than 1,000) operating in the Italian electricity industry and thereafter became the public monopolist working on a national scale. Even local municipal enterprises operated on the basis of ENEL's authorizations granted to each of them by contracts enforced on the basis of the above mentioned Law, whereas import/export activity was entirely reserved to ENEL. This organisation of the electricity sector lasted till the beginning of the 1990s when the legal right for monopolistic activity in the generation segment was withdrawn, the former legal status of ENEL was modified to create an incorporated company listed in the stock market and other firms were authorised to operate as producers, delivers and importers/exporters of electricity. Nowadays ENEL is a (partially) private group operating in the generation, delivery and retail markets alongside other entirely private groups performing the same activities. In the following sections a brief history of ENEL is outlined.

1.1. ENEL and the Development of the Electricity Sector in Italy

Due to the scarcity of coal, the Italian electricity industry was built on hydro technology at the end of the 19ᵗʰ century but thermoelectric production soon replaced the old hydroelectric generation sources. In fact, hydro technology became rapidly unfit to guarantee the huge necessities connected to the supply of public lighting in tows and roads and, above all, to support the massive industrialisation of the Northern part of the country as well as the expansion of the national public railways system after the end of World War I. Production was in the hands of private companies but the main overall shareholdings was concentrated in the private banking sector. Then, when a new State Agency (IRI) was established in 1933 and forced to incorporate many private firms belonging to several productive sectors, the above mentioned banks were nationalised and consequently, as banks belonging to the Agency, they became the effective large public co-owners of the electric companies. To some extent we may say that 1933 represented a first indirect partial nationalisation of the Italian electricity sector.

Producers were classified in three groups: i) "Private" producers; ii) City Hall public producers; iii) Self-producers. Specifically:

i) Immediately after the end of World War II there were 259 companies belonging to six private groups that had emerged from a concentration process that took place during the 1920s. Their activities were vertically integrated and allocated along a chain of command and responsibility with activities going from generation to final delivery. They were: a) *Gruppo Edison*; b) *Gruppo SIP*; c) *Gruppo SADE*; d) *Gruppo La Centrale*; e) *Gruppo SME*; f) *Gruppo Bastogi*. Each group was dominant in a specific geographical area.

ii) City Hall Municipal public producers were a conquest of the early Italian socialist movement particularly in Milan, Turin and Rome since the beginning of the 20ᵗʰ century. They were part of a larger political program of socialization of services (assets and management) at the local level in Italy which it was explicitly endorsed by a Law approved in 1902. They never gained ground in the South of the country but in the

North-Centre they represented a viable and fair alternative to the above mentioned private local natural monopolies.

iii) Self-producers were a residual category. They were private firms and produced electricity for their industrial use only. They never reached the maximum allowed production limits.

Table 1 shows the development of production and consumption of electricity in Italy from the birth of the industry until nationalisation.

Table 1. Production and Consumption in Italy
Until Nationalisation (GWH)

Years	Gross production	Energy for auxiliary services	Net Imp/Exp	Energy consumed
1883	0.7	-	-	0.7
1884	1.8	0.1	-	1.7
1885	2.5	0.1	-	2.4
1890	8	0.4	-	7.6
1895	45	1.5	-	43.5
1900	160	3	-	157
1905	550	10	-	540
1910	1,500	20	-	1,480
1915	2,925	30	-	2,895
1920	4,690	32	-	4,658
1925	7,260	55	-	7,205
1930	10,670	70	164	10,764
1935	13,800	89	218	13,929
1940	19,431	176	252	19,507
1945	12,648	83	7	12,572
1950	24,681	246	129	24,564
1955	38,124	967	16	37,173
1960	56,240	1,363	-128	54,749
1961	60,565	1,608	168	59,125
1962	64,859	2,274	1,269	63,854

Source: Italian GRTN.

As a result of the fact that the national territory was fragmented in "zonal" monopolistic markets, prices were also strongly differentiated across zones. Table 2 reports some data referred to households and industrial consumption in some large Italian towns. A common decreasing trend can be observed in each case.

Table 2. Prices (Cents of Italian Lira per kWh)

		Domestic consumption		Industrial use	
	1898	1908	1913	1898	1908
Bologna	-	100	70	-	25/40
Firenze	100	65/80	75	-	20/30
Genova	90	60	59	20	-

		Domestic consumption		Industrial use	
	1898	**1908**	**1913**	**1898**	**1908**
Milano	80	40	40	-	4-40
Napoli	-	30/70	70	-	12/40
Palermo	70/100	70/100	64	-	55
Roma	70	65//0	50	30	20
Torino	73/100	40/90	60	11-15	28/15
Venezia	100	50	50	40/60	25

Source: Barluzzi, 1962.

Between 1947 and 1956 tariffs were regulated by a Government Committee (CIP). In 1948 tariffs increased by 24 times their 1942 level and in 1961 a national tariff system was introduced. Long-term investment programs were recommended but never implemented by the private firms. Indeed, a collusive behaviour simplified by cross shareholdings lead to an insufficient conversion of profits into investments, as Table 3 shows.

Table 3. Total Installed Power of Private Companies (MWH)

Group	1946	%	1954	%	1962	%
Edison	2,137	25.3	3,073	21.9	3,870	16.8
SIP	857	10.1	1,385	9.9	2,791	12.1
SADE	526	6.2	1,138	8.1	1,477	6.4
La Centrale	261	3.1	961	6.9	1,835	7.9
SME	446	5.3	1,084	7.7	2,137	9.3
Bastogi	188	2.2	412	2.9	567	2.5
AEM	426	5.0	739	5.3	1,637	7.1
Others	1,137	13.5	1,569	11.2	2,066	8.9
Total	5,977	70.7	10,362	73.8	16,380	70.9
Self-producers	2,474	29.3	3,669	26.2	6,722	29.1
Total	8,451	100	14,031	100	23,102	100

Source: Authors' elaboration from Gianetti, 1989 and ANIDEL data.

Not only private generation activity was open to criticisms but also distribution and delivery were alleged of being inefficient since the integrated activities could not benefit from the existence of a national unified grid. Lacking a national and completely unified high-tension grid, economies of scale could not be exploited and a balance of supply and demand across different areas could not be realised. Nonetheless, this shortcoming of the market structure did not represent an obstacle to the cashing of significant private profits.

1.2. The Budget Performance of the Private Firms

Starting with the profit/loss data, the following tables summarise the budget performance of the private producers for the years before nationalisation.

**Table 4. Profit/Loss Results of Some Firms
(Millions of Current Italian Liras)**

Year	Edison	Idroelettrica Piemonte	Società Romana elettricità	SADE	Società generale elettrica della Sicilia
1959	8,870	7,120	3,836	5,383	2,316
1960	9,240	7,491	3,839	6,694	2,691
1961	10,718	9,376	7,240	8,130	3,867
1962	12,327	12,457	6,641	11,057	3,844

Source: data from Castronovo, 1994, *Storia dell'industria elettrica*, Vol. IV.

Profits were increasing in the period immediately before nationalisation as a result of high tariff rates (see above) and low investment activity that permitted to maintain a non-increasing burden of debt. The following Figure 1 shows the series of Debt and Return on Capital for the period following the end of World War II. The series are calculated as average values for the first four companies operating in Italy (*Edison, Sip, SADE, SME*). As one can see, the return on capital increased sharply in the five years before nationalisation and shows a greater variability (Variance is 0.019) than Debt (Variance is 0.0068).

**Figure 1. Debt on Capital (AVD) and Return on Capital (AVR)
Before Nationalisation (Average Values)**

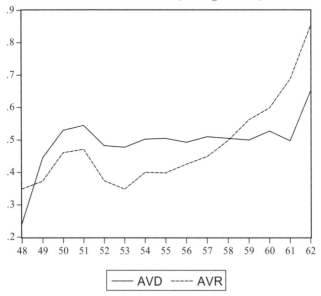

Similar information is provided by the values of ROI and, particularly, ROE for the same time period.

Table 5. ROI for a Group of Private Companies

Firms	1959	1960	1961	1962
Sip	4.86	5.90	7.25	10.68
Edisonvolta	7.98	8.35	10.35	10.77
SADE	7.93	9.04	9.43	14.83
SRE	8.42	8.49	8.87	16.59
SME	6.42	6.25	7.20	10.16
SGES	7.85	7.28	8.47	8.92
SES	4.07	5.43	6.19	5.96
Average	6.79	7.25	8.25	11.13

Source: data from Castronovo, 1994, *Storia dell'industria elettrica*, Vol. IV.

Table 6. After tax ROE for a Group of Private Companies

Firm	1948-52	1953-58	1959-62	1948-62
Sip	3.50	4.45	6.18	4.71
Edisonvolta	-	-	6.57	-
SADE	3.97	4.42	6.81	5.07
SRE	3.83	6.05	9.08	6.32
SME	3.54	4.51	6.72	4.92
SGES	2.80	3.17	5.84	3.94
SES	2.03	2.41	4.47	2.97

Source: data from Castronovo, 1994, *Storia dell'industria elettrica*, Vol. IV.

Summing up we may stress that before nationalisation the electricity sector was characterised by low fix investment activity (high tension grid) and high tariffs. This generated high profit margins and permitted only a partial matching of the potential industrial and household demands.

1.3. The Nationalisation of ENEL and its Economic and Financial Performance

The nationalisation of the Italian electricity industry followed similar policies previously implemented, for example, in 1946 in France (Electricité de France for generation and E.d.F., Service de Distribution for transport and delivery) and in 1947 in the UK (British Electricity Authority, B.E.A, and 14 Areas Electricity Boards for delivery). Italy was forced to wait until December 1962 when the nationalisation was approved by the Law 1643 and ENEL was created to carry on, as a public (*quasi*)monopolist, the activities of producing, importing, exporting, transporting and delivering of electricity. ENEL incorporated in a single productive structure 1,243 previously private firms and was responsible for the activities of the remaining producers, such as the Municipal firms. Law 1643 explicitly indicated the main goals and management policies to be pursued by the newly created entity: welfare oriented – as opposite

378

to private profit maximisation – tariff policies and uniform – across nation – infrastructure investments. Those goals would represent ENEL's inspiration for the entire 30 years of its existence.

The following plot gives the idea of the economic results of ENEL from its first operational year (1963) to the beginning of the privatisation process (1992), and beyond.

Figure 2. Annual Current Net Profit/Loss of ENEL (Billions of Italian Liras) Before and After Privatisation

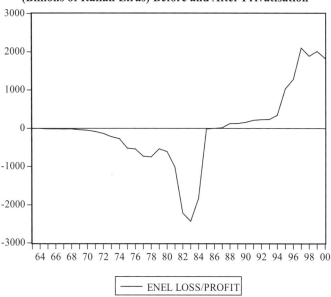

The profit/loss performance of ENEL during the entire period when it was a SOE was heavily affected by the approach chosen by the Government of 1962 to finance the compensation to the granted to be former private owners. Contrary to the policy followed by France and the UK, the Italian Government decided to assign directly to ENEL and not to the Treasury the burden of that debt. The debt totalled more than 1500 billion of 1963 Italian Liras (equivalent to 17.5 Euro billions) to be paid in 20 semi-annual balances to the private former owners and each balance was inflated by an (inconceivable, for those years) 5.5% interest. This implied an immediate undercapitalisation of ENEL which started with a nominal liability of more than 2200 billion Liras. The burden of the debt prolonged somehow beyond the 1970s and affected the financial performance of ENEL till the beginning of the 1990s, when, curiously enough, ENEL was reorganised in order to be privatised. It is worth recalling that the French and the British Governments followed a more advisable policy of granting a small interest (up to 3.3%) and diluting these payments over a much longer time span. The following Table 7 summarises the compensation schemes adopted by the Italian Government.

Table 7. Direct Compensations Paid till 1978

Compensation criterions	Number of firms	Value (Billions of Italian Liras)
Share Values (if listed)	26	1,251.6
Balance Sheet	275	243.6
Technical estimates	809	151.1
Total	1,110	1,646.3
Less: Rounding		-3.6
Plus: Extra Compensation to be paid		1,642.7
Plus: Interest, integrative payments, etc.		567.9
Net Total		2,210.6

Source: Castronovo, 1994.

The Italian Government did not immediately create the usual capital fund specific for public firms (*Fondo di Dotazione*, i.e. the equivalent to the equity capital for private firms) to be used for facing and compensating exceptional revenue/costs circumstances. This Fund was created only in 1986 and, since tariff remained (by law) fixed till 1974, this implied that ENEL had to resort to the financial market to fulfil its debt obligations with the inevitable result that the debt burden hardened through time. In turn this implied that even more debt was needed to finance the huge fix investments – never realised before by the generously compensated private owners. The management was made even more complicated by governmental and trade unions' pressures as well as by somewhat opaque budget decisions probably induced by covered requests on the part of the major ruling political parties of the time, namely the Christian Democrats and the Socialists who had recently formed a new government coalition block that lasted for almost thirty years.

The oil crisis of the early 1970s led ENEL into an even harder financial distress since in that period the thermoelectric generation was already the main source of electricity (about 69% in 1973) and the production of electricity required sources mainly imported from abroad (67% in 1973). Under these conditions the budget imbalance of ENEL was inevitable. Still, the industrial results were remarkable. The following Table 8 summarises some of the main achievements.

Table 8. Industrial Results (1963-1992)

	1963	1970	1980	1992
Population not served	1,210,000	900,000	500,000	100,000
Available power (MW)	10,000	23,137	31,693	46,759
Gross production (bn of kWh)	48	82.7	147	184
Net return of thermoelectric plants %	33.3	34.2	35.5	37.3
Leaks on the grid %	11	9.50	8.50	7
Energy sold per employee (millions of kWh)	0.63	0.90	1.20	1.84
Customers per employee	192	200	215	259
Cost of each kWh sold (index 1963=100)	100	90	80	60

Source: Castronovo, 1994.

When it was founded ENEL received a clear public mission consistent with the main targets of welfare enhancement and allocative efficiency. Indeed, data presented in Table 8 show that under public ownership the firm's efficiency increased. It was responsible for generation, transmission, delivery, import and export of electricity in Italy with the explicit purpose of expanding national production and supporting the growing electricity demand of families and firms. Moreover, it was recognised that the natural monopoly conditions of the market required the full exploitation of scale economies at the national level and the long term planning perspective for investment, both physical and financial. Indeed, total Italian production increased from a 48 billion of kWh in 1963 to 184 in 1992 and the number of persons not connected to the grid fell from 1.2 million in 1962, when the private companies were nationalised, to a mere 100,000 in 1992. ENEL was also in charge for the coordination and planning of the energy reserves (hydro-geological reserves, for example) even when these reserves belonged to other firms such as the municipal public producers. The policy of ENEL was dictated by the National Energy Plans which were prepared by the Ministry of Industry and approved by the Government. Tariff policy was based on a marginal cost pricing perspective, in order to allow households to buy electricity at the minimum charge and to expand their consumption.

1.3.1. The Incorporation of ENEL (S.p.A.)

As recently as the 1970s, many major industries in OECD countries were owned by the State, in keeping with the Fabian Society's dictum that the "commanding heights" of the economy should be in government hands. The first organised effort to divest SOEs took place during the 1970s in Chile under the influence of the "Chicago boys" who masterminded the Pinochet's era of economic "reforms". But the largest and best-known effort was that of Margaret Thatcher's government in the United Kingdom during the 1980s (Florio, 2004). Thatcher succeeded in making privatisation politically popular while selling off the commanding heights of the British economy: British Airways, British Airports Authority, British Petroleum, British Telecom, and several million units of public housing, to name only a few examples. Thatcher's political strategy emphasised widespread public share offerings rather than auctions to other private firms. Over the decade, this approach tripled the number of individual shareholders in Britain, giving the policy some popular base of support.

By the end of the 1980s governments in Italy, France, Germany, Japan, Australia, Argentina, and Chile all sold numerous SOEs, and global privatisation proceeds ran in the tens of billions of dollars each year. Generally speaking, companies that moved into the private sector were restructured (often, but not always, without considerable loss of jobs) and turned into value-adding enterprises. In the case of public utilities (airports, electricity, water, etc.), privatisation generally led to the creation of some form of regulatory oversight if the company remained a monopoly provider. The privatisation wave expanded further in the 1990s, encompassing the countries emerging from the former socialist systems and many more developing countries. By the end of the decade, privatisation proceeds in the EU were well above $100 billion per year, and the cumulative total for the two decades exceeded $1 trillion.

In Italy the privatisation of ENEL and other similar public entities started with the abolition of the previous *sui generis* legal form of the "enterprise-ENEL" (D.L. 11/7/1992 No. 333; Law 30/7/1994, No. 474). The "enterprise-ENEL" was converted into an ordinary corporation whose share capital was initially entirely owned by the Treasury and then partially sold to private shareholders by an IPO followed by a series of public offers. This process was accompanied by measures aimed: i) at introducing competitive conditions in the generation segment by eliminating the legal monopolistic condition of ENEL as a sole authorized generator and ii) at breaking-up ENEL in order to create private generators operating with plants previously owned by ENEL. Then, an auction market for the exchange of bulk electricity was planned and then finally introduced in 2004 (see below). At the same time regulations were introduced for operators active in the wholesale and retail market, particularly in terms of their obligation to sell to ENEL any excess production and at what price (CIP, No. 6/1992). Many alternatives were postulated for the full privatisation of the new company. A vigorous move towards a new electricity market's architecture was represented by the adoption of a Legislative Decree on 16 March 1999 which was directed at splitting the previous vertically integrated public monopolist and to separate the different stages of the activity. Moreover, a cap to total production of any single operator was introduced and ENEL Spa (that is the new company name) was invited to dismiss a substantial portion of its generation capacity. A separate public company (*Gestore della Rete, GSE*) was established to manage the dispatching activity in the whole national transmission system. A Single Buyer (*Acquirente Unico*) was constituted by the GSE in 1999 with the responsibility of guaranteeing the supply of electricity to all the non-eligible customers. In the same Decree, the road was paved for the organisation of the wholesale physical electricity market as a pool market (operational as an auction since 2004), following the examples of other European countries. Nowadays, ENEL Spa is controlled by the Treasury by means of minority quota (around 30%) of the capital and operates in the Italian IPEX as a dominant producer (see below).

The group to which ENEL Spa now belongs (ENEL group, from now on) is organised in several separate entities (legally structured as incorporated companies) each one responsible for one of the production and distribution activities, namely generation, transmission, distribution and final sale of electricity. As already noticed, immediately after the start of the privatisation process the former ENEL organisation was subjected to a breaking-up process that generated a new legal configuration of the group. In particular, the ENEL group is composed by companies operating in the energy (and, immediately after privatisation, telecommunication too) sector and it is organised in five main subgroup of companies. They are: a) Generation and Energy Management (ENEL production Spa; ENEL green power Spa.; ENEL trade S.P.A., etc.); b) Market Activity (ENEL distribution-Market area Spa.; ENEL gas Spa.; ENEL energy Spa.; etc.); c) Infrastructures and grid (ENEL distribution-network area Spa.; ENEL distribution gas Spa.; d) Telecommunication (Wind Spa.; now dismissed); e) Services to firms and other activities (ENEL real estate Spa.; ENEL power Spa.; Sfera Spa.; etc.). At the beginning of the privatisation process ENEL group included also a company (*Terna*) which owned and managed the nation-wide grid system for the transmission of energy which, before an unbundling policy was adopted, was a segment of the previous vertically integrated public enterprise.[1] In the last ten years this structure of the group has evolved but the main characteristics have remained. The legal breaking-up of the former vertically integrated public firm was motivated by the expectation that separate entities would compete on a liberalised market

---

[1]   The unbundling of previously vertically integrated operator was established at the EU level by the Third Energy package (2009) which requires separation of generation and sale companies from the transmission operators.

and that competition would foster efficiency. ENEL Spa now operates in almost 40 countries worldwide and has an installed capacity of more than 97,000 MW. It sells electricity and gas at more 61 million customers. It is listed (Milan stock exchange) since 1999 and it is the Italian company with the highest number of shareholders (about 1.4 million including retailers and institutional). The main shareholder is still the Treasury (about 31% of share capital) but among shareholders there are insurance companies, international investments funds, pension funds and ethical funds. In 2011 the group realized 4,148 million EUR of consolidated profit (4,390 in 2010) corresponding to EUR 0.44 per share.

2. The New "Market Oriented" Mission and Governance

It is difficult to define a post-privatisation mission for ENEL since the privatisation was accompanied by the creation of a new wholesale pool market for bulk energy open to a plurality of producers (some virtually created by the breaking up of ENEL itself), So, the (privatised) ENEL was given no specific mission other than to participate in this market alongside other competitors. In a sense it was the very participation to the established-by-decree wholesale market (called IPEX) the new mission for the privatised company. That mission was defined under the expectation that the already mentioned welfare and efficiency targets could be better achieved by many competing producers rather than by a fully integrated public monopolist. Yet, when actual market behaviour of ENEL is observed, it is difficult to assess how successful the above described policy has been. Using market data, an investigation of actual behaviour is needed in order to evaluate in practice in which way privatisation has affected ENEL's behaviour and performances and as a consequence, energy pricing and production results in the IPEX. The operation of ENEL will be analysed by confronting, once again, the periods before and after privatisation. Specifically, a detailed description of the activities, both in Italy and abroad, and their evolution after privatisation can be found in the annual Reports presented in recent years to the shareholders meetings. The most interesting part of the analysis of the operation on the "New" ENEL is, however, represented by the study of its activity on the Italian pool market. Having still in its control several generation units, ENEL participates to IPEX with a plurality of combined price/quantity pairs each representing an independent bid. According to the rules governing the Pool market, each bid (MWh of electricity and price asked) received by the Market Operator (GME) is ordered in an increasing supply function and generating units are selected on the basis of a cost minimization plan (see below the Regulation section). Being the dominant producer ENEL is frequently in a position to exploit market power more than what even casual analysis shows.

Privatisation, however partial, brought about enormous changes in the governance of ENEL. Since 1991 the governance was a mix of political – mainly government – patronage and civil service structure and was subjected to the accountancy control on the part of the public accounting judiciary system (*Corte dei Conti*) like any structure belonging to the public administration of the State. The Government was the only final claimant of revenues and losses as well as of any economic and social success/failure of the enterprise, and as such it exercised the controlling powers, *de jure* and *de facto*.

After privatisation the group has acquired the physiognomy implicit in the 2006 Code of Self-Discipline adopted by Italian listed companies and whose main structure is reproduced below.

Figure 3. Stakeholder's Meeting

Then, ENEL's corporate governance system is inspired by the principles of highest standards of transparency and correctness in corporate management. This system complies with legal provisions and with CONSOB (Italian National Commission for Companies and the Stock Exchange) regulations and, as already stressed, is in line both with the recommendations of the Corporate Governance Code of Italian listed companies and with international best practices. According to the company's statements, ENEL's corporate government system not only represents an essential tool for ensuring an effective and efficient management and controlling corporate activities, but is essentially aimed at the creation of shareholders' value while being aware of the social importance of the activities performed by the ENEL Group and of the ensuing need to adequately consider all the interests involved when performing such activities.

Every year ENEL submits to the market detailed information on the corporate governance system that it has adopted and the strict observance of the recommendations contained in the Corporate Governance Code of Italian listed companies. Such information is included in the "Report on corporate governance and ownership structure" published jointly with the financial report and published in the website.

3. The New Market Regulation

The reorganisation of the Italian electricity industry started at the beginning of 1991 (Law 9/01/91, No. 9) when, on the one hand, the independent power producers were allowed to produce and inject electricity into the system and, on the other hand, ENEL was obliged to buy the surplus. Starting in 1991 and in particular in 1992 a new regulation was issued providing economic and regulatory incentives to the building of new generation plants, with emphasis on those based upon renewable technologies. In 1995 the Italian Authority for Electricity and Gas (AEEG) was established with responsibilities ranging from the design of the new market architecture, to unbundling, regulation, pricing and antitrust activity. The market liberalisation was designed and then implemented after the Directive 96/92/CE and the *Bersani Decree* of 16/3/99 which defined a new market structure in the generation, import, export and supply of electricity. The main innovation introduced was the unbundling of the previously vertically integrated market structure in a way that generation, transmission, distribution and retail were separated and managed by different entities. Generation was opened to competition with suppliers subjected to a merit order dispatching whereas GRTN was a newly established (public) entity responsible for the transmission on the national grid. A new operator named *Acquirente Unico (AU)* was made responsible for the purchasing of electricity for non-eligible customers. A new platform managed by the GME was designed as the market place where power producers and buyers were required to submit bid/offers for physical quantities of electricity. The wholesale electricity market was established in 2000 but started its operations on April 2004 (supply side only) and on January 2005 (supply and demand side).

Starting from April 2000 GRTN was in charge of the transmission activity, without owing directly the grid (which was still in the possession of ENEL), with the mission of allowing access to electricity producers in a non-discriminatory way. Producers paid regulated tariffs for the access to the essential facility. GRTN was established as an incorporated company belonging entirely to the Italian government. GRTN owned the whole shares of both AU and GME.

The *Marzano Decree* of December 2003 made some further steps on the way of liberalisation of the electricity industry and of privatisation of its main actors. First, the GRTN was granted the ownership of the transmission grid and then privatised as TERNA S.p.A. The distribution activity was managed by local monopolists rewarded under a regulated tariff regime. The retail market was opened to competition gradually, first setting an eligibility threshold for those customers who were allowed to buy directly electricity in the wholesale market and then lowering that threshold progressively until July 1st 2007 when all customers were free to sign contracts for the delivery of electricity with the preferred retailer. Therefore from the second semester of 2007 there were two different segments on the demand side of the market. A first segment, called *mercato tutelato*, included all customers who did not exercised yet the option of choosing a new retailer; they continued to buy electricity from the local distributor at a regulated tariff. A second segment, called *mercato libero*, included all customers who decided to change supplier; they were served by the new supplier at a market price (energy component of the electricity bill).

Following the full market opening, the AEEG implemented a new tariff scheme designed to reward separately the different components of the electricity supply activity. The electricity bill (regulatory period 2008-2011) comprises three tariff components for the reward of the transmission, distribution and measure activities (for 2008, the first year after the full liberalisation, the three components totalled to 2,152 c€/ kWh on average) and a price component for the electricity consumed. The price component is therefore the part of the electricity bill which should be influenced by the competitive process. The whole unbundling procedure and the introduction of competition in the wholesale and in the retail market had first the objective of lowering the wholesale price. In a second phase the competition among retailers was expected to drive down commercial costs and to pass through to final consumers the cheaper wholesale prices.

For the above mentioned reasons it is extremely interesting to place a close look at the results obtained in the liberalised portions of the electricity market. In particular we want to evaluate what the role of

ENEL has been in the first years of market opening and liberalisation. At the moment however some conclusions can be drawn for the wholesale market only, whereas the retail market has started to become more competitive in the last few years since in the first period after full liberalisation only a small portion of customers switched to the free market. More reactive consumers with respect to price conditions would make the market demand more elastic and this would reduce market power on the supply side.

3.1. The Italian Electricity Industry and the Wholesale Market

The liberalised Italian power generation industry is characterized by a high quota of thermal production with figures ranging from 80% in 2004 to 71% in 2011. Thermo production includes technologies based on oil, gas and carbon. Hydro production remained stable during the period covered in Table 9 and it is around 15%. Hydro production is mainly concentrated in the North Zone near the Alpi. The South Zone on the contrary shows a productive mix more concentrated on thermal (90.2%) than on hydro (6.2%) with some increasing share of wind production (3.5%). Finally both islands, Sardinia and Sicily, show a productive mix more concentrated on thermal technologies: 91.6% in Sicily (of which 69.1 on CCGT) and 91.4% in Sardinia (of which 51.3% from carbon and 38% from CCGT). Hydro production has a low share in both islands but wind production is growing considerably, having attracted new investments in the last years.

Table 9. Production by Technology

Technology	2004	2011	Share 2004	Share 2011
Thermo	241,626	213,676	0.80	0.71
Renewable	11,787	37,884	0.18	0.28
Hydro	49,908	48,812	0.17	0.16
TOTAL	303,321	300,373		

Source: AEEG Annual Report 2012.

The total generation capacity increased markedly since 2001. In particular in the ten years period from 2001 to 2010 new capacity came from thermal units (+37.6 GW, against 7.5 GW from renewable) whereas from 2011 new capacity came from renewable sources (+10.7 GW). Starting from 2005 a new incentive mechanism for renewable sources has been introduced by the Italian Government. The mechanism, which has been recently revised in 2012, offers a fixed tariff to energy produced and injected into the grid by photovoltaic, wind, hydro, biogas and biomass units. A number of 1874 small plants took advantage from this incentive policy which caused an expenditure of around €1bn to the Italian budget.

Before liberalisation and privatisation, a portion of ENEL's generation capacity (around 15,000 MW of mainly mid-merit units) has been sold to newcomers with the purpose of creating a more levelled playing field in the wholesale market. Notwithstanding this pro-competitive measure, when IPEX transactions started in 2004, ENEL maintained a dominant position in the market. Table 10 summarises the production data for the Italian electricity industry contrasting 2004 with 2012.

Table 10. Production Data

Main Companies	Production %		Capacity 2012		
	2012	2004	Thermo	Hydro	Ren
ENEL	25.4	43.9	26,439	12,384	1,647
Eni	9.5	6.0	6,222	0	5
Edison	7.2	12.1	5,404	1,040	501
Endesa (from 2008 E.On)	4.4	7.4	4,637	649	357
Edipower	3.9	9.0	7,711	692	3
Tirreno Power	3.1	2.2	3,313	80	0
A2A (AEM Mi + Asm BS)	3.2	1.5+0.9	3,176	1,277	219
GdF Suez	3.6		1,801	0	166
Erg	2.9	1.9	1,142	3	969
Sorgenia	1.9		3,290	0	50
Iren	2.2		1,335	516	24
Axpo Group	1.7		1,537	0	66
Saras	1.6	1.6			
Others	29.6	9.0			

Source: AEEG Annual Report 2012.

We notice that ENEL's market share in electricity production steadily decreased starting from a dominant position of around 49% to a still relevant but less dominant position[2] of 25.4%. The reduction of market share went partly to the advantage of some newcomers but most importantly it was absorbed by small competitive producers in the segment of green generation.

The Italian electricity market (IPEX) was established in April 2004 (supply side only) and started to be fully operational from January 2005. In 2012, the volume of energy demanded in Italy was of 298.7 TWh of which 59.8% was negotiated on the day-ahead market. Electricity is exchanged through bilateral contracts under the control and authorization

---

[2] The HHI Index of market power decreased to 884 in 2012 starting from a value of 1,097 in 2010.

of AEEG. Below we reproduce the structure of the Italian Electricity Market as it emerged from the implementation of the Legislative Decree 79/99 and of the European Union Directive on the internal market in electricity (96/92/EC).

Figure 4. Structure of IPEX

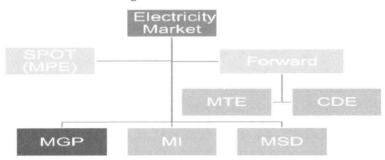

The market operator, GME, manages energy markets, spot and forward. The spot market (MPE), includes a day-ahead market (MGP), an infraday market (MI) and a real time market (MSD). The forward market (MTE) is a platform where long term contracts for physical delivery of energy are exchanged. GME also manages the physical delivery related to financial contracts exchanged in the segment of energy futures[3] of the Italian Stock Exchange, IDEX.

The spot market starts the day ahead of physical delivery with MGP which provides a preliminary supply program. Sessions of Infraday marked correct the initial allocations and finally the real time market (MSD) is implemented by Terna to continuously match demand and supply. Starting from 2004, the participation in the IPEX markedly increased: the maximum number of registered operators has been attained in 2010 with 198 active firms whereas at the date of 31st December 2011 we observed 181 operators.

The increased competition in the IPEX did not have much influence on wholesale prices. On the contrary, electricity prices showed an increasing trend from 2004 to 2008 and a slight decrease in the last three years. The average purchasing price in 2012 was 75.53 €/MWh against much lower values registered in the other European exchanges, as it can be observed in Figure 5.

---

3   The IDEX segment has been created in 2008.

Figure 5. Series of European Electricity Prices

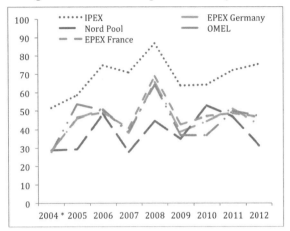

Source: AEEG Annual Report 2012.

The comparison between the Italian market and other European markets shows that there exists a significant gap in price levels. We notice that the French and the German markets (Powernext and EEX, respectively) generated prices which are very close both in levels and in their dynamics (Bosco *et al.*, 2010). For that reason European central markets merged in 2008. EPEX SPOT is the exchange for the power spot markets at the heart of Europe. It covers France, Germany, Austria and Switzerland. Together, these countries account for more than one third of the European power consumption.

The market monitoring activity of AEEG guided the evolution of the wholesale market towards better competitive conditions. In particular, the Italian regulator, with the Decision 254/2004, implemented a set of rules to prevent the occurrence of monopolistic conditions in the power market. The regulatory activity was accompanied by an industrial planning that, on the one hand, tried and eased the building of new plants (mainly gas fired CCGT, but also wind and solar plants) and, on the other hand, programmed new interconnecting lines between zones where bottlenecks frequently occurred.

The monitoring of the evolution of competitive conditions in the power market was realised through the public diffusion of some standard measures of market power, like market shares, Herfindal Index, the index of competition at the margin (IOM) and an index similar to the RSI, named IOR, that measures the degree of pivotality (both with respect to hours and quantities). In particular the IOM is defined, for each firm and for each zone, as the ratio of volumes on which the operator was the price setter over total volumes sold in the same zone. The dominant operator was marginal from 80% to 90% of the hours during the year 2005, whereas it was marginal only from 10% to 30% of the hours in 2010. The IOR is defined as the ratio between residual supply and total supply. As such, IOR is considered an ex-post measure of pivotality. When a pivotal operator exists, the IOR is less than 1 and it approaches 0 as residual demand increases. Two versions of the IOR are usually calculated and published by the AEEG: the IORh measures the percentage of hours in which one operator was pivotal and the IORq measures the share of volumes on which one operator was pivotal.

Table 11. Price-setting Operator Index

IOM (%)			
	2005	**2007**	**2010**
ENEL	89	77	22
Edison	4	7	14
E.on	1	2	9
Tirreno power	0	1	5
A2A	2	4	8
Others	3	9	42

Source: AEEG Annual Report 2012.

Table 11 shows how pro-competitive policy measures introduced at the beginning of IPEX negotiations were successful in limiting ENEL market power. It is extremely important to notice that from year 2010 small competitive producers set the price with the highest frequency as compared to larger oligopolistic competitors.

4. The Behaviour of Privatised ENEL on the Market

In this part of the paper we want to focus on the behaviour of ENEL in the wholesale electricity market. To this end a model of optimal bidding in multi-unit auctions can be considered the benchmark of the analysis. To make the theoretical model closer to reality, it is standard to assume uncertainty about competitors' costs/quantity supplied. Moreover, the model must incorporate the hypothesis that some firms might be vertically integrated[4] and might hold forward contract positions. Three research questions have been addressed in the applied research: i) how competitive the IPEX is in its first years of operation and after the worldwide crisis; ii) is ENEL really behaving as a private profit maximising firm or can we

---

[4] Vertical integration considered is the ownership of both producer and retailer firms by the same group. This for example the case of ENEL (*ENEL Produzione* for generation and ENEL trade) which has two branches acting independently on the two sides of the electricity market.

discover some element of pro-social behaviour; iii) is vertical integration between production and retailing beneficial to consumers. To answer these questions we refer to previous empirical analyses conducted by Authors using the GME public database of the day-ahead market (MGP).

To evaluate the competitiveness of the Italian Power Exchange we estimated[5] price-cost margins and Lerner Indexes for a set of Italian companies operating from 2005 to 2011. In this connection, we evaluate the extent of their market power by first estimating generation costs from supply bids and demand elasticity and then we derive Lerner Indexes accordingly. The incorporation of vertical integration and forward contract commitments strongly improves the adaptability of existing theoretical models of bidding behaviour to the data generated in electricity markets. Estimates[6] of marginal cost functions for non-dominant firms appear to be positively correlated with supplied quantities and convex. On the contrary, estimated marginal costs of ENEL are flatter and generally decreasing with respect to quantities. This result indicates that the theoretical profit maximisation model accurately reflects the actual behaviour of non-dominant firms, but not that of ENEL. Estimated Lerner Indexes are almost equal to zero for non-dominant firms and suggest the existence of a strong market power of the (vertically integrated) dominant firm both when she is net supplier and net buyer. Figure 6 plots estimated values of Lerner Index for ENEL in period 2005-2008.

Figure 6. Lerner Index *vs.* Net Quantities ENEL 2005-08

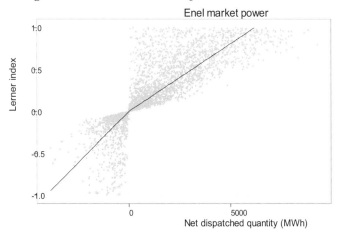

Source: Bosco *et al.*, 2012.

---

[5]   Bosco *et al.* (2012).

[6]   Bosco *et al.* (2012).

The main results that emerged from the applied analysis of bidding behaviour in the Italian day-ahead market are that ENEL is not fully exploiting its very high degree of market power. In particular, Italian wholesale electricity prices are higher than European averages (see Figure 5 above), but lower than the level implied by the application of a standard profit maximising model. The main reason is that ENEL, especially during the first years of functioning of the Italian IPEX, was very often in a pivotal position. A firm is pivotal if its capacity is necessary to satisfy the market demand whatever the equilibrium price, when competitors have already exhausted theirs. When market demand is price-inelastic and there are barriers to entry in the short run, then the pivotal operator can in theory exploit its market power setting an equilibrium price arbitrarily high. In this case regulatory authorities should take price-capping policies and/or other pro-competition policies into consideration to restrict monopoly power. However, the typical bidding behaviour of ENEL was "socially responsible" in the sense that even under extreme non-competitive conditions it set a price much lower than theoretically possible. An example[7] of this behaviour can be observed from Figure 7.

Figure 7. Socially Responsible Price Policy

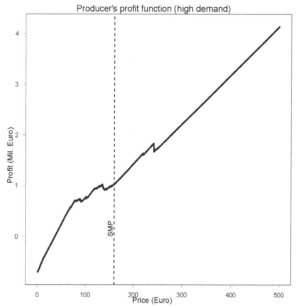

Source: Bosco *et al.*, 2013.

---

[7]   See Bosco *et al.*, 2013.

Figure 7 shows the shape of the profit function for a pivotal operator. Profit function is not concave but it looks like a straight line. Profit maximization then would require setting a price equal to infinity (or equal to the cap, if any), but as it can be seen from the dotted line in Figure 7, ENEL set a high – but reasonable – price level. Since the starting of the exchange through year 2008 there were many hours characterized by the above situation. The evolution of the market outlined above and the regulatory intervention of AEEG promoted more pro-competitive conditions so that the estimated profit function of ENEL from year 2009 until today appears to adjust towards a more standard concave shape. It is important to remark that the ex-monopolist displayed its still (partly) public mission in limiting the extent of price spikes in periods when competitive conditions alone were not able to restrict the occurrence of extreme monopolistic conditions.

Another characteristic of ENEL which proves to be very helpful in limiting price spikes in the market is vertical integration. The Third Package of the European Regulation, containing measures for the integration of electricity markets of member States, introduced unbundling measures relative to generation and the possession of (portions of) national grid, specific protections to green sources and new rules for Third Party Access. Even if the ownership and management of the grid have been transferred to the independent transmission system operator, TERNA, ENEL maintain a degree of vertical integration between production and distribution. The ENEL group includes both the generation company, *ENEL Produzione*, and a sale company, ENEL Trade. Both firms are active in the wholesale market one among suppliers and the other among buyers. Economic literature has studied vertical integration of firms belonging to a group as a possible explanation of generators' supply price moderation in wholesale electricity markets. Generators sell in the wholesale auction and retailers buy in the auction and resell at regulated prices to final consumers. The retailers' profits are therefore determined by the difference between the selling price (which is regulated by AEEG or by a contract, see below) and the SMP and the quantity they buy is predetermined by their contract obligations. Usually competitive conditions are such that market power benefits upstream firms whereas downstream sellers have restricted profit opportunities. Thus generators could set a very high price in the wholesale market shifting profits at their own advantage. When producer and sellers are vertically integrated however, there is an issue of profit allocation within the group. We can think that the holding firm tries and coordinates the branches in a way to redistribute profits among them. If the holding firm is able to perfectly coordinate the divisions then the optimal wholesale price is set at a level that maximises the group profit (and not the seller's profit). This price level is obtained[8] by maximising profits with respect to the net group quantity (namely quantity sold minus quantity bought) exchanged in the wholesale market. When the holding firm is not able to perfectly control divisions due, for example, to asymmetric information about private characteristics of the branches, then coordination is imperfect and the resulting equilibrium price higher than the one prevailing under perfect coordination. However, the main result of this kind of models is that even under partial coordination the equilibrium price is lower with respect to the case in which there are no vertical relationships between buyers and sellers. Vertical integration therefore proves to be pro-competitive.[9]

4.1. Tariffs and Distributional Issues in the Liberalised Electricity Industry

Due to the full liberalisation of the retail segment of the electricity market which took place on July 1st 2007, now consumers belongs to one of two possible groups: on the one hand, households who decided to access the competitive market now pay a free market price for the energy component of their bill, whereas households who did not switch from the regulated market still pay an energy price component which is under the AEEG regulation. The following Table 12 reports data about switching of consumers to the free market.

Table 12. Switching Rate 2012

Customer	Vol. (%)	No. of Withdrawal points (%)
Domestic	8.3	6.4
Low	23.2	11.9
Medium	36.4	27.7
High and very high voltage	34.3	17.7
TOTAL	26.4	7.6

Source: AEEG Annual report 2012.

We notice from Table 12 that, after some initial years in which customers adopted a quite conservative behaviour, now they appear to be more attracted by new commercial offers. The 7.6% of customers changed supplier and this figure amounts at 26.4% of total volumes sold.

Tariffs have shown a tendency to increase in the last years, following the increasing price trend of the IPEX (see above). The retail average price calculated by AEEG in 2012 is equal to 113.06 €/MWh whereas

---

[8] See Bosco *et al.*, 2013.

[9] The cases of negative prices that sometimes are registered in the wholesale market are explained by the position of net buyer of the price-setting firm.

the same figure calculated for the protected market results to be equal to 107.93 €/MWh.

As for the other regulated components of the electricity bill, the Authority is in charge of defining the conditions of all the tariff system and in particular the ones concerning the access to the network. For year 2012 the tariff components for transmission, distribution and measure were set at 2,655 c€/kWh.

Figure 8 shows electricity prices (both with taxes and net of taxes) for final consumers in Italy, UK and Germany for different classes of consumption.

Figure 8. Electricity Prices for Final Customers (2012)

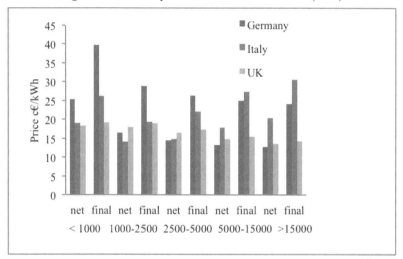

Source: Authors' elaboration from AEEG Annual report 2012.

The issue of tariff policies is a subject that must be adequately investigated since it incorporates both a universal service issue and a market incentive-regulatory issue. The increased competition in the IPEX did not have much influence on wholesale prices but we notice from Figure 8 that Italian retail prices are lower than average EU prices. For domestic consumers in the second class (yearly consumption between 1,000 and 2,500 kWh) Italian prices net of taxes are 7.6% lower than European average, whereas they are 6.2% lower including taxes. On the contrary Italian prices are higher that the European average for classes of high consumption. In the second class of consumption (2,500-5,000 kWh), for example, Italian prices including taxes are 15% higher than EU average. This reflects a tariff policy that favours low consumptions

397

levels at the expense of high consumption levels. There is in fact a sort of redistribution that implicitly assumes that low consumption is strictly correlated with low-income levels. This must not be true however since high consumption can be explained by other reasons like for example the number of family members. More recently a new scheme that favours poor people or people with special needs has been introduced (the so-called Social Tariff).

Industrial consumers pay higher tariffs as compared to the EU average: in the consumption range of 500-2,000 MWh prices are 37% higher (47% higher including taxes).

Conclusion

In this paper we analysed the history of ENEL and the related evolution of the Italian electricity industry. Starting from the beginning of the 20th century, we traced the path that conducted to the creation of a vertically integrated public monopolist who was responsible of all the phases of the electricity industry. In this connection ENEL sustained the investments necessary to create a production and distribution system adequate to the needs of a rapidly growing industrial nation more than the previous fragmented markets each lead by a "zonal" private monopolist with prices for long time strongly differentiated across zones. When it was founded ENEL received a clear public mission consistent with the main targets of welfare enhancement and allocative efficiency.

We then analysed the new phase that started with the season of privatisation of SOEs. In Italy the privatisation of ENEL started at the beginning of the 1990 when it was transformed into an ordinary corporation whose share capital was initially entirely owned by the Treasury and then partially sold to private shareholders. This process was accompanied by measures which introduced competitive conditions in two segments of the electricity industry (generation and sale) and a new industrial architecture in which transmission remained a national monopoly under the control of an independent TSO. Generation was open to competition and a newly created wholesale electricity market was established to coordinate the activity of independent private producers. Since it is not possible to analyse the new ENEL without referring to the new regulatory structure in which now it operates, we described the new mission of ENEL which successfully accompanied the first steps of the new market with clear examples of what we called a "socially responsible" behaviour. In the meanwhile, various factors affected the electricity market, such as the entrance and empowerment of new producers, the reduction of bottlenecks on the grid due to better line interconnections and the decrease in demand due to the economic downturn. Altogether, better competitive conditions emerged as the result of a new market environment and of the regulatory activity of AEEG. Still, an overall evaluation of the privatisation and market restructure is not easy to make. Italian prices are still higher than European averages and transmission capacity is still insufficient. Huge private investments and massive technological improvements have not been realized whereas the new transaction costs – related to the organisation and management of the new markets – are at an unknown level. Further analysis will be needed in order to draw a balance of the net results of the privatisation policy adopted for the Italian electricity sector. The history of ENEL however, proved to be an interesting case to be analysed since it illustrated how a an influential government may still hold a partial control of a newly privatised firm and use its special powers to pursue its welfare objectives.

References

Barluzzi, F., *La tariffcazione dell'energia elettrica*, Vallecchi (ed.), Firenze, 1962.

Bortolotti, B., Faccio, M., "Reluctant Privatisation", in *Working Paper*, University of Torino, 2004.

Bosco, B., "Privatisation, Reproduction and Crisis: the Case of Utilities", in E. Brancaccio, and G. Fontana (eds.), *The Global Economics Crisis*, 2011, London: Routledge Taylor & Francis Group, pp. 231-249.

Bosco, B., Parisio, L., Pelagatti, M., "Deregulated wholesale electricity prices in Italy. An empirical analysis", *International Advances in Economic Research*, 2007, Vol. 13, No. 4, pp. 415-432.

Bosco, B., Parisio, L., Pelagatti, M., "Estimating Marginal Costs and Market Power in the Italian Electricity Auctions", in *Energy Market (EEM)*, 2010, 7th International Conference on the European Electricity Market, Madrid.

Bosco, B., Parisio, L., Pelagatti, M. e F. Baldi, "Long Run Relations in European Electricity Prices", in *Journal of Applied Econometrics*, 2010, Vol. 25, No. 5, pp. 805-32.

Bosco, B., Parisio, L., Pelagatti, M., "Strategic bidding in vertically integrated power markets with an application to the Italian electricity auctions", in *Energy Economics*, 2012, Vol. 34, No. 6, pp. 2046-57.

Bosco, B., Parisio, L., Pelagatti, M., "Optimal pricing behavior of vertically integrated utilities: theory and evidence from the Italian electricity wholesale market", in *Energy Market (EEM)*, 2013, 10th International Conference on the European Electricity Market, Stockholm.

Castronovo, V. (ed.), *Storia dell'industria elettrica in Italia. Dal dopoguerra alla nazionalizzazione, 1945-1962*, Bari, Laterza, 1994.

Florio, M., *The great divestiture*, Cambridge, MIT Press, 2004.

Giannetti, R., "I sistemi elettrici regionali privati: dal secondo dopoguerra alla nazionalizzazione", in AAVV, *La nazionalizzazione dell'energia elettrica*, Laterza, Roma-Bari, 1989.

Mori, G. (ed.), *Storia dell'industria elettrica in Italia. 1. Le origini (1882-1914)*, (2 Vols.), Bari, Laterza, 1992.

Parisio, L., Bosco, B., "Market Power and the Power Market: Multi-unit Bidding and (in) efficiency of the Italian Electricity Market", in *International Tax and Public Finance*, 2003, Vol. 10, No. 4, pp. 377-401.

Parisio, L., Bosco, B., "Electricity Prices and Cross-border Trade: Volume and Strategy Effects", in *Energy Economics*, 2008, Vol. 30, No. 4, pp. 1760-1775.

Rossi, E., *Elettricità senza Baroni* (Electricity with no Barons), 1962, Bari, Laterza.

Zanetti, G. (ed.), *Storia dell'industria elettrica in Italia. 1. Le origini (1882-1914)*, (2 Vols.), Bari, Laterza, 1995.

13. The Transformation of Milan's City Energy Enterprise in a Leading National Industrial Group

Laura DELPONTE, Maddalena SORRENTINO,
Matteo TURRI & Daniela VANDONE*

University of Milan

Introduction, Research Context and Rationale

Traditionally, in Northern Italy, electricity and gas services were supplied by municipal enterprises. Changes in the regulatory framework for the provision of local public services, along with opening to competition of the energy sectors, favoured the involvement of private capital in these companies and led to an accelerated process of corporatization and ultimately privatisation.

The opening of the energy markets was seen as a necessary step to offer users better services at a lower price, as liberalisation was expected to eliminate subsidies and monopoly rents. The reformed markets' structure resulted from different combinations of competitive and administrative mechanisms. These arrangements aimed at setting minimum standards for the quality of the service delivered and at ensuring universal access to the service, while introducing some degree of competition in specific segments of each industry (Glachant, 2002). The removal of entry barriers in the competitive segments of the two industries opened up several opportunities for the former municipal energy companies that consolidated their position along the energy value chain while expanding in other network services.

The most dynamic once public enterprises modified their ownership, governance structure and business models. In these companies the

---

* We would like to thank Professor Giuseppe Bognetti and Professor Massimo Florio for their helpful suggestions and thoughtful guidance. We are also grateful to Enrico Cerrai, the AEM president from 1976 to 1981 and from 1992 to 2002, who shared with us his experience with making the AEM a successful public enterprise, and to the Fondazione AEM for providing many enterprise's documents.

restructuring process followed a similar path. Structural separation was first achieved by establishing joint-stock companies as independent legal entity governed by private law. The largest municipal energy enterprises were then listed and partially privatised while being kept under public control because of their public service mission (Bognetti, Robotti, 2007). In parallel, these enterprises engaged in sectorial and geographical diversification to tap into scale economies that arose from by putting together network services. Finally, most of these enterprises engaged in different forms of inter-municipal cooperation that ended up into broader industrial projects and the establishment of multi-utility groups with a larger geographical base and a diversified ownership structure (Grossi, 2007).

As a result of these transformations, in the largest cities of Northern and Central Italy, the provision of network services, including energy, water and environmental services, is currently provided by a restricted number of semi privatised multi-utility enterprises, such as A2A (Milan and Brescia), IREN (Genoa and Turin), HERA (Bologna and Modena) and ACEA (Rome), along with the two former national monopolists, the ENI and ENEL Group and number of new private operators.

In the city of Milan, prior to liberalisation of the 1990s, energy services were supplied by the AEM, the in-house energy enterprise that was established in 1910. While being part of Milan' city administration, the AEM was an example of efficient management and dynamic entrepreneurship in the public sector. Following the removal of legislative constraints and the gradual opening to competition of network industries, the AEM undertook an impressive process of business growth, where vertical and horizontal restructuring were pursued as a way to adapt to changing regulatory environments and increased competition. At the same time the enterprise was partially privatised and listed. As a way to strengthen the AEM's market position in Italy and in Europe, the A2A Group was established in 2008 out of the merger between the AEM Milan and the ASM Brescia, another former municipal utility of Lombardy region.

Presently, the A2A Group is the largest Italian multi-utility that operates in different network industries, including energy, water and waste. In spite of having being partially privatised, the A2A remains under public control and ended up having a hybrid ownership structure that resulted in various conflict between public and commercial interests. The current corporate governance structure and arrangements protect the public ownership, but do not insulate the enterprise's management from political interferences (Citroni, Lippi, Profeti, 2013) that often clash with competitive market rules. Despite being publicly owned and controlled the A2A cannot any more define its public mission, but it rather pursue the general public interest within a less transparent framework that is based upon the influence the mayors of the cities of Milan and Brescia exert on the company.

By looking at the A2A case history, this paper seeks to understand to what extent the original objectives of privatisation and liberalisation of local public services and energy markets have been achieved. It explores the underlying reasons of the public ownership and how this materializes in the enterprise's business choices and conflicts with commercial interests. The study also looks at the sustainability of this hybrid model that pushed the enterprise towards riskier industrial operations and an increased exposure to the international financial markets, while keeping the commitment to providing quality public services in the local jurisdictions in which it has traditionally operated.

This study draws on an extensive review of the A2A recent and past corporate documents and of the relevant literature concerning various liberalization issues of energy services in Europe and of local public services in Italy. Interviews with the enterprise and municipal representatives were also organised to bring into the study the perspective of the key stakeholders. A press review of articles concerning the A2A and other similar utilities was also performed to report about important events that affect the enterprise's performance and behaviour in terms of its relationship with the public owner, Milan's citizens and the market.

The paper is organised as follows. Sections 1 and 2 briefly present the A2A from its origins to its current structures. Section 2 and 3 addresses issues related to the A2A public mission and corporate governance arrangements. Section 4 describes the enterprise's economic and financial performance following the structural separation from Milan city's administration. Section 6 concludes.

1. The Largest Italian Multi-Utility Enterprise

AEM has been for over a century the electricity company of Milan's municipality. Today, the AEM's legacy has been taken over by the A2A Group, the Italian largest multi-utility company established in 2008 out of the merger between Milan's energy (AEM) and waste (AMSA) companies with the multi-utility of city of Brescia (ASM). Both the AEM and the ASM are two former public local enterprises, supplying energy services, with a history stretching back more than 100 years and strong local roots.

A2A is a listed joint stock company and its controlling shareholders are the Municipality of Milan and of Brescia, respectively with a participation of 27.5%, while other minority shares (less than 2%) are in the hands of the municipality of Varese and Bergamo, two other important cities of Lombardy's region.

A2A Group operates in the following sectors: i) energy (i.e., production, sale and distribution of electricity, sale and distribution of gas), which accounts for 67.3% of total revenue; ii) environment (i.e., management of waste) (13%); iii) heat and services (5%); iv) district heating networks (11%); and v) other services and corporate (3.6%) (figure 1).

Figure 1. A2A's Sectors of Activity

Energy	Environment	Heat and services	Networks	Other services and corporate
Thermoelectric and hydroelectric plants	Collection and street sweeping	Cogeneration plants	Electricity networks	Other services
Energy management	Treatment	District heating networks	Gas networks	Corporate services
Sale of electricity and gas	Disposal and energy recovery	Sales of heat and other services	Integrated water cycle	

Source: A2A Interim Report on operations 2013.

The current A2A Group's structure is rather complex and resulted from a twenty year long process of acquisitions, mergers, divestures and restructuring operations. As long as the enterprise grew in new sectors, the company's structure had to adapt to integrate new businesses and comply with changing regulations. Presently, thirty-two enterprises constitute the A2A Group. Fourteen operate in the energy business, four in the environmental services, two in the district heating business, eight in the network services and four provide various corporate services. The energy business, and especially power generation, has remained the A2A's core business in spite of various attempts to diversify in other network industries.

Amongst the Italian once public utility enterprises, A2A Group is the largest multi-utility company in terms of revenues and market capitalization (Table 1). However, the A2A Group can be considered a medium size energy company as compared to the largest European energy enterprises, such as ENEL (Italy), RWE (Germany) or EdF (France). As an example, the ENEL group, the second electric company in Europe in terms of installed capacity, in 2011 reached revenue of 79,514 million euro that is by far higher than the sum of the revenues of the four largest Italian multi-utilities.

**Table 1. Comparing the A2A's Key Figures with Those
of Other Italian Local Multi-Utilities (2011)**

Indicators	A2A	HERA[1]	ACEA[2]	IREN[3]
Market capitalization (million €)	2,274	1,349	1,041	552
Revenues (million €)	6,198	4,105	3,464	3,254
Gross operating income (million €)	942	644	655	591
Net operating income (million €)	301	334	222	308
Profit (million €)	(420)	104	86	(107.9)
Employees (units)	11,886	6,484	5,114	4,655
Electricity portfolio (GWh)	48,843	9,996	16,539	13,816
Gas portfolio (million mc)	5,567	3,321	96	3,108
Heat sold (GWht)	2,874	499.3	n.a.	2,572
Water distributed (million mc)	69	254	774	181
Waste treated (tons)	2,626	5,107	579	1,017

Sources: author's elaboration from A2A, HERA, ACEA and IREN web sites and Annual Reports.

The A2A's customer base is rooted in the Lombardy region, where the A2A sells 85% and 92% of its volume of electricity and gas respectively. However, the enterprise pursued a geographical market diversification strategy that resulted in asset investments in other Italian and European regions.

2. The History of a Successful Public Enterprise

2.1. A Public Response to a Private Monopoly in the Electricity Sector

The official foundation of the AEM took place in 1910, following a referendum which saw nearly 91% of favourable votes of Milan's citizens for establishing a municipal electric company. In terms of material and financial assets, it was the largest Italian municipal company.

At that time, the city of Milan was laying the foundation to become the most important Italian industrial and financial centre. Provision of reliable and low-cost source of horse power was perceived by the local administrators as a major impediment toward the industrial development of the city. Electricity was supplied by the Edison, a local Italian private company that succeeded in establishing a dominant position in both power generation and electricity distribution. This allowed the company to benefit from a substantial rent that came from charging users with prices that were above the national average.

---

[1]   Municipality of Bologna and other cities of Emilia Romagna.

[2]   Municipality of Rome.

[3]   Municipality of Turin, Genoa and Reggio Emilia.

The electricity produced by Edison's pioneering investment in power generation was promptly absorbed by the development of the city's tramway lines, and by the increased electrification of the city's productive activities. The municipality of Milan was Edison's major client, so that the City's Council was looking for alternatives to purchasing electricity from Edison. The opportunity came in 1903, when the State passed a new law[4] concerning the provision of local public services through municipal companies.

Given the urgent need to break Edison's monopoly, Milan's City Council undertook the acquisition of hydraulic power sites in the nearby Alpine valleys of Valtellina, and the in-house building of a thermoelectric (Piazzale Trento) and a hydroelectric (Grosotto) power generation plants. The official foundation of the AEM took place some years later, when the complex bureaucratic process foreseen by the Giolitti Law was completed.

In less than two years, electricity prices decreased of about 35%-50% and in 1910 the lightening prices were the lowest amongst Italian cities. However, given that at that time the municipality's generation facilities were less efficient that those of Edison because of their less favourable location, the municipality soon came to sign agreements with its competitor on tariffs and allocation of users' connection. The agreement also included a subsidised tariff for housing projects and small shops.

The first fifteen years of the AEM operations were rather difficult. First, the outbreak of the First World War temporarily interrupted the company's growth. Secondly, the rise to power of Fascism in the early 1920s created a hostile political environment for municipal companies. An attempt to divest the AEM and the newly established municipal transportation company (ATM) was deemed so unpopular that the fascist regime had to review its position and opportunistically proceeded to use the AEM as a tool to build political consensus.

In the aftermath of World War I, the Italian electricity system was characterized by vertically integrated and regionally-based private monopolies, the so-called Edison system. Seven private companies had a regional dominant position, whereas municipal electricity companies were established in the largest cities to cope with an increasing demand for industrial and domestic use. Between 1917 and 1931, Milan's population grew at an average annual rate of 3%, while medium and large size industrial companies prospered in the mechanical, chemical and steel

---

[4]   The Giolitti law of 1903 shaped the provision of local public services in Italy for almost a century and set a number of legal and operational constraints that accompanied the development of these municipal companies. For instance, municipal companies couldn't be established as independent legal entities, were ruled as public administration bodies, and couldn't operate outside the city boundaries.

sectors. The AEM's electricity generation capacity was undersized as compared to the city's needs and urged the company to expand further, given that all new capacity would have been absorbed by the market. Investments were geared towards increasing the AEM's hydroelectric generation capacity up to 211 MW.

Investments were self-financed through the use of unusually high annual depreciation charges that allowed the AEM to keep its earning that would have had otherwise been transferred almost entirely to the city of Milan. In parallel with financing its investments, the AEM was also providing a stable stream of revenues to Milan's municipality in the form of interest rates on the enterprise's endowment capital. Specifically, between 1915 and 1940 the recorded annual return of the AEM was in the range of 5-7%, while from 1925 to 1940, the AEM's endowment capital grew almost six times in nominal value, increasing thus the revenues provided to Milan's municipality.

2.2. Backing Milan's Economic Miracle

The AEM growth continued in the immediate post-war reconstruction. During the years of the Italian economic miracle, Milan became the most important national industrial hub and the city population grew considerably. These two factors led to a continuous increase in electricity consumption for domestic and industrial uses that the AEM met through the implementation of three four-year plans aiming at doubling its electricity generation capacity. Between 1951 and a 1962 the AEM's sales grew up to an impressive 121%. The highest share of the AEM's revenue finally came from private users and this allowed the company to sell electricity for public uses at production cost.

In the same years, at the national level, the Italian parliament was elaborating a project for nationalising the electricity sector. The proposal was underpinned by several arguments, including the strategic relevance of electricity supply, and the need to better pursue the collective interest, to reduce regional unbalances and overcome the existing fragmentation of the regional networks, and to limit the high rents and lobbying power of the private electricity companies. In 1962, a national law established the ENEL, the national public monopolist for the generation and provision of electric services.

The nationalization achieved the development of a national electricity production and transmission system and the universalization of the service. It also shifted the electricity generation technology in favour of fuel-based power generation. The nationalisation had a heavy impact on municipal companies that were left with the option to operate as concessionaire with no autonomy for setting tariffs.

In 1964 Milan's City Council unanimously established to keep the AEM concession from ENEL. As a matter of fact, the licensing agreement was more profitable for the city's administration given that ENEL would have provided a 12 billion liras compensation for 10 years, whereas in 1964 the AEM was already providing 8 billion liras of annual revenue to the municipality. In addition, the electricity supplied by the AEM to the municipality allowed the city to save up to 1.5 billion liras each year. The behaviour of the ENEL was initially hostile and the two companies had to come to an agreement to allocate the distribution of electricity in the different districts of the city.

The oil shocks of the 1970s had a negative impact on the AEM's balance sheets. In 1975, for the first time, the AEM had to use its reserve fund to meet its payment obligations with the city of Milan. Despite the AEM was less exposed to the oil shock because of the predominance of hydro-based energy sources, the introduction of a national compensation for thermal-generated electricity reduced its revenues as compared to other producers. In addition, the cost of labour rose quickly, as a result of national automatic wage adjustments, whereas increases of public services' tariffs were blocked to control inflationary pressures. At the same time, electricity demand in Milan was increasing at lower rates, as a result of a gradual decrease in the urban population and the resettlement of most industrial activities outside the city boundaries.

At the beginning of the 1980s many municipal companies, including the AEM, undertook a diversification strategy in other network industries and became multi-utility companies. The AEM was transformed in Milan's energy company by taking over the municipal gas services from the Edison and by initiating experimental investments in district heating. Investments were geared towards laying down an extensive network of natural gas pipelines in the city of Milan, where, in 1981, nearly 97% of house heating came from the burning of more pollutant petroleum products.

In this decade, the company's profitability was satisfactory. The financial contributions to the municipality of Milan grew from 37 billion liras in 1981 to 200 billion liras in 1989. The gross operating margin of the electricity business grew from 29.32% in 1985 to 32-33% in the following years, while the gross operating margin of the gas business was nearly 26%.

2.3. Seizing the Opportunities of Reformed Local Public Service Provision and Liberalised Energy Markets

In the 1990s the combined effect of a reform in the provision of local public services and the progressive liberalisation of the electricity and natural gas markets, spurred an unprecedented process of growth and transformation of the largest municipal companies in Northern Italy. In two decades the AEM significantly modified its business model, ownership and corporate governance structure and the relationship with Milan's municipality and its citizens.

Amongst the many legislative changes that occurred in this period, two played a key role for the municipal energy companies. First, the national law 142 of 1990 transferred the model of State-owned enterprises to local public services by allowing the establishment of special companies as separate legal entity. The law aimed at opening local market services to competition, separating managerial and control functions, and improving the cost and quality of services. In addition, it opened new growth opportunities for municipal companies by removing the restriction to operate within the city boundaries.

Secondly, following a number of European Directives[5] that aimed at creating an integrated European market for energy services, the electricity and natural gas markets were gradually open to competition, while the national public monopolist, ENEL and ENI, were partially privatised. Despite the two national incumbents maintained a dominant position, a number of new operators entered in previously protected market segments. Taking advantage of their dominant positions in the local markets of the largest and wealthiest cities of Northern Italy, most municipal companies, including the AEM, quickly expanded their business activities beyond their traditional geographical jurisdiction.

In 1996 the AEM transformed in a joint stock company that was a necessary step towards privatization of the enterprise that was formally achieved in 1998 through the enterprise's listing in Milan's stock exchange. In 1999, following the transposition of the EU energy Directives, the AEM restructured into an industrial group with operative companies in each sector of activity. At the beginning of the liberalization, the expansion of the AEM business followed a path similar to other European energy utilities (Testarmata, 2009). In particular, the AEM's strategy aimed at vertical integration along the electricity value chain, horizontal investments in adjacent utility industries, including telecommunication, and geographical market diversification. At the same time the AEM started expanding its operations in the promising sectors of district heating and environmental services that will be reinforced in the following years.

---

[5] These were: for the internal electricity market: Directive 96/92/CE of 1996, Directive 03/54/CE of 2003, and Directive 2009/72/EC of 2009; for the internal market in natural gas: Directive 98/30/EC of 1998, Directive 2003/55/EC of 2003, and Directive 2009/73/EC of 2009.

The AEM strengthened its leading position in Lombardy region through the acquisition of stakes in other local utilities and private companies. In parallel, it undertook a large industrial investment in thermal-based generation facilities by purchasing a quota of the largest power plants divested by the ENEL group that led to the establishment of Edipower. Internationalization was pursued through technological partnerships with other European energy companies and participation in several international bids for the provision of local public services.

Overall, these years were marked by an impressive growth of the company's generation capacity, investments, sales and turnover. The AEM's electricity generation capacity increased from 3,086 GWh in 1997 up to a maximum of 36,293 GWh in 2007. Between 1997 and 2008, the AEM more than tripled its net profits, increased by nine times the invested capital, by five times its equity, and by twelve times its revenues, while employees decreased from 2,959 to 2,503 units. At the same time, Milan municipality collected annual dividends in the range of 38 and 75 million Euros (see the Appendix).

Following a series of mergers and acquisitions in European and Italian utilities (The Economist, Nov. 30th 2006), the AEM also intended to consolidate its market position in Italy and launched a merger project with ASM, Brescia's municipality multi-utility company that led to the establishment of the A2A Group in 2008.

The challenges posed by the global financial crisis in 2008 and the persisting national economic downturn, along with structural problems of the Italian energy markets, abruptly interrupted this period of accelerated growth. In 2011, for the first time in its history, the A2A registered high losses up to 420 million Euros. These were due, amongst other factors, to extraordinary events, such as the write-down of assets and investments related to the reorganisation of the shareholdings in Edison and Edipower[6] and the losses registered by the Montenegrin subsidiary EPCG.[7]

---

[6] In 2005, together with the EDF Group, the AEM gained control over Edison Spa, the old private rival that shared with the AEM the control over Milan's electricity market. In 2012, following a controversial reorganization that lasted almost a year, Electricité de France acquired sole control of Edison. The selling of the A2A shareholding in Edison was followed by a consolidation of the A2A position in Edipower and a loss of 627 million euros.

[7] In 2009 the A2A Group decided to participate in an international bid for acquiring control of Montenegro state-owned electric company (EPCG). This operation pursued two business objectives: to acquire new capacity from renewable sources in view of the planned interconnection between Italy and Montenegro, and to spot new business areas in energy and environmental services in these markets.

At the end, the rapid expansion in the domestic market, along with the integration with new companies, had a cost that could not be compensated in the context of a falling national demand for gas and electricity. The recent deterioration of the enterprise's capitalisation and debt structure, together with a reduced profitability, have induced the A2A management to put in place a more caution corporate strategy that is based on further consolidation in core business areas and deleveraging. An example of this new business orientation, that is also common to other European energy utilities, such as ENEL or RWE, is provided by the divesture of all assets in the telecommunication sector.

3. Towards a Large Number of Loosely Defined Public Missions

3.1. The A2A Public Missions: the Enterprise's Perspective

When it was established over a century ago, AEM had a clear public goal which consisted of providing the municipality of Milan with a low-cost and reliable source of horse power. In 1910, *Corriere della Sera*, a national newspaper, wrote: "Special attention was devoted to the design of low electricity tariffs for small retailers, private customers and of subsidized flat rate for social housing. By doing this AEM achieved the main objective of the municipalisation program that consisted of lowering the price of electricity". Electricity supplied by AEM was used for the lightening of streets and municipal buildings, but was also instrumental to the development of the municipal transportation system that was based on tramways and metro lines.

Till the AEM was part of the city's public administration its public mandate was determined by the local politics and oriented towards anticipating the development needs of a growing city with expanding industrial activities. As a result, its original public mission was added with various mandates over the years for the purpose of providing an efficient public response to specific city' needs. For instances, in the 1970s malcontents over the functioning of the municipal traffic lightening system led the AEM to take up this new responsibility. In the 1980s the AEM changed its statute to include gas services and became Milan's Energy Enterprise (*Azienda Energetica Milano* and was subsequently assigned with the important mandate of developing Milan's gas distribution network. In spite of these changes, the public missions of the AEM remained limited to the provision of energy services and oriented towards producing well-defined and tangible outputs.

Although it was not formally stated, another non negligible contribution of the AEM to Milan's municipality was its ability to generate profits out of the sale of electricity to private clients and its capacity to cross-subsidise other less profitable municipal services, including Milan's public transportation services.

When structural separation from the city's public administration was pursued at the beginning of the 1990s, the AEM's public mission was subject to radical change. A separation between a formal and a multitude of informal public missions emerged. While the formal enterprise's mission is established in the A2A's corporate documents and has to fulfil the interests of both its public and private owners, the A2A public mission is related to the public nature of the services provided and the relationship between the enterprise and the local jurisdictions in which the company has its historical roots.

When in 1996 the AEM was transformed in a public joint-stock enterprise, the AEM's chairman recalls that this was "an enormous change (...) because from that moment the link between politics and industrial activity was less strong" (AEM President Zuccoli's speech at the opening of the new Canale Viola, 2004). The creation of a joint-stock company represented the end of "a municipal phase" and made it necessary "to begin (...) developing outside the city's walls, moving in the direction of the open sea of the markets" (letter to the AEM's shareholders, 1996).

Since the enterprise's listing in 1998, following the example of private corporates' communication strategies, the AEM's formal mission became simply that of "creating value for its shareholders" (A2A web site). This statement oversimplified the enterprise's mission towards achieving financial targets, but it also spelt out clearly that profit generation had to be a relevant objective both for the private and the public owners. More specific corporate objectives were geared towards seizing the opportunities of liberalised energy markets and becoming an industrial group of national relevance (letter to the AEM's shareholders, 1999). As the AEM increased its electricity production capacity by purchasing generation plants on the national scale, the enterprise became more interested into national and international energy market developments expressing the willingness to become an important national player (letter to the AEM's shareholders 2004 and 2005). The enterprise's management set increasing growth targets, which were based on the assumption that in liberalised energy markets only a limited number of large players would have survived to competition (the AEM Group's Report on Operations 2005).

These strategic objectives were successfully achieved, given that at the end of this expansionary phase of the business cycle the AEM was an established national industrial group. Interestingly, despite the AEM's growth has been driven by investments outside its traditional regional jurisdiction, the corporate documents still attach great importance to the local roots of the enterprise and to the peculiar relationships between the AEM, Milan's administration and citizens, and the mountain communities of the alpine valleys of Valtellina, where AEM first developed its hydroelectric generation facilities. By contrast, there are no references to the original public mission of the enterprise that was based on controlling the price of electricity in the city of Milan (Pavese, 2011).

It was on the basis of this growth path that in 2007 AEM approached the merger with ASM, Brescia's former public multi-utility company. The main industrial goals of the merger were set out as follows: i) expand sufficiently to be able to compete with other national and international competitors; ii) strengthen integration both upstream and downstream in the value chain of its activities; iii) exploit opportunities deriving from economies of scale; and iv) strengthen the local roots of the new company (the A2A web site).

From the private investor's perspective, the merger was expected to provide higher returns for the A2A's shareholders by "exploiting the advantages and benefits that derive from reaching an adequate size in order to successfully compete in the local public services' markets that are undergoing rapid deregulation" (letter to the A2A's shareholders, 2009) and was also considered instrumental to "establish A2A not only as one of the leaders in the Italian energy market but also seeks to play a leading role in Europe" (letter to the AEM's shareholders 2007).

As for the AEM, the A2A's corporate documents follow a business rhetoric that does not explicitly address the issue of the public functions of the enterprise and overemphasises the profit goals. The A2A's Articles of Association do not include any reference to the company's public mission.

The A2A's annual reports attach great importance to the local roots of the newly established enterprise that, according to its management, would have been reinforced by the merger. Given the ownership structure of the A2A, the annual letters to its shareholders are full of references to the advantages of the local public ownership and to the existence of a privileged relationship with the local administrations that would guarantee that the interests of the local communities are pursued.[8]

---

[8] Examples of this commitment are the following statements: "in these Municipalities, the heart of Lombardy, A2A, having made major acquisitions and purchased new shareholdings in local utility companies, works closely with local authorities for the development of projects that can guarantee a higher quality of life in these cities" (letter to the A2A's shareholders, 2007) or "the presence of the Municipalities in the A2A shareholding composition are an additional protection for the interests of the communities in the areas served by A2A" (letter to the A2A's shareholders, 2009).

As A2A keeps expanding beyond the regional boundaries, a number of new public missions of national relevance emerged. These were not conceptualised or formalised, but are rather documented by the enterprise's actions. Within this context, can be explained the 2007 acquisition of a significant shareholding in EPCC, the Montenegrin state energy company. "It is primarily an economic operation of national interest in which A2A is participating together with Terna (...), creating, as per the intention of the two Governments, an energy bridge between Italy and Montenegro" (letter to the A2A's shareholders, 2007). Another business operation in Southern Italy was also pursued as a public national interest as the A2A President wrote "taking responsibility for the management of the Acerra waste-to-energy plant, we have been able to provide the Italian Government with concrete support in order to resolve the rubbish problem in Campania" (letter to the A2A's shareholders, 2007).

In spite of the business rhetoric of the official documentation, an analysis of the operations of A2A reveals how the enterprise interprets and carries out its public mission, providing thus tangible benefits to the local communities. This is well documented in the A2A's Annual Sustainability Reports that provide detailed information about a number of projects that promote energy efficiency, reduction of pollution and better network infrastructures. In this respect, it is worth mentioning the A2A's commitment to further developing district heating projects for the city of Milan, Brescia and Bergamo that are expected to contribute to lowering households' costs for heating and to reduce emissions of air pollutants. Other relevant environmental targets refer to improving the energy efficiency of municipal and public buildings and to increasing the separate collection of waste.

3.2. The A2A Public Missions: the Municipality's Perspective

The public mandate of the enterprises controlled by Milan's City Council is defined by a specific department (*Settore Enti Partecipate*). However, this does not apply to the listed enterprises. Supply of local public services is regulated through service contracts (*Contratto di Servizio*) that set a number of quantitative and qualitative targets to be satisfied by the tenderer. These contracts define the public functions of specific public services, but are not enterprise specific and cannot thus be associated to the public mission of an enterprise.

Beyond the service contract, there are no other public documents that formally set the public goals of the A2A. This does not mean that the public owner ignores the public functions of the A2A, but it is rather a consequence of the legal status of the enterprise. Because the enterprise is listed and has to compete in open markets it cannot have public missions that would dislike private investors. However, although it is not formalised, the public owner exercises its property rights through specific and contextualised interventions that are intended to preserve the public interest. For instance, this emerged prominently when in 2012 the mayor of Milan repeated its commitment to safeguard jobs of waste collector workers in the city of Milan and undertook to establish a dialogue with the A2A's management and trade unions.

An analysis of the minutes of Milan's Council meetings between 2007 and May 2013, reveals the existence of diversified political interests with regard to the A2A's activities and the lack of a clear political orientation. At the time of the establishment of the A2A, at least three dominant public missions were noticed. Specifically:

a) maintaining the public investment in the utility sectors during the troubled phase linked to the deregulation process "defending against the aggressive policies of competitors and creating new professional and technological development opportunities" (*Deliberazioni del Consiglio Comunale 45/07*);

b) the production of "growing economic resources for the city of Milan" (*Deliberazioni del Consiglio Comunale 44/07*) through the "increase of dividends which can be used in the development policies of the Municipality" (*Deliberazioni del Consiglio Comunale 45/07*);

c) maximising network services, for example "developing and implementing – also thanks to the availability of greater financial resources – innovative energy diversification projects in the area of the Municipality of Milan, such as the extension of the network and district heating services" (*Deliberazioni del Consiglio Comunale 45/07*).

In spite of so many different approaches towards the A2A, it is clear that the enterprise is considered a strategic asset for the public owner, both in terms of its capacity to generate profits that support other local services and investments, but also for its ability to operate in strategic sectors and to provide the city of Milan and Brescia with high quality infrastructure and innovative environmental technologies.

As compared to the past, when affordability of electricity supply for Milan's citizens was a key issue, social themes, such as energy poverty, appear to be less prominent in the local political debate. It is rather perceived that the (semi) private nature of the enterprise doesn't allow for the explicit set of social targets that could come at the expense of profits. In line with private corporate practices, social objectives are pursued by charitable and corporate and social responsibility initiatives. To this end, the A2A Group supports through sponsorships cultural and social initiatives, especially in the territories in which it operates.

3.3. Open Issues in the A2A's Public Mission

An understanding of the A2A's public mandate requires to investigate underneath the surface of the corporate's rhetoric that strives to strike a balance between private and public interests. Generally, this study highlights an atrophy of the public debate about the public mission assigned to the A2A, and a structural weakness in clearly delineating what should be the enterprise's priorities with respect to its public owners.

As the enterprise grew, diversified its business areas and modified its ownership and governance structure, its public missions become more complex and multi-faceted. Whereas profitability is firmly established as the overarching enterprise's goal, a number of social and environmental targets that affect the quality of living of citizens are also included in the enterprise's mission.

A number of contradictions are due to the public nature of the service supplied and the private corporate form adopted by the enterprise. For instance, there is an intrinsic contradiction between promoting energy saving practices and making profits out of gas and electricity sales. As a publicly controlled enterprise, A2A cannot disregard environmental and social issues that are relevant for its customers and ultimate owners. However, these targets have to be pursued with a private corporate approach that prioritizes profits.

The current ownership structure of A2A also poses some challenges in terms of the assigned public mission, given the asymmetry between the two public owners. In 2012 the two municipalities prepared provisional accounts with respectively 8.4 billion (Milan) and 476 million (Brescia) euros of revenues. This large difference resulted in a different approach towards the A2A's dividend policy. While for the municipality of Brescia the A2A's dividends are essential to finalise the municipal budget, the municipality of Milan is less dependent on these transfers. This has resulted in a permanent debate about the amount of annual dividends that the A2A has to distribute, regardless of the enterprise's performance (Scarpa, 2012).

Although it can be generally concluded that A2A remains loyal to its customer base in spite of the diversified geographical nature of its business, the enterprise's growth beyond the regional jurisdiction also proved to affect the enterprise's public mission. As a consequence, local public debates arise whenever there is the perception that national interests are pursued at the expense of the local interests. It also appears that the role of the City Council is marginalized when decisions of national interests have to be taken.

4. Keeping Public Control through Corporate Governance Arrangements

4.1. From Public to Mixed Ownership

For nearly a century the AEM has been a municipal company entirely owned by Milan's municipality. Functional separation was not enough to ensure that there was not confusion between the powers and autonomy of the AEM with respect to the city's political orientations. Income generating companies, such as the AEM, were often forced to contribute to the municipal budget beyond their statutory obligations. Political interferences were reported to be pervasive, especially with respect to the enterprise's recruitment and investment policies. Furthermore, the complex system of administrative and formal controls posed several limits to the company's operations and was deemed unfit to support the enterprise's growth in the energy market.

In the early 1990s, new public management principles (Pollitt, 1990; Stewart and Walsh, 1992) were gradually introduced in the Italian context. These principles were oriented towards improving efficiency and effectiveness of public interventions, improving relationships with citizens, ensure financial sustainability of public services, adopting business-oriented practices and reducing political interferences. The means for achieving these objectives were identified in deregulation, privatization, decentralisation and a shift from a bureaucratic model based on norms to a managerial model based on performance. A number of important judicial scandals, related to episodes of pervasive corruption and mismanagement of public funds, also urged to separate politics from business administration.

The national reform of local public services at the beginning of the 1990s, allowed for a structural separation of municipal companies from administrative bodies and triggered a process of corporatisation of local utilities (see Galanti and Moro, 2013). Partial privatisation was also pursued to allow access to international capital markets and attract private investors. The municipality of Milan initially held a 51% majority share that was subsequently lowered below the absolute majority. However, public control was ring fenced by shareholder's agreements that limited individual shareholding with a 5% ceiling and constrained the voting rights of minority shareholders below the 5% threshold.

The merger with ASM Brescia brought about another substantial change in the enterprise's ownership structure. As laid down in the A2A's Articles of Association, the fundamental principles concerning the ownership structure and control of A2A are based on a number of principles that guarantee public control and a perfect balance of power. In particular, these include: i) an equal distribution of shares between the two municipalities (approximately 27.5%), ii) limitations on ownership of shares with voting rights, iii) the same roles and identical powers for the two municipalities, and iv) a public majority constraint.

The AEM and the A2A have never had a strong industrial shareholder, but the floating has been rather distributed amongst institutional investors including Italian and foreign banks. At the end of 2011, retail investors had about 17.6% of the share capital. Interestingly, nearly 57% of small shareholders are from Lombardy region where the enterprise has its historical roots.

4.2. From a Traditional to a Two-Tier Corporate Governance Model

At the time the AEM became an independent municipal enterprise, it adopted a traditional corporate governance model which is based on three entities, including the Shareholders Meeting, the Board of Directors and the Board of Statutory Auditors. Following the establishment of the A2A, a change in the corporate governance structure was needed. The merger raised important political issues related to the choice of the governance arrangements, the renewal of the management positions and the loss of the historical local roots for the respective enterprises.

Unlike other Italian multi-utilities that were established through integration of different local utilities, the A2A decided on a dual board structure. This governance structure originated in Germany and is characterized by the interposition of a body (the supervisory board) between the shareholders' meeting and the management board. Diffusion of this model has taken place in Italy thanks to an increased number of corporate mergers, both in the private and public sector, given that the dual system allows a better integration between different enterprises' cultures (Oriolo, 2008). In publicly controlled enterprises, the use of the dual model is justified by the need to separate the political and the managerial sphere by creating a filter between the public ownership and the leadership of the enterprise (Mele, 2009).

In the current corporate governance structure (figure 2), the Supervisory Board is composed of 15 members, including a chairman and a vice-chairman, who are appointed by the shareholder's meeting on the basis of a voting list.

Figure 2. The A2A Governance Structure

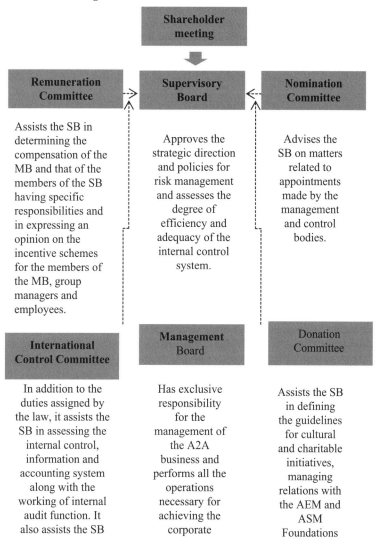

Source: Author's elaboration from A2A's 2011 Sustainability Report.

Twelve out of fifteen members are appointed by the two majority public shareholders. The right to appoint the offices of the chairman and vice-chairman is attributed in rotation to the municipality of Milan and Brescia. Members of the Supervisory Board must meet the requirements of honesty and professionalism, as well as the requirements of independence. At least two members of the Supervisory Board must be chosen from statutory auditors. The lists presented must be made available to the public according to the procedures for listed companies and must provide full information regarding the personal and professional characteristics of the candidates.

Unlike the German dual board model, within the Italian legislative context the supervisory board carries out many other important duties besides general supervisory activities. In particular, upon the Management Board's proposal, the Supervisory Board defines the general planning and strategic guidelines of the enterprise. In relation to this, it approves the A2A multi-year strategic, industrial and financial plans and the A2A strategic transactions.[9]

The Management Board is composed of eight members, including a chairman and a vice-chairman. Four members are appointed by the municipality of Milan and Brescia, out of lists prepared by the Supervisory Board. As for the chairmanship of the Supervisory Board a mechanism of alternation of the power of appointment between Milan and Brescia is foreseen. The Management Board appoints up to two managing directors in charge of financial and technical functions respectively. One more time, this mechanism ensures the perfect balance of power between the two public majority shareholders.

4.3. How the Public Owner Controls the A2A

The four main ways in which the Municipality of Milan controls the A2A are the following: i) the appointment of representatives in the shareholders' meeting, ii) the control activities of the department of the municipal shareholdings (*Settore Enti Partecipate*), iii) the service contracts, and iv) the control activities of the City's Council.

The Municipality of Milan's primary source of influence over the enterprise materialises into its right to appoint representatives in the shareholders' meeting and, through them, to appoint representatives on the A2A's Supervisory Board and Management Board. By appointing top managers, the mayor indirectly exerts its influence over the enterprise. This form of control mainly takes place at the informal level, in the trusting relationship between the mayor and the appointee, given that neither the representatives in the shareholders' meeting nor the A2A's top-managers receive any formal mandate in terms of pursuing specific strategic goals. According to Milan's Municipality's Statute (art. 57), appointments in municipally controlled enterprises have to be assessed by

---

[9]   These include capital transactions, investments and companies' operations exceeding the value of 100 million euro, establishment of joint ventures, allocation of profits and dividend policies.

a committee of experts that control compliance with formal requirements. The Committee is appointed by the Local Council by a majority of three fifths of its members. Candidacies can be submitted by local councillors, professional association, local universities, trade unions, registered local or national associations and a group of at least one hundred citizens. It is also stated that at least 25% of the directors of corporation, special companies, and institutions, organisations owned or controlled by the municipality have to be chosen from candidates proposed by civil society.

A second form of control is exercised through Milan's public administration and its Settore Enti Partecipate, which is assigned a variety of objectives with reference to the enterprises in which the municipality holds a stake. Despite its highly complex assignments, which spread over more than one hundred shareholdings, the Settore Enti Partecipate only employs fourteen staff. With reference to the A2A, the department's activities are limited to providing technical documentation for the representatives of the mayor for their participation in the annual shareholders' meeting.

A third control tool is the service contract that regulates the procurement arrangements between the enterprise and the Municipality. The design of the service contract gives Milan's municipality an instrument for determining and regulating the supply of the service. Because of the size of the city, the local authority has significant negotiating power when establishing the details of the service. As for the relevance of this control instrument for the A2A, it has to be noted that it is limited to activities related to the provision of local public services, whereas energy production, where the enterprise has its core business, is not included.

A fourth and final instrument of control is represented by the activities of the Local Council and its thematic committees. However, from this study it appears that this body is oriented towards debating issues that attract media attention and that might have a political impact on the short-term, while the A2A strategic plans are not questioned before being implemented.

Citizens have also their instruments to control the performance of the A2A. These include the service charter for service delivery that establishes homogeneous quality standards. Although citizens can vote with their consumption choices, by selecting a different provider of energy services, they do not have this alternative for other protected services, such as waste collection and disposal. Local political elections appear to be the ultimate instrument to express citizens' satisfaction for the services they receive. However, electoral outcomes are influenced by a number of heterogeneous factors that are hardly entirely attributable to the performance of the A2A, especially considering that other important public services such as water management and local transportation are provided by different enterprises.

4.4. Unresolved Issues

Although the dual governance structure is used to further separate ownership from management, this model, along with ring-fenced public control, has introduced a number of inefficiency in the A2A corporate governance functioning. First, separation is weakened given that the Supervisor Board has some strategic direction functions and minority shareholders are underrepresented in this body.

Secondly, independency of the Supervisory Board remains questionable. Although formal selection requirements are met, political affiliation still plays an important role. Despite the mechanism in place in Milan's municipality can be generally considered a national good practice (IRS, 2009), it is still based on political designation given the prominent role of local councillors in submitting a candidacy and considering that the three fifth majority reflects the balance of power in the Local Council. For instance, recent episodes showed that changes in the composition of the A2A governance bodies followed changes in local political majorities along a spoil system logic.

Thirdly, in spite of recent talks about a possible change of the existing governance system, the two municipalities seem unwilling to redress the inefficiencies generated by the duplication of roles and powers. As a matter of fact, the existing model seems to be the best configuration to ensure a perfect balance of power between Milan and Brescia municipalities, also in view of a possible merger with other similar utility enterprises.[10]

Fourthly, formal control mechanisms in place in Milan's municipality are weak and undersized with respect to the number of enterprises in which the city has a shareholding. The role of control and strategic guidance of the Local Council is also reduced as compared to the past, whereas more powers are attributed to the city's major. Within this context, accountability of the A2A managers and public officers is sometimes hard to disentangle. The chain of transmission of public mandates and decisions of public interest is based upon informal and personal relations between the mayor and the representatives of the municipality in the shareholders' meeting. This also creates a fertile ground for opportunistic behaviours in local politicians where unpopular decisions, that include layoff of employees or incinerators' site location, can be passed on to the corporate level, whereas local politics can benefit from the business success of the enterprise (Citroni, Lippi, Profeti, 2013).

Finally, external controls based upon market mechanisms and regulatory institutions have brought about some progress as compared to past

---

[10] The media reported several times about possible mergers with IREN or HERA. This process is supported by the Government as a way to establish a stronger energy company following the model of the German RWE.

practices. This includes an increased quantity and quality of information available for the general public on the once public utilities' operations and performance. However, these mechanisms have several limitations with reference to the corporate governance structure and arrangements that are ruled by the Italian Civil Code and enterprises statue.

5. A Mixed Economic Performance

5.1. Beefing up Milan's City Budget

Prior to becoming a joint stock company, AEM was undoubtedly the cash cow enterprise of the city of Milan and did not require transfers from the city's administration. Time series of the enterprise's revenue show that AEM was profitable and capable to self-finance its investments. The enterprise had a low level of indebtedness, which was constrained by legal requirements, and adequate cash reserves that were invested in Italian treasury bonds.

Previous reports and economic data show that the process of corporatisation and restructuring was already in place in the period before the enterprise went public. An evidence of this trend can be found in the enterprise's profitability and productivity data. In particular, the ratio value added to turnover increased from 52.92% in 1990 to 53.91% in 1995. In the same period the Ebitda to turnover raised from 23.19% to 28.85% and the ratio net income to total assets increased from 1.85% to 2.73%.[11]

Following the enterprise's listing, the economic and financial strategy of AEM adapted to the new competitive context. Dividends were used to remunerate the public and private shareholders, investments were supported through capital markets financing, turnover and profits increased at stunning rates as a result of several acquisitions and business expansion. At the same time, at the end of the expansion phase of the business cycle, the enterprise's indebtedness grew and reached critical levels whereas profitability gradually decreased. As a result, A2A is currently prioritising debt reduction and business rationalisation, whereas future investments are expected to focus in the waste and district heating business areas, in view of an unfavourable evolution of the macroeconomic scenario for the electricity and gas markets (Kepler Cheuvreux, May 2013).

5.2. Profits, Losses and Debt Structure: Two Sides of the Same Coin

For the purpose of assessing the A2A's performance, we use the most common ratio applied in financial and economic analysis. Given

---

[11] A similar trend was also observed in other Italian public enterprises prior to privatisation (see Florio, 2000).

that the enterprise changed several times the perimeter of consolidation of its balance sheets, as a result of major mergers and acquisitions, the use of ratios reduces problems of data comparability of nominal values across time. Information and data for the following analysis are from the company's consolidated annual reports, the Amadeus Bureau Van Dijk databank, and Datastream.

Profitability is measured by the Return on Equity ratio (ROE), defined as net income divided by total equity. This analysis highlights a stable fall in A2A's profitability after 2007. The ratio shows a progressive drop from 10.04% in 2007 to -25% in 2011. The strong decrease in 2011 is mainly due to a deterioration in the operating margin caused by lower returns from sales of electricity, to capital losses from the sale to EdF of 50% of Transalpina, and to impairment charges in Edipower and EPCG. The unexpected negative performance of 2011, was reversed the following year when profits bounced back to 260 million euros. Before the decline, the ROE was fairly stable around 10%, with a positive peak in 2003 (+21.79%) due to a positive effect on net income of extraordinary events, i.e. capital gains from the sale of the stake in Fastweb SpA.

In order to further investigate such a negative trend we break down the ROE into various factors influencing the company's performance, according to practices widely discussed in the literature. To highlight the contribution of the different management areas to the company's profitability we use the Miller-Modigliani equation.[12] Two main trends emerge from this analysis: a reduction in the operating profitability and the growing level of financial debt. The analysis also highlights the volatility of non-recurring items, such as mergers and acquisitions, disposals of business units.

As for the operating performance, there has been a drop in the ROI ratio from 6.27% in 2008 to 2.64% in 2011. This drop in the profitability of the company's operations is due to macroeconomic and firm-level factors. In one hand, the economic downturn brought about a slowdown in industrial dynamics and reduced demand for electricity and gas consumption, on the other hand, some investments delivered unexpected low performance (e.g. EPCG in Montenegro).

---

[12] ROE = [(ROI-I/D)*D/E+ROI]*NI/GI. The operating performance is measured by the Return on Investments ratio (ROI), defined as earnings before interests and taxes divided by total assets. ROI is a synthetic indicator of the effectiveness and efficiency with which the company handles its operations. The contribution of the financial area is measured by two indicators: the interest burden, defined as interests divided by debt (I/D), and the debt ratio, defined as debt divided by equity (D/E). The contribution of the non-current area is given by the ratio of net income (NI) and earnings before tax and extraordinary items (GI).

We further investigate the operating performance by calculating the Return on Sales ratio (ROS), defined as Earning before interests and taxes divided by turnover. The A2A's ROS confirms the above mentioned trend: the percentage of sales revenue still available after covering all operational costs has strongly decreased due to increasing competition and shrinking margins, especially from the sales of electricity, one of the main business of the company.

The financial structure of the enterprise has significantly changed over time. Particularly, there has been a strong increase over time in the level of leverage that can be measured by the debt to equity ratio. From the A2A listing in 1998, the leverage has risen from 44.60% to 211.93% in 2011, with a peak in 2005 when the level of debt was almost three times the level of capital. Similarly, other Italian once public utilities saw a worsening of their debt exposure as compared to their capital. From 2004 to 2010, the leverage of ACEA and HERA increased up to approximately 300% and 150% respectively (IFEL, 2012).

The A2A's debt began to grow significantly in 2002. It consists mostly of medium and long-term debt aimed to finance the acquisition and development of new investments. In particular, in 2005 the growth in leverage is due to the acquisition of control of Edison and the resulting debt consolidation of the group, while in 2009 the increase in debt is mainly attributable to the acquisition of the Montenegrin company EPCG. Over time, the non-current to current liabilities ratio has grown, while the liquidity ratio, measured by current assets divided by current liabilities, highlights mounting imbalances as current liabilities start to become far superior to current assets.

The problem of excessive exposure to debt has become a serious issue also in other regulated network industries. In the UK, a 2004 survey by the Department of Trade and Industry (DTI) has shown a considerable increase of the debt by the British utilities operating in the telecommunications, energy and water sectors. Similarly, in Italy, a Court of Auditors' evaluation study about the processes of privatisation of public enterprises showed that the evolution of the debt of Italian utilities is critical. Specifically, it appears that in the case of some regulated utilities the level of debt could have been intentionally increased to strengthen enterprises' negotiating power vis-à-vis the regulator, that might have granted tariff increases in order to contain the risk of insolvency (*Corte dei Conti*, 2010).

At the same time, the company faced increased average cost of debt that reaches the highest levels in 2010 and 2011, 4.83% and 3.29% respectively. This is a consequence of the financial crisis that started in 2008 and that made financing of Italian companies more costly, but is also due to a downgrade of the A2A's credit ratings. The revision of the company's rating was mainly driven by its electricity generation activities that expose the A2A to instability of margins in the electricity industry.

5.3. Subject to Market Scrutiny

The Italian Court of Auditors (*Corte dei Conti 2010*), reckons that privatisation of utility enterprises has brought a substantial increase in the Italian stock exchange capitalisation. In particular, these shares worked as a substitute of more traditional investments in Italian Treasury Bonds and the initial public offering were generally successful. Given that control of some of these enterprises remained in public hand, investors perceived a lower level of risk as compared to other fully private enterprises. Public ownership was also seen as a guarantee for getting a generous annual dividend, because of the severe budget constraints of public finances.

We analyse the share price of the A2A and compare it with a benchmark company, Acea, a multi-utility operating in central Italy, the utility market index measured by the Italian FTSE Utilities and the market index measured by the FTSE-MIB. Share prices are daily observations from January 2000 to March 2013 and, for easy of comparison, each series is normalised and set equal to 100 on January 3, 2000 (Figure 3). Visual inspection of the plot reveals, as expected, that the two share price series tend to move together over time and to follow the market trends. Although the trend is similar, the performance of the A2A is below the sector level, the market level and the competitor for almost all the time considered.

Figure 3. Stock Price Trends (2000-2013)

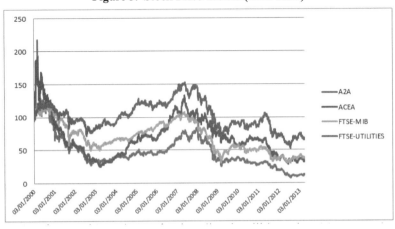

As the stock's prices of other listed utilities, the A2A's stock performance shows a high volatility. In 2003, all listed utilities in Milan's Stock Exchange, with the exception of HERA, were below their initial public offering (IPO) price, and in the case of ACEA and AEM Torino their values almost halved. In 2006 this negative trend was reversed and utilities' stock prices went above their IPO levels. One more time, the financial crisis in 2008 pushed down stock prices of utilities below their IPO levels.

While in 2003 the A2A stock prices were 23% below their IPO levels, in 2007 they were nearly 60% above the same values and dropped again significantly in 2008. However, as compared to the utility market index (FTSE IT Utility) the drop was steeper for the A2A. Specifically, the share price of the A2A lost 87% of its value between January 2000 and March 2013, while for ACEA and the market index the reduction was far less, respectively 65% and 64%. Noticeably, for the utility sector index, the reduction was much smaller, less than 34%. It appears that the A2A's stock prices are greatly exposed to stock market fluctuations as compared to other peers.

Generally, dividend payout ratios from utility enterprises have been higher than the market average, reflecting the lower risk of operating in protected markets. The dividend policy of the Italian former public utilities has been influenced by the critical conditions of the local public finances. Many articles in the Italian local media report how these revenues have become necessary even to keep running essential local services. From 2008 to 2011, the city of Brescia financed up to 36% of its current annual expenditures from the dividends paid by the A2A.

6. Conclusion

During the 1990s and 2000s various reforms of network industries have been made in Italy for introducing competition and participation of private investors in local public service supply. As in other European countries, the reformers' effort run more or less in parallel in three directions: i) liberalisation of markets, ii) changes in the regulatory systems, and iii) privatization of the incumbent national or local monopolists (Joskow, 1996). These radical changes of network industries were deemed necessary to improve service delivery, achieve higher efficiency and increase the amount of investments for new or renovated infrastructures. They also responded to the need to create an integrated market for network services within the European Union.

In Italy, the combined effect of reformed local public service provision and liberalisation of network industries, led to the establishment of large multi-utility enterprises with a mixed ownership structure. This process brought about many changes at the firm and market level, but the outcomes, in terms of improved efficiency and profitability, reduced tariffs for consumers and limited political interferences are mixed (Asquer, 2011). This study, which is focused on the evolution of the A2A from 1990s to 2012, shows that the key objectives of privatizing the enterprise, including increased managerial autonomy and efficiency and reinforced capital structure, haven't been achieved. More importantly, the hybrid nature of the enterprise has brought about a number of contradictions that undermine the long-term sustainability of the A2A.

The existing corporate governance's arrangements, that are set to establish a dominant public ownership and control over the enterprise, seem to disguise past forms of direct public interventions into the local economy, but are unable to express a clear public mandate in terms of increased welfare outcomes for Milan's and Brescia's citizens. The public owner, that in the past was able to set a model of successful entrepreneurship for delivering energy services within the public administration, is jeopardizing the enterprise's businesses in several ways.

In the context of increasingly constrained local finances, the need to contribute to the municipal budgets of the cities of Milan and Brescia has come to the detriment of the financial strength of the company. A further sell of the A2A shares, that would however keep unchanged the dominant position of the public shareholders, is currently debated by the two city's mayors as a mean to temporarily relieve local budget constraints. It seems that decisions about changing A2A's shareholding structure are determined by current financial needs rather than being based on a long-term industrial vision.

The establishment of the A2A generated too large costs for integrating the two enterprises of Milan and Brescia, especially because these are mainly justified by parochial interests. The current corporate governance arrangements, that are based on a perfect balance of powers between the two public owners, are unsuitable for running a private business in a fast changing environment and proved to be unappreciated by the market.

Political affiliation, that was supposed to be substantially reduced in the privatized enterprise, still plays a determinant role in appointing and dismissing the enterprise's managers. At the same time, Municipal Councils seems to have reduced their capacity to control the enterprise, whereas the role of mayors has become more prominent. This has led to a loss of transparency and accountability, along with a poor capacity to elaborate a consensual vision about the advantages of the public ownership and the public mission of the enterprise.

The current financial situation of the A2A reached an unsustainable level and forced the enterprise to re-focus on its core business and undertake a deleveraging strategy. Such a high level of debt is the result of substantial investments for expanding in new business areas and increasing outputs, even when industrial considerations would have pointed to a more prudent investment strategy. While the national macroeconomic scenario for energy consumption remains negative, the enterprise devises expanding in the more protected markets of waste services and district heating, where the public owner has a higher degree of autonomy for tariff setting.

Finally, the national politics has also played a key role in delineating the current scenario. The limitation of the existing ownership and governance arrangements of the Italian local multi-utilities are well-known. Current talks about creating a larger industrial group by aggregating the largest multi-utility of Northern Italy, including the A2A, are based on a reduced power of the local public shareholders that could be replaced by private investors or by the Italian Government through the Cassa Depositi e Prestiti.[13] Clearly, this would move again the electricity and gas markets towards a more concentrated structure where the supposed gains from increased competition, that have not materialised yet for the end-users, would be further uncertain.

References

AEEG, *Annual report to the European Commission on regulatory activities and the state of services in the electricity and gas sectors*, 2006 and 2011 issues.

AEEG, *Annual report on the state of services and regulatory activities*, from 2005 to 2013.

Asquer, A., "Liberalization and regulatory reform of network industries: A comparative analysis of Italian public utilities", in *Utilities Policy*, 2011, p. 19.

A2A S.P.A., *15 anni nel mercato dell'energia e dei servizi ambientali*, A2A publication, 2011.

A2A S.P.A., *Signori Azionisti – raccolta delle lettere agli azionisti di Giuliano Zuccoli dal 1996 al 2010*, A2A publication, 2012.

A2A S.P.A., *Codice Etico*, 2009.

A2A S.P.A., *Bilancio di sostenibilità*, A2A publication, from 2008 to 2011.A2A S.P.A., *Relazione sul Governo Societario e sugli Assetti Proprietari relativa all'esercizio chiuso al 31 dicembre 2009*, A2A, 2010.

A2A S.P.A., *Articles of Association*, text amended on July 2011.

Bianco, M., Sestito, P., *I servizi pubblici locali – Liberalizzazione, regolazione e sviluppo industriale*, Bologna, il Mulino, 2010.

---

[13] See Luca Pagni in *La Repubblica* of 28th May 2012 or Massimiliano Del Barba in *Corriere della Sera* of 18th September 2013.

Boffa, F., Cervigni, G., D'Orazio, A., Piacentino, D., Poletti, C., Spalletta, S., *La generazione di energia elettrica in Italia a 10 anni dal Decreto Bersani Risultati raggiunti e agenda futura*, IEFE The Centre for Research on Energy and Environmental Economics and Policy at Bocconi University research paper, 2010.

Bognetti, G., Robotti, L., "The provision of local public services through mixed enterprises: the Italian case", in *Annals of Public and Cooperative Economics*, 2007, Vol. 78, No. 3, pp. 415-437.

Bolchini, P., "Le aziende elettriche municipali", in V. Castronovo, *Storia dell'industria elettrica in Italia. Dal dopoguerra alla nazionalizzazione, 1945-1962*, Roma-Bari, Laterza, 1992.

Bortolotti, B., Scarpa, C., Pellizzola, L., "Comuni al bivio: assetti proprietari, performance e riforme nei servizi pubblici locali" in *L'Industria*, 2011, No. 1, January-March 2011.

Calabrò, A., Torchia, M., "Conflitti di interesse e meccanismi di governance nelle public utilities italiane", in *Banca, Impresa e Società*, 2011, pp. 105-136.

Cambini, C., Rondi, L., "La moderna regolazione e le public utilities: quale evidenza empirica nell'Unione europea?" in *l'Industria*, 2011, No. 1, January-March 2011.

Cassa Depositi e Prestiti, *Il mercato del gas naturale in Italia: lo sviluppo delle infrastrutture nel contesto europeo*, 2013.

Capano G., Gualmini, E., *Le pubbliche amministrazioni in Italia*, Bologna, il Mulino.

Cassese, S., *Il sistema amministrativo italiano*, Bologna, il Mulino, 1983.

Collin, S.O., "Governance Strategy: A Property Right Approach Turning Governance into Action", in *Journal of Management and Governance*, 2007, Vol. 11, No. 3, pp. 215-237.

Citroni, G., Lippi, A., Profeti, S., "Remapping the State: Inter-Municipal Cooperation through Corporatisation and Public-Private Governance Structures" in *Local Government Studies*, 2013, Vol. 39 No. 2, pp. 208-234.

Corte dei Conti – Sezione centrale di controllo sulla gestione delle amministrazioni dello Stato Collegio di controllo sulle entrate, *Obiettivi e risultati delle operazioni di privatizzazione di partecipazioni pubbliche*, Roma, 2010.

Cristofoli, D., Valotti, G., "Proprietà e corporate governance delle public utilities: tra autonomia d'impresa e tutela dell'interesse pubblico", in *Economia & Management*, 2007, No. 4.

Del Bo, C., Florio, M., *Electricity Investment: An Evaluation of the New British Energy Policy and its Implications for the European Union*, DEEM working paper, April 2012.

Department of Trade and Industry and HM Treasury, *The Drivers and Public Policy Consequences of Increased Gearing*, 2004 London.

European Commission, *Directive 96/92/EC of the European Parliament and of the Council of 19 December 1996 Concerning Common Rules for Internal Market in Electricity*, in "*Official Journal*", L.027, 30/01/1997 P. 0029-0029.

– *Directive 2003/54/EC of the European Parliament and of the Council of 26 June 2003 Concerning Common Rules for Internal Market in Electricity and Repealing Directive 96/92/EC*, in "*Official Journal*", L.176, 15/07/2003 P. 0037-0056.

– *Directive 2003/55/EC of the European parliament and of the Council of 26 June 2003 concerning common rules for the internal market in natural gas and Repealing Directive 98/30/EC.*

European Commission – Market Observatory for Energy, DG Energy, *Quarterly report on the European gas market* various volumes from 2008.

Florio, M., "Lo Stato senza proprietà", in L. Bernardi, *Finanza Pubblica Italiana. Rapporto 2000*, Bologna, il Mulino.

Florio, M., "Il declino dell'impresa pubblica: cause, effetti, prospettive", in *Democrazia e Diritto*, 2008.

Florio, M., *Network industries and social welfare – The experiment that reshuffled European Utilities*", Oxford, Oxford University Press, 2013.

Florio, M., *The Great Divesture – Evaluating the welfare impact of the British Privatization 1979-1997*, MIT Press, 2004.

Fondazione Civicum, *Le società controllate dai maggiori comuni italiani: costi, qualità ed efficienza*, 2009.

Fondazione Civicum, *Le società controllate dai maggiori comuni italiani: bilanci*, 2009.

Fraquelli, G., "Aspetti dimensionali ed efficienza nei servizi di pubblica utilità in Italia", in *L'Industria* special edition 2007.

Glachant, J.-M., "Why regulate deregulated network industries?", in *Journal of Network Industries*, 2002, Vol. 5.

Grossi, G., "Governance of Public-Private Corporations in the Provision of Local Utilities in the Italian Case", in *International Public Management Review*, 2007, Vol. 8, No. 1, pp. 130-151.

IFEL – Fondazione ANCI, *Le partecipazioni dei Comuni nelle public utilities locali – Il quadro delle regole, la dimensione del fenomeno e la percezione delle collettività*, 2012.

IRS – Fondazione Civicum, *La trasparenza delle nomine nei comuni capoluogo di regione*, 2009.

Istituto Bruno Leoni, *Privatizzare Asm: Perché Brescia può star meglio senza A2A*, 2008 IBL pamphlet.

Joskow, P., "Introducing competition into regulated network industries", in *Industrial & Corporate Change*, 1996, Vol. 5, No. 2, pp. 341-382.

Kickert, W. J.M., "Public Governance in the Netherlands: An Alternative to Anglo-American Managerialism", in *Public Administration*, 1997, Vol. 75, pp. 731-752.

Lanza, S., Silva, F., *I servizi pubblici in Italia: il settore elettrico*, Ed. il Mulino, 2006.

Marzi, G., *Concorrenza e regolazione nel settore elettrico*, Roma: Carocci, 2006.

Mele, R., Mussari, R., *L'innovazione della governance e delle strategie nei settori delle public utilities*, Bologna: il Mulino, 2009.

OECD, *OECD Guidelines on Corporate Governance of State-Owned Enterprises*, Paris, 2005.

OFWAT, *Regulatory issues associated with multi-utilities: A joint paper by the Directors General of Electricity Supply, Gas Supply, Telecommunications and Water Services, the Director General of Electricity Supply (Northern Ireland) and the Director General of Gas (Northern Ireland)*, available on Internet, 1998.

Oriolo, C. M., "Le criticità del sistema dualistico della corporate governance", in *Magistra Banca e Finanza*, 2008, Milano.

Pavese, C., *Un fiume di luce. Cento anni di storia della AEM*, Milano: Rizzoli, 2011.

Pollitt, C., Bouckaert, G., *La riforma del management pubblico*, EGEA, Milano, 2002.

Pollitt, C., "Bureaucracies Remember, Post-bureaucratic Organizations Forget?", in *Public Administration*, 2009, Vol. 87, No. 2, pp. 198-218.

Polo, M., Scarpa, C., *The liberalization of energy markets in Europe and Italy*, IGIER Working Paper 230, 2002.

Polo, M., Scarpa, C., "Liberalizing the gas industry: Take-or-pay contracts, retail competition and wholesale trade", in *International Journal of Industrial Organization*, 2013, Vol. 31, pp. 64-82.

Ranci, P., "Le infrastrutture energetiche: l'Italia ed il mercato unico europeo", in P. Manacorda, *I nodi delle reti: infrastrutture, mercato ed interesse pubblico*, 2010, Astrid.

Scarpa, C., *A2A, più che il dolor poté il digiuno*, 2012, available on the Internet www.lavoce.info.

Shepherd, W. G., "Public Enterprise: criteria and cases", in H. W. de Jung, *The structure of European Industry*, Kluwer Academic Press, Dordrect, 1989.

Testarmata, S., *The Strategies of Local Utilities After the Liberalization of the European Energy Sector: Which Is the Emerging Business Model? The Case Study of Italy*, DSI Essays Series, Milano, McGraw-Hill, 2009.

Vagliasindi, M., "Governance Arrangement for State Owned Enterprises", in *the World Bank Policy Research Working Paper*, 2008, 4542, pp. 1-36.

Valotti, G., *La riforma delle autonomie locali: dal sistema all'azienda*, Milano, Egea, 2000.

Walsh, P., Todeva, E., *Vertical and Horizontal Integration in the Utilities Sector: the case of RWE*, University of Surrey Working paper.

Williams, I., Shearer, H., "Appraising public value: past, present and futures", in *Public Administration*, 2011, Vol. 89, pp. 1367-1384.

Zorzoli, G. B., *Il mercato elettrico italiano*, Ed. Energia Viva, 2007.

Appendix

Statistical data about AEM/A2A development 1997 to 2011

AEM and A2A, electricity produced and electricity sales

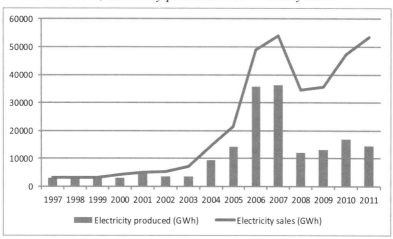

AEM and A2A, gas distributed and gas sales

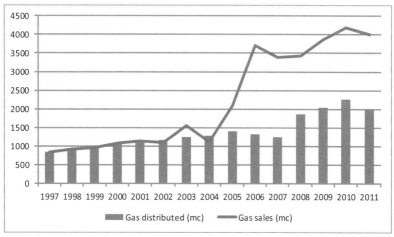

AEM and A2A, heating services sales

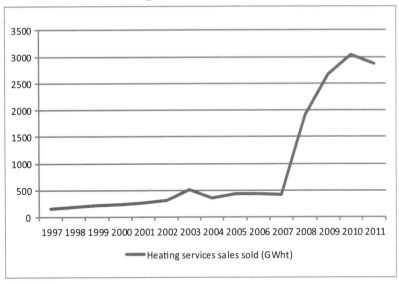

AEM and A2A, number of clients by business lines

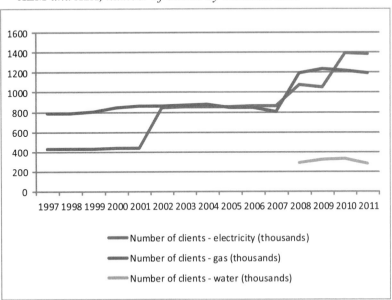

AEM and A2A economic performance from 1997 to 2011

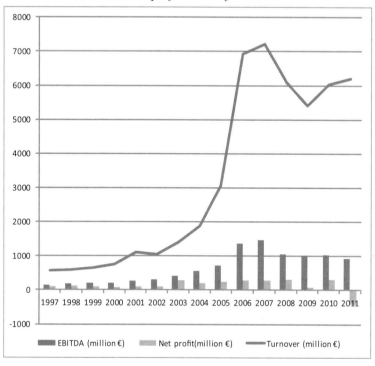

14. La Caisse de Dépôt et Placement du Québec
Straddling Between Two Worlds

Luc Bᴇʀɴɪᴇʀ

ENAP

"The current year was one of achievement, as the *Caisse* continued to reposition itself." The Board of Directors is pleased to note that the strategic orientations defined in co-operation with the depositors is taking shape and that major changes are in progress." Robert Tessier, Chairman of the Board, Annual Report, 2012.

Identification of the Enterprise

This study is about *la Caisse de dépôt et placement du Québec (CDPQ)* or, in English, the "Québec Deposit and Investment Fund" that is known in short in Canada as "*la Caisse*". When the time of the idea came to create a public pension system that was to be managed by the *Régie des Rentes du Québec*, the Government decided to create a second institution where the money accumulated would be managed. It is *la Caisse*. The idea to capitalise the money instead of a system of pay as you go was a major difference between Québec and the rest of North America at the time (Maisonneuve, 1998, p. 56). *La Caisse* was to be an important instrument for the modernisation of the Québec economy and the development of the Québec State (Morin and Megas, 2012). It has now 29 depositors for pension and insurance plans. As of December 2012, it had net asset of 176.21 billion dollars (Canadian) of which 27.6 is invested in Québec's private sector. Its credit rating is AAA. It has a double mandate of profitability for its depositors and has to contribute to the growth of the Québec economy. The dual mandate is important. As explained in this chapter, since 1966 profits have been better when *la Caisse* was also working on economic development. In other words, having more than one objective does not lead to a diminished financial performance but to the contrary to better results. The worst disaster of its history came in 2008 when its only mission was to make profits (Morin and Megas, 2012, p. 93). So, as the chairman of the Board quoted above writes, the *Caisse* has to reposition itself and find the strategy to guide its future.

When giving the speech at the National Assembly (the then Québec lower House of Parliament) on June 9, 1965 for the bill that would create *la Caisse*, Premier Jean Lesage said that it would be the most important and powerful financial instrument the Québec State has never had. This speech is still referred to by officers of *la Caisse* and quoted in annual reports. The *Caisse* was to be a financial instrument making good returns as a trust but also as already mentioned a tool of economic development. Since then, the *Caisse* has been navigating between both objectives. Some of its CEOs have insisted more on the return on investment, some on Québec's economic development, some have said the first objective is essential to the second, the last one that the issue is an exercise of casuistry as Jesuits used to practice.

The CDPQ was a huge success for many years although in the 1960s and 1970s, its managers were rather cautious in their investments. It had built a good reputation on the markets although a State actor was initially suspicious in the world of finance. Later, the CDPQ was even asked to manage pension money for third parties (Pelletier, 2002). At its peak, the CDPQ managed 250 billions of Canadian dollars. The total assets have followed the movement described by the following table taken from its 2012 annual report presenting the depositors' net assets in billions of Canadian dollars:

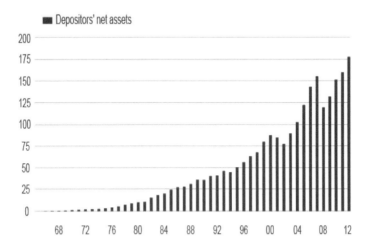

As the curve of the total assets illustrates, there have been two very difficult years in 2002 and 2008. The last decade has been the time when the *Caisse* neglected its economic development role to focus on profitability. This makes of the *Caisse* an interesting case to study. When its managers have argued for the economic development role, the financial performance has been better than when the focused on one objective only. Although, it is generally argued that public enterprises are less efficient than private enterprises because they have conflicting roles, *la Caisse* might be the counter example.

History

La Caisse was created during what has been described as the Quiet Revolution, an era of rapid modernisation when the State apparatus rapidly developed to catch up with development elsewhere in North America (Bernier, Bouchard and Lévesque, 2003). The transformation of the Québec economy wanted by the Government in the 1960s was confronted to the capacity of the English-speaking elites to resist the initiatives of the State (McRoberts, 1993, p. 135). The *Caisse* was created in an era when other public enterprises were created or radically transformed. Hydro-Québec, for example, had been created in the 1940s but the additional nationalisations of the 1960s made it the second largest public utility in North America by 1977 (McRoberts, 1993, p. 174).

The *Caisse de dépôt* was created by a provincial law sanctioned on July 15, 1965. The *Caisse* took office, as its first annual report says, on January 20, 1966. A first deposit by the Québec Pension Board (*Régie des Rentes*) on February 16 marked the beginning of its operations. The second year, they already had three more depositors: the Québec Agricultural Marketing Board, the Québec Crop Insurance Board and the Québec Deposit Insurance Board. It was also the beginning of a stock portfolio and of investment in real estate (CDPQ, Annual Report 1967). They were to be 15 depositors by 1990. The annual reports of the first decade saluted the rise of the total assets and of the annual income. The climb was spectacular: over a billion of total assets in 1970, over two in 1972, 4 in 1975. In 1976, 1977 and 1978, the assets increased by over a billion per year. In early 1980, *la Caisse* was at 10 billion and at 20 in 1984, 25 a year later, 36 in 1990, over 50 in 1995, over 100 in 1999. From 1985 to 2003, the total asset of the *Caisse* went from 20 to 40% of the GDP of Québec (Hanin, 1985, p. 26).

La Caisse was based on the model of the French *Caisse de dépots et consignations*, Belgium's *Caisse générale d'épargne et de retraite* and Sweden's National Provident Fund for Retirement Pensions. It was so suggested by the Dupont Committee that led to the creation of the *Régie des Rentes* and the pension system. The committee saw the *Caisse* as necessary to change the existing pattern on investment in Québec (Brooks and Tanguay, 1985, 102-3). The State that emerged in the 1960s was not only a welfare State but also an entrepreneurial State (Bernier *et al.*, 2003,

p. 323). In Québec, the modernisation of the State that was done in the 1960s and early 1970s is known as the Quiet Revolution. The term "Quiet Revolution" refers to three processes: an ideological revolution that led to the birth of a new nationalism; a transfer of power and responsibilities to the State; and a confrontation between the State and the elites that had dominated the society thus far: the Church, the federal Government and the English-speaking bourgeoisie (McRoberts, 1993).

Because of a lack of well-trained civil servants, most of the reforms were conducted by a small team of young technocrats. It was true for the *Caisse*. We can name the "founding fathers" among whom Jacques Parizeau who later became Minister of Finance in 1976 and later in the 1990s briefly Prime Minister of Québec. Among them was Claude Castonguay, an actuaire (Maisonneuve, 1998), a lawyer who was to be a judge of the Supreme Court of Canada and Claude Morin who also became Minister later and a banker Douglas Fullerton (Côté and Dussault, 1995, p. 27). They negotiated even directly with the Prime Minister of Canada (Maisonneuve, 1998, p. 55). The *Régie des rentes du Québec* is created following the Wheeler Dupont report on the state of pension plans (Côté and Dussault, 1995) that needed *la Caisse* to manage the money. At a time when the Government needed a pool of money for economic development while the private sector controlled by the English-speaking community did not want to lend to the Government, the *Caisse* emerged as a necessary instrument. It was a time of institutional building, an attempt to build a network of organisations to extend the limits of the Québec State. Using public enterprises, the State moved in two sectors of the economy; natural resources and finance (Bernier *et al.*, 2003, p. 324).

> The conscious use of State capital to advance industrial development in Québec dates from the 1960s, when new nationalism took institutional expression through an array of State-owned enterprises. In the same historical transition period the Québec Government set up the two agencies that today serve as formidable vehicles of investment policy – the *Société générale de financement (SGF)* and the *Caisse de dépôt et placement* (Laux and Molot, 1988, p. 144).

Québec was not the only province doing so: an inescapable feature of the provinces' growing economic role is their expanded and aggressive use of public enterprises as a policy instrument (Tupper, 1983, p. 3).

In the 1960s, the *Caisse* became an important purchaser of Québec Government bonds (McRoberts, 1993, p. 135) thus reducing the Government's dependence on English-Canadian and American financial institutions for the sale of its bonds. The *Caisse* as the SGF were created to enhance provincial autonomy (Laux and Molot, 1988, p. 144). In the fourth and fifth annual reports, it is stressed that the Fund knows that it has to play a vital role in both the primary and secondary markets for Québec and Hydro-Québec bonds. "As for the *Caisse*, the very creation of an agency to manage pension contributions in Québec was a political triumph for the province which had emerged from fractious federal-provincial negotiations in 1964 as the only jurisdiction in Canada to have independent control over such funds" (Laux and Molot, 1988, p. 145).

In the 1970s, the *Caisse* helped to finance the development of the French business class in various sectors: groceries, cable television, pulp and paper etc. Rapidly it outgrew the Québec borders and became an important investor in Canadian companies such as Noranda mining industry and the Canadian Pacific. *La Caisse* which has been in the middle of confrontations with the federal Government since its beginning has a dual mandate of managing properly the funds deposited and of economic development. The worst crisis with the federal Government was in 1981 when the owners of the then largest Canadian private company, the Canadian Pacific, were afraid that by buying shares as discussed later, the creation of the *Caisse* was seen by both French and English speaking businessmen as "galloping socialism" (McRoberts, 1993, pp. 163 and 168).

In the eighth annual report, it is reported that Marcel Cazavan who had been the deputy Minister of Finance and Board member replaced Claude Prieur who died suddenly. By 1974, over 40% of the revenues came from the income on the deposits and the remaining from the new deposits. Despite its cautious approach, by then, *la Caisse* had the largest individual portfolio of Canadian equities in the country. Cazavan was very careful in his investment policies (Arbour, 1993, pp. 23-24).

In the late 1980s, as elsewhere, privatisation became popular or rolling back the State. Québec did the same and a special group was constituted to analyse what should be sold. For the group, the Quiet Revolution was dead and most public enterprises should be privatised but not the *Caisse de dépôt* (McRoberts, 1993, 406-7). In short, the committee sought to reduce drastically the network of public enterprises and through that many of them had outlived their usefulness. For the others, among whom *la Caisse*, the structures had to be changed.

Public Mission: Economic Development

The pension system in Québec is like an insurance system. Employees and employers contribute to ensure that at retirement age, workers will have a minimum income. *La Caisse* is the fiduciary of the pension system. The mission of the *Caisse* is not in the law of 1965 but in the speech of Jean Lesage and for a long time new employees at the *Caisse* were given a copy of the speech.

If the law did not specify the mission, it contained various technicalities limiting what the *Caisse* could do. According to Roland Parenteau who then was the President of the *Conseil d'orientation économique*, some of the restrictions in the law were built in because at the time, it was not believed that French-Canadians could manage a huge financial organisation and they had to be protected from themselves. These constraints such as the percentage of the total assets that could be invested in stock actions have been diminished over the years. Officially, it was to limit the risk associated with the portfolio of investments and to avoid interference with market rules (Morin and Megas, 2012, p. 97).

As stated in the first annual report (p. 5) in the section on investment policy that was the first task to be addressed y the board of directors, there was a "Manifest intention on the part of the legislators to create an institution to which a role would be given in the financing of the economic development of Québec." And further in the same page "Thus, when choosing between two investments of equal quality and price, preference will be given to that which seems more likely to favour the economic development of the Province even if it should entail some relative reduction in the diversification of the portfolio."

In the third annual report, *la Caisse* (AR, 1968, p. 8) is already more cautious: "(…) the investment policy of the Fund must give primary consideration to the security and growth of the capital. Without compromising the foregoing principles, the Fund must also use its best endeavours to promote the economic development of Québec". That year, the report also mentions corporate financing and direct placements. That year, although the ceiling for the stock portfolio is at 30% of the total assets, the *Caisse* remains in practice at 14.5%. In the seventh annual report, again the primary role of the protection of capital is reaffirmed together with the structuring impact of the *Caisse* on financial and monetary markets and an impact on the Canadian market. The annual report also mentions the role of the *Caisse* in helping Québec companies that enter or will enter the stock exchange.

In the 1976 Annual report, the investment policy was presented in "four primary objectives: protection of capital, attainment of a return compatible with the risk taken, sound diversity in investments, and promotion of the economic growth of Québec" (p. 9). As for the previous year, the annual report in 1978 starts its investment policy section by referring to the speech to the Legislative Assembly of June 9, 1965, but the first section that year is about economic and social objectives, not only the fiduciary role. There is an explanation that economic development and the fiduciary roles are compatible. And the four previous principles or objectives are reaffirmed but there is a sub-section on economic promotion that gives a few examples of what has been accomplished and again referring to the 1965 speech (p. 15). Such a list of examples was given also in 1980.

The 1979 Annual report is the one of a new departure. Marcel Cazavan is replaced by Jean Campeau as CEO. The new investment policy for the 1980s is planned. The report suggests that *la Caisse* is now strong enough to play a more innovative role. And be more involved in the financing of Québec private enterprises. The 1981 annual report talks of economic development first (p. 8) and that the fiduciary role should not be neglected. "The reorientation of the *Caisse* into an aggressive player in the marketplace shows that provincial Governments, unlike the federal Government, can target investments to shape industrial development" (Laux and Molot, 1988, p. 148). In their study, Brooks and Tanguay (1985) found that there was little evidence to support claims that the investment policy of this agency is influenced in a direct and systematic way by the political objectives of the PQ Government. In 1986, it is clearly a double mission after celebrating, a year before, the extraordinary financial results obtained. In 1990, after Campeau has left, the double mandate is again spelled out in the annual report.

In the early 1980s, *la Caisse* became more aggressive in its investment policy (McRoberts, 1993, p. 377). As explained in the 1981 Annual report, *la Caisse* flexes its muscles. It becomes an important owner of Noranda, the giant mining enterprise in association with a private holding. It also becomes a major owner of Domtar, the pulp and paper company, this time in association with another public enterprise, la Société Générale de Financement. It was the first visible sign of a more active investment policy although from 1973 until 1983, private sector equity proportion in *la Caisse*'s portfolio did not increased (Brooks and Tanguay, 1985, p. 108). The Caisse was to become a more proactive stockholder in a number of companies (Annual report 1985). This participation to boards of private companies by managers of the *Caisse* or by businessmen sympathetic to *la Caisse* is a way to coordinate economic activities but a very weak one. At the time of the Brooks and Tanguay study, *la Caisse* had representatives on 15 boards but return on investment remained the priority (1985, pp. 117-119). If we go back in time, the most important and revealing crisis that the *Caisse* faced on its investment policy was around a federal bill name S-31 in the early 1980s. *La Caisse* had wanted to invest and have representatives on the board of Canadian Pacific, then the largest company in Canada. The bill was initiated by the Government in the Senate in order to have immediate effect. The federal Minister in charge of the S-31 bill claimed in his testimony at the Canadian Senate that *la Caisse* was a tool of "socialism", the instrument for the covert nationalisation of major sectors of Québec's and Canada's economies (Brooks and Tanguay, 1985, p. 100). For a long time, the *Caisse* statute placed the ceiling for a shareholding in any one company at 30%. As Laux and Molot (1988, p. 146) noted, this was an ambiguous figure: "It conforms to the notion that the *Caisse* should remain a passive financier, but in today's corporate world it is a proportion that often translates into control."

In the 1993 and 1994 Annual reports, in a difficult period for *la Caisse*, the mission presented insists on the rate of return and the contribution to the dynamism of the Québec economy, more financial again. The President of the Board in his messages then states that the mission should not be reconsidered but that confronted to evolving financial markets, the ways of achieving it have to be reinvented. Among the elements he looks at is the increasing role of institutional investors such as *la Caisse* that contribute to transform the relations between managers and stockholders. In 1995, under the new CEO who for the first time comes from the ranks of the institution, the maximisation of the financial performance is presented as the *raison d'être* of *la Caisse* with a second mandate, *les bénéfices économiques accessoires* (the incidental economic fallouts).

In annual reports, the evolution of the double mandate can be followed as Morin and Megas (2012) did for the years 1985 until 2008. Over the years, the economic development mission was neglected in favour of the maximisation of profits that was the rule when the 2008 *debacle* hit. It was the second time in a decade that a financial disaster struck the *Caisse*. In 2003, the new CEO starts his message in the annual report by saying that the institution has recentered itself on managing assets for its depositors. In 2004 and 2005, optimal returns and economic development in annual reports are stressed. In 2004 with the new law, the mission of the *Caisse* was specified:

> The mission of the Fund is to receive moneys on deposit as provided by law and manage them with a view to achieving optimal return on capital within the framework of depositors' investment policies while at the same time contributing to Québec's economic development.

Although it was neglected over the 2002-2008 period, the need to contribute to economic development came back with Michael Sabia after the difficulties of 2008. The double mission had been clear under Jean Campeau (1980-1990) and Delorme-Savard (1990-1994) (Morin and Megas, 2012). According to the message of the Chairman of the Board in the 2012 Annual report, what the *Caisse* does for the Québec economy is to:

– make investments (loans and equity) in companies;

– support well-managed small and medium-sized businesses in partnership with Desjardins;

- support the well-established companies that want to expand internationally;
- invest in small mining companies;
- provides venture capital for technology companies;
- helps new entrepreneurs, in cooperation with several partners.

The CEO, in his message in the same report insists on four key words: balance (between returns and risk), performance, flexibility (to seize investment opportunities) and Québec. He presents five priorities:

- absolute-return management: invest on the basis of strong convictions rather than major stock-market indexes by selecting high quality companies and foster long-term relationships with promising companies;
- less-liquid assets: invest in assets whose value is directly linked to the real economy and increase investments in private equity, infrastructure and real estate;
- Québec: invest in the market we know best: seek out and seize the best business and investment opportunities, serve as a bridge between Québec companies and global markets and strengthen the next generation of entrepreneurial and financial leadership;
- emerging markets: capitalise on growth in these markets; understand emerging markets better by drawing on the expertise of local partners with in-depth understanding of them and increase direct and indirect investments in these regions;
- depth of expertise and processes: 1) deepen the understanding of assets and sectors: emphasize in-house portfolio management, develop multidisciplinary research, strengthen operational and sector expertise and continue to integrate risk management and investment decisions, and 2) simplify approaches: improve systems and processes to achieve greater operational efficiency.

La Caisse has, of course, a responsible investment policy and a sustainability policy, and produce annual reports on these matters.

Operations

During the first year of operations, the portfolio was composed primarily of long-term bonds (CDPQ, AR 1966, p. 6). The deposits received that year amounted to $ 178.5 million (Canadian). There were then 23 employees. In the early years of *la Caisse*, it was managed with excessive caution. It was not until the 1970s that the *Caisse* had begun to play a more effective role (McRoberts, 1993, p. 174). In its second annual report, the *Caisse* stressed that it invested in "good quality stocks with a defensive potential". The 1978 annual report indicates that the return on investment has been improving every year since 1966 (p. 12). The auto insurance becomes that year the biggest depositor, surpassing the *Régie des Rentes* for the first time. In 1979, the annual report states that the salary reform was necessary because the *Caisse* was losing too many employees to the private sector.

In 1980, according to the Annual report, *la Caisse* was allowed, as the Albertan Heritage Fund, to lend to the Québec Government at a rate equivalent to the best rate available to a Canadian province (Annual reports, Brooks and Tanguay, 1985). The quality of the investments of *la Caisse* could also be debated. Comparing the Alberta Heritage Fund which had a purely passive investor behaviour with *la Caisse*, Pesando (1985), looked at how having secondary objectives such as economic development could influence the risk-returns trade-offs. This author considered it difficult to empirically establish whether pursuit of the second objective conflicted with the standard fiduciary objective. The portfolio of 1982 was not efficiently enough diversified and thus risky.

By 1983, for the first time, the *Régie des Rentes* stopped depositing money to pay pensions. So the growth had to come from revenues generated. Also a first that year, the *Caisse* started an international portfolio. At the same time, *la Caisse* developed minority participations in several small and medium size enterprises in Québec, initially above 500 000 dollars and later under this line (Annual report 1990, p. 6). It was certainly one of the main actors on the Montreal Stock Exchange as long as it existed. According to its 2012 Annual report, *la Caisse* has decided to reinforce its management support functions, an initiative started in 2011. The information technology, human resources and financial control, as well as monitoring of major investments have been improved.

An important operation for *la Caisse* is to manage its collaboration with its depositors. The eight main depositors (out of a total of 29) represent 97.25% of the total net assets: the Government and public employees retirement plan, the retirement plans sinking fund, the *Régie des rentes du Québec*, the Supplemental pension plan for employees of the Québec construction industry, the *Commission de la santé et sécurité du travail*, the *Société de l'assurance automobile du Québec*, the Pension plan of management personnel and the Generation Funds.

According to the 2012 Annual report, the *Caisse* offers depositors to allocate their funds to various specialised portfolios according to an investment policy with target returns, objectives for value added, benchmark indexes and risk monitoring. *La Caisse* reorganised in 2009 its portfolio offering and risk management (Annual Report 2012).

According to its 1998 Annual report, *la Caisse* has become the most important owner of real estate in Canada as well as having the largest portfolio of stock actions. It is by then active in 40 countries with offices around the world. By 2005, after the technology bubble, the reference was Canada and in his message, the CEO stressed that he wanted Quebeckers to be proud of *la Caisse*.

Over the years, the structure of *la Caisse* has evolved often. In 1996, *la Caisse* decided to create subsidiaries. The idea was to concentrate the expertise on specific areas such as telecommunications. In 2001, there was another remodelling with the creation of CDP Capital where the activities of managing investments would be regrouped whereas the corporate activities such as relations with depositors, human resources, audit, institutional relations where to remain with *la Caisse*. A structure was created in which Michel Nadeau, who had been with *la Caisse* for 17 years, was made number two (Bourdeau, 2001). Without separating the Presidence of the board from the job of CEO, it made possible to create a position responsible for operations distinct from strategic planning.

The 1988 Annual report mentions the sophistication of the financial instruments *la Caisse* is playing with. By 2000, *la Caisse* considers capable of being a world leader. Reuters Survey 2000 considered that it was the best financial manager in Canada among 292 comparable enterprises in Canada. It was managing funds for various customers outside its depositors. It was also the greatest Canadian investor on world markets. Québec was now too small for *la Caisse* who had expanded its network of offices around the world. It had also heavily invested in technology and communications companies, accompanying the movement of mergers then in vogue in this industry (in terms of contents and supporting devices). In the annual reports of 2002 and 2003, there are references to the necessity to reduce the cost of operations. Also, the management of risks has become a reality.

The 2010 Annual report presents the collaboration with the depositors as an essential element. The other three objectives are profitability, risk management and be more active in Québec. In the 2011 annual report, it is mentioned that *la Caisse* has invested that year more in Québec than in the United States. The 2011 report starts with a comment about the rebuilding of the institution.

Performance

As said earlier, excluding more ordinary results in the early 1990s, *la Caisse* had been a success story for many years. For most of its history, *la Caisse* has been achieving interesting results, generally above its "indices of reference" (Morin and Megas, 2012: 113). For 2012, the weighted average return was 9.6% and since the reorganisation in July 2009, an annualised return of 10.7%. Before the end of the technology bubble, the CDP had a rate of return of 20% on its investment. In 2000, the then CEO Jean-Claude Scraire decided to present his global strategy. It was to improve the performance of the *Caisse*, nothing was said about economic development (Morin and Megas, 2012, p. 106). In order to generate more profits, *la Caisse* developed international activities over the years 1990 and early 2000. The CDPQ opened offices around the world.

In 2003, it was back making profits. Part of the problem in 2002 was due to large investments in the new economy. Other problems arose. The Auditor general had to review the building of the new facilities of *la Caisse* in Montréal in 2003. The project was poorly managed according to the report. The building appeared too costly compared to similar examples in Montreal (VGQ, 2003). Around 2000, *la Caisse* decided to invest in "Montréal Mode" that was rapidly closed down after another audit by the Auditor General. It was more than investing, it was getting into the management of fashion companies. The idea was to help create in Montréal an internationally competitive high fashion industry and give the administrative support the businesses in the sector lacked. *La Caisse* was not able to find a business partner with whom to share the risk. The adventure lasted three years and a half. Financially, it was negligible for *la Caisse* but detrimental to its image.

The question was how to do better than the banner years of the end of the 1990s. Involvement in China and Hollywood began. A sense of invincibility existed among managers. Then, it had two years of negative returns: -4.99 and -9.57%. 8.5 billions of dollars were lost that year. When things turned sour, the initial reaction was to reconsider how the organisation had been governed for a number of years. A new world required a radical change in the organisation. Confidence had disappeared and a new skill set was required internally to work on more sophisticated markets as the then new CEO presented in his speeches. Over time, the operations of *la Caisse* became more complex but the mechanisms to control them were not improved (Castonguay, 2002). After 2004, a culture of financial innovation became the new culture (Pineault, 2009). For Hanin (2005), after 2002, the model of *la Caisse* was to concentrate exclusively on the fiduciary role. One of the issues raised was that the board of directors did not know what was going on. Another issue was that the board could not fire the CEO because he had a mandate for ten years from the Government. Another issue considered was that the regulations over how to invest the money had been abandoned over the years. Initially, stock in private companies could not represent more than 30% of the total assets. It had been moved to 70%. Was that too much? A new governance system was established. In the end, the role of the board of directors was reconsidered and the independence of the members strengthened. The focus on third parties was changed for a reorientation and focusing on the institutional clients that were the core business. The *Caisse* looked for new models such as the Norvegian Petroleum Fund for examples of how to reorganise its activities. Managing by projects has become a tool of management. Above everything else, the team of managers was radically changed. Several managers who had allowed the CDP to achieve the impressive results before the crisis were considered obsolete and fired. The questions about the existence of the CDP have stopped. Other organisations from around the world now visit the CDP to learn lessons.

In 2008, at the height of the financial crisis, again *la Caisse* had a disastrous year. The total assets went down by 35.2 billion $ (Canadian). The year before, the assets managed were of 227 billion $ (Morin and Megas, 2012, p. 92). According to Morin and Megas (2012, p. 100), between 1985 and until the nomination of Henri-Paul Rousseau as CEO in 2002, the *Caisse* had been able to both achieve good returns and contribute to economic development. What was going to be an important element of the problem in 2008 were third-party asset-backed commercial papers that were not properly managed (Morin and Megas, 2012, p. 103). In 2008, *la Caisse* lost 39.8 billions $ (Canadian). The rate of return was of minus 25 while other retirement funds in Canada were at plus 18.4. The total assets went down from 155.4 billion to 120.1 including the new deposits. The previous worst year was 2002 at minus 9.57. It was poor management when for that year *la Caisse* was doing worst than anyone else on bonds, stock, etc. (Bérubé, 2009).

Governance

According to the Lesage speech of 1965, there were to be two essential principles in the governance of the CDPQ: independence of the management *vis-à-vis* the Government and coordination of the operations with the overall economic policy of the State. This was to be achieved through the board of managers (Morin and Megas, 2012, p. 96). Lesage also said that no member of the board or their companies could borrow from the CDPQ. Until the 1980s, there were interlocking directorates for coordination but the practice stopped to be used since then (Bernier and Burlone, 2000). Policy coordination has been weak in general as discussed further. For the independence of *la Caisse*, it has always been debated.

As the first annual report indicates (p. 4), the Board of Directors counted seven members and three associate members. The board is chaired by the manager general. The vice-chairman is the President of the Québec Pension Board. The other members were two senior civil servants, the President of a labour union and two representatives of the financial community, one English-speaking and the other one French-speaking. The associate members were the Deputy Minister of Finance (the highest civil servant in the department), the employee in charge of Finance at Hydro-Québec at that time (later, Hydro-Québec's treasurer), and the vice-President of the Québec Municipal Commission. There have been variations since then but the general idea has persisted.

In 1977, the Bill 97 (Chapter 62 of the laws of the province of Québec) specifies that the board of directors is constituted of the CEO of the *Caisse*, the President of the *Régie des rentes* and 7 other members nominated for three years among whom are two officers of the Government or the directors of a Government agency, a representative of associations of employees and another to be chosen from among the directors of cooperative associations. The law specifies that no member of the board shall have an interest in a security business. The year after, the annual report presents that following the law the number of board members is now of 9 voting members and 3 non-voting (the civil servants and the President of the Municipal Commission). For the first time, the employees of *la Caisse* are not civil servants and thus their salaries can be closer to those of the private sector. The law was changed again in 1987 to give more flexibility to *la Caisse* in its investment policy.

There is more to governance than the board of directors. "Government direction thus comes through an informal, interpersonal path and by way of management and board appointments that insure compatibility of objectives" (Laux and Molot, 1988, p. 146). This summary is still accurate. Campeau was frequently on the phone with the Minister of Finance (Arbour, 1993, p. 27). For many critics of the *Caisse*, its autonomy remained controversial over time (Laux and Molot, 1988, p. 146). For some, more direction from Government was necessary for improved economic development. The closest relation between the Minister of Finance and the CEO of the *Caisse* could have been when Jacques Parizeau was Minister and Jean Campeau was the head of the *Caisse*. Campeau who was maintained by the Liberals after 1985 had been a student of Parizeau at HEC in Montreal and had before entering the *Caisse* a career that prepared him well for the job. It was a time when "strategic" enterprises for the Québec economy were targeted and board members replaced at the end of their terms.

Over the years, this public enterprise has had to manage several deposits related to the activities of the Québec State: car insurance for example. It has had over the years an excellent record on returns on investment on the assets it managed. This, until the technology bubble ended and September 11, 2001 created turmoil on the market. It undertook then a review of its governance, seriously considering changing the length of the mandate of its CEO and who is to be nominated on its board. It has returned to profitability over the last two years.

After the technology bubble crisis, the governance of the CDPQ was transformed. The model borrowed from the private sector developed for the *Caisse* in 2004 was to be generalised in 2006 to the other public enterprises in Québec (Morin and Megas, 2012, p. 99; Bernier and Pelletier, 2008). The effective division between a President of the board and the CEO was suggested in 2002 by the then President and CEO, Jean-Claude Scraire. In 2002, the new structure of the board became effective with three committees: audit, human resources and risk management (later governance and ethics) when Henri-Paul Rousseau arrived as CEO. By 2004, two third of the directors were to be independent. When the disaster struck in 2008, members of the audit committee of the board complained that they knew nothing of the commercial papers (Couture, 2009). As Morin and Megas (2012, p. 111) have calculated, from 1985 until 2005, the percentage of board members coming from the Government oscillated generally between 40 and 50 while board members from the private sector represented between 30 and 40 until 2007 when they climbed above 50%.

After years avoiding the issue, the question was raised in 2009 about the participation of the President of the cooperative movement Desjardins at the board of directors of *la Caisse*. Is it a conflict of interest (Desjardins, 2009)? The question was also asked about the President of the union movement who also is the President of the worker's fund, *le Fond de Solidarité*. Some could see useful interlocking directorates to coordinate the activities of these organisations. Some of the potential investments could also interest the cooperative bank. At the same time, the Minister of Finance asked for her deputy Minister to be reintegrated on the board. The previous reform had omitted him in 2004. The independent members of the board are paid to participate. They have an annual compensation of 17,385 dollars. Committee chairs receive an additional 5,433 dollars and there are attendance fees. The total compensation varies for an average of 33,209 dollars. It is not bad for the boards on Québec public enterprises but far lower than in the private sector.

In theory, the CEO is selected according to a process that is in the law. In 2009, the choice of the new CEO was made more in the premier's office than by the board (Cousineau, 2009C). Some have argued such as Sophie Cousineau (2009B), an economic columnist for the Montreal based newspaper *La Presse*, that other candidates would have been better than the current CEO. He was selected after the President of the board was selected and with ties to the chief of staff of the Prime Minister with whom he had worked for the federal Government. In 2009, former board members considered that the nomination of the new CEO was improvised (Desjardins, 2009). This said, the results thus far have been good.

Until the last decade, the CEO of the *Caisse* was nominated for ten years. Only Jean Campeau completed his term. Claude Prieur died while in charge and the others were removed after difficult years such as the ones under the Delorme-Savard team. In 1990 for the first time, the CEO is not the President of the board. The experience lasted for four years. Now, in Québec's public enterprises, there is a President of the board of directors separate from the CEO. Before, this model had thus been attempted at the *Caisse* with Delorme and Savard.

YEARS	PB	CEO
1966-1973		Claude Prieur
1973-1980		Marcel Cazavan
1980-1990		Jean Campeau
1990-1995	Jean-Claude Delorme	Guy Savard
1995-2002		Jean-Claude Scraire
2002-2008	Pierre Brunet	Henri-Paul Rousseau
	(2005-2008)	
2008		Intérim Guay
2009-	Robert Tessier	Michael Sabia

Most of these Presidents had experience in finance. The only one recruited from the inside was Scraire who had been working at *la Caisse* for 15 years before getting promoted. For a long time, salaries were quite low at *la Caisse*. Jean Campeau believed that these employees were "missionaries". Lately, the top salary has climbed. Henri-Paul Rousseau was making around close to two million $ (Canadian) per year with a very generous retirement plan to hide part of his income (Morin and Megas, 2012, p. 108). The authority to fix the income of the CEO has been delegated by the Government to the board according to the 2004 law. The salaries of the top managers were also climbing quickly, closer to the market ones in the private sector. In 2009, after the crisis hit *la Caisse*, salaries were brought back down. The new CEO, Michael Sabia, was making half a million $ (Canadian), not over a million like Rousseau's salary and will not receive a pension plan as his predecessor (Morin and Megas, 2012, p. 109). When do you replace CEOs? According to the following table taken from the 2012 Annual report, it is when you have financial difficulties. Delorme and Savard left after 1994, Scraire left after 2002 and Rousseau in 2008. The 1980s when the *Caisse* was interventionist was also clearly a time of excellent financial results. Cazavan was replaced by Campeau in 1980 because the Government wanted a more proactive CDPQ.

The Caisse's overall return. 1966-2012
(for period ended December 2012)

Year	Overall return (in %)	Total assets under management (in millions of dollars)*	Year	Overall return (in %)	Total assets under management (in millions of dollars)*
1966	6.4	179	1990	0.5	37,304
1967	(1.2)	383	1991	17.2	42,061
1968	4.4	653	1992	4.5	42,370
1969	(4.4)	866	1993	19.4	48,022
1970	12.8	1,321	1994	(2.1)	46,491
1971	14.1	1,783	1995	18.2	52,899
1972	10.8	2,312	1996	15.6	61,533
1973	3.4	2,895	1997	13.0	70,959
1974	(5.6)	3,168	1998	10.2	86,695
1975	12.5	3,949	1999	16.5	106,003
1976	18.3	5,210	2000	6.2	124,708
1977	10.9	6,448	2001	(5.0)	131,657
1978	9.9	7,910	2002	(9.6)	129,673
1979	7.2	9,254	2003	15.2	139,209
1980	9.9	10,965	2004	12.2	175,518
1981	(1.9)	11,448	2005	14.7	216,153
1982	32.8	16,110	2006	14.6	236,953
1983	17.0	19,004	2007	5.6	257,745
1984	10.1	20,785	2008	(25.0)	220,424
1985	24.0	25,243	2009	10.0	201,245
1986	13.5	28,080	2010	13.6	199,130
1987	4.7	28,914	2001	4.0	204,178
1988	10.5	31,798	2012	9.6	259,136
1989	16.9	37,493			

Since 1993, the Caisse has recorded its investments and other related assets and liabilities at market value. Previously, investments were recorded at cost, at amortized cost, or at the amount determined by the equity method. Total assets from 1966 to 1992 inclusively have been adjusted to reflect this change in accounting method.

Officially, the *Ministère de tutelle*, the Ministry responsible for *la Caisse* is Finance. But as one of the higher civil servants we interviewed said: "They don't have problems with the department, they go directly to the office of the Prime Minister." As for Hydro-Québec, *la Caisse* is too important for the Prime Minister not to be informed of what is going on there. It is part of the arm's length relation. The informal discussions have varied over time. Some Prime Ministers such as Robert Bourassa spent hours every day on the phone and often with the CEO of the *Caisse*.

La Caisse and Coordination. Is There a *Modèle Québécois*?

For Laux and Molot (1988, pp. 145-146), it could once be argued that the public enterprises in Québec constituted a network. *La Caisse* invested in joined projects with other State-owned enterprises. The control of Domtar, the giant pulp and paper company was achieved with the SGF (*Société générale de financement*). Investments in *Gaz métropolitain* were done jointly with another public enterprise, Soquip. The *Caisse* was holding bonds and mortgages and sometimes took minority equity shares. It was still a fiduciary agent and an underwriter of the established public sector. Improved coordination among the *Caisse*, the SGF and the *Société de Développement Industriel* that was to become Investissement Québec was required to improve state direction over Québec's economic development. For Brooks and Tanguay quoted by Laux and Molot, there was only a broad coincidence between *la Caisse* investments and Government policy.

The CDPQ's activities are completed by other public enterprises: *la Société générale de financement* and Investissement Québec. In addition to these agencies, there are in Québec's social economy sector, the credit union movement Desjardins and workers union financial arms: *Fonds de solidarité* and *Fondaction*. Together they constitute a complementary network of financial institutions (Bernier *et al.*, 2003). There are partnerships between *la Caisse* and Desjardins for small and medium-sized enterprises.

How strongly are they coordinated is more open for debate but there is convergence in their actions. For Hanin (2005), using the theory of institutional complementarities of Bruno Amable, the answer is yes. Being an active shareholder allows to receive information useful to improve the profitability of *la Caisse*. The public enterprises are supposed to have specialised missions that do not overlap. For various reasons, the SGF and *Investissement Québec* have been merged resulting in better coordination and the Québec Government is currently considering transforming it in a development bank. It could be argued that the overall system or model is a way to defend the general interest in an era where governance is shared between the State and various groups in society (Bernier *et al.*, 2003, p. 339).

Regulation

The new more active profile that was backed by an increasing capital was not well accepted in English-Canada in the early 1980s. The *Caisse*'s request for membership of the board of directors of Canadian Pacific in which *la Caisse* had a 9% holding was rejected by the President of the company. The federal Government convinced by him that a national company should not be controlled by a provincial enterprise introduced what is known as bill S-31: An Act to Limit Shareholding in Certain Corporations. The specific prohibition was that no Government shall hold or beneficiary own more than 10% of the shares. The federal Government could but not the provinces (Laux and Molot, 1988, p. 149). A particularity was that, contrary to the tradition, the bill was initiated in the Senate instead of the House of Commons and thus effective immediately. For Brooks and Tanguay (1985, p. 113), it was clearly the request by the *Caisse* for representation on the board of Canadian Pacific, then the largest private company in Canada that prompted the bill, a federal bill that targeted a single public enterprise owned by a Canadian province. If it had become a law, *la Caisse* could have pleaded discriminatory treatment (Brooks and Tanguay, 1985, p. 115).

> A richer explanation sees S-31 as resulting from a confluence of corporate and state interests. For corporations, the Bill provided a bulwark against provincial Government influence in profitable, nationally significant firms. For the federal Government, S-31 promised to curb provincial Government investment strategies, enhance federal control over such strategies, and strengthen federal jurisdiction over transportation. In this alliance, corporations were defending themselves against threatening provincial interventions while Ottawa was once again on the offensive in its continuing struggle with the provinces (Tupper, 1983, p. 19).

For Tupper (1983, p. 29), Bill S-31 was "a mixture, par excellence, of bad politics and inadequate economics." He adds that it was paternalistic and that it was an offensive against province-building. Tupper (1983, p. 7) quotes a ruling from the Québec Superior Court that the *Caisse* is immune from certain provisions of Canada Business Corporations Act but has to obey the Ontario Securities Commission regulations.

Other elements concerning the governance or the regulation of *la Caisse* has to do with the role of the Auditor General. Since 2006, the Auditor general has an increased role concerning public enterprises in Québec (see Bernier and Pelletier, 2008). In 2004, during the parliamentary commission on the new law, he had complained that the new law did not increase his power over *la Caisse*. Several restrictions were initially applied to the *Caisse* investment policy. For equity investments, "the fund could not hold more than 30% of any single corporation's equity, nor could it invest more than 30% of its total assets in common shares" (Brooks and Tanguay, 1985, 104-5). In other words, the *Caisse* was not to become a holding company. These controls have been diminished by changes to the law of *la Caisse*. The other controls such as parliamentary commissions (standing committees), obligations on strategic plans, annuals reports, etc. are normalised in Québec (Bernier and Pelletier).

Conclusions and Lessons Learned

In an early evaluation, Fournier (1978) considered that *la Caisse* surpassed expectations regarding the yield of its investments, doing better than most other pension funds. For its economic policy function, its greatest success was in reducing the Government's dependence on the financial syndicate and in stabilising Québec's capital markets in times of crisis (Brooks and Tanguay, 1985, p. 106). For Fournier, the *Caisse* was too autonomous from the Government to participate into coordinated economic policy. For business leaders surveyed in 1984, *la Caisse* was not sufficiently independent of the Québec Government (Côté and Courville, 1984). The Prime Minister of Canada expressed concerns about the *Caisse* (Brooks and Tanguay, 1985, p. 112).

Pierre Arbour (1993) who managed the portfolio of *la Caisse* from 1967 until 1976 published a book to explain that *la Caisse* and the other public enterprises in Québec have been failures. The positive result he saw was in the profitability mission. Most of his examples of poor decisions by public enterprises are in other institutions but he also covers the most publicised acquisitions by *la Caisse* that went wrong. He concludes (p. 112) that in all Governments, all that could be privatised should be. Gagnon (1996) wrote an article to contradict the financial analysis done by Arbour as very bad science.

All this said, *la Caisse* has become the powerful instrument Jean Lesage dreamed of. It was that power that made the business community and the federal Government so nervous in the early 1980s. By 2002, *la Caisse* had become a very complicated organisation that the new President decided to simplify. Financially, *la Caisse* has been a success but the technology adventure and the very bad 2008 financial results make wonder if it was not managed by apprentice sorcerers. In the years between 2002 and 2008, *la Caisse* used very sophisticated policy instruments that backfired. The depositors were not pleased with the methods used (Dutrisac, 2009). But over the 1980s, clearly the years when the *Caisse* was more interventionist, it also got excellent financial results.

In Québec where the French-speaking workers were economically considered as second-class citizens until the 1960s, the development of public enterprises was important to change who was in control of the economy. The *Caisse* first allowed the Québec Government to escape the colonialist control it had known until then. *La Caisse* was to have a role to "help stabilise and deepen the market for Québec issues" and to loosen the control of the English-speaking financial establishment (Brooks and Tanguay, 1985, p. 104). Despite all the help from the Québec Government, French-speaking businessmen have remained very critical of its economic role (McRoberts, 1993, p. 361; Laux and Molot, 1988, p. 149). Is *la Caisse* too far or too close to political power? For Brooks (1987, p. 323), *la Caisse* had greater formal autonomy than the Alberta Heritage Fund. It could also have been a more active stockholder but even a rather passive role made the private sector nervous. And in a sector not much discussed here, *la Caisse* has been doing very well at managing its portfolio of real estate.

In 2004, when the new law was voted, commentators, editorialists, analysts concluded that the mistakes of the past would now be avoided (see Pratte, 2004). It was true until 2008. *La Caisse* was also supposed to be more independent and thus further from political pressures. Also, the economic development mission disappeared, profit was to be the new mission (Dutrisac, 2004). It failed because of poor risk management (Cousineau, 2009A). By 2008, *la Caisse* had become a manager of funds like the others. Rates of return and the market were the only rationale (Morin and Megas, 2012, p. 113). The changes to the governance of *la Caisse* over the years have not made possible to avoid the disasters of 2002 and 2008. The commercial paper crisis should have been avoided but the technology bubble and the 2008 crisis were beyond control for any financial organisation. New coming Presidents have been able to restore the profitability of *la Caisse* for a while. Before the 2002 disaster, under Jean-Claude Scraire, *la Caisse* had been very profitable. Under Rousseau after him, there were good years too before lightning struck again. But the Campeau years in the 1980s remain perhaps the most interesting years (Rouzier, 2008). One graph illustrates this conclusion.

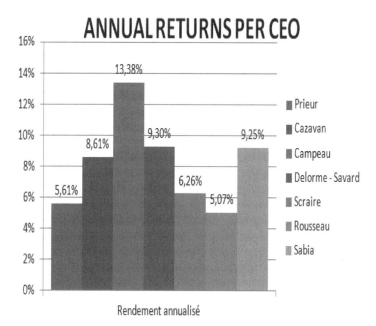

The profit years that were to be Rousseau's are by far not as good as the Campeau years when the *Caisse* was accused of intervening too much in the economy. A more sophisticated economic analysis would be necessary to test the lesson suggested here (see Wilmer, 2001 for example). Nevertheless, it could be argued that *la Caisse de dépôt* is an interesting example of a public enterprise doing well with a more complex mission than only profit. The public mission years were more profitable than the poor risk management years of the maximisation thesis. Interesting lessons could also be learned from comparative studies of the Alberta Heritage Fund but also of Ontario's Teachers and Omers. What the case of *la Caisse* teaches us is that when the institution tried to focus on profit, it had poorer results than when it tried to fulfil its dual mandate. It is an interesting case of complex rationality.

References

Arbour, Pierre (1993), *Québec Inc. et la tentation du dirigisme*, Montréal: L'Étincelle.

Bernier, Luc, Bouchard, Marie et Benoît Lévesque (2003), "Attending to the general interest: new mechanisms for mediating between the individual, collective and general interest in Québec", in *Annals of Public and Cooperative Economics*, Vol. 74, pp. 321-347.

Bernier, Luc and Burlone, Nathalie (2000), "Les conseils d'administration des sociétés d'État québécoises à l'époque des privatisations", in, *Gestion*, Vol. 24, pp. 57-62.

Bernier, Luc and Pelletier, Marie-Louise (2008), "La gouvernance des sociétés d'État", in *Canadian Journal of Administrative Law and Practice*, Vol. 21, No. 2, juillet, pp. 151-192.

Bérubé, Gérard (2009), "La maladie du gestionnaire", in *Le Devoir*, Montreal, pp. A-1 and 8.

Bourdeau, Réjean (2001), "La Caisse regroupe ses activités de gestion sous CDP Capital inc.", in *La Presse*, Montreal, August 30, p. D1.

Brooks, Stephen (1987), "The State as Financier: a comparison of the Caisse de dépôt et placement du Québec and Alberta Heritage Savings Trust Fund", in *Canadian Public Policy*, Vol. 13, pp. 318-329.

Brooks, Stephen and Tanguay, A. Brien (1985), "Québec's Caisse de depot et placement: tool of nationalism?", in *Canadian Public Administration*, Vol. 28, pp. 99-119.

Caisse de dépot et placement du Québec, *Annual Reports*, 1966 to 2012.

Castonguay, Claude (2002), *La Caisse de dépôt et placement: Un succès au-delà des espoirs formulés à l'origine*, Troisième Grande conférence anniversaire de l'Institut de recherche en politiques publiques (IRPP), le mardi 7 mai, à Montréal, dans le cadre des célébrations entourant le 30ᵉ anniversaire de la fondation de l'Institut.

Côté, Marcel and Dussault, Gaston (1995), *Claude Castonguay: architecte social et gestionnaire*, Ste-Fo: PUQ.

Cousineau, Sophie (2009A), "Repenser la Caisse", in *La Presse*, Montreal, February 2009, p. A-1.

Cousineau, Sophie (2009B), "Sabia à la Caisse: pincez-moi quelqu'un", *La Presse*, Montreal, March 13, blog.

Cousineau, Sophie (2009C), "Mascarade: comprendre la nomination de Michael Sabia à la Caisse", in *La Presse*, Montreal, March 17.

Couture, Pierre (2009), "Si on avait su: le C.A. de la Caisse ignorait tout des placements dans les PCAA", in, *Le Soleil*, Québec, Marsh 13, p. 25.

Desjardins, François (2009), "Malaise autour du conseil de la Caisse de depot", in *Le Devoir*, Montreal, March 18, p. B-1.

Dutrisac, Robert (2004), "Nouvel objectif: le rendement optimal", *Le Devoir*, Montreal, November 2004, p. A-1.

Dutrisac, Robert (2009), "Les demi-vérités d'Henri-Paul Rousseau", in *Le Devoir*, Montreal, May 23, p. C-2.

Forget, Claude E. ed. (1984), *La Caisse de dépôt et placement du Québe: sa mission, son impact et sa performance*, Toronto, CD Howe Institute.

Fournier, Pierre (1978), *Les sociétés d'État et les objectifs économiques du Québe: une évaluation préliminaire*, Québec, Éditeur officiel.

Gagnon, Jean-Marie (1996), "La Caisse sous le microscope", in *Recherches sociographiques*, Vol. 37, pp. 131-145.

Hanin, Frédéric (2005), *Fonds de pension du secteur public et modèles de développement au Canada; une étude comparative de la CDPQ et du CPIBB*, Cahier de recherche du Crises ET0506, UQAM.

Laberge, Mathieu, Marcelin, Joanis and Vaillancourt, François (2009), "Caisse de dépôt et placement du Québe: le calme après la 'tempête parfaite'?", in Joanis, Marcelin and Luc Godbout (eds.), *Le Québec économique 2009: le chemin parcouru depuis 40 ans*, Québec, PUL, pp. 295-319.

Laux, Jeanne Kirk and Maureen Appel Molot (1988), *State Capitalism: public enterprise in Canada*, Ithaca, Cornell University Press.

Lévesque, Benoît, Malo, Marie-Claire and Rouzier, Ralph (1997), "The Caisse de dépôt et placement du Québec and the Mouvement des Caisses populaires et d'économie Desjardins", in *Annals of Public and Cooperative Economics*, Vol. 68, pp. 485-501.

Maisonneuve, Pierre (1998), *Claude Castonguay: un artisan du Québec moderne*, Montréal, Novalis.

McRoberts, Kenneth (1993), *Quebec: Social Change and Political Crisis*, Toronto, McClelland and Stewart.

Morin, Danielle and Megas, Sarah (2012), "Caisse de dépôt et placement du Québec: je me souviens...", in *Canadian Public Administration*, Vol. 55, pp. 91-123.

Pelletier, Mario (2009), *La Caisse dans tous ses États*. Montréal: Carte blanche.

Pesando, James E. (1985), *An Economic Analysis of Government Investments Corporations, with attention to the Caisse de depot et placement du Québec and the Alberta Heritage Fund*, Discussion paper No. 277, Economic Council of Canada.

Pratte, André (2004), "Une Caisse plus solide", in *La Presse*, Montreal, December 16, p. A-22.

Puineault, Éric (2009), "Que faire de la Caisse en temps de crise?, Montréal", in *Le Devoir*, 25 février, p. A-9.

Rouzier, Ralph (2008), *La Caisse de dépôt et placement du Québec: portrait d'une institution d'intérêt général (1965-2000)*, Paris, L'Harmattan.

Simeon, Richard (2006), *Federal-provincial diplomacy*, Toronto, University of Toronto Press.

Tupper, Allan (1983), *Bill S-31 and the Federalism of State Capitalism*, Discussion Paper 19, Institute of InterGovernmental Affairs, Queen's University.

Vérificateur général du Québec (2003), "Rapport du Vérificateur général à l'Assemblée nationale pour l'année 2002-2003, Rapport de vérification sur le projet de construction 'Complexe CDP Capital'".

Vérificateur général du Québec (2003), "Rapport du Vérificateur général à l'Assemblée nationale pour l'année 2002-2003, Rapport de vérification sur Montréal Mode inc. Et Montréal Mode Investissements inc".

Wilmer, Johan (2001), "Ownership, efficiency and political interference", in *European Journal of Political Economy*, Vol. 17, pp. 723-748.

15. Stadtwerke Köln
A Market-Based Approach
Towards Public Service Provision

Dorothea GREILING

University Professor, Johannes Kepler University Linz, Austria

Introduction

During the last 20 years, the provision of Services of General Economic Interest (SGEIs) has changed considerably. A starting point for these changes was the Single Market Act which was enacted in October 1992. In general, European Union legislation on SGEIs is influenced by the belief that regulation is an adequate substitute for public ownership in those areas where market failure occurs. The substitution of public ownership by sector-specific regulations is fully in line with the privatisation agenda of NPM with its promises of greater allocative efficiency and better customer orientation. These changes in the regulatory framework led to the situation that utilities in public ownership are under pressure to demonstrate that they create value added for the society. The European Union market liberalisation policy has brought along that the provision of public services by public enterprises is no longer taken for granted.

Traditionally, public enterprises were seen as an instrument of the public owners for achieving commonweal objectives in Germany. Their existence has not been limited to areas of market failures, they are rather seen as an instrument used by the public owners to achieve a variety of economic and non-economic policy objectives, as expressed by the "Instrumentalthese" by Thiemeyer (1975) According to this author, public enterprises were regarded as an effective instrument for fulfilling a variety of economic policy objectives ranging from competition policy (monopoly control and simulating competition), through regional policy, industry-specific stabilisation and growth policy, labour market and social policy to environmental and supply policy.[1] Additionally, public enterprises were also seen as a tool for stimulating innovations and economic growth.[2]

---

[1] Thiemeyer, 1975; Greiling, 1996.
[2] Greiling, 1996.

Conduct regulation and intensive interference by the public owners were regarded as appropriate instruments for ensuring that public enterprises acted in line with the public owners' objectives. This brief enumeration of the common good objectives of German public enterprises shows that the public mission went far beyond providing public services in those areas were the market offered no efficient allocation.

Unlike in other European Union-countries (e.g. in France or Italy) the local provision of SGEI has a long tradition in Germany. This fact served as rationale why a local public utility was chosen. Against this background a longitudinal case study of the *Stadtwerke Köln GmbH* (SWK group – Stadtwerke Cologne group) was conducted in order to observe the development of focus, public missions, governance structure including owner's policy, regulatory framework and entrepreneurial policies over the past 20 years. The SWK group was selected because it is among the biggest public utility providers at the local level. According to the annual report 2011, the SWK group had 11,348 employees and the turnover of the SWK group added up to EUR 5.3007 million in 2011.

In order to provide an in-depth insight, a qualitative research design was chosen. Based on a documentary analysis and expert interviews with managers of the SWK group, conducted in January 2013, the results were compiled. The case-study approach allows addressing the issues at hand from an evolutionary perspective. The time span of the analysis ranges from 1990 to 2011. The collection and analysis of the material was carried out between October 2012 and April 2013.

Portrait of the SWK Group

The SWK GmbH is situated in the City of Cologne. It has the legal form of a *Gesellschaft mit beschränkter Haftung* (GmbH – private limited liability company). As a legal form under private law GmbHs exist independent of individual shareholders. The liability is limited to the capital invested. For the establishment of a GmbH at least one shareholder is required. In the case of the SWK group the sole owner is the City of Cologne.

In its present legal form the SWK Group has existed for 52 years. The Stadtwerke Köln GmbH was founded in 1960 by the Council of the City of Cologne as a 100% city-owned enterprise. Cologne's public ownership goes back much longer.[3] Already back in 1849 the city built a modern city port, followed by the first water works in 1872. In 1873 a formerly privately operated gas company was municipalised. The city's activities regarding public swimming baths started in 1887 and its involvement in

---

[3]   SWK, 2010, p. 49.

street cleaning and waste collection began in 1890. It was followed by the first electricity company in 1891 and in 1900 by the municipalisation of a formerly privately owned streetcar company. This brief review of the history does not take into account Cologne's Roman times when municipal infrastructure (e.g. ports, bathing houses, water supply) was provided to an amazing extent.

The SWK Group, including the many subsidiary companies, offers quite a variety of public services in the areas of energy supply (gas, electricity) mobility and public transport, waste collection and street cleaning. The SWK GmbH as the parent company provides central services for the subsidiary companies. Employee-wise the SWK GmbH as the holding company is quite small with only 164 employees according to the annual report 2011. The SWK GmbH is an example of a merely financial holding – not of an operating holding – offering a small number of centralised services for the SWK group such as legal services, insurance, central personnel services, central management accounting services and central policies towards the subsidiaries.

The most important subsidiaries within the SWK group are:

GEW Köln AG (*Gas, Elektrizitäts- und Wasserwerke Köln AG* – gas, electricity, and water works Cologne public limited company) as an intermediate holding company with its holdings *RheinEnergie AG, NetCologne GmbH, BRUMATAGmbH* and additional shares and holdings under the umbrella of *RheinEnergie AG.*

The *Kölner Verkehrsbetriebe AG* (KVB AG – Cologne public transport public limited company) transports more than 850,000 passengers per day in streetcars –, busses and via the public underground system.

The HGK Köln AG – *Häfen und Güterverkehr Köln AG* (ports and freight transport Cologne public limited company) offers a huge variety of logistic services in the Cologne region. After Duisburg the HGK AG is the second largest inland port operator in Germany. The SWK GmbH holds 54.5% of the shares of the HGK Köln AG, the City of Cologne 39.2% and the Rhine-Erft-County 6.3%.

Köln Bäder GmbH (Cologne public swimming baths private limited company) and

WSK GmbH – *Wohnungsgesellschaft der Stadtwerke Köln GmbH* (housing society of the local municipal public utility Cologne private limited company) mainly provides housing for the employees of the SWK group.

In the area of waste collection and street cleaning there are three fully consolidated subsidiary companies. The AWB – *Abfallwirtschaftsbetriebe Köln mbH & Co KG* (waste management services Cologne private limited company & limited partnership) is in the sole ownership of the SWK

Gmbh. AWB's slogan is "always to work for a clean Cologne". Another 100% subsidiary is the AWB *Verwaltung-Abfallwirtschaftsbetriebe Köln Gmbh* which is the management company of the waste management services Cologne private limited company. For household waste collection and recycling a third subsidiary, the AVG GmbH – *Abfallentsorgungs- und Verwertungsgesellschaft Köln mbH* (waste collection and recycling Cologne private limited company) is responsible. Here the SWK GmbH owns 50.1%. 49.9% of the shares are held by the REMONDIS GmbH Rhineland, a subsidiary of the globally operating REMONDIS Group.

The *Moderne Stadt-Gesellschaft zur Förderung des Städtebaus und der Gemeindentwicklung mbH Köln* (Moderne Stadt Köln GmbH – modern city company for urban and local development private limited company Cologne) is a small subsidiary wholly-owned by the SWK GmbH, focusing on urban and regional development within the SWK group and providing consultancy services.

Table 1 provides a divisional overview of the turnover in the main areas of activities within the SWK group:

Table 1. Divisional Turnover 2011

In million EUR	2011
Energy and water	3,863.9
Telecommunication	253.7
Cleaning and waste collection	245.4
Public transport	201.1
Port and freight transport	214.6
Heat-metering service	80.0
Revenues from services	41.3
Public swimming baths	10.1
Income from letting company flats	8.9
Total	4,919.0

Source: author's compilation based on the SWK annual report 2011.

The ownership structure of major daughter companies is displayed in table 2.

Table 2. Shareholding Structure (in per cent)

Subsidiary	SWK	Cologne city
GEW Köln AG	90	10
Kölner Verkehrsbetriebe AG (KVB AG	90	10
Häfen und Güterverkehr AG (HGK AG)	54.5	39.2
KölnBäder GmbH	74	26
Wohnungsgesellschaft der Stadt Köln mbH (WSK)	100	
AWB Abfallwirtschaftsbetriebe Köln GmbH & Co. KG (AWB)	100	
AWB Abfallwirtschaftsbetriebe Köln Verwaltung GmbH (AWB Verwaltung)	100	

Subsidiary	SWK	Cologne city
AVG Abfallentsorgungs- und Verwertungsgesellschaft Köln mbH (AVG)	50.1	
Moderne Stadt Gesellschaft zur Förderung des Städtebaues und der Gemeindeentwicklung mbH	100	

Source: SWK (2012), Annual report 2011, p. 8.

Within the subsidiaries the GEW Köln AG acts as an intermediate holding company. Back in 1992 the operating part of the GEW Köln AG was integrated in the RheinEnergie AG which is a regional public utility provider. Tab. 3 lists all the subsidiary companies of the GEW Köln AG which are fully consolidated.

Table 3. Fully Consolidated GEW Subsidiaries

Subsidiary	Equity in EUR	GEW's share
RheinEergie AG Köln	400 million	80%
BRUMATA GmbH & Co KG Hürth	129,000	100%
METRONA GmbH & Co KG	25,000	100%
NetCologne Köln	9.21 million	100%

Source: SWK (2012), Annual report 2011, p. 16.

According to the interview partners, the SWK group is also an enterprise which, from the very beginning, embraced a market approach combined, on the one side, with a strong commitment to improving the quality of life of all citizens and to acting as a stimulus for the regional economy, on the other side. The market-orientation also manifests itself in the creation of economic value added for the City of Cologne. From 1996 onwards the SWK Group had a surplus which was used for reinvestment and was partly transferred to the City of Cologne.

The SWK group is also a typical example of a local public municipal company where the surpluses of one division are used for cross-subsidising the deficits in other areas. Such cross-subsidisation can be found among others in many local public-owned public utilities in Germany. Historically, tax advantages and the fact that direct transfers by the owners are minimised, are the main reasons for this construction.

The 1960s were the founding years of the present SWK group. In November 1960 the legal form of the *GEW Köln AG* and the KVB AG was changed to that of a public limited company. Already then intergroup agreements specified that any profits from the GEW Köln AG and the KVB AG belong to the SWK GmbH. The losses of the subsidiaries have to be covered by the SWK GmbH. As early as at that time the profits of the GEW AG were used to cover the losses in the public transport section (KVB AG). The 1960s were also years of huge investment in the modernisation of the public infrastructure. In 1964 the WSG housing company of the SWK group was established. Documents from this time show that one central reason behind this move was to provide and improve the city's attractiveness as an employer by providing adequate, modern and comfortable flats for the employees of the SWK group.[4] The labour market of the 1960s, which were also the boom years of the German *Wirtschaftswunder* (economic miracle) was a market, where private and public employers competed for employees. In the sector of waste collection and street cleaning personnel was recruited in Southern Europe. As early as 1964 one third of the personnel working in this sector were immigrants.[5]

The 1970s and 1980s did not bring any new subsidiaries. The 1970s were years when the enlargement of the city boundaries following the local municipal reform resulted in the fact that for the first time Cologne had one million citizens in 1975. Infrastructure-wise the high commitment of providing up to date infrastructure continued. Huge sums were invested in the public transport network. In energy and water production investments were made in order to expand the networks and to provide these services in an ecologically efficient way. The focus on safe and eco-efficient energy production facilities was strengthened further by an energy concept in 1980.[6] Already in 1981 the *GEW Köln AG* developed a strategic concept which put the focus on long-distance heating and natural gas as main energy sources. In 1985 the GEW Köln AG and partner companies presented a concept of energy-saving measures for Cologne, including incentives for thermal insulation in private households, which aimed at reducing the total amount of energy used for heating by 20% till 2000. In 2000 this target was exceeded by 12%.

In the area of waste collection the AWB GmbH & Co. KG started to expand the separate collection of glass bottles by providing additional containers for the collection of waste paper back in 1984. In 1989 the city and the SWK GmbH passed the first integrated waste management concept.

Also in line with the promotion of ecological objectives were the investments made in the area of public transport. The regional expansion and the provision of park and ride facilities helped to increase the annual number of passengers by 20%[7] in 1980.

Intensifying the market-orientation of the public-owned ports was a very relevant topic in the mid 1980s. To improve their efficiency the city council decided to increase the managerial and legal autonomy

---

4   SWK, 2010, p. 9.
5   SWK, 2010, p. 6.
6   SWK, 2010, p. 50.
7   SWK, 2010, p. 27.

of the ports in Cologne in 1985.[8] In the 1990s three subsidiaries were integrated into the SWK group. In 1992 a new logistics company was founded. The HWK AG was established as a merger of two regional train freight companies and the port of Cologne. The KölnBäder GmbH was included as a subsidiary into the SWK group in 1998. This was seen as a step leading out of the permanent crisis of the public swimming pools in Cologne.[9] With the KölnBäder GmbH a second area of activities was integrated into the SWK group which is still not profitable but offers services improving the quality of life for the citizens of Cologne. According to the interview partners, it was a strategic decision by the city council to use the management experience and the economic potential for internal subsiding within the SWK group for integrating the loss-generating public swimming pools. This decision was carried by the trust that the management of the SWK group and the surpluses of the GEW AG would be the most advantageous solution and that it would be also a step towards a professionalization of the management of the KölnBäder GmbH. At the time of the integration of KölnBäder GmbH the public swimming pools also had a severe investment backlog. As "functional" buildings in line with a swimming pool design of the 1960s they did not meet the needs for fun pools with extensive wellness facilities. With the integration into the SWK group a modernisation process of the swimming pools was started aiming at creating modern leisure facilities.[10]

In 1998 the GEW Köln AG also acquired a stake in the BRUMATA METROMA Hürth GmbH.[11] The involvement of the GEW Köln AG in the area of broadband telecommunication also dates back to the 1990s. The integration of new companies has continued through the first decade of this century. Already in 2001 the AVG GmbH & Co KG and the AVG Verwaltung Köln GmbH were integrated as fully consolidated subsidiaries into the SWK group.[12] In 2002 a major reorganisation took place at the GEW Köln AG. Until then the GEW Köln AG had been an operating company. In 2002 this changed as the GEW Köln AG became an intermediate holding company within the SWK group. As a regionally-oriented energy company the *GEW RheinEngergie AG* (GEW RhineEnergy public limited company) was established. The stakes in this *GEW Köln AG* subsidiary belong to 80% to the GEW AG and to 20% to *the Rheinisch Westfälische Elektrizitätsgruppe AG* (RWE group – Rhineland and Westphalia Electricity Group public limited company).

---

[8] SWK, 2010, p. 25.
[9] SWK, 2010, p. 27.
[10] SWK, 2010, p. 27.
[11] SWK, 2011, p. 7.
[12] SWK, 2010, p. 7.

The involvement of the GEW Köln AG in the telecommunication sector increased in 2004. Since then the GEW Köln AG has been the sole shareholder of NetCologne AG. A minority share of 20% of the local municipal enterprise in Düsseldorf was acquired by the GEW Köln AG in 2005. As a regional enterprise the SWK group also holds shares in companies outside NRW. The biggest involvements can be found within the subsidiaries of the GEW Köln AG; outside North Rhine – Westphalia the RheinEnergie AG holds shares of a wind-park operator in South Germany and Spain. In 2011, 49.62% of the highly ecologically efficient coal-heat plant in Rostock were acquired. The interview partner stressed that this acquisition is seen as a strategic investment in modern technology and as a step towards being less dependent on the highly volatile energy trading market. The RheinEnergie AG is also a minority share-holder (16.3%) of the MVV Energie AG, a municipal public utility in Mannheim.[13]

Public Mission

The scope of the SWK group as mentioned in the annual report 2011 (SWK 2012) is the following:

- electricity, natural gas, water and heat supply,
- participation in to companies that run telecommunication networks, including telecommunication services,
- running charitable foundations to promote science, research, education, culture and family,
- operating public and non-public transport,
- operating ports,
- implementation of functions including the collection and disposal of waste, street cleaning and winter maintenance, and the provision of services in the sector of waste management,
- development and promotion of real estate, primarily of properties of affiliates,
- advertising and broadcasting,
- and the running of public swimming pools and ice sports facilities in Cologne.

This enumeration of the SWK group's objectives shows that the scope of the SWK goes well beyond a traditional local public multi-utility. The involvement in the areas of telecommunication, radio broadcasting and city planning may serve as an example. The involvement in the area of telecommunication has to do with Cologne's profile as a media city. The range of public services offered by the SWK group is rather comprehensive.

---

[13]   SWK, 2012, p. 11.

Only wastewater treatment is missing among the municipally provided public infrastructure services.

The mission statement of the SWK GmbH gives an idea of the key external stakeholders. It states the following:

> We are a fundamental contributor to the quality of life of the citizens and provide an important stimulus for the economy in Cologne and the region.

> The SWK group creates a substantial value added for the City of Cologne

> We work for Cologne and the region.

Key Performance Data

Table 4 provides an overview of key service provision indicators from 1995 to 2011. For 1990 no data were available.

Table 4. Service Provision Indicators (1995-2011)

SKW	1995	2000	2005	2011
Electricity sales (incl. trading) in GWh	5,855	7,773	38,405	37,407
Heat sales in GWh	4,889	4,863	1,523	1,161
Steam sales in GWh	n.d.a.	554	631	617
Gas sales (incl. trading) in GWh	9,143	8,667	10,367	11,098
Water sales in 1,000 m³	54,866	54,216	99,144	88,814
KVB passengers in million	218.2	230.9	247.1	274.4
Freight transport in million t	4.7	5.8	21.6	22
Visitors in public baths in 1,000	n.d.a.	2,117	1,999	2,269

Source: author's compilation based on the annual reports of the SWK GmbH.

The development of the number of employees is displayed in Figure 1.

Figure 1. Employees (1990-2011)

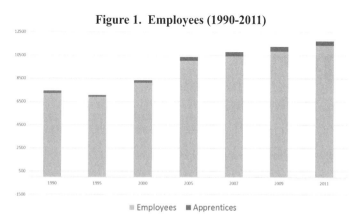

Source: author's compilation based on the annual report of the SWK group.

469

Figure 2 presents the development of key financial ratios over time and figure 3 the annual results of the SWK GmbH group.

Figure 2. Key Financial Ratios (1990-2001)

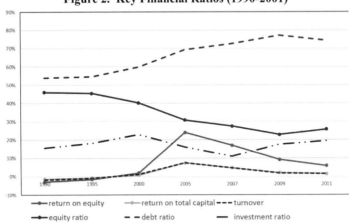

Source: author's compilation based on the annual report of the SWK group.

Figure 3. Annual Results

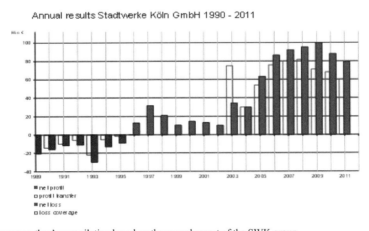

Source: author's compilation based on the annual report of the SWK group.

Continuous investments in eco-efficiency and network enlargement, in line with the growth of the City of Cologne and regional expansion have determined the investment policy since the 1970s. Between 1988 and 2008 the SWK group invested more than EUR 5.2 billion in the region.[14] The development of investments over time is displayed in Figure 4. The lowest investment quota was 11% in 2007 the highest level was 23% in 2000. In 2012 the SWK group invested EUR 727.8 million in energy production facilities, distribution networks (energy, water, and telecommunication) and public transport infrastructure.

Figure 4. Investments (1990-2011)

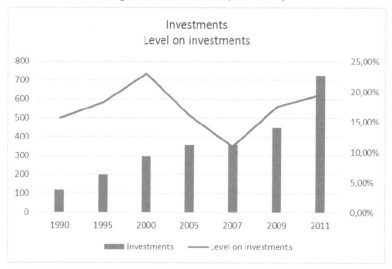

Source: author's compilation based on the annual report of the SWK group.

Regulation

As stated above, the SWK group has been affected by the EU market liberalisation in the area of the provision of Services of General Economic Interest since the 1990s, in particular in the energy markets and public transport. Within the SGEIs water provision has so far been the least liberalized one in Germany.

In an European Union 27 comparison the European Commission comes to the conclusion that the electricity market in Germany is reasonable well developed (European Commission, 2012). Unlike in other countries a national electricity monopoly has never been established in Germany. The ownership structure of the four super-grid providers is a mixed one. The majority of shareholders of EnBW AG are the State of Baden-Wurttemberg (46.75%) and Swabian local communities (46.75%). The State-owned Swedish Vattenfall group holds 89% of

---

[14]   SWK, 2010, p. 42.

Vattenfall Europe.[15] Local authorities own one-third of RWE AG, which holds 20% of the RheinEnergie.[16] The GEW Köln AG holds 5.03% of the RWE AG (equity EUR 74,363 million). On the second tier of the German electricity provider system there are 54 regional utilities,[17] one of them is the RheinEnergie AG. These regional suppliers transmit the energy which they have produced themselves in their own power plants or which they have bought.[18] On the third tier one finds the vast majority of local providers (about 800 municipal distributors).[19]

In 2011 the German gas market had 18 transmission system operators, 27 regional network operators and 743 local distribution operators.[20] Again the RheinEnergie AG is a regional network operator. There have been significant developments towards more competition in the last few years but competition is not as intense as on the electricity market.[21] The starting point of the liberalisation of the energy market in Germany was the year 1998 when a new *Energiewirtschaftsgesetz* (Energy Industry Act 1998) came into force. Its major objectives were the promotion of competition, the reduction of energy costs, the improvement of energy efficiency and an increase in the market share of renewable energies.[22] The amendments in European Union and national legislation also affected the structure of the GEW Köln group. In 2002 the GEW Köln AG became an intermediate holding company. As a regional operating company the RheinEnergie AG was established. The second energy directive led to a fundamental amendment of the Energy Industry Act on 13 July 2005. The unbundling of networks from other areas of activities was stringently enforced. In the case of the RheinEnergie this led to the establishment of the *RheinEnergieNetz GmbH* in 2005. The Energy Industry Act also substantially changed the conditions for the access to networks and the regulation of the tariffs for network access. It put an end to the German option that network access and access tariffs were determined by the "consensus of the sector" where network access conditions and tariffs were determined by a private agreement between the German industry association and associations of the energy suppliers. Since 2005 the calculation of tariffs for network access has been based on the costs of an efficiently operating network provider of a comparable size. This

15 von Danwitz, 2006, p. 428.
16 von Danwitz, 2006, p. 428.
17 European Commission, 2012, p. 73.
18 von Danwitz 2006, p. 428.
19 European Commission 2012, p. 73.
20 European Commission 2012, p. 73.
21 European Commission 2012, p. 73.
22 Rotaru 2013, p. 105.

includes an adequate and risk-appropriate return on the invested capital stock.[23] The German regulation of access tariffs is based on the idea of an incentive regulation where upper limits for tariffs for networks access or the resulting revenues are determined ex ante for a fixed period of time.[24] Since 2005 access tariffs have been on a decline.

With the Energy Industry Act 2005 the structure of the regulatory agencies changed in Germany. Traditionally, the supervision of energy suppliers was carried out by state authorities of the German *Länder* (States). In 2005 the Federal Network Agency for Electricity, Gas, Telecommunications, Post and Railways was founded as a federal regulator. The Federal Network Agency performs tasks that have not been assigned to the Land regulatory authorities. The Land regulatory authorities regulate supply companies with fewer than 100,000 electricity and gas network customers und those companies whose grids do not extend beyond a federal State's borders. Today's main regulatory tasks of the Federal Network Agency are to ensure non-discriminatory network access, the monitoring of the unbundling activities, the control of network usage rates and the supervision of anti-competitive practices. A major current challenge on the markets for energy and gas is the fact that the majority of the more than 20,000 concession contracts for electricity and gas will expire in 2015 and 2016.[25] In recent years more than 170 private concession contracts for energy distribution networks have returned to public hands.[26] In the case of the RheinEnergie AG most concession agreements will run out in 2014.

A second major influence on the regulation of the energy market is caused by the German policy for the promotion of renewable energy as a move against the climate change. In 2011 the Fukushima tragedy caused a revision of this "exit from the exit" as a binding political solution. Immediately afterwards eight nuclear power plants were shut down. Already in 2001 the Renewable Energy Sources Act (EEG), served as the starting point of a massively subsidized expansion of renewable energy production. Compared to other countries, Germany has quite ambitious objectives with respect to climate protection which bear the German label *"Energiewende"* (energy turnaround). The Energiewende is having its impact on the SWK Group. The program "Energy & Climate 2020" will lead to investments in the area of climate protection of approximately EUR 100 million. The City of Cologne has committed itself to very ambitious CO_2 emission objectives. Here the SWK group is an important partner.

---

[23] von Danwitz 2006, p. 447.

[24] van Danwitz, 2006, p. 447.

[25] Reck, 2013.

[26] Reck, 2013.

Eco-efficient investments have a long tradition in the SWK group. This does not go along with a total rejection of coal as an energy provider but the SWK group has a policy of investing in highly ecologically efficient coal-heat plants. The above mentioned new acquisition in Rostock stands for this policy.

The second sector of the SWK group which is most affected by market liberalisation is the *local public transport* sector. Providing good public transport within the cities is also a core element of the *Energiewende*. In the past decade European Union directives on local public transport led to amendments in the German Local Public Transport laws. Already in 2001 the European Commission (2001) published a white paper "*European transport policy for 2010: Time to decide*" which contained basic principles. The main objective is to guarantee a safe, efficient and high-quality passenger transport service through regulated competition.

As not all local public transport services that are required in the general economic interest can be operated profitably, there is a public services obligation. The relevant public authority, which is in the case under review the City of Cologne, can award exclusive rights to public service operators. The selection process for the enterprise which is granted exclusive rights must be based on the principles of transparency, equal treatment of the competitors and proportionality. For the public service obligation a financial compensation is granted. The local public authority either has the option to entrust a third party with the provision of local public transport services or it can chose to entrust it to an internal operator without competitive tendering. By city council decisions on 15 December 2005 and 24 June 2008 the KVB AG was mandated with the fulfilment of the public service obligations till 2019. The decision of 2005 was necessary because of a decision by the European Court of Justice (case C/280/00 Altmark Trans GmbH). This ruling specified the criteria under which the provisions of Art. 87 of the European Community (EC) Treaty are not applicable for local public transport. The four Altmark criteria are (European Commission staff working paper, 2011):

Firstly, the receiving enterprise must actually have a clearly defined public service obligation to discharge.

Secondly, the parameters for the compensation of the public service obligation must be established in advance in an objective and transparent manner to avoid that an economic advantage for the provider is created.

Thirdly, the compensation cannot exceed the sum that is necessary to cover the costs incurred in the discharge of public service obligations. This includes a reasonable profit.

Fourthly, the compensation is limited to the costs which are incurred by a well-run provider.

Whether these criteria are met, needs to be audited every three years by an auditor. A further milestone for the regulatory framework of local public transport was EU Regulation No. 1370/2007 of the European Parliament and the Council of 23 October 2007 on public passenger transport services by rail and road. The purpose of the regulation is the following: to define, in accordance with the rules of the Community, how a competent authority may act in the field of public passenger transport to guarantee the provision of SGEIs in a safer, qualitative better way than market forces would do. The European Union regulation also specifies the conditions under which public service obligations are to be compensated. Since the enforcement of the EU regulation 1370/2007 in 2009, the City of Cologne has had to publish an aggregated report on the public service obligations once a year. The respective report of the City of Cologne as commissioning authority can be found on the homepage of the KBV AG. The report provides key figures with respect to the amount of transport lines (2011: 11 city railway lines, 43 bus lines and 8 on-demand lines – taxis and busses), the compensation by public authorities for local public transport and the service quality. Key figures are compiled in Table 5.

Table 5. Compensations to the KVB (EU Regulation 1370/2007)

Compensations	2009	2010	2011
Compensation busses	29.8 Mio €	31.3 Mio €	31.8 Mio €
Compensation city railways	78.97 Mio €	66.4 Mio €	58.7 Mio €
Lump-sum compensation by the state of NRW for investments and service quality (§ 11 PBefG NRW)	12 Mio €	12.0 Mio €	4.8 Mio €
Compensation for transport of pupils and disabled persons by the state of NRW	13.1 Mio €	13.9 Mio €	14.6 Mio €
Total	133.87 Mio €	123.6 Mio €	109.9 Mio €
Total expenditures KVB AG	326.5 Mio €	363.22 Mio €	330.7 Mio €
Share of compensations in %	41.00 %	34.03 %	33.23 %
Passengers transported	265.8 Mio	272.4 Mio	274.4 Mio
Km of bus service lines	536 km	553 km	548 km
Km of city railway lines	237 km	240 km	240 km
Km of total network	775 km	793 km	788 km

Source: author's compilation based on the reports by the Stadt Köln (2010-2012).

With respect to the promotion of market liberalisation the interview partners regarded the Federal Ministry of Economy and Technology

(BMWi) as more radical than the European Commission. Compared to the initiatives from Brussels the BMWi is a much more difficult partner to cooperate with. Literally translated one interview partner said: "The EU Commission is as meek as an orphan child in comparison to the BMWi".

Governance

The SWK is organised in the legal form of a private limited company as discussed previously. As compulsory organs the German GmbH law requires the establishment of a shareholder meeting and a management board. A supervisory board must be established in GmbHs with a workforce above 500 full-time employees. According to the German co-determination laws there must be employee representatives on the supervisory board.

From an owner's perspective, the GmbH offers more opportunities to interfere in the management board's decision-making, compared to the Aktiengesellschaft (public limited company). The better chances to intervene in the decision-making process are the reason why the legal form of the private limited company is the preferred one for local enterprises in public ownership. Compared to other cities, Cologne can be regarded as pioneer in choosing a legal form under private law. On a larger municipal scale such legal forms for public utilities started to become popular in the 1970s. At that time they were seen as an important step to increase the management board's autonomy and to limit the liabilities of the public owners.

Looking at the present supervisory board of the SWK GmbH, we find the following composition. 10 out of 20 positions are held by employee representatives. This is in line with the German law for co-determination in large companies. The employee representatives on the supervisory board either come from the companies within the SWK group or are trade union representatives. The chairperson of the supervisory board is a member of the city council of Cologne. The annual reports show that there is a long tradition that the vice-chair is an employee representative. Looking at the present supervisory board of the SWK group we see that eight out of 10 board members also belong to the city council.[27] The other two non-employee positions are taken by the mayor of Cologne and an entrepreneur.

The current management board of the SWK GmbH has three members, all of them male. The Chief Executive Officer (CEO) is at the same time CEO of the three biggest subsidiaries the GEW Köln AG and also CEO of the biggest operating company within the GEW Köln AG, the RheinEnergie AG. Another member of the management board of the

---

[27]   SWK 2012, p. 6.

SWK GmbH is at the same time CEO of the public transport company, the KVB AG. The third member of the management board is at the same time CEO of the HGK AG. He is also the director for personnel of the SWK group. All three members of the management board spend most of their time as CEOs of subsidiary companies.

An informal but nevertheless highly important coordination organ is the monthly meeting of all managing boards of the SWK group. All sides attach great importance to these meetings. These meetings are used for coordinating the activities throughout the group.

Earlier than many other owners of municipal companies the City of Cologne made the providers of public transport and energy legally independent and granted them entrepreneurial freedom. This went along with the demand that the SWK group should act in a market-oriented way. This market-orientation became a trademark well before the EU market liberalisation. Therefore the SWK group had an early mover advantage.

Throughout these more than five decades, the city has never questioned public ownership. Around the year 2000 there was a minority within the city council who wanted to privatize parts of the SWK group. However, this group did not succeed with their plans. Currently it is not part of the City of Cologne's policy to sell the family silver. The sole ownership of the City of Cologne has always been the backbone of the SWK group. The perquisite is that the SWK group meets its annual financial and service provision targets.

Asked about the benefits of public ownership in the perception of the SWK group and the City of Cologne, the interview partners stressed that there is a shared understanding on both sides. The main benefits are:

- Private for-profit companies clearly have to prioritise the generation of shareholder value. Therefore service provision always has to take a profit margin into account.
- Private for-profit companies have an incentive to under-invest in the maintenance of network infrastructure.
- Contracting-out SGEIs produces additional transaction costs.
- There is a high commitment on both sides and a trusting relationship.
- The security of service provision is higher in the case of public ownership.
- The SWK group creates a value added because there are economies of scope within the SWK group. Contracting-out services individually could not provide the same /results.
- Water is regarded as public service which should not be privatised.

With respect to economies of scope the interview partners mentioned the transport of waste by the HGK AG as it can operate a railway network which would not be profitable for a private investor. There is also a clear policy that the AWB does not charge the City of Cologne for street cleaning in the case of mega events. The expertise of the SWK in the areas of integrated public transport planning (KVB AG), city development planning (Moderne Stadt Gmbh) and management expertise for providing public services in an entrepreneurial way is highly valued by the City of Cologne.

The relationship between the SWK group and the City of Cologne is described by the interview partners as close. On the one side there is a strong commitment of the city towards the SWK group. On the other side the SWK group clearly sees its obligation to provide an economic value added for the City of Cologne. According to the interview partners, the city trusts the SWK group that it will not use information asymmetries to outsmart the city. There is a clear preference of the city for public ownership instead of structural regulation. Under transaction cost aspects the first is preferred. The SWK group is regarded by the city as the entrepreneurial arm for infrastructure provision. The city trusts r that the SWK group will act in entrepreneurial and professional way in accordance with the city's interests. The internal cross-subsidisation within the SWK group is seen as an asset.

Although there is a clear preference for public ownership and therefore for the SWK group as a multi-public utility company, the interview partners stressed that it is essential that the SWK group creates an economic value added for the City of Cologne. Throughout the SWK group cost-efficiency is a key objective. Fulfilling the public mission in the most efficient and effective way is important for SWK group, according to the interview partners.

As the sole owner the City of Cologne negotiates every year with the SWK Gmbh financial and service provision targets for the public services to be provided. The financial targets are ambitious but achievable with a stringent focus on a cost-efficient provision of the services. The interview partners stressed that while the city sets ambitious annual financial targets, it does not squeeze out the SWK group like a lemon. Taking into account the current public debts such a policy can be found in many other German cities.

The management team of the SWK group uses these targets in their annual planning rounds with its subsidiaries, which are responsible for meeting these targets in their respective markets.[28]

The financial obligations of the subsidiaries are regulated by executive contracts. Since 1996 the SWK group has been profitable. The transfer

---

[28]   SWK 2010, p. 43.

of profits to the City of Cologne has been possible since 2003. Between 1996 and 2003 net profits have been employed for strengthening the self-financing capacity.

Asked about the importance of financial objectives, the interview partners differentiated between the subsidiaries. For the GEW Köln AG Group and the HGK AG a clear priority of financial objectives exists. Asked about the relationship between financial objectives and service provision objectives, the interview partners came up with a relation of 70% to 30% in favour of financial objectives. This shows that both enterprises within the SWK group have to generate a profit to make the business model sustainable. While the GEW Köln AG has always been profit-generating, the HGK AG had to undergo some restructuring before it became profit-generating.

The relationship between financial objectives and public service provision objectives changes from 10% to 90% in the cases of the KVB AG and the Köln Bäder GmbH. Here a clear dominance of public service provision objectives is apparent. Both subsidiaries went through phases of reorganization. In the cases of local public transport, the Köln Bäder GmbH and the WSK GmbH, there is a clear commitment to social pricing. Reductions are granted to children, students and pensioners with the intention to make these services affordable. The amount of seasonal tickets in public transport is high. Although the KBV and the Köln Bäder are cross-subsidised, this policy is not called in question.

The documentary analyses as well as the interviews showed that in addition to the (economic) value-creation for the city, the value added for the citizens and the region is likewise accorded high priority. This is also expressed by the SWK group's slogan which is *"Da sein für Köln"*. Literally translated this means "Be there for Cologne". The expression *Da sein* is also a play of words on the term *Daseinsvorsorge*, a German notion for services of general interest.

Table 6 displays the financial value added for the City of Cologne.

Table 6. Transfers within the group SWK in millions

In million EURO	2012
SWK group dividend to the City of Cologne	70.0
Internal loss coverage KVB	81.5
Internal loss coverage KölnBäder	18.9
SWK group total (subtotal)	170.4
Licence duty RheinEnergie	73.8
Licence duty (advertising fees)	2.7
Local business tax to the city of Cologne	15.4
Total financial value added for the City of Cologne	262.3

Source: information provided by SWK group.

The SWK is a typical example of a municipal multi-utility. Profits made in one subsidiary are used to cover losses in other areas. Table 7 provides a differentiated picture of internal cross-financing within the SWK group.

Table 7. Transfers within the group SWK in millions

SWK	Deutsche Mark			EURO			
	1990	**1995**	**2000**	**2005**	**2007**	**2009**	**2011**
Profit transfer GEW	106.1	190.6	219.9	180.5	225.4	195.6	152
Profit transfer HGK	1.6	0.8	-3.9	0.1	-	-	3.5
Loss compensation KölnBäder	-	-	15	10.9	12.4	14.1	18
Loss compensation. KVB	135.5	197.9	179.9	108.8	104.5	97	73
Profits AWK	-	-	-	-	7.7	12.2	12
Profits AVG	-	-	-	-	5.8	6	5.3
Profits KAW	0.1	-	-	-	-	-	-
Other shareholdings	-	-	-	-	2.4	1.8	2
Annual results	-31.3	-18.5	28.5	63	151.8	99.7	79.5

Source: author's compilation based on the annual report of the SWK group.

Looking at the KVB as the biggest recipient of subsidiaries, the following can be said: While the average percentage of cost coverage in all local public transport providers was 77.9% in 2011, the KVB slightly outperformed this figure with 79% (see Fig. 5).

Figure 5. Cost recovery rates (2002-2011)

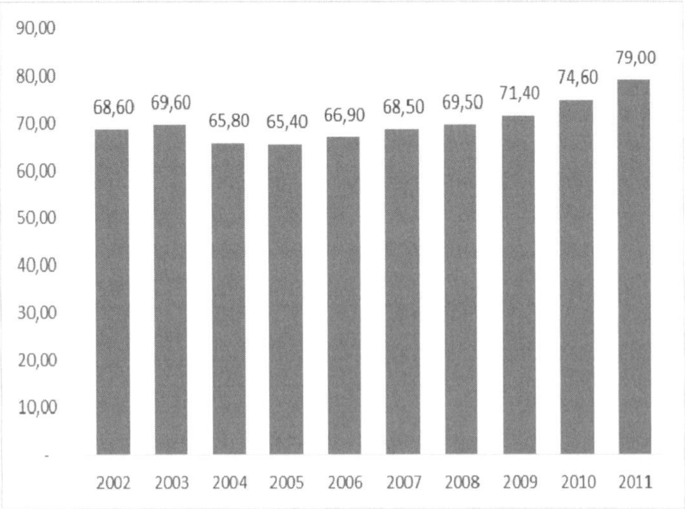

Source: KVB 2012.

480

The risks and chances section in the annual report 2011 highlights the fact that the environment for the SWK group is getting more complex and more volatile. Major drivers for this development are:[29]

- a substantial increase in competition in nearly all areas,
- the consequences of globalization, trade liberalisation and the crisis of the financial markets,
- a growing scarcity of important natural resources,
- more extreme environmental risks with global warming as the most important one,
- very fast and resource-intensive technological developments,
- an increase in structural regulation,
- the growing influence of European Union legislation on national legislations and its consequences for enterprises and
- demographic changes.

In the upcoming decades demographic change will in many German municipalities lead to a situation requiring the down-sizing of service provision networks; Cologne is an exception of trend as the city will be growing over the next 10 years.

With respect to the development of energy tariffs within the GEW group, the interview partners stressed that before the German Energy Industry Act 1998 came into force, profit margins were not so high. From 1998 onwards things changed due to the policy of high prices pursued by the super grid providers. At that time they produced energy with depreciated production facilities. Compared to the 1990s it is today much more difficult for the RheinEnergie AG to make profits. For the coming years there are some doubts whether the GEW Köln group will achieve the same surplus. According to the interview partners the years when electricity provision was a fat cash cow are over. The changes in the energy markets, the reduction of the prices of the electricity nets and the large amount of money that will be needed for multi-grid technologies pose some risks. The EU plans regarding service concessions are seen as a substantial risk for the business model of the SWK group.

Conclusions and lessons learned

The SWK group is an example where public service provision and market orientation go hand in hand. In an institutional logic perspective the SWK group combines in a value-creating way a market logic with a clear commitment towards the public interest. The City of Cologne has

---

[29] SWK 2012, p. 51.

clear expectations with respect to the economic value added to be created by the SWK group for the City of Cologne. Earlier than many other cities Cologne granted the SWK entrepreneurial autonomy by choosing private-law legal forms. From its foundation onward, the SWK, as the parent company, has been a private limited company and its first two subsidiaries, the GEW Köln AG and the KVB AG, were public limited companies, this clear preference for private-law companies continues till today. The main subsidiaries are either public or private limited companies.

The SWK group is seen as the entrepreneurial arm of the City of Cologne for the provision of infrastructure services. There is a marked preference on the part of the City of Cologne in favour of providing SGEIs in public ownership. That the SWK group is municipal and will remain municipal is a policy which is not questioned. The commitment of the City of Cologne shows a clear long-term orientation and there is a very high degree of taken-for-grantedness of public ownership. The public service obligations in the field of local public transport are fulfilled by the KVB AG. Third party provision of SGEIs is not regarded as a viable option for the metropolitan area of Cologne. The provision by its own public utility provider is seen as advantageous with respect to transaction costs, the dangers of being outsmarted by a private for-profit provider, safety reasons and the quality of service provision. Furthermore, it is assumed that there is less risk of under-investment.

In the past two decades the portfolio of the SWK Group has been expanded. The city has always used the SWK group for integrating financially problematic fields of public service provision for enhancing their market-orientation and for professionalising the management of the new subsidiaries.

There is a clear commitment by the SWK group to the creation of value added for the citizens and the region as well as for the City of Cologne. This is reflected by the commitment to delivering high quality public service provision with energy, drinking water, public transport, street cleaning and waste collection and other service areas. The SWK is one of the largest employers in Cologne. The fringe benefits for the employees include company flats and group-wide health promotion at the workplace. The SWK group is also one of the biggest investors in the region.

From the 1960s onward it was the guiding principle for investments in the infrastructure to invest in modern and up to date infrastructure. The policy of the SWK group can be characterised that of an early mover in the field of eco-efficiency. The first combined heat-power production plant started its service in the 1960s. Today the RheinEnergie AG invests above average amounts in renewable energy production and smart grid technology. Green technology and highly efficient energy production is an important investment area for the GEW group.

Environmental protection and sustainability are also firmly anchored in other SWK subsidiaries. As stated above, there is a long-term policy safeguard sustainability. The KVB AG has a long history of EMAS certificates. The integration of the Köln Bäder GmbH in 1998 was motivated by the necessity to modernise and enlarge the facilities which resulted in the next 15 years in an ambitions investment policy. The three foundations of the RheinEnergie AG are important sponsors in Cologne. Activities aiming at being a good employer date back to the 1960s when the WSK AG was established.

The SWK is a typical example of a German multi-utility provider with a high degree of internal cross-subsidising. This reduces the financial subsidies from the City of Cologne. The business model is regarded as sustainable as long as the GEW Köln group remains an economically powerful subsidiary. A further benefit of the SWK as a multi-utility provider is that of economies of scope.

In conclusion it can be said that the SWK group is an example of a profitable provider of SGEIs with a clear focus on economic, ecological and social sustainability. Looking at the financial results which improved considerably in the last decades the SWK group is among the most successful municipal multi-utility providers in Germany. As states by the interview partners as well as the annual statements there is a clear commitment for creating added value for Cologne's citizens, the region and the City of Cologne. This policy ensures the city's continuous commitment to the SWK group. The example of the SWK group shows that even more than 20 years after the Single Market Act local public utility providers can position themselves in a way that there existences is not questioned if they combine market-orientation with a strong commitment towards local and regional welfare. In the eyes of the key stakeholders the combination of welfare and financial objectives secures the legitimacy of the SWK Group in the liberalised market for SGEI.

References

BMWI (Federal Ministry of Economics and Technology) and BMU (Federal Ministry for the Environment, Nature Conservation and Nuclear Safety), *First monitoring report "Energy of the future"*, Bonn, 2012.

Bundesnetzagentur and Bundeskartellamt (eds.), *"Monitoring report 2012 – Development of the electricity and gas markets in Germany"*, Bonn, 2012.

European Commission, *"European transport policy for 2010: Time to decide"*, Luxembourg: Office for Official Publications of the European Communities, 2001.

European Commission, *"Energy market in the European Union in 2011"*, SWD (2012) 368 final of 15, November, 2012.

European Commission staff working paper, *"The Application of EU State Aid rules on Services of General Economic Interest since 2005 and the Outcome of the Public Consultation"*, SEC (2011) 397, 23, March, 2011.

Greiling, D., *"Öffentliche Trägerschaft oder öffentliche Bindung"*, Baden-Baden, Nomos, 1996.

Reck, H. J., "Practioner Statement: The municipal companies (Stadtwerke) as an example for public entrepreneurship", in *Zoegu, special issue* No. 43, 2013, pp. 13-20.

Rotaru, D. V., *"A glance at the European energy market liberalisation"*, Centre for European Studies, working paper, University of Iasi (Romania), 2013.

Thieneyer; Th., *"Wirtschaftlehre öffentlicher Betriebe"*, Reinbek bei Hamburg, Rowolt, 1976.

Von Danwitz, Th., "Regulation and liberalisation of the European Electricity Market – a German view", in *Energy Law Journal* 2008, Vol. 27, No. 2, pp. 423-450.

Annual reports and other documents by the SWK group

AWB Abfallwirtschaftsbetriebe Köln GmbH & Co. KG (2012): *"Da sein für Köln. Geschäftsbericht 2011"*: http://www.stadtwerkekoeln.de/index.php?id=195, accessed: May 2013.

Häfen und Güterverkehr Köln AG, *"Da sein für Köln. Geschäftsbericht 2011"*, Köln: http://www.stadtwerkekoeln.de/index.php?id=195, accessed: May 2013.

KölnBäder GmbH, *"Da sein für Köln. Geschäftsbericht 2011"*: http://www. stadtwerkekoeln.de/index.php?id=195, accessed: May 2013.

Kölner Verkehrs-Betriebe AG, *"Da sein für Köln. Geschäftsbericht 2011"*: Köln http://www.stadtwerkekoeln.de/index.php?id=195, accessed: May 2013.

KVB, *"Mobilität in Köln: regionaler Nutzen der Kölner Verkehrs-Betriebe"*, Köln, 2011.

RheinEnergie AG, Da sein für Köln. Geschäftsbericht 2011: http://www. stadtwerkekoeln.de/index.php?id=195, accessed: May 2013.

Stadt Köln, *"Gesamtbericht der Stadt Köln für 2009 gemäß Artikel 7 der Verordnung 1370/2007 der Europäischen Union"*, Köln, 2010.

Stadt Köln, *"Gesamtbericht der Stadt Köln für 2010 gemäß Artikel 7 der Verordnung 1370/2007 der Europäischen Union"*, Köln, 2011.

Stadt Köln, *"Gesamtbericht der Stadt Köln für 2011 gemäß Artikel 7 der Verordnung 1370/2007 der Europäischen Union"*, Köln, 2012.

Stadtwerke Köln GmbH, *"Geschäftsbericht und Konzerngeschäftsbericht"*, Köln, 1991.

Stadtwerke Köln GmbH, *"Geschäftsbericht und Konzerngeschäftsbericht 1995"*, Köln, 1996.

Stadtwerke Köln GmbH, "*Geschäftsbericht 2000*", Köln, 2001.
Stadtwerke Köln GmbH, "*Geschäftsbericht 2005*", Köln, 2006.
Stadtwerke Köln GmbH, "*Geschäftsbericht 2007*", Köln, 2008.
Stadtwerke Köln GmbH, "*Geschäftsbericht 2009*", Köln, 2009.
Stadtwerke Köln GmbH, "*Da sein für Köln: Geschäftsbericht 2011*", Köln, 2012.
SWK, "*50 Jahre Stadtwerke Köln. – leben in Köln*", Köln, 2010.
SWK, "*Stadtwerke Cologne: Economic power for the common good*", Köln, 2011.
SWK (n.y), "Unser *Leitbild: Wir sind die Stadtwerke Köln*", Köln.

Conclusion
Les entreprises publiques, aujourd'hui et demain

Luc BERNIER

ENAP

Ce livre a présenté des études de cas sur des entreprises publiques dans neuf pays qui œuvrent dans des secteurs aussi diversifiés que l'eau, l'électricité, la finance, les infrastructures immobilières, la poste, le transport aérien, local ou maritime, les services d'ingénierie. Certaines sont des organisations complexes qui remplissent une mission d'intérêt public tout en étant des opérateurs efficaces dégageant des performances financières assez robustes. Ces entreprises publiques fonctionnent dans des systèmes politiques aussi différents que ceux du Pérou, de la Suède, de la tradition d'origine britannique au Canada et en Irlande ou dans des systèmes continentaux européens en France, en Belgique ou en Italie. Elles fonctionnent dans des pays de grande taille comme l'Allemagne ou plus petits comme l'Autriche ou l'Irlande.

Dans ces entreprises, tout n'est pas parfait : SEDAPAL n'offre pas d'eau aux familles les plus défavorisées de Lima (9,55 % de la population) et même à Paris, des familles doivent encore aller chercher l'eau à des fontaines publiques. Mais comme dans le projet de recherche précédent du CIRIEC qui portait sur les entreprises publiques locales[1], ces entreprises peuvent présenter des éléments intéressants permettant d'argumenter face aux tenants de la privatisation et de faire avancer le débat scientifique. Pendant longtemps, il s'est fait peu de recherche sur les entreprises publiques. Les derniers ouvrages importants sur le sujet datent des années 1980 (Aharoni, 1986 ; Hafsi, 1989). Il y a eu certes depuis d'autres articles, des livres consacrés à des cas intéressants mais l'essentiel de la recherche dans le domaine a été publié sur les privatisations. De grandes

---

[1] Cette recherche menée par la Commission scientifique internationale du CIRIEC « Services publics/Entreprises publiques » (2008-11) a donné lieu à trois synthèses sectorielles (déchets, transports, eau) publiées dans les *Annales de l'économie publique, sociale et coopérative*, vol. 83, n° 4, décembre 2012.

synthèses comme celle de Megginson et Netter (2001) ont célébré l'entreprise privée et sa supériorité sur l'entreprise publique. En 2000, on pensait que les entreprises publiques avaient vécu, étaient dans un déclin qui risquait peu d'être inversé (Toninelli, 2000). Pourtant, les quinze cas réunis dans ce livre témoignent que des entreprises publiques ont toujours une place, qu'elles offrent des services importants d'intérêt général et qu'elles fonctionnent bien sous des régimes de gouvernance très variés.

Ce chapitre de conclusion revient dans un premier temps sur les leçons apprises au moyen des études de cas présentées dans les chapitres qui précèdent, en fonction des questions posées en introduction et en cherchant les éléments communs à plus d'un cas. Nous n'avions pas la prétention de « réinventer » avec ces études de cas la théorie sur les entreprises publiques ce qui constituera peut-être un futur projet du CIRIEC. Néanmoins, nous croyons que les matériaux empiriques que constituent les études de cas présentées ici offrent un portrait intéressant d'une nouvelle réalité de ces entreprises où, entre autres, la gouvernance a été transformée, que ce soit la gouvernance corporative ou leur régulation par des organismes créés à cette fin, et que l'intérêt général peut être porté à travers diverses formules où contractualisation et propriété publique se mêlent. Dans un deuxième temps, il fait ressortir d'autres enjeux soulignés par ces analyses. Il faudra évaluer à plus long terme dans des contextes socio-économico-politiques variés et changeants comment les leçons apprises à la lecture de ces cas résistent au passage du temps. Une troisième section se penche sur la méthode des études de cas. Le tout est fait dans la perspective de proposer des questions pour poursuivre la recherche réalisée et présentée dans cet ouvrage, dont il faut ici remercier les auteurs et louer la qualité de leur travail.

Les entreprises publiques aujourd'hui

On peut retenir de la lecture de ce livre que les entreprises publiques ont encore un rôle à jouer. Elles ne sont pas actives dans des secteurs en déclin comme jadis le charbon mais dans des secteurs essentiels d'infrastructure comme l'électricité, la distribution de l'eau, les services de transport en commun qui facilitent la vie en collectivité que ce soient les traversiers sur la côte ouest canadienne ou les transports publics à Bruxelles ou à Vienne. Certaines entreprises publiques répondent à des nécessités d'intervention de l'État dans l'économie ou des besoins d'infrastructure qu'on leur confie comme en Ontario ou en Irlande. L'État ne se retire plus pour laisser la place au secteur privé, sauf dans quelques cas suite à de graves difficultés budgétaires, comme la Grèce par exemple. L'actualité économique du printemps 2014 a été marquée par la lutte entre *Siemens* et *General Electric* pour le contrôle de la compagnie française Alsthom où l'État sera désormais un actionnaire important. Il semble se dessiner une intervention accrue de l'État français dans cette entreprise, même si elle ne devrait être que temporaire. La renationalisation ou la remunicipalisation de divers services publics se situe dans le même esprit. Si les nationalisations face à la crise de 2008 étaient faites sans stratégie et souvent temporaires (Bance et Bernier, 2011), ce n'est pas le cas des entreprises analysées dans ce livre-ci.

Certaines entreprises publiques existent depuis le milieu du 19ᵉ siècle, voire avant. À Paris, la ville a acheté 80 % de l'entreprise de distribution d'eau en 1788 à la veille de la Révolution française. Les grands réseaux d'aqueduc comme celui de la ville de New York ont été créés dans leur forme actuelle dès 1842. L'histoire de la compagnie des eaux de Berlin (BWB) remonte à 150 ans, celle de Milan à 1888. À Vienne, la première ligne de tramway tiré par un cheval date de 1865. Ce sont souvent les entreprises nationalisées après 1945 qui ont été privatisées depuis comme Bosco *et al.* (chapitre 12) le soulignent. D'autres présentées dans ce livre sont très récentes, comme Infrastructure Ontario par exemple. Elles correspondent à une nouvelle manière d'organiser les services publics et participent à l'évolution de leur société, étant modelées par les grands changements de notre époque comme la chute du mur de Berlin. Et entre ces deux époques, certaines – comme la Caisse de dépôt et placement du Québec – ont été lancées au début des années 1960 dans la phase de rapide modernisation de la société québécoise. En Colombie britannique, BC Ferries relève de la même logique de province-building et à la même époque (Bernier, 2011). Si Crespi Reghizzi (chapitre 3) emploie « corporatisation », Dutil (chapitre 10) utilise « agencification » pour parler de la création d'une nouvelle entreprise publique. En Ontario, il s'agit d'un phénomène important, des centaines d'agences ont été créées : des agences « *at arm's length* » pour reprendre l'expression de l'Angleterre d'Herbert Morrison mais pour de nouvelles entreprises publiques.

La mission de service public

Paradoxalement, circonscrire la définition de la mission de service public a été difficile dans plusieurs études de cas même si une entreprise publique sans mission de service public n'est pas vraiment une entreprise publique selon la définition retenue pour la recherche présentée dans cet ouvrage (Florio, 2014). C'est comme dans la pièce de Molière où *Le bourgeois gentilhomme* faisait de la prose sans le savoir. Contribuer à l'intérêt général en distribuant de l'eau potable à l'ensemble d'une population, assurer le ramassage des ordures, organiser un système de collecte et de traitement des eaux usées (même si cela apparaît tardivement dans certaines grandes villes comme à Milan depuis 2005 seulement et en opération par le secteur privé), distribuer de l'électricité, assurer un système de traversiers fiable, etc. sont des missions qui semblent aller de soi dans plusieurs pays et qui sont d'intérêt général. La protection de l'environnement et la responsabilité sociale sont une façon de définir l'intérêt général.

Les infrastructures de transport sont jugées souvent essentielles pour le développement régional. Ce sont les missions que remplissent les entreprises étudiées. La Caisse de dépôt et placement (chapitre 14) a eu un rôle essentiel dans l'économie de la province de Québec et la transformation sociale de cette société qui était en rattrapage sur le reste de l'Amérique du Nord. Pour Greiling, les entreprises publiques allemandes ont toujours eu un rôle qui dépasse de loin la simple fourniture de services publics. Ainsi, dès le début, le holding municipal de Cologne SWK (chapitre 15) a eu une vocation commerciale et s'est fortement investi pour améliorer la qualité de vie des citoyens, tout en favorisant le développement économique. Pour son actionnaire, la valeur de l'entreprise ne se limite pas à son poids économique ou financier qui permet le financement croisé de diverses activités. L'entreprise est surtout considérée comme véritable « valeur » à préserver et capitaliser pour des développements et bénéfices futurs. C'est lorsque ces services font défaut qu'on réalise à quel point ils sont essentiels aux collectivités desservies. Nous sommes à la fois clients des services publics et propriétaires. De tels services existent pour satisfaire leurs utilisateurs mais assurent également, du moins dans la tradition française mais certainement aussi ailleurs, un fondement de cohésion de la société.

Au Pérou, la plus grande entreprise d'eau et d'épuration du pays SEDAPAL (chapitre 4) offre des tarifs très bas qui doivent être financés par l'État ; un des principes de sa tarification est en effet celui de l'équité sociale pour permettre à la majorité de la population de bénéficier du service. Paris offre également un système de solidarité pour ses citoyens aux revenus les plus faibles. Le transport en commun est quant à lui un service d'intérêt général réduisant la congestion automobile, la pollution, etc. Il doit donc, comme indiqué par Kostal *et al.*, être offert en quantité et qualité suffisantes. À Bruxelles, les transports publics sont reconnus en tant que contributeur à la qualité de vie. Outre la livraison classique de lettres et de colis, la Poste française délivre les journaux et participe à l'aménagement du territoire. Par contre, avec la privatisation de A2A (chapitre 13) la mission d'intérêt général a été réduite, avant de réapparaître peu à peu lorsque l'entreprise prenait de l'expansion et, là comme ailleurs, elle est à présent spécifiée par contrat. Delponte *et al.* proposent une explication fort intéressante de l'évolution de la mission de service public.

Dans le cas de certaines entreprises publiques, les obligations de service public sont explicitées dans des plans stratégiques ou d'investissement et dans des contrats. De plus, le cas de la compagnie des eaux de Berlin (chapitre 1) est illustratif du fait qu'outre la mission de base, l'entreprise a également un rôle financier. À Milan l'entreprise publique réussit mieux que la moyenne des services de distribution d'eau d'Italie (chapitre 3) et d'après Crespi Reghizzi, la corporatisation n'a pas mené à négliger les objectifs de service public qui existaient auparavant.

La préoccupation pour la clientèle, soulignée dans l'étude sur les transports en commun à Vienne (chapitre 6), est une dimension récente. Elle existe aussi dans les traversiers étudiés par Malcolm Bird (chapitre 8) au niveau de la sécurité des passagers par exemple, ou encore pour la Poste française (chapitre 11). Les usagers sont des clients qui méritent un bon service, même si selon Dutil (chapitre 10), l'expression « Crown corporation » utilisée au Canada pour désigner les entreprises publiques témoigne que celles-ci sont dans la sphère de la puissance et de l'autorité étatique.

Opérations et performance

Avoir une mission publique n'empêche pas de bien fonctionner. Au contraire, les meilleures années de rentabilité de la Caisse de dépôt (chapitre 14) furent celles durant lesquelles elle s'occupait aussi de développement économique. À Cologne, le groupe SWK réalise des surplus depuis 1996. En pratique, pour remplir leur mission publique et asseoir leur légitimité, les entreprises publiques d'aujourd'hui sont efficaces et rentables. À Berlin, les BWB ne perdent que 2 % de l'eau qu'elle transporte, ce qui est bien moindre que les chiffres habituels dans son industrie. La qualité du service offert par les Wiener Linien est en progression depuis vingt ans malgré des pertes opérationnelles couvertes par la ville de Vienne. La STIB à Bruxelles fait face à une augmentation de sa clientèle impressionnante avec un certain succès, et ce dans la limite de ses moyens. L'Ontario doit gérer une croissance de population très soutenue depuis 20 ans. L'aéroport de Dublin a dû faire face à une montée en flèche de la clientèle.

Pour Berlin comme pour Paris, va se poser la question de la capacité de production alors que la consommation d'eau diminue. Comment maintenir et rentabiliser les équipements ? La survie à long terme des infrastructures va demander des sommes colossales qui risquent de ne pas toujours être disponibles. Le problème de la baisse de clientèle ou de consommation n'est pas uniquement un enjeu pour les compagnies des eaux, BC Ferries fait face à la même situation. La Poste française, par exemple, prévoit une baisse pour le courrier de 30 % sur huit ans. À Milan, les auteurs concluent qu'A2A (chapitre 13) est une entreprise bien gérée qui a su s'adapter à une baisse de la demande de gaz et d'électricité. À l'époque où ENEL (chapitre 12) était une entreprise publique, l'efficience avait augmenté. Le groupe SWK s'attend à devoir faire face au déclin démographique dans les années à venir à Cologne.

Les entreprises publiques sont des entreprises aux tâches parfois complémentaires et nombreuses. L'entreprise milanaise des eaux fournit l'eau potable, traite les eaux usées et développe un service d'ingénierie. Infrastructure Ontario a étendu sa mission par la tenue d'un registre du diabète pour compenser les lacunes d'une autre agence gouvernementale ; cette entreprise publique participe par ailleurs à un projet de centrale nucléaire. De la même manière, DAA exporte son expertise en gestion aéroportuaire et commerciale dans divers aéroports autour du monde. Cahill, Palcic et Reeves présentent l'aéroport de Dublin comme une entreprise de développement économique désormais en concurrence avec les autres aéroports irlandais, ce qui permettra de juger ses résultats par comparaison. Il serait également intéressant de comparer comment ce service d'une entreprise publique est compétitif avec le secteur privé. Dans le cas de BC Ferries, l'entreprise publique a remplacé des entreprises privées peu efficaces. Par ses besoins en équipement, elle contribue au maintien de l'industrie de la construction navale sur la côte ouest canadienne. La Poste a réussi à développer avec des résultats intéressants son secteur bancaire. Elle est même l'institution préférée des Français. La Caisse de dépôt et placement du Québec a connu des hauts et des bas comme plusieurs organisations dans le secteur financier depuis 1990 ; elle a suivi les mêmes cycles accentués par ses décisions parfois trop risquées mais demeure un cas relativement réussi. Et ce qui est dit pour l'aéroport de Dublin est aussi décrit historiquement pour le nord de l'Italie (chapitre 13) : la vitalité industrielle de Milan s'explique en partie historiquement par l'accès à une électricité moins chère qu'ailleurs.

Le cas suédois (chapitre 2) décrit par Mattisson et Ramberg offre une autre idée intéressante. Dans des sociétés vieillissantes, il se peut que le recrutement d'employés doive être plus attractif. Créer une plus grande entreprise conjointe qui succède à de petites entreprises municipales offre plus de possibilités aux employés recrutés même si la standardisation des processus peut mener à une impression de bureaucratie accrue. Cette dimension n'est pas négligeable dans certaines entreprises publiques. La Poste est en France le deuxième employeur après l'État et d'autres entreprises publiques comme le groupe SWK sont de très grandes entreprises.

Les études de cas présentées ici témoignent dans l'ensemble d'une bonne performance des entreprises publiques. VA Syd illustre aussi les gains systémiques d'efficacité qui ont été obtenus dans le sud de la Suède. À Paris, après la remunicipalisation, les tarifs pour l'eau ont baissé de 8 %. La qualité des services offerts par les transports en commun viennois a été soulignée dans plusieurs classements internationaux. Dans le cas de la STIB, Goethals explique que si la performance a été assez mauvaise avant 1990, les chiffres sont depuis en net progrès alors que la clientèle qui utilise les transports en commun bruxellois augmente rapidement et de manière importante. Les chiffres présentés dans son chapitre sont éloquents.

La gouvernance et la régulation

Le cas des BWB (chapitre 1) est intéressant sur le plan de la gouvernance. Comme Schaefer et Warm l'écrivent, la renationalisation des eaux de Berlin vient d'un mouvement populaire sans l'appui d'aucun parti politique après des débats sur les tarifs qui étaient jugés trop élevés. Les tarifs ont baissé d'ailleurs depuis la remunicipalisation. On peut aussi retenir de ce cas une demande pour une transparence accrue comme c'est noté pour d'autres cas étudiés dans ce livre.

Au niveau de la gestion de l'eau, la population réclame de manière croissante des actions en faveur de la qualité de l'environnement. Le traitement des eaux usées est un domaine où les pressions sociales existent autant à Milan que dans le sud de la Suède mais moins à Paris où la propriété de la gestion de l'eau est un sujet pratiquement tombé dans l'oubli. Pour la population, il semble normal que ce soit une entreprise publique qui s'occupe de tels services. Quant au transport en commun, le cas de Vienne est intéressant en ce qu'il documente la présence dans l'environnement de l'entreprise du gouvernement fédéral, de la chambre de commerce mais aussi du mouvement ouvrier et des consommateurs. À Cologne et en fonction de la loi allemande, les employés sont nombreux au conseil de supervision. Trop souvent dans le passé, les études sur les entreprises publiques ont négligé les « stakeholders ».

Une dimension qui mériterait plus de recherche est le degré de gouvernance politique. Est-ce que, par exemple dans les services d'eau, les élus locaux doivent être au conseil d'administration ? Les réponses mises en exergue dans les études de cas varient selon les traditions. Au Canada, on a créé des entreprises publiques pour éloigner leur gestion du politique mais ce n'est pas vrai partout. Dans le cas de l'eau à Paris (chapitre 5) la trop grande proximité du politique ne laisse pas assez de marge de manœuvre à l'entreprise. Pour le transport public local à Bruxelles (chapitre 7), la question du lien avec les partis politiques se pose également, les membres du conseil d'administration de la STIB ayant un lien avec les partis au pouvoir. Certaines des décisions les plus controversées dans le cas traité par Bird (chapitre 8) étaient celles prises par le conseil des ministres de la province dans le passé. On y a adopté depuis un modèle plus moderne : une régie indépendante, une entreprise commerciale pour gérer les traversiers avec un conseil d'administration autonome, un régulateur indépendant et un contrat de service. Le cas de l'Ontario (chapitre 10) est intéressant à cet égard : dans le système politique de tradition britannique, les politiciens tiennent habituellement à annoncer les nouveaux investissements immobiliers pour accroître leur visibilité et montrer qu'ils s'occupent de leurs mandants tout en recueillant des contributions électorales des entrepreneurs qui érigent les immeubles. La création d'une agence a rompu cette façon de faire.

Le cas de la remunicipalisation de l'eau à Paris traité par Bauby et Similie est intéressant sous l'angle de la gouvernance d'une autre manière. Dans la tradition française, il y a de grands opérateurs privés qui sont devenus des entreprises multinationales. Elles ont forcément les ressources et le savoir-faire pour convaincre les gouvernements de leur accorder la gestion de systèmes d'aqueducs. Si elles ont renoncé à combattre la remunicipalisation, faut-il y voir une estimation de leur part qu'il s'agit désormais d'un secteur peu rentable pour les entreprises privées ? La dimension politique du débat est bien expliquée dans le chapitre 5. Inversement, les entreprises privées sont souvent hostiles aux entreprises publiques. Le cas décrit au chapitre 14 de la Caisse de dépôt en est un excellent exemple.

Les entreprises publiques contemporaines ont des structures de gouvernance qui sont souvent celles popularisées par l'OCDE en particulier avec des administrateurs généralement indépendants. Cette normalisation fait que par exemple dans le cas d'ENEL, le changement de propriétaire n'a pas entraîné de changement fondamental de structure de propriété de l'ancienne entreprise publique. Sa gouvernance correspond aux standards attendus. Ce n'est pas le cas à la STIB mais ce l'est maintenant pour BC Ferries. Dans le cas de l'aéroport de Dublin, la gouvernance est jugée efficace, comme dans plusieurs autres cas. Pour A2A à Milan, selon un modèle qui existe aussi en Allemagne, on a créé un système avec un conseil d'administration et un conseil de gestion pour éloigner les opérations de la politique. Delponte, Sorrentino, Turri et Vandone (chapitre 13) décrivent d'ailleurs un système de gouvernance très sophistiqué de cette entreprise italienne, quoique pas toujours idéal. Mais de telles entreprises publiques ont des conseils d'administration avec toutefois un principal qui n'est pas un actionnariat dispersé. On est plus proche du modèle des investisseurs institutionnels. Le contrôle parlementaire dans certains cas est une illustration de cette situation.

La dimension stratégique de ces organisations est importante. Dans le cas suédois, c'est elle qui va permettre de résoudre les tensions entre les intérêts des villes concernées et de gérer l'entreprise en fonction de son activité principale, plus loin des intérêts politiques. Dans le cas de la gestion de l'eau à Paris, il y a un contrat précis qui décrit les dix objectifs principaux de l'entreprise. La Poste étudiée par Bance et Rey a aussi des contrats à remplir. Pour les transports en commun de Vienne, il y a un plan de transport avec des objectifs clairs. À Bruxelles pour la STIB, même chose où on en est à la cinquième génération de contrats, contrats qui sont de plus en plus sophistiqués grâce à l'expérience acquise. Ces contrats régissent le lien entre le principal et l'opérateur.

Une autre dimension à retenir est la création de conglomérats publics. C'est le cas de SEDAPAL qui est dans un groupe d'entreprises de l'État péruvien. Si l'entreprise a une mission relativement claire, le plan stratégique de l'ensemble est encore à préciser. Aragón et Bonifaz (chapitre 4) concluent que la gouvernance d'ensemble du secteur est inadéquate. À Vienne, les transports en commun sont incorporés dans la Wiener Stadtwerke Holding AG. Infrastructure Ontario remplace trois anciennes entreprises publiques. A2A (chapitre 13) et le groupe SWK (chapitre 15) sont des illustrations de groupes multi-activités, même si pour A2A la diversification est surtout géographique. Le groupe A2A est le plus grand groupe italien multi-activités : énergie, eau et déchets. L'entreprise publique de Cologne est active dans le gaz, l'électricité, le transport en commun, les services logistiques (portuaires et autres), les bains publics, le logement, la collecte des ordures, les télécommunications ainsi que le recyclage, le planning urbain, etc. Et si ce n'est pas un conglomérat, comment convient-il de gérer la coordination d'un tel réseau d'entreprises publiques, comme la question est posée aux chapitres 13 et 15 ? Doit-on utiliser des « interlocking directorates » ou avoir une politique industrielle ou économique explicite avec des objectifs précis ? Il existe une littérature scientifique importante sur les holdings privés mais que savons-nous des holdings dans le secteur public ? Il s'agit sans doute d'un sujet de recherche à poursuivre.

Parler de conglomérat dans le cas de la Poste française serait exagéré mais on assiste à une diversification des activités des entreprises publiques pour répondre à divers objectifs. Ainsi, pour éviter l'exclusion sociale, la dimension « banque des pauvres » est un ajout important aux fonctions classiques de la Poste, innovation qui l'a rendue plus légitime dans la société française et correspond à l'idée de service public à la française. Il faudrait aussi reprendre le thème de la filialisation par les entreprises publiques. Ont-elles tendance, comme ce fut le cas jadis, à créer des filiales pour échapper au contrôle gouvernemental ? Doit-on voir ainsi l'évolution de la poste française ?

L'histoire de ENEL est fascinante en ce qu'elle permet d'étudier comment l'État peut demeurer un actionnaire influent dans une entreprise privatisée et comment il peut instaurer des mécanismes de régulation extérieurs à la firme pour la réguler. Le chapitre 13 complète l'explication sur la transformation des entreprises publiques en Italie et les privatisations partielles. Dans le cas des entreprises publiques établies en Europe, la régulation est faite à la fois par des organismes nationaux mais aussi par des instances européennes. Dans le domaine de l'eau, il faut ainsi se conformer à une Directive-cadre européenne dans ce domaine. À Milan, toujours dans le secteur de l'eau, il faut considérer le régulateur local et le national. Le chapitre 3 conclut cependant que le régulateur local n'a pas la capacité de contrôler l'entreprise mais que ce manque est compensé par la culture de service public des employés de celle-ci. Tandis qu'en France, l'eau est le seul grand secteur où il n'y a pas de régulateur national, au Pérou par contre, la régulation se fait par un organisme indépendant. Au Canada, la régulation est partagée entre les provinces et le gouvernement fédéral. Pour l'aéroport de Dublin s'ajoutent les contrôles des organismes internationaux de sécurité aérienne. Pour le transport en commun comme à Vienne, c'est le régulateur national qui stipule les services à offrir. La Poste doit de son côté répondre à une autorité indépendante.

En fait, la régulation des entreprises de réseaux est devenue un domaine de recherche à part entière comme leur gouvernance. Nonobstant le nouveau management public et l'idéologie néo-libérale qui le sous-tendait, il fallait résoudre des besoins de transparence envers les parties prenantes mais aussi d'efficience. Par ailleurs, il faut aussi considérer une nouvelle situation, comme les chapitres 3, 10, 12 et 13 en témoignent où les pouvoirs publics n'ont plus toujours l'expertise qu'ils avaient dans le passé pour interagir avec leurs entreprises publiques et participer à leur gouvernance. Régulation et gouvernance corporative doivent aller de pair mais exigent que tous soient capables de jouer leur rôle respectif.

L'aspect financier

On peut retenir de l'analyse des BWB (chapitre 1) que la gestion financière des entreprises publiques est devenue très sophistiquée avec des mesures strictes et beaucoup de benchmarking. On peut aussi en retenir qu'une entreprise publique rentable peut utiliser ses profits pour financer d'autres services publics. Du moins était-ce vrai en Europe avant certaines limitations introduites par la législation européenne de non-distorsion de concurrence. Ce fut ainsi longtemps vrai à Milan pour l'entreprise qui a précédé A2A. La privatisation de BWB dans les années 1990 satisfaisait des impératifs financiers à court terme mais ne réglait en rien le déficit plus structurel de la région berlinoise. En Suède, la création d'une plus grande entreprise a permis des économies d'échelle. DAA à Dublin est devenue plus commerciale avec le temps. Ceci dit, ce n'est pas toujours le cas, Infrastructure Ontario n'est pas mandatée pour générer des surplus même si celle-ci a un système de gestion financière très sophistiqué. La Poste française a une gestion bien développée de sa tarification.

Une formule qui semble se dessiner et qui explique par exemple la « corporatisation » du service d'eau à Milan est l'idée que les entreprises publiques doivent couvrir leurs coûts. À Vienne de la même manière, l'entreprise publique a développé au fil du temps une autonomie relative plus grande. Par exemple, autrefois, les tarifs étaient fixés par le conseil municipal ce qui n'est plus le cas. En fait, à Milan, la ville reçoit des revenus de son entreprise publique pour financer les autres services municipaux quoique le modèle dans ce cas soit à risque. Ceci dit, des menaces externes pèsent sur la viabilité du secteur, comme par exemple le Pacte européen de Stabilité qui menace les bas tarifs pratiqués en ce moment. Dans les cas étudiés ici comme par exemple celui de l'entreprise péruvienne SEDAPAL, Aragón et Bonifaz considèrent que la performance financière est saine.

La performance financière est devenue un élément important dans la stratégie comme la mission publique et la qualité des services. C'est explicite pour les transports publics à Vienne. Les équipes qui se sont succédé à la tête de la Caisse de dépôt et placement sont jugées sur la base du rendement qu'elles obtiennent, ce qui est normal dans une entreprise financière mais c'est vrai aussi ailleurs. Les gouvernements aujourd'hui ne veulent plus compenser pour les pertes de leurs entreprises publiques mais dans certains secteurs comme le transport en commun à Bruxelles ou les traversiers au Canada, ils doivent continuer à verser des subsides surtout si des contraintes sur les tarifs sont imposées. Il y a les tarifs pour les usagers mais il faut également tenir compte de la dimension compétitivité. Pour l'aéroport de Dublin, il faut s'assurer que les tarifs aéroportuaires d'une part ne rendent pas les voyages trop onéreux, d'autre part permettent à Dublin de rester compétitif vis-à-vis d'aéroports similaires en Europe, et ce afin que la mission de développement économique soit et reste possible.

Autres enjeux

Ce qui ressort également des études de cas rassemblées dans ce livre mais qui n'était pas forcément prévu dans le canevas de base est la sophistication des arrangements institutionnels tant au niveau de la gestion et des opérations que pour la gouvernance de ces entreprises. Par exemple, la création de la VA SYD dans le sud de la Suède avait été précédée par quatre études dans les villes concernées et des discussions dans les conseils municipaux. En d'autres mots, les connaissances pour une bonne gouvernance et un fonctionnement optimal existent et sont utilisées. Les décisions sur la tarification relèvent aussi de calculs qui bénéficient d'une longue expérience acquise. La gouvernance est une question relativement bien étudiée et résolue et c'est sans doute plus sur l'entreprenariat des dirigeants de ces entreprises qu'il faut à présent pousser la recherche. La compagnie qui a précédé le groupe A2A (chapitre 13) était l'exemple d'une entreprise publique où on retrouvait des entrepreneurs dans le secteur public. C'est une notion encore à explorer en grande partie (Bernier, 2014).

Outre ces éléments, on peut retenir que les entreprises publiques sont une forme d'institution malléable, adaptable. Il n'y a pas de portrait-robot de ces entreprises. Les BWB (chapitre 1) sont le résultat de la fusion d'organisations existant des deux côtés du mur de Berlin. C'est une organisation qui a été partiellement privatisée en 1999 avant d'être complètement remunicipalisée en 2014, illustrant ainsi la flexibilité ou la plasticité de la formule des entreprises publiques et la nécessité des capitaux privés au moment de la réunification de Berlin ; ce qui a conduit à la formule en PPP dans les années 1990 quoique celle-ci ait démontré ses limites. Les structures du holding ou des conseils n'ont pas été changées suite à cette transformation de la propriété qui jusque-là était dans un « consortium agreement » confidentiel. Le chapitre 2 documente le cas d'une entente entre gouvernements locaux pour créer une entreprise publique conjointe. Les chapitres 3 et 13 illustrent le passage à la « corporatisation » d'un service municipal qui devient une entreprise publique. À Vienne, l'opérateur est public mais il lui arrive d'impartir une partie des lignes à desservir. Infrastructure Ontario présente aussi un excellent exemple : cette entreprise est restructurée et soumise à de nouvelles régulations, adopte des méthodes du secteur privé et, sous un gouvernement de centre gauche, poursuit des politiques habituellement favorisées par la droite.

Les entreprises publiques existent aujourd'hui aux niveaux local, régional et national et offrent une qualité de service qui puisse faire douter que de meilleurs arrangements de gouvernance, de régulation, etc. pourraient mieux faire. L'absence de débat autour de la municipalisation de l'eau à Paris ou le manque de questionnement sur l'arrangement institutionnel actuel à Vienne pour le transport en commun peuvent être des indications de la légitimité de ces entreprises publiques. Le cas de l'entreprise de Cologne est représentatif de la légitimité que peuvent avoir ces entreprises pour lesquelles il n'y a pas de velléité de privatisation ni au conseil municipal ni dans la population.

Si les programmes de privatisation n'ont pas été faits pour des motifs d'intérêt général, bien au contraire (Florio, 2004), les entreprises publiques actuelles se situent sur une très fine ligne de démarcation entre le privé et le public. On constate en effet que le mouvement dans une direction ou l'autre n'est pas irréversible. Si la nationalisation peut être temporaire comme ce fut le cas pour les banques suédoises dans les années 1990 ou les banques et entreprises automobiles dans la crise de 2008 (Bance et Bernier, 2011), on peut aussi renationaliser, privatiser temporairement et revenir au public. On peut aussi comme le décrivent Bosco, Pelagati et Visconti Parisio (chapitre 12), ne privatiser que partiellement et conserver à l'État une portion suffisante du capital pour garder le contrôle.

Il y a clairement un enjeu de noyau technologique (Hafsi, 1989) dans ces entreprises publiques. Tant les entreprises de transport que d'eau connaissent des expériences similaires d'un pays à l'autre bien que les traditions étatiques soient très différentes. L'économie et la technologie ont plus d'importance que l'idéologie pour expliquer les choix faits (Millward, 2005). La création d'ENEL en 1962 ressemble à ce qui a été fait au Québec (Bernier, 2011) au même moment avec la complétion de la nationalisation des entreprises d'électricité. Il s'agissait alors de rationaliser le secteur et créer un quasi-monopole étatique comme ce fut fait en Angleterre et en France après 1945. Puis la nouvelle configuration où production, distribution, etc. sont faites par des entités séparées a eu lieu aussi pour tenir compte de l'évolution de l'industrie et de la réglementation autant en Europe qu'en Amérique du Nord. C'est ce qu'explique également le chapitre 13 par Delponte et ses collègues.

Une autre dimension qui revient est celle de la commercialisation des entreprises publiques. Celles-ci sont parfois devenues des entreprises internationales importantes dont le rôle dans l'économie mondiale doit être mieux compris (Florio, 2014).

Que retenir d'études de cas ?

La recherche par études de cas permet d'avoir des analyses riches et détaillées de certains phénomènes. Comme Flyvbjerg (2006) le proposait, la recherche par études de cas permet d'établir les fondements des connaissances. C'est ce que nous espérons ici pour relancer la recherche sur les entreprises publiques et créer une nouvelle communauté épistémique sur cet enjeu. C'est aussi pourquoi cette conclusion propose autant de thèmes possibles de recherche. Dans la cadre de ce projet de recherche qui était dirigé par Philippe Bance, Massimo Florio, Gabriel Obermann et l'auteur de ces lignes, nous avons pu demander aux auteurs de suivre le même canevas ce qui a permis de confirmer nombre d'intuitions et présupposés initiaux. En ce sens, les études de cas présentées dans ce livre sont expérimentales en ce qu'elles sont des exemples d'enjeux importants. Si les études de cas multiples sont plus rares dans la littérature (Stewart, 2012), elles sont néanmoins intéressantes parce qu'elles offrent un portrait à partir duquel il est possible de généraliser un certain nombre d'éléments.

Certains de ces chapitres apportent des leçons qui sont de portée plus générale (Flyvbjerg, 2006, p. 228). Ce qui est dit sur la Poste française vaut pour les services postaux dans d'autres pays. Le Postal Service américain ou la Poste canadienne font face de la même manière aux transformations du secteur. La Caisse de dépôt et placement a des équivalents en France, en Belgique, en Suède, en Norvège, en Californie. Ceci dit, nous ne prétendons pas ici avoir développé des inférences causales au sens où Yin (2009) l'entend mais offrir un certain nombre de propositions pour des recherches futures sur les entreprises publiques. Nous avons ici une variation sur les cas choisis et des contextes assez similaires dans plusieurs cas pour penser que les leçons apprises sont valables et permettront aux coordinateurs de ce projet de recherche du CIRIEC d'en diriger une suivante sur des bases plus formalisées (Stewart, 2012). Nous en avons quinze ici mais ils peuvent être liés à plusieurs autres. Les étudiants en statistique apprennent que pour avoir une courbe normale, il faut 30 cas dans un échantillon. Avons-nous un échantillon représentatif ? Les phénomènes dont nous parlons ici ont des portées plus générales dans d'autres domaines que la poste. La remunicipalisation de l'eau à Paris ou à Berlin a aussi eu lieu à Hamilton au Canada, à Buenos Aires en Argentine, à Dar Es Salaam en Tanzanie et en Malaisie (Pigeon *et al.*, 2012).

Nous croyons que le biais existait lors de la sélection des cas mais qu'il était relativement mineur (Flyvbjerg, 2006). Les cas nous ont été proposés lors d'un appel de communication lancé dans le réseau international du CIRIEC puis propagé à travers divers réseaux de recherche comme l'Economics Research Network (ERN), POLCAN de l'association canadienne de science politique et l'American Society of Public Administration. Des chercheurs en Europe, en Afrique, dans les Amériques mais aussi en Australie et en Asie ont reçu cet appel et y ont répondu. Les cas présentés ici ont l'avantage de la richesse de l'analyse en profondeur par des auteurs bien au fait des nuances contextuelles dans chaque pays considéré. Bien que la méthode comparée de cas ait ses limites (Dion, 1998), nous croyons que ceux présentés ici méritaient de l'être et apportent des leçons intéressantes sur les entreprises publiques. Pour la suite, nous proposons un nouveau cycle d'études des entreprises publiques afin d'étendre l'analyse à davantage de cas, permettant de confirmer ou infirmer ce qui a été avancé ici et de favoriser une approche plus sectorielle. Pourraient aussi se faire d'autres études sur les mêmes cas pour voir si les résultats peuvent être répliqués. De ces études de cas, nous pourrons dégager des hypothèses pour des vérifications empiriques plus larges. Une prochaine étape possible est l'utilisation de banques de données. Peut-on modéliser à partir des cas ici présentés ? Une connaissance à la fois plus large et plus approfondie des modes de fonctionnement effectifs des entreprises publiques et de leurs relations avec l'ensemble des « parties prenantes » (*stakeholders*) est un prérequis indispensable pour aller plus loin dans la compréhension des entreprises publiques contemporaines. Pour ce faire, une banque de données a été initiée par Massimo Florio à Milan avec le projet SuPER[2] où certaines des

---

[2] SuPER – *Survey of Public Enterprise Return* : http://www.publicenterprise.unimi.it/.

idées présentées ici pourront être testées (Clò *et al.*, 2014). Cette banque de données (via une enquête en ligne) systématise les transformations récentes encourues par les entreprises publiques. Arrimée à d'autres données statistiques économiques et financières, cette banque de données apportera un autre éclairage aux études de cas et permettra de généraliser (ou non) les analyses faites dans ce livre.

Pour la suite

Nous n'avons pas repris ici plusieurs éléments intéressants des chapitres qui précèdent. Par exemple, Schaefer et Warm développent une section très intéressante sur la tarification de l'eau. La présentation sur les tarifs et la performance des Wiener Linien mériteraient aussi d'être reprises. De la même manière, la subtilité de la couverture de ses coûts par la STIB (chapitre 7) et l'importance du financement extérieur nécessaire se doit d'être soulignée. La formule de gestion des infrastructures de l'Ontario pourrait être utilisée ailleurs. On pourrait multiplier les exemples. Ce que ces études de cas démontrent également est que l'étude des entreprises publiques bénéficie des progrès de diverses disciplines des sciences humaines depuis vingt ans. L'analyse économique a évolué pour comprendre des phénomènes plus variés. Le management stratégique offre de nouvelles explications sur la vision des organisations et l'inclusion des « stakeholders » dans l'analyse en plus de la compréhension du jeu politique dans la gouvernance de ces entreprises. Il faut comprendre la gouvernance d'entreprise autant que la régulation complexe actuelle. Les entreprises publiques sont au cœur d'un nœud complexe de relations. Il faut relier les études de cas présentées ici aux divers travaux plus théoriques qui ont été développés dans ce projet de recherche du CIRIEC mené de 2012 à 2014 et qui ont été publiés dans *le Journal of Economic Policy Reform* en 2014, dans la *International Review of Applied Economics* (voir Florio, 2013 et 2014) ainsi que dans le numéro à venir dans les *Annales de l'économie publique et coopérative* (2015).

La littérature scientifique ancienne, surtout dans des secteurs fortement réglementés, ne concluait pas à des différences dans la performance des entreprises publiques ou privées (Aharoni, 1986). Qu'en serait-il aujourd'hui ? Dans son livre *From Good to Great* sur les entreprises privées à succès, Colins (2001) établissait sa norme à 15 ans de succès continu au-dessus du marché. Ce livre a été un grand best-seller vendu à plus de quatre millions d'exemplaires et enseigné dans de nombreuses écoles de gestion. Les entreprises célébrées en 2001 par Collins n'ont toutefois pas toutes bien passé la dernière décennie. Revenons par comparaison un instant au dernier cas de ce livre-ci, le groupe SWK. Cette entreprise réussit à concilier bonne performance financière et mission publique, et ce depuis 1960, pas seulement durant 15 ans, a des surplus depuis presque vingt ans. C'est une entreprise complexe et de grande taille active dans de nombreux secteurs essentiels au bien commun. Il y a dans les entreprises publiques présentées ici un test de durée que plusieurs ont remporté haut la main. On peut retenir de A2A que la formule des entreprises mixtes a certaines limites. Devrait-on retourner à des entreprises seulement publiques ? Se pourrait-il que les entreprises privées qui, dans la littérature sur les privatisations ont été tant vantées comme étant supérieures aux entreprises publiques, devraient prendre des leçons de ces dernières ? Les entreprises publiques sont des organisations hybrides (Pache et Santos, 2013), aux logiques complexes (Greenwood, 2011) qui doivent internaliser les missions d'intérêt général qui leur sont confiées et ont démontré qu'elles en sont capables. On peut combiner efficacité et mission d'intérêt général. Les entreprises publiques ont su se renouveler dans un contexte changeant. C'est ce que continuent à faire les entreprises publiques aujourd'hui et il est possible qu'elles soient un modèle pour demain que le CIRIEC va continuer d'étudier.

Note : pour les références bibliographiques, voir version anglaise dans le chapitre suivant.

Conclusion
Public Enterprises Today and Tomorrow

Luc BERNIER

ENAP

This book presents case studies on public enterprises in nine countries active in sectors as diverse as water, electricity, finance, real estate infrastructures, postal services, air, local or maritime transport and engineering services. Some are complex structures pursuing a general-interest mission at the same time as being efficient operators delivering rather solid financial performances. These public enterprises function in political systems as different as those of Peru or Sweden, or the British parliamentary tradition of Canada and Ireland, or those of continental European systems such as France, Belgium and Italy. They function in large countries, such as Germany, or small ones such as Austria or Ireland.

Not everything is perfect in these enterprises; SEDAPAL does not supply water for the poorest families in Lima, (9.55% of the population) and, even in Paris, families still have to get their water from public fountains. However, as in the previous CIRIEC research project on local public enterprises,[1] these enterprises provide interesting elements allowing to argue against the advocates of privatisation and to further the scientific debate. For a long time, little has been done in the way of research on public enterprise. The more significant works on the subject date from the 1980s (Aharoni, 1986; Hafsi, 1989). True, there have been some other articles since, books devoted to interesting cases, but the nub of the research in the field is published around privatisation. The sweeping meta-analysis by Megginson and Netter (2001) blased the name of private enterprise and its alleged superiority over public enterprise. In 2000, it was found that public enterprises were in a state of decline that could barely be remedied (Toninelli, 2000). That said, the fifteen case

---

[1] This research conducted by CIRIEC's International Scientific Commission "Public services/Public enterprises" (2008-11) did result in the publication of three sectorial monographies (waster, transport, water) in the *Annals of Public and Cooperative Economics*, Vol. 83, No. 4, December 2012.

studies in this book attest to the fact that public enterprises still have their place, that they offer important general-interest services and that they continue to operate under many and various systems of governance.

This concluding chapter initially ponders the lessons learnt from studying the cases presented in the previous chapters with reference to the questions raised by way of introduction, seeking the elements that emerge in more than one case. With these case studies we did not pretend to "reinvent" the theory on public enterprises, what could become a future CIRIEC research endeavour. Nonetheless we think that the empirical material from the case studies do give an interesting portrait of a new reality of those enterprises: their governance has been transformed, be it the corporate governance or its regulation by institutions set up to do so, and the general interest can be carried by various formula where contractualisation and public property mingle. In a second movement, we map the other potential research questions brought out in those analyses. It will be necessary to evaluate over the longer term how the lessons learnt via those case studies stand the test of time within various and changing social, economic and political contexts. A third section considers the method behind the case studies. The whole exercise is undertaken in order to raise research questions in order to pursue the work conducted and presented in this book, for which we must therefore offer our thanks to the authors and praise them for the quality of their work.

Public Enterprises Today

If this book tells us one thing then it is that public enterprises still have a part to play. They are not active in waning sectors such as once the coal industry, but in key infrastructure sectors such as electricity or water distribution. Local public passenger transport services that facilitate everyday life, be they the ferryboats on the west coast of Canada or the trams and buses of Brussels or Vienna. Public enterprises also answer needs for State intervention in the economy or in the infrastructure, as so entrusted in Ontario or in Ireland. The State no longer pulls out to let the private sector in, apart from some situations due to heavy budgetary problems as in Greece for instance. The economic landscape of spring 2014 was marked by the battle between Siemens and General Electric for control of the French company Alsthom, in which the State, will now be a major shareholder. It looks like a stepped-up involvement in this company on the part of the French State, even if it should be of temporary nature. The renationalisation or remunicipalisation of various public services was cut from the same cloth. Where the nationalisations countering the 2008 crisis were made without strategy and often on a temporary basis (Bance and Bernier, 2011), such is not the case for the enterprises analysed in this book.

Certain public enterprises have been around since the mid-19th century, or even earlier. In Paris, the city bought 80% of the water distribution company in 1788, on the eve of the French Revolution. The big water supply networks, such as those of the city of New York, were created in their present form as early as 1842. The history of the Berlin water company (BWB) goes back 150 years, the Milan water company to 1888. In Vienna, the first horse-drawn tramway line dates from 1865. It is often the enterprises nationalised after 1945 that were since privatised, as Bosco *et al.* (chapter 12) point out. Others presented in this book are very recent, such as *Infrastructure Ontario*. They correspond to a new way of organising public services and participate in the evolution of their society, being shaped by the big changes of our times, such as the fall of the Berlin Wall. And, between those two eras, some of them – such as the *Caisse de dépôt et placement du Québec* – were launched in the early 1960s in the phase of rapid modernisation of Québec society. In British Colombia, BC Ferries falls within the same logic of province building and the same period (Bernier, 2011). If Crespi Reghizzi (chapter 3) uses "corporatisation", Dutil (chapter 10) uses "agencification" to speak of the creation of a new public enterprise. In Ontario, this is an important phenomenon, hundreds of "arm's length" agencies have been created, to use the expression of the England of Herbert Morrison, but for new public enterprises.

The Public Service Mission

Paradoxically, defining the mission of the public service has been difficult in several case studies, even if a public enterprise without a public service mission is not really a public service according to the definition adopted for the research presented in this book (Florio, 2014). It is like the play by Molière where *Le bourgeois gentilhomme* wrote prose without knowing it. Contributing to the general interest by distributing drinking water to an entire population, waste disposal, organising a wastewater collection and treatment system (even if this appears quite late in some large cities such as Milan, where it is in place since 2005 only and run by the private sector), distributing electricity, providing a reliable ferry boat system, etc., are missions that seem to be self-evident in several countries and are in the general interest. For this public enterprise as for others, protection of the environment and social responsibility are a way of defining the general interest.

The transport infrastructures are often thought essential for regional development. These are the missions undertaken by the enterprises studied here. The *Caisse de dépôt et placement* (chapter 14) had an essential role in the economy of the province of Québec and in the transformation of Québec society, which was catching-up with the rest of North America. For

Greiling, the German public enterprises have always had a role that goes far beyond the simple provision of public services. Since the beginning, the Cologne municipal holding SWK (chapter 15) has had a commercial vocation and a strong commitment to improving the quality of life of citizens while promoting economic development. For its shareholder, the value of the company is not limited to its economic or financial weight allowing the cross-financing of various activities. The enterprise has also a vocation of true "value" to be preserved and capitalised for future developments and benefits. It is when these services fail that we realise the extent to which they are essential to the communities that they cover. We are clients of public services but also their owners. Such services exist to satisfy their users but also provide, at least in the French tradition but certainly also elsewhere, a foundation for the cohesion of society.

In Peru, the biggest enterprise in the country for water and sewage SEDAPAL (chapter 4) offers very low prices that must be financed by the State, one of its price-setting principles being indeed that of social equity, to allow the majority of the population to get the service. Paris also offers a system of solidarity for its citizens on the lowest incomes. Public passenger transport on its side is a general-interest service, reducing road traffic congestion, pollution, etc., and should, as pointed out by Kostal *et al.*, be offered in sufficient quantity and quality. In Brussels, public transport is considered as contributing to the quality of life. Besides the conventional delivery of letters and parcels, *La Poste française* delivers newspapers and participates in town and country planning. However, with the privatisation of A2A (chapter 13), the general-interest mission has slowly been eroded, before gaining back consistence as the enterprise followed the path of expansion and, there as elsewhere, is now specified by contract. Delponte *et al.* put forward a very interesting explanation concerning the evolution of the public service mission.

In the case of certain public enterprises, the public service obligations are explicated in strategic plans or in investment plans, and in contracts. Moreover, the case of the Berlin water company (chapter 1) illustrates that in addition to the basic mission, the enterprise has a financial role too. In Milan, the public enterprise is more successful than average in Italian water distribution services (chapter 3) and, for Crespi Reghizzi, corporatisation has not led to the abandoning of the public service objectives that existed earlier.

The concern for the clientele, underlined in the study on public passenger transport in Vienna (chapter 6), is a recent dimension. It also exists in terms of safety of passengers for instance for the ferries studied by Malcolm Bird (chapter 8), or for *La Poste française* (chapter 11). The users are also clients who deserve a good service even if, as Dutil points out (chapter 10), the expression "Crown corporation" used in Canada to describe public enterprises attests to the fact that they are in the sphere of State power and authority.

Operation and Performance

Having a public mission does not preclude good functioning. On the contrary, the best years of cost-effectiveness of the *Caisse de dépôt* (chapter 14) were those when it also occupied itself with economic development. In Cologne, the SWK group has been showing profit since 1996. In practice, to accomplish their public mission and ensure their legitimacy, the public enterprises of today are efficient and profitable. In Berlin the *Berliner Wasserbetriebe* lose only 2% of the water that it transports, which is well below the usual figures in its industry. The quality of service offered by the *Wiener Linien* has been improving for twenty years, despite operational losses which are covered by the City of Vienna. The STIB in Brussels is coping with a substantial increase in its clientele with a certain success, and this within the limits of its means. Ontario has been dealing with a very sustained growth of population over the past 20 years. Dublin airport has had to contend with a sharp rise of its clientele.

For Berlin as for Paris, there is the question of production capacity while water consumption continues to decline. How maintain and secure a return on the equipment? The long-term survival of infrastructures will require huge sums of money that have an unfortunate habit of not always being there when needed. The problem of the reduction of clientele or consumption is not only a cause of concern for the water companies, BC Ferries faces the same situation. The French post, for example, foresees a downturn in mail estimated at 30% over eight years. In Milan, the authors conclude that A2A (chapter 13) is a well managed enterprise that has had to adapt to a reduction of demand for gas and electricity. At the time when ENEL (chapter 12) was a public enterprise, efficiency had increased. The SWK group expects to have to contend with a demographic decline in the years to come in Cologne.

The public enterprises are enterprises whose tasks are sometimes complementary and numerous. The Milan water company supplies drinking water, treats wastewater and develops a public works service. Infrastructure Ontario has extended its mission by adding the keeping of a register of diabetes to fill the gaps of another governmental agency; this public enterprise on the other hand participates in a nuclear power plant project. In the same way DAA exports its expertise in airport and commercial management in different airports around the world. Cahill, Palcic and Reeves present the Dublin airport as an enterprise of economic development now in competition with other Irish airports, so its results may now be judged by comparison. It would also be interesting to compare how this public enterprise service competes with the private sector. In the case of BC Ferries the public enterprise has replaced low-efficiency private enterprises. Through its needs in terms of equipment, it contributes to maintaining the naval construction industry on the west coast of Canada. *La Poste* has succeeded in developing with interesting results in its banking sector; it is even the financial institution that the French prefer. The *Caisse de dépôt et placement* has had some ups and downs like several other organisations in the financial sector since 1990; it has followed the same cycles punctuated by sometimes rash decisions but is still a relatively successful case. What has been said for Dublin airport is also described historically for the north of Italy (chapter 13): historically, the industrial vitality of Milan is partially explained by access to electricity that is less expensive than elsewhere.

The Swedish case (chapter 2) described by Mattisson and Ramberg offers another interesting idea. In aging societies it may be the case that the recruitment of employees has to be made more attractive. Creating a bigger joint enterprise that takes over from small municipal enterprises offers the recruited employees more possibilities, even if the standardisation of processes may lead to an impression of increased bureaucracy. This dimension is not inconsiderable in certain public enterprises. In France, *La Poste* is the second biggest employer after the State, and other public enterprises such as the SWK group are very large enterprises.

On the whole, the case studies presented here acknowledge of good performance of public enterprises. VA Syd also illustrates the systemic efficiency gains obtained in the South of Sweden. In Paris, after remunicipalisation, the cost of water fell 8%. The quality of the services provided by the public transport in Vienna has been underlined in several international ratings. In the case of the STIB Goethals explains that if performance was rather poor before 1990, the figures now indicate a clear improvement while the clientele using the Brussels public transport is increasing rapidly and appreciably. The figures presented in his chapter speak volumes.

Governance and Regulation

The BWB case (chapter 1) is interesting as regards governance. As Schaefer and Warm report, renationalisation of the Berlin water is sprung from a popular movement without the support of any political party after debates on charges considered being excessively high. The charges have incidentally been reduced since remunicipalisation. We may also mention the case of a demand for greater transparency as noted for other case studies in this book.

For water management there is increasing demand from the population as regards quality of the environment. The treatment of wastewater is an area where social pressures exist, in Milan and in the South of Sweden, but less so in Paris where the ownership of the management of water is a subject that has practically fallen into oblivion. The population finds it normal that a public enterprise takes care of such services. For public passenger transport, the case of Vienna is interesting in that it documents the presence in the environment of the federal Government enterprise, of the chamber of commerce, but also of the workers' movement and its consumers. In Cologne, under German law, employees are numerous on the supervisory boards. Too often in the past studies on public enterprises have forgotten the "stakeholders".

One dimension that deserves more research is the degree of political governance. Should, in the water services, for example, local elected representatives serve on the board of directors? The answers brought out in these case studies vary according to tradition. In Canada, public enterprises have been created to distance their management from politics, but this is not true everywhere. In the case of water in Paris (chapter 5) the undue proximity of politics does not allow the enterprise sufficient room for *manoeuvre*. For the public transport in Brussels (chapter 7), the question of the link with political parties arises too; the members of the STIB board of directors have ties with the parties in power. Certain of the most controversial decisions in the case discussed by Bird (chapter 8) were those taken by the Council of Ministers of the province in the past. A more modern model has since been adopted: an independent management, a commercial enterprise to manage the ferries with an autonomous board of directors, an independent regulator and a service contract. The case of Ontario (chapter 10) is interesting in this respect. In the political system of the British tradition politicians make a point of announcing new property investments to increase their visibility and to show that they concern themselves with their electorate while collecting electoral contributions from the entrepreneurs who erect the buildings.

The case of remunicipalisation of water in Paris discussed by Bauby and Similie is interesting in another way from the governance perspective. In the French tradition there are large private operators that have become multinational enterprises. They necessarily have the resources and know-how to convince Governments to entrust them with the management of water supply systems. If they gave up fighting remunicipalisation, must we here see an estimation on their part that this is now a low-profit sector for private enterprises? The political dimension of the debate is well explained in chapter 5. Conversely, the private enterprises are often hostile to public enterprises. The case of the *Caisse de dépôt* (chapter 14) is an excellent example.

The contemporary public enterprises are governance structures that are often those popularised by the OECD in particular, with generally independent directors. This standardisation means that, for example, in the case of ENEL, the change of owner has not trigged any essential change of structure of ownership of the former public enterprise. Its governance corresponds to the expected standards. This is not the case in the STIB but it now is for BC Ferries. In the case of Dublin airport, governance is judged efficient, and in several other cases. For A2A in Milan, on a model that also exists in Germany, a system has been created with a board of directors and a management council to distance operations from politics. Delponte, Sorrentino, Turri and Vandone (chapter 13) describe besides a system of governance of this Italian enterprise that is highly sophisticated although not always ideal. But such public enterprises have management councils with, however, a principal that is not a dispersed shareholder. This is closer to the model of institutional investors. The parliamentary control in certain cases is an illustration of this situation.

The strategic dimension of these organisations is important. In the Swedish case it is this that will allow the resolution of tensions between the interests of the town concerned and the management of the enterprise according to its main activity, farther away from political interests. In the case of the management of water in Paris there is a precise contract that sets out the ten main objectives of the enterprise. *La Poste*, studied by Bance and Rey, also has contracts to fulfil. For public passenger transport in Vienna there is a transport plan with clear objectives. The same for the STIB in Brussels, where there is now a fifth generation of contracts, contracts that are increasingly sophisticated thanks to the acquired experience. These contracts govern the link between the principal and the operator.

Another dimension to consider is the creation of conglomerates. It is the case for SEDAPAL, which is in a group of enterprises of the Peruvian State. The enterprise may well have a relatively clear mission, but the strategic plan of the whole is yet to be defined. Aragón and Bonifaz conclude that the governance of the sector as a whole is inadequate. In Vienna, the public passenger transport is incorporated in the *Wiener Stadtwerke Holding AG*. Infrastructure Ontario replaces three former public enterprises. A2A (chapter 13) and SWK (chapter 15) even are illustrations of multi-activity group, even if, in the A2A case, the diversification is mostly geographical. The A2A group is the largest Italian multi-utility group: energy, water and waste. The public enterprise in Cologne is active in gas, electricity, pubic passenger transport, logistics services (docks and harbours, etc.), public baths, housing, waste collection, telecommunications and recycling, town planning, etc. And, if not through a conglomerate, how should the coordination of such a network of public enterprises be managed, as the question is raised in chapter 13 and 15? Should use be made of "interlocking directorates", should there be an explicit industrial or economic policy with precise objectives? There is a substantial scientific literature on the private holdings, but what do we know about holdings in the public sector? This is certainly a subject that invites future research.

To talk of a conglomerate in the case of French *La Poste* would be exaggerated, but public enterprises diversify their activities to meet various objectives. So, to avoid social exclusion, its "bank of the poor" dimension is an important addition to classical functions of the postal operator, an innovation that has rendered it more legitimate in French society and corresponds to the idea of public service the French way. We should therefore talk rather of filiarisation by the public enterprises. Do they tend, as was once the case, to set up branches to escape Government control? Is this therefore to be regarded as the evolution of *La Poste française*?

The story of ENEL is fascinating in that it allows a study of how the State can remain an influential shareholder in a privatised enterprise and how it can install mechanisms external to the firm to regulate it. Chapter 13 completes the explanation of the transformation of public enterprises in Italy and the partial privatisations. In the case of public enterprises established in Europe, regulation is affected by national bodies but also by European agencies. In the water sector, one needs to conform to the European Water Framework Directive. In Milan, still in the water sector, we must consider the local regulator and the national regulator. Chapter 3 concludes, however, that the local regulator does not have the capacity to control the enterprise, but that this lack is compensated by the public service culture of its employees. While in France, water is the only sector for which there is no national regulator, in Peru on the contrary, regulation rests with an independent organisation. In Canada, regulation is shared among the provinces and the federal Government. For Dublin airport there is the added factor of inspections by international air transport safety organisations. In the case of public transport, as in Vienna, it is the national regulator that stipulates the services to offer. *La Poste* must on, its side, answer to an independent authority.

In fact, the regulation of network enterprises has become a field of research in its own right, as is their governance. Notwithstanding the new public management and the neo-liberal ideology underpinning it, more transparency towards stakeholders and efficiency required due answers. Further, a new situation must be considered, as shown in chapters 3, 10, 12 and 13, namely that public authorities no longer always hold the expertise they had in the past to interact with their public enterprises and participate in their governance. Regulation and corporate governance must go hand in hand but require everyone to be able to play their respective roles.

The Financial Aspect

It may be recalled from the analysis of the BWB (chapter 1) that the financial management of public enterprises has become highly sophisticated, with strict measures and much benchmarking. It may further be recalled that a cost-effective public enterprise can use its profits to finance other public services. At least, this was true in Europe before certain limitations were introduced by European Union legislation aiming at not distorting competition. This was thus long true for Milan, for the enterprise that went before A2A. The privatisation of the BWB during the 1990s satisfied the short-term financial imperatives but did nothing to settle the more structural deficit of the Berlin region. In Sweden, the creation of a larger enterprise has allowed economies of scale. DAA in Dublin has become more commercial over time. That said, such is not always the case; Infrastructure Ontario is not mandated to generate surplus, even if this is a highly sophisticated system of financial management. *La Poste française* has a well-developed management of its scheduled rates and charges.

One formula that seems to suggest itself and explains, for example, the "corporatisation" of the water service in Milan is the idea that the public enterprises must cover their costs. In Vienna, in the same way, the public enterprise over the years has developed greater relative autonomy. For example, tariffs were once fixed by the Municipal Council, which is no longer the case. In fact, in Milan, the city receives revenues from its public enterprise to finance other municipal services, even though the model in this case may be at risk. That said, external risks weigh upon the viability of the sector, for instance with the European Internal Stability Pact threatening the low tariffs applied at present. In the cases studied here, for example, the case of Peruvian enterprise SEDAPAL, Aragón and Bonifaz consider that the financial performance is sound.

Financial performance has become as important an element in strategy as the public mission and quality of services. It is explicit for public passenger transport in Vienna. The teams who have risen to the head of the *Caisse de dépôt et placement* are appreciated basing on the return they obtain, which is normal for a financial enterprise but is also true elsewhere. Governments today wish no longer to offset the losses of their public enterprises but, in certain sectors such as public transport in Brussels or the ferries in Canada, they must continue to pay subsidies, especially if limits are imposed on the tariffs. There are tariffs for the users, but there is also the dimension of competition. For Dublin airport it is necessary to ensure that the airport does not make flights too expensive, but equally to ensure that the costs of landing in Dublin are competitive with those of similar airports in Europe, and this in order that the mission of economic development may remain possible and be realised.

Other Issues

What also emerges from the case studies collected in this book but does not necessarily feature in the basic framework is the sophistication of institutional arrangements made for management and operations and for the governance of these enterprises. For example, the creation of VA SYD in the South of Sweden was preceded by four studies in the towns and cities concerned and discussions in municipal councils. In other words, the knowledge for an optimal governance and running exists and is being used. The decisions regarding price-setting also have to do with calculations that benefit from long years of acquired experience. Governance is an issue that is largely studied and resolved and it is perhaps more on the entrepreneurship of directors of these enterprises that research must now press forwards. The company that preceded the A2A group (chapter 13) was an example of a public enterprise with entrepreneurs in the public sector. It is a notion that is largely yet to be explored (Bernier, 2014).

Besides these elements, we may recall that the public enterprises are a malleable, adaptable form of institution. There is no identikit for these enterprises. The BWB (chapter 1) are the result of the merger of organisations once either side of the Berlin Wall. It is an organisation that was partially privatised in 1999 before being completely remunicipalised in 2014, this way illustrating the flexibility or plasticity of the public enterprise formula and how it needed private capital at the time of the reunification of Berlin; *ergo* the PPP formula during the 1990s, although it also revealed its limits. The holding structures, or the boards, did not change after this transformation of ownership which, up until that point, had been a confidential "consortium agreement". chapter 2 documents the case of an entente between local Governments to create a joint public enterprise. Chapters 3 and 13 map out the "corporatisation" movement of a municipal service on the way to becoming a public enterprise. In Vienna, the operator is public but also has to contract out part of the lines that it covers. Infrastructure Ontario is another excellent example: in 2011 this public enterprise underwent reorganisation and was subjected to new regulations, adopted private-sector methods and, under a centre-left Government, pursues policies usually favoured by the right.

Public enterprises today exist at local, regional and national level and offer such a quality of service such that might suggest that no better arrangements of governance, regulation, etc. exist to offer the same services. The lack of debate around the municipalisation of water in Paris or the absence of questioning on the current institutional in Vienna for public passenger transport may be indications of the legitimacy of these public enterprises. The case of the enterprise in Cologne is representative of the legitimacy that these enterprises might enjoy, enterprises for which there is no inclination towards privatisation in the Municipal Council, nor among the population.

The privatisation programmes, then, may not have been pursued for general-interest reasons; quite the contrary (Florio, 2004), however, the present-day public enterprises tread a very fine line between private and public. In point of fact it can be seen that no movement this way or that is irreversible. If nationalisation can be temporary, as was the case for the Swedish banks during the 1990s, or for the banks and car manufacturers during the crisis of 2008 (Bance and Bernier, 2011), they can just as easily be renationalised, temporarily privatised and returned to the public sector. And, as Bosco, Pelagati and Visconti Parisio (chapter 12) describe it, you may also privatise only partially and let the State in any case holds on to a sufficient slice of the capital to keep control.

There is clearly a vested interest in the core technology (Hafsi, 1989) in these public enterprises. The transport companies have had experiences not unlike those of the water companies in this country and that, even if they happen to work within very different state traditions. Economy and technology are more important than ideology in explaining the choices made (Millward, 2005). The creation of ENEL in 1962 bears a family likeness to what was done in Québec (Bernier, 2011) at the time of the completion of nationalisation of the electricity companies. So it is a matter of rationalising the sector and setting up a State quasi-monopoly, as in England and France post-1945. Then the new configuration where production, distribution, etc., are handled by separate entities to accommodate the evolution of the industry and the regulations in Europe and North America. The subject is also examined in chapter 13 by Delponte and colleagues.

Another dimension that arises is that of the commercialisation of public enterprises. These have often become sizeable international enterprises whose role in the world economy really needs to be better understood (Florio, 2014).

What do the Case Histories Tell Us?

Research by case studies yields rich and detailed analyses of certain phenomena. As Flyvbjerg (2006) suggests, research by case studies allows us to lay the foundations of knowledge. We hoped here to relaunch research on public enterprises and to have created a new epistemic community around this interest. This is also why this conclusion proposes as many subjects for research as possible. In the framework of this research project, led by Philippe Bance, Massimo Florio, Gabriel Obermann and the author of the present text, we were able to ask the authors to follow the same master plan that allowed us to have confirmation of numerous intuitions and initial presuppositions. In that sense, the case studies presented in this book are experimental in as much as they are examples of important issues. The multiple case studies may well be fewer and farther between in the literature (Stewart, 2012), but they are nonetheless interesting because they paint a portrait from which we might infer a certain number of elements.

Certain of these chapters bring about lessons of more general outreach (Flyvbjerg, 2006, p. 228). What has been said regarding *La Poste française* applies likewise in respect of the postal services in other countries. The American Postal Service or Canada Post are squaring up to changes in the sector in the same way. The *Caisse de dépôt et placement* has equivalents in France, Belgium, Sweden, Norway and California. That said, we do not pretend here that we have developed any causal inferences within the meaning of Yin (2009), but rather offer a certain number of ideas for future research on public enterprise. Here we have a variation on the cases chosen and rather similar contexts in several contexts to think that the lessons learnt are valid, and will allow the coordinators of this CIRIEC research project to prepare a sequel on more formalised bases (Stewart, 2012). We have fifteen here, but they could be linked to several others. The statistics students have learnt that it takes 30 cases in a sample to have a normal curve. Do we, in fact, have a representative sample? The phenomena of which we speak here have more general range in fields other than the postal services. The remunicipalisation of water in Paris or Berlin also took place in Hamilton Canada, Buenos Aires Argentina, Dar-Es-Salaam Tanzania and in Malaysia (Pigeon *et al.*, 2012).

We feel that a bias existed in the selection of cases but that it was only a relatively minor one (Flyvbjerg, 2006). The cases were proposed to us in a call for communication put out on the international CIRIEC network and then broadcast on various research networks, such as the Economics Research Network (ERN), POLCAN of the Canadian Political Science Association and the American Society of Public Administration. Researchers in Europe, Africa, the two Americas and also in Australia and Asia received the call and answered it. The cases presented here have the advantage of wealth and depth of analysis by authors well in touch with the contextual nuances of each of the countries examined. The case comparison method may well have its limits (Dion, 1998), but we do feel that the cases presented have their rightful place here and teach interesting lessons about public enterprises. To go on, we propose a new cycle of research on public enterprises, the addition of new cases that might confirm or invalidate what is advanced here and favour a more sectorial approach. Other studies of the same cases could also be done to see whether the results can be replicated. Basing on these case studies we can then form hypotheses for broader empirical verifications. A possible next step is the use of data banks. Can we modelise on the basis of the cases presented here? A broader and deeper knowledge of the effective functioning modes of public enterprises and their relations with all the stakeholders is a necessary prerequisite to advance in the understanding of contemporary public enterprises. To do so, a data bank has been launched by Massimo Florio in Milan with the SuPER[2] project in which certain of the ideas presented here could be tested (Clò *et al.*, 2014). This data bank (via online questionnaire) systematises the recent changes undergone by public enterprises. Docked to other economic and financial statistics, this data bank will provide a different light on the case studies and allow to generalise (or not) the analyses in this book.

And for the Future

We have not included here a number of interesting elements from the preceding chapters. For example, Schaefer and Warm develop a very interesting section on the pricing of water. The presentation on the tariffs and performance of the *Wiener Linien* also deserved to be included. In the same way, the subtlety of the coverage of its costs by the STIB (chapter 7) and the scale of outside financing necessary deserve mention. The infrastructure management formula in Ontario could also be used elsewhere. The examples could be multiplied. What these case studies moreover show is that the study of public enterprises benefits from progress in various disciplines in the human sciences over the past twenty years. Economic analysis has come to understand more varied phenomena. Strategic management offers new explanations for the vision of organisations and the inclusion of "stakeholders" in the analysis besides the comprehension of the political game in these enterprises. We must understand corporate governance and the current complex regulation. Public enterprises are at the heart of a complex tangle of relations. We must connect the case studies presented here to various more theoretical works that have been developed in this CIRIEC research project conducted from 2012 to 2014 and that have been published in the *Journal of Economic Policy Reform* in 2014, in the *International Review of Applied Economics* (see Florio, 2013 and 2014) and in the coming issue of the *Annals of Public and Cooperative Economics* (2015).

The aged scientific literature, especially in highly regulated sectors, did not see any differences in the performance of public or private enterprises (Aharoni, 1986). How do things stand today? In his book *From Good to Great* on private enterprise success stories, Collins (2001) established his standard of 15 years of continued success above the market. This book

---

[2]   SuPER – *Survey of Public Enterprise Return*: http://www.publicenterprise.unimi.it/.

was a big bestseller, selling more than four million copies and is required reading in numerous management schools. However, the enterprises celebrated by Collins in 2001 have not all fared well during the past decade. By way of comparison, let us return a moment to the last case in this book, the group SWK. This enterprise succeeded in reconciling good financial performance and a public mission, and this since 1960 – not just during 15 years – with surpluses for nearly twenty years. It is a complex, large-scale enterprise involved in numerous sectors essential to the general interest. In the public enterprises presented here there is a life expectancy test that many have passed with flying colours. We may mention A2A, whose mixed-enterprise formula has certain limits. Should we return to solely public enterprises? Is it possible that the private enterprises that, according to the literature on privatisations, are vaunted as superior to public enterprises have lessons to learn from the latter? Public enterprises are hybrid organisations (Pache and Santos, 2013), with complex logics (Greenwood, 2011) that have to internalise the general-interest missions assigned to them; they have demonstrated that they are up to the task. Efficiency and the general-interest mission can be combined. Public enterprises succeeded in renewing themselves in a changing environment. That is what the public enterprises are still busy doing and they may even be a model for tomorrow that CIRIEC will go on studying.

References

Aharoni, Yair (1986), *The Evolution and Management of State-Owned Enterprises*, Cambridge, Mass.: Ballinger.

Bance, Philippe et Bernier, Luc (2011), *Crise contemporaine et renouveau de l'action publique*, Bruxelles: Peter Lang.

Bernier, Luc (2011), "The Future of Public Enterprises: perspectives from the Canadian Experience", in *Annals of Public and Cooperative Economics*, Vol. 82, pp. 399-419.

Bernier, Luc (2014), "Public enterprises as policy instruments: the importance of public entrepreneurship", in *Journal of Economic Policy Reform*, advanced publication.

Clò, S., Del Bo, C., Ferraris, M., Fiorio, C., Florio, M. and Vandone, D., "Publicization versus Privatization: Preliminary Findings 2000-2012", in *CIRIEC working papers*, (2014/03).

Collins, Jim (2001), *Good to Great*, New York: Harper, Collins.

Dion, Douglas (1998), "Evidence and Inference in the Comparative Case Study", in *Comparative Politics*, Vol. 30, pp. 127-145.

Florio, Massimo (2004), *The Great Divesture*, Cambridge, Mass: MIT Press.

Florio, Massimo (2013), "Rethinking on public enterprise: editorial introduction and some personal remarks on the research agenda", in *International Review of Applied Economics*, Vol. 27, pp. 135-149.

Florio, Massimo (2014), "Contemporary public enterprises; innovation, accountability, governance", in *Journal of Economic Policy Reform*, advanced publication.

Flyvbjerg, Bent (2006), "Five Misunderstandings About Case-Study Research", in *Qualitative Inquiry*, Vol. 12, pp. 219-245.

Greenwood, R., Raynard, M., Kodeih, F., Micelotta, E.R. and Lounsbury, M., (2011), "Institutional Complexity and Organizational Responses", in *The Academy of Management Annals*, Vol. 5, pp. 317-371.

Hafsi, Taïeb, directeur (1989), *Strategic Issues in State-Controlled Enterprises*, Greenwich, Conn.: JAI Press.

Megginson, William L. and Jeffrey M. Netter (2001), "From State to Market: a survey of empirical studies on privatization", in *Journal of Economic Literature*, Vol. 39, pp. 321-389.

Millward Robert (2005), *Private and public enterprise in Europe*, Cambridge: Cambridge University Press.

Pache, Anne-Claire and Filipe Santos (2013), "Inside the Hybrid Organization: Selective Coupling as a Response to Competing Institutional Logics", in *Academy of Management Journal*, Vol. 56, pp. 972-1001.

Pigeon, Martin, McDonald, David A., Hoedeman, Olivier and Satoko, Kishimoto (2012), *Remunicipalisation*, Amsterdam: Transnational Institute.

Stewart, Jenny (2012), "Multiple-Case Study Methods in Governance-Related Research", in *Public Management Review*, Vol. 14, pp. 67-82.

Toninelli, Pier Angelo (2000), *The Rise and Fall of State-Owned Enterprises in the Western World*, Cambridge: Cambridge University Press.

Yin, R. (2009), *Case Study Research Design and Methods* (4th edition), Thousand Oaks: Sage.

About the Authors / À propos des auteurs

Gisella Aragón Peñaloza holds a Master and is Bachelor in Economics from Universidad del Pacífico (Lima, Peru). Her main fields of study are related to microeconomics: regulation and competition in public services, infrastructure and extractive economies. She has been Analyst of the Economic Research Department of the National Institute for Defence of Competition and Protection of Intellectual Property of Peru, Senior Research Assistant of the Economical Regulation, Competition and Infrastructure Area of Universidad del Pacífico Research Centre and has been part of consultancies for national and international institutions. She currently works at the Analysis Office of the National Fishing Society of Peru and as a Professor of the Faculty of Economics and Finance at Universidad del Pacífico.

Philippe Bance is deputy director of the laboratory CREAM (Centre for Research in Applied Economics Globalisation) at the University of Rouen – Normandy University. He was Chairman of the Department of Economics from 1997 to 2002 and Vice-President of the University of Rouen from 2007 to 2010. Scientific Delegate at the Evaluation Agency for Research and Higher Education (AERES) since 2010, he chaired the Scientific Commission "Public Economics" CIRIEC France since 2011 and the International Scientific Council of CIRIEC since 2014. He runs the collection "Public Economics and Social Economics" of Presses Universitaires de Rouen et du Havre (PURH). His research focuses on services of general interest, the European economy, public policy and evaluation of public action.

Pierre Bauby, member of the International Scientific Commission of CIRIEC International on Public Economy, researcher and professor in Political science (Paris 8 University, Science Po, CNFPT, etc.) is specialist on public services (services of general interest) and public action. He is expert for the Public Services Intergroup of European Parliament and for the European Economic and Social Committee and participates in several European networks. He is (co)author of several studies, particularly, the chapter on "Europe" in UCLG (ed.), *Basic Services for All in an Urbanizing World*, Routledge, 2014; *(Re)légitimer l'action publique en Europe*, Fondation Jean Jaurès, 2014; *Providing High-Quality Public Services in Europe based on the Values of Protocol 26 TFEU*, CESI Brussels, 2012; *L'européanisation des services publics*, Presses de SciencePo, Paris, 2011; *Service public, services publics*, La Documentation Française, Paris, 2011; *Mapping of the Public Services* *in the European Union and the 27 Member States*, Brussels, 2010; *Les services publics en Europe, Pour une régulation démocratique*, Publisud, 2007; *Reconstruire l'action publique*, Syros, 1998; *Le service public*, Flammarion, 1997; *L'Etat-stratège*, Editions ouvrières, 1991.

Luc Bernier is professor of public policy at l'École nationale d'administration publique where he is also the director of the research centre on governance (CERGO). From 2001 until 2006, he was director of research and education at l'ÉNAP. In 2005-6, he was president of the institute of Public Administration of Canada. He was president of CIRIEC'S International Scientific Council from 2011 until 2014. After completing his PhD at Northwestern University in Illinois where his dissertation was on public enterprises, he was assistant professor in political science at Concordia University in Montreal before moving to l'ENAP. His research interests are on the impact of organizational variables such as entrepreneurship or corporate governance on the implementation of public policy. He has published frequently on public enterprises, central agencies, complex organizations and administrative reform.

Malcolm G. Bird is an assistant professor of political science at the University of Winnipeg who is fascinated by the evolution of Canadian state-owned enterprises. His research focuses on examining the modernization efforts of contemporary Crown corporations and how they are adapting both their internal operations and governance regimes to remain pertinent in the current era. His case studies span the breadth of English Canadian public enterprises in a number of sectors including alcohol distribution, auto insurance, financial services, logistics as well as land and marine transportation, among others. It is the complexity of the challenges that public firms face on a day-to-day basis that make them such interesting public policy instruments. In contrast to profit maximizing private firms, public enterprises must balance a whole host of divergent and, in some cases, conflicting demands from many different interests such as their political superiors, the public and various stakeholder groups.

Jose Luis Bonifaz Fernández is Civil Engineer from the Pontificia Universidad Católica del Peru and Master of Arts in Economics at Georgetown University. His main fields of study include regulation and competition in public services, infrastructure concessions and transport logistics. He has been Head of the Department of Economics at Universidad del Pacífico, General Manager of the National Superintendence of Sanitation Services (SUNASS), and consultant to the IDB, CAF, GIZ, KfW and World Bank. He currently holds the position of Associate Dean of the Faculty of Economics and Finance and Director of the Master of Public Service Regulation and Infrastructure Management of the Universidad del Pacífico. Also, he is Member of the Board of the

Competition Agency (INDECOPI) and Member of Pro-Development Committee in PROINVERSIÓN.

Bruno Bosco is Full Professor of Public Finance at the University of Milan-Bicocca and has previously held the positions of Associate Professor at the State University of Milan and of Contract Professor at the L. Bocconi University of Milan. He has received his Ph. D. in economics from the University of Oxford. His main research interests are in field of the economics of regulation and regulated markets as well as in the economics of institutions. He is author of various papers published in international journals on topics belonging to the above mentioned fields.

Catríona Cahill is a PhD candidate at the University of Limerick where she is a member of the Privatisation and PPP Research Group. Her research covers the impact of market orientated reforms such as corporatisation, commercialisation, and liberalisation on the productivity of Irish state owned enterprises in a comparative context.

Olivier Crespi Reghizzi is an analyst at *Eau de Paris* and PhD candidate in Economics at the *Centre International de Recherche sur l'Environnement et le Développement (CIRED) – AgroParisTech* and at the *Centro di Economia Regionale, dei Trasporti e del Turismo (CERTET) – Bocconi University*. His research interests are focused on public finance and particularly on infrastructure financing issues in urban water and sanitation services in Europe. Previously he spent more than two years in Dakar, Senegal, working as a project officer (water and energy) for the *Agence Française de Développement* and as a consultant for the *World Bank*. Olivier holds a *MSc in Civil Engineering* from *Politecnico di Milano* and from *Ecole Centrale de Nantes*.

Laura Delponte, researcher with the Department of Economics, Management, and Quantitative Methods of the University of Milan, holds a university degree in Public Administration and International Institution Management from L. Bocconi University (Italy) and a Master of Arts in Economic Science from Louvain-la-Neuve university (Belgium). A professional consultant for more than ten years, she carried out several evaluation studies of public policies and investments on behalf of international organisations, including the European Parliament, the African Development Bank and the European Commission.

Patrice Dutil is Professor in the Department of Politics and Public Administration at Ryerson University. Before joining the department in August 2006, he was the Acting Executive Director and Director of Research at the Institute of Public Administration of Canada. In addition to multiple articles published in scholarly journals, magazines and newspapers, he is the co-author and editor of many books including *The Service State: Rhetoric, Reality and Promise* (2010); *Searching for*

Leadership: Secretaries to Cabinet in Canada (2008); *The Guardian: Perspectives on the Ontario Ministry of Finance* (2011) and *Canada 1911: The Decisive Election that Shaped the Country* (2011). He earned a Ph.D. at York University in Toronto. His website is patricedutil.com.

Massimo Florio is Professor of Public Economics and *Ad Personam* Jean Monnet Chair of EU Industrial Policy, University of Milan, Italy. His most recent books include *Network Industries and Social Welfare. The Experiment that Reshuffled European Utilities* (Oxford University Press, 2013) and *Applied Welfare Economics. Cost-Benefit Analysis of Project and Policies* (Routledge, 2014).

Christophe Goethals has a master's degree in Economics and has a complementary master's degree in transportation management. Between 2008 and 2011, he worked as a consultant for an engineering consulting firm specialized in transportation and socio-economic studies. Since 2011 he is the coordinator of the Economics Department of the Centre for socio-political research and information (CRISP). Meanwhile, he is teaching assistant at the Université Libre de Bruxelles (ULB) and associated fellow at the Centre Emile Bernheim (SBS-EM – ULB). His main research interests are transport economics, public management, public economics, corporate ownership and governance.

Dorothea Greiling is a full professor at the Johannes Kepler University Linz, Austria and head of the Institute for Management Accounting at the Faculty of Social Sciences, Economics and Business Administration at the Johannes Kepler University, Linz (Austria). Before that she held academic positions at the Protestant University of Applied Sciences Darmstadt (Germany), and at the Faculty of Business Administration of the University of Mannheim (Germany. In 1990 Dorothea Greiling graduated in business administration (University of Mannheim) and received her doctorate in 1995 with a theses on "Regulation versus Public Ownership of Public Enterprises" from the same University. Her engagement within CIRIEC dates back to 1999. Her current research focuses on accountability, integrated reporting and performance management in the public and nonprofit sector.

Thomas Kostal is assistant professor and deputy chair at the Institute for Public Sector Economics, Department of Economics, WU Vienna University of Economics and Business. He holds a PhD in economics from the WU Vienna University of Economics and Business. His research interests and teaching experience are in public sector economics and economic and fiscal policy. He is member of CIRIEC Scientific Commission "Public Services/Public Enterprises".

Ola Mattisson is an associate professor of Strategy and Public management at the Department of Business Administration, School of

Economics and Management at Lund University. Ola received a PhD in Business Administration in 2000 and he is now a researcher at Public Management Research in Lund (PUMAR). The research interest is directed towards strategy and management control in both public and private contexts with a special focus on competition and cooperation. Another interest is service management and service organizations. Ola is the author of a number of books and articles on strategy and public management.

Verena Michalitsch is a PhD student at the Institute for Public Sector Economics at WU Vienna University of Economics and Business. Her research and teaching activities focus on infrastructure economics and quality management in the public sector.

Gabriel Obermann is retired Full Professor for Public Finance and Public Sector Economics at the Institute for Public Sector Economics at WU Vienna University of Economics and Business. He served from 2005 to 2013 as president of the International Scientific Commission on "Public Services/Public Enterprises" of CIRIEC International. His research and teaching activities are focussed on various fields of the economics of the public sector, on issues of public enterprises and the provision of public services, especially in the context of the process of European integration. He contributed to studies for the European Parliament, the European Commission, national public institutions and authorities, and published numerous articles in journals and books.

Dr. Dónal Palcic is a Lecturer in Economics at the University of Limerick. His primary area of research is in public sector economics with a particular focus on the privatisation of state-owned enterprises. Dónal recently co-authored a book on the Irish privatisation experience (*Privatisation in Ireland: Lessons from a European Economy*, Palgrave Macmillan, 2011) and has also published a number of refereed journal articles and book chapters on the same topic.

Lucia Parisio is Full Professor of Public Finance at the Department of Economics, Management and Statistics of the University of Milan-Bicocca. She is Member of the Senate of the University of Milan-Bicocca. She has been Head of the Department of Law and Economics in the same institution (2009-2012) and Associate Professor of Public Economics (2001 to 2005). She holds a PhD in Economics from the University of Pavia. Her research interests and publications in international journals are in the fields of Auction theory and applications, Electricity wholesale markets (theory and empirics), Regulation and Public firms behaviour in liberalized markets.

Matteo Pelagatti is Assistant Professor of Economic Statistics at University of Milan-Bicocca and holds a PhD in Statistics from

University of Milan. His main fields of research are time series analysis, energy econometrics, robust statistics and forecasting, and he is author of various articles covering these topics in international scholarly journals. He also does some training and consulting for public institutions and private companies in the abovementioned fields.

Ulf Ramberg is an associate professor of Management control and Public management at the Department of Business Administration, School of Economics and Management at Lund University. He is also the director of The Council for Local Government Research and Education (KEFU). Ulf received his PhD in Business Administration in 1997. He is a researcher at Public Management Research in Lund (PUMAR) and the author of several books and articles on management control and public management.

Eoin Reeves is a Senior Lecturer in Economics at the University of Limerick where he is also the Director of the *Privatisation and Public Private Partnerships Research Group* (www.p4.ul.ie). His research interests focus on market-based reform of the public sector. He has published over thirty papers (journal articles and book chapters) on these topics and recently co-authored a book on the Irish privatisation experience, which was published by Palgrave Macmillan in 2011.

Nathalie Rey is Assistant Professor at the University of Paris 13, Sorbonne Paris Cité, Deputy Director of the Faculty of Economics, and Director of the Master "Financial Engineering and Modeling". She was Financial Controller in a bank and senior designer in a financial software company. She teaches Financial Theory, Portfolio Theory, and Risk Management. Her research focuses on financial integration, bank restructuring, and financials markets in the laboratory CEPN University Paris 13, Sorbonne Paris Cité.

Christina Schaefer is full professor for Public Administration and Management at the Helmut-Schmidt University/University of the Armed Forces in Hamburg. After graduating in mathematics she worked as research assistant (1997-2004) for the chair of Public Management at the University of Hamburg, where she earned her PhD with a thesis on organizational management and qualified for a university-professorship with a thesis on Public Financial Management. During 2004-2009 she was professor for Public Management at the University of Applied Sciences Berlin. Her main research interests are Public Financial Management and Public Corporate Governance with a focus on public enterprises.

Mihaela M. Similie (Popa), member of Ciriec France, is PhD in Law and researcher in administrative sciences. She is (co)author of several studies and reports on services of general interest in Europe: the "Europe" chapter in UCLG (ed.), *Basic Services for All in an Urbanizing World*,

Routledge, 2014; "Quelle contribution des services d'intérêt général à la politique de cohésion de l'UE", in *L'action publique dans la crise. Vers un renouveau en France et en Europe?*, dir. Philippe Bance, PURH, 2012; *Providing High-Quality Public Services in Europe based on the Values of Protocol 26 TFEU*, report for CESI Brussels, 2012; *La mise en oeuvre de la politique européenne de cohésion en régions françaises: Limousin, Lorraine and Rhône-Alpes*, 2011, on-line publication for Coesionet network SciencePoParis; *Mapping of the Public Services in the European Union and the 27 Member States*, report for CEEP Brussels, 2010.

Maddalena Sorrentino is a Business Organization researcher at the Department of Economics, Management and Quantitative Methods (DEMM) of the University of Milan. Her main research interests are Organization Theory, Public Management, eGovernment, and Public Partnerships. She is a cofounder and Director of Centro ICONA, the Inter-departmental Centre for organizational innovation in public administrations, which was established by the University of Milan in 2006. Maddalena Sorrentino is the author and editor of numerous publications and her articles appear regularly in leading international journals and conference proceedings.

Matteo Turri holds a PhD in Management. Since 2006 he is assistant professor of public management at the Department of Economics, Management and Quantitative Methods (DEMM) – University of Milan. The research and relevant scientific production of Matteo have centred on: (a) Evaluation and control systems in European public administration, focusing attention on the organisational effects of their implementation (the use of output, organisational consequences and degeneration); (b) Management aspects in the higher education sector with particular reference to quality assurance, governance systems, funding, change and the relationship between government bodies and universities; (c) Management of public sector organisations.

Daniela Vandone is Associate Professor of Economics of Markets and Financial Intermediaries at the University of Milan (Italy). She graduated in Banking, Financial and Insurance Science at the Catholic University of Milan (Italy). She earned a MSc in International Banking and Financial Studies at the University of Southampton (United Kingdom) and a PhD in Banking and Finance at the Catholic University of Milan (Italy). She has been visiting PhD student at the Pompeu Fabra University in Barcelona (Spain). Her research interests include: microeconomics of banks, corporate governance, stock market analysis, commodity derivatives, households' indebtedness, wholesale and retail payment systems.

Stephanie Warm is research assistant at the chair for Public Administration and Management at the Helmut-Schmidt University/

University of the Armed Forces in Hamburg. She is currently following her PhD project with a thesis on public enterprises in the water sector. She graduated in public management in Berlin, Germany and in business administration in Chambéry, France. Her main research interests are Public Financial Management and the governance of public enterprise.

Social Economy & Public Economy

The series "Social Economy & Public Economy" gathers books proposing international analytical comparisons of organizations and economic activities oriented towards the service of the general and collective interest: social services, public services, regulation, public enterprises, economic action of territorial entities (regions, local authorities), cooperatives, mutuals, non-profit organizations, etc. In a context of "large transformation", the scientific activity in this field has significantly developed, and the series aims at being a new dissemination and valorization means of this activity using a pluri-disciplinary approach (economics, social sciences, law, political sciences, etc.).

The series is placed under the editorial responsibility of CIRIEC. As an international organization with a scientific aim, CIRIEC undertakes and disseminates research on the public, social and cooperative economy. One of its main activities is the coordination of a large international network of researchers active in these fields. Members and non-members of this network are allowed to publish books in the series.

Series titles / Titres parus

www.peterlang.com